First Published in 2012

Standard Edition ISBN : ISBN 978 967 11018 0 3

Perpustakaan Negara Malaysia. COPYRIGHT @2012BY Colour Box Publishers House, Melaka

EXCELLENCE IN CLINICAL CASE PRESENTATION IN MEDICINE: 51+ Examination Cases Illustrated first edition 2012

DISCLAIMER

Whilst the advice and information is believed to be true and accurate at the date going to press, neither authors nor the publishers can accept any legal responsibility or liability for any errors or omissions that may be made. In particular every effort has been made to check the drug dosages: however it is still possible that errors have been missed. Furthermore dosage schedules are constantly being revised and new side effects being recognised. For these reasons the reader is strongly urged to consult the drug companies' printed instructions before administering any of the drugs recommended in this book. In view of on-going research, equipment development, changes in governmental regulations and rapid accumulation of information relating to the biomedical sciences, the reader is urged to carefully review and evaluate the information provided herein.

Distributed by Kamal Medical Book Supplies Sdn Bhd
134, Jalan Pahang, Next to Hotel Grand Season. Opp GENERAL HOSPITAL –KUALA LAMPUR main Entrance Ground Floor, Kuala Lumpur 53000, Kuala Lumpur
Phone no +6(03)-40210575 Fax: +6(03)-40214612
Email : http://kmedical@streamyx.com

Publisher: COLOUR BOX PUBLISHING HOUSE
No.54, Jalan Jati 6, Taman Jati,
75350 Batu Berendam, Melaka.

Printer: Colour Box Enterprise
28, Jalan TTC 15, Taman Teknologi
Cheng, 75250 Melaka, Malaysia
First printed in Melaka, Malaysia.

PREFACE

EXCELLENCE IN CLINICAL CASE PRESENTATION IN MEDICINE: 51+ Examination Cases Illustrated (First Edition) is intended to assist medical students to perform professionally at undergraduate assessment both at summative examinations and at the end of posting evaluations. The objective of this book is to outline the salient features encountered in clinical case presentation of common diseases seen in Internal Medicine that would enable medical students to perform at par excellence. The cases illustrated are based on the fundamentals of andragogy sharpening clinical skills and what students would be assessed on in an examination setting. The book should also undoubtedly serve as a convenient tool for physicians to teach and assess students in clinical reasoning and professional practice. The 51+ Examination Cases discussed are essentially similar to those used for the clinical examinations for undergraduates either as Long Case, OSLER or as OSCE. Some of the investigations mentioned could also be utilized as OSPE questions for data interpretation.

Each case begins with an overview of the clinical condition, highlighting vital information that would eventually pave the way for subsequent discussion. A typical case vignette in questionnaire format follows. Specific information is given to the student to assist him in eliciting an excellent history and perform an accurate clinical examination. The subsequent discussion revolves in developing a differential diagnosis. Clinical reasoning skills are incorporated wherever relevant to enable the student to understand how the diagnosis is confirmed after requesting and reviewing the clinical findings and relevant investigations.

Subsequently, additional information is provided to assist the student as to how only relevant investigations should be requested thus avoiding listing of investigations without discriminating their value in diagnosis and assessment of complications of the disease. This discriminative approach paves the way to nuture higher reasoning skills and higher cognitive thinking .

In discussing the management of the clinical condition, the student is taken through several aspects of management although not all may be relevant especially if the case is presented as a short OSCE. By being comprehensive in explaining the management of the case, students should be able to appreciate the holistic approach towards clinical management.

The authors have painstakingly elaborated the vital points that students should address in the course of their clerking and presentation through check lists. Each of the case discussed has three important sections that students need to take note of: Must know facts, common omissions and

2

questions that may be asked. The inclusion of advanced level questions for high achievers should motivate students to read further on the subject so that clinical performance can be further enhanced to a higher level.

Both students and their teachers should use the material presented in each of the cases to prepare the candidate for clinical examinations by incorporating time constraints befitting the assessment tool, either as OSCE (short and long) or OSLER/LONG CASE.

EXCELLENCE IN CLINICAL CASE PRESENTATION IN MEDICINE: 51+ Examination Cases Illustrated features a concise approach equipping medical students with necessary skills to excel in the undergraduate clinical examination. It is also a useful teaching tool for physicians involved in preparing students for excellent performance at high stake examinations.

Sivalingam Nalliah & Sachchithanantham. K

July 2012

ACKNOWLEDGMENT

'EXCELLENCE IN CLINICAL CASE PRESENTATION IN MEDICINE: 51+ Examination Cases Illustrated ' is the product of the relentless work of fourteen experienced and seasoned physicians from various sub-specialities of Internal Medicine, all from the academic sector of Universities, both locally and abroad . This comprehensive, evidence based textbook will meet the current needs of medical undergraduates to perform at par excellence at the various clinical examination in Internal Medicine.

First and foremost we would like to thank the medical students, who have over the years expressed the need for a comprehensive textbook to guide them in their clinical presentation
To all the authors listed in the contributors page, and to several colleagues whose names we cannot continue listing and who have assisted us in one way or another, we feel very much indebted. We wish to thank all contributors for submitting their contributions within the short time frame given. We also wish to thank them for their cooperation in both agreeing to write and having painstakingly made changes to their original draft as required by the editorial panel.

We certainly would like to acknowledge and thank Associate Professor Rumi R. Khajotia for his meticulous approach taken in presenting the largest number of contributions in Respiratory Medicine. The comprehensive approach to the common problems in his field would appeal to both undergraduates and postgraduates. Our gratitude to Professor Sethuraman , Dean of the Faculty of Medicine , AIMST University, Malaysia in encouraging his faculty to generously contribute to this book. A special mention of thanks to Dr.Upali Marasinghe who has take time to proof read this book and Dr.Mohamed Najimudeen who initially requested his Sri Lankan colleagues to participate in this project

Chiang Graphic Advertising and Marketing from Malacca is to be complimented for their cover designs. Chong Sean Hoon from Colour Box Publishing House & Colour Box Printing Press is acknowledged for the excellent print and in enabling the book to be printed on time

Prof Sachchithanantham

Dr.Kavitha Nagandla

Prof Dato'Dr.N.Sivalingam

Prof Dr Rifdy Mohideen

4

CONTRIBUTORS

Dr A P Singh,
MD(Genera Medicine), DM Neurology
Professor of Medicine & Neurology,
Head of Department
Department of Medicine,
AIMST University,
Bedong 08100,
Kedah Darul Aman
Malaysia.

Dr.Champica Kasmari Bodinayake
MBBS (Ruhuna) MD (Colombo) MRCP (UK)
Senior Lecturer
Department of Medicine
Faculty of Medicine
University of Ruhuna
Galle
Sri Lanka

Professor Dr Esha Das Gupta
MBBS (India), MRCP (Ireland), FRCPI (Ireland), FRCP (London), AM (Malaysia)
Associate Professor and Head of Department
Department of Medicine
Clinical School
International Medical University.
Seremban,
Malaysia

Dr.Kyaw Min
MBBS, DTM&H, MCTM, MPH, PhD, FACTM, FRSTMH
Associate Professor of Tropical Medicine,
Faculty of Medicine AIMST University
Kedah
Malaysia

Dr. Koh Kwee Choy,James
BSc (Hons) (UKM), MBBS (Manipal), MMed (Malaya)
Senior Lecturer & Infectious Diseases Physician
Department of Medicine
Clinical School
International Medical University
Seremban

Professor Mohamed Rifdy Mohideen
MBBS (Col), MD (Col), MRCP (UK), FRCP (Lond), FCCP, FRACP
(Hon)
Senior Professor in Medicine
Faculty of Medicine
University of Ruhuna
Galle P.O.Box 70
Sri Lanka

Dr. Rumi R. Khajotia,
MBBS (Mumbai), MD (Mumbai), Facharzt (Vienna), FAMA (Vienna),
FAMS (Vienna)
Associate Professor in Internal Medicine and Pulmonology
Department of Medicine
Clinical SchoolInternational Medical University
Seremban
Malaysia
Consultant Pulmonologist, Hospital Tuanku Ja'afar
Seremban
Malaysia

Dr.Sangeetha Poovaneswaran
MBChB (UK), MRCP(UK), FRCR (UK),AM (Mal)
Clinical Oncologist and Senior Lecturer
Department of Medicine
Clinical School
International Medical University
Seremban
Malaysia

Professor Saroj Jayasinghe
MBBS (Col), MD (Col), MD (Bristol), FRCP (Lond), ?FCCP
Professor in the Department of Clinical Medicine
Faculty of Medicine
University of Colombo
Sri Lanka
Hon Consultant Physician
National Hospital of Sri Lanka
Colombo,
Sri Lanka

Dr Shivanan Thiagarajah
MBBS (IMU), MRCP (UK)
Physician in Charge
Department of Medicine
Hospital Port Dickson,
Negeri Sembilan, Malaysia

Prof.Dr.S.Nandakumar
MBBS., MD.
Additional Professor,
AIMST University,
Alor Setar
Kedah
Malaysia

Professor Dato Dr Sivalingam Nalliah
MBBS (Mal), MCGP (Mal), FRCOG, FAMM (Mal), M Ed
Consultant Obstetrician and Gynecologist
Department of Obstetrics and Gynecology
Clinical School
International Medical University
Seremban
Malaysia

Dr Suresh Ponnusamy,
Associate Professor
Faculty of MedicineAIMST University
Sungai Petani
Kedah
Malaysia

Dr. Usha Rani Singh
M.D. (Pediatrics),
Associate Professor,
Department of Pediatrics,
AIMST University,
Sungai Petani,
Kedah
Malaysia.

Dr Vaani Valerie Visuvanathan
MBBS (Malaya) MRCP (UK)
Physician and Lecturer,
Clinical School
International Medical School
Seremban
Malaysia

CONTENTS

INTRODUCTION: THE CLINICAL EXAMINATION

Sivalingam Nalliah & Sachchithanantham .K

Introduction

The clinical examination is integral to assessment in Internal Medicine. The 'apprentice model' is ideal for the medical student as he sharpens his clinical skills through mastery learning. He learns to adopt the manner and attitude of practising clinicians to patient care, fine tuning his skills through experiential learning. Historically role modelling has has served well to mould the student to mature from a being a novice to become an expert clinician. Observation, performance under supervision and demonstrating clinical techniques require both exposure to a variety of learning opportunities and practice in performing clinical examinations. Certainly practice makes perfect and hence a variety of learning tools have been incorporated to master the clinical examination. Clinical techniques involves going through the process of inspection, palpation, percussion and auscultation. Undeniably the novice student requires rigorous training in the clinical setting to rationalise the steps adopted in clinical examination to arrive at a diagnosis after history taking and physical examination. The senior years of clinical training requires clinical reasoning and ability to draw a management plan once a diagnosis is established.

Skills based assessment could be used to evaluate a combination of learning domains such as cognitive, psychomotor and affective aspects. The design of the appropriate assessment tool would dictate if one or all aspects of the skills are to be evaluated. In assessing skills, the primary concern is if the test that is utilised is reliable. The traditional LONG CASE, often utilised in examinations are frequently quoted as lacking reliability and not being a good assessment of clinical skills. In order to decrease bias and increase objectivity and validity of assessment , medical educationalists have introduced newer assessment tools over the last two decades. It is agreed that by sampling across a range of cases, measures of reliability inevitably improves. Hence assessment of clinical skills should have excellent reliability and validity.

Types of Clinical Skills Assessment

The clinical case that the student is assessed could be a LONG CASE or SHORT CASE. To improve reliability newer tools like the OSCE, Modified OSCE and PACES have been introduced. The OSLER is a modification of the LONG CASE where objectivity is factored in to improve assessment. The Mini-Clinical Evaluation Exercise (MiniCEX) is coming into vogue as a formative assessment. The Mini-CEX is useful in that specific areas of the case are evaluated after directly observing the candidate and immediate feedback is given so that remediation is possible and the candidate can improve his skills to achieve a desired set standard of performance.

The traditional bedside teaching provides enormous opportunities for the student to perfect his/her techniques in all aspects of clinical learning i.e knowledge, skills and attitude, in real life situations. By definition bedside teaching, extends to beyond learning in the hospital set up as it generally implies learning in the 'presence of a real patient'. The dynamism of bedside teaching is realised as soft skills like professionalism, communication skills, breaking serious illness news and attitude can be evaluated. In bedside teaching, not infrequently the patient is desirous of involvement in the discussion providing yet another opportunity to seek patient feedback on the student's performance.

Having completed a period of learning the student should have adequate knowledge and psychomotor skills before appearing for a summative clinical examination like OSCE and OSLER. Students who do not perform well either have not had adequate clinical learning or have not understood the objectives of case discussion as a means of assessment. Apart from the formal aspects of assessment pertaining to the clinical case the student is also assessed on his personal appearance and approach to patient during a clinical encounter signifying the importance of professionalism in the practice of Medicine. Irrespective of the type of clinical examination that the student is tested hand washing before touching the patient and seeking permission to examine are essential steps.

These steps are intentionally repeated in many of the cases discussed.

Bedside Manner

As enshrined in the Medical Code of Good Clinical Practice, bed side manner is important and is fundamental to the clinical examination. The dynamic nature of bed side manner is shown by the way the student adapts to changing needs of the patient during the clinical examination. Medicine is the only field where the patient allows one to touch him/her as part of the clinical management, hence using the correct language without being judgemental and having the correct attitude are vital. The student needs to be aware of the dynamism involved in the clinical encounter and the role of the patient in the whole encounter. Inconvenience to the patient should be minimized and anxiety and discomfort should be reduced to a tolerable and acceptable level. It is fundamental to state that you are not going to cause pain or discomfort in the course of the palpation, rather than warn the patient to 'shout out if an area on the tummy you palpate is painful!' The patient may need to expose his/her body; it is incumbent on the student is to explain the need for such and to ensure that the patient is not unduly distressed or embarrassed. At the end of the examination, though the student would be deeply engaged with the examiner in answering questions, he/she should not fail to address the patient's concern, especially if the patient feels that the clinical discussion between the student and examiner has cast some queries on his own treatment for which he needs clarification.

History and Physical Examination

In writing the cases, the authors in this book have been thorough in detailing how the history is to be taken and have indicated possible areas that need to address based on the clinical problem. Leading questions should be avoided and open questions like 'how are you' and 'tell me about the 'loose stools' you are having' are advised. Always try to terminate the questioning by giving time for the patient to ask you any question that bothers him/her especially in the Long Case where the student may be with the patient for 45 mins to 60 mins. Before leaving the patient, thank him and terminate the encounter with, 'Are there any queries you have that I need to know?'

Techniques on physical examination have to be methodical and should they deviate from the conventional method the student should be able to tell the examiner why such deviations are necessary. If the patient is distressed or in pain, do not proceed with the examination but let the examiner know so that the examination could be halted without causing further pain to the patient.

Intimate examinations like per rectal examination and pelvic examination may not be tested during the clinical examination except in certain instances. Students should seek clarification should such examinations be done before undertaking them on their own.

The check list provided in the clinical cases included in the book should be an aid for the student to learn from and be familiar with. Common pitfalls in clinical examination have been highlighted based on experiences in examining clinical students. Again reading through and practising the techniques of physical examination would lead to a degree of 'professional automation' that would be aligned to good clinical practice.

Clinical Reasoning

In establishing a clinical diagnosis one needs to elicit a detailed history and clinical findings. It is good wisdom to refresh our minds on the elements of problem based learning (PBL) where a trigger is provided to work on so that possible differential diagnoses are established. In the clinical examination the patient's chief complaint provides the 'clinical trigger'. For example if the history relates to 'vomiting of a short duration' a probable list of clinical diagnoses is drawn. This list of diagnoses is done before getting a detailed history of present illness and investigations. In narrowing this list more questions are asked so as reduce the original list for' vomiting' which may include neuropsychiatric disorders , poisoning and gastrointestinal disorders to a shorter list focussing on intestinal obstruction because the patient had an abdominal surgery done and there was no CNS history. Having a new and shorter list of differential diagnoses, the physical examination is done focussing on developing yet a shorter probable diagnosis /diagnoses. The latter examination should permit re-ordering the differential diagnosis list, perhaps from four diagnoses to two. Many a time, in undergraduate examination one can make a final diagnosis with near 100 % certainty if we adopted this approach.

Some of the cases illustrated in this book include 'Interpretation of the history and physical examination'. This is based on clinical reasoning, a useful tool for good practice. Deductive reasoning is based on sound basic science knowledge, ability to relate patient's complaints to functional disorders and justifying the final diagnosis. Investigations that are done need to be relevant as they should either increase or decrease the probability of the final diagnosis. In some of the cases described, it is reiterated that students should avoid giving a 'grocery list' of investigations without detailing the relevance of the test. Health economics and distributive justice are elements of medical ethics that the doctor should uphold. Investigations add to health costs apart from causing undue anxiety to the patient. No test should be 'routine' in clinical practice.

Clinical experience in the formative years adds to excellence in establishing the diagnosis and outlining the clinical management. Pattern recognition is fundamental to diagnosis. The quality of the student's diagnosis is based on his/her clinical reasoning. The prevalence of the disease and the epidemiology of the disease impacts a great deal on diagnosis. Should the protean clinical manifestation be perplexing and there are two possibilities i.e tuberculosis and sarcoidosis, then one would select 'tuberculosis' in this country because of the resurgence of this tropical disease rather than sarcoidosis. Experience does count as one moves from being a novice through to an intermediate and expert in medicine. Medical students who have obtained the clinical experience expected of them as they progress from junior to senior medical students should have little difficulty in all areas expected in a case presentation viz. history taking, clinical examination, establishment of the diagnosis with clinical reasoning and clinical management.

The cases described in this book could be used to prepare students to walk through the way they usually perform in the ward setting and to understand how one can enhance learning. Each case begins with an 'overview'. This is not meant to be exhaustive but adequate to alert the student on some essential points about the disorder. When the respiratory and cardiovascular cases are read the student would appreciate the elements of applying basic science to understanding the dysfunctional status of the sick patient. The case vignettes have been kept short so that the student could draw the 'probable' list of differential diagnoses and then work through so as establish the provisional diagnosis. Should the student get the diagnosis wrong then he/she should re-trace the clinical reasoning pathway. Additional reading is expected after going through the questions at the end of each case so as to supplement information that would make learning current. The student is advised to consult current clinical practice guideline in management of the case apart from learning what is mentioned in each case presented.

Investigations and Management

Investigations are meant to either increase or decrease the probable final diagnosis. Mention is made about both relevance and usefulness. Some investigations are done to assist in confirming the diagnosis e.g. blood film for falciparum malaria. Others are done to assess the general status of the patient e.g. FBC, urine analysis. Yet others are done to help in management e.g. renal function test for chronic renal failure. It is incumbent on the student to clearly state as to what the investigations relate to i.e. confirming diagnosis, evaluate a complication or assess response to treatment.

An outline of the clinical management is essential in a LONG CASE. When drawing the outline, the student should include treatment directed to the disease and also address concerns that are bothering the patient e.g. psychological distress and depression, nutrition and appetite, anaemia etc.

Co-morbid disease that is present like hypertension, stroke and diabetes mellitus, impact on the treatment of the current disease. Attention should be given to optimizing these chronic diseases while drawing an outline of management of the current disease. Such a holistic approach is essential to score high marks. Should time be a factor, the student should clarify if he /she needs to address co-morbid disease management during the examination apart from addressing the main disease.

Types of Cases in Clinical Examination

LONG CASE Examination

The student is given a case for him to clerk for an hour. He works by himself drawing the history and performing the clinical examination. He would attend to time management. He would then have written the points he would like to share with the examiners who would come at an appointed time assessing the history he has taken and physical examination. Time will be allocated for the types of investigations he would do and how he would manage the case. Should time permit he may be asked to interpret relevant blood investigations, ECG, CT scans etc.

Marks are given for each portion by the team of two to three examiners. The objectivity of marking in the long case is shadowed by the imprecise global marking that categorizes the performance into 'distinction, pass, borderline and fail'. For more objectivity some have broken the assessment into components (history -10%, developing a diagnosis with reasoning -20%, requesting relevant investigations giving reasons-15%, outlining management-25%, application of basic science to discussion 20%, professional approach and patient safety issues - 5%).

Most teams of examiners would have examined the case before hand and would have arrived at some agreement as to what would constitute a pass mark; in other words , what is expected of the student regarding the case. Because the LONG CASE largely suffers from not being structured some suspect its validity and reliability of being a fair examination tool. Further, students may not be tested on the same case because of patient fatigue contributing to variations in assessment.

Tips for the Long case

Practice is essential and time management would put the student in a comfortable position. Preliminary introductions and establishment of rapport should not be more than 5 minutes with adequate time of about 15 minutes for history taking. Focussed questions and clarifications may be needed after having drawn the list of differential diagnosis. The physical examination should take about 20 minutes leaving another twenty minutes to document the findings and draw a plan of management.

Table 1:

Types of Questions that should go through your mind in LONG CASE

- *Can I summarize the salient points?*
- *What is my provisional diagnosis?*
- *What is the differential diagnosis, if any?*
- *What are the risk factors of this patient?*
- *What investigations are relevant for confirming the diagnosis and in determining complications and progress of disease?*
- *What is your immediate or short term plan of management?*
- *What is your long term plan of management?*
- *What do the results of investigations mean?*
- *What is the prognosis?*
- *Is my communication and attitude good?*

Ensure the following are included:

- Detailed introductory overview of the case.
- Chief complaint and associated conditions.
- Past history, medications, allergies, family history, occupational history and
- Social history.
- Physical examination, provisional diagnosis and differential diagnosis
- Management outline

Management plan

- Review the main problem and co-morbid disease
- Provisional and differential diagnosis giving reasons why the probability is high on the list of a chosen diagnosis
- Relevant investigations and the expected results
- Proposed treatment or management

Objective Structured Long Examination Record (OSLER)

The limitation of the LONG CASE is that the encounter between the student and the patient is not directly observed. This major criticism is overcome by the OSLER type of clinical examination.. Often a 10-item analytical record of the traditional long case is drawn and objectivity is improved, so are validity and reliability. All candidates are assessed over 20–30 minutes by the examiners on the same 10 items. The items reflect on assuring construct or face validity. Soft skills like communication skills, professional practice and difficulties in the case are taken into account. Having a minimum of 10 items provides the range of components to be assessed (as stated under LONG CASE). For example four items could focus on history (pace and clarity of presentation, communication skills process, systematic approach and establishment of the case facts) and three items on physical examination would include systematic approach, examination technique and establishment of the correct physical findings. Clearly by direct observation the candidate's affective behaviour can also be evaluated. Three items would focus on prioritizing investigations giving reasons and justifying cost-benefit in a logical sequence, outlining appropriate management and demonstrating confidence in the management of the case. The last three items would carry a good proportion of the marks in the final year as it would demonstrate the preparedness for the student to function as a professional. Problem solving skills and designing appropriate strategies in management are tested in the last portion of the 10 items. The 10 item OSLER permits both global marking and categorized marking. The examiner has the liberty to be descriptive in specific areas of strengths and weaknesses and such marking helps in giving feedback to stakeholders. Agreeably there is still weakness in LONG CASE and OSLER examinations as one tries to factor in objectivity, validity and reliability on one hand and practicality on the other.

Table 2: MARKING SCHEME FOR OSLER

CANDIDATE'S NAME:

EXAMINATION NO. :

Examiners are required to GRADE each of the ten items below and assign an overall GRADE and MARK concerning the candidate prior to discussion with their co-examiner as follows

GRADES /MARKS
P+ = VERY GOOD/EXCELLENT (60-80+), P = PASS/BORDERLINE PASS (50-55), P– = BELOW PASS (35-45) mark details

PRESENTATION OF HISTORY

GRADE / AGREED GRADE

PACE/CLARITY.
COMMUNICATION PROCESS:
(History, e.g., CVS; investigation,
e.g. Endoscopy; Management, e.g., patient education).

SYSTEMATIC PRESENTATION
CORRECT FACTS ESTABLISHED
PHYSICAL EXAMINATION
SYSTEMATIC
TECHNIQUE
(including attitude towards patient)
CORRECT FINDINGS ESTABLISHED
APPROPRIATE INVESTIGATIONS IN A LOGICAL SEQUENCE
Communication Process option)
APPROPRIATE MANAGEMENT
CLINICAL ACUMEN.
(Problem identification/Problem-solving ability

ADDITIONAL COMMENTS:
Please Tick (X) For CASE DIFFICULTY

INDIVIDUAL EXAMINER

PAIR OF EXAMINERS

Examiner   Difficulty
Standard   OVERALL MARK
AGREED

GRADE   P-, P, P+   MARKS _____ /100%
Difficult
Very Difficult

Objective Structured Clinical Examination (OSCE)

As you read the case illustrations you would realize they are written to be comprehensive along what is expected during the LONG CASE. However there are several elements within the discussion that are applicable to OSCE/OPSE and OSLER.

The OSCE examination is a multi-station multi-task assessment which tests both clinical and practical skills contributing to both variety and case-mix. Based on the Miller's Triangle of Learning, the OSCE focuses on 'SHOW HOW' while MCQS and MEQs test cognitive functions (KNOWS and KNOWS HOW).

The Objective of the OSCE examination is to examine ALL students using the same assessment tool hence contributing to improved reliability and validity. Specific skill modalities tested are: history taking, reasoning skills, clinical examination skills, procedures, communication, breaking serious illness news, X-rays and counselling skills. Structured marking scheme lends to the objectivity of the OSCE. The primary aim is for the student to demonstrate his clinical skills rather than describe the theoretical aspect alone. Because of multi-station and multitasks in the OSCE a wider sampling is possible unlike the LONG CASE/ OSLER LONG CASE. Hence, reliability is assured provided the construct of the stations are good. Each OSCE may be short (5-8 mins) or long (10-20 mins). By providing several stations (of about 12-15) on a variety of topics, focused areas or tasks are tested. All students have to go through all the stations.

Table 3
Set up of the OSCE
- Number of stations 12-15 (may be combination of SHORT and LONG OSCE)
- A short case vignette is provided and the task is clearly specified e.g.
  Take a focused history, examine his precordium, examine the hands and feet etc.
- Both 'standardized' and real patient s may be provided.
  Specified clinical skills are tested. Communication skills, professional practice and counselling may also be tested.
- Scoring is done using a task specific check list that makes the test objective in nature.

Objectivity is ensured by using a prepared marking sheet. In most instances the examiner plays a small role apart from being largely an observer when he is tasked to ask a few questions. . By being an observer most of the time, anxiety is expected to be taken out of the encounter while clinical skills that are tasked to be done are evaluated.

In some OSCE stations it may end with one or two minute oral questions. The student should look at the instruction pertaining to the need to answer some questions so that adequate time is allotted after completing the assigned task. During this time, you are not allowed to talk to the real or simulated patient but only to the examiner.

Objective Structured Practical Examination (OSPE)

The OSPE is a method of objectively testing both practical knowledge and procedural skills required of undergraduate medical students. This constitutes the psychomotor domain in the medical curriculum, apart from cognitive and affective domains. Students should demonstrate competency in performance of basic technical skills, interpretation of laboratory investigations and radiographs applying theory to practice, in the process. Apart from learning in the wards, the Clinical Skills Unit is an excellent place for learning many of these skills. Currently multimedia has contributed enormously to learning and authenticated learning materials (CDs, YouTube,) recommended by the medical school enhances learning.

Practical skills students need to be competent in include venepuncture, inserting a cannula into a peripheral vein, suturing a wound, vaginal bimanual exam, rectal digital exam, PAP smear, breast and testes exam, prostate exam, ophthalmoscopy, diagnostic procedures like endometrial biopsy, basic cardio-pulmonary resuscitation (adult and child), performing urinary catheterisation in both male and female, use of inhalers , giving injections(intramuscular and subcutaneous), safe disposal of sharps, resuscitation using manikins etc. Data interpretation (laboratory results), ECG tracings, Ultrasound pictures, CT/MRI scans, growth charts of children, CTG and partograph and voiding cystometry are commonly utilized.

Again all students are expected to complete multi-stations in the OSPE. Questions are set for each station which usually should be completed in 5 minutes.. A good degree of objectivity is derived from this assessment and reliability is high.

The Mini-Clinical Evaluation Exercise (Mini-CEX)

The Mini-Clinical Evaluation Exercise (Mini-CEX) is a clinical examination intended to facilitate formative assessment of core clinical skills. Students are evaluated for periods of 15-20 minutes in the real setting so as to get a 'quick view' of the student under direct observation of the clinical encounter. It is incumbent on the faculty to provide immediate feedback so that remediation is possible to improve performance. The Mini-CEX can be conducted in both outpatient and inpatient set up. The types of clinical skills evaluated could be history taking, clinical examination, taking informed consent, problem solving and clinical reasoning. Marking scheme can be global with 1-3 being unsatisfactory, 4-6, satisfactory and 7-10 being excellent. Clearly a borderline mark of 4-5 or lower would require remediation. For each task tested the marking scheme could be broken up to assess specific skills.

For example in history taking the following could be assessed:

- Thorough history pertinent to case
- Non directive or open questions for accurate information
- Responds appropriately to non-verbal cues
- Proper attitude and approach (respect, , empathy and rapport)
- Considers patient comfort, modesty, confidentiality and needs

The mini-CEX assessment is becoming a popular formative assessment tool in many medical schools. As it utilises a range of cases focussing on specific aspects of the clinical encounter (e.g. history taking, or physical examination) it lends to reliability. The formative nature and compulsory feedback at the end of the encounter assists student to gauge their performance and permits time for remediation should gaps be apparent.

Conclusion

Assessment of clinical skills would continue to change as more effective tools are designed to make them reliable and valid. However, the more vital aspect of clinical learning is observation and practice following the master teacher's techniques exhibiting professionalism and deductive decision making based on history and physical findings. Formative assessment like the Mini-CEX provides opportunities for feedback and time for improving performance and mastery learning. The Miller's triangle should be visited in this respect. Periodic visits to the clinical skills unit would complement clinical learning acquired in the hospital, clinics and operation theatres where students would be have few opportunities to perform clinical skills on real patients even under supervision. It is the view of most clinical teachers that with good clinical teaching and meaningful learning, students would perform well irrespective of the evaluation tool

REFERENCES

1. Seems. Skill based assessment. BMJ. 2003;326(7391):703-706

2. Sood R. Long Case Examination-can it be improved? Ind J Acad Cl Med 2001;2(4):263

3. Regher G, MacRae H,Reznick R, David S. Comparing the psychometrics of checklist and global rating scale for assessing performance on the OSCE –format examination. Acad Med 1998; 73(9):993-997

4. American Board of Internal Medicine   Mini-Clinical Evaluation Exercise (Mini-CEX), www.abim.org/program-director-admin/assessment-tool/mini-cex asp Reference

5. Gleeson Assessment of clinical competence using OSLER.AMEE Medical Education Guide 9. 1997; 19(1):7-14 (Assessment Table on OSLER derived from this source)

SECTION1 :RESPIRATORY SYSTEM

RUMI R KHAJOTIA

Pleural Effusion is a good clinical case for testing history taking and physical examination skills and assessing the knowledge of procedural skills (aspiration and drainage of fluid)

A case of pleural effusion follows.

DEFINITION:

Pleural effusion is defined as an abnormal collection of fluid in the pleural space due to excessive fluid production or decreased absorption.[1]

Pathophysiology of Pleural effusion:

The pleural space, under normal circumstances has a small amount of fluid which serves as a lubricant allowing the lung surface to smoothly glide within the thorax during the respiratory cycle. Normally, approximately, 15 ml of fluid enters the pleural space daily via the capillaries within the parietal pleura and is reabsorbed by the parietal pleural lymphatics. As a result, at any given time there is normally 15-20 ml of fluid in each hemithorax and the layer of fluid is 2-10 mm thick.[2]

Pleural fluid is produced at parietal pleural level, mainly in the less dependent regions of the cavity while reabsorption is accomplished by parietal pleural lymphatics in the most dependent part of the cavity on the diaphragmatic surface and in the mediastinal regions. Miserocchi G,[3] has explained that the flow rate in pleural lymphatics can increase in response to an increase in pleural fluid filtration, thereby acting as a negative feedback mechanism to control pleural liquid volume. When filtration exceeds maximum pleural lymphatic flow, pleural effusion occurs.

Pleural Effusion may be transudative or exudative

TRANSUDATIVE PLEURAL EFFUSION

It occurs mainly due to an increase in hydrostatic pressure or a decrease in the colloid osmotic pressure. The fluid appears clear with a specific gravity of <1.012. The protein content is <25g/l while the fluid protein: serum protein ratio is less than 0.5.

COMMON CAUSES OF A TRANSUDATIVE PLEURAL EFFUSION:

(handwritten: ↳) ↑ hydrostatic P
↳ ↓ oncotic

They include:

- Left ventricular failure ✔
- Cirrhosis of Liver ✔
- Nephrotic syndrome ✔
- Hypothyroidism ✔
- Pulmonary embolism (20% cases) ✔

(handwritten:
• specific gravity
• protein contain
• fluid : serum protein)

Exudative Pleural Effusion:

Unlike transudative effusions, exudative pleural effusion is caused by alterations in local factors affecting the pleural surfaces, leading to an imbalance between the formation and absorption of pleural fluid. The main cause is inflammation. An exudative pleural effusion is usually cloudy in appearance and has a specific gravity of > 1.020. The protein content of the fluid is >35g/l and the ratio of fluid protein: serum protein is >0.5 g/l.

☞ Note: *Differentiating transudative and exudative pleural effusion is a common examination question.*

Common causes of an Exudative Pleural Effusion:

- ✔ Pneumonia
- ✔ Malignancy- commonly, lung or breast cancer, leukemia and lymphoma.
- ✔ Tuberculosis (TB)
- ✔ Fungal infection
- Collagen vascular disorders such as Rheumatoid Arthritis, Systemic Lupus Erythematosis
- Trauma (Haemothorax
- Post-cardiac injury syndrome
- Oesophageal perforation
- Pulmonary embolism
- Asbestos-related pleural diseases
- Drug-induced

Sensitivity of tests to distinguish exudative from transudative effusions [4]

	Sensitivity for Exudate	Specificity for Exudate
Light's criteria	%	
(one or more of the foll. three)	**98**	**83**
1) Ratio of pleural-fluid protein level to serum protein level >0.5	86	84
2) Ratio of pleural fluid LDH level to serum LDH level >0.6	90	82
3) Pleural fluid LDH level >two thirds the upper limit of normal for serum LDH level	82	89

Table adapted from N Engl J Med, Vol. 346, No. 25. June 20, 2002.
www.nejm.org

CASE VIGNETTE:

A 65-year-old man who is a chronic heavy smoker for the past 28 years comes to the out-patient department with complaints of fresh blood in his sputum (5-6 episodes) since the past 15 days. He is an office worker, non-tobacco chewer and non- alcoholic. He also complainsof hoarseness of voice and significant weight loss of 15 kilograms over the past 2 months. He gives history of a persistent cough and acute shortness of breath since the past 15 days. This is accompanied by unrelenting, right-sided chest pain which is of a boring character and which severely disturbs his sleep. He also complains of anterior right chest wall tenderness. There is history of progressively increasing breathlessness over the past 6-7 years accompanied by mucoid expectoration. There is no history of fever.

There was no history of hypertension, diabetes mellitus, malignancy or pulmonary tuberculosis in the family.
There was no past history suggestive of occupational exposure to asbestos, toxic fumes or other dusts.

The student is expected to have in his mind some pertinent questions at this stage

Q 1.Based on the history provided , what is the provisional diagnosis?

Q 2. Which systems should you examine to help in firming the diagnosis?

On general physical examination, the patient appeas underweight. His vital parameters (temperature, pulse and blood pressure) are within normal limits. However, he is tachypnoeic with a respiratory rate of 28 breaths per minute. His fingers showed grade III clubbing and the finger nails had nicotine stains. There is no cyanosis, pallor, icterus or oedema of feet. . There are three cervical lymph nodes palpable on the right side, varying in diameter from 1 cm to 3 cm. They arediscrete, hard, non-tender and fixed to the underlying structures. On systemic examination, the trachea is shifted *slightly to the right side.* The chest appears barrel-shaped with significantly reduced chest wall movements on the right side. Tactile vocal fremitus is increased posteriorly in the right interscapular region but is absent in the right inframammary and right infrascapular regions. There is a stony dull note on percussion below the right 3rd interiscostal space anteriorly, and posteriorly in the right infrascapular region. On auscultation, expiration is prolonged over the left side of the chest. There is absent air entry in the right inframammary region anteriorly and in the right infrascapular region posteriorly. Localised rhonchi and tubular bronchial breath sounds are heard in the right interscapular region and vocal resonance is increased in the same area. Vocal resonance is absent in the right inframammary and right infrascapular regions.

Cardiovascular, abdominal and central nervous systems are normal..

Note: The student is expected to be thorough in reporting the respiratory system findings and should report on relevant negative findings in the other systems mentioned.

Note:

In eliciting the history, the student should bear in mind the differential diagnosis mentioned:

Ask for cardinal symptoms of the respiratory system:

- **Cough:** inquire whether cough is dry or productive.
- **Expectoration:** if the cough is productive (expectoration is present), inquire whether it was admixed with blood. If the sputum was blood-tinged, ask whether there was:
- Frank blood or streaks of blood. Bright red blood would be indicative of active bleeding in the tracheobronchial tree while dark red or altered blood is indicative of an earlier bleed. In such a case pulmonary tuberulosis, bronchogenic carcinoma and bacterial pneumonia should be considered as possible aetiological causes.
- **Breathlessness:** to describe whether the breathlessness was progressively worsening. eg. 'initially the patient became breathless on climbing 4-5 flights of steps (Grade I), but the breathlessness had since progressed and now the patient became breathless even on performing his day-to-day household activities (Grade IV).'
- **Chest Pain:** to determine the character of the chest pain, eg. whether it is dull aching, crushing, stabbing or piercing, boring or burning in nature.
    - If the chest pain is persistent, severe and 'boring in character,' disturbing his sleep and accompanied by chest wall tenderness, *malignancy* should be seriously considered. In such cases, the pain is due to the tumour infiltrating the chest wall and mediastinum.
- **Fever:** if fever is present, determine whether it is high-grade or low-grade. A low-grade fever with an evening rise of temperature is indicative of pulmonary tuberculosis, while a high grade fever is indicative of a bacterial infection which may be the primary aetiological factor or which may be secondary to another underlying cause, namely, malignancy. In malignancy, a tumour mass may block a part of the tracheobronchial tree. As a result, the lung parenchyma distal to the blockage may collapse and infection may set in resulting in fever.)
- **Weight Loss:** inquire whether the patient has lost weight. Gradual loss of weight over a longer duration of time is usually suggestive of tuberculosis eg. 5 kg. weight loss over 6

29

months. However, if a large amount of weight is lost in a short duration of time eg. 15 kgs. in 2 months, it is highly suggestive of malignancy.

Past Medical History:

- Past history of smoking if he is an ex-smoker. History of passive smoking (second-hand smoke) should also be elicited. *Smoking is the single-most important cause of lung cancer*
- Chronicity and severity of the present illness: When breathlessness is progressive and there is increased severity and production of cough, loss of weight, loss of appetite, increasing doses of medication and frequent visits to the physician's clinic are required, increased frequency of admissions to the hospital and increased absenteeism from work occurs, it is indicative of a progressive disease process as seen in tuberculosis or malignancy.
- *History of respiratory tract infection in the recent past:* Very commonly, the patient gives a history of being diagnosed with lower respiratory infection a few months prior to the present episode. In such cases if the patient is middle-aged or older and a chronic smoker with the above-mentioned symptoms and signs, *it is imperative to consider malignancy* as a serious differential diagnosis.

Family History:

Enquire about smoking in the family, history of tuberculosis in a family member, neighbour or colleague at work, malignancy in the family, especially breast cancer, lung cancer or gastrointestinal malignancies.

Personal History:

Inquire about bladder, bowel, sleep and dietary habits. A patient with progressively increasing breathlessness will have a significantly reduced appetite and significant sleep disturbances. It is important to remember *that chest pain occurring due to a tumour infiltrating the chest wall and mediastinum is usually very severe and unrelenting, resulting in significant sleep disturbances.*

Social and Occupational History:

Inquire in detail about:

- Smoking habits: number of cigarettes smoked per day and for how many years.
- Tobacco chewing or betel nut chewing
- Drug abuse

- Alcohol intake

Occupational history is relevant to the patient's condition, hence details need to be elicited. If the patient is in a 'high-risk' occupation such as working in a paint industry, rubber factory, plastic factory, tile factory (grinding or chipping departments), ship-building or ship-breaking yards, insulation factory or working with asbestos, then the exact duration and severity of exposure must be determined. Tile-factory workers are at a particular risk of developing silicosis[5] which in turn is known to increase the risk of pulmonary tuberculosis. People working in insulation factories, ship-building and ship-breaking yards may stand the risk of exposure to asbestos which is known to be highly carcinogenic.   *silicon*
asbestos

Surgical History: −sec met.

History of abdominal or breast surgery for suspected malignancy. History of surgical procedures undertaken in the past such as colonoscopy should also be elicited because the chief cause of metastatic lung tumours in males is primary colonic carcinoma while in females it is primary breast carcinoma.

Summarizing the History:

Student should be adept at summarizing the history in 2-3 sentences *highlighting* the *salient clinical features relevant to the case.*

Systemic Review of Symptoms:

- To confirm whether the symptoms are primarily due to an underlying infective process such as pulmonary tuberculosis, bacterial, viral or fungal infection or due to a malignancy such as primary or metastatic lung cancer.
- On systemic review of symptoms it is necessary to rule out other causes such as bronchiectasis, lung abscess, pulmonary embolism or interstitial lung disease.
- To determine whether the primary problem is infective or neoplastic. If infective, to determine the aetiological facotr. If neoplastic, to determine whether it is a primary or metastatic lesion in the lung. If the lesion is metastatic, it is important to determine the location of the primary lesion
- To determine whether the patient had been treated for similar complaints in the past and his response to past medication. This is particularly important in a suspected case of pulmonary tuberculosis as it would help determine the likelihood of drug-resistance.

Check list for History in a suspected case of Pleural Effusion:

- Cough with or without expectoration

- Breathlessness, whether slowly progressive or rapid

- Chest pain, its severity, location and whether it disturbs the patient's sleep

- Whether the patient is coughing out blood, since how long, its quantity and colour.

- Weight loss, whether gradual or rapid

- History of exposure to cigarette smoke (active or passive)

- Occupational history (whether significant or not)

- Medication taken in past, its dosage and response to treatment taken. This is particularly important in suspected cases of multi-drug resistant tuberculosis (MDR-TB) and extremely-drug resistant tuberculosis (XDR-TB)

- Whether patient was compliant to treatment in the past

Bed-side manners:

Student introduces himself/herself to the patient and politely asks permission to examine. Student is polite and courteous throughout the examination and has a gentle and caring demeanour. The patient is thanked at the end of the examination and helped into the position he was in before the examination.

The entire Physical examination should be conducted from the right side of the patient.

General Physical Examination:

- Comment on the general condition of the patient, particularly his weight
- Vital parameters: Temperature, Pulse, Respiratory Rate, Blood Pressure
- Respiratory rate: to observe from the foot-end of the bed on the right side.

Look for:
- respiratory rate

- whether the chest is moving equally on both sides
  - intercostal retraction
  - movement of the subcostal angle
  - whether accessory muscles of respiration are active or not. Particularly important if you are suspecting malignancy
- Jugular Venous Pressure (JVP): may be raised in 'superior vena cava (SVC) obstruction.' Pancoasts tumour is an important cause of SVC obstruction. Comment on the 'waveforms' of the JVP
- Cyanosis: Central and Peripheral
  - Clubbing: If present, mention the grade. In malignancy there may be severe clubbing and even pulmonary hypertrophic osteoarthropathy may occur.
- Oedema of feet: If present, pitting or not, unilateral or on both legs
- Cervical lymphadenopathy: ideally to be palpated from the back with the patients neck slightly flexed. Comment as you examine. In tuberculosis the lymph nodes are usually matted, while in malignancy they are hard, discrete, non-tender and usually adherent to the underlying structures.
- Flaps; if present, suggestive of CO2 retention. This may occur due to severe endobronchial obstruction by a tumour.
- Facial swelling, swelling over the neck, upper arms and trunk (SVC obstruction).
- Headache, dizziness, reddish face and cheeks, shortness of breath, decreased alertness, fainting and visual changes are all signs of SVC obstruction.
- Dupytrens contractures, spider naevi, wasting of small muscles of hands, reddish palms (SVC obstruction), scratch marks
- Pallor, Icterus,
- Examine the nose: look for:
  - deviated nasal septum
  - nasal polyps
  - enlarged nasal turbinates
- Examine the mouth for: oral hygiene
  oral ulcerations
  glossitis, angular
  stomatitis
  injected throat

Systemic Examination of the Respiratory System:

Inspection:

- ❖ Position of the trachea: whether perceived or not. If perceived, comment on its position. In cases of massive pleural effusion if the trachea is not significantly shifted to the opposite side, it is indicative of a large underlying lung collapse on the side of pathology, in addition to the presence of fluid. In this case, while the fluid pushes the mediastinum to the opposite side, the collapse tends to pull it to the same side. As a result there is no significant shift in the trachea. *This is highly indicative of underlying malignancy.* In case of a tuberculous pleural effusion, the mediastinum is usually shifted to the opposite side as there is no significant underlying collapse. This is an important clinical indicator for the discerning physician which helps him suspect an underlying malignancy.

- ❖ Shape of the chest: whether normal (elliptical) or barrel shaped (hyperinflated) especially in smokers.

- ❖ Movement of chest wall: usuallly reduced on the side of pathlogy in case of pleural effusion, intercostal retraction may be present , whether subcostal angle moving well with respiration or not.

- ❖ Respiratory rate: Breaths per minute.

- ❖ Presence of scars, sinuses, seen veins, visible pulsations, apex beat perceived or not.

- ❖ Accessory muscles of respiration: Active or not. They may be active in case of a significanly large pleural effusion.

- ❖ Kyphosis, scoliosis, kyphoscoliosis, spino-scapular distance.

- ❖ Level of shoulder girdles, supraclavicular and infraclavicular fullness and indrawing. In case of tuberculosis with apical scaring, the shoulder girdles would not be at the same level and there may be supraclavicular and infraclavicular 'indrawing.' Conversely, in case of an apical tumour and/or SVC obstruction, there may be significant supraclavicular and infraclavicular 'fullness' on the side of the lesion.

Palpation:

- • Confirm the position of the trachea, mention the cricosternal distance,
- • examine for tracheal tug: main causes include:
  - • aortic arch aneurysm
  - • malignant lymphomas, and
  - • COPD - predominantly emphysema
- • Position of the cardiac apex

- Chest wall movements, anteriorly and posteriorly
- Chest wall tenderness, bony tenderness, sternal tenderness. In lung malignancies, significant chest wall and bony tenderness may be elicited. In such cases, tenderness is indicative of a tumour infiltrating the chest wall and mediastinum.
- Tactile fremitus (symmetrically checked). It is decreased or absent over a pleural effusion but may be increased over a tumour or collapsed lung if there is a patent bronchus underlying it.

Percussion:

- ❖ Apical percussion. May be dull in case of a massive pleural effusion or apical lung fibrosis
- ❖ Direct clavicular percussion
- ❖ Anterior and posterior percussion
- ❖ Determine the liver span using the method of tidal percussion. This is a particularly important method of percussion if right-sided pleural effusion is suspected.
- ❖ **Tidal Percussion:** It is of importance in a suspected case of right-sided pleural effusion. Start percussion from the right 2nd intercostal space in the mid-clavicular line. Percuss downwards till you encounter dullness, usually in the right 5th or 6th intercostal space. When dullness is encountered, while still keeping the finger in the intercostal space, ask the patient to take a deep breath and then hold it, at the depth of inspiration. Percuss again. If the dull note has changed to resonant then ask the patient to exhale and again hold the breath at the depth of expiration. If the resonant note again changes back to a dull note (ie. dull-to-resonant-and-back-to-dull), it implies that it is liver dullness and that the diaphragm is moving well with respiration. However, if on taking a deep inspiration the dull note does not change to a resonant note, it implies that there is a supradiaphragmatic pathology, *most commonly pleural effusion,* other causes being right lower lobe lung collapse, right lower lobe tumour mass or right lower lobe consolidation. In such situations, it is difficult to comment on the 'liver span' as the upper border of liver dullness is not elicitable.

- ❖ Determine the cardiac dullness: whether obliterated or not. In case of a left-sided pleural effusion, cardiac dullness may be obliterated.

Note: To percuss the interscapular region, the hands should be folded over the shoulders so as to get the scapulae out of the way. To percuss in the axillary region the hands should be folded over the head.

Note to the HIGH ACHIEVER:

A Special Percussional Finding:

S-shaped curve of Ellis: [6] In moderate-sized pleural effusions, the upper border of dullness or flatness, which is highest in the axilla and lowest at the spine, tends to assume the shape of the letter 'S.' Hence it is referred to as the S-shaped curve. It is believed to occur due to 'capillary suction.' The possible mechanism suggested is that, in a moderate pleural effusion the lung tends to retract towards the hilum. However, since the part of the lung below the hilum is fixed by the pulmonary ligament, the fluid tends to rise in the axilla, as in this region the lung is more free to collapse.

Auscultation:

Auscultate for:

- Normal vesicular breath sounds
- Bronchial breath sounds. Usually tubular (high-pitched) bronchial breath sounds are heard over a tumour mass, collapsed lung (if a patent bronchus is present below it) or a consolidation

- Rhonchi,rales and pleural rub

- Other adventitious breath sounds such as Bronchophony, Aegophony and Whispering Pectoriloquy

Relevant Cardiovasular System Examination:

Relevant to the above case, look for:

- ❖ Evidence of co-existent pericardial effusion. A common cause is tuberculosis which may be associated with a tuberculous pleural effusion
- ❖ Deviated cardiac apex (in case of pleural effusion the cardiac apex may be shifted to the opposite side or may not be palpable).
- ❖ *Note:* if a moderately large (occupying > 25-50% of the hemithorax) or massive pleural effusion is suspected to be present and in spite of this, the heart does not appear to be shifted to the side opposite to the effusion, it implies that there is possibly a massive collapse underlying the effusion which is 'pulling' the mediastinal structures (heart) to the same side as the effusion. The commonest cause in such cases is usually an

underlying malignancy. In such instances, an underlying tumour obstructing a bronchus results in a collapse of the lung distal to the site of obstruction.

❖ Obliteration of cardiac dullness due to a left pleural effusion

Relevant abdominal examination:

❖ Palpate for the liver: look for a palpable, mildly tender liver with positive hepatojugular reflux

❖ An enlarged liver with rock-hard or nodular consistency is suggestive of hepatic neoplasm.

❖ Liver dullness is obliterated in case of a massive right-sided pleural effusion. In such cases, it is difficult to comment on the liver span as the upper border of the liver may not be detectable on percussion. In order to determine this, 'Tidal Percussion' needs to be resorted to (see above).

To summarise:

The patient was an elderly man who is a chronic heavy smoker. He comes with complaints of blood in his sputum, cough, persistent chest pain(which also disturbed his sleep), hoarseness of voice and significant weight loss which occurred in a short duration of time. There iss no history of fever orf contact with a tuberculosis patient. On examination, a right-sided pleural effusion is suspected. However, the trachea and lower mediastinum (heart) are shifted to the same side as the effusion (right side). Cervical lymph nodes are palpable which are discrete, hard and non-tender.

QUESTION:

Taking into consideration the above clinical symptoms and signs what would be the differential diagnosis?

Does this list differ from that first mentioned after history- taking?

Differential Diagnoses :

1) Malignant Pleural Effusion

2) Tuberculous Pleural Effusion

3) Bacterial Pleural Effusion

4) Pleural Effusion due to Pulmonary Embolism

5) Pleural Effusion due to Cardiac Failure (Left Ventricular Failure)

6) Other less likely causes: Hypothyroidism, Drug-induced, Nephrotic Syndrome, Cirrhosis of Liver and Pancreatitis

Note: At this stage a Provisional Diagnosis should be elicited so that the student is ready to suggest RELEVANT INVESTIGATIONS. One must consider that the investigations listed below are for both diagnosis and management.

Investigations:

Non-invasive Investigative Procedures:

- *Chest Radiography-*Postero-anterior (PA) and lateral views: helps to determine the extent of the pleural effusion and may also help in detecting an underlying lung collapse.
- *NOTE: This is readily done in most centres and provides the student with enormous amount of information. Expertise must be shown in interpreting chest radiographs*

- *Arterial Blood Gas investigations (ABG):* helps to determine the pH of the blood, extent of hypoxia and CO_2 retention or washout.

- *Electrocardiogram (ECG):* It is essential in suspected cases of breathlessness of cardiac origin. However, it is advisable to have an ECG done for every patient with breathlessness. ECG changes are also seen in cases of breathlessness of non-cardiac origin such as pulmonary embolism (S1,Q3,T3 pattern).

- *Full Blood Count:* It is raised in case of bacterial infections where there is a neutrophilic leucocytosis. In case of pulmonary tuberculosis, the differential cell count may show predominant lymphocytosis.

  Note: It should be remembered that *the presenting feature of a Bronchogenic Carcinoma* is frequently an infection.

- *Erythrocyte Sedimentation Rate (ESR):* In case of active pulmonary tuberculosis the ESR is usually between 80-100 mm at the end of one hour. However, if the ESR is above 100 mm/ 1 hour, malignancy should be suspected. In case of Hodgkin's lymphoma, gastric carcinoma, breast carcinoma, renal cell carcinoma and colorectal cancer an ESR >100 mm per hour is indicative of metastatic disease.

- *Sputum Examination:* Sputum should be   examined for:
    - *Acid-Fast Bacilli (AFB)-smear and culture:* Preferably six early-morning sputum samples should be collected on consecutive days and tested.

    - *TB-PCR qualitative test:* this is a rapid test which helps to detect the presence of *live* acid-fast bacilli within 48 hours.

    - *Malignant cells (cytology):* early-morning sputum samples collected on four consecutive days should be tested for malignant cells.

    - *Bacterial smear and culture:* should be tested for gram-positive, gram-negative and anaerobic organisms.

    - *Fungal culture:*sSputum should be tested for spores and hyphae of *Aspergillus Spp.* which is a common cause of respiratory tract infection.

    - *Ultrasonography of the chest:* usually done to detect very small (<25 ml) pleural effusions which are not seen on conventional chest radiographs. It is also useful in diagnosing suspected *loculated* pleural efusions.

- *High-resolution Computed Tomography (HRCT) chest scan:* It is useful in diagnosing:

    - ❖ Suspected malignancies.
    - ❖ Lung cavities especially in the upper zones
    - ❖ A fungal ball (aspergilloma) in a tuberculous cavity
    - ❖ Bronchiectasis, when the plain chest radiograph is normal.
    - ❖ ILD: May show the typical ground-glass appearance of early involvement, reticulo-nodular patterning or honey combing

Invasive Investigative Procedures:

These include:

> *Pleural Aspiration and Pleural Biopsy:* Initially a *diagnostic* pleural tap may be undertaken to obtain fluid for examination.
>
> The pleural fluid once tapped should be sent for the following laboratory investigations:
>
> ✓ AFB smear and culture
> ✓ Bacterial culture and antibiotic sensitivity
> ✓ Examination for Malignant cells (cytological examination)
> ✓ Fungal culture
> ✓
>
> A pleural biopsy is a rather specific procedure which is usually reserved for the diagnosis of conditions such as tuberculosis or malignant disease, particularly malignant mesothelioma.[7] Connective tissue disorders such as rheumatoid disease may also have pleural involvement, requiring pleural biopsy to confirm the diagnosis.

> *Transthoracic percutaneous needle biopsy:* This procedure is usually undertaken under CT-guidance in patients with a peripherally located tumour mass.

> *Fibreoptic/Video Bronchoscopy:* In case of a centrally located tumour mass and/or an accompanying underlying lung collapse, a fibreoptic/video bronchoscopy must be carried out to determine the location and extent of tumour infiltration into the tracheobronchial tree.

> *Excision biopsy of palpable cervical and/or axillary lymph nodes:* In patients with palpable lymph nodes an excision biopsy is recommended in order to establish a definitive diagnosis.

Note: The student should have written a management plan as this often follows investigations and diagnosis especially in a long case examination

Management:

Note: The discussion below is largely on pleural effusion. The student should be reminded that this would form only part of the examination in a long case

I) Management of a pleural effusion depends on the *quantity of fluid* present in the pleural cavity and *the rapidity with which it refills* in the pleural space.

a) If there is a small quantity of fluid in the pleural cavity (occupying <25% of the hemithorax), it may be easily aspirated.

b) If the quantity exceeds 1500-2000 ml, the fluid may still be aspirated, though care should be taken that not all fluid is aspirated at one sitting, to prevent re-expansion pulmonary oedema.[8]

c) If a large amount of fluid is present in the pleural cavity (occupying >50-75% of the hemithorax), it may be preferable to drain the fluid rather than undertake repeated aspirations.

d) If the pleural fluid rapidly refills after aspiration, it may become necessary to perform a *Chemical Pleurodesis.*

II) Treatment of the underlying condition:

If the pleural efusion is due to tuberculosis, anti-tuberculous treatment must be instituted at the earliest.

If the patient has a *malignant pleural effusion,* palliative treatment with chemotherapy and radiotherapy needs to be considered. In case of severe pain, pain management forms an important part of palliative treatment in these patients.

Complications of a Pleural Effusion:

- ❖ If the fluid is not adequately removed, it will eventually organize, leading to pleural thickening and fibrosis.
- ❖ This can eventually lead to contraction of one hemithorax and consequent restrictive lung impairment.
- ❖ A rapidly increasing pleural effusion may cause severe breathlessness due to collapse of the underlying lung caused by the enlarging fluid.
- ❖ Malignant pleural effusions are commonly haemorrhagic. This can result in a significant loss of blood into the pleural cavity.
- ❖ The effusion if long standing, may get secondarily infected leading to the formation of an *Empyema.*

❖ A pleural effusion may itself be the result of an underlying complication such as a ruptured lung abscess, bronchiectasis, trauma, pulmonary embolism, oesophageal perforation, hypothyroidism or nephrotic syndrome. In such cases, the underlying cause must be promptly detected and treatment instituted accordingly.

Learning Outcomes:

- Able to define 'Pleural Effusion,' and identify the various potential causes.

- Able to 'suspect' the underlying cause of the pleural effusion based on quantity, colour and consistency of the fluid *(physical attributes of the fluid).*

- Be well-versed with the investigations that need to be done in order to arrive at a diagnosis regarding
- the cause of the pleural effusion.

- Know how to manage the patient on admission to the hospital.

- Know the modalities of long-term management especially in cases of malignant and tuberculous pleural effusions.

- Understand the potential complications of a long-standing, infected or recurrent pleural effusion.

- Understand the measures to be undertaken to improve the quality of life in case of malignant pleural effusion.

NOTE: The relevant areas of the case that the student should know are discussed:

The above clinical presentation of a gentleman who had a *malignant pleural effusion*, warrants long-term treatment plans and a multidisciplinary approach.

The treatment essentially includes reducing the volume of fluid in the pleural cavity and preventing its recurrence.

The fluid can be aspirated or drained. If it rapidly reforms, as is common with malignant pleural effusions, other treatment options may be considered such as chemical pleurodesis.

Other treatment options that need to be considered are palliative chemotherapy and/or radiotherapy.

Note: Chest radiographs are frequently produced at examinations. Have a good knowledge of the radiological features of a Pleural Effusion:

❖ If a very small amount of effusion accumulates in a subpulmonic location, it causes a slight elevation of the hemidiaphragm.

❖ Sometimes a very small pleural effusion (10-25 ml) may only be detectable on a *lateral decubitus view.* The fluid is detected as a dependent, linear and sharply defined opacity.

❖ Fluid accumulating posteriorly is seen in the lateral view first before becoming visible on the postero-anterior (PA) view.

❖ When the fluid is slightly more (150-175 ml), *blunting of the costophrenic angle* is seen. This is the earliest sign of a pleural effusion on a PA-view.

❖ Presence of a moderately large pleural effusion appears as an opacity with lateral upward sloping of a *meniscus-shaped contour.*

❖ If the mediastinal shift (as represented by the trachea and cardiac shadow) is less prominent or even absent, an underlying pulmonary pathology such as a collapse must be considered. This is particularly observed in cases of *malignant* pleural effusions.

❖ A *subpulmonary effusion* is more common on the right side. On PA-view, it presents as an elevated diaphragm (pseudodiaphragmatic contour). It is due to fluid accumulating in a subpulmonary location.

Ethical issues include:

In case the above patient decides to discontinue all forms of treatment due to a sense of hopelessness, it is essential for the doctor (in the capacity of the primary health-giver) to explain to the patient the potential disadvantages of such a decision.

Treating the effusion as and when it recurs would reduce the breathlessness, and palliative chemotherapy and/or radiotherapy may also help to reduce the mass of the tumour-burden, thereby reducing pain, breathlessnes (endobronchial obstruction) and improving the quality of life.

References:

1) Diaz-Guzman E, Dweik RA. Diagnosis and management of pleural effusions: a practical approach. *Compr Ther*. Winter 2007; 33(4):237-46.

2) Light RW. Pleural diseases. Third edition. Baltimore, MD: Williams and Wilkins; 1995.

3) Miserocchi G. Physiology and pathophysiology of pleural fluid turnover. Eur Respir J 1997; 10(1): 219-225.

4) Light RW. Pleural Effusion. N Engl J Med 2002; 346 (25): 1971-1977.

5) Khajotia R, Das Gupta E. A tile-factory worker presenting with breathlessness and dry cough. Australian Family Physician 2009; 38 (10): 803-804.

6) Vakil RJ, Golwalla AF. Physical Diagnosis. A textbook of Symptoms and Physical Signs. Media Promoters and Publishers Pvt. Ltd. Bombay; 1980.

7) Prakash UB, Reiman HM. Comparison of needle biopsy with cytologic analysis for the evaluation of pleural effusion: analysis of 414 cases. *Mayo Clin Proc*. Mar 1985;60(3):158-64.

8) Sivrikoz MC, Tunçozgur B, Cekman M et al: The role of tissue reperfusion in the reexpansion injury of the lungs. Euro J Cardiothorac Surg 2002;22:721-7.

CASE 2: CHRONIC OBSTRUCTIVE PULMONARY DISEASE (COPD)
RUMI R KHAJOTIA

OVERVIEW:

The Global initiative for Chronic Obstructive Pulmonary Disease (GOLD) defines COPD as a disease state characterized by airflow limitation that is not fully reversible, usually progressive, and associated with an abnormal inflammatory response of the lungs to inhaled noxious particles or gases.[1]

COPD essentially consists of two groups of patients, one of which predominantly shows symptoms and signs suggestive of chronic bronchitis while the other shows predominant emphysematous changes.

Chronic bronchitis is clinically defined as cough with expectoration for 3 months of a year for two consecutive years, wherein other conditions have been excluded. Emphysema is pathologically defined as abnormal, permanent dilatation of the airways distal to the terminal bronchioles with destruction of their walls.

CASE VIGNETTE:

A 60-year-old man presents to the accident and emergency department with complaints of progressively increasing breathlessness accompanied by cough and fever for a week. He is a chronic smoker ,smoking 40 cigarettes a day for the past 40 years. There is no history of paroxsysmal breathlessness in childhood.

On examination, the patient appears drowsy and cyanosed with a respiratory rate of 18 breaths per minute. His pulse is 94 beats per minute and bounding. Flaps are noted. On auscultation, prolonged expiration is heard bilaterally over both lungs with scattered rhonchi. Fine early inspiratory crepitations are heard over both lung bases. A loud pulmonary second sound (P2) is heard in the pulmonary area. Pulmonary function testing done one month ago shows moderate obstructive impairment.

HISTORY OF PRESENTING ILLNESS:

To include the cardinal symptoms of the Respiratory System, namely:

Cough: Inquire whether cough is dry or productive.

Expectoration: If the cough is productive (expectoration is present), ask about the

- ✓ **Quantity:** Slight, 5-10 ml, half-a-cupful, one-cupful, etc.

- ✓ **Colour:** Whether it is whitish, greenish, yellowish or blackish in colour.

- ✓ **Consistency:** Whether it is mucoid, watery, thick or viscid in consistency.

- ✓ **Odour:** Odourless or foul smelling (indicative of anaerobic infection)

- ✓ **Blood tinged:** Frank blood or streaks of blood.

  Bright red blood is indicative of active bleeding while dark red or altered blood is indicative of having bled earlier on.

Breathlessness: To *describe* the grade of breathlessness eg. breathlessness on climbing 4-5 flights of steps (heavy exertion) is indicative of Grade I breathlessness, breathlessness on doing day-to-day household activities is indicative of Grade IV breathlessness, while breathlessness at rest is Grade V. To determine whether the patient has orthopnoea, paroxsysmal nocturnal dyspnoea which could indicate cor pulmonale with biventricular failure.

Chest Pain: **In an acute exacerbation of COPD,** to determine whether the chest pain is cardiac, respiratory, musculoskeletal or gastrointestinal in origin.

Fever: Would be indicative of an upper or lower respiratory tract infection and consequently the likely underlying triggering factor for the acute exacerbation.

Weight Loss: Inquire whether the patient has lost weight. Loss of weight in a COPD is considered a poor prognostic sign. Also, if there is a large amount of weight lost in a short duration of time eg. 15 kgs. in 2 months, underlying malignancy must be ruled out. Co-existent tuberculosis would usually result in a more gradual weight loss.

PAST MEDICAL HISTORY:

Past history of paroxsysmal breathlessness, cough with or without expectoration. Past history of smoking if he is an ex-smoker. History of passive smoking (second-hand smoke) should also be elicited.

History of wheezing in the past, whether he has taken any medication from a family physician or a specialist for it.

Chronicity and severity of the present illness: Whether the breathlessness is progressive, increased severity of cough, loss of weight, loss of appetite, increasing doses of medication required including nebulisation at home, increasing visits to the physician's clinic, increased frequency of admissions to the hospital and increased absenteeism from work.

History of respiratory tract infection in the recent past as a precipitating cause of the exacerbation.

FAMILY HISTORY:

History of similar illness in the family (suggestive of alpha-1 antitrypsin deficiency). History of smoking in the family.

PERSONAL HISTORY:

Inquire about bladder, bowel, sleep and dietary habits. A patient with progressively increasing breathlessness will have a reduced appetite and significant sleep disturbances.

SOCIAL HISTORY:

- Smoking habits: number of cigarettes smoked per day and for how many years.

- Tobacco chewing or betel nut chewing

- Drug abuse

- Alcohol intake

OCCUPATIONAL HISTORY:

It is important to enquire whether the patients occupation contributes adversely to the progression and exacerbation of his respiratory problem. If the patient is in a 'high-risk' occupation such as working in a paint industry, rubber factory, plastic factory, ship-building or ship-breaking yards, insulation factory, working with animals, or exposed to wood dusts or asbestos, then the exact duration and severity of exposure must be determined.

For example: "The patient works in a factory and is exposed to welding fumes for 8 hours a day, 6 days a week, for the past 20 years."

SURGICAL HISTORY:

Chronic cough can lead to abdominal and inguinal hernias for which the patient may have been treated. An acute exacerbation may have caused a pneumothorax in the past for which an intercostal drain (ICD) tube may have been inserted into the peural cavity.

SUMMARIZING THE HISTORY:

Student should be adept at summarizing the history in 2-3 sentences *highlighting* the *salient clinical features relevant to the case.*

SYSTEMIC REVIEW OF SYMPTOMS:

- To confirm that cough and expectoration is primarily due to underlying chronic bronchitis and not due to other causes such as pneumonia, tuberculosis, bronchiectasis, lung abscess or interstitial lung disease.

- To determine whether the patient has predominant chronic bronchitis or emphysema.

- To determine whether there is a likelihood of co-existing morbidities such as, bronchogenic carcinoma, interstitial lung disease, left ventricular failure, ischaemic heart disease.

  To determine his response to past medication and whether the symptoms subside following treatment, ie. to determine whether the patient has been responsive to past treatment or not.

✓ CHECK LIST FOR HISTORY IN COPD:

- Cough with expectoration for 3 months of a year for 2 consecutive years

- History of exposure to cigarette smoke (active or passive)

- Occupational history (whether significant or not)

- Presence of co-morbidities such as Ischaemic Heart Disease, Lung Cancer, Tuberculosis

- Medication taken in past, dosage and response to treatment

- Whether patient is compliant to treatment

BED-SIDE MANNERS:

Student introduces himself/herself to the patient and politely asks permission to examine. Student is polite and courteous throughout the examination and has a gentle and caring demeanour.

The patient is thanked at the end of the examination and helped into the position he was in before the examination.

Note: The entire Physical examination should be conducted from the right side of the patient.

GENERAL PHYSICAL EXAMINATION:

- Comment on the general condition of the patient
- Vital parameters: Temperature, Pulse, Respiratory Rate, Blood Pressure
- Respiratory rate: To observe from the foot-end of the bed on the right side.
- Look for: respiratory rate, whether the chest is moving equally on both sides, intercostal retraction, movement of the subcostal angle, whether accessory muscles of respiration are active or not
- Jugular Venous Pressure (JVP): raised in 'cor pulmonale.' Comment on the 'waveforms' of the JVP
- Cyanosis: Central and Peripheral
- Clubbing: If present, mention the grade
- Oedema of feet: If present, pitting or not, unilateral or on both legs
- Cervical lymphadenopathy: ideally to be palpated from the back with the patients neck slightly flexed. Comment as you examine
- Flaps; if present, suggestive of CO_2 retention in a COPD
- Tremors: if present, could be due to long-term use of salbutamol
- Dupytrens contractures, spider naevi, wasting of small muscles of hands, palmer erythema, scratch marks
- Pallor, Icterus,
- Examine the nose: look for:
  - deviated nasal septum
  - nasal polyps
  - enlarged nasal turbinates
- Examine the mouth for: Oral hygiene, oral ulcerations, glossitis, angular stomatitis, injected throat

SYSTEMIC EXAMINATION OF THE RESPIRATORY SYSTEM:

Inspection:

- ❖ Position of the trachea: whether perceived or not. If perceived, comment on its position
- ❖ Shape of the chest: whether normal (elliptical) or barrel shaped (hyperinflated)
- ❖ Movement of chest wall: equal on both sides or not, intercostal retraction present or not, subcostal angle moving well with respiration or not.
- ❖ Respiratory rate: Breaths per minute
- ❖ Presence of scars, sinuses, seen veins, visible pulsations, apex beat perceived or not
- ❖ Accessory muscles of respiration: Active or not
- ❖ Kyphosis, scoliosis, kyphoscoliosis, spino-scapular distance.
- ❖ Level of shoulder girdles, supraclavicular and infraclavieular fullness and indrawing

Palpation:

- ❖ Confirm the position of the trachea, mention the cricosternal distance,
- ❖ Examine for tracheal tug: main causes include:
- ❖ Aortic arch aneurysm
- ❖ Malignant lymphomas, and
- ❖ COPD - predominantly emphysema
- ❖ Position of the cardiac apex
- ❖ Chest wall movements, anteriorly and posteriorly
- ❖ Chest wall tenderness, bony tenderness, sternal tenderness
- ❖ Tactile fremitus (symmetrically)

Percussion:

- ❖ Apical percussion
- ❖ Direct clavicular percussion
- ❖ Anterior and posterior percussion
- ❖ Determine the liver span
- ❖ Determine the cardiac dullness: whether obliterated or not

☞ *Note: To percuss the interscapular region, the hands should be folded over the shoulders so as to get the scapulae out of the way. To percuss in the axillary region the hands should be folded over the head.*

Auscultation:

Auscultate for: the normal vesicular breath Sounds, Bronchial breath sounds, Rhonchi, Rales and Pleural Rub other adventitious breath sounds such as Bronchophony, Aegophony and Whispering Pectoriloquy

Relevant cardiovasular system examination:

Relevant to a case of COPD, look for:

❖ A loud P2 in the pulmonary space suggestive of pulmonary hypertension
❖ Gallop rhythm
❖ Murmurs (pan systolic murmur of tricuspid regurgitation)
❖ Parasternal heave (suggestive of right ventricular hypertrophy)
❖ Deviated cardiac apex (in case of RVH the cardiac apex is deviated upwards and outwards)
❖ Obliteration of cardiac dullness due to hyperinflation

Relevant abdominal examination:

❖ Liver dullness is pushed downwards in case of hyperinflation (emphysema)
❖ Palpate for the liver: look for a palpable, mildly tender liver with hepatojugular reflux

INVESTIGATIONS:

❖ *Chest radiograph:* to look for hyperinflation, consolidation, pneumothorax, cardiac size, signs of pulmonary oedema (parenchymal and interstitial)
❖ *Arterial Blood Gase Analysis:* To look for hypoxia, CO2 retention, CO2 washout, metabolic acidosis
❖ *Electrocardiogram:* Look for right axis deviation, 'p' pulmonale, right ventricular hypertrophy, right bundle branch block (complete or incomplete)
❖ *Full blood count:* to detect infection
❖ *Sputum examination:* sample should be sent for AFB smear and culture, bacterial culture and sensitivity, fungal culture and malignant cells (cytology)
❖ *Spirometry:* to determine presence and severity of obstructive impairmeent(reduced FEV1 and FEV1/FVC ratio) and evidence of air trapping (increased RV and the RV/TLC ratio, in emphysema)
❖ *HRCT chest scan:* Occasionally done to determine severity of emphysema and parenchymal lung destruction
❖ *Diffusion studies:* May be impaired in severe emphysema

- ❖ **_Random blood sugar levels:_** to <u>rule out</u> underlying hypoglycemia due to irregular oral intake
- ❖ **_Electrolyte abnormalities,_** such as :
- ❖ <u>Water retention</u> and <u>Hyponatremia</u> in(advanced cases of COPD)
- ❖ <u>Hypokalemia</u> may be present if the patient is on diuretics or certain antihypertensive agents
- ❖ Raised <u>Bicarbonate</u> levels due to chronic carbon dioxide retention (chronic hypercapnia)

CLINICAL CASE DISCUSSION

This patient presents with clinical symptoms suggestive of an acute exacerbation of COPD with signs of CO_2 retention. He appears to be predominantly a case of 'Chronic Bronchitis.' On admission, it is essential that his chest radiograph, arterial blood gas analysis (ABG) and electrocardiogram (ECG) be urgently done. The ABG will likely show 'Hypoxia with Respiratory Acidosis.' His chest radiograph may show evidence of infection and the ECG may show changes of 'cor pulmonale.'

It is essential to determine whether the patient is in respiratory fatigue, distress and impending respiratory failure, so that the further plan of management can be determined accordingly:

Plan of Acute Management:

- ❖ Hospitalise the patient as there is evidence of CO_2 retention

- ❖ Start the patient on '<u>controlled oxygen</u> therapy.' This may be achieved with nasal prongs or a face mask.

- ❖ Intravenous Hydrocortisone

- ❖ Intravenous Aminophylline

- ❖ <u>Intravenous Antibiotics</u>

- ❖ Nebulisation with <u>Beta-2 a</u>gonists alternating with Steroids

- ❖ Nebulisation with <u>sodium bicarbonate</u> nebulising solution (diluted with distilled water), in order to liquefy tracheobronchial secretions

- ❖ Strictly 'No Sedation,' while patient is not on ventilator

If patient fails to respond to above management:

- ❖ To consider non-invasive ventilatory management using either

CPAP or BiPAP

❖ To consider invasive ventilatory management using volume-cycled ventilators.

Home Management:

Long Term Oxygen Therapy (LTOT):

❖ It is known to help slow the progression of the disease

❖ Slow the progression and development of cor pulmonale and pulmonary hypertension

❖ Reduces breathlessness and improves quality of life, reduces depression, improves exercise tolerance

Note: A minimum duration of 15 hours a day of LTOT is required to render a beneficial effect.[2]

❖ Oral theophylline

❖ Beta-2 agonists (terbutaline or salbutamol), administered orally or via. metered-dose inhalers

❖ Steroids: orally or via. metered dose inhaler

❖ In severe cases, nebulisation with beta-2 agonists alternating with steroids

❖ Steam inhalation to clear airways of impacted secretions

❖ Pulmonary rehabilitation

Note: In long-term management, terbutaline is preferred over salbutamol, as salbutamol causes palpitations and tremors, which can be quite discomforting for the patient.

LEARNING OUTCOMES

By the end of this case review the student should be:

1. Able to define COPD and its subsets viz., Chronic Bronchitis and Emphysema
2. Able to distinguish between a 'Blue Bloater' and a 'Pink Puffer'
3. Know the main investigations that need to be done and their interpretation
4. Know clearly the modalities of acute management
5. Able to explain to the patient the long-term management required in these cases
6. Understand the potential complications of this condition and how to manage them

THE RELEVANT AREAS OF THE CASE THAT THE STUDENT SHOULD KNOW ARE DISCUSSED:

The above clinical presentation of a gentleman, who had an established diagnosis of COPD, warrants long-term treatment plans and a multidisciplinary approach called pulmonary rehabilitation.
Early institution of pulmonary rehabilitation is very essential and ideal, but may not be achievable in all patients of COPD.

Our patient needs further evaluation at later date and three specific therapy strategies to be applied in his management include:

1. Smoking cessation [nicotine supplement, Varnecline and Bupropion if no contraindications]
2. Home oxygen therapy [if Spo2 less than 88% and Pao2 less than 55mmHg during reassessment after recovery]

3. Pulmonary rehabilitation

Remember, COPD is second only to heart disease as a cause of disability that forces people to stop working.
ETHICAL ISSUES INCLUDE:

1) Whether oxgen therapy should be recommended to a patient who refuses to stop smoking since oxygen is highly inflammable, and hence there is a real risk to life and property in such a situation.

2) Ethical issues involved in stopping ventilatory management (on request of close relatives), in a COPD who is on invasive ventilation.

MUST KNOW FACTS ABOUT COPD:

Subsets of COPD:

Chronic Bronchitis	Emphysema
Also known as 'Blue Bloater'	Also known as "Pink Puffer"
Radiological signs of hyperinflation absent	Radiological signs of hyperinflation present such as hyperluscent lung fields, low, flat diaphragms, 'tear-drop' heart, widened intercostal spaces, straightening of the ribs and absence of bronchovascular lung markings towards the periphery of the lung fields
	Patient is usually 'tall and thin'
Patient has the typical 'Pickwickian' body habitus	
	Usually alert
May be drowsy	
	Usually very breathless and tachypnoeic
Does not appear to be breathless or tachypnoeic	
	Usually pink in appearance
Dusky or cyanosed	
	Usually there is CO_2 washout
ABG shows CO_2 retention	

Important Note:

Type II Respiratory Failure:

It occurs in patients having predominant 'Chronic Bronchitis' and is characterised by the following:

- ✓ Drowsiness or unconsciousness
- ✓ Cyanosis (central and peripheral) or a dusky appearance
- ✓ ABG showing CO_2 retention
- ✓ CO_2 retention clinically presents with headache, drowsiness, warm hands, bounding pulse, flaps, conjuctival oedema, papilloedema

An ABG picture in a case of Type II Respiratory Failure:

Parameters	Patients values	Normal values
pH	↓ 7.280	7.35-7.45
PaO2	↓ 55 mm Hg	80-100 mmHg
PaCO2	↑ 60 mm Hg	35-45 mmHg
HCO3	↑ 32 mmol/l	22-26 mmol/l
Sat (SaO2) %	↓ 88%	95%-100%
Base excess (BE)	↑ +7	+/-. 2

Interpretation of the above ABG:

"Moderate Hypoxia with chronic respiratory acidosis."This ABG picture could be classically seen in a chronic bronchitic patient.

✓ **CHECK LIST FOR FINDINGS IN COPD**

Exposure to cigarette smoke

Chronic cough with expectoration

Progressively increasing breathlessness

Fever suggestive of an underlying respiratory tract infection

Gradually increasing weight loss

Hyperinflated chest

Prolonged expiratory phase

Scattered rhonchi heard bilaterally

Fine early inspiratory crepitations at both lung bases

In Emphysema, radiological signs of hyperinflation

Differential Diagnosis of an "Acute Exacerbation of COPD"

In the D/D the following should be considered:

- ❖ Acute Exacerbation of Bronchial Asthma
- ❖ Congestive Cardiac Failure
- ❖ Pulmonary Embolism
- ❖ Pneumothorax
- ❖ Acute Coronary Syndrome (ACS)
- ❖ Pneumonia (Lobar Consolidation)
- ❖ Lobar Atelectasis
- ❖ Obliterative Bronchiolitis
- ❖ Diffuse Panbronchiolitis

It is not possible to 'cure' a patient of his /her COPD but it is to some extent preventible (stopping cigarette smoking).

Management involves reducing the progression of the disease process and improving the quality of life

Chronic Bronchitis is treated with 'controlled oxygen therapy' as, in these patients there is chronic CO_2 retention which consequently blunts the hypercapnic stimulus in the respiratory center. As a result, the only drive available is the hypoxic drive which could get blunted if high-flow oxygen is administered to the patient. Therefore, in chronic bronchitis, *'controlled-oxygen' therapy* is essential.

LTOT requires that the patient completely ceases to smoke and his family members too should not smoke in the presence of the patient as oxygen is highly inflammable.

Invasive ventilatory management is resorted to only in severe unrelenting cases of COPD as it is very difficult to 'wean' a COPD off the ventilator.

While on the ventilator, if the patient is non-compliant and restless, the patient may be sedated in order that he does not injure himself, especially since he is either intubated or has a tracheostomy in place which could damage the trachea if the patient 'fights' the ventilator.

COMPLICATIONS OF COPD:

- ❖ Respiratory fatigue leading to consequent respiratory failure and CO_2 retention
- ❖ Cor pulmonale with pulmonary hypertension
- ❖ Left ventricular failure
- ❖ Bullae formation (in emphysematous patients)
- ❖ Occurrence of pneumothorax

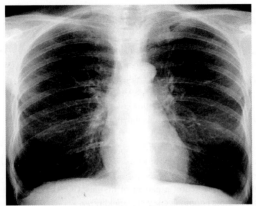
Fig. 1: Chest Radiograph of COPD

Chest radiograph of a patient with predominant emphysema showing hyperluscent lung fields, low, flat diaphragms, 'tear-drop' heart, widened intercostal spaces, straightening of the ribs and absence of bronchovascular lung markings towards the periphery of the lung fields

REFERENCES:

1) GOLD - The Global Initiative for Chronic Obstructive Lung Disease. Available at http://www.goldcopd.com/.

2) Katsenos S, Constantopoulos SH. Long-Term Oxygen Therapy in COPD: Factors Affecting and Ways of Improving Patient Compliance. Pulmonary Medicine Volume 2011 (2011), Article ID 325362, 8 pages doi:10.1155/2011/325362

Hyperinflated sign. < ant rib
                      post rib.
- hyperlucent lung field
- ↑ intercostal space
- straitening of the rib
- tear drop heart
- ↓ bronchopulmon. vascular marking towards the periphery
- flat diaphragm

Bronchogenic Carcinoma is a clinical case often used in clinical examinations to assess history-taking, physical examination and assessing the students knowledge of its pathogenesis, clinical management and relevant procedural skills.

DEFINITION:

Bronchogenic Carcinoma is is defined as malignancy of the lung arising from the epithelium of the bronchial tree and its prevalence is second only to that of prostate cancer in men and breast cancer in women.

Bronchogenic carcinomas (also known as lung cancer), are broadly classified into two types: small cell lung cancers (SCLC) and non-small cell lung cancers (NSCLC). This classification is based upon the microscopic appearance of the tumor cells.

SCLC constitutes approximately 20% of lung cancers and is the most rapid growing of all lung cancers. SCLC has a strong correlation with cigarette smoking, exceptionally 1% occurrs in non-smokers. Small cell lung cancers metastasize rapidly to various organs within the body, the most common sites being the liver, brain, bones, gastrointestinal tract and the adrenal glands.

NSCLC is the commonest lung cancer, accounting for aproximately 85% of all lung cancers. NSCLC can be divided into three main types, namely, adenocarcinoma, squamous cell carcinoma (SCC), and large cell carcinoma.

Adenocarcinoma arises from the bronchial mucosal glands and is the most frequent non-small cell lung cancer accountable for 50% of NSCLC and 35-40% of all lung cancers. While adenocarcinomas are seen in smokers, this is the subtype most commonly seen in non-smokers. Most adenocarcinomas arise in the outer, or peripheral, areas of the lungs.

Broncholoalveolar carcinoma is a subtype of adenocarcinoma that arises from type II pneumocytes and grows along alveolar septa. This subtype may manifest as a solitary peripheral nodule or in a rapidly progressing pneumonic form. A characteristic finding in patients with advanced bronchoalveolar carcinoma is voluminous watery sputum.

Squamous cell carcinomas were previously more common than adenocarcinomas; currently, they account for about 30% of NSCLC and 25-30% of all lung cancers. Also known as epidermoid carcinomas, squamous cell carcinomas are more centrally located and may present as a cavitary lesion. SCC is characterized histologically by the presence of keratin pearls and has a tendency to exfoliate.

Large cell carcinomas, sometimes referred to as undifferentiated carcinomas, are the least common type of NSCLC. They account for 10-15% of all lung cancers. Large cell carcinoma typically manifests as a large peripheral mass on the chest radiograph and histologically shows sheets of highly atypical cells with focal necrosis, with no evidence of keratinization (typical of SCC) or gland formation (typical of adenocarcinomas).

Mixed histological types of the various forms of NSCLC are also seen.

SCLC is divided into pure small cell, mixed small cell, and combined small cell lung carcinoma. SCLC is more rapidly spreading than NSCLC and usually presents as a central lesion with hilar and mediastinal invasion along with regional adenopathy. Usually patients have evidence of metastasis at the time they first present with the disease, the most common sites of metastasis being the brain, bones, liver, adrenal glands, and spinal cord.[1]

Other types of cancers can arise in the lung; these types are much less common than NSCLC and SCLC and together comprise only 5%-10% of lung cancers:

Bronchial carcinoids account for up to 5% of lung cancers. These tumors are generally small and occur most commonly in people under 40 years of age. Carcinoid tumours generally grow slower than bronchogenic carcinomas, but can metastasize. Because of their slow growth, many are resectable at initial diagnosis.

Cancers of supporting lung tissue such as smooth muscles and blood vessels can also rarely occur in the lungs.

Metastatic cancers from other primary sites in the body are often found in the lung. They usually spread to the lungs via the bloodstream, through the lymphatic system, or by direct spread from nearby organs. Metastatic tumours usually appear as multiple lesions scattered throughout the lungs, sometimes giving the typical *'cannon-ball appearance.'*

Note: Metastatic lesions to the lungs most commonly arise from a primary from the colon in males, and from the breast in females.

Aetiology of Bronchogenic Carcinoma:

> **Smoking:** 90% of primary lung malignancies are believed to be due to tobacco use, the risk increasing with the number of cigarettes smoked and the duration of smoking. Alternatively pipe and cigar smoking can also cause lung cancer.

Note: Passive smoking too increases the risk of lung cancer with studies showing a 24% increased risk of lung cancer in non-smokers regularly exposed to cigarette smoke as compared to non-smokers who are not exposed.

> **Asbestos exposure:** The silicate form of asbestos fibre is a carcinogen which can persist for life in lung tissue following exposure to asbestos, leading to malignancy. Occupationally, asbestos exposure may occur in ship-building yards, thermal and acoustic insulation factories, construction sites, power plants, etc. Consequently, asbestos use has now been banned in many countries around the world due to its carcinogenic properties. Asbestos exposure is strongly associated with the development of lung cancer, malignant pleural mesotheliomas, asbestosis and pulmonary fibrosis.

Ironically, tobacco smoking and asbestos exposure synergistically increases the risk of lung cancer in patients, with incidencs rising to 80 to 90 times that of the control population.

> **Radon exposure:** Radon gas exposure in uranium miners is known to increase the risk of lung cancer.

> **Other environmental factors:** Berylium, nickel, chromium, cadmium, arsenic, chloromethyl ethers and mustard gas are also believed to be aetiological factors in the causation of lung cancer.

> **Familial predisposition:** It is believed that genetic susceptibility plays a role in the causation of lung cancer. Studies have shown that lung cancer is more likely to occur in both smoking and non smoking relatives of those who have had lung cancer, than in the general population.

> **HIV infection:** State of Texas Health Department has suggested a 6.5-fold increase in lung cancer incidence in patients infected with HIV.[2] However, other studies have failed to establish such a corelation.

> **Air pollution:** Air pollution from vehicles, industry, and power

plants is believed to increase the likelihood of lung cancer in exposed individuals. Prolonged exposure to highly polluted air can carry a risk for the development of lung cancer similar to that of passive smoking.

➢ **Lung Diseases:** Certain lung diseases such as Chronic Obstructive Pulmonary Disease (COPD), are associated with an increased risk for developing lung cancer. Patients with COPD have a risk of developing lung cancer that is four to six times greater than a non-smoker. This may also be due to the common association with cigarette smoking in this patient population.

CASE VIGNETTE:

A 61-year-old male, smoking 25 cigarettes per day for the past 35 years comes to the out-patient department with complaints of fresh blood in his sputum (5-6 episodes) since the past 15 days. He is a non-tobacco chewer and non- alcoholic. He also complains of hoarseness of voice and significant weight loss of 12 kilograms over the past 2 months. He gives history of a persistent cough with mucopurulent expectoration and acute shortness of breath since the past 3 weeks. This is accompanied by right-sided chest pain which is unrelenting and of a 'boring' character, severely disturbing his sleep. He also complains of anterior right chest wall tenderness. There is history of progressively increasing breathlessness over the past 5-7 years accompanied by mucoid expectoration. There is no history of fever.

There is no history of hypertension, diabetes mellitus, malignancy or pulmonary tuberculosis in the family.

His bladder and bowel habits are normal.

+ relevent negative

The patient is an office worker. There is no past history suggestive of occupational exposure to asbestos, toxic fumes or other dusts.

The student is expected to have in his mind some pertinent questions at this stage:

Q 1.Based on the history provided , what is the provisional diagnosis?

Q 2. Which systems should you examine to help in firming the diagnosis?

The student should then proceed to conduct the General Examination and the Systemic (Local) Examination of the Respiratory System.

General Examination: The patient appears underweight. His temperature, pulse and blood pressure) are within normal limits. However, he is tachypnoeic with a respiratory rate of 28 breaths per minute. His fingers show grade III clubbing and the finger nails have nicotine stains. There is no cyanosis, pallor, icterus or oedema of feet. Cervical lymph nodes are palpable on the right side. There are three nodes palpable, varying in diameter from 1 cm to 3 cm. They are discrete, hard, non-tender and fixed to the underlying structures.

Systemic (Local) Examination: The chest appears barrel-shaped with significantly reduced chest wall movements on the right side, on inspiration. Tactile vocal fremitus is increased posteriorly in the right interscapular and infrascapular regions and there is also a dull note on percussion in the same area. On auscultation, expiration is prolonged over the left side of the chest. There is diminished air-entry over the right interscapular and infrascapular regions. Localised rhonchi are heard in the right interscapular region. Tubular bronchial breath sounds are heard in the right interscapular and infrascapular regions posteriorly and vocal resonance is increased in the same area.

Cardiovascular system examination is normal. Abdominal examination is normal. Liver and spleen are not palpable, there is no abdominal tenderness, no evidence of free fliud in the abdomen and peristalsis are well heard. The central nervous system examination is also normal.

Note: The student is expected to be thorough in reporting the respiratory system findings and should report on relevant negative findings in the other systems mentioned.

In eliciting the history, the student should bear in mind the various differential diagnosis:

Ask for cardinal symptoms of the respiratory system:

Cough: inquire whether cough is dry or productive.

Expectoration: if the cough is productive (expectoration is present), inquire whether it was admixed with blood. If the sputum was blood-tinged, ask whether there was:

Frank blood or streaks of blood. Bright red blood would be indicative of active bleeding in the tracheobronchial tree while   dark red or altered blood is indicative of an earlier   bleed. In such a case, bronchogenic carcinoma should be considered a possible diagnosis.

Breathlessness: to describe whether the breathlessness was progressively worsening.

Chest Pain: to determine the character of the chest pain: If the chest pain is persistent, severe and 'boring' in character, disturbing sleep and accompanied by chest wall tenderness, ***malignancy*** should be seriously considered. In such cases, the pain is due to the tumour infiltrating the chest wall and mediastinum.

Fever: if fever is present, determine whether it is high-grade or low-grade. A high grade fever is indicative of a bacterial infection which may be the primary aetiological factor or which may be secondary to another underlying cause, namely, malignancy. In malignancy, a tumour mass may block a part of the tracheobronchial tree. As a result, the lung parenchyma distal to the blockage may collapse and infection may set in resulting in fever.

Weight Loss: inquire whether the patient has lost weight. A large amount of weight loss in a short duration of time eg. 15 kgs. in 2 months, is highly suggestive of malignancy.

PAST MEDICAL HISTORY:

- Past history of smoking if he is an ex-smoker. History of passive smoking (second-hand smoke) should also be elicited. ***Smoking is the single-most important cause of lung cancer***

- Chronicity and severity of the present illness: When breathlessness is progressive and there is increased severity and production of cough, loss of weight, increased frequency of admissions to the hospital and increased absenteeism from work, it is indicative of a progressive disease process such as malignancy or tuberculosis.

- *History of respiratory tract infection in the recent past:* Very commonly, the patient gives a history of being diagnosed with lower respiratory infection a few months prior to the present episode. In such cases if the patient is middle-aged or older and a chronic smoker with the above-mentioned symptoms and signs, ***it is imperative to consider malignancy*** as a serious differential diagnosis.

FAMILY HISTORY:

Enquire about smoking in the family, history of malignancy in the family, especially breast cancer, lung cancer or gastrointestinal malignancies.

PERSONAL HISTORY:

Inquire about bladder, bowel, sleep and dietary habits. A patient with progressively increasing breathlessness will have a significantly reduced appetite and significant sleep disturbances. It is important to remember *that chest pain occurring due to a tumour infiltrating the chest wall and mediastinum is usually very severe and unrelenting, resulting in significant sleep disturbances.*

SOCIAL AND OCCUPATIONAL HISTORY:

Inquire in detail about:

- Smoking habits: number of cigarettes smoked per day and for how many years.

- Tobacco chewing or betel-nut chewing

- Drug abuse

Occupational history is relevant to the patient's condition, hence details need to be elicited. If the patient is in a 'high-risk' occupation such as working in a paint industry, rubber factory, plastic factory, ship-building or ship-breaking yards, insulation factory, power plants or working with asbestos, then the exact duration and severity of exposure must be determined.

People working in insulation factories, power plants, ship-building and ship-breaking yards may stand the risk of exposure to asbestos which is known to be highly carcinogenic.

SURGICAL HISTORY:

History of abdominal or breast surgery for suspected malignancy.

History of surgical procedures undertaken in the past such as colonoscopy should also be elicited because the chief cause of metastatic lung tumours in males is primary colonic carcinoma while in females it is primary breast carcinoma.

SUMMARIZING THE HISTORY:

Student should be adept at summarizing the history in 2-3 sentences *highlighting* the *salient clinical features relevant to the case.*

SYSTEMIC REVIEW OF SYMPTOMS:

- To confirm whether the symptoms are primarily due to an underlying infective process or due to a malignancy such as primary or metastatic lung cancer.

- On systemic review of symptoms it is necessary to rule out other causes such as bronchiectasis, lung abscess, pulmonary embolism or interstitial lung disease.

- To determine whether the primary problem is infective or neoplastic. If neoplastic, to determine whether it is a primary or metastatic lesion in the lung. If the lesion is metastatic, it is important to determine the location of the primary lesion

- To determine whether the patient had been treated for similar complaints in the past and his response to past medication. If the patient has had repeated treatment with antibiotics for 'recurrent' or 'non-resolving' pneumonia, underlying malignancy must be suspected.

BED-SIDE MANNERS:

Student introduces himself/herself to the patient and politely asks permission to examine. Student is polite and courteous throughout the examination and has a gentle and caring demeanour. The patient is thanked at the end of the examination and helped into the position he was in before the examination.

In a female patient a chaperone should be present and due care to modesty should be given.

The entire Physical examination should be conducted from the right side of the patient.

GENERAL PHYSICAL EXAMINATION:

- Comment on the general condition of the patient, particularly his weight
- Vital parameters: Temperature, Pulse, Respiratory Rate, Blood Pressure
- Respiratory rate: to observe from the foot-end of the bed on the right side.

Look for:
- respiratory rate

66

- whether the chest is moving equally on both sides
- intercostal retraction
- movement of the subcostal angle
- whether accessory muscles of respiration are active or not. Particularly important if you are suspecting malignancy

- Jugular Venous Pressure (JVP): may be raised in 'superior vena cava (SVC) obstruction.' Pancoasts tumour is an important cause of SVC obstruction. Comment on the 'waveforms' of the JVP.
- Cyanosis: Central and Peripheral
- Clubbing: If present, mention the grade. In malignancy there may be severe clubbing and even pulmonary hypertrophic osteoarthropathy may occur.
- Oedema of feet: If present, pitting or not, unilateral or on both legs
- Cervical lymphadenopathy: ideally to be palpated from the back with the patients neck slightly flexed. Comment as you examine. In malignancy, the lymph nodes are hard, discrete, non-tender and usually adherent to the underlying structures.
- Flaps; if present, suggestive of CO_2 retention. This may occur due to severe endobronchial obstruction by a tumour.
- Facial swelling, swelling over the neck, upper arms and trunk (SVC obstruction).
- Headache, dizziness, reddish face, cheeks and palms, shortness of breath, decreased alertness, fainting and visual changes are all signs of SVC obstruction.
- Pallor

SYSTEMIC EXAMINATION OF THE RESPIRATORY SYSTEM:

Inspection:

- ❖ Position of the trachea: whether perceived or not. If perceived, comment on its position. If there is an underlying lung collapse (partial or complete), the trachea is shifted to the side of the collapse. In such cases malignancy must be ruled out. However, in case of a large tumour mass, the trachea and lower mediastinum may be pushed to the opposite side.
- ❖ Shape of the chest: whether normal (elliptical) or barrel shaped (hyperinflated) especially in smokers.
- ❖ Movement of chest wall: is reduced on the side of an underlying lung collapse, tumour mass.

- ❖ Respiratory rate: Patient may be tacchypnoeic in case of bronchial narrowing due to a tumour mass, which may be pressing on or infiltrating the bronchial lumen.
- ❖ Accessory muscles of respiration: Active or not. They may be active in case of endobronchial obstruction due to a tumour mass.
- ❖ Level of shoulder girdles: In case of an apical tumour and/or SVC obstruction, there may be significant supraclavicular and infraclavicular 'fullness' on the side of the lesion.

Palpation:

- • Confirm the position of the trachea, mention the cricosternal distance,
- • examine for tracheal tug: main causes include:
    - • aortic arch aneurysm
    - • malignant lymphomas, and
    - • COPD - predominantly emphysema
- • Position of the cardiac apex: May be shifted in case of an underlying lung collapse or a large tumour mass.
- • Chest wall movements, anteriorly and posteriorly
- • Chest wall tenderness, bony tenderness, sternal tenderness. In lung malignancies, significant chest wall and bony tenderness may be elicited. In such cases, tenderness is indicative of a tumour infiltrating the chest wall and mediastinum.
- • Tactile fremitus (symmetrically checked). It is increased over a tumour or collapsed lung if there is a patent bronchus underlying it.

Percussion:

- ❖ Apical percussion. May be dull in case of a Pancoast's tumour.
- ❖ Direct clavicular percussion
- ❖ Anterior and posterior percussion
- ❖ Determine the liver span: The liver may be enlarged in case of primary hepatocellular carcinoma or in case of hepatic metastasis arising from a primary bronchogenic carcinoma.

Note: To percuss the interscapular region, the hands should be folded over the shoulders so as to get the scapulae out of the way. To percuss in the axillary region the hands should be folded over the head.

Auscultation:

Auscultate for:

- Normal vesicular breath sounds
- Bronchial breath sounds. Usually tubular (high-pitched) bronchial breath sounds are heard over a tumour mass, collapsed lung (if a patent bronchus is present below it) or a consolidation
- Rhonchi, rales and pleural rub: Commonly, co-existent signs and symptoms of COPD are present in a patient with suspected bronchogenic carcinoma due to heavy smoking.

Relevant abdominal examination:

- ❖ Palpate for the liver: An enlarged liver with rock-hard or nodular consistency is suggestive of hepatic neoplasm.

Differential Diagnosis:

Based on the above history and physical examination findings, a comprehensive 'differential diagnosis' should now be arrived at.

These should include the following:

- ➢ Bronchogenic carcinoma
- ➢ Pulmonary tuberculosis or tuberculous granuloma
- ➢ Bacterial pneumonias
- ➢ Endobronchial obstruction due to bronchial adenomas (rare slow-growing tumours) or due to foreign body aspiration
- ➢ Lung abscess (as some neoplastic lesions may cavitate)
- ➢ Bronchiectasis

Other differential diagnosis of bronchogenic carcinoma are:

- ➢ Obstructive disorders such as: Chronic Obstructive Pulmonary Disease, Bronchial asthma

    Note: Patients with bronchial narrowing due to a tumour or foreign body aspiration are sometimes mistakenly diagnosed as COPD or bronchial asthma due to the presence of rhonchi. However, in such cases the rhonchi tend to be *'localised'* to a particular location and are not generalised. It should therefore be remembered that if the rhonchi are not generalised, but rather 'localised,' *a focal pathology* such as tumour or foreign-body obstruction is more likely. In contrast, in COPD and bronchial asthma **generalised rhonchi** are present bilaterally over the lung fields.

- ➢ Sarcoidosis (bilateral hilar prominence)
- ➢ Arteriovenous malformations
- ➢ Pulmonary hamartoma
- ➢ Encysted effusions

INVESTIGATIONS:

Non-invasive Investigative Procedures:

- 🔱 **Chest Radiography-**Postero-anterior (PA) and lateral views: to determine the presence of a tumour mass and its location, hilar and mediastinal enlargement, and an underlying lung collapse, if present. In case of metastasis in the lung, multiple rounded tumour masses may be seen diffusely present throughout both lung fields, giving the typical **'cannon-ball appearance.'**

- 🔱 **NOTE:** *This is readily done in most centres and provides the student with enormous amount of information. Expertise must be shown in interpreting chest radiographs*

- 🔱 **Arterial Blood Gas investigations (ABG):** helps to determine the pH of the blood, extent of hypoxia and CO_2 retention. In case of severe endobronchial obstruction by an infiltrating tumour, hypoxia with respiratory acidosis may be seen, which if severe may require ventilatory management.

- 🔱 **Full Blood Count:** It is raised in case of infection in the lung distal to the site of obsstruction.

  Note: It should be remembered that **a common presenting feature of Bronchogenic Carcinoma** is **infection.**

- 🔱 **Erythrocyte Sedimentation Rate (ESR):** If the ESR is above 100 mm/ 1 hour, malignancy should be suspected. In case of Hodgkin's lymphoma, gastric carcinoma, breast carcinoma, renal cell carcinoma and colorectal cancer an ESR >100 mm per hour is indicative of metastatic disease.

- 🔱 **Sputum Examination:** Sputum should be examined for:

Malignant cells (cytology): early-morning sputum samples collected on four consecutive days should be tested for malignant cells. If the sputum quality is not satisfactory, sputum may be induced using an ultrasonic nebuliser and hypertonic saline. In some studies, induced sputum has been shown to be qualitatively superior to normal sputum in the cytological diagnosis of lung cancer.[3]

Bacterial smear and culture: sputum should be tested for gram-positive, gram-negative and anaerobic organisms, as bronchogenic carcinomas commonly present with underlying lung infections.

Ultrasonography of the chest: Ultrsonography will help differentiate a solid mass (tumour) from a cystic lesion (loculated effusion).

- ***High-resolution Computed Tomography (HRCT) chest scan:*** HRCT chest scan would show the presence of a solid tumour mass in the thorax which may be extending upto and infiltrating the chest wall. It would also determine whether there is endobronchial obstruction. Involvement of the hilar, mediastinal and subcarinal lymph nodes too may be determined on HRCT chest scan.

- ***Pulmonary Function Testing:*** It may show obstructive impairment with a fall in the FEV1 and the FEV1/FVC ratio. Residual volume (RV) and the RV/TLC ratio may be increased indicative of hyperinflation and air-trapping.

- ***Invasive Investigative Procedures:***

These include:

- ➢ ***Percutaneous transthoracic needle biopsy:*** This procedure is usually undertaken under CT-guidance in patients with a peripherally located tumour mass.

- ➢ ***Fibreoptic/Video Bronchoscopy:*** In case of a centrally located tumour mass and/or an accompanying underlying lung collapse, a fibreoptic/video bronchoscopy must be carried out to determine the location and extent of tumour infiltration into the tracheobronchial tree. A bronchoscopy could also determine whether the carinal angle is widened, indicative of subcarinal lymph node enlargement.

Note: Procedures normally undertaken at the time of bronchoscopy (in a suspected case of lung cancer) include: endobronchial tumour biopsy, transbronchial lung biopsy, hilar lymph node biopsy, subcarinal lymph node biopsy, bronchial brushings and brochial washings.

Students should be well-acquainted with the anatomy of the tracheobronchial tree and the bronchopulmonary segments so that there is a better understanding of HRCT chest scans and bronchoscopic procedures during the internal medicine posting.

> **Pleural fluid aspiration and pleural biopsy:**
Pleural fluid aspiration is done in case of malignant pleural effusion and a pleural biopsy is undertaken in case of suspected malignant involvement of the pleura, especially in case of malignant mesothelioma.

> **Excision biopsy of palpable cervical and/or axillary lymph nodes:** In patients with palpable lymph nodes an excision biopsy is recommended in order to establish a definitive diagnosis.

Note: The student should have written a management plan as this often follows investigations and diagnosis especially in a long case examination

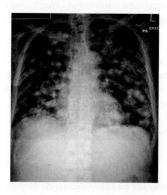

Chest radiograph PA-view showing multiple, rounded, well-defined (clearly demarcated) opacities in both lung fields, depicting the typical **'cannon-ball' appearance.** This is a chest radiograph of multiple metastatic lesions in the lung (metastatic lung carcinoma), in a man with primary colonic carcinoma.

MANAGEMENT:

Note: The discussion below is largely on bronchogenic carcinoma. The student should be reminded that this would form only part of the viva in a long case

I) Management of a case of bronchogenic carcinoma depends on a multiplicity of factors, namely,

> whether it is a primary or a metastatic lesion.

- whether there is hilar and mediastinal infiltration by the malignant tumour mass.
- whether there is chest wall involvement.
- whether there are associated complications such as massive pleural effusion, SVC obstruction, collapse-consolidation of the surrounding lung parenchyma.
- whether there is phrenic nerve involvement
- whether there is spread of the malignancy to other organs such as liver, brain, bones, gastrointestinal tract and adrenal glands.
- whether there are accompanying paraneoplastic syndromes.

Note: It must be remembered that it is indeed unfortunate that primary bronchogenic carcinomas are usually detected late in the stage of the disease. The first time the lesion is seen on the chest radiograph as a hilar opacity, it has usually spread to the mediastinum and is commonly Stage IIIA or IIIB at the time of diagnosis. Consequently, management of a case of bronchogenic carcinoma usually revolves around palliative care.

Treatment Options in primary lung cancer:

- Surgical resection of the tumour mass
- Chemotherapy (palliative or curative)
- Radiotherapy (palliative or curative)
- Treatment for endobronchial tumours such as debulking of an intraluminal mass, tracheobronchial stenting and endobronchial radiotherapy
- Treatment of symptoms such as infection and breathlessness
- Pain management and quality of life
- Adequate hydration and food intake

Complications of Lung Cancer:

- Haemoptysis, which may be massive
- Acute breathlessness due to endobronchial narrowing,
- Massive, recurrent, haemorrhagic pleural effusion,
- Superior vena cava obstruction,
- Severe, unrelenting chest pain due to the tumour infiltrating the chest wall,
- Paraneoplastic syndromes, and,
- Complications arising from metastatic spread of the malignancy.

Summarising Bronchogenic Carcinoma:

The history is usually more acute with the patient complaining of a persistent cough, rapid and significant weight loss, haemoptysis, chest pain and breathlessness. Smoking history is of vital importance as smoking is the single most important aetiological cause of lung malignancies. Occupational history too is very essential. The patient may give history of exposure to asbestos or other inhaled carcinogens. The patient may sometimes present with symptoms suggestive of a "non-resolving pneumonia." This is usually due to an endobronchial tumour obstructing a bronchus with parenchymal lung infection distal to it, which presents as a consolidation (pneumonia). The clinical signs in lung cancers are usually those suggestive of solid lesions, large pleural effusions or lung collapse. The presence of a malignant pleural effusion is suggestive of a poor prognosis. Chest radiography, sputum examination for malignant cells, HRCT scan of the chest, bronchoscopy, percutaneous lung biopsy, pleural aspiration and pleural biopsy usually help to arrive at a definitive diagnosis.

Prognosis of Lung Cancer:

Knowledge of prognosis is essential while managing the patient and addressing his concerns and those of his family members.

Generally, the overall prognosis in lung cancer is poor. Usually, the patient is already in Stage III B when the lesion is first detected on a chest radiograph. Small cell lung cancer (SCLC) has a 5-year survival rate of 5-10%. However, non-small cell lung cancers (NSCLC) if detected early (Stage 1) have a 5-year survival rate as high as 75%. Overall, the 5-year survival rates for lung cancer are generally lower than those of most cancers, with an overall 5-year survival rate of about 15% as compared to 63% for colon cancer, 88% for breast cancer and 99% for prostate cancer.

MUST KNOW FACTS

Deleterious effects of smoking:

There should be complete awareness of risk factors underlying the development of bronchogenic neoplasms. It should be amply clear that cigarette smoking is the single most important causative factor in bronchogenic carcinoma. Deleterious effects of both active and passive (second hand) smoking must also be known.

Students should be aware of the deleterious effects of passive smoking (second-hand smoke) and should be able to emphatically convey the same to the patient, his friends and his relatives.

Student should be aware that second-hand smoke is composed of side stream smoke (the smoke released from the burning end of a cigarette) and exhaled mainstream smoke (the smoke exhaled by a smoker). They should be aware that second-hand smoke has been designated as a "known human carcinogen" (cancer-causing agent) as it contains more than fifty cancer-causing chemicals. Non-smokers exposed to second-hand smoke are known to inhale many of the same cancer-causing chemicals that smokers inhale.

ETHICAL AND PROFESSIONAL ISSUES INCLUDE:
Competence in the following is essential:

Breaking 'serious illness' news
Informed consent for procedures required for diagnosis of Brochogenic carcinoma
Discussing prognosis and palliative care
Cost-benefit of management of terminal illness.

In case the patient decides to discontinue all forms of treatment due to a sense of hopelessness, it is essential for the doctor (in the capacity of the primary health-giver) to explain to the patient the potential disadvantages of such a decision.

The patient should be explained that treating the lung cancer with palliative chemotherapy and/or radiotherapy helps to reduce the mass of the tumour-burden, thereby reducing pain, breathlessnes (endobronchial obstruction) and improving the quality of life. It also helps to reduce the incidence of recurrent pleural effusion.

References:

1) Sher T, Dy GK, Adjei AA. Small cell lung cancer. *Mayo Clin Proc*. Mar 2008;83(3):355-67.

2) Parker MS, Leveno DM, Campbell TJ, et al. AIDS-related bronchogenic carcinoma: fact or fiction?. *Chest*. Jan 1998;113(1):154-61.

3) Khajotia RR, Mohn A, Pokieser L et al. Induced sputum and cytological diagnosis of Lung Cancer. Lancet 1991; 338: 976 -977.

Recommended reading:

- Murray and Nadel's Textbook of Respiratory Medicine, 4th edition.

- Egan's Fundamentals of Respiratory Care. 8th Edition. Mosby Publications.

- Health consequences of involuntary exposure to tobacco smoke: A report of the Surgeon General, U.S. Department of Health and Human Services (June 2006)

http://www.surgeongeneral.gov/library/secondhandsmoke/factsheets/factsheet1.html

CASE 4: BRONCHIECTASIS
RUMI R KHAJOTIA

[handwritten margin note: emphysema - permanent dilation of air space distal to TB & destruction of their wall. distal to terminal bronchiole.]

DEFINITION:

It is an abnormal, permanent dilatation of the bronchi (> 2mm in diameter) with accompanying destruction of the muscular and elastic tissue within the walls.

As a result, the bronchi are dilated, thinned, inflamed and easily collapsible, resulting in stagnation and impaired clearance of secretions. At times, peribronchial alveolar tissue is also damaged, resulting in diffuse peribronchial fibrosis.[1]

Though there are a wide range of disorders causing bronchiectasis, the most common cause is chronic, persistent infection, and the most common organisms include *Staphylococcus aureus, Klebseilla and Bordetella Pertussis.*

PATHOPHYSIOLOGY OF BRONCHIECTASIS:

As a result of the abnormal, permanent dilatation of the bronchi with accompanied destruction of their walls, transmural inflammation sets in, resulting in severe alteration of the bronchial anatomy. This results in stagnation and poor clearance of secretions leading to further damage of the bronchial walls.

Hence, when left untreated this results in progressive bronchial wall damage.[2]

CLASSIFICATION OF BRONCHIECTASIS:

Bronchiectasis is usually characterised as:[3]

Saccular or Cystic
Cylindrical
Varicose

'Saccular or Cystic' bronchiectasis is usually characterised by ulceration and bronchial neovascularisation, resulting in ballooning of the bronchial walls and air-fluid levels.

'Cylindrical' bronchiectais is characterised by dilated bronchi that have straight and regular outlines that end squarely and abruptly.

'Varicose' bronchiectasis is characterised by dilated bronchi with bulbous

appearance interspersed by areas of relative constriction.

CAUSES OF BRONCHIECTASIS:

Bronchiectasis can occur due to a variety of causes.

They include:

- Bacterial or viral infections
- Tuberculosis
- Aspiration of foreign bodies or gastric contents
- Inherited disorders such as Cystic Fibrosis (CF)
- Allergic Bronchopulmonary Aspergillosis
- Primary ciliary dyskinesia
- Alpha 1-antitrypsin deficiency
- Autoimmune disorders
- Immunodeficiency states
- Connective tissue disorders
- Congenital anatomical defects such as Williams Campbell Syndrome, Swyer-James Syndrome and Mounier-Kuhn Syndrome

Infective causes commonly include:

- Staphylococcus aureus
- Klebsiella
- Mycobacterium tuberculosis
- Mycoplasma pneumonia
- Pertussis virus
- Measles virus
- Respiratory syncytial virus (RSV)
- Herpes Simplex virus

CASE VIGNETTE:

A 38-year-old man came with complaints of cough and greenish-yellow expectoration accompanied by fever off-and-on, over the past five years. The expectoration is about half-a-cupful a day. He is an office worker, non-smoker, non-tobacco chewer and non- alcoholic. He also complained of weight loss of 10 kilograms over the past 3 years. He complains that since the last 2 years the cough was worsened on lying in the left-lateral position and had noticed progressively increasing breathlessness since the past 18 months.

There was no history of hypertension, diabetes mellitus, malignancy or pulmonary tuberculosis in the family.

His bladder and bowel habits were normal. His sleep had been disturbed since the past 2 years due to cough accompanied by expectoration whenever he sleeps in the left-lateral position.

He gave history of having been hospitalised for pneumonia 6 years ago, and claims that he had had a relapse of the condition a few weeks later, for which he had to be re-hospitalised.

On general physical examination, the patient appears underweight. He was febrile. His pulse was 94 beats/minute and blood pressure was 134/86mmHg. He was tachypneic with a respiratory rate of 26 breaths per minute. His fingers showed grade IV clubbing (drum-stick appearance). There was no cyanosis, pallor, icterus or oedema of feet. Cervical lymph nodes were not palpable.

collaps o ?

On systemic examination, the trachea was shifted *to the right side.* The chest appeared hyperinflated with reduced chest wall movements in the right infrascapular and infra-axillary regions. Tactile vocal fremitus was diminished posteriorly in the right infrascapular and infra-axillary regions. There was a dull note on percussion in the same area. On auscultation, expiration was prolonged bilaterally over the chest. There was diminished air entry in the right infrascapular and infra-axillary regions. Coarse mid-to-late inspiratory crepitations *('leathery rales')* were heard in the infrascapular and infra-axillary regions on the right side and vocal resonance was decreased in the same area. *VRↆ*

Mediastinal Shift

Cardiovascular system examination was normal. The cardiac apex was in the 5th left intercostal space 1 cm *medial* to the mid-clavicular line. First and second heart sounds were well heard. There was no gallop and no murmur was heard. On abdominal examination, liver and spleen were not palpable, there was no abdominal tenderness, no evidence of free fluid in the abdomen and peristalsis were well heard. The Central Nervous System examination was normal.

HISTORY OF PRESENTING ILLNESS:

To include the cardinal symptoms of the Respiratory System, namely:

Cough: inquire whether cough is dry or productive. In bronchiectasis the cough is productive.

Expectoration: in bronchiectais, there is usually a large amount of expectoration. Due to presence of underlying infection, the cough is usually yellowish or greenish, large in quantity and may sometimes be admixed with blood. If the sputum was blood-tinged, ask whether there was:

Blood in the sputum: frank blood or streaks of blood. Bright red blood would be indicative of active bleeding in the tracheobronchial tree while

dark red or altered blood is indicative of an earlier bleed. In a suspected case of bronchiectasis blood in the sputum is usually indicative of tuberulosis, bacterial or fungal infections.

Breathlessness: to describe whether the breathlessness is progressively worsening. This would be indicative of increased secretions in the bronchiectatic cavities or progressive lung parenchymal destruction .

Chest Pain: if chest pain is present, to determine the character of pain. In bronchiectasis, a pleuritic pain could be present if there is surrounding consolidation extending to the lung periphery. Sometimes, a generalised dull-aching chest pain may be present. This may be of muscular origin due to chronic, persistent coughing.

Fever: if fever is present, determine whether it is high-grade or low-grade. A low-grade fever with an evening rise of temperature is usually indicative of pulmonary tuberculosis while a high-grade fever is indicative of a bacterial infection.

Weight Loss: inquire whether the patient has lost weight. In bronchiectasis patients usually complain of weight loss as there is usually an accompanying loss of appetite and a significant loss of protein in the expectorated sputum.

Generalised fatigue: This is a common complaint in long-standing cases of bronchiectasis and may be attributed to loss of sleep due to chronic coughing.

Aspiration: An attempt should be made to elicit history of foreign-body aspiration or vomiting, which could be the underlying cause of bronchiectasis in the patient.

PAST MEDICAL HISTORY:

Past history of smoking if he is an ex-smoker. History of passive smoking (second-hand smoke) should also be elicited.

History of recurrent or persistent respiratory tract infection in the past: This is a strong indicator of chronic cavitary lung disease.

FAMILY HISTORY:

History of smoking in the family. History of tuberculosis in a family member, neighbour or colleague at work.

PERSONAL HISTORY:

Sleep may be disturbed due to coughing in a patient with bronchiectasis, especially when the patient lies in a particular position, as stagnant secretions present in bronchiectatic cavities may then be drained out.

SOCIAL HISTORY:

Inquire in detail about:

Smoking habits: number of cigarettes smoked per day and for how many years.
Tobacco chewing or betel nut chewing
Drug abuse
Alcohol intake

OCCUPATIONAL HISTORY:

It is imperative to inquire whether the patient's occupation contributes adversely to the progression and exacerbation of his respiratory condition. Sweepers, cleaners and people working in garbage-dumping areas are more prone to repeated lower respiratory tract infections which in turn could lead to chronic respiratory illnessess such as bronchiectasis and lung abscess.

SUMMARIZING THE HISTORY:

Student should be adept at summarizing the history in 2-3 sentences *highlighting* the *salient clinical features relevant to the case.*

SYSTEMIC REVIEW OF SYMPTOMS:

- To confirm whether the symptoms are primarily due to an underlying infective process such as pulmonary tuberculosis, bacterial, viral or fungal infection.

- To determine whether the patient had been treated for similar complaints in the past and his response to past medication. This indicates whether a persistent infection is present; a common cause of which is bronchiectasis.

✓ **CHECK LIST FOR HISTORY IN A SUSPECTED CASE OF BRONCHIECTASIS:**
- Duration of cough and the amount of expectoration
- Breathlessness
- Blood in the sputum
- Chest pain, weight loss
- Occupational history (whether significant or not)
- Treatment taken in past, and its response..

BED-SIDE MANNERS:

Student introduces himself/herself to the patient and politely asks permission to examine. Student is courteous throughout the examination and has a gentle and caring demeanour. The patient is thanked at the end of the examination and helped into the position he was in before the examination.

The entire Physical examination should be conducted from the right side of the patient.

GENERAL PHYSICAL EXAMINATION:

- Comment on the general condition of the patient, particularly his weight, which is usually reduced in bronchiectasis.
- Breath Odour: The breath may be foul-smelling if the bronchial secretions are due to anaerobic infection.
- Vital parameters: Temperature, Pulse, Respiratory Rate, Blood Pressure
- Respiratory rate: to observe from the foot-end of the bed on the right side.Whether the chest is moving equally on both sides, intercostal retraction. Whether accessory muscles of respiration are active or not.
- Cyanosis: Central and Peripheral cyanosismay be present in widespread bronchiectasis
- Clubbing: Commonly present in bronchiectasis, mention the grade.
- Oedema of the feet: If present unilateral or bilateral,pitting or not.. In bronchiectasis it may be due to hypoproteinemia.
- Cervical lymphadenopathy: In tuberculous bronchiectasis, the lymph nodes are usually matted.
- Pallor, Icterus,
- Examine the nose: look for:
  - deviated nasal septum

- nasal polyps
- enlarged nasal turbinates
- Examine the mouth for: oral hygiene, oral ulcerations, glossitis, angular stomatitis, injected throat

SYSTEMIC EXAMINATION OF THE RESPIRATORY SYSTEM:

Inspection:

- Position of the trachea: whether perceived or not. If perceived, comment on its position. In case of bronchiectasis, the trachea may be pulled to the side of the lesion as bronchiectasis usually results in fibrosis and scarring of the surrounding lung parenchyma.
- Shape of the chest: whether normal (elliptical) or barrel shaped (hyperinflated). Bronchiectasis leads to obstructive impairment which may lead to hyperinflation.
- Movement of chest wall: usuallly reduced on the side of bronchiectasis.
- Respiratory rate: Breaths per minute.
- Presence of scars, sinuses, seen veins, visible pulsations, apex beat perceived or not.
- Accessory muscles of respiration: Whether active or not, active in cases of extensive bilateral lung destruction due to bronchiectasis..
- Kyphosis, scoliosis, kyphoscoliosis, spino-scapular distance.
- Level of shoulder girdles, supraclavicular and infraclavicular indrawing. In case of tuberculosis with apical scaring, the shoulder girdles would not be at the same level and there may be supraclavicular and infraclavicular 'indrawing.'

[handwritten margin note: signs of hyperinflation — reduce cricosternal D, ↑ AP Diameter, Intercostal indrawing, Apex beat not palpable, Hyper resonance percussion note]

Palpation:

- Confirm the position of the trachea, mention the cricosternal distance.
- Position of the cardiac apex.
- Chest wall movements, anteriorly and posteriorly. May be reduced in the area of bronchiectasis.
- Chest wall tenderness, bony tenderness, sternal tenderness.
- Tactile fremitus (symmetrically checked). It is decreased or absent over an area of bronchiectasis.

Percussion:

- Apical percussion.
- Direct clavicular percussion.

83

- Anterior and posterior percussion: The percussion note may be frankly dull or impaired in an area of bronchiectasis.

Note: To percuss the interscapular region, the hands should be folded over the shoulders so as to get the scapulae out of the way. To percuss in the axillary region the hands should be folded over the head.

Auscultation:

Auscultate for:

- The normal Vesicular Breath Sounds
- Bronchial Breath Sounds: may be heard over bronchiectatic cavities   coarse crepitaten .
- Rhonchi, Rales and Pleural Rub: Coarse 'leathery' rales (crepitations) are a characteristic feature of bronchiectasis when the bronchiectatic cavities are filled with secretions. Expiratory rhonchi may be present due to progressive obstructive impairment. A pleural rub may be present if there is a surrounding consolidation extending to the lung periphery.

CLINICAL CASE DISCUSSION

The patient is a middle-aged man who came with the chief complaints of cough accompanied by half-a-cupful of expectoration per day. He also complained of fever, weight-loss and progressively increasing breathlessness. The cough disturbs his sleep especially when he was lying in the left-lateral position. He notices that in this position he expectorated out a large quantity of sputum.

Taking into consideration the above clinical symptoms and signs;

The *Differential Diagnoses* in the above case would include:

1. Right lower-lobe bronchiectasis
2. Right lower-lobe consolidation due to bacterial or tuberculous infection
3. Aspiration pneumonia involving the right lower lobe
4. Right lower-lobe lung abscess
5. Chronic obstructive Pulmonary Disease with right lower lobe pneumonia

Note: End-stage interstitial lung disease (ILD) may mimic bronchiectasis, as in this condition there is extensive honey-combing and fibrosis. However, since ILD is a bilateral lung disease, the clinical findings too are bilateral. In the above case, the clinical signs are confined to the right side indicating that the patient has right lower lobe bronchiectasis.

INVESTIGATIONS:

Non-invasive Investigative Procedures:

***Chest Radiography*-**Postero-anterior (PA) and lateral views: areas of cavitation with multiple air-fluid levels and peribronchial fibrosis may be seen in a particular part of the lung. Tram-line appearance may be seen. The trachea may be pulled to the side of the lesion. Chest radiography helps to determine the location and extent of the bronchiectatic lesion.

Note: A normal chest radiograph does not exclude bronchiectasis. If there is a high-index of clinical suspicion, an HRCT chest scan must be undertaken.

Arterial Blood Gas investigations (ABG): In severe, extensive bilateral bronchiectasis gas-exchange could be significantly impaired leading to hypoxia and carbon dioxide retention.

Electrocardiogram: may show evidence of cor pulmonale   Right ventricular Strains

Full Blood Count: It is raised in cases of bacterial infections where there is a neutrophilic leucocytosis. In case of pulmonary tuberculosis, the differential cell count may show predominant lymphocytosis. (↑ h)

Erythrocyte Sedimentation Rate (ESR): In case of active pulmonary tuberculosis the ESR is usually between 80-100 mm at the end of one hour.   consolidation due to TB infection

Sputum Examination: Sputum should be   examined for:

- *Acid-Fast Bacilli (AFB)-smear and culture:* Preferably six early-morning sputum samples should be collected on consecutive days and tested.
- *Bacterial smear and culture:* sputum should be tested for gram-positive, gram-negative and anaerobic organisms.
- *Fungal culture:* Sputum should be tested for spores and hyphae of *Aspergillus Spp.* Bronchopulmonary aspergillosis is a common cause of bronchiectasis.
- *High-resolution Computed Tomography (HRCT) chest scan:* It is useful in:
    - o Confirming the presence of bronchiectasis, especially when the chest radiograph is doubtful.

o   Determining the exact location of the cavitations.
o   Determining the presence of a fungal-ball (aspergilloma) in a bronchiectatic cavity

- **Pulmonary Function Testing:** Usually shows an obstructive impairment

Other tests include:

[handwritten: AR - defect CFTR defective Cl secretion ↑ Na absorption ↓ thick mucus]

- **Sweat Chloride levels:** to rule out Cystic Fibrosis
- **Serum Immunoglobulin Electrophoresis**
- **Alpha 1-antitrypsin levles**
- **Aspergillosis precipitin test**

Invasive Investigative Procedures:

These include:

Fibreoptic/Video Bronchoscopy: To look for tumours and embedded foreign bodies in the bronchial tree. To determine the cause of the underlying infection by doing a broncho-alveolar lavage (BAL). To diagnose suspected malignancy in long-standing bronchiectatic cavities by doing bronchial brushings and washings.

Excision biopsy of palpable cervical and/or axillary lymph nodes: In patients with palpable lymph nodes an excision biopsy is recommended in order to establish a definitive diagnosis. In a case of bronchiectasis ,one of the common causes of enlarged cervical lymph nodes is tuberculosis.

MANAGEMENT:

I) Medical Management:

- Antibiotic coverage: Whenever the patient has evidence of infection, appropriate antibiotics are recommended.
- Chest Physiotherapy: It is esssential in order to help patients expectorate out the secretions.
- Postural Drainage: It helps patients to drain the cavities of the secretions. This could be a source of inconvenience to the patient but the patient should be encouraged to perform it regularly so that secretions do not collect and there is no spread of the infection.
- Bronchodilators may be useful to reduce breathlessness
- Expectorants: used to clear tracheobronchial secretions
- Mucolytics: to liquefy secretions

- Adequate Hydration: it helps to prevent secretions from becoming thick and viscid and also helps to keep the airway mucosa moist.
- Well-balanced diet: This is essential as the patient looses a lot of vital proteins in the expectorated sputum.
- Prophylactic antibiotics has sometimes been recommended. However, in such cases there is a risk of developing drug-resistant infections.
- Oxygen therapy in case of severe, extensive bronchiectasis with accompanying respiratory failure
- Regular immunizations

II) *Surgical Management:*

- Drainage of secretions using fibreoptic/video bronchoscopy: In some patients the secretions are not easily expectorated out even after chest physiotherapy and good postural drainage as the secretions may be thick or the opening to the bronchiectatic cavities may be very narrow. In such cases suction may be employed through a bronchoscope in order to clear the cavities of secretions.
- Surgical removal of the infected area: Depending on the extent of involvement a pneumonectomy, lobectomy or a segmentectomy may be done. This is recommended early in the disease process when the lesion is still localised so as to prevent further spread of infection.

COMPLICATIONS OF BRONCHIECTASIS:

- Spread of the infection to healthy parts of the same lung or to the contralateral lung.
- Development of superadded fungal infection in bronchiectatic cavities
- Haemoptysis, which may at times be massive. Massive haemoptysis may be caused by an aspergilloma in a tuberculous cavity.
- Recurrent pneumonia
- Atelectasis due to secretions blocking the bronchial passages
- Cor pulmonale, pulmonary hypertension and heart failure
- Hypoprotenemia due to chronic expectoration of secretions which are rich in proteins.
- Amyloidosis
- Cerebral absces
- Respiratory failure in patients with bilateral, extensive bronchiectasis

RADIOLOGICAL FEATURES OF BRONCHIECTASIS:

Chest radiography may sometimes be normal in patients with bronchiectasis.

Common bronchiectatic changes seen on radiography include prominent bronchovascular markings which occur due to peribronchial fibrosis and intrabronchial secretions. Tram-lines which are parallel lines outlining dilated bronchi and areas of cystic changes with air-fluid levels may also be visualised.

High-resolution computed tomographic (HRCT) findings include cysts with air-fluid levels, dilated bronchi usually situated at the periphery of the lungs and bronchial wall thickening is due to peribronchial fibrosis.

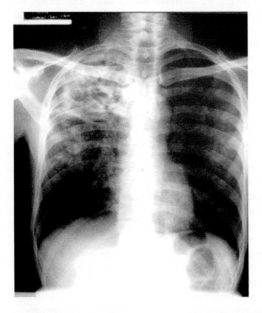

Fig 1: This is the chest radiograph of a patient with pulmonary tuberculosis

It shows multiple cavitations (tuberculous bronchiectasis) in the right upper and mid zones with non-homogenous infiltrates in the surrounding pulmonary parenchyma, suggestive of active tuberculosis. Ill-defined infiltrates are also seen in the upper and mid zones on the left side.

ETHICAL ISSUES INCLUDE:

1) In case the above patient decides to discontinue all forms of treatment due to a sense of hopelessness, it is essential for the doctor to explain to the patient the potential disadvantages of such a decision.

The patient should be informed that regular chest physiotherapy and postural drainage are essential cornerstones in the treatment of this condition as they help in keeping the cavities free of secretions and therefore prevent recurrence and consequent spread of infection.

Treating the infection as and when it recurs is vitally important in reducing the spread of the disease and would also help in combating breathlessness.

If surgery is required, the patient should be explained that resection of the affected part is essential in order to prevent the progression of bronchiectasis to healthy parts of the same lung and to the contralateral lung, which would eventually help to decrease the morbidity associated with this condition.

REFERENCES:

1) Morrissey D. Pathogenesis of Bronchiectasis. *Clin Chest Med*. 2007;28:289-296.

2) Cole PJ. A new look at the pathogenesis, management of persistent bronchial sepsis: A 'viscious circle' hypothesis and its logical therapeutic connotations. In: Davies RJ. *Strategies for the Management of Chronic Bacterial Sepsis*. Oxford: Medicine Publishing Foundation; 1984:1-20.

3) Reid LM. Reduction in bronchial subdivision in bronchiectasis. *Thorax*. Sep 1950;5(3):233-47.

Interstitial Lung Disease (ILD) is a clinical case commonly presented for medical examinations at both undergraduate and postgraduate levels. In clinical practice, ILD should be considered as a possible diagnosis following history-taking and physical examination in a patient with typical symptoms and signs. It should then be confirmed by relevant invasive and non-invasive investigative procedures.

DEFINITION:

Interstitial lung disease (ILD) by definition, involves abnormalities of the interstitium. It is also known as *diffuse parenchymal lung disease (DPLD)*.[1]

ILD refers to a group of lung diseases affecting the interstitium of the lungs. The interstitium includes the alveolar epithelium, pulmonary capillary endothelium, basement membrane, perivascular and perilymphatic tissues. DPLD may be idiopathic, when it is also known as 'Idiopathic Pulmonary Fibrosis' (IPF). The underlying histopathology of IPF is Usual Interstitial Pneumonitis (UIP), which is characterized by progressive scarring (fibrosis) involving the interstitium of both lungs.[2] UIP is thus a form of interstitial lung disease. It is also known as 'Cryptogenic Fibrosing Alveolitis' (CFA), in British literature.

Other major histopathologic forms of idiopathic interstitial pneumonias include the following:

- desquamative interstitial pneumonia (DIP)
- acute interstitial pneumonitis (AIP) (also known as Hamman-Rich Syndrome)
- nonspecific interstitial pneumonia (NSIP)
- cryptogenic organizing pneumonia (COP)

INCIDENCE OF INTERSTITIAL LUNG DISEASE: There are limited data available regarding the incidence and prevalence of various ILD's. It has been estimated that common ILD's (such as idiopathic pulmonary fibrosis, sarcoidosis and occupational lung diseases) together affect about 40 individuals per 100,000 population per year. Although various ILD's affect individuals at any age; most occur in adults. Some, such as IPF are uncommon under the age of 50, and demonstrate increased incidence with each subsequent decade.

AETIOLOGY OF INTERSTITIAL LUNG DISEASE:

➤ In most cases, the aetiology is unknown.

➤ Known causes include:

1. *Occupational and environmental exposure* to silica dust, asbestos fibres, beryllium, grain dust, bird and animal droppings.

2. *Exposure to radiation treatment* in lung and breast cancers resulting in lung damage involving the lung interstitium, months to years after the initial treatment. Severity of the lung damage depends on pre-existing underlying lung disease, amount and duration of exposure to radiation, amount of lung tissue exposed to radiation and whether chemotherapy was also prescribed.

3. *Rheumatoid arthritis*

4. *Sarcoidosis*

5. *Systemic Lupus Erythematosis*

6. *Systemic Sclerosis*

7. *Polymyositis*

8. *Dermatomyositis*

9. *Medications,* such as: chemotherapeutic agents (cyclophosphamide, methotrexate), cardiac drugs (propranolol, amiodarone, statins) and antibiotics (nitrofurantoin, sulphasalazine)

10. *Infections:* atypical pneumonia, pneumocystis pneumonia (PCP), tuberculosis, respiratory syncytial virus (RSV), chlamydia trachomatis

11. *Lymphangitic carcinomatosis*

PATHOGENESIS OF INTERSTITIAL FIBROSIS: A fibrous thickening of the lung interstitium is the hallmark of chronic interstitial lung disease. In this condition two mechanisms play a role:

❖ Primary interstitial widening: In this case oedema

and fibrosis form directly within the interstitial compartment. Classic examples of this include, interstitial edema and sarcoidosis (thickening of interstitium initially by granuloma formation)

❖ organization of exudate within the alveolar space that is converted to fibrous connective tissue and is incorporated into the interstitium; in some cases the exudate is cleared by resolution, eg. organizing pneumonia

End Stage Lung Disease: This is characterised by:

❖ A diffusely fibrotic pattern
❖ Honeycombing, which is a porous network of fibrous-walled cysts that resembles a bee-hive.

▪ *Pathological features:*

✓ alveolar destruction, bronchiectasis, and formation of fibrous septa between widely separated airspaces
✓ vascular intimal sclerosis due to surrounding inflammation and morphological changes induced by hypoxia and hypertension
✓ right ventricle hypertrophy and cor pulmonale resulting from prolonged pulmonary hypertension (PH).

CASE VIGNETTE:

A 55-year-old female, non-smoker, comes to the out-patient department with complaints of cough and progressively increasing breathlessness over the past 7 years. She is a non-tobacco chewer and non- alcoholic. There is no history of blood in the sputum, chest pain or fever. The cough is dry (non-productive) and persistent even at night.

She has also noticed a gradual change in the shape of her fingernails which she says have become 'beak-like.' The patient complains of fatigue, weakness, loss of appetite and loss of weight (5 Kg) since the past 10 months. There is no history suggestive of rheumatoid arthritis, scleroderma or other connective tissue disorders. There is no past history of diabetes, hypertension or tuberculosis. There is no history of hypertension, diabetes mellitus, malignancy or pulmonary tuberculosis in the family. There is also no history of similar symptoms in her family.

Her bladder and bowel habits are normal.

The patient works in the grinding department of a tile-factory, since the past 15 years. Prior to that, she worked for 10 years in the chipping department of the same factory.

At this stage the student is expected to have in his mind some pertinent questions :

Q 1.Based on the history provided , what is the provisional diagnosis?

Q 2. Which systems should I examine to help in confirming the diagnosis?

The student should then proceed to conduct the General Examination and the Systemic (Local) Examination of the Respiratory System.

General Examination: The patient appears underweight. She is afebrile and her blood pressure is within normal limits. However, she has tachycardia, with a pulse rate of 108 beats per minute and tachypnoea, with a respiratory rate of 28 breaths per minute.

Her fingernails show grade III clubbing with the classic 'parrot-beak' appearance.

She appears mildly cyanosed.

There is no pallor, icterus or oedema of feet.

Cervical lymph nodes are not palpable.

Systemic (Local) Examination:

The shape of the chest appears to be normal (elliptical). However, chest wall movements appear to be significantly reduced on both sides, on inspiration.

Tactile vocal fremitus is decreased bilaterally in the 4th and 5th intercostal spaces anteriorly and in the axilla and also in the infrascapular regions.

There is also a dull note on percussion in the same area.

On auscultation, mid-to-late inspiratory crepitations ('velcro rales') are heard bilaterally in the infrascapular and lower axillary regions and vocal resonance is decreased in the same area.

On cardiovascular system examination, S1 and S2 are heard. A loud P2 (pulmonary second sound) is heard in the pulmonary area. A protodiastolic gallop (third heart sound, S3) is heard.

Abdominal system examination is normal. Liver and spleen are not palpable, there is no abdominal tenderness, no evidence of free fliud in the abdomen and peristalsis are well heard.

The Central Nervous System examination is also normal.

Note: In this case, the student is expected to be thorough in reporting the respiratory and cardiovascular system findings, and should also report on relevant negative findings in the other systems mentioned.

In eliciting the history, the student should bear in mind the various differential diagnoses.

Ask for cardinal symptoms of the respiratory system:

- **Cough:** inquire whether cough is dry or productive.

  Note: In ILD the cough is usually *dry (non-productive).*

  However, in end-stage interstitial lung disease when 'honey-combing' develops, the cough may become productive due to infection in the underlying cavities. Presence of a persistent, dry cough is usually indicative of active ILD.

- Blood in the sputum: haemoptysis is not seen in the early stages of ILD. However, once honey-combing sets in bleeding may occur from the underlying cavities.

  - **Breathlessness:** to determine whether the breathlessness is progressively worsening.

  - In ILD the breathlessness is characteristically 'slowly-progressive.'

- **Chest Pain:** Usually absent. However, sometimes the patient may complain of chest pain which may be of muscular origin due to the chronic, persistent cough and progressive breathlessness.

- **Fever:** if fever is present, determine whether it is high-grade or low-grade. A high-grade fever is indicative of a bacterial infection. This may be seen in 'end-stage' interstitial lung disease when honey-combing' (cavitation) sets in, which in turn may get secondarily infected. The infection may be bacterial, fungal or tuberculous in origin.

- **Weight Loss:** inquire whether the patient has lost weight. Seen in later stages of the disease process due to breathlessness leading to anorexia and consequent weight loss.

PAST MEDICAL HISTORY:

- Chronicity and severity of the present illness: Dry, non-productive cough with progressively increasing breathlessness accompanied by weight loss, increased frequency of admissions to the hospital and increased absenteeism from work, is indicative of a progressive disease process such as ILD.

- *History of respiratory tract infection in the recent past:* In end-stage ILD, infection can frequently occur in the multiple cavities which develop usually at the lung bases, leading to repeated lower respiratory tract infections.

FAMILY HISTORY:

- Enquire about similar illness in the family and also history of rheumatoid arthritis, scleroderma and other connective tissue disorders, as they are commonly associated with co-existent ILD.

PERSONAL HISTORY:

Inquire about bladder, bowel, sleep and dietary habits. A patient with progressively increasing breathlessness will have a significantly reduced appetite and significant sleep disturbances. A persistent dry cough of active ILD may also disturb sleep.

SOCIAL AND OCCUPATIONAL HISTORY:

Inquire in detail about:

- Smoking habits: number of cigarettes smoked per day and for how many years.

- Tobacco chewing or betel-nut chewing

- Drug abuse

Occupational history is relevant to the patient's condition, hence details need to be elicited.If the patient is in a 'high-risk' occupation such as working in a tile factory (exposed to silica dust) or working with asbestos fibres, then the exact duration and severity of exposure must be determined.

People working in insulation factories, power plants, ship-building and ship-breaking yards stand the risk of exposure to asbestos which is known to be an aetiological factor in the development of ILD, besides being a known carcinogen.

SUMMARIZING THE HISTORY:

Student should be adept at summarizing the history in 2-3 sentences *highlighting* the *salient clinical features relevant to the case.*

In this case the history could be summarized as follows:

"A 55-year-old female patient presents with complaints of dry, persistent cough and progressively increasing breathlessness over the past 7 years. She also complains of loss of appetite and loss of weight (5 kg) since the past 10 months. The patient is a non-smoker and non-tobacco chewer. She is working in a tile-factory over the past 25 years."

SYSTEMIC REVIEW OF SYMPTOMS:

- To confirm whether the symptoms of cough and progressively increasing breathlessness are due to an obstructive lung disease such as COPD or due to a 'restrictive lung disorder' such as ILD.

- On systemic review of symptoms it is necessary to rule out other causes such as bronchiectasis. In end-stage interstitial lung disease, when honey-combing with fibrosis is present bilaterally at both lung bases, it may be difficult to differentiate it from 'bilateral basal bronchiectasis.'

- To determine whether the patient had been treated for similar complaints in the past and the response to past medication. In case of ILD, the patient may give history of being treated with corticosteroids and/or immunosuppressants, in the past.

BED-SIDE MANNERS:

Student introduces himself/herself to the patient and politely asks permission to examine. Student is polite and courteous throughout the examination and has a gentle and caring demeanour. The patient is thanked at the end of the examination and helped into the position he was in before the examination.

In a female patient a chaperone should be present and due care to modesty should be given.

The entire physical examination should be conducted from the right side of the patient.

GENERAL PHYSICAL EXAMINATION:

- Comment on the general condition of the patient, particularly his weight
- Vital parameters: Temperature, Pulse, Respiratory Rate, Blood Pressure
- Respiratory rate: to observe from the foot-end of the bed on the right side.

Look for:
- Respiratory rate
- Whether the chest is moving equally on both sides.
- Intercostal retraction
- Movement of the subcostal angle
- Whether accessory muscles of respiration are 'active' or not.
- Particularly important if you are suspecting 'end-stage' interstitial lung disease.

- Jugular Venous Pressure (JVP): may be raised in a patient with ILD if cor pulmonale and pulmonary hypertension have set in. Comment on the 'waveforms' of the JVP.
- Cyanosis: Central and Peripheral. Seen in patients with extensive honey-combing and fibrosis.
- Clubbing: If present, mention the grade. 40%-75% of patients with ILD show various grades of clubbing, usually late in the disease course.

Note: In an examination, student should not forget to mention if clubbingis present. If not present, student should mention that he looked for clubbing in the patient.

- Oedema of feet: If present, state if pitting is present, whether, unilateral or on both legs. Patient with end-stage ILD may develop cor pulmonale (right ventricular failure) leading to bilateral pitting oedema.
- Cervical lymphadenopathy: ideally to be palpated from the back with the patient's neck slightly flexed. Comment as you examine.

97

- Flaps; if present, suggestive of CO_2 retention. This may occur in end-stage ILD with extensive honey-combing and fibrosis.
- Pallor, icterus

SYSTEMIC EXAMINATION OF THE RESPIRATORY SYSTEM:

Inspection:

- ❖ Position of the trachea: whether perceived or not. If perceived, comment on its position. If there is underlying pulmonary fibrosis, the trachea is pulled to that side.
- ❖ Shape of the chest: whether normal (elliptical) or barrel-shaped (hyperinflated) especially in smokers.
- ❖ Movement of chest wall: in ILD there is usually ***bilaterally reduced*** chest wall movements especially in the infrascapular and lower axillary regions.
- ❖ Respiratory rate: Patient's with ILD are usually tachypnoeic. The tachypnoea increases as the disease progresses, with the development of extensive honey-combing and fibrosis. In extensive (end-stage) disease, this may finally lead to respiratory failure.
- ❖ Accessory muscles of respiration: Active or not. They may be active in case of extensive fibrosis.

Palpation:

- Confirm the position of the trachea, mention the cricosternal distance,
- examine for tracheal tug: main causes include:
  - aortic arch aneurysm
  - malignant lymphomas, and
  - COPD: predominantly emphysema
- Position of the cardiac apex: May be shifted in case of pulmonary fibrosis.
- Chest wall movements, anteriorly and posteriorly
- Chest wall tenderness, bony tenderness, sternal tenderness.
- Tactile fremitus (symmetrically checked). It is decreased over areas of fibrosis and honey-combing.

Percussion:

- ❖ Apical percussion.
- ❖ Direct clavicular percussion
- ❖ Anterior and posterior percussion. In case of extensive fibrosis and honey-combing, a dull note on percussion may be elicited.

Note: *To percuss the interscapular region, the hands should be folded over the shoulders so as to get the scapulae out of the way. To percuss in the axillary region, the hands should be folded over the head.*

Auscultation:

Auscultate for:

- Normal vesicular breath sounds
- Bronchial breath sounds. Tubular (high-pitched) bronchial breath sounds may be heard over areas of honey-combing.
- Mid-to-late inspiratory crepitations *('velcro rales')* are heard over areas of fibrosis and honey-combing. It is therefore sometimes difficult to distinguish from bronchiectasis especially in cases of end-stage ILD when there is extensive honey-combing.

Note:

The profuse rales present in IPF patients are believed to be due to retained secretions in the ectatic bronchioles. Their characteristic quality ("Velcro rales") may be due to the loss of attenuation provided in healthy lungs by surrounding air-filled alveoli. High-pitched, end-inspiratory wheezing accompanying the profuse rales (i.e. chirping rales) may aid in the differential diagnosis of diffuse parenchymal lung disease by directing attention to a bronchiolitic component as in, extrinsic allergic alveolitis.[3]

Cardiovascular system examination:

In the mid-to-late stages of the disease, the patient usually develops signs of cor pulmonale and pulmonary hypertension, with a loud P2, right-ventricular heave and a S3 (protodiastolic) gallop.

DIFFERENTIAL DIAGNOSIS:

Based on the above history and physical examination findings, a comprehensive 'differential diagnosis' should now be arrived at.

These should include the following:

- Idiopathic Pulmonary Fibrosis (IPF)
- Bronchiectasis: It may be unilateral or bilateral. Usually seen as multiple cystic lesions.

- Sarcoidosis: bilateral symmetrical mediastinal and/or hilar lymphadenopathy. Skin and/or eye lesions too may be present.
- Asbestosis: calcified and non-calcified pleural plaques with bilateral basal interstitial shadowings
- Lymphangioleiomyomatosis/ tuberous sclerosis: women in the child-bearing age group with numerous cystic areas diffusely present throughout both lungs. May be accompanied by pneumothorax, chylothorax, renal and hepatic angiomyolipomas.
- Pulmonary alveolar protenosis: diffuse mosaic ground-glass crazy paving pattern without fibrosis.
- Chronic hypersensitivity pneumonitis (extrinsic allergic alveolitis): Ill-defined non branching centrilobular nodules with an upper lobe predominance or a diffuse distribution with or without ground-glass opacities are characteristic for acute or subacute hypersensitivity pneumonitis. These findings are diagnostic in an appropriate clinical setting.
- Rheumatoid arthritis: Bilateral basal reticular shadowing. There may be honeycombing and fibrosis. Ground-glass appearance is usually less than reticular shadowing.
- Scleroderma/ systemic sclerosis: Bilateral basal ground-glass opacities seen. Honeycombing is rare.
- Polymyositis: Bilateral basal ground-glass opacities seen. Honeycombing is rare.
- Sjogren's: Bilateral ground-glass appearance seen, thin perivascular cysts, centrilobular nodules and mild reticular shadowing are also seen.
- Dermatomyositis/ polymyositis: Bilateral basal ground-glass opacities seen. Honeycombing is rare.
- Mixed collagen vascular disorder: Bilateral basal ground-glass opacities seen. Honeycombing is rare.
- Bronchogenic carcinoma: should be considered as a possible differential diagnosis in smokers.
- Histiocytosis X: centrilobular fine nodules and cysts in upper zones with relative sparing of lower zones.
- Chronic eosinophilic pneumonia
- Granulomatous vasculitis

INVESTIGATIONS:

Based on the history elicited and findings on clinical examination the student is expected to discuss the value of relevant investigations in establishing a diagnosis. He is expected to be competent in discussing findings of a chest radiograph especially in a 'long case'.

It would be appropriate to categorize investigations into those for diagnostic purposes and for those that are relevant in assessing severity of the underlying disease.

Results of ABG are common discussion points in the management of the patient.

Non-invasive Investigative Procedures:

Chest Radiography-Postero-anterior (PA) and lateral views: it shows characteristic ***"interstitial"*** infiltrates which affect the lung bases more than the apical regions.

In most ILDs, the plain chest radiograph reveals reduced lung volumes with bilateral reticular or reticulonodular opacities. The plain radiograph in IPF shows bilateral, peripheral disease predominantly at the lung bases with reticulonodular infiltrates and/or honeycombing. The radiographic abnormalities are predominantly present in the subpleural and dependent areas of the lung. Ground-glass appearance is absent or minimal in classic IPF. Pleural disease and significant lymphadenopathy are also not seen, although up to two-thirds of IPF patients have mild mediastinal adenopathy.[4] As the disease progresses, the chest radiograph shows multiple tiny cysts (honeycombing), predominantly at the lung bases. Honeycombing reflects end-stage ('burnt-out') fibrosis and is a classical presentation of end-stage ILDs.

In contrast, some diseases cause an inflammatory abnormality with a differing radiographic image. In cellular nonspecific interstitial pneumonia (NIP), the predominant abnormality is a 'ground-glass' appearance in the mid-zones, without distortion of the lung architecture or loss of lung volume.

NOTE: *Chest radiography is readily done in most centres and provides the student with enormous amount of information. Expertise must be shown in interpreting chest radiographs*

Arterial Blood Gas investigations (ABG): helps to determine the pH of the blood, extent of hypoxia and CO2 retention. In case of extensive disease (end-stage ILD) severe hypoxia with respiratory acidosis and oxygen desaturation may be present. Early on, respiratory alkalosis may be present due to tachypnoea. There may also be ***increased alveolar-arterial partial pressure of oxygen gradient.*** All these findings may also be worsened with exercise, and exercise-testing may demonstrate decreased exercise capacity with exercise-limiting impairment in ventilation and gas exchange. Patients with extensive lung damage (end-stage ILD) may finally require invasive ventilatory management.

Full Blood Count: It is raised in case of superadded bacterial infection, usually in patients with multiple cystic changes (honeycombing).

Sputum Examination: Sputum should be examined for:

Bacterial smear and culture: sputum should be tested for gram-positive, gram-negative and anaerobic organisms, as cysts in ILD may get secondarily infected.

- **Fungal culture:** Fungal infection may be present in long-standing cysts (honeycombs).

- **Acid-fast bacilli (AFB) smear and culture:** sputum should be tested for AFB smear and culture to rule out presence of tuberculous infection in long-standing cysts.

- **Malignant cells (cytology):** early-morning sputum samples collected on four consecutive days should be tested for malignant cells.

High-resolution Computed Tomography (HRCT) chest scan: In IPF, the HRCT chest scan reveals bilateral, peripheral disease, predominantly at the lung bases with reticulonodular infiltrates. In later stages of the diseases process, honeycombing and fibrosis with distortion of the lung architecture and traction bronchiectasis are seen, predominantly at the lung bases. Ground-glass appearance is absent or minimal in classic IPF. Pleural disease and significant lymphadenopathy are not seen. However, two-thirds of IPF patients have mild mediastinal adenopathy.[4] With progression of the disease, HRCT chest scan may reveal multiple tiny cysts (honeycombs) in the lower zones which reflect the presence of end-stage ILD.[5]

In cellular nonspecific interstitial pneumonia (NIP), the predominant abnormality is ground-glass appearance in the mid-zones, without distortion of the lung architecture.

Pulmonary Function Testing: It shows a *restrictive impairment* on lung function. Both, the forced expiratory volume in one second (FEV1) and forced vital capacity (FVC) are diminished, and the FEV1/FVC ratio is preserved or even increased.

Lung volumes and the diffusing capacity of the lung for carbon monoxide (DLCO) are both reduced. The *reduction in diffusing capacity* reflects damage to the alveolar-capillary interface. In ILD the lungs have *reduced compliance* and require supranormal transpleural pressures to ventilate. This lack of compliance results in *small lung volumes* and *increased work of breathing.*

DLCO — reflect in reduction in diffusing capacity.

Note: In patients with concomitant ILD and significant emphysema, the opposing physiologic effects of the two diseases can result in deceptively normal spirometry and lung volume measurements, as well as apparently normally compliant lungs. However, because both emphysema and ILD result in impaired gas exchange, the DLCO is significantly decreased.

An obstructive defect may be present in patients with coexistent chronic obstructive pulmonary disease, sarcoidosis, LAM, and tuberous sclerosis.

Serologic testing for rheumatologic disease or vasculitis: These include antinuclear antibodies, rheumatoid factor, erythrocyte sedimentation rate, C-reactive protein, anticitrulline antibody, antineutrophil cytoplasmic antibodies, antiglomerular basement membrane antibodies and serum precipitins for common hypersensitivity antigens.

Invasive Investigative Procedures:

These include:

> ➤ ***Bronchoalveolar lavage (BAL):*** Though bronchiolar lavage findings are not diagnostic for ILD, it is useful in evaluating the possibility of infection or malignancy. It can also be useful in diagnosing eosinophilic pneumonia. BAL has also been used to assess the 'activity' of the disease process. A BAL sample rich in cells (predominantly lymphocytes) is suggestive of active disease, with response to treatment expected to be good. However, if the BAL sample shows a paucity of cells, the diagnosis goes more in favour of end-stage or 'burnt-out' disease, with an expected poor response to treatment.

> ➤ ***Fibreoptic/Video Bronchoscopy:*** Transbronchial and endobronchial lung biopsies are diagnostic for sarcoidosis and lymphangitic spread of carcinoma but may not help in the diagnosis of ILD. This is due to the patchy distribution of the lesion in ILD.

> ➤ Hence, ***Open Lung Biopsy or Thoracoscopic Lung Biopsy*** are considered the ***'gold standard'*** in the definitive diagnosis of ILD. However, at present, video-assisted thoracoscopic lung biopsy is the procedure of choice due to convenience and easy accessibility.

> Even so, the role of lung biopsy in the presence of characteristic high-resolution CT scan findings remains controversial.[5,6] Clinicians believe that biopsy may not be

necessary when typical clinical and high-resolution CT scan features of UIP/IPF are present.

Note: Students should be well-acquainted with the anatomy of the tracheobronchial tree and the bronchopulmonary segments so that there is a better understanding of HRCT chest scan findings and bronchoscopic procedures, during the internal medicine posting.

Note: The student should have written a management plan as this often follows investigations and diagnosis especially in a long case examination

MANAGEMENT:

Note: The discussion below is largely on interstitial lung disease. The student should be reminded that this would form only part of the viva in a long case

Possible Questions:

- *Briefly outline the non-surgical management of the patient.*

Suggested aspects to cover:

i.	Breaking 'serious illness' news
ii.	Medical Management
iii.	Continued management
iv.	Counselling patients who decline care

Outline of Medical Management:

This includes:

➢ **Cessation of exposure to occupational agents** such as silica dusts, asbestos fibres. etc. This may require change of occupation which may not always be easy due to financial compulsions.

➢ **Corticosteroids**

➢ **Immunosuppressants/cytotoxic agents** such as cyclophosphamide, azathioprine, methotrexate

➢ Other immunosuppressive or antifibrotic agents such as colchicine, cyclosporine, and D-penicillamine

- ➤ Approaches based on altering signalling pathways (e.g., interruption of endothelin or TNF-directed pathways, or augmentation of interferon gamma-1b pathways)
- ➤ **Supportive treatment** with oxygen supplementation, antibiotics for lower respiratory tract infections and pulmonary rehabilitation is often useful in optimizing function, reducing morbidity and prolonging life.
- ➤ **Vaccinations and Infection Avoidance**
- ➤ **Non-invasive and invasive ventilatory management** (usually needed in later stages of the disease)

Some patients with ILD respond well to conventional immunosuppressive or anti-inflammatory therapy, such as corticosteroids, cyclophosphamide, or azothioprine. This is especially so in cases where there is good cellular infiltration of the interstitium by lymphoid or monocyte-lineage cells (e.g., cellular NSIP), or those that involve granulomatous inflammation (e.g., sarcoidosis).

However, cases of ILD that have a paucity of inflammatory cells, or a predominance of fibrosis, are less likely to respond to anti-inflammatory or immunosuppressive therapy. In such cases, alternative treatment approaches have been tried to combat the poor prognosis. Approaches based on altering signalling pathways (e.g., interruption of endothelin or TNF-directed pathways, or augmentation of interferon gamma-1b pathways) are currently being tested.

Pulmonary rehabilitation is important in building aerobic fitness, maintaining physical activity and improving quality of life.

Since ILD patients are treated with immunosuppressants, they are at an increased risk for development of infections. Hence, patients with ILD should receive pneumococcal vaccination and a yearly influenza virus vaccine. Additionally, these patients should be taught to practice good hand hygiene (frequent hand washing).

POSSIBLE QUESTION:
Discuss briefly the role of lung transplantation in Interstitial Lung Disease

Surgical Management:

Lung transplantation is often the only available long-term option for selected patients with advanced disease refractory to medical therapy,[7] provided they are in an appropriate age group (generally, less than 65 years) and lack other comorbid diseases that could limit success after transplant (e.g., heart or kidney failure).

Moreover, it is the only surgical form of management that has been shown to increase survival in patients with UIP/IPF. Survival rates worldwide after single lung transplantation are approximately 74% at 1 year, 58% at 3 years, 47% at 5 years, and 24% at 10 years. Survival rates are lower for bilateral lung transplantation.

Note:

In the case discussed students are expected to consider complications and be adept at requesting for relevant investigations and suggest specific treatment for such complications. In the long run they should also discuss prognosis and preventive aspects of the disease (e.g. occupation disease, notification to health authorities).

Complications of Interstitial Lung Disease:

- ❖ Haemoptysis
- ❖ Increasing breathlessness due to the progressive nature of the disease process
- ❖ Superadded bacterial, fungal or tuberculous infection within the cystic spaces (honeycombs)
- ❖ Severe hypoxia with respiratory acidosis (CO2 retention)
- ❖ Cor pulmonale with right-sided heart failure
- ❖ Pulmonary Hypertension
- ❖ Respiratory failure which may require invasive ventilatory management
- ❖ Opportunistic infections due to long-term treatment with immunosuppressants and corticosteroids, such as PCP pneumonia
- ❖ Complications of video-assisted thoracoscopic lung biopsy
- ❖ Post surgical (lung transplant) complications

Prognosis of Interstitial Lung Disease:

Knowledge of prognosis is essential while managing the patient and addressing his/her concerns and those of the family members.

Pulmonary function studies and the 6-minute walk study is of prognostic value in IPF with histopathologic findings of UIP and NSIP. A reduced diffusion capacity (DLCO) on initial evaluation is a poor prognostic indicator, regardless of histologic type, with advanced versus limited disease based on a cutoff value of DLCO greater or less than 40%.[8] Similarly, oxygen saturation of less than 88% during a 6-minute walk test is believed to be a predictor of poor prognosis. In addition, serial reductions in forced vital capacity and DLCO over time are also associated with increased morbidity and mortality.

Ethical and Professional issues:
Competence in the following is essential:

- Breaking 'serious chronic illness' news

- Informed consent for procedures required for diagnosis and management of Interstitial Lung Disease
- Discussing prognosis and 'long-term' management plans

- Cost-benefit of management of this chronic progressive illness.

- Notification of occupation hazards and compensation

In case the patient decides to discontinue all forms of treatment due to a sense of hopelessness over the chronic, progressive nature of the disease, it is essential for the doctor (in the capacity of the primary health-giver) to explain to the patient the potential disadvantages of such a decision.

The patient should be explained that treating ILD with corticosteroids, immunosuppressive agents and other supportive therapies helps to *curtail progression of the disease process,* thereby reducing the cough, breathlessness and incidence of other potential complications. Active management reduces the incidence of repeated respiratory infections, cor pulmonale, pulmonary hypertension and respiratory failure, thereby improving the quality and span of life and reducing mortality.

MUST KNOW FACTS

- ILD is characterised by the presence of a 'dry' cough with progressively increasing breathlessness.
- It is most commonly seen in the 50-60 year age group.
- On physical examination the most common findings include, *clubbing and 'velcro' rales.*
- Tests used to diagnose ILD include, chest radiograph, HRCT chest scan, BAL, pulmonary function testing and ABG.
- However, the *'gold standard'* in the diagnosis of ILD is *open lung biopsy or video-assisted thoracoscopic lung biopsy.*
- Medical treatment includes *corticosteroids and immunosuppressants,* along with supportive management.
- Surgical treatment involves single or bilateral *Lung Transplantation.*

REFERENCES:

1) King TE. Clinical advances in the diagnosis and therapy of the interstitial lung diseases. Am. J. Respir. Crit. Care Med 2005; 172 (3): 268–79.

2) Travis WD, King TE, Bateman ED, et al. "ATS/ERS international multidisciplinary consensus classification of idiopathic interstitial pneumonias. General principles and recommendations." American Journal of Respiratory and Critical Care Medicine 2002; 165 (5): 277–304.

3) Reich JM. Genesis of some histologic, BAL, and auscultatory features of Idiopathic Pulmonary Fibrosis. Chest **2008;** 133 **(2): 585-586.**

4) Souza CA, Muller NL, Lee KS, et al: Idiopathic interstitial pneumonias: Prevalence of mediastinal lymph node enlargement in 206 patients. AJR Am J Roentgenol. 2006, 186: 995-999.

5) Lynch DA, David Godwin J, Safrin S, Starko KM, Hormel P, Brown KK, et al. High-resolution computed tomography in idiopathic pulmonary fibrosis: diagnosis and prognosis. Am J Respir Crit Care Med 2005;172(4):488-93.

6) Hunninghake GW, Zimmerman MB, Schwartz DA, King TE Jr, Lynch J, Hegele R, et al. Utility of a lung biopsy for the diagnosis of idiopathic pulmonary fibrosis. Am J Respir Crit Care Med 2001;164(2):193-6.

7) Alalawi R, Whelan T, Bajwa RS, Hodges TN. Lung transplantation and interstitial lung disease. *Curr Opin Pulm Med* 2005; 11(5):461-6.

CASE 6 : PNEUMOTHORAX
RUMI R KHAJOTIA

Pneumothorax is an important clinical case with which medical students must be acquainted, both at undergraduate and postgraduate levels. In clinical practice, pneumothorax should be considered as a possible diagnosis following history-taking and physical examination in a patient with typical symptoms and signs. It should then be confirmed by relevant investigative procedures.

❧ DEFINITION: Pneumothorax is defined as the presence of air or gas in the pleural cavity, (the pleural cavity being the potential space between the visceral and parietal pleura) with concomitant collapse of the underlying lung tissue.

Classification of Pneumothorax:

There are various classifications available, namely:

A) Based *on cause:*

- *Primary spontaneous pneumothorax:* is one which is idiopathic (without apparent cause) and without significant underlying lung disease.[1] Usually, it is seen in patients who are tall, thin and smokers between

- 19-30 years of age *In some cases it has been attribu*ted to a sharp first or second rib injuring the lung. In one study, 57% of patients with benign spontaneous pneumothorax were found to have a sharp first or second rib.[2] This has also been termed as the *'sharp rib syndrome.'*

- *Secondary spontaneous pneumothorax:* It is a pneumothorax which occurs as a result of an underlying lung pathology.[1]

- *Traumatic:* It is usually due to *a blunt or a penetrating* injury to the chest wall.[3] It may occur due to a variety of causes such as:

  ➢ Rib fractures penetrating the parietal pleura and damaging the underlying lung tissue

  ➢ Penetrating lung injuries with a sharp object such as a knife or sharpnel following an explosive blast.

  ➢ Following medical procedures such as pleural fluid aspiration, percutaneous lung biopsy, internal jugular vein catheterisation and mechanical ventilation. It is then known as *'Iatrogenic pneumothorax.'*

B) Based on the pathological abnormality:

- **Open pneumothorax:** In this case the pneumothorax occurs due to the development of a **bronchopleural fistula** which results in a partially collapsed lung. The lung usually remains in a 'partially-collapsed' state. The patient may be clinically stable as air freely moves in and out of the pleural cavity with each successive respiratory cycle.

  Open pneumothorax is usually resistant to conventional methods of treatment such as intercostal drainage and suction. In these cases, **surgical intervention** to close the fistulous opening is absolutely required.

- **Closed pneumothorax:** In this condition the tear in the lung parenchyma (which led to air leaking out into the pleural cavity and the consequent development of a pneumothorax) heals (closes) spontaneously, with no further air-leak into the pleural cavity. In these patients the pneumothorax may resolve spontaneously without any intervention or if large, may require intercostal tube drainage, when the lung usually re-expands well.

- **Tension pneumothorax:** A tension pneumothorax occurs when the intrapleural pressure exceeds atmospheric pressure throughout expiration and often during inspiration. It is a life-threatening condition that develops due to the trapping of air in the pleural cavity under positive pressure. This is because of the development of a one-way valve mechanism in the traumatised lung parenchyma, which allows air to enter the pleural cavity on inspiration but does not allow it to escape out on expiration. As a result, there is an increased build-up of air in the pleural cavity with each inspiration causing a displacement of the mediastinal structures and compromising cardiopulmonary function.

  A high-index of clinical suspicion of this condition results in early detection, which may be life-saving. Immediate decompression is essential to relieve the rising pressure in the pleural cavity and this should not be delayed for radiographic confirmation.

  Delay in diagnosis may lead to an abnormally high pressure developing in the intrapleural space causing a sudden drop in the venous return to the heart, leading to a fall in the blood pressure, cardiogenic shock and consequent death.

☆ ↑ Intrapleural P
   ↓
   ↓ Venous return   110
   ↓ BP → cardiogenic shock → death

Causes of tension pneumothorax include:

➢ traumatic chest injuries (blunt or penetrating) ✓

➢ trauma due to high-pressure mechanical ventilation

➢ sudden lifting of heavy weights

➢ a harsh bout of coughing.

Tension pneumothorax should be considered a serious differential diagnosis in patients who develop acute breathlessness and chest pain following a harsh bout of coughing.[4]

AETIOLOGY OF PNEUMOTHORAX:

➢ Idiopathic, spontaneous. 1°
2°

➢ Known causes include:

Underlying lung diseases such as, tuberculosis, pneumonia (esp. staphylococcal), emphysema (usually due to ruptured subpleural blebs), cystic fibrosis, bronchogenic carcinoma, pulmonary fibrosis, sarcoidosis, lymphangioleiomyomatosis (LAM), Pneumocystis carinii (PCP) pneumonia.

Note: Chronic obstructive pulmonary disease (COPD), tuberculosis and *Pneumocystis carinii* pneumonia (PCP) related to infection with the human immunodeficiency virus (HIV) are the most common conditions which are associated with secondary spontaneous pneumothorax.

LAM is a diffuse cystic disease seen almost exclusively in women of child-bearing age groups. It has rarely been reported in males. It is usually accompanied by other lesions such as tuberous sclerosis and renal and hepatic angiomyolipomas. The pneumothorax that occurs in this case is usually '***open***' and resistant to treatment with intercostal drainage and suction. Surgical closure of the air-leaks is usually required in such patients. bronchopleural fistula

✓ ***Traumatic chest wall injuries:*** Tension Pneumothorax

❖ Blunt trauma from a blow or car crash

❖ Knife wounds

❖ Fractured ribs

❖ Gunshot wounds

✓ **Iatrogenic:** due to medical procedures such as:

  ❖ Percutaneous lung biopsy

  ❖ Insertion of intercostal drainage tubes

  ❖ Internal jugular vein catheterisation

  ❖ Cardiopulmonary resuscitation (CPR)

  ❖ Mechanical ventilation _(High Pressure) →TP

✓ **Occupational and other causes:**

  ❖ Flying in unpressurised aircrafts

  ❖ Scuba diving

  ❖ Mountain climbing at high-altitudes

Note: **Catamenial pneumothorax,** is pneumothorax which occurs in conjunction with the menstrual periods of women. It is believed to be caused primarily by endometriosis of the pleura. ?

Risk factors in the development of pneumothorax:

They include:

> *Gender:* Males have a greater chance of developing a pneumothorax as compared to females.

> *Smoking:* The risk increases with the amount of cigarettes smoked and the duration of smoking, even in the absence of emphysema.

> *Age:* Idiopathic spontaneous pneumothorax is more common in young men between 20-40 years of age who are tall and of asthenic build.

> *Underlying lung disease:* Coexistent lung diseases such as emphysema, pulmonary fibrosis, sarcoidosis, cystic fibrosis or LAM increases the risk of developing pneumothorax.

> *A previous history of pneumothorax:* increases the chances of developing a second pneumothorax especially within 1-2 years of the first episode. This may occur in the same lung or the contralateral lung.

PATHOPHYSIOLOGY OF PRIMARY SPONTANEOUS PNEUMOTHORAX:

Even though patients with primary spontaneous pneumothorax are believed not to have clinically apparent lung disease, studies have shown that subpleural bullae were present in 76 to 100 percent of patients during video-assisted thoracoscopic surgery.[5] The mechanism of bulla formation is not exactly known. However, it is believed that degradation of elastic fibers occur in the lungs, induced by the smoking-related influx of neutrophils and macrophages. Consequently, this leads to an imbalance in the protease–antiprotease and oxidant–antioxidant systems.[6] Once the bullae have formed, inflammation-induced obstruction of the small airways increases alveolar pressure, resulting in an air leak into the lung interstitium. This air then moves to the hilum, causing pneumomediastinum, and as the mediastinal pressure rises, rupture of the mediastinal parietal pleura occurs, causing pneumothorax.[7]

PATHOPHYSIOLOGY OF SECONDARY SPONTANEOUS PNEUMOTHORAX:

When alveolar pressure is greater than the pressure in the lung interstitium, as may occur in patients with chronic obstructive pulmonary disease and airway inflammation after coughing, air from the ruptured alveolus moves into the interstitium and then along the bronchovascular bundle to the hilum of the ipsilateral lung, resulting in pneumomediastinum. The air then moves through the mediastinal parietal pleura into the pleural space causing a pneumothorax.[7] Secondary spontaneous pneumothorax may also occur if air from a ruptured alveolus or lung cavity leaks directly into the pleural space as a result of necrosis of the lung tissue. This is usually the mechanism seen in *P. carinii* pneumonia or pulmonary tuberculosis.

ruptured alveoli → leak to pleura space .

Size of pneumothorax:

Various method have been proposed to determine the size of a pneumothorax.

The new BTS guidelines divide the size of a pneumothorax into "small" or "large" depending on the presence of a visible rim of air <2 cm or ⩾2 cm between the lung margin and the chest wall.

Henry et al[8] explain that they have attempted to use a variation of the method described by Axel based on the largest distance from the chest wall to the pleural line and using the assumption that, because the volume of the lung and the hemithorax are roughly proportional to the cube of their diameters, the volume of pneumothorax can be estimated by measuring an average diameter of the lung and the hemithorax, and by cubing these diameters, thus finding the ratios.[9]

The American College of Chest Physicians has proposed a different arbitrary system for estimating pneumothorax size. They suggest that "small" pneumothoraces should be defined by distances of <3 cm from the apex to cupula of the lung and "large" pneumothoraces by distances of >3 cm.[10]

CASE VIGNETTE:

A 22-year-old male, non-smoker, of asthenic build, comes to the out-patient department with complaints of sudden, 'sharp' right-sided generalised chest pain and acute breathlessness over the past two hours. There is no history of cough, blood in the sputum and not associated with fever. There is no history of loss of appetite or loss of weight.

There is no past history of diabetes, hypertension or tuberculosis.

There is no history of hypertension, diabetes mellitus, malignancy or pulmonary tuberculosis in the family.

His bladder and bowel habits are normal.

The patient is a college student and is not involved in any strenuous activities.

At this stage the student is expected to initiate and formulate some pertinent questions :

Q 1.Based on the history provided , what are the possible differential diagnoses?

Q 2. Which systems should I examine to help me in confirming the diagnosis?

The student should then proceed to conduct the General Examination and the Systemic (Local) Examination of the Respiratory System.

General Examination: The patient appears to be of asthenic build. He is afebrile and his blood pressure is within normal limits. He has tachycardia, with a pulse rate of 112 beats per minute. His right hemithorax moves less with respiration as compared to the left. He is not cyanosed. His JVP is not raised. There is no pallor, icterus or oedema of feet. Cervical lymph nodes are not palpable.

Systemic (Local) Examination:

On inspection, the right hemithorax appears to be hyperinflated as compared to the left and chest wall movements appear to be significantly reduced on the right side.

Reduced chest wall movements are confirmed by palpation.

Tactile vocal fremitus is decreased on the right side in the 3rd to 6th intercostal spaces anteriorly, the entire axilla and also in the interscapular and infrascapular regions posteriorly, on the right side.

There is also a hyperresonant percussion note in the same area on the right side.

On auscultation, air entry is absent in the right 3rd to 6th intercostal spaces anteriorly, the right axilla and posteriorly in the right interscapular and infrascapular regions. Vocal resonance is also absent in the same area.

On cardiovascular system examination, S1 and S2 are normal. There is no gallop or murmur heard. The cardiac apex is shifted outwards and downwards and is palpable in the 6th intercostal space in the anterior axillary line.

Abdominal system examination is normal. Liver and spleen are not palpable, there is no abdominal tenderness, no evidence of free fluid in the abdomen and peristalsis are well heard.

The Central Nervous System examination is normal.

Note: In this case, the student is expected to be thorough in reporting the respiratory and cardiovascular system findings.

In eliciting the history, the student should bear in mind the potential differential diagnosis.

Ask for cardinal symptoms of the respiratory system:

Cough: may or may not be present in case of an idiopathic spontaneous pneumothorax. However, in case of a secondary pneumothorax cough may be present depending on the underlying pathology,e.g. emphysema, pulmonary tuberculosis, cystic fibrosis, *Pneumocystis carinii* pneumonia. A harsh bout of coughing is also known to precipitate the development of a pneumothorax.[4]

Blood in the sputum: haemoptysis may be present in case of secondary spontaneous pneumothorax depending on the aetiological cause, namely, pulmonary tuberculosis, cystic fibrosis, LAM.

Breathlessness: The breathlessness is usually of sudden onset and then slowly progresses as observed in primary spontaneous pneumothorax.

If the breathlessness is rapidly progressive with coexistent cyanosis, fall in blood pressure and deterioration of the patients overall general condition, **_tension pneumothorax_** must be considered a serious possibility.

In secondary spontaneous pneumothorax the patient may give history of progressively increasing breathlessness over months or years. In such cases, an underlying cause such as emphysema, pulmonary fibrosis, pulmonary tuberculosis or cystic fibrosis must be considered.

Chest Pain: Usually present. It is usually **_'sharp' or 'stabbing'_** in character (pleuritic pain). The pain is believed to be due to stretching of the parietal pleura due to increasing air in the pleural cavity. The pain may later settle as a **_'steady ache.'_**

Fever: usually absent ~~in~~ _may or may not_ in idiopathic primary spontaneous pneumothorax. However, fever may be present in cases of emphysema with lower respiratory tract infections, cystic fibrosis or end-stage pulmonary fibrosis. A low-grade fever may be present in cases of pulmonary tuberculosis.

Weight Loss: inquire whether the patient has lost weight. Seen in progressive emphysema, cystic fibrosis and pulmonary tuberculosis.

PAST MEDICAL HISTORY:

History of repeated respiratory tract infection in the past: This could be indicative of conditions such as cystic fibrosis, LAM, and other cavitary lung diseases.

History of similar illness in the past: Incidence of pneumothorax increases in patients who have had an earlier episode. This is more common within 1-2 years of the initial episode of pneumothorax and may occur in the same lung or in the contralateral lung.

FAMILY HISTORY:

Enquire about similar illness in the family. Certain types of pneumothorax may run in families, e.g. (Alpha 1-antitrypsin deficiency causing emphysema) or cystic fibrosis which may lead to pneumothorax.

History of tuberculosis in the family.

PERSONAL HISTORY:

Inquire about bladder, bowel, sleep and dietary habits. In case of progressive emphysema, the patient may have progressively increasing breathlessness which may significantly reduce his appetite and also cause significant sleep disturbances.

SOCIAL AND OCCUPATIONAL HISTORY:

Inquire in detail about:

- Smoking habits: number of cigarettes smoked per day and for how many years. Tobacco chewing or betel-nut chewing

- Drug abuse

Occupational history is important in pneumothorax, hence details need to be elicited. *Aircraft pilots, scuba divers and mountain guides* have a higher risk of developing pneumothorax than the general population.

SUMMARIZING THE HISTORY:

Student should be adept at summarizing the history in 2-3 sentences, *highlighting* the *salient clinical features relevant to the case.*

In this case the history could be summarized as follows:

"A 22-year-old male patient, non-smoker, of asthenic build, presents with complaints of a 'sharp' right-sided chest pain and sudden onset breathlessness over the past 2 hours. He is a college student not involved in any strenuous activities. There is no history of cough, fever or blood in the sputum.

SYSTEMIC REVIEW OF SYMPTOMS:

- To determine the possible cause of a sharp, sudden-onset chest pain and acute breathlessness over 2 hours. For this, it would be essential to consider potential causes such as *pulmonary embolism, a rapidly enlarging emphysematous bulla or a spontaneous pneumothorax.*

- On systemic review of symptoms it is necessary to determine the cause of the pneumothorax, whether it is *idiopathic or due to a secondary underlying cause such as emphysema, pulmonary tuberculosis, cystic fibrosis or sarcoidosis.*

To determine whether the patient had been treated for similar complaints in the past and the response to past treatment. This could indicate presence of chronic diseases such as pulmonary tuberculosis, cystic fibrosis, pulmonary fibrosis.

BED-SIDE MANNERS:

Student introduces himself/herself to the patient and politely asks permission to examine. Student is polite and courteous throughout the examination and has a gentle and caring demeanour. The patient is thanked at the end of the examination and helped into the position he was in before the examination.

In a female patient a chaperone should be present and due care to modesty should be given.

The entire physical examination should be conducted from the right side of the patient.

GENERAL PHYSICAL EXAMINATION:

- Comment on the general condition of the patient, particularly his weight

- Vital parameters: Temperature, Pulse, Respiratory Rate, Blood Pressure

- Respiratory rate: to observe from the foot-end of the bed on the right side.

  Look for:

  - respiratory rate

  - whether the chest is moving equally on both sides. In unilateral pneumothorax, the chest wall movements are significantly reduced or absent on the affected side.

  - intercostal fullness and/or hyperinflation may be noticed on the affected side. This is especially evident in case of a *tension pneumothorax.*

  - movement of the subcostal angle

- whether accessory muscles of respiration are 'active' or not. In case of a large or rapidly increasing pneumothorax, the patient may be in respiratory distress, resulting in active use of accesssory muscles of respiration.

- Jugular Venous Pressure (JVP): may be raised in a patient with a rapidly-increasing pneumothorax. This is especially so in case of a tension pneumothorax as the intrapleural pressure is very high leading to a reduced venous return to the heart. Comment on the 'waveforms' of the JVP.

- Cyanosis: Central and Peripheral. Seen in patients with large or tension pneumothorax.

- Clubbing: If present, mention the grade. May be indicative of cystic fibrosis. 40%-75% of patients with pulmonary fibrosis also show various grades of clubbing, usually late in the course of the disease.

- Oedema of feet: If present, state if pitting is present or not, and whether the oedema is unilateral or on both legs. Patient with end-stage pulmoary fibrosis may develop cor pulmonale (right ventricular failure) leading to bilateral pitting oedema.

- Cervical lymphadenopathy: ideally to be palpated from the back with the patient's neck slightly flexed. Comment as you examine. Matted lymph nodes may be present, indicative of tuberculosis.

- Flaps: if present, are suggestive of CO2 retention.

- Pallor, icterus

SYSTEMIC EXAMINATION OF THE RESPIRATORY SYSTEM:

Inspection:

- ❖ Position of the trachea: whether perceived or not. If perceived, comment on its position. In case of a large pneumothorax or tension pneumothorax, the trachea is pushed to the opposite side.
- ❖ Shape of the chest: whether normal (elliptical) or barrel-shaped (hyperinflated), especially in smokers. In case of a rapidly increasing pneumothorax (as occurs in tension pneumothorax) one hemithorax may appear to be enlarged and hyperinflated.
- ❖ Movements of the chest wall: the hemithorax on the side of the pneumothorax moves less with respiration as compared to the contralateral side.
- ❖ Respiratory rate: Patient with pneumothorax may become tachypnoeic in order to maintain blood oxygen concentration (PaO2 and oxygen saturation). However, the hemithorax on the affected side (side of the pneumothorax) moves less than the normal side. In case of a large pneumothorax or a tension pneumothorax, the hemithorax on the affected side may show *absent chest wall movements.*
- ❖ Accessory muscles of respiration: Active or not. They may be active in case of a large pneumothorax or a tension pneumothorax.

Palpation:

- Confirm the position of the trachea, mention the cricosternal distance,
- examine for tracheal tug: main causes include:
  - aortic arch aneurysm
  - malignant lymphomas, and
  - COPD: predominantly *emphysema*
- Position of the cardiac apex: May be shifted to the side opposite the pneumothorax.
- Chest wall movements, anteriorly and posteriorly
- Chest wall tenderness, bony tenderness, sternal tenderness.
- Tactile fremitus (symmetrically checked). It is decreased or absent over area of pneumothorax.

Percussion:

- ❖ Apical percussion.
- ❖ Direct clavicular percussion
- ❖ Anterior and posterior percussion. In case of a pneumothorax, a hyper resonant note is heard on the affected side.

> ***Note:*** *To percuss the interscapular region, the hands should be folded over the shoulders so as to get the scapulae out of the way. To percuss in the axillary region, the hands should be folded over the head.*

Auscultation:

Auscultate for:

- Normal vesicular breath sounds on the opposite side.
- Bronchial breath sounds: bronchial breath sounds may be heard in an open pneumothorax over the site of a broncho-pleural fistula.
- Absent or diminished breath sounds and absent or diminished vocal resonance on the affected side, due to presence of air in the pleural cavity and an underlying collapsed lung.

Cardiovascular system examination:

In case of right-sided pneumothorax, the cardiac dullness and cardiac apex are shifted further to the left side and may be in the anterior axillary line or even beyond. In case of a left-sided pneumothorax the cardiac dullness may be completely obliterated (if the pneumothorax is large) and the apex will be shifted to the right side.

Differential Diagnosis of Pneumothorax:

Based on the above history and physical examination findings, a comprehensive 'differential diagnosis' should now be arrived at.

These should include the following:

> Pneumothorax *(it is always important to mention the side)*
> Emphysematous bulla
> Pulmonary embolism
> Acute coronary syndrome (ACS)/ Myocardial ischaemia
> Emphysema
> Acute exacerbation of bronchial asthma with 'silent chest.'
> Foreign body obstructing the trachea or a large bronchus/aspiration pneumonia
> Mediastinal emphysema
> Acute respiratory distress syndrome (ARDS)
> Oesophageal rupture and tears
> Pericarditis and cardiac tamponade
> Congestive heart failure and pulmonary oedema
> Aortic dissection
> Rib fracture
> Subcutaneous emphysema

Underlying causes of a 'secondary spontaneous pneumothorax' which need to be considered include:

✓ Pulmonary tuberculosis
✓ Emphysema
✓ Cystic fibrosis
✓ Ruptured lung abscess
✓ Bronchogenic carcinoma with a cavitating lesion which has ruptured
✓ Pulmonary fibrosis
✓ Sarcoidosis
✓ Lymphangioleiomyomatosis/ tuberous sclerosis
✓ Pneumonia: especially, staphylococcal and pneumocystis carinii pneumonia

INVESTIGATIONS:

Based on the history elicited, and findings on clinical examination, the student is expected to discuss the value of relevant investigations in establishing the diagnosis of a pneumothorax. He is expected to be competent in discussing findings of a chest radiograph especially in a 'long case'. It would be appropriate to categorize investigations into those for diagnostic purposes and for those that are relevant in assessing severity of the underlying disease.

Chest radiographic and computed tomographic findings are common topics of discussion in this case.

Investigative Procedures:

- **Chest Radiography-**Postero-anterior (PA) and lateral views: it shows the presence of air in the pleural cavity with the margin of the collapsed lung clearly seen. In a pneumothorax the lung collapses medially and towards the hilum of the lung. In contrast, in case of a large upper-zone emphysematous bulla, the wall of the bulla may be clearly demarcated and the lung appears to be sandwiched between the bulla above and the hemidiaphragm below.

  Note: In case of an emphysematous bulla, the compressed lung does not collapse medially towards the hilum but collapses upwards or downwards, depending on the location of the bulla and its size.

  NOTE: Chest radiography is readily done in most centres and provides the student with enormous amount of information. Expertise must be shown in interpreting chest radiographs, especially in cases of pneumothorax where a chest radiograph is usually diagnostic of the condition.

  In case of a very small pneumothorax it is important to clemarcate the visceral pleural line in order to detect the pneumothorax. In some cases it may be necessary to take a chest radiograph in expiration in order to detect a very small quantity of air in the pleural cavity.

  Points to remember:
  - ❖ In erect patients, pleural gas first collects over the apex, and the space between the lung and the chest wall is most notable at that point (see the image below).

  - ❖ In the supine position, air collects in the juxtacardiac area, the lateral chest wall, and the subpulmonic region. The presence of a deep costophrenic angle on a supine film has been termed the *'deep sulcus sign.'* In some patients this is sometimes the only sign of a pneumothorax.

  - ❖ In order to detect a small pneumothorax, a lateral decubitus film may sometimes be required.

  - ❖ The most common radiographic features of a *tension pneumothorax* are a significant mediastinal shift to the opposite side, diaphragmatic depression, and rib cage expansion with the affected hemithorax appearing distinctly larger than the normal side.[4] This is highly suggestive of a tension pneumothorax in a symptomatic and clinically compromised patient.

- *Arterial Blood Gas investigations (ABG):* helps to determine the pH of the blood, extent of hypoxia and CO2 retention. In case of tension pneumothorax, severe hypoxia with respiratory acidosis and oxygen desaturation may be present.

- *Full Blood Count:* It is raised in patients with pneumonia, cystic fibrosis or other bacterial infections.

- *Sputum Examination:* In case of a suspected secondary pneumothorax, sputum should be examined for:

    - *Bacterial smear and culture:* sputum should be tested for gram-positive, gram-negative and anaerobic organisms, as cavities in cystic fibrosis may get secondarily infected.

    - *Fungal culture:* Fungal infection may be present in long-standing cysts.

    - *Acid-fast bacilli (AFB) smear and culture:* sputum should be tested for AFB smear and culture to rule out presence of tuberculous infection.

    - *Malignant cells (cytology):* early-morning sputum samples collected on four consecutive days should be tested for malignant cells. Malignant tumours are also known to cavitate and these cavities may rupture leading to the occurrence of a pneumothorax.

- *High-resolution Computed Tomography (HRCT) chest scan:* CT scanning of the chest has been increasingly used in patients with pneumothorax. CT scanning may be especially useful in detecting the underlying pathological lesion in the partially collapsed lung tissue and the contralateral lung, thereby predicting the rate of recurrence in patients with spontaneous secondary pneumothorax. It has been observed that patients having multiple, large, subpleural blebs are more prone to develop recurrent pneumothorax. With the help of an HRCT chest scan the underlying lung pathology can be detected early on during the first episode of pneumothorax, thereby mitigating the chances of a recurrence by adopting correct management techniques.

Note: HRCT chest scan has been shown to demonstrate areas of focal emphysema in more than 80% of patients with primary spontaneous pneumothorax. These focal areas of emphysema have been found to be situated predominantly in the peripheral regions of the apex of the upper lobes. In one study of 35 patients with primary spontaneous pneumothorax, localized emphysema with or without bulla formation was identified on CT in 31 patients (89%) and on radiographs in 15 patients (43%).[11]

⦿ ***Other tests to determine the underlying cause:*** These may include: erythrocyte sedimentation rate, mantoux test, alpha 1-antitrypsin levels, sweat sodium and chloride levels.

☞ *Note: The student should have written a management plan as this often follows investigations and diagnosis especially in a 'long-case' examination*

MANAGEMENT:

☞ *Note: The discussion below is largely on spontaneous pneumothorax. The student should be reminded that this would form only part of the viva in a long case*

Outline of Management:

This includes:

➢ ***Medical observation:*** If the primary spontaneous pneumothorax is small (one involving <15 percent of the hemithorax or as per the new BTS guidelines), patients may have symptoms of mild chest pain and minimal breathlessness . In such cases, supplemental oxygen may be given as it accelerates by a factor of four the reabsorption of air by the pleura, which normally occurs at a rate of 2 percent per day in patients breathing room air.[12] It is recommended to hospitalize patients even with a small pneumothorax for observation, so as to make sure the pneumothorax does not worsen.

➢ ***Simple aspiration:*** Primary spontaneous pneumothoraxes that are large (involving ≥15 percent of the hemithorax) or progressively increasing, may be drained by simple aspiration with a plastic intravenous catheter, or small-bore (7 to 14 French guage) catheter. Simple aspiration is successful in 70 percent of patients with moderate-sized primary spontaneous pneumothorax. However, it has been observed that if the patient is more than 50 years old, or if more than 2.5 liters of air needs to be aspirated, this method is likely to fail.[13]

> ***Insertion of intercostal drainge tube in the pleural cavity:*** *Primary spontaneous pneumothorax* if large(≥15 percent of the hemithorax) usually requires intercostal drainage. Since persistent air-leak from the puncture site is minimal or absent, a small-bore (7 to 14 French gauge) chest catheter is usually used.[14] The catheter is either attached to a one-way Heimlich valve or to an underwater seal.[14] The advantage of using the one-way Heimlich valve is that it allows the patient to remain ambulatory. Routine use of suction has not been shown to improve lung expansion and is not recommended in these patients. However, underwater seal devices are preferred in patients who have comorbid conditions that reduce the ability to tolerate a recurrent pneumothorax. Drainage through a chest tube has a success rate of 90 per cent for treatment of a first pneumothorax, but the rate decreases to 52 per cent for treatment of a first recurrence and to 15 per cent for treatment of a second recurrence.[1,15]

> *Secondary spontaneous pneumothorax* is usually managed with a chest tube (20 to 28 French gauge) attached to an underwater seal. Suction is sometimes used in patients with on going air leaks from the lung puncture site, and also in those in whom the lung fails to re expand after drainage with an underwater seal.

Complications of chest-tube drainage include pain, intrapleural infection, incorrect placement of the tube leading to the development of subcutaneous emphysema, haemorrhage due to trauma, lung contusion, and pulmonary edema[16] during lung re-expansion.

Removal of the intercostal drainage tube after successful lung re-expansion:

Once the lung has fully re-expanded and the patients underlying symptoms have resolved, removal of the drainage tube may be considered. It is however important to remember that certain precautions must be adhered to, prior to removal of the intercostal drainage tube. It is therefore recommended to first *clamp the tube for 24-48 hours prior to removal.* After clamping the tube, the patients clinical parameters must be regularly monitored and a chest radiograph must be repeated after 12 hours of clamping, to confirm continued lung expansion. If the lung continues to remain fully expanded and the patient is clinically stable with no evidence of tachycardia, tachypnoea, cyanosis, chest pain or hypotension, 48 hours after clamping, the tube can be removed. If the clamping procedure is followed carefully, chances of reinsertion of the drainage tube for recurrent lung collapse is minimal.

Note:A common question the student can anticipate is how tension pneumothorax is treated. Clinical competence in both technique and speed should be acquired by drills in the clinical skills unit and observation of a number of cases in the clinical setting.

Treatment of Tension Pneumothorax: [4]

➢ Tension pneumothorax, when suspected, requires urgent decompression with needle thoracostomy, followed by intercostal drainage. In an emergency situation, confirmation of the diagnosis with imaging studies might not be possible and it is considered unwise to delay chest decompression in such cases.[17]

➢ Needle thoracostomy is usually performed followed by tube thoracostomy (intercostal drainage), which is the definitive treatment of tension pneumothorax. The tube is usually inserted in an area under the axilla known as the *safe triangle.* This is done to avoid damage to internal organs. The safe triangle is formed by a horizontal line extending from the nipple and the borders of the latissimus dorsi and pectoralis major muscles.

➢ However, if a large-bore tube (no. 28 French gauge, 9.3-mm diameter) is required to be inserted, the chest tube is usually inserted under surgical guidance by dissecting through the soft tissue down to the rib using a curved hemostat.

➢ **Surgical treatment of Open Pneumothorax:**

❖ In case of an open pneumothorax there is a persistent air-leak due to the presence of a *bronchopleural fistula*. This usually occurs if a tuberculous lung cavity ruptures causing a pneumothorax. Such a cavity, being lined by granulation tissue fails to collapse and a patent fistulous tract persists, leading to a persistent air-leak.

In such cases even an intercostal drainge tube with underwater seal and suction usually fail to re-expand the lung. Therefore, surgical treatment is indicated for closure of the bronchopleural fistula.

Note:In the case discussed, students are expected to consider complications of pneumothorax and be adept at requesting for relevant investigations and suggest specific treatment for such complications. In the long-run, they should also discuss prognosis and preventive aspects of the disease (e.g. pleurodesis, occupational aspects).

Complications of Pneumothorax:

- ❖ Recurrence of a pneumothorax
- ❖ Persistent air leak
- ❖ A large pneumothorax or a rapidly increasing tension pneumothorax may lead to severe hypoxemia, CO_2 retention (due to massive lung collapse), respiratory failure, diminished venous return to the heart, hypotension and finally cardiogenic shock leading to death.
- ❖ Mediastinal emphysema especially if the pneumothorax develops while the patient is on mechanical ventilation
- ❖ Surgical (subcutaneous) emphysema
- ❖ Direct pressure on the cardiac chambers leading to reduced venous return and ejection fraction. This may occur in case of a rapidly-increasing left-sided tension pneumothorax.
- ❖ Pulmonary oedema

Prognosis of Pneumothorax:

Knowledge of prognosis is essential while managing the patient and addressing his/her concerns and those of the family members.

Prognosis in pneumothorax depends on whether it is an idiopathic spontaneous primary pneumothorax or secondary to an underlying cause.

- ❖ In a compilation of 11 studies of primary spontaneous pneumothorax the rate of recurrence was between 16 to 52 percent.[19] Most recurrences occur within six months to two years after the initial episode.[20] Asthenic habitus, history of smoking, and younger age have been reported to be independent risk factors for recurrence.

❖ The rates of recurrence for spontaneous secondary pneumothorax is similar to those for primary spontaneous pneumothorax, ranging from 39 percent to 47 percent.[19] However, underlying aetiological causes do play a role in the determination of incidence of recurrence, eg. in patients with multiple subpleural blebs or diffuse cystic lung disease (cystic fibrosis, LAM) recurrence rate may be significantly increased.

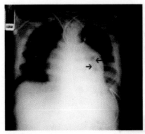

Fig 1: Semi-expanded left lung with areas of hyperluscency suggestive of lung parenchymal cavitation

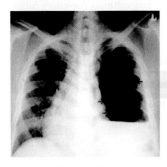

Fig 2 :A left-sided hydropneumothorax (black arrow) with complete collapse of the left lung (red arrows).

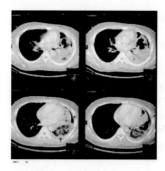

Fig 3: High-resolution (HRCT) scan of the chest showing areas of cavitation in the semi-expanded left lung and presence of a left-sided pleural effusion.

<u>**Ethical and Professional issues: Competence in the following is essential:**</u>

- **Breaking 'serious illness' news**

- **Informed consent for procedures required for diagnosis and management of Pneumothorax**

- **Discussing prognosis and 'long-term' management plans**

- **Cost-benefit of management of this chronic progressive illness.**
- **Notification of occupation hazards and compensation**

In case of primary or secondary spontaneous pneumothorax the patient should be informed of the *incidence of recurrence* and how best he may avoid it. If he is in a high-risk profession such as *aircraft pilot, scuba diver or a mountain guide,* he would need to change his profession.

In other circumstances, some patients would need to alter their hobbies such as sky-diving, scuba-diving, mountaineering, which considerably increase the chances of a recurrent pneumothorax.

In case the patient is on mechanical ventilation and develops a pneumothorax, the relatives of the patient would need to be explained the seriousness of the situation and the potential life-threatening consequences.

related to pneumothorax:

It is defined as the presence of fluid and air in the

It is defined as the presence of chyle and air in the
e seen in cases of LAM.

Pyopneumo... It is defined as the presence of pus and air in the
pleural cavity. This is most commonly seen in case of a ruptured lung
absces wherein pus and air leak into the pleural cavity.

Haemopneumothorax: It is defined as the presence of blood and air in the
pleural cavity. It is most commonly seen following blunt or penetrating
chest wall injuries.

HIGH ACHIEVER QUESTIONS:

a) What is the pathophysiology behind the development of cardiogenic
shock and consequent death in a case of tension pneumothorax?

b) Why is the *'deep sulcus sign'* of significant clinical importance?

c) Which type of pneumothorax is the one most resistant to treatment?

d) Why is a patient with an 'open pneumothorax' clinically quite stable?

e) How do you determine the size of a pneumothorax? Explain the two
methods commonly used.

Radiology quiz:

Describe in detail the following chest radiograph?

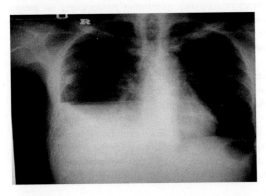

(Patients history: *Chest radiograph of a 32-year-old male with cough,
right-sided chest pain, weight loss and haemoptysis.*

Answer :

A right-sided hydropneumothorax with areas of consolidation

at the left apical region.

Diagnosis of 'hydropneumothorax' is established by the following radiological markers: collapsed lung with visceral pleural line distinctly seen.

fluid within the right pleural cavity having an upper 'straight' border, indicative of air above it. This is commonly termed as an *'air-fluid' level.*

presence of fluid in the right pleural cavity is also evident by the obliteration of the underlying rib markings, obliteration of the right costophrenic and cardiophrenic angles, and obliteration of the contour of the right hemidiaphragm.

Likely aetiological cause: Pulmonary tuberculosis

REFERENCES:

1) Sahn SA, Heffner JE. Spontaneous pneumothorax. *N Engl J Med*. Mar 23 2000; 342(12):868-74.

2) Stephenson SF. Spontaneous pneumothorax: the sharp rib syndrome. Thorax 1976; 31: 369-372.

3) Noppen M, De Keukeleire T . "Pneumothorax". Respiration 2008; **76** (2): 121–7.

4) Khajotia R, Somaweera N. Acute breathlessness and chest pain following a harsh bout of
    coughing Canadian Family Physician 2012; 58: 276-279.
5) Inderbitzi RG, Leiser A, Furrer M, Althaus U. Three years' experience in video-assisted thoracic surgery (VATS) for spontaneous pneumothorax. Thorac Cardiovasc Surg 1994;107:1410-1415.

6) Fukuda Y, Haraguchi S, Tanaka S, Yamanaka N. Pathogenesis of blebs and bullae of patients with spontaneous pneumothorax: an ultrastructural and immunohistochemical study. Am J Respir Crit Care Med 1994;149:Suppl:A1022-A1022 abstract.

7) Sahn SA, Heffner JE. Spontaneous pneumothorax. N Engl J Med 2000; 342:868-874.

8) Henry M, Arnold T, Harvey J. BTS guidelines for the management of spontaneous pneumothorax. Thorax 2003; 58 (Suppl II): ii 39-52.

9) Axel L. A simple way to estimate the size of pneumothoraces. Invest radiol 1981; 105: 1147-1150.

10) Archer GJ, Hamilton AAD, Upadhyag R, et al. Results of simple aspiration of pneumothoraces.
Br J Dis Chest 1985; 79:177–82.

11) Mitlehner W, Friedrich M, Dissmann W. Value of computer tomography in the detection of bullae and blebs in patients with primary spontaneous pneumothorax. *Respiration*. 1992;59(4):221-7.

12) Northfield TC. Oxygen therapy for spontaneous pneumothorax. BMJ 1971;4:86-88.

13) Soulsby T. British Thoracic Society guidelines for the management of spontaneous pneumothorax: do we comply with them and do they work? J Accid Emerg Med 1998;15:317-321.

14) Conces DJ Jr, Tarver RD, Gray WC, Pearcy EA. Treatment of pneumothoraces utilizing small caliber chest tubes. Chest 1988;94:55-57.

15) Jain SK, Al-Kattan KM, Hamdy MG. Spontaneous pneumothorax: determinants of surgical intervention. J Cardiovasc Surg (Torino) 1998;39:107-111.

16) Rozenman J, Yellin A, Simansky DA, Shiner RJ. Re-expansion pulmonary oedema following spontaneous pneumothorax. Respir Med 1996;90:235-238.

17) Watts BL, Howell MA. Tension pneumothorax: a difficult diagnosis. Emerg Med J
2001;18(4):319-20.

18) Khajotia R, Kew ST, Cham YL. Left-sided hydropneumothorax in a young male: Importance of clinical and radiological markers in arriving at an aetiological diagnosis. Malaysian Family Physician. 2009;4(1):41-43

19) Schramel FM, Postmus PE, Vanderschueren RG. Current aspects of spontaneous pneumothorax. Eur Respir J 1997;10:1372-1379.

20) Lippert HL, Lund O, Blegvad S, Larsen HV. Independent risk factors for cumulative recurrence rate after first spontaneous pneumothorax. Eur Respir J 1991;4:324-331.

CASE 7 : LUNG COLLAPSE
VAANI VALERIE VISUVANATHAN

OVERVIEW

Lung collapse occurs due to proximal occlusion of a bronchus, causing loss of aeration. The most common causes of lung collapse are:

- bronchogenic carcinoma – intrinsic occlusion by the tumour or compression by enlarged mediastinal lymph nodes

- inhaled foreign objects – frequently among young children

- mucous plug – patients with bronchial asthma and cystic fibrosis tend to develop mucous plugs which occlude the bronchus

- retention of secretion – common following thoracic or upper abdomen surgery (chest expansion is limited by pain and posture)

- aortic aneurysm – external compression on major airway

- iatrogenic – occurs in intubated patients when the endo-tracheal tube is inserted too deep, entering a bronchus but occluding another

Types of cases for clinical examination:

1) Short /long case
2) OSCE
3) OSPE

CASE VIGNETTE

A 65-year-old gentleman presents with complains of cough for the past one year. The cough is progressively becoming more disturbing and interrupts his sleep at night.

He is a chronic smoker, smoking 20 sticks of cigarette a day.

A chest radiograph was performed, which reveals collapse of the right upper lobe.

Obtain a full history from the patient and perform a focused physical examination.

(Note: further discussion of this topic will be focussed on bronchogenic carcinoma as the aetiology of lung collapse)

Bronchogenic carcinoma is classified according to the histologic types:

i) Small cell carcinoma – aggressive with strong relation to smoking, accounts for 1/5 of lung cancers

ii) Non-small cell carcinoma – consists of adenocarcinoma (commonly occurs in non-smokers and located in lung peripheries), large cell carcinoma and squamous cell carcinoma (high incidence among smokers)

History of Presenting Illness

- Cough – onset, progression, severity, aggravating and relieving factors, sputum production (amount and viscosity), haemoptysis, associated symptoms of chest pain, fever, shortness of breath or wheezing

Systemic Review

Regional effects:

- Hoarseness of voice (due to vocal cord paralysis or invasion of recurrent laryngeal nerve)
- Horner's syndrome (ipsilateral miosis, ptosis and anhidrosis - involvement of the sympathetic ganglion by the tumour)
- Dysphagia – compression of oesophagus
- Ipsilateral shoulder/arm pain (result of brachial plexus invasion) – may result in weakness of hand muscles
- Distension of neck veins and/or swelling of ipsilateral arm and face – compression or thrombosis of superior vena cava
- Orthopnoea – phrenic nerve palsy

(Note: Pancoast tumour refers to lung carcinomas at the apical chest wall. These tumours, which are almost always malignant, produce characteristic presentation in view of their location at the thoracic inlet and adjacency to the cervical sympathetic nerve and brachial plexus)

Metastatic effect:

- Depends very much on the organ and extent of spread eg. headache or seizures in brain metastases

Paraneoplastic effects:

(Note: Paraneoplastic syndromes refer to collection of clinical symptoms that occur remote to the tumour due to substances produced by the tumour. The more common paraneoplastic syndromes are:
i) Small cell carcinomas – syndrome of inappropriate anti-diuretic hormone production, adrenocorticotropic hormone secretion and Eaton Lambert syndrome.
ii) Non-small cell carcinomas - hypercalcaemia (due to increased parathyroid-like hormone production) and hypertrophic pulmonary osteoarthropathy (HPOA).
Patients with paraneoplastic syndromes may present with:

- Painful swelling of extremities (HPOA)
- Abdominal pain, constipation – hypercalcaemia
- Weakness that improves with activity – Eaton Lambert syndrome

Past Medical History

- Recurrent pneumonia – obstruction of the bronchus may lead to infection and the persistence of symptoms may have led to the misdiagnosis of recurrent or unresolved pneumonia

Social history

- Smoking – may suggest co-existing chronic bronchitis or emphysema
- Family support
- Financial status

CHECK LIST FOR HISTORY TAKING

- ✓ Cough – duration, haemoptysis, severity
- ✓ Other symptoms – dyspnoea, chest pain, wheeze
- ✓ Local effects – change in voice, dysphagia, weakness of hands, pain of shoulders, ptosis, distension of neck veins, swelling of upper limb
- ✓ Metastatic effects – headache, backache, paraparesis, seizures
- ✓ Paraneoplastic syndromes
- ✓ Smoking history
- ✓ Financial status

✓ Family support

EXAMINATION

Professionalism

Introduce yourself to the patient. Explain that you would like to examine him and briefly state what the examination would involve. Proceed to examination after obtaining consent from the patient. Hoarseness of voice may be noted during conversation with the patient.

General examination and vital signs

Observe and comment on usage of supplementary oxygen by the patient, if any. Look for sputum pots and metered-dose inhalers at the bedside. Determine the respiratory rate of the patient. Ensure that the patient is not tachypnoeic or cyanosed, if so state this to examiners so as to make a decision about suitability of the patient for clinical exams.

The patient might appear to be cachectic.

Examination of the hands might reveal clubbing, tar staining (nicotine is colourless, the staining of fingers among smokers is caused by tar), HPOA or muscle wasting. Swelling of the whole arm suggests obstruction of the superior vena cava. Loss of sensation along C8 and T1 dermatome occurs in Pancoast tumours.

Head and neck

Examine for pallor and jaundice (liver metastases). Patients with superior vena cava obstruction will appear plethoric with distended neck veins. Stridor might be audible.

Look for ptosis and pupil size asymmetry (Note: Horner's syndrome is characterised by unilateral miosis, ptosis and anhidrosis).

Determine position of trachea. Trachea will be shifted towards the side of lung collapse.

Feel for enlarged cervical lymph nodes and look for scars due to lymph node biopsy.

Lungs

Look for scars from previous thoracocentesis or percutaneous lung biopsy. Reduced breath sounds and vocal resonance would suggest lung collapse.

Bronchial breathing would be heard if there was an underlying consolidation.

☞ *(Note: A patient with a pleural effusion will have reduced breath sounds as well, but the trachea will not be deviated to the side of the effusion, unless the effusion was associated with collapse of the lung)*

Cardiovascular

Metastases to the pericardium may result in pericardial effusion which causes muffled heart sounds.

Abdomen

Ascites, hepatomegaly and splenomegaly may present in patients with advanced lung carcinoma with metastases to the abdomen.

Neurological

Brain or spinal metastases may cause weakness or paralysis. Therefore, examine the limbs for weakness and sensory deficit.

CHECK LIST FOR CLINICAL EXAMINATION

- ✓ General – cachexia, signs of respiratory distress
- ✓ Hands – clubbing, tar staining, upper limb swelling, muscle wasting
- ✓ Face – pallor, jaundice, Horner's syndrome
- ✓ Neck – distended veins, lymph nodes, trachea position
- ✓ Lungs – scars, breath sounds, vocal fremitus
- ✓ Abdomen – hepatosplenomegaly
- ✓ Limbs - weakness

INVESTIGATIONS

1. Chest radiograph

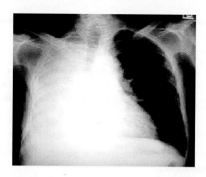

The chest radiograph provides vital information in this case. There is shift of the trachea and mediastinum to the right. Other features to support lung collapse are crowding of the ribs and loss of lung volume on the right with compensatory hyperinflation of the left lung. The right hemidiaphragm and mediastinum are obscured (silhouette sign). Raised hemidiaphragm suggests phrenic nerve involvement.

(Note: 98% of patients with lung cancer have an abnormal chest radiograph)

2. Sputum cytology

Least invasive test in a patient suspected to have lung carcinoma but the accuracy is dependent on quality of sputum sample and number of samples. The highest yield is obtained in large, centrally located tumours. Malignant cells are looked for in the sputum.

3. Contrast-enhanced Computed Tomography (CECT) scan

CECT of thorax is a useful tool to confirm diagnosis and for staging. Involvement of mediastinal lymph nodes can be assessed and used for staging.

4. Flexible bronchoscopy
Patients with centrally-located tumours, who are otherwise fit, should undergo a flexible bronchoscopy. This allows visualization of the airways and biopsy of the tumour mass for histopathology examination. Broncheoalveolar lavage can also be sent for cytology examination.

5. Transthoracic percutaneous fine needle aspiration (FNA) and biopsy
This procedure is usually performed for patients with peripherally located tumours. It is performed with guidance of ultrasonography or computed tomography, enabling localization of the tumour.

6. Thoracocentesis

Lung carcinomas that involve the pleura will lead to pleural effusion. Thoracocentesis may be performed for symptomatic relieve of shortness of breath, which accompanies massive effusions, or to obtain a cytologic diagnosis. Pleural fluid is classically noted to be haemorrhagic and exudative. Thoracocentesis can be followed by pleurodesis for recurrent malignant pleural effusions.

(Note: Pleurodesis is a procedure that is aimed at obliteration of the potential space for reaccumulation of pleural effusion. An irritant is usually administered into the space between the parietal and visceral pleura to cause inflammation and hence adherence via fibrosis. However, prior to pleurodesis the pleural effusion has to be fully drained. The commonly used sclerosing agents are talc, doxycycline and bleomycin.)

7. Computed Tomography scan of abdomen, pelvis and brain
Required to adequately stage the disease

8. Radionuclide bone scan
Bone metastases from lung carcinomas are predominantly osteoblastic and radionuclide bone scans are superior to plain radiographs in detecting these lesions.

9. Lung function test
Lung function test is a vital preoperative assessment for patients who are planned for lung resection. Patients with forced expiratory volume (FEV1) of less than 1L are not considered suitable candidates for surgery.

10. Arterial blood gas
Arterial blood gas should be performed for all patients in whom surgery is contemplated. Patients with underlying chronic obstructive airway disease may develop type 2 respiratory failure or require long term oxygen therapy.

11. Laboratory investigations
Liver function test - Liver enzymes may be raised if there were metastases to the liver.
Renal profile - Renal profile should be reviewed before initiation of any treatment, as these may require dose adjustment in renal failure. SIADH should be suspected if there was hyponatremia.
Serum calcium - Hypercalcaemia may be a result of metastatic lesions to the bone or increased parathyroid-like hormone production.
Serum lactate dehydrogenase - Raised serum lactate dehydrogenase (LDH) indicates an increased tumour mass and cell turnover.

CASE SUMMARY

This 65-year-old gentleman who is a chronic smoker presents with chronic cough and significant weight loss. He is not breathless at rest but requires supplementary oxygen via nasal prong. His fingers are clubbed with tar staining noted. There is wasting of the small muscles of the right hand. There is a non-tender supraclavicular lymph node palpable on the right, measuring 2x2cm. Trachea is deviated to the right. Chest expansion is reduced on the right with decreased vocal fremitus and breath sounds. The history and clinical examination findings are suggestive of collapse of right lung secondary to lung carcinoma.

CLINICAL DISCUSSION OF THE CASE

The student should be able to

- take a relevant history with pertinent questions regarding effects of the tumour
- recognise the relevance of the smoking history
- assess whether patient is in respiratory distress
- perform a focused physical examination to assess the extent of the tumour
- discuss the investigations that should be performed and the rationale for performing the investigations

MANAGEMENT

A multidisciplinary approach involving the respiratory physician, oncologist, cardiothoracic surgeon, nutritionist and palliative team is advocated.

Chemotherapy
Chemotherapy is the treatment of choice for most small cell carcinomas, since these tumours are usually advanced at the time of diagnosis. Chemotherapy may be given as an adjuvant to surgery or in combination with radiotherapy for non-small cell carcinomas.

Radiotherapy
Radiation therapy may be beneficial for both small cell carcinomas and non-small cell carcinomas. Radiation therapy causes shrinkage of the tumour and limits its growth. Therefore, it is used as an adjuvant to surgery (shrink the tumour before resection) or as palliative therapy (reduce symptoms in tumours which are inoperable).

Surgical resection

Lobectomy is usually performed for non-small cell carcinomas which are diagnosed early and have not metastasized. Prior to surgery, patients are carefully assessed for lung reserve volume and cardiac diseases.

Palliative

All patients should be assessed regularly regarding pain. Analgesics, including opioids, may be necessary for pain relief.

Opioids can also be used to relieve bothersome cough and relieve dyspnoea.

Anti-depressant and anxiolytics may be required by some patients.

Patients should be encouraged to remain active and avoid prolonged immobilization.

Radiation may be beneficial for patients with painful bone metastases, not responding to analgesics.

Stenting may be necessary for patients with symptomatic superior vena cava obstruction.

LEARNING OUTCOMES

By the end of this case review the student should be able to:

1. Obtain a history from a patient with lung collapse due to lung carcinoma

2. Perform physical examination with attention to relevant findings

3. Interpret the chest radiograph of a patient with lung collapse

4. Discuss the relevant investigations that should be performed to confirm the diagnosis and determine extent of disease

5. Discuss management options of the patient

COMMONLY ASKED QUESTIONS

1. What is a Pancoast tumour?
Pancoast tumours are tumours that occur in the lung apex. They grow at the thoracic inlet, invading the lower part of the brachial plexus and cervical sympathetic ganglion. Horner's syndrome is present in combination with wasting of the small muscles of the hand and loss of sensation in the C8 and T1 dermatome. Pain along the involved dermatomes is also a significant feature.

2. What are the factors associated with increased risk of lung cancers?
Smoking, asbestos exposure, interstitial lung disease, prior radiation exposure

HIGH ACHIEVER QUESTIONS

1. List some of the non-metastatic dermatologic manifestations of lung carcinoma.
Acanthosis nigricans
Dermatomyositis
Migrating venous thrombophlebitis
Ichthyosis

2. What is Trousseau's syndrome?
Trousseau's syndrome is a cancer associated hypercoagulability. In most cases, the malignancy is occult. There is spontaneous recurrent or migratory vascular thrombosis

COMMON MISTAKES

- Mistaking lung collapse for pleural effusion upon clinical examination
- Not familiar with the classification of lung carcinoma
- Assessment of distant spread and paraneoplastic manifestations not addressed
- Not familiar with relevant investigations

MUST KNOW FACTS ABOUT LUNG COLLAPSE

1. Malignancy is the most common cause of lung collapse among adults.

2. Bronchogenic carcinoma can be divided into small cell and non-small cell carcinoma.

3. Effects of the carcinoma may be regional, metastatic and paraneoplastic.

4. The relevant investigations include chest radiograph, CECT thorax, CT abdomen, CT brain, biopsy via bronchoscopy or percutaneous transthoracic approach and sputum cytology.

5. Pulmonary function test is mandatory if surgical resection is contemplated

REFERENCES:

1. Diagnosis and Management of Lung Cancer Executive Summary: ACCP Evidence-Based Clinical Practice Guidelines (2nd Edition)

CASE 8 : PNEUMONIA
RUMI R KHAJOTIA

OVERVIEW

Pneumonia is a clinical condition commonly encountered by undergraduate and post-graduate medical students. It is also a common clinical case seen in medical 'End-of-Posting' (EOP) examinations. Students may also be tested on various aspects of this condition in their clinical viva and OSPE examinations.

Definition:

It is defined as an inflammatory consolidation of the pulmonary parenchyma typically caused by pyogenic organisms. However, though pneumonia is usually caused by an infection, there may be other causes as well, such as aspiration, inhalation of chemical contents and trauma to the chest wall.[1,2]

Infective agents usually responsible as causative agents include bacterial, viral, fungal, parasitic and protozoal organisms.

Classification of Pneumonia:

Pneumonia is usually classified depending on:

I) where and how it is acquired, or,

II) the part of the lung affected (anatomic distribution of consolidation)

I) This classification includes:

a) Community-acquired pneumonia (CAP):

It is defined as pneumonia which develops in the outpatient setting or within 48 hours of admission to a hospital.
Community-acquired pneumonia (CAP) is a very common infectious disease encountered by physicians worldwide. Moreover, CAP assumes wide importance as it is responsible for significant morbidity and mortality.

Causative pathogens for CAP include:

Streptococcus pneumoniae (penicillin-sensitive and resistant strains),

Haemophilus influenzae (ampicillin-sensitive and resistant strains), and,

Moraxella catarrhalis (all strains penicillin-resistant).

These three pathogens are the most common causes of CAP and account for approximately 85% of CAP cases.[3]

CAP is usually contracted by the patient via inhalation or aspiration of the pulmonary pathogens into a lung segment or lobe.

Less commonly, CAP may occur due to secondary bacteremia from sources such as urinary tract infection or septicaemia.

Aspiration pneumonia is also considered a form of CAPusually caused by anaerobic organisms. It is frequently observed in elderly individuals who are bed-bound at home either due to generalised debility or long-standing illnesses.

Severe CAP:

Severe CAP is usually seen in patients with co-existent cardiopulmonary disease, post-splenectomy, or infection due to a highly virulent organism. Common examples include, severe acute respiratory syndrome (SARS), Hantavirus pulmonary syndrome (HPS), and Legionnaires disease.[4]

Complications in CAP include:

Empyema: usually occurs in infection with Streptococcus pneumoniae, Klebsiella pneumoniae, and group A beta-hemolytic streptococcus.

Cavitation: usually occurs in infection with Klebseilla pneumoniae.

Myocardial infarction: is known to be precipitated by fever due to community-acquired pneumonia (CAP).

Pneumococcal sepsis: Seen in patients with impaired splenic function or post-slenectomy, and is a potential cause of death in these cases.

b) Institutional-acquired pneumonia (IAP):

This includes healthcare-associated pneumonia (HCAP) and nursing home–associated pneumonia (NHAP).

HCAP is defined as pneumonia which develops *within* 48 hours of admission to a hospital in patients with increased risk of exposure to multi-drug resistant (MDR) organisms, as a cause of infection. Risk factors for exposure to MDR organisms in HCAP include:

- Exposure to antibiotics, chemotherapy, or wound care within 30 days of current illness
- Hospitalization for 2 or more days in an acute care facility within 90 days of current illness
- Hemodialysis at a hospital or clinic
- Residence in a nursing home or long-term care facility
- Home nursing care (infusion therapy, wound care)
- Contact with a family member or other close person with infection due to MDR bacteria

Note: In patients with NHAP there is a high incidence of infection with gram-negative bacilli and *Staphylococcus aureus*. Hence it is included in this category.

Some believe that pneumonia in patients in nursing homes and long-term care facilities is associated with greater mortality than in patients with CAP. This may be due to significant reduction in functional status of patients in nursing homes, greater likelihood of exposure to infectious agents, and exposure to virulent organisms, amongst others.

Note: These patients are less likely to present with classic signs and symptoms of consolidation such as fever, chills, chest pain, cough and purulent expectoration, but instead these individuals often present with delirium and altered mental status. Hence, it is as yet debatable whether such patients can be included under the definition of HCAP.[5]

c) Nosocomial pneumonia:

Nosocomial infections are those which are acquired in the hospital setting. Nosocomial pneumonias may be further divided into:

- Hospital-acquired pneumonia (HAP), and,
- Ventilator-associated pneumonia (VAP)

Hospital-acquired pneumonia (HAP)
Definition: It is pneumonia that develops at least 48 hours *after* admission to a hospital. It is also characterized by an increased risk of exposure to MDR organisms, as well as gram-negative organisms.[6]

Ventilator-associated pneumonia (VAP)
It is defined as pneumonia that develops *more than* 48 hours after

endotracheal intubation or within 48 hours of extubation. Risk factors for exposure to MDR bacteria that cause VAP are the same as those for HCAP and/or HAP.-VAP may occur in as many as 10-20% of patients who are on ventilators for more than 48 hours.[7]

II).Anatomic classification of pneumonia:

This includes:

- **Lobar:** It involves an entire lobe of the lung It is also known as focal or nonsegmental pneumonia.

- **Segmental, subsegmental, multifocal or lobular:** Commonly referred to as bronchopneumonia, it usually involves a segment of the lung and not the entire lobe.

- **Interstitial:** It involves predominantly the lung interstitium. *Idiopathic interstitial pneumonias* comprise usual interstitial pneumonia (UIP), nonspecific interstitial pneumonia (NSIP), desquamative interstitial pneumonia (DIP), respiratory bronchiolitis–associated interstitial lung disease (RB-ILD), cryptogenic organizing pneumonia (COP), acute interstitial pneumonia (AIP), and lymphoid interstitial pneumonia (LIP).

<u>**Causes of Pneumonia:**</u>

Pneumonia can occur due to a variety of causes.

These include:

- ***Bacterial pneumonia*** due to S. pneumoniae, H. influenzae, staphyllococcus aureus, M. catarrhalis, gram-negative bacilli, mycoplasma pneumoniae, legionella pneumoniae

- ***Viral pneumonia*** due to influenza virus, parainfluenza, rhinovirus, coronavirus, respiratory syncytial virus, adenovirus, herpes simplex virus, cytomegalovirus

- ***Tuberculous pneumonia*** due to infection with mycobacterium tuberculosis.

- ***Fungal pneumonia:*** It is rare, but may occur in patients who are immunocompromised due to AIDS or long-term treatment with steroids or immunosuppressants. Fungal pneumonia is most commonly caused by aspergillus fumigatus, cryptococcus neoformans, histoplasma capsulatum, pneumocystis jiroveci and coccidiodomycosis.

- ***Parasitic pneumonia:*** Common parasites causing pneumonia include, toxoplasma gondii, strongyloides stercoralis, and ascariasis.

- ***Idiopathic interstitial pneumonia:*** (as above)

- ***Aspiration pneumonia:*** usually occurs following aspiration of foreign bodies, oropharyngeal or gastric contents.

- ***Chemical pneumonia:*** caused by aspirating or inhaling irritants. These include vomitus, ingested gasoline, petroleum distillates, ingested pesticides, gases from electroplating and smoke.

- ***Benign tumours:*** a benign tumour such as a bronchial adenoma may cause endobronchial obstruction leading to infection in the lung parenchyma distal to the obstruction, resulting in the development of parenchymal consolidation (pneumonia).

- ***Malignant lung tumours:*** cause bronchial narrowing either due to external compression by the tumour mass or from endobronchial tumour infiltration, resulting in endobronchial narrowing and infection in the lung distal to the obstruction, leading to consolidation (pneumonia).

- ***Trauma:*** Inflammation of the lungs following a violent injury such as a severe blow or compression of the chest, leading to lung contusion.

CASE VIGNETTE:

A 62-year-old man comes with complaints of cough and greenish-yellow expectoration accompanied by high-grade fever since the past 2 weeks. The expectoration is about 25-30 ml. a day. He is an office worker. He has been smoking 25 cigarettes per day for the past 35 years but is a non-tobacco chewer and non- alcoholic. The cough is present throughout the day and also disturbs his sleep. Since the past 10 days he has noticed a sharp, stabbing pain in the right infrascapular region which is aggravated on coughing and taking a deep breath. The pain is also worse when he sleeps in the right-lateral position and is relieved on lying on the opposite side. Since the past one week he has also noticed occasional streaks of blood in his sputum. Further, there is progressively increasing breathlessness since the past 2 weeks. He also complains of 15 kgs weight loss since the past one month.

There is no history of hypertension, diabetes mellitus, malignancy or pulmonary tuberculosis in the family.

He gives history of having been hospitalised for 'pneumonia' 4 months ago, for which he had been treated with antibiotics .

His bladder and bowel habits are normal. His sleep has been disturbed since the past 10 days due to the pain in the right infrascapular region and persistent coughing.

Physical Examination

On general examination, the patient appears underweight. He is febrile. His pulse is 102 beats/minute and blood pressure is 134/86mmHg. He is tachypnoeic with a respiratory rate of 32 breaths per minute. There is no cyanosis, clubbing, pallor, icterus or oedema of feet. Cervical lymph nodes are not palpable.

On systemic examination of the respiratory system, the trachea is *central.* The chest appears normal in shape with reduced chest wall movements in the right infrascapular and infra-axillary regions. Tactile vocal fremitus is increased posteriorly in the right infrascapular and infra-axillary regions. There is a dull note on percussion in the same area. On auscultation, expiration is prolonged bilaterally over the chest. Coarse mid-inspiratory crepitations are heard in the infrascapular and infra-axillary regions on the right side and vocal resonance is increased in the same area. Tubular bronchial breath sounds are heard in the right infrascapular region.

Cardiovascular system examination is normal. The cardiac apex is in the 5th left intercostal space in the mid-clavicular line. First and second heart sounds are well heard. There is no gallop and no murmurs are heard.

On abdominal examination, liver and spleen are not palpable, there is no abdominal tenderness, no evidence of free fliud in the abdomen and peristalsis are well heard. The central nervous system examination is normal.

HISTORY OF PRESENTING ILLNESS:

To include the cardinal symptoms of the Respiratory System, namely:

- **Cough:** inquire whether cough is dry or productive. In

pneumonia the cough is productive.

- **Expectoration:** in pneumonia, cough is usually accompanied by expectoration. Due to underlying infection, the cough is usually yellowish or greenish in colour and may sometimes be admixed with blood. If the sputum is blood-tinged, inquire about its characteristics, namely:

- **Rusty sputum:** it is a reddish-brown, blood-stained expectoration which appears like 'rust.' It is typically seen in pneumonococcal pneumonia.

   Bright red blood: usually seen in bacterial, tuberculous and fungal infections

- **Breathlessness:** to describe whether the breathlessness is progressively worsening. This would be indicative of the extent of the consolidation, whether it is bilateral, and would also be a good indicator of the underlying aetiology, eg, aspiration or endobronchial obstruction.

- **Chest Pain:** if chest pain is present, to determine the character of pain. In pneumonia, a pleuritic pain is present if the consolidation is extending to the lung periphery. Sometimes, a generalised dull-aching chest pain may be present. This may be of muscular origin due to chronic, persistent coughing.

   Fever: if present, determine whether it is high-grade or low-grade. A low-grade fever with an evening rise of temperature is usually indicative of a tuberculous pneumonia, while a high-grade fever is indicative of a bacterial infection.

- **Palpitation:** commonly noticed by the patient due to tachycardia.

- **Weight Loss:** inquire whether the patient has lost weight. In bacterial pneumonia the weight loss may not be significant. However, if the weight loss has been gradually increasing over weeks to months a chronic aetiology such as tuberculosis must be considered. In contrast, if a large amount of weight loss has occurred in a short period of time, an underlying malignancy must be ruled out.

- *Generalised fatigue and malaise:* This is a common complaint in acute bacterial pneumonia, and may be attributed to loss of appetite and loss of sleep.

- **Aspiration:** An attempt should be made to elicit history of foreign-body aspiration or vomiting, which could be the underlying cause of pneumonia in the patient.

- **Nausea, vomiting and diarrhoea:** are also commonly seen.

PAST MEDICAL HISTORY:

- Past history of smoking if he is an ex-smoker. History of passive smoking (second-hand smoke) should also be elicited. This could help decide whether the underlying cause of the pneumonia is malignancy.

- *History of recurrent or persistent respiratory tract infection in the recent past:* Recurrent pneumonia or a non-resolving pneumonia could be indicative of foreign-body aspiration or malignancy.

FAMILY HISTORY:

- History of smoking in the family. History of tuberculosis in a family member, neighbour or colleague at work.

PERSONAL HISTORY: Sleep may be disturbed due to coughing and chest pain, in a patient with pneumonia.

SOCIAL HISTORY: Inquire in detail about:

- Smoking habits: number of cigarettes smoked per day and for how many years.

- Tobacco chewing or betel nut chewing

- Drug abuse

- Alcohol intake: chronic alcoholics are more prone to suffer from aspiration pneumonia following binge drinking.

OCCUPATIONAL HISTORY:

It is imperative to inquire whether the patient's occupation contributes adversely to the progression and exacerbation of his respiratory condition. Sweepers, cleaners and people working in garbage-dumping areas are more prone to develop repeated lower respiratory tract infections leading to pneumonia.

SUMMARIZING THE HISTORY:

Student should be adept at summarizing the history in 2-3 sentences, *highlighting* the *salient clinical features relevant to the case.*

SYSTEMIC REVIEW OF SYMPTOMS:

- To confirm whether the symptoms are primarily due to an underlying infective process such as pulmonary tuberculosis, bacterial, viral, fungal or parasitic infection.

- To determine whether the patient has been treated for similar complaints in the past and his response to past medication. This indicates whether the pneumonia is recurrent or non-resolving, giving an indication of the likely aetiology.

☞ *Note:* Common causes of a recurrent or non-resolving pneumonia include foreign-body aspiration and malignancy.

CHECK LIST FOR HISTORY IN A SUSPECTED CASE OF PNEUMONIA:

- Duration of cough and the amount of expectoration
- Breathlessness   *Rusty – pneumoccal pr*
- Blood in the sputum

Consolidation extending to lung periphery

- Chest pain, weight loss if present
- Occupational history (whether significant or not)
- Treatment taken in past, and the response to it.

BED-SIDE MANNERS:

Student introduces himself/herself to the patient and politely asks permission to examine. Student is polite and courteous throughout the examination and has a gentle and caring demeanour. The patient is thanked at the end of the examination and helped into the position he was in before the examination.

The entire Physical examination should be conducted from the right side of the patient.

GENERAL PHYSICAL EXAMINATION:

- Comment on the general condition of the patient, particularly his weight, which is usually normal or slightly reduced.
- Breath odour: The breath may be foul-smelling if the pneumonia is due to an anaerobic infection.
- Vital parameters: Temperature, pulse, respiratory Rate, blood pressure
- Respiratory rate: to observe from the foot-end of the bed on the right side.

  Look for:
  - respiratory rate: is usually increased in case of acute pneumonia
  - whether the chest is moving equally on both sides. Chest wall movements are usually diminished on the side of the consolidation (pneumonia).
  - intercostal retraction. May or may not be present, depending on the size of the consolidation.
  - whether accessory muscles of respiration are active or not.

- Cyanosis: central and peripheral. May be present in case of severe pneumonia.
- Clubbing: if present, mention the grade. If present, should rule out an underlying aetiology such as bronchiectasis or malignancy.
- Oedema of feet: if present, pitting or not, unilateral or on both legs
- Cervical lymphadenopathy: in tuberculosis, the lymph nodes are usually matted, while in malignancy they are hard, non-tender and firmly adherent to the underlying structures.
- Pallor, Icterus,
- Examine the nose: look for:
  - deviated nasal septum
  - nasal polyps
  - enlarged nasal turbinates
- Examine the mouth for: oral hygiene
  - oral ulcerations
  - glossitis, angular
  - stomatitis
  - injected throat

SYSTEMIC EXAMINATION OF THE RESPIRATORY SYSTEM:

Inspection:

- ❖ Position of the trachea: whether perceived or not. If perceived, comment on its position. In case of pneumonia, the *trachea is central in position.* If the trachea is shifted to the same side, it is usually indicative of an underlying collapse. This is commonly termed, *'collapse-consolidation.'*
- ❖ Shape of the chest: whether normal (elliptical) or barrel shaped (hyperinflated).
- ❖ Movement of chest wall: usually reduced on the side of consolidation.
- ❖ Respiratory rate: in case of pneumonia, the respiratory rate is usually increased.
- ❖ Presence of scars, sinuses, seen veins, visible pulsations, apex beat whether perceived or not.
- ❖ Accessory muscles of respiration: whether active or not. They may be active in case of extensive consolidation.
- ❖ Kyphosis, scoliosis, kyphoscoliosis, spino-scapular distance.
- ❖ Level of shoulder girdles, supraclavicular and infraclavicular indrawing. In case of tuberculosis with apical scaring, the shoulder girdles would not be at the same level and there may be supraclavicular and infraclavicular 'indrawing.'

Palpation:

- • Confirm the position of the trachea, mention the cricosternal distance.
- • Position of the cardiac apex. Normally located in case of consolidation (pneumonia)
- • Chest wall movements, anteriorly and posteriorly. May be reduced in the area of consolidation.
- • Chest wall tenderness, bony tenderness, sternal tenderness.
- • Tactile fremitus (symmetrically checked). It is increased over an area of consolidation.

Percussion:

- ❖ Apical percussion.
- ❖ Direct clavicular percussion.
- ❖ Anterior and posterior percussion: The percussion note may be *dull or impaired* over an area of consolidation.

Note: To percuss the interscapular region, the hands should be folded over the shoulders so as to get the scapulae out of the way. To percuss in the axillary region the hands should be folded above the head.

Auscultation:

- ❖ Auscultate for:
- normal vesicular breath sounds
- Bronchial breath sounds: *tubular bronchial breath sounds may be heard over an area of consolidation.*
- Rhonchi, rales and pleural rub: Coarse rales (crepitations) are a characteristic feature of pneumonia and are heard over an area of consolidation. If expiratory rhonchi are present it could be indicative of endobronchial narrowing or obstruction. A pleural rub may be present if the consolidation extends to the lung periphery.

To summarise:

The patient is an elderly man who comes with the chief complaints of cough accompanied by purulent expectoration, right-sided pleuritic chest pain and blood in the sputum. He also complains of high-grade fever, weight-loss and progressively increasing breathlessness. The chest pain worsens when he is lying in the right-lateral position and is relieved when he is sleeping on the opposite side.

Taking into consideration the above clinical symptoms and signs, the *Differential Diagnoses* in the above case would include:

- Right lower lobe pneumonia due to an infective aetiology

- Right lower lobe pneumonia due to an underlying malignancy

- Right lower lobe bronchiectasis

- Aspiration pneumonia involving the right lower lobe

- Right lower lobe lung abscess

- Chronic obstructive pulmonary disease with right lower lobe pneumonia

Note: End-stage interstitial lung disease (ILD) may mimick a consolidation, as in this condition there is extensive honey-combing and fibrosis. However, since ILD is a bilateral lung disease, the clinical findings too are bilateral. In the above case, the clinical signs are confined to the right side, indicating that the patient has right lower lobe pathology.

INVESTIGATIONS:

Non-invasive Investigative Procedures:

- *Chest Radiography:* Postero-anterior (PA) and lateral views: area of consolidation may be seen. The consolidation may involve the entire lobe (lobar) or may be segmental or subsegmental. When the interstitium is predominantly involved, it is termed 'interstitial pneumonia.'

    Radiographic features of a consolidation: A consolidation presents as a homogenous opacity with '*air-bronchogram*' seen within the area of opacity. The trachea and lower mediastinum (heart) are central. The consolidation may involve the entire lobe (lobar), or may be segmental, subsegmental or interstitial. The fissures bordering the consolidation (oblique or transverse fissure), usually maintain their normal contour and position.

    Note: If the consolidation is accompanied by an underlying collapse, it is termed 'collapse-consolidation.' In such a case, the trachea is shifted to the side of the lesion and the surrounding fissure is pulled to the affected side.

    In order to definitively diagnose a pneumonia, it is essential to demonstrate the presence of a consolidation on chest radiography which may be confirmed by an HRCT chest scan.

- *Arterial Blood Gas investigations (ABG):* In severe, extensive pneumonia gas-exchange could be significantly impaired leading to hypoxia and carbon dioxide retention. In early stages however, there is usually hypoxia with hypocapnia, due to increased respiratory rate.

- *Full Blood Count:* It is raised in case of bacterial pneumonia where there is a neutrophilic leucocytosis. In case of pulmonary tuberculosis, the differential cell count may show predominant lymphocytosis.

- *Erythrocyte Sedimentation Rate (ESR):* In case of active pulmonary tuberculosis the ESR is usually between 80-100 mm at the end of one hour.
    If there is an underlying malignancy, the ESR may be significantly elevated to > 100 mm at the end of one hour.

Sputum Examination: Sputum should be examined for:

- **Acid-Fast Bacilli (AFB)-smear and culture:** Preferably six early-morning sputum samples should be collected on consecutive days and tested.

- **Bacterial smear and culture:** sputum should be tested for gram-positive, gram-negative and anaerobic organisms.

- **Fungal culture:** Sputum should be tested for spores and hyphae of *Aspergillus Spp.* Bronchopulmonary aspergillosis is a common cause of fungal pneumonia and bronchiectasis.

- **Chest ultrasonography:** If a small 'reactive pleural effusion' is suspected in a patient with pneumonia, a USG may be done to determine its quantity and location.

High-resolution Computed Tomography (HRCT) chest scan: It is useful in:

- ❖ Confirming the presence of consolidation, especially when the chest radiograph is unclear or doubtful.
- ❖ Determining the exact location of the consolidation.
- ❖ Determining whether there is an accompanying collapse
- ❖ Determining whether there is endobronchial obstruction due to a foreign body or a tumour process.

Invasive Investigative Procedures:

These include:

- ➢ **Fibreoptic/video bronchoscopy:** To look for tumours and embedded foreign bodies in the bronchial tree. To determine the cause of the underlying infection by doing a broncho-alveolar lavage (BAL). To diagnose suspected malignancy in recurrent and non-resolving pneumonias, by doing bronchial brushings and washings.

> *Excision biopsy of palpable cervical and/or axillary lymph nodes:* In patients with palpable lymph nodes an excision biopsy is recommended in order to establish a definitive diagnosis. In a case of pneumonia, common causes of enlarged cervical lymph nodes include tuberculosis and malignancy.

> *Pleural fluid aspiration:* If the consolidation extends to the lung periphery, a 'reactive pleural effusion' may develop, which may be aspirated for diagnostic purposes.

MANAGEMENT:

I) *Medical Management:*

> Antibiotic therapy: whenever the patient has evidence of infection, appropriate antibiotics are recommended.
> Chest physiotherapy: It is essential in order to help patients expectorate out the secretions.
> Bronchodilators may be useful to reduce breathlessness in acute pneumonia
> Expectorants: used to clear tracheobronchial secretions
> Mucolytics: to liquefy secretions and aid in expectoration
> Good hydration: it helps to prevent secretions from becoming thick and viscid and also helps to keep the airway mucosa moist.
> Well-balanced diet: This is essential as the patient looses a lot of vital proteins in the expectorated sputum.
> Prophylactic antibiotics has been recommended in patients with impaired splenic function or following splenectomy, to combat MDR-pneumococcal pneumonia.
> Oxygen therapy in case of severe, extensive or bilateral pneumonias, where a large amount of the pulmonary parenchyma is affected. Generally aim to keep the $PaO_2 > 8.0$ and saturation>92%
> Regular immunizations with pneumococcal vaccine in patients with impaired splenic function or following splenectomy.
> Anlagesics, in case of persistent pleuritic pain.

II) *Surgical Management:*

> Drainage of secretions using fibreoptic/video bronchoscopy: In some patients the secretions are not easily expectorated out even after chest physiotherapy as the secretions may be thick and viscid. In such cases, suction may be employed through a bronchoscope in order to clear secretions from the affected parts of the lung.

> ➢ Removal of foreign body: this may be necessary in case of foreign-body aspiration. Usually it is removed by suction using a fibreoptic bronchoscope. If the foreign-body is large, a rigid bronchoscope may be needed to suction out the contents from the tracheobronchial tree.

III) *Follow up management:* It is essential to closely follow up a patient with pneumonia in order to ensure that the consolidation fully resolves following treatment. Clinical and radiological resolution of the consolidation is essential in order to ensure successful treatment. Radiological resolution of the consolidation is usually complete within 21 days of treatment with appropriate antibiotics. Failure of the consolidation (opacity) to completely resolve following appropriate treatment would indicate a 'non-resolving' pneumonia. In such cases, an underlying aetiology such as foreign body aspiration or malignancy must be ruled out.

Complications of Pneumonia:

❖ Spread of the infection to healthy parts of the same lung or to the contralateral lung, resulting in bilateral pneumonia.

❖ Development of cavitations (lung abscess), usually following staphylococcal or gram-negative bacterial infections.

❖ Haemoptysis, which may at times be massive.

❖ Recurrent pneumonia
❖ Non-resolving pneumonia
❖ Atelectasis due to secretions blocking the bronchial passages, resulting in a 'collapse-consolidation.'
❖ Pleural effusion may develop if the consolidation extends up to the lung periphery ('reactive' pleural effusion) or if the pneumonia is caused by highly virulent organisms. Usually the pleural effusion is small in quantity and resolves following appropriate antibiotic treatment. Rarely, the fluid may increase in quantity and may get secondarily infected.
❖ Septicaemia, which if severe may be life-threatening.
❖ Respiratory failure in patients with bilateral or extensive pneumonia.

Radiological Features of Pneumonia:

Chest radiography is essential in diagnosing a case of pneumonia. A consolidation presents as a homogenous opacity usually involving an entire lobe or a segment of the lung. Air-bronchogram may be seen in an area of consolidation. The mediastinum (upper and lower) is central in these cases. If the consolidation borders a fissure, the position of the fissure is not altered. If the consolidation extends to the periphery of the lung, a 'reactive pleural effusion' may develop, which is usually small and presents as a 'blunting' of the costophrenic angle.

High-resolution computed tomographic (HRCT) chest scan helps in confirming the diagnosis and may also shed light about the underlying aetiology, eg. endobronchial narrowing due to a tumour mass or foreign body.

MUST KNOW FACTS

- ✓ Pneumonia is an inflammatory consolidation of the pulmonary parenchyma caused by pyogenic organisms.
- ✓ Besides infection, other causes include foreign-body aspiration, malignancy, aspiration, chemical pneumonitis and trauma.
- ✓ *In elderly individuals (persons above 50 years) presenting with pneumonia, malignancy must be ruled out as an underlying aetiology.*
- ✓ An untreated, inadequately treated pneumonia or a pneumonia caused by virulent organisms may cavitate giving rise to long-term complications such aa bronchiectasis and lung abscess.
- ✓ *A consolidation (pneumonia) may not be easily detectable on clinical examination. In such cases, chest radiography and HRCT chest scan examination may be necessary in order to arrive at a definitive diagnosis.*

Ethical issues include:

1) In case of recurrent or non-resolving pneumonia the patient and his relatives should be counselled as to the potential causes and their long-term implications, especially in case of suspected malignancy.

2) In case an elderly bed-bound patient is being treated at home, relatives should be made aware of the possibility of 'aspiration pneumonia' and how to prevent it. They should be informed that aspiration pneumonia is the commonest cause of morbidity and mortality in these patients and is a 'harbinger of death' in such cases.

3) Relatives of patients admitted to nursing homes for long-term palliative care must be cautioned about the possibility of the patient contracting nursing home-associated pneumonia (NHAP), and should also be informed that this condition is associated with greater mortality than CAP, due to significant reduction in the functional status of patients in nursing

homes, greater likelihood of exposure to infectious agents, and increased predisposition of exposure to virulent organisms.

4) Cost analysis is currently vital in clinical medicine. Student should be adept in discussing the relevance of investigations along these lines, when requesting for investigations.

REFERENCES:

1) McLuckie, [editor] A. (2009). Respiratory disease and its management. New York: Springer. p. 51. ISBN 978-1-84882-094-4.

2) *Stedman's Medical Dictionary.* 27th ed. Baltimore, Md: Lippincott, Williams and Wilkins; 2003.

3) Howard LS, Sillis M, Pasteur MC, Kamath AV, Harrison BD. Microbiological profile of community-acquired pneumonia in adults over the last 20 years. J Infect 2005; 50(2):107-13.

4) Alvarez-Lerma F, Torres A. Severe community-acquired pneumonia. Curr Opin Crit Care 2004; 10(5):369-74.

5) El Solh AA. Nursing home-acquired pneumonia. *Semin Respir Crit Care Med* 2009; 30(1):16-25.

6) Gaynes R, Edwards JR. Overview of nosocomial infections caused by gram-negative bacilli. *Clin Infect Dis*

2005;41(6):848-54.

7) Peleg AY, Hooper DC. Hospital-acquired infections due to gram-negative bacteria. *N Engl J Med* 2010; 362(19):1804-13.

CASE 9 : LUNG FIBROSIS
VAANI VALERIE VISUVANATHAN

1. Lung fibrosis occurs when normal lung parenchyma is replaced by fibrotic tissue as a reaction to chronic interstitial inflammation. There are many causes of lung fibrosis, including:

- idiopathic pulmonary fibrosis – most common, no identifiable cause for fibrosis

- connective tissue disease – respiratory manifestation in rheumatoid arthritis, systemic lupus erythematosus, ankylosing spondylitis and other connective tissue disease

- environmental and occupational pollutant exposure – asbestosis, silicosis and farmer's lung

- infection - tuberculosis

- radiation therapy – post radiation therapy for lung or breast malignancy

- medications – amiodarone, nitrofurantoin, bleomycin, busulfan

-inherited conditions – tuberous sclerosis, neurofibromatosis, Gaucher's disease

Types of cases for clinical examination:

Short /long case
OSCE
OSPE

CASE VIGNETTE

A 55-year-old gentleman presents with gradually worsening shortness of breath for the past one year. The shortness of breath is worse upon exertion but there is no orthopnoea or paroxysmal nocturnal dyspnoea. He also has a chronic cough that is non-productive.

He was diagnosed to have pulmonary tuberculosis 14 years ago, and had completed treatment for 6 months. He has no other medical problems and has not been on any medications. He smokes 1-2 cigarettes a day and has been doing so for the past 30 years. He is a teacher.

Obtain a detailed history from patient and perform a focused physical examination.

History of Presenting Illness

- Shortness of breath – onset, progression, severity, aggravating and relieving factors, limitation of daily activities, diurnal variation, ability to work
- Cough – onset, progression, severity (disturbs sleep?), sputum production, presence of haemoptysis (quantify if present), aggravating and relieving factors, presence of associated chest pain?
  (Note: dyspnoea is the most common complaint, however, do keep in mind that some patients may present with haemoptysis, chest pain or no complaints at all!)
- Associated symptoms eg. wheeze, pleurisy or haemoptysis
  (Note: haemoptysis may be a manifestation of Wegener's granulomatosis or Goodpasture's syndrome, may also suggest development of lung carcinoma, pneumonia or pulmonary embolism)
- Symptoms suggestive of connective tissue disease eg. painful joint swelling, joint stiffness, rash, acid reflux, sicca symptoms and Raynaud's phenomenon
- Symptoms in relation to exposure of possible irritants eg. worsening of shortness of breath when at the farm with improvement of symptoms during off days (not applicable in this case though)

Past Medical History

- Previous lung infections eg. tuberculosis (including treatment duration and outcome)
- Haematuria – suggestive of vasculitis
- Previous pneumothorax – suggestive of cystic lung disease eg. lymphangioleiomyomatosis, tuberous sclerosis
- Previous radiation(radiation pneumonitis usually develops within a few weeks)
- Previous illness which was treated with medication that could have led to interstitial lung disease eg. recurrent urinary tract infections treated with nitrofurantoin

Family History

- Family history of respiratory disorders (Sarcoidosis may be familial, albeit rare)

Social history

- Smoking – may suggest co-existing chronic bronchitis or emphysema
  (Note: Langerhans' Cell Histiocytosis and Goodpasture's syndrome are more common among smokers)
- A detailed occupational history regarding relevant exposure, its duration and usage of protective gear
- Hobby – hobbies such as, bird rearing, must be actively sought for
- Financial status (if patient is unable to work who will be supporting the family, would the patient require welfare assistance)
- Family support

Medication history

- Previous and current drug exposure, including, dose and duration

Check list for history taking

- ✓ Shortness of breath – onset, duration, progression, severity
- ✓ Cough – onset, duration, sputum
- ✓ Other symptoms – haemoptysis, wheeze, pleurisy
- ✓ Symptoms of connective tissue disease
- ✓ Exposure to irritants
- ✓ Occupation history
- ✓ Previous and current medications
- ✓ Radiation
- ✓ Financial and family support

Examination

Introduce yourself and confirm the identity of the patient. Explain the examination that you would like to perform and obtain consent.

General examination and vital signs

Ensure that patient is not tachypnoeic, dyspnoeic or cyanosed. Determine the respiratory rate and look for usage of accessory muscles. The student should comment on usage of supplementary oxygen, if any.

Hands should be examined for clubbing, digital ulcers, sclerodactyly and Raynaud's phenomenon. Joint swellings, deformities and skin nodules should be sought for. Presence of pedal oedema may suggest the development of pulmonary hypertension.

Sarcoidosis or malignancy should be suspected if there was lymphadenopathy.

Patients with ankylosing spondylitis will have a stooped forward-flexed posture.

Head and neck

Malar rash and mouth ulcers would be present in systemic lupus erythematosus. Microstomia with tight, mask-like skin would be noted in scleroderma. Uveitis would again be suggestive of connective tissue diseases.

Determine position of trachea. Trachea may be shifted in the presence of lung collapse, pneumothorax or apical lung mass.

Jugular venous pressure must be measured with patient satisfactorily positioned. A prominent a wave can be observed in pulmonary hypertension.

Lungs

There may be scars caused by previous chest tube insertion for treatment of pneumothorax. Look for post radiotherapy skin changes eg. hyperpigmentation, telangiectasia. Chest expansion may be reduced. Fine inspiratory basal crackles, which are present despite getting the patient to cough, is characteristic in lung fibrosis. Wheeze may be present in some patients.

Cardiovascular

Pulmonary hypertension may have developed in patients with lung fibrosis. The signs that would suggest the presence of pulmonary hypertension are a palpable right ventricular heave, loud palpable pulmonary component (P2) of the second heart sound and an ejection systolic murmur along left sternal border. A tricuspid regurgitation murmur may be noted if there was right ventricular failure.

Abdomen

The other signs of cor pulmonale are ascites, hepatomegaly, pulsatile liver and ascites.

Check list for clinical examination

✓ Lungs
  - reduced chest expansion
  - fine, inspiratory crackles, usually at bases
  - wheeze (occasionally)
✓ Signs of underlying cause
  - Connective tissue disease eg. joint swelling/deformity, uveitis, digital ulcers
  - Radiotherapy skin changes
  - lymphadenopathy
✓ Signs of pulmonary hypertension
  - Right ventricular heave
  - Loud P2 or widely split S2
  - Pulmonary regurgitation
  - Pulsatile liver with ascites
  - Ankle swelling

INVESTIGATIONS

Investigations

1.Chest radiograph

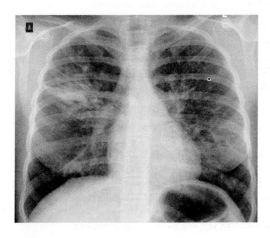

Reticular or reticular nodular infiltrates are the hallmark findings on chest radiograph. The chest radiograph above shows diffuse bilateral reticular interstitial pattern. Progressive fibrosis leads to cystic dilatation of distal air spaces, which is visible as "honeycombing".

Lung fibrosis secondary to connective tissue diseases tends to be bibasal. The mnemonic SCHATE and BRASIO can be used to remember the possible causes based on lung involvement.

Upper lung fibrosis:
S silicosis/sarcoidosis
C coal-worker pneumoconiosis
H histocytosis
A ankylosing spondylitis/ABBA
T tuberculosis
E extrinsic allergic alveolitis

Lower lung fibrosis:
B bronchiectasis
R rheumatoid arthritis
A asbestosis
S scleroderma
I idiopathic pulmonary fibrosis/intrinsic fibrosing alveolitis
O others: drug, irradiation

Besides the typical changes of lung fibrosis, other findings may suggest the underlying condition:
Asbestosis – pleural plaques
Sarcoidosis - bilateral hilar lymphadenopathy
Silicosis – nodular lesions which may coalesce causing contraction of lung volume and egg-shell calcification
(Note: All previous chest radiographs should be reviewed as well)

2. Arterial blood gas

pH	7.47	(7.35-7.45)
pO2	65	(80-100mmHg)
pCO2	27	(35-45mmHg)
HCO3	18	(22-26mmol/L)
BE	1	(+/- 2)
SpO2	85	(95-100%)

Performing an arterial blood gas will help to determine whether the patient is in respiratory failure and the type of respiratory failure (type 1 or 2). The blood gas analysis will also be of aid to decide on the requirement of long term oxygen therapy.

When analyzing blood gases, first look at the pH. In the example given, the pH is more than 7.45, therefore there is alkalosis. The pO2 and oxygen saturation are both low, indicating hypoxaemia. The pCO2 is reduced and is the cause of alkalosis. As compensation, the plasma bicarbonate level is reduced. This is Type 1 Respiratory Failure which is partially compensated.

Dyspnoea, a common complaint of patients with lung fibrosis, should be addressed. There is no evidence that oxygen therapy improves the quality of live or long term survival in patients with lung fibrosis, but dyspnoea has been known to contribute to depression in these patients.

3. Pulmonary function test

Pulmonary function test reflects severity of disease. A restrictive defect is expected, however, this may not be evident in patients with coexistent chronic obstructive airways disease or lymphangioleiomyomatosis. A reduced vital capacity with normal or raised FEV1/FVC ratio can be expected. Carbon monoxide transfer factor (TLco) would be reduced in patients with lung fibrosis.

4. High-resolution Computed Tomography (HRCT) scan

HRCT is a sensitive tool for detecting lung fibrosis in patients with normal chest radiograph and for disease severity staging. The typical HRCT findins are reticular opacities, subpleural honeycombing and traction bronchiectasis.

5. Bronchoalveolar lavage (BAL)

Bronchoalveolar lavage does not contribute much to confirm the diagnosis of lung fibrosis but it has a small role in ruling out other possible diagnosis, for example, malignancy or infection.

6. Transbronchial /surgical lung biopsy

Lung biopsies are diagnostic, especially with certain conditions with patchy distribution. Surgical lung biopsy can be performed by thoracotomy, thoracoscopic techniques or video-assisted. However, the role of biopsies in the era of HRCT is debatable.

7. Laboratory investigations

Full blood count may be ordered if a superimposed infection or infective cause is suspected. In the event of connective tissue diseases being the prime suspect, C-reactive protein, anti-nuclear antibody and Rheumatoid factor sent for. In patients whom sarcoidosis is contemplated, serum angiotensin-converting enzyme (ACE) may provide further evidence. In hypersensitivity pneumonitis, precipitating antibody to suspected antigen would be present.

CASE SUMMARY

This 55-year-old gentleman presents with chronic cough and progressively worsening dyspnoea which has been present for the past one year. Physical examination reveals that the trachea is shifted to the right and there are fine inspiratory crackles over the right upper and middle lobes. In the absence of features to suggest a connective tissue disease and history of exposure to possible irritants, he most probably has lung fibrosis as a result of the previous tuberculosis infection.

CLINICAL DISCUSSION OF THE CASE

The student should be able to

- take a detailed occupational history, with attention to exposure to asbestos, silica, and other toxins
- recognise the relevance of the previous lung infection
- elicit history that would suggest other underlying diseases undetected thus far
- assess whether patient is in respiratory distress
- appreciate lung findings
- suggest a possible diagnosis, integrating details obtained from history and clinical findings

MANAGEMENT

Specific management of lung fibrosis is determined by the underlying cause. A multidisciplinary approach is advocated.

Supportive care and general measures include:

- oxygen therapy – for patients with significant hypoxia
- pulmonary rehabilitation
- oral opioids – relieve distress of dyspnoea
- smoking cessation
- treatment of respiratory infections
- avoidance of inhalational exposure (in hypersensitivity pneumonitis)
- cessation of offending medication (if drug induced fibrosis)
- influenza and pneumococcal vaccination

- Lung transplant – only for those who fulfil established selection criteria eg. age < 65years old, advanced disease (TLCO < 40% predicted) or progressive disease

Idiopathic pulmonary fibrosis (IPF)
- several trials have shown that corticosteroids and immunosuppressive agents are beneficial for IPF
- antifibrotic agents that inhibit fibrogenesis, eg. colchicine and pirfenidone have been studied with no conclusive data for now

LEARNING OUTCOMES

By the end of this case review the student should be able to:

1. Obtain a complete history from a patient with lung fibrosis

2. Perform physical examination with attention to relevant findings

3. Present a comprehensive list of differential diagnosis

4. Discuss the relevant investigations that should be performed to confirm the diagnosis

5. Discuss further management of the patient including respiratory failure and prognosis

COMMONLY ASKED QUESTIONS

1. What would be the expected findings on chest radiograph in a patient with idiopathic pulmonary fibrosis?
Bilateral reticular (net like) densities at the lung bases with volume loss

2. What are the other causes of clubbing?
Bronchiectasis, congenital cyanotic heart disease, familial, primary biliary cirrhosis

3. What are sequelae of IPF?
Increased incidence of small cell and non-small cell carcinoma, spontaneous pneumothorax, chronic intractable cough, haemoptysis and pulmonary hypertension

HIGH ACHIEVER QUESTIONS

1. Explain the pathogenesis of lung fibrosis in rheumatoid arthritis.
In patients with rheumatoid arthritis, development of lung fibrosis may be related to idiopathic pulmonary fibrosis, atypical lung infections, drugs

used in the treatment of rheumatoid arthritis (methotrexate) or co-existent medical disorders (sarcoidosis)

2. Which group of patients should be considered for long term oxygen therapy (LTOT)?

Patients with persistent resting hypoxaemia with PaO2 ≤ 7.3 kPa (55 mm Hg) or below 8 kPa (60mmHg) with clinical evidence of pulmonary hypertension are candidates for long term oxygen therapy.

3. What are the characteristic features seen on chest radiograph in Caplan's syndrome?

Caplan's syndrome is the combination of pneumoconiosis and seropositive rheumatoid arthritis. It occurs in patients with a history of exposure to coal mine dust. On the chest radiograph, typical features are multiple, well-defined, nodules ranging from 0.5cm to 2.0cm which may coalesce and cavitate. These nodules typically occur in the lung peripheries involving the upper lobes.

COMMON MISTAKES

- Mistaking lung fibrosis for bronchiectasis
- Not assessing for pulmonary hypertension
- Not asking a detailed occupational and exposure history
- Unable to interpret ABG result

MUST KNOW FACTS ABOUT LUNG FIBROSIS

1. Idiopathic pulmonary fibrosis is the most common cause of fibrosis.

2. Lung fibrosis may be secondary to certain connective tissue diseases, drugs and exposure to pollutants.

3. Reticular shadowing or honey combing may be noted on the chest radiograph of a patient with lung fibrosis.

4. HRCT is performed to assess disease severity

5. Pulmonary function test will reveal a restrictive defect.

References:

1. Interstitial Lung Disease Guideline by the British Thoracic Society

SECTION 2: CARDIOVASCULAR SYSTEM

CASE 10 : HEART FAILURE
CHAMPIKA BODINAYAKE

OVERVIEW

Heart failure is an important cause of morbidity and mortality all over the world. Prevalence of heart failure rapidly rises with aging, with the mean age of the heart failure in the general population being 74 years. Heart failure is defined as a condition in which, in the presence of adequate venous return, a cardiac abnormality makes this organ unable to pump blood at a rate that satisfies the metabolic needs of tissues.

Heart failure is defined by the following three criteria; and criteria 1 and 2 should be fulfilled in all cases.

1. Symptoms of heart failure at rest or during exercise
2. Objective evidence of cardiac dysfunction at rest
3. Response to treatment directed at heart failure

The commonest form of heart failure (HF) is left ventricular (LV) dysfunction. LV dysfunction is usually the end result of coronary artery disease (CAD), either following myocardial infarction or chronic under perfusion but yet viable myocardium or both. Other causes of LV dysfunction include hypertension, valvular heart disease, congenital heart disease and cardiomyopathy.

Right ventricular failure (RVF) is rare, and commonly follow left ventricular failure (LVF). When there is evidence of both left and right ventricular failure the term congestive cardiac failure (CCF) is used. Left ventricular systolic dysfunction is assessed by measuring left ventricular ejection fraction (LVEF). Chronic heart failure with preserved systolic function is known as diastolic dysfunction of the ventricles. Diastolic dysfunction is associated with LV hypertrophy as in hypertensive heart disease and hypertrophic cardiomyopathy. Diastolic dysfunction has the similar clinical features as left ventricular dysfunction but is managed differently.

Heart failure is a popular clinical exam topic. Students may be tested on a number of formats including long and short cases.

CASE VIGNETTE

A 58-year-old male presents with progressive dyspnoea on exertion and palpitations of three months duration. He has orthopnoea, paroxysmal nocturnal dyspnoea and oedema of both feet for one week. He has stable angina noticed on walking 1 Km for several years. He has no diabetes or hypertension but was advised to reduce fat in his diet. He smokes 10 cigarettes a day for several years and consumes 30 units of alcohol per week for the past five years. There is no family history of IHD.

On examination he is propped up and dyspnoeic with a respiratory rate of 25/min. There is no pallor or cyanosis. Bilateral pedal oedema is present. Both his parotids are enlarged, but no features of chronic liver disease are noted. The pulse is 100 beats/min, irregularly irregular, low volume and all peripheral pulses are present. Blood pressure is 100/70 mmHg and jugular venous pressure is elevated 5 cm above sternal angle with normal wave pattern. The apex beat is diffusely enlarged and felt at the left sixth intercostal space 2 cm lateral to the mid-clavicular line. There was no parasternal heave. On auscultation, grade 3/6 pansystolic murmur radiating to axilla is heard with no thrill at the cardiac apex. Bilateral fine crepitations are present at both bases.

CLINICAL REASONING

The clinical features in this middle aged man are compatible with CCF. There is gross cardiomegaly and bilateral fine basal crepitations suggestive of LVF and peripheral oedema and raised JVP suggestive of RVF. A pansystolic murmur at cardiac apex suggests the presence of mitral regurgitation. He has stable angina and two major risk factors, smoking and hyperlipidaemia. He is in atrial fibrillation (AF). There is a history of excess alcohol consumption with enlarged parotids but no clinical evidence of chronic liver disease is present. The most likely cause of CCF in this case is CAD, the differential diagnosis being alcohol related cardiomyopathy. At present, he is severely incapacitated with functional class IV according to NYHA classification (discussed below).

History of the presenting complaint

- Shortness of breath: Establish when it was first noticed and the rate of progression
- Paroxysmal nocturnal dyspnoea: Are you awakened suddenly by difficulty in breathing or coughing? Do these symptoms improve when you sit up or walk? (suggestive of left ventricular dysfunction)
- Orthopnoea: Do you find it more comfortable to sleep flat or with several pillows? How many pillows do you use?
- Chest pain: Do you have any pain or discomfort in the chest? Does it occur at rest or with activity? How long does it last? Do you use relief medication as GTN? (suggestive of angina)
- Palpitations: Suggestive of arrhythmias. Do you experience your heart racing or skipping a beat? If so when does it occur, how long does it last and are there associated symptoms as vomiting and blackouts

- **Syncope:** Have you experienced light headedness or blackouts (suggestive of arrhythmias)
- **Cough?** Do you have a cough? Is there sputum? If so what is the colour? (in pulmonary oedema there is pink frothy sputum and the patient is very unwell with dyspnoea)
- **Swelling of feet:** Is there pedal swelling? Does it improve with lying flat for several hours?
- **Wheeze:** Are the symptoms associated with wheeze (musical sounds generated mainly in expiration)? Sometimes in LVF a wheeze may be present.(cardiac asthma)
- Weight loss: This is a feature of severe HF
- Functional assessment of activities of daily living is assessed at the same time and patient is classified to a NYHA class according to the symptoms

Past medical history
- Previous admissions for worsening symptoms of heart failure, sudden arrhythmias, angina etc
- History of myocardial infarction/angina- duration, control, complications, investigations, treatment
- History of diabetes – duration, control, complications, ,investigations, treatment
- History of hypertension: duration, control, treatment
- Valvular heart disease and rheumatic fever: if present duration, treatment including surgical correction, penicillin prophylaxis etc. → ppt heart failure
- History of asthma: (for beta-blocker use)
- History of thyroid disease: thyrotoxicosis a well known cause of high output failure
- Other (co morbidities) chronic lung disease as obstructive airways disease, obstructive sleep apnoea, anaemia, renal disease, liver disease,
- Recent viral infections: Viral myocarditis may lead to dilated cardiomyopathy.
- Allergy to drugs (angioneurotic oedema following ACEI)
- Pregnancy, recent delivery and breast feeding: Peripartum cardiomyopathy is a cause of CHF in young females, and has an immune aetiology.

Family history

- Size of family and children
- Are there any family members having heart disease eg: CAD, diabetes hypertension, dyslipidemia, familial cardiomyopathy and other hereditary disease

Social history

- Employment history: current and past employment and ability to continue work
- Income: able to afford hospital visits, medication. Check if insured and how much of the medical expenses are covered.
- Smoking: quantity and duration of use
- Alcohol: quantify and assess if dependent
- Other illicit drugs
- Amount of exercises √
- Family support and other support available

Dietary history

Inquire whether the patient is on a modified low salt diet
Inquire about fluid restriction
Inquire on dietary fat intake
Nutrition: Inquire on intake of a balanced diet which include iron, thiamine, trace elements ?

Treatment history

- Obtain a list of drugs the patient is taking and the dosage (diuretics, angiotensin converting enzyme (ACE)inhibitors, spironolactone, beta-blockers,digoxin, nitrates and antiplatelet drugs)
- Inquire if on anticoagulants and monitoring, bleeding episodes
- Long term use of cardiotoxic drugs e.g.:anthracyclines,abstruzimab
- Surgical treatment, implanted devices, pacemakers
- (Check adherence)to therapy
- Assess if follow up is satisfactory

CHECK LIST FOR HISTORY IN HEART FAILURE

- Assess current and past cardiac symptoms with onset and duration
- Identify the precipitating factors for heart failure as infection, noncompliance with drugs, ongoing ischemia, uncontrolled hypertension, arrhythmia, pulmonary embolus, renal failure, thyrotoxicosis etc.
- Presence of other disease as CAD, diabetes, hypertension, COPD, renal disease, thyroid disease
- Inquire on patient's lifestyle to detect progressive changes in the daily activity and functional disability in an objective manner
- Review the most likely underlying causes
- Review if current medications are appropriate and adequate with special reference to ACE inhibitors, diuretics, digoxin,

antiplatelet drugs, anticoagulation and concurrent treatment with cardio toxic drugs

- Review dietary modification and nutritional adequacy and adherence to such
- Inquire regarding implanted devices, pacemakers, coronary stents
- Assess the quality of the follow up and check adherence to medication
- Assess patient's understanding of the illness and family and other social support received

Examination

- Explain to patient what you intend doing before starting to examine
- Make sure the curtains are drawn and males should ask for a chaperone when examining a female patient
- Position patient for adequate viewing of jugular veins
- Expose the chest adequately

General examination

- Observe patient. Note if he looks well, dyspnoeic or distressed. Count respiratory rate
- Note pedal and sacral oedema
- Examine colour of mucosae for cyanosis, pallor or plethora.
- Inspect tongue for pallor, plethora, cyanosis and for macroglossia (amyloid)
- Inspect face for xanthelasma, cornea for premature arcus, palmar xanthoma and tendon xanthoma at elbows, Achilles tendons suggestive of hyperlipidemia
- Inspect skin for pigmentation (pigmented in haemochromatosis, chronic renal failure)
- Inspect lower limb for oedema
- Examine the back for sacral oedema

Cardiovascular and other system examination

- Examine radial pulse for rate, regularity, volume, character and presence of AF.
- Examine all other accessible peripheral pulses for volume, pulsation and bruits (carotids, femoral, popliteal, dorsalis pedis, posterior tibial arteries)
- Inspect jugular veins; measure height and observe waveform. Note giant V waves in tricuspid regurgitation
- Measure blood pressure
- Localise and characterise apex (heaving) & determine tracheal position
- Feel for a left parasternal pulsation
- Feel for thrills over the precordium; time with carotid pulse

- Auscultate for heart sounds (identify additional3rd and 4th heart sounds, 3rd and 4th together summation gallop). Note if the sounds are normal, soft, loud, split or single *grade*.
- Auscultate for murmurs; note timing, site best heard, loudness, radiation, character, variation with posture, position and other manoeuvres. Use the bell for low-pitched sounds and the diaphragm for high-pitched sounds.
- Auscultate lung bases for fine basal crepitations and check for dullness.
- Palpate liver for enlargement and pulsation; note other features
- Palpate the spleen for enlargement:(haemochromatosis, amyloidosis)
- Examine other systems (respiratory, nervous, musculoskeletal, abdomen) depending on the instructions, case format (OSCE, long case etc.), relevance and availability of time.
- Thank the patient at the end of the examination and cover patient up

Checklist for examination findings

- General examination: Observe for dyspnoea, pallor, plethora, cyanosis, pedal and sacral oedema, features of hyperlipidemia
- Pulse: Palpate for rate, rhythm (AF, ectopy), volume, character, peripheral pulse
- Jugular veins: Inspect height and waveform, notice giant V waves in tricuspid regurgitation
- Blood pressure
- Apex:Palpate apex for displacement and nature (diffuse heave)
- Left parasternal heave:note the presence of right ventricular hypertrophy
- Palpate for thrills in the precordium
- Heart sounds:Auscultate for softS1,S2, additionally S3 and S4 or both together causing a gallop rhythm.
- Murmurs:Auscultate for pan systolic murmurs of mitral and tricuspid regurgitation and other murmurs which are etiologically important
- Auscultate lung bases for fine basal crepitations and check for dullness.
- Palpate liver for enlargement and pulsation

Investigations

- ECG: Findings of LV hypertrophy, left bundle branch block, intra ventricular conduction delay, and nonspecific ST-segment and T wave changes support a diagnosis of heart failure. In acute heart failure sinus tachycardia is present.

- Q waves in contiguous leads strongly suggest previous myocardial infarction and CAD as the cause. Rhythm abnormalities as ventricular ectopy and ventricular tachycardia may indicate severe LV disease.

  NOTE: Student should be competent in reading an ECG, these can appear in OSPE or be asked at the clinical examination.

- Chest radiograph: Chest radiographic findings of heart failure include cardiomegaly, pulmonary vascular redistribution to upper lobes, pulmonary venous congestion, Kerley B lines, alveolar oedema, and pleural effusions.

- Echocardiography:Most useful investigation in HF. Distinguishes between systolic and diastolic dysfunction. Regional wall motion abnormalities or LV aneurysm suggest CAD as underlying cause, whereas global dysfunction suggests a non ischemic cause. Echo will detect valvular heart disease, cardiac tamponade, pericardial constriction, infiltrative and restrictive cardiomyopathies, and provides clues about diastolic function and prognosis.

- B type natriuretic peptide (BNP) assay and N terminal pro BNP (NT- pro BNP): Levels correlate with severity of heart failure and decrease in compensated state. BNP useful in distinguishing CHF from other causes like pulmonary disease) which may present similarly.

- Cardiac catheterization: Angiography detects the presence of CAD as the cause of heart failure, and if found, revascularization can be performed if myocardium is viable. Coronary computed tomographic angiography (CTA) is an alternative to angiography.

- Exercise testing: Underlying CAD may be diagnosed. Metabolic exercise testing is used as a prognostic aid and discriminate between CAD and pulmonary causes (pulmonary conditions causes desaturation on exercise)

- Cardiac catheterization: to exclude coronary artery disease: Left ventricular angiography is an accurate measure of LV systolic function

- 24 hour Holter monitor: Detects arrhythmias specially in asymptomatic patients.

- Lung function tests:FVC and FEV1 reduced in HF. Reversibility testing may be useful for beta blocker use

- Routine blood tests (heart failure screen): Complete blood count, blood glucose, urea and electrolytes, creatinine, thyroid function, lipids, liver functions

- Additional investigations may be required to identify the underlying cause e.g.: serum ferritin level, viral titres, HIV testing, genetic testing etc.
- Cardiac MRI is useful in assessing myocardial viability, infiltrative cardiomyopathy
- Myocardial perfusion scanning: SPECT (single photon emitting CT) is useful to detect inducible ischemia and hibernating myocardium
- Stress echocardiography: Exercise or dobutamine stress can detect inducible ischemia and hibernating myocardium
- Endomyocardial biopsy: Indicated in suspected cases when specific treatment is available

Management

The management of CHF include establishing the diagnosis, assessment of clinical features and severity, precipitating factors, likely aetiology and looking for the presence other co morbidities. The prognosis should be assessed and the likely complications should be anticipated. The patient and relatives should be counselled and appropriate management strategy should be chosen for the patient considering availability and cost. The patient should be regularly monitored.

Non pharmacological management: Smoking and alcohol cessation, low salt diet, exercises and achieving optimum body weight are important lifestyle modifications. The patient and family should be educated regarding illness.

Pharmacological management:

ACE inhibitors: All patients with LV systolic dysfunction are treated with ACE unless contraindicated or intolerant. ACEI reduce mortality and symptoms; improve exercise tolerance and LVEF and hospital readmission. In ACE intolerance, angiotensin receptor blocker (ARB) can be used.

Beta-blockers: They are recommended for the treatment of all patients with stable, mild, moderate or severe heart failure.Three drugs have proven to reduce mortality namely bisoprolol, carverdilol and sustained release metoprolol. Diuretics: diuretics are essential to reduce fluid overload and cause rapid improvement in symptoms, despite no survival advantage. They are concomitantly started with ACE inhibitors.

Spironolactone: Recommended in advanced heart failureand is shown to reduce morbidity and mortality.

Digoxin: Only indicated in symptomatic heart failure and atrial fibrillation. In patients who are in sinus rhythm with no symptoms the risk may outweigh the benefit.

Hydralazine and nitrates are venodilators and can be used reduce preload. When combined they will not cause nitratre tachyphylaxis (loss of effect). They can be add on therapy (specially for African Americans) for severe HF or used when ACE and beta blockers cannot be given.

Intravenous therapies: Intravenous therapies like dobutamine, nitrates, hydralazine, sodium nitroprusside, nesiritide (synthetic BNP) has been tried as therapy with limited evidence of success

Revascularization:

Coronary artery bypass grafting or percutaneous intervention may improve cardiac function in areas of myocardium that are non-functioning (hibernating) because of inadequate blood supply. Hibernating myocardium is identified by stress echocardiography and other nuclear imaging techniques

Device therapies Pacemaker

Cardiac resynchronization therapy (biventricular pacing): Right and left ventricles are paced in a synchronous fashion to improve ventricular contraction, mitral regurgitation and reverse re-modelling. Indicated for patients with NYHA class III or IV heart failure with EF less or equal to 35% and wide QRS complex (equal or more than 0.12 sec)

As 50% of heart failure patients die suddenly, implantation of ICD (implantable cardioverter defibrillator) can improve survival and sudden death. They are shown to be superior to anti arrhythmic drugs. ICD are indicated as secondary prevention following cardiac arrest, ventricular fibrillation or tachycardia and primary prevention for severe symptomatic HF despite optimal medical therapy.

Ultra filtration therapy: removal of sodium and water in volume overloaded patients who are resistant to diuretic therapy reduces hospitalization.

LV assisted devices (LVAD): These temporarily provide mechanical support till cardiac transplant is performed

Cardiac transplantation:

Cardiac transplantation is considered for otherwise healthy patients with severe refractory cardiac failure who fail to respond to medical therapy. Median life expectancy after transplant is 10 years.

Case summary

This middle aged patient presents with severe CCF. He has stable CAD with smoking and hyperlipidemia as risk factors. He has been taking alcohol well exceeding the maximum limits. Examination reveals features typical of CCF. There is atrial fibrillation and mitral regurgitation. The likely cause of CHF is CAD but excess alcohol causing dilated cardiomyopathy also appears contributory. The diagnosis should be confirmed by chest radiograph, ECG, and echocardiography. Further investigations are needed to assess severity, complications, underlying cause and co morbidities to aid further therapy.

CLINICAL DISCUSSION OF THE CASE

Starts with the summary of the patient which highlights the symptoms and abnormal signs
The patient has all the clinical features of severe NYHA class IV heart failure. He has CAD which is the commonest cause of HF. In addition heavy alcohol consumption can be a causally related to the HF, and which is a well recognized cause of dilated cardiomyopathy.
His cardiac rhythm is consistent with AF which is a feature of many cardiac conditions as mitral valve disease, congenital heart disease, cardiomyopathy and thyrotoxicosis. Alcohol can cause AF specially in binge drinking and atrial fibrillation is a typical arrhythmia seen in alcoholic cardiomyopathy.

Parotid enlargement is a sign associated with chronic alcohol abuse, though signs of chronic liver disease are absent in this case. The presence of a pan systolic murmur of mitral regurgitation may be explained as either cause or effect but more likely the effect following a dilated mitral valve ring associated with a large left ventricle.

The diagnosis of CCF should be confirmed and underlying cause established; the extent of the disease and functional disability should be determined to plan treatment options. In the index case, CCF is complicated by atrial fibrillation which needs rate control and prophylactic anticoagulation.
Important non pharmacological interventions in this case are total abstinence from alcohol and cessation of smoking. Low salt diet and fluid restriction is also adviced.

Medical therapy should be aimed at symptom relief and reducing the progression of left ventricular dysfunction. The patient is dyspnoeic at rest with evidence of volume overload specially in the lungs. Intravenous frusemide will reduce overload reliving symptoms.

The patient should be started on ACE inhibitor (or ARB if ACE inhibitor intolerant) which is of proven benefit. Beta blocker such as bisoprolol, carverdilol or sustained release metoprolol should be added starting from a low dose titrating up.

Spironolactone may be added considering the severity of HF.

The patient is in atrial fibrillation hence digoxin will be of added benefit to control ventricular rate. The patient should be monitored for hyperkalemia (ACE inhibitors, spironolactone) and bradycardia (beta blocker) with regular monitoring of renal function. As he has CAD, anti platelet drugs as aspirin and clopidogrel as well as statins (e.g.atorvastatin) should be commenced to reduce lipid level to prevent further atherosclerosis.

Symptomatic angina can be treated with nitrates. There is an increased risk of atrial thrombosis in the presence of AF and severe heart failure, therefore oral anticoagulation with warfarin should be commenced. There is an added risk of bleeding when concomitant anti platelets are used. Liver function tests are mandatory prior anticoagulation as the patient can have asymptomatic chronic liver disease.

Further assessment with angiography may reveal concomitant CAD which may be treatable with improvement of LV function. Risk of arrhythmia can be assessed and further treatment may be needed.

The patent and his family should be counselled regarding the illness, psychological issues, treatment and prognosis.

NYHA (New York Heart Association) Classification of heart failure

Class I	No limitation: ordinary physical activity does not cause fatigue, dyspnoea or palpitation
Class II	Slight limitation of physical activity: comfortable at rest but ordinary activity results in fatigue, dyspnoea and palpitation
Class III	Marked limitation of physical activity: comfortable at restbut less than ordinary activity results in dyspnoea and symptoms
Class IV	Unable to carry out any physical activity without discomfort; symptoms present at rest

Once the diagnosis of heart failure is established, symptoms may be used to classify the severity and to assess the response to therapy. NYHA classification is in widespread use.

Causes of chronic heart failure

Common	Less common
→ Ischemic heart disease	Drugs eg:adriamycin

→ Valvular heart disease

→ Hypertension

→ Congenital heart disease

→ Alcohol

→ Viral myocarditis,Chaga'sdisease, HIV

→ Peripartum cardiomyopathy

Haemochromatosis

Deficiencies eg:thiamine, selenium.

Infiltrations eg; sarcoid, amyloid

Eosinophilic cardiomyopathy

High output e.g.:thyrotoxicosis

Tachycardia induced eg: A-V fistulae

LEARNING OUTCOME

The student should be able to

- Elicit a focussed history in a patient with suspected cardiac failure
- Perform a complete examination of the cardiovascular system and detect the abnormal physical signs
- Explain the clinical features on a physiological and pathological basis
- Make a clinical diagnosis or provide a differential diagnosis based on the history and examination findings
- Select the relevant investigations that would confirm the diagnosis, aetiology, complications and functional capacity for overall management of the patient
- List the common causes of cardiac failure
- Discuss the principles of management of cardiac failure
- Discuss new therapies available in severe cardiac failure
- Communicate to the patient about the nature of the illness, important lifestyle changes, compliance with therapy, avoiding precipitants and coping with daily living .

COMMONLY ASKED QUESTIONS

How is the diagnosis of heart failure confirmed?

HF is confirmed by echocardiogram which measures systolic function by assessing the EF. In systolic dysfunction the LV is dilated and the EF is low. The findings are supported by chest radiographic findings of cardiothoracic ratio >50%, and evidence of pulmonary congestion and oedema. BNP levels are elevated in HF. ECG may show tachycardia, arrhythmia, LVH, ischemia or nonspecific changes.

What are the causes of right ventricular failure?
RVF commonly result from chronic pulmonary hypertension following chronic lung disease, chronic pulmonary embolism, mitral valve disease and ASD. Acute right ventricular failure can occur in RV infarction, acute respiratory distress syndrome in acute pulmonary embolism and following thoracic surgery

What are the causes of high output failure
Conditions associated with a very high cardiac output such as anaemia, beriberi, thyrotoxicosis and large AV fistula are well known to cause high output failure

What are the characteristic changes in the chest radiograph in heart failure?
Cardiomegaly, pulmonary vascular redistribution to upper lobes, pulmonary venous congestion, Kerley B lines, alveolar oedema, and bilateral pleural effusions are Fluid in the fissure may appear as a homogenous opacity which disappears after diuretics

What are the common factors which precipitate heart failure?
Anaemia, fever and infection, onset of arrhythmia, ongoing ischemia, drugs causing salt and water retention, alcohol, renal disease, thyrotoxicosis and poor compliance to drugs and diet are well known to precipitate heart failure

What are the causes of dilated cardiomyopathy? Ischemic heart disease and valvular heart disease, familial cardiomyopathy, hypertension, following myocarditis, peripartum cardiomyopathy, haemochromatosis, alcohol, nutritional (beriberi, selenium and zinc deficiency),neuromuscular dystrophy, infection related (HIV, lyme, Chagas)and storage disorders (Fabry's disease, Pompe's disease)are some examples

What are the clinical markers of poor prognosis heart failure?
Worsening NYHA class, worsening heart rate, low BP, low body weight, anaemia, presence of S3 and elevated JVP are markers of poor prognosis

Distinction level questions

What are the poor prognostic markers in the ECG in heartfailure?
Wide QRS,Left bundle branch block, ventricular arrhythmia, T-wave alternans indicate a poor prognosis.

What are the indications for myocardial biopsy in heart failure?
Biopsy is indicated in infiltrative cardiomyopathies as sarcoidosis, haemochromatosis, amyloidosis and endomyocardial fibrosis, cardiac allograft rejection and in anthracycline induced cardiomyopathy

What are the surgical treatments available for heart failure?
Left ventricular resection (Batista surgery), left ventricular reconstruction by Dor procedure, mitral valve repair, autologus skeletal muscle cardiac assist and splint and compression devices are available as surgical procedures. What about heart transplant?

RED FLAG ENCOUNTERS

The following are situations that may be overlooked:
- Failure to examine the jugular venous pulse in 45^0reclined position therefore elevated JVP is not detected
- Slow AF can be easily missed unless pulse is felt for one minute with attention to rhythm
- Cardiac apex may be quite shifted and diffuse therefore it is important to feel the left precordium in left lateral position if not felt in supine position
- Failure to detect 3rd and 4th heart sounds using the bell as they are low pitched at the cardiac apex
- Failure to detect fine crepitations at lung bases
- Failure in detecting a congested liver which is soft and gentle palpation with deep respiration is advised as it may be tender

MUST KNOW FACTS OF HEART FAILURE

→ HF is not a complete diagnosis unless the cause is found
→ Cardiomegaly and pulmonary fine basal crepitations are signs of LVF and jugular venous distension and peripheral oedema are signs of RVF
→ Peripheral oedema may be absent in well treated heart failure and lungs may be clear to auscultation in chronic heart failure
Heart failure with preserved systolic function (normal ejection fraction) is known as diastolic dysfunction and is associated with ventricular hypertrophy as in hypertension
Symptoms are used to assign an NYHA class to patients
→ BNP assay improves accuracy of diagnosis of heart failure
Echocardiography is the single most useful investigation
→ All patients should receive ACE and beta blocker unless contraindicated
→ Spironolactone is indicated in NYHA class III and IV while digoxin is mainly for patients with AF
→ There are poor prognostic markers which are clinical, ECG, blood tests and imaging

REFERENCES

ACCF/AHA guidelines available online from onlinejacc.org
2009Focused update: ACCF/AHA guidelines for the management of Heart failure in adults

OVERVIEW

Definitions:

Rheumatic Fever

It is a non-suppurative sequelae of Group A, ß-haemolytic streptococcal throat infection. The disease involves the joint (hence the word "rheumatic"), heart, skin, subcutaneous tissue and the brain. It is considered as acute when the illness lasts for less than 6 months or chronic, if it is greater than 6 months in duration.

Rheumatic heart disease:

Rheumatic heart disease is the major long-term sequel of acute rheumatic fever, which involves the cardiac valves leading to stenosis or regurgitation with resultant hemodynamic disturbance.

Epidemiology:

Rheumatic fever is a major cause of acquired heart disease in children worldwide, with the disease occurring most frequently in developing countries where access to medical care is limited and children live in poverty and unsanitary crowded conditions. The epidemiology of rheumatic fever is identical to that of group-A streptococcal upper respiratory tract infection. It is most common in children aged between 5-15 years, which also correlates with peak incidence of streptococcal throat infection. This streptococcal pharyngitis is transmitted through droplet spread and the attack rate of acute rheumatic fever following untreated sporadic and endemic group-A streptococcal pharyngitis is 0.3% and 3% respectively. Out of this a good number of them (40-60%) develop rheumatic heart disease

Pathogenesis of Rheumatic heart disease:

If a patient gets streptococcal pharyngitis, along with other risk factors like genetic susceptibility, poor nutrition and overcrowded conditions, after 2-3 weeks, the patient may get acute rheumatic fever with arthritis, carditis, etc. This occurs on an auto-immune basis based on the theory of antigen mimicry. Further, it leads to initiation of tissue (cardiac valvular) damage and turns into an established rheumatic valvular heart disease over a period of 5-10 years time.

Rheumatic heart disease with mutivalvular involvement:

Carditis is the late sequel of acute rheumatic fever . It can occur in the acute form of rheumatic fever. Approximately 50% of those with evidence of carditis develop organic valvular damage. Mitral valve is the most commonly affected (90%) valve With regards to the relative frequency of valvular involvement in rheumatic heart disease:

- Isolated mitral valve = 50% (either stenosis or regurgitation or both)
- Mitral valve + aortic valve = 40% (either stenosis or regurgitation or both)
- Mitral valve + aortic valve + tricuspid valve = 5% (either stenosis or regurgitation or both)
- Aortic valve alone = 3% (either stenosis or regurgitation or both)
- Others = 2%

Types of cases for clinical examination:

Short case – as an isolated mitral stenosis, mitral regurgitation or as an isolated aortic stenosis or aortic regurgitation with or without pulmonary hypertension

OSPE – Chest radiograph of a patient who has mitral valve disease or aortic valve disease (and aortic valve calcification)

Long Case/OSLER – students would be expected to take a detailed history and perform a focused clinical examination of a patient who presents with features of either/both mitral and aortic valve disease with or without the complications such as pulmonary hypertension and/or congestive cardiac failure.

MITRAL STENOSIS:

CASE VIGNETTE

A 38-year-old labourer presents with a 3-month history of progressive shortness of breath on effort. Exertion is frequently associated with central chest pain and regular palpitations. He has, on two occasions, e woken from sleep with attacks of 'feeling frightened', breathless and being unable to lie flat. His general health is good, with no weight loss or anorexia. He has been told that he had suffered *rheumatic fever* when he was 9 years old.

History of Presenting Illness

- Breathlessness – onset, duration, frequency, severity, precipitating factors (exertion), history suggestive of paroxysmal nocturnal dyspnoea or orthopnoea (due to pulmonary venous congestion)

- Associated symptoms for eg. Syncope (as happens in Atrial Fibrillation or severe Mitral Stenosis -MS), fatigue (low cardiac output, chest pain (due to pulmonary hypertension)
- Complications – Palpitations, Transient ischemic attacks-TIA and stroke often due to atrial fibrillation,
- Compression symptoms – hoarseness of voice and dysphagia (due to left atrial dilatation secondary to severe MS)
- Hemoptysis – due to elevated bronchial pressure

The student should be able to reason as to why these symptoms are present based on the pathophysiology of Mitral Stenosis

Systemic Review

- Symptoms of lower respiratory tract infection – to rule out winter bronchitis
- Symptoms to suggest an alternative underlying cardiac disorder eg. angina, orthopnoea
- Recent evidence of infection e.g. High grade fever, chills, rigor (which may suggest a complication or sequel of infective endocarditis)

Past Medical History

- History of rheumatic fever during childhood or any history of previous administration of Benzathine Penicillin injection IM every 3 weeks during childhood days
- Previous cardiac valvular disease
- History of connective tissue disorders
- History of intake of drugs such as Methysergide
- Concurrent pregnancy status
- History of coexisting illnesses – diabetes, hypertension and ischaemic heart disease

Surgical history

- Recent thoracic or cardiac surgery

Social history

- Alcohol intake – quantify amount of alcohol
- Smoking – chronic lung diseases tend to worsen the valvular heart disease

Medication history

- Has the patient been on anorexiants/anti-obesity drugs such as fenfluramine and also history of methysergide usage (for migraine)

Check list for history taking

- ✓ Determine the duration of rheumatic fever and heart disease to enable progression of it and severity
- ✓ Assessment of symptoms (to know the severity) and precipitating factors
- ✓ Identify the complications of MS such as infective endocarditis, AF, pulmonary hypertension, etc.
- ✓ Determine the presence of other cardiovascular disease such as hypertension, ischaemic heart disease
- ✓ Evaluate the possibility of complications that may occur from treatment
- ✓ Prior usage of prophylaxis for recurrence of rheumatic fever, prophylaxis of infective endocarditis
- ✓ Relevant drug history

EXAMINATION

Introduce yourself and explain your intentions to the patient. Obtain consent before you proceed. Ensure that you have a chaperone, if required.

General examination and vital signs

Perform a visual survey and proceed to determine patient's haemodynamic stability.

Determine if the patient is dyspnoeic, tachypnoeic, febrile or cyanosed. Measure her blood pressure (suspect low systolic BP) and count her respiratory rate.

Feel her peripheral pulses to determine rate, regularity, low volume pulse for evidence of atrial fibrillation

Patients with mitral stenosis are usually in AF. Sometimes an irregular pulse may be difficult to ascertain especially if there is bradycardia. The pulse volume is often variable in AF. The pulse volume can be low in mitral stenosis, as this is a low cardiac output state, and you may expect a narrow pulse pressure in this situation.

Always look for presence/absence of markers of infective endocarditis in any patient with physical signs of valvular heart disease. More than often, they are absent, but this is an important negative finding.

Face and neck

A malar flush signifies a low cardiac output state with pulmonary hypertension and is often seen in patients with severe mitral stenosis. Remember, there are other causes of appearances that may resemble a malar flush. A malar flush should always be looked for in the CVS examination; its absence or presence should be commented on in the final presentation in the presence of mitral valve disease.

Look for a raised jugular venous pressure. This would suggest cardiac failure and/or pulmonary hypertension. The presence of systolic 'v' waves should prompt you to look for other signs of pulmonary hypertension: parasternal heave, parasternal thrill (tricuspid regurgitation), loud pulmonary component of the second heart sound, the pan-systolic murmur of tricuspid regurgitation, Graham-Steel murmur of pulmonary regurgitation).

On examination of Precordium and Chest

1. Look carefully for previous mitral valvotomy scar on the left lateral chest wall.

2. A tapping apex beat is a palpable first heart sound, and in this setting the first heart sound will be loud. In cases where the first heart sound is not loud, the first heart sound will not be palpable and thus the apex beat will not demonstrate a tapping quality.

3. With a raised venous pressure, you would expect to find signs of pulmonary hypertension and right sided cardiac failure. A parasternal heave signifies right ventricular pressure overload. A parasternal thrill signifies underlying 'functional' tricuspid regurgitation (if present, don't miss the systolic 'v' waves in the venous pressure)

4. A loud first heart sound is usually heard, that reflects mobile and pliable valve leaflets. However, if the mitral valve leaflets themselves are calcified and immobile, then the first heart sound will be soft and the opening snap will be lost. Calcification of valve leaflets does not indicate severity, thus a soft first heart sound and absence of an opening snap cannot be used as markers of severe mitral stenosis.

5. The pulmonary component of the second heart sound will be loud with pulmonary hypertension. If present do not miss the other signs of pulmonary hypertension.

6. The opening snap will be heard with a loud first heart sound, and indicates the mitral valve leaflets are mobile and pliable.

This will be lost if the leaflets are calcified. The opening snap follows the second heart sound and occurs in early diastole. The earlier the opening snap, the greater the left atrial pressure, thus the greater the severity of mitral stenosis.

7. The murmur of mitral stenosis can be difficult to hear. It is a low-frequency murmur, and is heard best in expiration with the patient in the left lateral position, using the bell of the stethoscope. If unsure of the murmur, it can be accentuated with exercise. Ask the patient to touch the toes and recline back and forth 10 times, or ask the patient to hop on one foot 10 times (this will usually not be expected in the examination, but is important to know for discussion). If the patient is in sinus rhythm, the murmur has pre-systolic accentuation, i.e. increases in intensity before the first heart sound is heard.

8. Mitral stenosis will initially lead to pulmonary venous hypertension, pulmonary congestion and then pulmonary arterial hypertension, and right sided cardiac failure. In the presence of signs of pulmonary hypertension, look carefully for bibasal crepitations (pulmonary congestion) and peripheral oedema. The lung fields can be clear, and peripheral oedema can be minimal especially if the patient is on diuretics.

9. This is the murmur of 'functional' tricuspid regurgitation and is associated with systolic 'v' waves in the venous pressure and a parasternal thrill. The murmur is louder in inspiration (Carvollo's sign). If present, look carefully for other signs of pulmonary hypertension.

10. This is the Graham-Steel murmur of pulmonary regurgitation. This signifies elevated pulmonary arterial pressures, and is a marker of severe mitral stenosis. This is often a very short murmur in early diastole, usually in the pulmonary area, and only radiates a few intercostals spaces down the left sternal edge. It is differentiated from aortic regurgitation by being much shorter and louder in inspiration. This murmur is almost always associated with a loud and often palpable pulmonary component of the second heart sound look for other signs of pulmonary hypertension.

11. Once having given a diagnosis of mitral stenosis, it is important to assess severity. Remember the markers of severe mitral stenosis

Gastrointestinal system:
Gastrointestinal

Signs of chronic liver disease, as well as, enlargement of liver and abdomen should be sought for.

A positive hepatojugular reflex and pulsatile liver is consistent with liver congestion due to right heart failure secondary to Mitral stenosis.

Neurology:

Look for signs of Syncope, TIA or stroke due to severe MS, AF or due to infective endocarditis as complication

Check list for clinical examination

- ✓ Vital signs – determine the haemodynamic stability
- ✓ Examine pulses – irregularity, low volume status
- ✓ Look for signs of pulmonary hypertension and heart failure
- ✓ Neck – jugular venous pressure
- ✓ Heart – apex beat, murmurs, additional sounds
- ✓ Lungs – bibasal crackles, pleural effusion/pulmonary oedema, signs of recurrent bronchitis
- ✓ Gastrointestinal system – signs of chronic liver disease and assess for hepatosplenomegaly
- ✓ Neurology – focal neurological deficits if any

CASE SUMMARY AND CLINICAL DISCUSSION OF THE CASE

This 38-year old man presents with shortness of breath with features of Paroxysmal Nocturnal Dyspnoea and orthopnoea. His vital signs show pulse rate of 100beats /min, regular, low volume and normal character. The blood pressure is 108/90mmHg. The venous pressure is elevated with systolic 'v' waves. There is a malar flush. On examining the Precordium, there is a lateral thoracotomy scar. The apex beat is undisplaced and has a tapping quality. There is a loud parasternal pulmonary component to the second heart sound. There is an opening snap in early diastole followed by a mid-diastolic rumbling murmur at the apex, heard best in expiration with the patient in the left lateral position. In addition, there is pansystolic murmur at the lower left sternal edge which is louder in inspiration, and a short early diastolic murmur in the pulmonary area radiating down the left sternal edge, louder in inspiration. On auscultation of the lung fields, there are bibasal crepitations, and there is peripheral oedema.

Provisional Diagnosis

Rheumatic Mitral Stenosis (severe) complicated with severe pulmonary hypertension and left ventricular failure

Summary of pathophysiology and the common complications of Rheumatic Mitral stenosis:
Elevated left atrial pressure, hence pulmonary venous and pulmonary capillary

pressure leads to:

- Exercise intolerance
- Dyspnoea
- Orthopnoea
- Pulmonary edema
- Haemoptysis and pulmonary haemorrhage
- Recurrent pulmonary infections

II. Dilated left atrium leads to

- Cardiomegaly
- Atrial fibrillation
- Systemic embolism

III. Pulmonary hypertension leads to

- Right ventricular failure with right ventricular and atrial dilatation, which

   may be complicated by pulmonary embolism.

IV. Abnormal valvular structure with roughened surface together with abnormal

hemodynamics leads to infective endocarditis.

Symptoms

Symptoms related to pulmonary congestion

- Dyspnoea
- Orthopnoea
- Paroxysmal nocturnal dyspnoea
- Haemoptysis
- Symptoms of right sided heart failure

   Right upper quadrant discomfort

   Leg swelling

- Symptoms of low cardiac out put

N.B: Symptoms of pulmonary congestion improves when right heart failsbecause of decreased pulmonary perfusion.

Signs

- Distended neck vein
- Silent precordium with epigastric pulsation
- Apical impulse is often localized
- Palpable P2
- Left para-sternal heave
- Diastolic thrill at apex
- S1 accentuation,
- Opening snap of the mitral valve
- Loud P2
- Mid diastolic rumbling murmur best heard at the apex with presystolic accentuation

NOTE:

A summary of the history and examination findings should be stated.

A likely diagnosis is then proposed with supporting factors explained.

Then, a reasonable list of relevant investigations should be compiled for further discussion.

Management:

Depending on the question posed the student is expected to outline management. Prioritizing the approach would be required of senior students based on the case presented beginning from urgent to short and long term care. Rehabilitation and care in the community after returning home would be holistic.

The content of the suggested management is outlined below:

Asymptomatic patients in sinus rhythm:

> Endocarditis prophylaxis
> Regular follow-up with echocardiography

Management of Atrial Fibrillation

> Adopt rhythm control or rate control strategy
> Patients with mitral valve disease should be anticoagulated with warfarin if no contraindication exist in view of atrial fibrillation

Management of symptomatic patients

> Diuretics to reduce left atrial pressure and relieve mild symptoms
> As symptoms worsen, and pulmonary hypertension begins to develop, these patients should be referred for surgery

What procedures can be used to treat mitral stenosis?

i. Closed commisurotomy: This can be achieved by closed mitral valvotomy (not done nowadays) or mitral valvuloplasty.

ii. Open commisurotomy: It requires open heart surgery with cardiopulmonary bypass and valve repair under direct vision.

iii.   Mitral valve replacement: if there is coexisting mitral regurgitation, then the valve is replaced requiring open heart surgery with cardiopulmonary bypass

LEARNING OUTCOMES

By the end of this case review the student should be able to:

1. Take a detailed history of a patient who presents with breathlessness

2. Identify cardiomegaly (left atrial dilatation) and straightening of the left heart border due to left atrial dilatation

3. Identifying signs of wide notched P waves due to left atrial hypertrophy and recognising atrial fibrillation in ECG.

4. Perform relevant and focused clinical examination of a patient who has mitral valve disease

5. Discuss the principles of management in patients with mitral stenosis

COMMONLY ASKED QUESTIONS

What are the causes of mitral stenosis?

➢   Rheumatic fever (most common)
➢   Congenital mitral stenosis
➢   Rheumatoid arthritis and Systemic lupus erythematosus
➢   Methysergide therapy
➢   Calcified mitral valve

What other conditions could give rise to mid-diastolic rumbling murmur?

➢   Left atrial mass (myxomas)
➢   Left atrial thrombus
➢   Cor triatriatum

How do you classify the severity of mitral stenosis?

The severity can be classified according to mitral valve area:

➢   Mild: >1.5cm^2
➢   Moderate: 1-1.5cm^2
➢   Severe: <1.0 cm^2

What are the clinical markers of severe mitral stenosis?

- ➢ Early opening snap (lost with calcified leaflets)
- ➢ Increasing length of murmur
- ➢ Signs of pulmonary hypertension
- ➢ Signs of pulmonary congestion
- ➢ Graham steel murmur (pulmonary regurgitation)
- ➢ Low pulse pressure

What are the complications of mitral stenosis?

- ➢ Left atrial enlargement
- ➢ Atrial fibrillation
- ➢ Left atrial thrombus formation
- ➢ Pulmonary hypertension
- ➢ Pulmonary oedema
- ➢ Right heart failure

What is the pathology underlying 'malar flush'?

A malar flush is seen in mitral stenosis with the development of severe pulmonary hypertension, leading to a low cardiac output state.

What are the differential diagnoses of a malar flush?

- ➢ Mitral stenosis
- ➢ Systemic sclerosis
- ➢ Cold weather
- ➢ SLE
- ➢ Irradiation
- ➢ Polycythaemia

If this patient develops hoarse voice, what would you be thinking?

An enlarged left atrium in mitral stenosis may compress the left recurrent laryngeal nerve leading to left vocal cord paralysis. This is called Ortner's syndrome.

HIGH ACHIEVER QUESTIONS

What are the expected findings in Chest Radiograph of a patient with severe mitral stenosis?

- • Left atrial enlargement (double shadow behind the heart in right heart border – shadow within shadow)
- • Straightening of the left heart border (due to prominent pulmonary artery and left atrial appendage)
- • Later mitral valve calcification

- Kerley B lines (dense, short, horizontal lines most commonly seen in the costophrenic angles when pulmonary venous pressure is between 20-30mmHg)
- Barium swallow in RAO view may demonstrate sickling of barium filled oesophagus due to compression by enlarged left atrium
- Splaying of carina
- Kerley A lines - dense straight lines up to 4cm in length and running towards the hilum when pulmonary venous pressure >30mmHg
- Rarely findings of pulmonary haemosiderosis and parenchymal ossification.

What are the expected findings in Echocardiography in patients with Mitral stenosis?
Thickened valve leaflets, especially at the tips, thickened chordate, diastolic doming of the leaflets, reduced orifice area and occasionally left atrial thrombi

What are the indications for surgery?

- Pulmonary congestion
- Pulmonary hypertension
- Hemoptysis
- Recurrent thrombo-embolic events despite therapeutic anticoagulation

What are the criteria for doing mitral valvuloplasty?

- Mobile valve (loud 1st heart sound and opening snap)
- Minimal calcification of the valve and subvalvular apparatus
- Absence of mitral regurgitation
- Absence of left atrial thrombus (on Transoesophageal echocardiography)

What conditions simulate mitral stenosis?
- Left atrial myxoma
- Cortriatriatum
- Aortic regurgitation with prominent Austin flint murmur
- Other causes of left heart failure and pulmonary hypertension
- Tricuspid stenosis
- Ball valve thrombus of left atrium
- Diastolic flow murmurs across normal mitral valve as in VSD, PDA, severe MR, etc

COMMON MISTAKES:
1. Failure to recognise the small volume pulse in a patient with mitral stenosis

2. Failure to appreciate the timing of the mid-diastolic murmur by using carotid pulse and often over diagnosing it as systolic murmur
3. Failure to recognize the calcified mitral valve causing soft S1 despite the presence of severe mitral stenosis
4. Failure to recognize the absence of pre-systolic accentuation of mid-diastolic murmur due to co-existent AF
5. Misinterpretation of functional TR murmur and Graham Steell murmur due to Pulmonary regurgitation both as a consequence of pulmonary hypertension as organic valvular lesions

MUST KNOW FACTS ABOUT MITRAL STENOSIS:

- Usually presents with exertional dyspnoea and features of left atrial failure.
- Essentials of diagnosis include tapping apex, loud first heart sound, presence of rough rumbling mid-diastolic murmur which is louder on expiratory apnoea and with the bell of the stethoscope. This murmur is associated with opening snap and presystolic accentuation
- More common in females and if it occurs with pulmonary hypertension can be deleterious and harmful to pregnancy.
- If untreated develops into atrial fibrillation, left heart failure, pulmonary hypertension, right heart failure and later sometimes gets infected leading to infective endocarditis.
- Close and careful follow-up with echocardiogram is essential to diagnose the severe forms of mitral stenosis which may prove fatal otherwise

CASE 12: HYPERTENSION WITH COMPLICATIONS (RESISTANT HYPERTENSION)
RIFDY MOHIDEEN

OVERVIEW

Hypertension is currently the single biggest contributor to deaths worldwide and remains the most important modifiable risk factor for coronary heart disease, stroke, congestive heart failure, renal disease, dementia and peripheral vascular disease. Suboptimal blood pressure control is responsible for 62% of cerebrovascular disease, 49% of ischemic heart disease, causing an estimated 7.1 million deaths a year. A significant proportion of patients with hypertension fail to achieve adequate blood pressure control despite multiple antihypertensive medications. These are the patients with resistant hypertension, a clinical condition frequently encountered in clinical practice.

Hypertension is considered to be resistant when the blood pressure remains elevated beyond 140/90 mmHg despite taking full doses of at least three antihypertensive medications which includes a diuretic. The approach to such a patient begins with careful history including an assessment of the patient's adherence to the management plan, including lifestyle modifications and medications and confirmation of true resistant hypertension. Careful physical examination and selected investigations may provide clues of a secondary cause.

CASE FOR EXAMINATION

Students may be tested on a patient with hypertension (with or without complications) mainly as a long case, unless there physical signs of a secondary cause when it may be given as a short case or OSCE.

CASE VIGNETTE

A 54-year-old male with a history of hypertension for two years is admitted to the hospital following a referral by his general practitioner who has difficulty in getting the patient's blood pressure controlled despite prescribing multiple medications. His medications include enalapril 10mg bid, atenolol 100mg daily and hydrochlorothiazide 25mg daily. He also receives treatment for a long-standing non-specific backache. The blood pressure measured in the clinic averaged 160/94 mmHg His BMI is 28 kg/m2.

OSCE, SHORT OR LONG:

The candidate may be asked to perform general examination or abdominal examination in a patient with resistant hypertension. The candidate should be alert to recognise important clues on general examination of a number of endocrine disorders (e.g. Cushing syndrome) and on abdominal examination of renal conditions (e.g. renal artery stenosis). If time permits, note the effects of hypertension on the heart, blood vessels, fundoscopy and brain.

LONG CASE or OSLER

Resistant hypertension requires a careful and tailored approach to identify modifiable causes and target organ damage. The candidate should take a detailed history of adherence to medication, compliance with lifestyle measures and potential secondary causes.

During clinical examination, the candidate should demonstrate clinical competence in identifying hypertension, the presence of cardiovascular, cerebrovascular and renal complications and detecting the presence of an underlying cause.

The candidate should also be able to discuss the rationale of the choice of investigations, plan of management and follow up including advice on lifestyle measures.

History
The history should focus on

- current symptoms if any, affecting the heart, brain, peripheral vessels and kidneys
- causes such as non-adherence to drugs and lifestyle measures, appropriateness of drug combination and drug-drug interference and the presence of a number of endocrine, renal and vascular causes.

- **Chest pain**: Do you have any pain or discomfort in the chest? Does it occur at rest or with activity? (suggestive of angina)
- **Shortness of breath**: Establish when it was first noticed and the rate of progression
- **Orthopnoea**: Do you find it more comfortable to sleep or rest in bed with several pillows? (suggestive of heart failure)
- **Paroxysmal nocturnal dyspnoea**: Are you awakened suddenly by difficulty in breathing or coughing? Do these symptoms improve when you sit up or walk? (suggestive of left ventricular dysfunction)

- Palpitations: Do you experience you heart racing or skipping a beat? If so find out when it occurs, how long does it last and what else occurs with it. (suggestive of arrhythmias)
- Syncope: Have you experienced light-headedness or blackouts (suggestive of arrhythmias)
- Intermittent claudication: Do you have to halt when walking due to pain in the calf? (peripheral vascular disease)
- Swelling of feet: Does your feet swell? (occurs in the severe lesions)

The candidate should be prepared to discuss the pathophysiology of the symptoms elicited e.g how to explain paroxyxmal nocturnal dyspnoea, the the mechanism behind syncopal attacks etc.

Review of systems
- Muscle weakness: Do you find difficulty is climbing stairs or fetching items from a height (suggestive of proximal muscle weakness)
- Urinary symptoms: nocturia, haematuria
- Excessive sweating: Do you have palpitations and sweating coming together? (phaeochromocytoma, hyperthyroidism)
- Gastrointestinal: Have you loose stools? (hyperthyroidism)
- Renal; Have you ever passed blood or stones with urine?
- Cerebrovascular; Have you suffered sudden weakness of limb or loss sight or had difficulty in speaking? (stroke)
- Excessive sleepiness and snoring: Find out if patient is likely to fall asleep during sitting, watching TV or during periods of inactivity.(if daytime sleepiness is present, the Epworth Sleepiness Scale is a more sensitive tool)

Past medical history
- Previous admissions (determine if these were for heart failure, arrhythmias, angina, or for investigations)
- History of hypertension (How long and if there was any difficulty in controlling blood pressure)
- History of asthma (for beta-blocker use), allergy to drugs (angioneurotic oedema following ACEI)
- Were you ever told by the doctor that an abnormal heart sound is heard? When was it?
- Do you have any one of the following conditions? (diabetes, elevated lipids, gout)

Family history
- Size of family and children

- Are there any family members having hypertension? (which member, severity and complications, age of death if any)

Social history
- Employment history: current and past employment and ability to continue work
- Income: able to afford hospital visits, medication and investigations on personal funds. Check if insured and how much of the medical expenses are covered.
- Alcohol: quantify and assess if intake is excessive and if dependent
- Smoking: quantity and duration of use
- Physical activity; type, frequency and intensity
- Salt: estimate if use is excessive

Treatment history
- Obtain a list of drugs the patient is taking and the dosage (antihypertensives)
- Inquire if on steroids, NSAIDs (in view of backache), nasal drops, oral contraceptives (women), cyclosporine and erythropoietin (if appropriate)
- Check adherence to therapy (non-threatening questioning, count remaining pills if medication is available)
- If adherence is poor, find out if this is because of poor instructions, adverse effects or economic reasons
- Assess if clinic follow up is satisfactory

CHECK LIST FOR HISTORY IN A 'DIFFICULT TO CONTROL HYPERTENSION'

- Assess if there are cardiac, renal, cerebral and vascular symptoms and comorbidities (e.g. diabetes, bronchial asthma, renal disease, dyslipidaemia)
- Assess the quality of the follow up and check adherence to medication
- Review if current medications are appropriate and in the right combination
- Inquire on patient's lifestyle to detect if diet and physical activity are at recommended levels
- Review possible underlying causes (e.g. Cushing syndrome)
- Assess patient's understanding of the illness

EXAMINATION

Professionalism

- Explain to patient what you intend doing before starting to examine
- Make sure the curtains are drawn and males should ask for a chaperone when examining a female patient
- Position patient for adequate viewing of abdomen
- Expose the chest adequately

General examination

- Observe patient. Note if well, dyspnoeic or distressed.
- Measure height, weight and waist circumference. Calculate BMI
- Inspect tongue for pallor and plethora
- Inspect face for puffiness (renal diseases), moon-shaped (Cushing)
- Inspect neck for goitre (thyroid disorders) and buffalo hump. Auscultate over thyroid if enlarged with the bell of stethoscope
- Inspect lower limb for oedema
- Examine the back for sacral oedema, abdomen for pigmented striae and for café au lait spots and neurofibromata (pheochromocytoma)

Cardiovascular examination

- Examine radial pulse for rate, regularity, volume, character (collapsing); time with femoral pulse.
- Examine the contralateral radial pulse at the same time. Note if any inequality in pulse characteristics
- Examine all other accessible peripheral pulses for volume, pulsation and bruits (carotids, femoral, popliteal, dorsalis pedis, posterior tibial arteries)
- Palpate the femoral artery at the same time as the radial pulse (delayed and smaller amplitude as seen in coarctation of aorta)
- Inspect jugular veins; measure height and observe waveform
- Measure blood pressure (record twice and also in contralateral arm)
- Localise and characterise apex (heaving) & determine tracheal position at the same time
- Feel for a left parasternal pulsation
- Feel for thrills over the praecordium; time with carotid pulse
- Auscultate for heart sounds (identify first, second & fourth heart sound). Note if the sounds are normal, soft, loud, split or single

- Auscultate for murmurs; note timing, site best heard, loudness, radiation, character, variation with posture, position and other manoeuvres. Use the bell for low-pitched sounds and the diaphragm for high-pitched sounds. If coarctation is suspected, auscultate over the back of chest near the fourth or fifth vertebra near the spine for a continuous murmur
- Auscultate lung bases for crepitations and check for dullness.
- Examine other systems (respiratory, nervous, musculoskeletal, abdomen) depending on the instructions, case format (OSCE, long case etc.), relevance and availability of time.

Abdominal examination

- Observe for abdominal fullness or bulging especially over flanks
- Note any surgical scars, puncture marks, visible veins and striae
- Palpate for enlarged kidneys placing one hand below the displacing the kidney anteriorly and the other above. Note its size, shape, consistency, mobility and its descent with inspiration.
- Palpate liver for enlargement and pulsation; note other features
- Look for other masses in the flanks (adrenals)
- Auscultate for a renal bruit below each costal margin

Nervous system

- Nervous system examination should focus on focal signs (e.g. hemiparesis) and fundal examination (hypertensive changes)
- Thank the patient at the end of the examination and cover patient up

CHECKLIST FOR EXAMINATION FINDINGS IN RESISTANT HYPERTENSION

- General examination; obesity, features of a secondary cause (e.g. Cushing syndrome)
- Pulse: radio-femoral delay, absent or weak peripheral pulses
- Blood pressure: elevated
- Apex: displaced to left, with a diffuse heave
- Heart sounds: normal S1, loud A2, S4
- Murmurs: Usually absent, continuous murmur over back in coarctation of aorta
- Abdomen: enlarged kidney(s), other masses(phaeochromocytoma), renal bruit
- Nervous system: evidence of stroke, hypertensive retinal changes on fundoscopy

☞ **Candidate should consider relevant investigations for specific diagnosis (complications) and for monitoring.**

Investigations

- Urine analysis; proteinuria, dysmorphic red cells (glomerular disease)
- Full blood count; anaemia (chronic renal disease), polycythaemia(Cushing
- Serum creatinine/blood urea; elevated in renal parenchymal disease and long-standing hypertension
- Serum electrolytes; hypokalaemia (Cushing syndrome, Conn syndrome, renal artery stenosis)
- Fasting blood glucose: co-morbid and risk factor
- Lipid profile: co-morbid and risk factor
- ECG: Cardiac axis, LVH, ischaemic and electrolyte changes
- Chest radiograph: enlarged cardiac shadow, pulmonary venous congestion, notching of the inferior rib margins
- Thyroid studies: ultrasensitive TSH, Free T4 (if clinically relevant)
- Ultrasound scan of abdomen: renal size (unequal in RAS), suprarenal mass
- Duplex ultrasonography of kidneys: renal artery stenosis
- Ambulatory blood pressure / home blood pressure recording; exclude "white coat hypertension"
- Echocardiography: LVH, left ventricular and left atrial dilatation in long-standing hypertension, EF usually preserved till late
- Additional investigations may be required if clinical features or preliminary investigations are suggestive

(e.g. Spiral CT angiogram and MR angiogram for RAS; aldosterone to renin ratio for Conn syndrome; urinary and plasma metanephrines for phaeochromocytoma; dexamethasone suppression test and urine cortisol for Cushing syndrome)

CLINICAL DISCUSSION OF THE CASE

This middle aged man has inadequate control of blood pressure despite being on adequate doses of three antihypertensive drugs. The inability to achieve target blood pressure in treated hypertensive patients has several potential causes.

Clinical clues in this patient are few except for obesity and a history of possible NSAID use that can interfere with the actions of antihypertensive medications. A systematic approach is required to identify some of the more common causes such as poor adherence to lifestyle measures and to prescribed medications. Suggestive clinical features may indicate an underlying secondary cause.

The candidate should suggest a plan of investigations based on confirming resistant hypertension, assessing extent of target organ damage and excluding likely secondary causes.

LEARNING OUTCOME

The student should be able to

- Elicit a focussed history in a patient with resistant hypertension
- Perform a general and systems examination to detect signs of secondary causes of hypertension and target organ damage
- Explain the clinical features on a physiological and pathological basis
- Identify potential drug-drug interactions and inappropriate combinations
- Select the relevant investigations that assess target organ damage, comorbidities, risk factors and secondary hypertension
- Discuss the non-drug and drug management of hypertension
- List secondary causes of hypertension
- Discuss the indications and expected findings of special investigations of common secondary causes of hypertension
- Communicate to the patient about the nature of the illness, general and specific preventive measures including diet, physical activity and the importance of drug adherence

COMMONLY ASKED QUESTIONS

What is meant by pseudo-resistant hypertension?
These are patients whose blood pressure levels are persistently above normal values at clinic measurements but who do not have resistant hypertension. Several factors such as poor blood pressure measuring techniques, white coat effect and poor compliance contribute to this situation.

Name clinical conditions that are examples of target organ damage of hypertension?

Left ventricular hypertrophy, myocardial infarction, renal impairment, retinopathy, peripheral vascular disease and stroke are the common examples.

What is pseudohypertension?

This is a condition seen sometimes in the older person where high blood pressure recordings are found but there is absence of target organ damage. The high recordings are due to a non-compressible sclerotic brachial artery where a higher pressure is needed to compress the artery.

What are the common drug related causes of resistant hypertension?

- Inadequate dose
- Inappropriate combination
- Inappropriate diuretic (hydrochlorothiazide in renal failure)
- Drug interactions

When should white coat hypertension be suspected in resistant hypertension?

White-coat should be suspected in a patient who is compliant to drugs with clinical features of overtreatment such as dizziness and postural hypotension present without evidence of target organ damage.

What are the principles of management of resistant hypertension?

Once the blood pressure is confirmed to be truly elevated and pseudo-resistance excluded, identify and address contributing lifestyle factors.
Discontinue any medications that may interfere with prescribed antihypertensive drugs and identify any secondary causes of hypertension. Optimise drug regimen which may often need additional diuretic use.
If these fail to achieve target, refer to a specialist dealing with hypertension.

HIGH-ACHIEVER LEVEL QUESTIONS

What is the DASH eating plan?

It is a diet rich in fruits, vegetables, and low-fat dairy products with a reduced content of saturated and total fat.

How does obstructive sleep apnoea cause hypertension?

Long term exposure to night-time hypoxia activates the sympathetic nervous system which leads to increase in peripheral vascular resistance and blood pressure. Additionally, there is a relative increase in serum aldosterone which promotes volume overload.

What are the novel therapies to treat resistant hypertension?

Carotid baroreceptor stimulation and catheter-based renal sympathetic nerve denervation are two very exciting therapies for selected patients whose blood pressure is difficult to control with medications. Both these therapeutic modalities suppress the influence of the sympathetic nervous system which plays a central role in elevated blood pressure.

RED FLAG ENCOUNTERS

The following are situations that may be overlooked:

- Failure to check blood pressure accurately and measure in both arms
- Failure to check non-adherence and drug interactions
- Failure to identify target organ damage
- Failure to identify a potentially correctible secondary cause of hypertension (e.g. renal bruit due to renal artery stenosis)

MUST KNOW FACTS OF RESISTANT HYPERTENSION

- Resistant hypertension of difficult to control hypertension is becoming increasingly common
- Uncontrolled blood pressure adds to the risk of cardiovascular, renal and cerebrovascular complications
- It is often associated with cardiovascular complications and target organ damage
- The murmur can be missed if patient is not examined in the seated position
- Leads to progressive decline in left ventricular function
- Require valve replacement in the asymptomatic stage for optimal outcome; appearance of symptoms may be too late for valve therapy
- Is a risk factor for infective endocarditis and should receive preventive treatment prior to high risk procedures

CASE 13 : MYOCARDIAL INFARCTION
CHAMPIKA BODINAYAKE

OVERVIEW

Acute myocardial infarction (MI) is a leading cause of morbidity and mortality worldwide. MI represents a life threatening manifestation of atherosclerosis, precipitated by an acute thrombus on a ruptured or eroded atherosclerotic plaque. Occlusion of the vessel leads to sudden and critical reduction of blood flow causing irreversible myocardial damage or death.

Myocardial infarction is classified according to Electrocardiographic (ECG) findings as ST elevation MI (STEMI) and non STEMI, which guides management. Non STEMI is more common and frequently occur in older patients. The incidence of MI increases with age, and the presence of risk factors for atherosclerosis. The primary risk factors include diabetes, hypertension, dyslipidaemia, smoking, family history and male gender. The presence of any risk factor doubles the relative risk of developing coronary artery disease (CAD)

CASE VIGNETTE

A 50-year-old male is brought in to emergency department with acute retrosternal tightening chest pain for one hour duration. The pain was radiating to his left arm and jaw. He was sweating profusely and complained of feeling faint. He had hypertension and elevated cholesterol for three years which was treated with losartan 50 mg/day and atorvastatin 10mg/day. There is no history of angina or myocardial infarction in the past. He is a teetotaller. His elder brother died of a MI at the age of 52 years.

On examination he is pale and sweaty and in severe pain. The pulse is110 beats/min, regular, low volume, Blood pressure is100/70 and Jugular venous pressure is normal. Auscultation of the heart and the chest are normal. Acute myocardial infarction is suspected and an urgent ECG confirms extensive anterior STEMI. The patient is given oxygen, aspirin, clopidogrel, intra venous morphine sulphate and thrombolysis with streptokinase is started. A few minutes later he has a cardiac arrest with ECG monitor showing ventricular fibrillation. Successful cardioversion reverts the rhythm back to normal. He then develops acute pulmonary oedema evidenced by bilateral fine basal crackles confirmed by chest radiograph. On the third day of illness, after apparent recovery he has syncope with a heart rate of 30/bpm with ECG evidence of complete heart block. A pacemaker is administered via the right internal jugular

Myocardial infarction is an important must know topic for clinical students. Students may be tested on a number of formats including OSCE, Long Case and viva.

The acute symptoms in this middle aged man are very suggestive of acute myocardial infarction. The patient presents with acute severe chest pain suggestive of myocardial ischemia. The ECG confirms acute ST elevation MI. The other criterion, the cardiac enzymes if elevated will further support the diagnosis. The patient survived following a ventricular tachycardia which is the most common life threatening complication of acute MI in the first few hours. He developed acute pulmonary oedema and complete heart block (CHB) which can follow a large infarction.

History of the presenting complaint
The patient is generally unwell therefore only a brief and focused history should be elicited during acute stage.
- Chest pain: How long did you have chest pain? What was the exact time of onset of severe pain? What is the nature? Is it tightening/crushing/ pressing? Where do you feel the discomfort? Does it radiate to left arm, neck, jaw or inter scapular area? Does it change with breathing (suggestive of pleurisy)? Does it relieve with GTN? Did you have similar bouts of pain in the recent past? If so, when?
- Autonomic symptoms: Is the pain associated with sweating? Nausea and vomiting?
- Dyspnoea: Are you finding it difficult to breathe?
- Orthopnoea: Are you finding it difficult to lie flat?
- Palpitations: Suggestive of arrhythmias. Do you experience you heart racing or skipping a beat? How long does it last? Are there associated symptoms as vomiting and blackouts
- Syncope: Have you experienced light headedness or blackouts (suggestive of arrhythmias)
- Cough? Is there a cough?(in pulmonary oedema there is pink frothy sputum and the patient is very unwell with dyspnoea)
- Confusion: confusion and impaired cognition may result from cerebral hypo perfusion

Past medical history
- Previous admissions for MI and angina: when, complications, investigations, treatment
- History of surgery: Coronary artery bypass grafting (CABG), stenting or balloon angioplasty, intracranial and bowel surgery,
- History of Diabetes – duration, control, complications as retinopathy, investigations, treatment
- History of hypertension: duration, control, treatment
- History of lipid abnormalities

- Other co morbidities: cerebrovascular accidents, bleeding peptic ulcers, malignancy, other bleeding diathesis, haematuria, asthma, chronic lung disease, renal disease, liver disease,
- Allergy to drugs: Angiotensin converting enzyme (ACE)inhibitors

Family history

- Are there any family members having heart disease eg: CAD, diabetes hypertension, dyslipidaemia, familial cardiomyopathy and other hereditary disease
- Size of family and children

Social history

- Employment history: current and past employment, Does work involve heavy manual work?
- Income: able to afford hospital visits, medication. Check if insured and how much of the medical expenses are covered.
- Smoking: quantity and duration of use
- Alcohol: quantify and assess if dependent
- Other illicit drugs
- Amount of exercises
- Family support and other support available

Dietary history

Inquire whether the patient is on a modified low salt diet
Inquire on dietary fat intake

Treatment history

- Obtain a list of drugs the patient is taking and the dosage (aspirin, statin, diuretics, ACE inhibitors , beta-blockers, calcium channel blockers, nitrates and antiplatelet drugs
- Inquire if on anticoagulants and monitoring, bleeding episodes
- Surgical treatment, CABG, coronary stents, implanted devices, pacemakers
- Check adherence to therapy
- Assess if follow up is satisfactory

Check list for history in acute MI

- Assess current and past cardiac symptoms with onset and duration
- Identify the possible risk factors
- Identify the possible complications like arrhythmia, angina, heart failure
- Identify presence of disease as diabetes, hypertension, dyslipidaemia which are directly related and other illnesses)
- Identify the precipitating factors for MI as non compliance with drugs, uncontrolled diabetes and hypertension, dyslipidaemia, current smoking etc.
- Review if current medications are appropriate and adequate with special reference to aspirin, beta blockers, statins,

antiplatelet drugs, oral hypoglycaemics, antihypertensives, anticoagulation
- Inquire regarding previous angiography, special investigations, CABG, coronary stents
- Inquire on smoking and alcohol current and past
- Inquire on patient's lifestyle to detect progressive changes in the daily activity and functional disability in an objective manner
- Review dietary modification
- Assess the quality of the follow up and check adherence to medication
- Assess patient's understanding of the illness and family and other social support received

Examination
- Explain to patient what you intend doing before starting to examine
- Make sure the curtains are drawn and males should ask for a chaperone when examining a female patient
- Position patient for adequate viewing of jugular veins
- Expose the chest adequately

General examination
- Observe patient. Note if well, dyspnoeic or distressed. Count respiratory rate
- Examine for cold and clammy extremities
- Note pedal and sacral oedema
- Examine colour of mucosa for cyanosis, pallor or plethora.
- Inspect face for xanthelasma cornea for premature arcus, palmer xanthoma and tendon xanthoma at elbows, Achilles tendons suggestive of hyperlipidemia

Cardiovascular and other system examination
- Examine radial pulse for rate, regularity, volume, character and presence of AF.
- Examine all other accessible peripheral pulses for volume, pulsation and bruits (carotids, femoral, popliteal, dorsalis pedis, posterior tibial arteries)
- Inspect jugular veins; measure height and observe waveform.
- Measure blood pressure
- Inspect chest for surgical scars, implanted devices
- Localise and characterise apex
- Feel for a left parasternal pulsation, thrills
- Auscultate for heart sounds; 1st and 2nd are soft due to poor contractility. There may be additional 3rd and 4th heart sounds which are also common.

- Auscultate for murmurs: New onset murmurs may signify ventricular septal rupture or acute mitral regurgitation following papillary muscle dysfunction
- Auscultate for pericardial friction rub
- Auscultate lung bases for fine basal crepitations and check for dullness.
- Palpate liver for enlargement and tenderness.
- Examine other systems eg:(respiratory, nervous, musculoskeletal, abdomen briefly guided by the history) depending on the instructions, case format (OSCE, long case etc.), relevance and availability of time.
- Thank the patient at the end of the examination and cover patient up

Checklist for examination findings
- General examination: Observe for dyspnoea, pallor, plethora, cyanosis, oedema, features of hyperlipidemia
- Pulse: Palpate for rate, rhythm (AF, ectopic beats), volume, character, peripheral pulse
- Jugular veins: Inspect height and waveform
- Blood pressure
- Apex: Palpate apex for displacement and nature
- Left parasternal heave: note the presence of right ventricular hypertrophy
- Palpate for thrills in the precordium
- Heart sounds: Auscultate for soft S1, S2, additionally S3 and S4 or both together causing a gallop rhythm.
- Murmurs: Auscultate for new onset murmurs
- Auscultate lung bases for fine basal crepitations
- Palpate liver for enlargement and tenderness

Investigations
- ECG: ECG is the most important investigation in the diagnosis of MI. ST segment elevation localizes area of infarction. (discussed below) Acute ST elevation is defined in men as 0.2mV in two contagious leads and 0.15 mV in V1-V3 and 0.1mV in all other leads in women (exception posterior MI). New onset left bundle branch block (LBBB) is also treated like STEMI. In non STEMI, ST segment depressions are seen.

Serum biomarker elevation in acute MI

Serum Biomarkers	Elevation (hours)	Peak(hours)	Normalization
CK-MB	4-6	14-36	48-72 hours

Troponin T and I	4-6	24-36	10-14 days
LDH	>48	72	10-14 days
Myoglobin	2	2	7-12

- Complete Blood count: Early rise in white cell count in MI.
- Routine blood tests: Blood glucose, urea and electrolytes, creatinine, lipids, liver function, INR, APTT
- Lipid profile: Unless one performed in one month
- HbA1C levels: Check glycaemic control in diabetics unless one performed within three months
- Chest radiograph: Chest radiography is useful in detecting pulmonary oedema and cardiomegaly.
- Echocardiography: Regional wall motion abnormalities indicate infracted area but cannot differentiate old from new. Echocardiography assesses ejection fraction, acute valvular regurgitation, mural thrombus etc.
- Cardiac catheterization: Assess the patient specially in STEMI for further intervention as PTCA (percutaneous transluminal coronary angioplasty) ,CABG and stenting
- Exercise testing: On discharge exercise testing is used as a prognostic aid.
- 24 hour Holter monitor: Detects arrhythmias especially asymptomatic ones.
- Cardiac MRI: Useful in assessing myocardial viability
- Myocardial perfusion scanning: SPECT (single photon emitting CT) is useful to detect inducible ischemia and hibernating myocardium
- Stress echocardiography: Exercise or dobutamine stress can detect inducible ischemia in areas of myocardium which are hibernating (dysfunctional myocardium following ischemia which can be reversed following restoration of blood flow).

Diagnosis

MI is characterized by the following three criteria and at least two should be present

- Severe chest pain lasting for at least 20 minutes
- Abnormal ECG
- Elevated cardiac enzymes

Management

The management of acute MI include establishing the diagnosis, acute management, assessment of complications, identification of risk factors, and follow up. Patient should be managed in a coronary care unit preferably at a place where angioplasty is an option. The patient should be on continuous monitoring.

Initial assessment and treatment

Re perfusion: Goal in management of STEMI is early re perfusion with primary PCI (percutaneous coronary intervention) or thrombolysis. If presented early (<3 hours) PCI is the choice. PCI is indicated in cardiogenic shock, failed thrombolysis and when thrombolytics are contra indicated.

Thrombolysis is indicated for all patients qualifying with ECG presenting within 12 hours unless there are contraindications. Thrombolysis target time (door to needle time) is less than 30 minutes of admission.

Indications for thrombolytics include, ST elevation>1mm in two or more contagious leads, ST depression > 1mm in true posterior MI and new onset bundle branch block. Available agents include streptokinase, tenecteplase, alteplase, retiplase.

Aspirin: non enteric coated aspirin 162-325mg is given immediately to follow 75-162 mg of enteric coated aspirin daily.

Morphine: 5-10 mg IV (may repeat) with IV anti emetic as metaclopramide

Beta-blockers: Unless bradycardia, acute heart failure or low BP is present oral beta blockers are started within 24 hours in all cases of acute MI.

Anticoagulation: IV unfractionated heparin, bivalirudin, enoxaparin or fondoparinux for at least 48 hours is recommended in acute MI.

ACE inhibitors: Initiated within 48 hours in anterior MI or in heart failure with EF<40% unless BP is low. If ACE inhibitors intolerant ARB can be used.

Nitrates: Contra indicated in right ventricular (RV) infarct and if sildenafil is used within 24 hours

Clopidogrel: Indicated if undergoing PCI as primary or secondary procedure.

Statins: May be started prior lipid panel being available.

Management of complications

Common complications such as ventricular arrhythmia, LVF and complete heart block is addressed during case discussion

Transfer from coronary care unit

Once the patient is pain free, stable, may be transferred (usually in 24-48 hrs. if pain and arrhythmia free) to a step down unit or telemetry unit according to the protocol of the hospital. Monitoring can be discontinued when electrically stabilized (usually in three days of MI).

Post discharge and follow up

Most patients are discharged within 5days of uncomplicated MI. Patient's General Practitioner should be informed.

All patients should have an exercise ECG performed prior returning for follow up visit at 6-8 weeks

Cardiac rehabilitation: support and advice for hospital based or home rehabilitation

Patient education, management of risk factors and lifestyle modifications:

Smoking and alcohol cessation, low salt diet, exercises and achieving optimum body weight are important lifestyle modifications.

Non diabetics need at least annual HbA1C and FBS

Drugs for secondary prevention: All patients who had an acute MI should be offered the following, unless contraindicated

- Aspirin and clopidogrel combination
- ACE inhibitor
- Beta blocker
- Statin

Return to work and driving: Patients with jobs involving minimal activity may return to job in 2-3 weeks, if more physically demanding jobs in 4-6 weeks, with complications longer as decided by the condition. Driving not permitted for 4 weeks and not permitted for unstable angina present at rest or emotion or at wheel

The patient and family should be educated regarding illness and the patient should receive psychosocial assessment and support

Case summary

This middle aged patient presented with an acute anterior MI. He develops ventricular fibrillation while being thrombolysed which recovers with cardioversion. He also has acute pulmonary oedema and CHB which are complications of a large anterior infarct. He has hypertension, hyperlipidaemia and positive family history as risk factors.

Clinical discussion of the case

Start with the summary of the patient which highlights the symptoms and abnormal signs

The patient has classical clinical features of an acute STEMI, which is confirmed by the ECG changes. There are four risk factors already identified as hypertension, hyperlipidaemia male gender and positive family history.

Important risk factors like impaired glucose tolerance may also be present on investigations.

The patient should be cared in a coronary care unit with continuous monitoring to detect complications. Standard treatment with inhaled oxygen, IV morphine, aspirin and clopidogrel and statins should be given.

Immediate reperfusion therapy should be started, ideally PCI. The patient should be treated with thrombolysis as PCI facility is not available as the first intervention as in many centres in the world. If thrombolysis fails the patient should receive rescue PCI within 12 hours.

Ventricular fibrillation is common in the first few hours of MI and accounts for the 25%mortality in MI which occurs within the first hour. Defibrillation quickly restores the rhythm but unless immediately performed, death is inevitable.

This patient has developed VT few hours after onset of symptoms and recovered with cardioversion. The patient should receive a bolus dose of IV lignocaine followed by an infusion for 24 hours following cardioversion. Alternatively IV amiodarone bolus followed by infusion can be used. IV magnesium is also indicated following VF. A prophylactic beta blocker reduces the risk of arrhythmia in STEMI.

Large area of anterior myocardium is infarcted leading to acute left ventricular failure and pulmonary oedema which is evident by the presence of basal crackles and radiographic changes.

ACE inhibitor is indicated early as the patient has LVF.

IV loop diuretic such as frusemide (50mg) reduces pulmonary congestion alleviating symptoms.

IV Nitrates also can be used if systolic BP is >100mm Hg.

In cardiogenic shock (SBP<90, oliguria and peripheral shutdown) IV inotropes as dobutamine is indicated. In LVF and cardiogenic shock an urgent echocardiogram is requested to look for acute mitral regurgitation or VSD. Early angiography and angioplasty should also be considered in patients with LVF and shock. NIPPV may be needed in severe pulmonary oedema leading to hypoxia.

CHB, which develops later, is likely to be following infarction involving conduction system, indicating the need for permanent pacing. (In inferior MI CHB is usually transient and self limiting)

Risk factors of CAD

Major risk factors	Other risk factors
Diabetes	Chronic kidney disease
hypertension	Central obesity
Smoking	Sedentary lifestyle
Dyslipidaemia : increased LDL,TG,Low HDL	Elevated lipoprotein a
Sex	Elevated Homocystine

	Stress, social isolation, depression
Age	
Family history of premature CAD	Elevated C-reactive protein
	Prothrombin factors, elevated fibrinogen
	HIV
	Cocaine

Localization of infarct by changes in ECG

localization	ST elevation	Reciprocal ST depression	Coronary artery
Anterior	V1-V6	none	LAD
Septal	V1-V4. Disappearance of septal Q in V5 V6	none	LAD
Lateral	L1,aVL, V5,V6	L11,L111, aVF	RCX or MO
Inferior	L11,L111, aVF	L1 aVL	RCA (80%or) RCX (20%)
Posterior	V7, V8, V9	Tall R and ST depression >2mm in V1-V3 (mirror image)	RCX

LAD- left anterior descending artery, RCX- Ramus circumflex, RCA- Right coronary, MO- marginal obtuse branch

Learning outcomes

The student should be able to

- Elicit a brief focussed history in a patient with suspected acute MI
- Perform a quick physical examination of the cardiovascular system to assess and detect the complications of AMI
- Explain the clinical features on a physiological and pathological basis
- Make a diagnosis or provide a differential diagnosis based on the history, examination and ECG findings
- Select the initial investigations and further investigations relevant in acute management and detecting complications
- List the common risk factors for CAD/MI and discuss the important lifestyle changes in prevention
- Discuss the acute and follow up management of acute MI
- Discuss the complications of acute MI
- Discuss the management of complications of acute MI

- Communicate to the patient about the nature of the illness, lifestyle changes, compliance with therapy and coping with daily living .

Commonly asked questions

What is the differential diagnosis of acute severe chest pain?

Acute aortic dissection, pericarditis , acute pulmonary embolus, pleurisy can cause severe chest pain and mimic acute MI. Similar though less acute pain may be caused by gastro oesophageal reflux disease, muscular pain and neuralgic pain of herpes zoster.

How is unstable angina differentiated from AMI?

Though the nature of pain is similar, the duration is less than 20 minutes. The ECG shows ST depressions and T wave inversions specially during pain (ECG changes are dynamic and may be absent when pain free).Generally the cardiac enzymes are not elevated

What are the absolute contraindications for thrombolysis?

Active bleeding or bleeding diathesis(except menstruation), prior haemorrhagic stroke, ischaemic stroke within 3 months, known structural cerebrovascular lesion or malignant intracranial neoplasm, suspected dissecting aneurism, significant closed head or facial trauma within 3 months

What are the complications of acute MI?

Acute arrhythmic complications: Atrioventricular block, bundle branch block, sinus bradycardia, ventricular ectopics, SVT (supra ventricular tachycardia) VT, Atrial flutter or fibrillation

Mechanical complications: Papillary muscle dysfunction with mitral regurgitation, VSD, LVF, pericarditis, ventricular aneurisms

Other complications: stroke, Dressler's syndrome (late and immune mediated)

Distinction level questions

What are the signs which suggest a right ventricular infarct?

RV infarct presents with hypotension in the context of inferior MI without pulmonary oedema. JVP is elevated. ECG may show ST elevation in V3R, V4R

What are the differences in managing a right ventricular infarct?

RV infarct is managed with IV fluid infusion (500ml 5% dextrose or haemacel). Diuretics are avoided.

What is an accelerated idioventricular rhythm?

Accelerated idioventricular rhythm is a harmless ventricular tachycardia with a rate of 100-120 bpm, often seen during myocardial re perfusion (reperfusion arrhythmia)

Red flag encounters

The following are situations that may be overlooked:

- Failure to detect 3rd and 4th heart sounds using the bell as they are low pitched at the cardiac apex
- Failure to examine the jugular venous pulse in 45^0 reclined position therefore elevated JVP is not detected (RV infarct)
- Failure to detect fine crepitations at lung bases
- Failure to detect new murmurs which can appear subsequently unless frequently auscultated
- Failure in detecting a congested liver which is soft, gentle palpation with deep respiration is advised as it may be tender

Must know facts of STEMI

- Most important initial treatment in MI is aspirin
- Treatment strategy is determined by ECG on presentation (STEMI or non STEMI)
- Early reperfusion of occluded artery is the mainstay of management of STEMI
- Primary PCI with stenting is the best perfusion strategy, and should be performed within 120 minutes of ECG diagnosis or within 90 minutes in a patient presenting within two hours with a large infarct.
- If primary PCI is not an option thrombolysis should be performed even while in ambulance
- Patients who had failed thrombolysis should receive rescue PCI within 12 hours of symptoms if infarct is large.
- Statins should be started to lower LDL <100mg/dL or 80mg/dL irrespective of previous value
- All patents should receive aspirin, clopidogrel, statin and a beta blocker unless contra indicated
- In patients with LV dysfunction ACE or ARB should be started and continued throughout
- All patients should have LV function evaluated prior discharge
- Secondary prevention include medication, smoking cessation, dietary modification, control of DM,HT, lipid and exercise

References:
ACC/AHA guidelines for the management of ST elevation MI 2009 focused update. available from circ.ahajournals.org
J.V.Nixon 2011 AHA clinical cardiac consult 3rd edition Wolters Kluver Lippincott Williams & Wilkins 2011

CASE 14: ATRIAL FIBRILLATION
VAANI VALERIE VISUVANATHAN

OVERVIEW

Atrial fibrillation is the most common cardiac arrhythmia, particularly in the elderly. It results in irregular and occasionally rapid heartbeat. The term atrial fibrillation is derived from the Latin words *atrium* which means "hall" and *fibrilla* which means "small fibre".

Normally the four chambers of the heart (two atria and two ventricles) contract in an organised rhythm, maintaining adequate cardiac output. The electrical impulse that modulates this organised contraction is initiated in the sinoatrial node (located in the right atrium). The electrical impulse from the sinus node travels through both the atria to the atrioventricular node, and then, to both the ventricles. In atrial fibrillation the electrical impulse is no longer initiated in the sinoatrial node, instead it begins in another part of the atrium or the adjacent pulmonary veins. The impulses spread through the atria in a disorganised pattern causing the atria to contract irregularly and rapidly. Impulses are transmitted to the ventricles via the atrioventricular node resulting in rapid contraction of the ventricles. However, not all the impulses are transmitted to the ventricles as the atrioventricular node limits the number of impulses that travel to the ventricles. Therefore, the ventricle contraction rate is not as rapid as that of the atria, but much more than normal. The ventricle contracts irregularly at the rate of 110-180 beats per minute in atrial fibrillation. The well-coordinated contraction of the atria and ventricles are lost and heart rhythm becomes irregular. In this situation, the heart does not pump out blood as well as it should and the amount of blood that flows from the atrium to the ventricle varies with each beat. This leads to a tendency for blood to pool in the atrium and form thrombi which can emboli.

Most patients with atrial fibrillation present with palpitations, breathlessness, chest pain and dizziness. Symptoms are more common with increased heart rate. Some patients who have atrial fibrillation may be asymptomatic but they face the same risks as those who are symptomatic.

Types of cases for clinical examination:

1.SHORT /LONG CASE – part of cardiovascular examination

2.OSPE – ECG of a patient who has atrial fibrillation

3.LONG CASE – students would be expected to take a detailed history and perform a focused clinical examination of a patient who presents with palpitations

CASE VIGNETTE

A 66-year-old lady presents to the Emergency Department with palpitations and chest discomfort of recent onset. She had been feeling dizzy since morning and had an episode of syncope at home. She has diabetes mellitus and dyslipidaemia for the past 12 years. Physical examination reveals that her blood pressure is 130/80 mmHg and capillary blood glucose is 5.1mmol/L. Heart rate is 180 beats per minute and irregular. Her ECG tracing is attached.

Obtain a full history from patient and perform a focused physical examination.

Differential Diagnoses:

Note:Atrial fibrillation(AF) is classified according to its temporal pattern.

1 *Paroxysmal AF – episodes terminate spontaneously within 7 days*

2 *Persistent AF – episodes persist beyond 7 days, requiring pharmacologic treatment or electrical cardio version for termination*

3 *Permanent AF – longstanding AF (more than 1 year), where cardioversion if attempted had been unsuccessful*

HISTORY OF PRESENTING ILLNESS

- Palpitations – onset, duration, frequency, precipitating factors (caffeine, exertion, medications), modes of termination
  It may be helpful sometimes to get the patient to tap out the rhythm of their heart beat during these episodes of palpitations.
- Associated symptoms (eg. syncope, lethargy, chest pain)
- Relation to exertion

The student should be able to reason as to why these symptoms are present based on the pathophysiology of AF

SYSTEMIC REVIEW

- Symptoms of thyroid disorder e.g. change in weight despite normal diet, hyperhidrosis, tremors, heat intolerance
- Symptoms to suggest an underlying cardiac disorder eg. angina, orthopnoea
- Recent infection e.g. fever, cough (pneumonia, myocarditis and pericarditis have been associated with AF)
- Polyuria and polydipsia – AF is found more frequently among diabetics
- Flushing, diaphoresis and headache – suggestive of phaeochromocytoma
- Symptoms of obstructive sleep apnoea
- Occult bleeding, if patient is already on anticoagulants

PAST MEDICAL HISTORY

- Diabetes mellitus, hypertension and hyperlipidaemia – ischaemic heart disease risk factors
- Previous cardiac valvular disease
- Peripheral vascular disease
- Cerebrovascular accident – intracranial lesions such as tumours and stroke can precipitate AF. A cerebrovascular accident may also be the presenting complaint of a patient with AF
- Pulmonary embolism
- Bleeding disorders e.g. peptic ulcer or cerebral haemorrhage – relevant when deciding on anticoagulation
  Note: 40% of those with AF are >60 years

Though not relevant to this patient, it is worthy of note that AF can occur without underlying heart disease (lone fibrillation).

SURGICAL HISTORY

- Recent thoracic or cardiac surgery

FAMILY HISTORY

- A familial association has been cited (sodium channel abnormalities)

SOCIAL HISTORY

- Alcohol intake – quantify amount of alcohol
  (excessive alcohol intake can trigger AF-'holiday heart')

- Stimulants eg. methamphetamines and cocaine usage (cocaine increases the incidence of stroke as well as arrhythmias)

- Smoking – chronic lung diseases has been associated with AF

MEDICATION HISTORY

- Has the patient been on anti-arryhythmics, rate control agents or anticoagulants

CHECK LIST FOR HISTORY TAKING

- ✓ Determine the duration and frequency of AF to enable classification
- ✓ Assessment of symptoms and precipitating factors
- ✓ Identify the aetiology of AF
- ✓ Determine the presence of cardiovascular disease
- ✓ Identify the presence of complications of AF
- ✓ Evaluate the possibility of complications that may occur from treatment
- ✓ Prior usage of anti-arrythmics and rate control medications, deciding on their efficacy
- ✓ Relevant drug history

Note: As this patient presents to the Emergency Department she could have severe symptoms. Student would not be presented with such an emergency case. However, they should be prepared to answer questions like:

When should a patient who has symptoms of AF call a doctor for advice?

In what situations would immediate intervention like cardioversion be warranted in the Emergency Department?

- Hypotension
- Evidence of angina and ischemia presenting as severe chest pain
- Decompensated state with congestive cardiac failure

EXAMINATION

Introduce yourself and explain your intentions to the patient. Obtain consent before you proceed. Ensure that you have a chaperone, if required.

General examination and vital signs

Perform a visual survey and proceed to determine patient's haemodynamic stability. Ensure that patient is not dyspnoeic, tachypnoeic, febrile or cyanosed. Measure her blood pressure and count her respiratory rate. Feel her peripheral pulses to determine rate, regularity and pulse deficit (difference in count between heart beat and peripheral pulse). Peripheral pulses may be absent in the presence of peripheral vascular disease. Calculate BMI [weight (kg) / height (m)^2].

Inspect for needle marks, if suspecting intravenous drug abuse. Also, look for signs of hyperthyroidism eg. tremors, exophthalmos. Examine for purpura and pedal oedema.

Head and neck

Examine the neck to determine presence of goitre and enlarged lymph nodes. Jugular venous pressure should be measured and an elevated pressure with loss of "a" wave looked for. The presence of carotid artery bruits may suggest underlying cerebrovascular disease.

Cardiopulmonary

Examination of the heart is of utmost importance in this case. A thorough examination should be performed to evaluate for the presence of heart failure, valvular pathologies, cardiomyopathies and pulmonary hypertension (loud P2). Locate the apex beat and auscultate for murmurs, and also additional heart sounds. A pericardial rub would suggest pericarditis.

Examination of the lungs should concentrate on looking for basal crepitation (heart failure or fibrosis), consolidations (tumour or pneumonia) and signs of chronic pulmonary disease.

Gastrointestinal

Signs of chronic liver disease, as well as, enlargement of liver and spleen should be sought for.

A positive hepatojugular reflex and pulsatile liver is consistent with liver congestion. Tenderness at the left hypochondrium may be elicited in the presence of splenic infarct.

Neurological

A cerebrovascular accident may be the result of embolism or may be the cause of the AF. The presence of focal neurological deficits should alert one to the possibility of intracranial tumours, too.

Brisk reflexes would suggest hyperthyroidism.

 Note:

While the focus is on AF and CVS the student would be expected to also perform relevant clinical examination of the patient in view of 12 years of diabetes mellitus and dyslipidaemia especially in OLSER or long case.

CHECK LIST FOR CLINICAL EXAMINATION

✓ Vital signs – determine the haemodynamic stability
✓ Examine peripheral pulses
✓ Look for signs of hyperthyroidism and heart failure
✓ Neck – goitre and jugular venous pressure
✓ Heart – apex beat, murmurs, additional sounds
✓ Lungs – pleural effusion/pulmonary oedema/consolidation/chronic obstructive pulmonary disease
✓ Gastrointestinal system – signs of chronic liver disease and assess for hepatosplenomegaly
✓ Neurology – focal neurological deficits

INVESTIGATIONS

2. Electrocardiogram – irregularly, irregular narrow complex tachycardia with discernible P waves would be typical in AF, might shed some light on the aetiology eg. previous myocardial infarction, pre-excitation syndromes. Attention should be paid to QT intervals in patients receiving anti-arrythmic medications

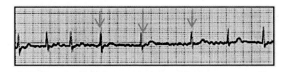

Irregular R-R intervals as shown on the ECG with fibrillatory baseline

3. 24-hour Holter monitor – may be required in paroxysmal AF (if the arrhythmia was not captured on initial ECG) or sick sinus syndrome

4. Echocardiogram – structural heart diseases and left ventricular dysfunction can be diagnosed using transthoracic echocardiography. Transesophageal echocardiography is a better means of identifying left atrial appendage thrombi and assessing left atrium size (significant left atrium enlargement is associated with long standing AF and increases the possibility of failure of cardioversion). Enables identification of patients with lone AF, ie; young (< 60 years) with no structural heart disease and normal echocardiography findings

5. Chest Xray – cardiomegaly and pulmonary plethora may be evident. Lung mass or lung parenchymal disease should be looked for.

6. Full blood count (infection) and renal profile (electrolyte imbalance and renal dysfunction)

7. Cardiac biomarkers – raised in acute myocardial infarction

8. B-type natriuretic peptide – raised in congestive cardiac failure

9. Coagulation profile – important to review coagulation profile before initiating anticoagulation therapy

10. Thyroid function test – TSH would be suppressed in hyperthyroidism. Thyroid function test is also of relevance if amiodarone had been prescribed. Amiodarone induced thyrotoxicosis.

11. Coronary angiogram – if deemed necessary after review of initial investigation results

12. Electrophysiology studies – if pre-excitation syndromes are suspected

CASE SUMMARY

This is a 66-year-old lady, known to have diabetes mellitus and hyperlipidaemia, who now presents with symptomatic fast atrial fibrillation. She is in heart failure as supported by the clinical findings of tachypnoea, raised jugular venous pressure, bilateral leg oedema and bibasal crepitations in the lungs. The apex beat is displaced.

Deduction:

This is most likely due to coronary artery disease as her dorsalis pedis and posterior tibialis pulses were absent and she has significant coronary artery disease risk factors. However, I would like to confirm the presence and aetiology of AF by performing an electrocardiogram, echocardiogram, cardiac enzymes, B-type natriuretic peptide and chest radiograph.

CLINICAL DISCUSSION OF THE CASE

A summary of the history and examination findings should be stated. A likely diagnosis is then proposed with supporting factors explained. Then, a reasonable list of relevant investigations should be compiled for further discussion.

Management:

Depending on the question posed the student is expected to outline management. Prioritizing the approach would be required of senior students based on the case presented beginning from urgent to short and long term care. Rehabilitation and care in the community after returning home would be holistic.

The content of the suggested management is outlined below:

Non-pharmacological management of patients in AF include correction of dehydration, electrolyte imbalance or thyrotoxicosis, if this is found to be the aetiology. Patients should also be advised to avoid precipitants, for example, caffeine, alcohol and undue exertion.

Management of patients with AF is aimed at reducing symptoms and preventing possible complications, mainly thromboembolic complications.

All patients with AF are at increased risk for thromboembolic events. Therefore aspirin or oral anticoagulants should be initiated, unless contraindicated. Patients with low risk for stroke should be started on aspirin and oral anticoagulants are preferred for those with increased risk. A simple and commonly used risk assessment score is the CHADS2 score, which evolved from the AF Investigators and Stroke Prevention in Atrial Fibrillation (SPAF) Investigators Score.

Risk factors	Points
Cardiac failure	1
Hypertension	1
Age > 75y	1
Diabetes mellitus	1
Previous stroke / TIA	2

Patients who have a CHADS2 score ≥ 2 are recommended to be on oral anticoagulant therapy with a target INR range of 2-3. A CHADS2 score of 0 is considered to be low risk and a score of 1 places the patient at moderate risk of developing thromboembolic events. In these patients, aspirin may be adequate.

As for determining between rate and rhythm control for the management of AF, much depends on the severity of patient's symptoms, the possibility of successful cardioversion and the preference of the patient.

Rhythm control

Cardioversion:

Patients who have intolerable symptoms during episodes of AF and those thought who have AF of recent onset (<7 days) are preferred candidates for cardioversion. Cardioversion may be performed electrically or pharmacologically. Patients who present with haemodynamic instability or ongoing myocardial infarction will require urgent cardioversion. However, elective cardioversion should only be performed after at least 3 weeks of anticoagulation prior to cardioversion.

Pharmacotherapy:

Common drugs used to achieve cardioversion to sinus rhythm are amiodarone and flecainide. Pharmacological cardioversion has the advantages of not requiring anaesthesia or sedation but poses an increased risk of other arrhythmias, for example, ventricular tachycardia.

Rate control

In patients who have failed rhythm control or have permanent AF, rate control by slowing the ventricular response rate may be the preferred option. Beta blockers, non-dihydropyridine calcium channel antagonist and digoxin are usually used. Clinical trials have shown that rate control is not inferior to rhythm control in mortality reduction. Adequate rate control

Other approaches

Catheter ablation of focal triggers of AF, pacemakers and surgical compartmentalization of the atria (MAZE procedure) are some of the approaches employed for AF that is poorly responsive to pharmacological treatment.

 Note:

The student needs to exhibit some practical knowledge of cardioversion as the patient given is seen in the Emergency Department.

- *Done under anaesthesia*
- *>80-90% would convert to sinus rhythm though can recur*

- *Best response in those who have AF recently (< few weeks old)*
- *Risk of stroke , hence need anticoagulation as pre-treatment)*

Some basic knowledge of radiofrequency ablation is worthy of note:

Aim to destroy abnormal conduction pathways in atria through a catheter

Best for those who have not responded to anti-arrhythmic medication or cannot tolerate medication

Some aspects of pacemaker placement and the need to carry identification tags should also be known

LEARNING OUTCOMES

By the end of this case review the student should be able to:

1. Take a detailed history of a patient who presents with palpitations.

2. Identify atrial fibrillation on ECG.

3. Perform a relevant and focused clinical examination of a patient who has atrial fibrillation

4. Discuss the principles of management in atrial fibrillation

COMMONLY ASKED QUESTIONS

1. How would one diagnose *Atrial fibrillation*?
   Irregular pulse on physical examination with ECG findings of irregularly irregular narrow QRS complexes and absent P waves.

2. What are the common non-cardiac causes of *Atrial fibrillation* F?
   Dehydration, pneumonia, thyrotoxicosis

3. Discuss the principles of management for *Atrial fibrillation*.
   Rhythm control, especially if, AF is of recent onset and patient has intolerable symptoms during episodes of AF. Rate control is an alternative option, especially if AF is permanent.

4. What do you understand by 'Lone *Atrial fibrillation*'?
   Lone AF occurs with no relation with any cardiac pathology or hypertension. It may be an isolated event or intermittent but is rarely chronic. The risk for thromboembolism is relatively low in

this group of patients and most do not require long term anti-arrhythmic medications.

HIGH ACHIEVER QUESTIONS

State one landmark trial regarding the management of *Atrial fibrillation*?

AFFIRM (Atrial Fibrillation Follow-up Investigation of Rhythm Management) trial concluded that rate control in the management of patients with AF is not inferior to rhythm control, and therefore should be considered as a primary approach.

1. What is the acute management of fast *Atrial fibrillation*?

Urgent cardioversion would be indicated if patient has severe hypotension, pulmonary oedema or ongoing myocardial ischaemia. Otherwise, rate control (resting ventricular rate <110bpm) would be the aim.

2. Name TWO (2) commonly used medications that potentiate the effects of warfarin.

Cotrimoxazole, erythromycin, omeprazole, amiodarone

3. How would you counsel her on prognosis?

Although most patients with AF have a fair to good prognosis especially with controlled heart rate (AFFIRM Trial), in this patient prognosis is guarded because:

She is 63 years and has congestive heart failure.

Patients with AF have a 3-5 X higher risk of stroke (a known complication of AF) and anticoagulant therapy (warfarin) is warranted to reduce the risk of stroke. Possible complications and the need for frequent monitoring when on warfarin should be explained as well.

MUST KNOW FACTS ABOUT ATRIAL FIBRILLATION

1. The incidence of AF increases with age.

2. All patients with AF have an increased risk of thromboembolic stroke.

3. Management of AF consists of rate control, rhythm control and anti-coagulation.

4. Assessment of thromboembolic risk is mandatory.

COMMON MISTAKES

Not attempting to classify AF according to temporality
Missing the irregularity of pulse during examination
Unable to diagnose AF on ECG
Not addressing anticoagulation as part of management

REFERENCES:
2011 ACC/AHA/ESC guidelines

CASE 15: ACUTE RHEUMATIC FEVER
KYAW MIN

- heart
- Jt
- brain
- sub cut. tissue

OVERVIEW

Acute Rheumatic Fever (ARF) is a delayed, non-suppurative sequela of a pharyngeal infection with group A beta-hemolytic streptococci or Streptococcus pyogenes. The acute phase of ARF is caused by a proliferative inflammatory reaction that involves the connective and/or collagen tissues and commonly affects the heart, joints, brain and subcutaneous tissues, although any organ may be involved.[1]

Worldwide, GAS infections and their postinfectious sequelae (primarily ARF and rheumatic heart disease) account for an estimated 500,000 deaths per year. Acute rheumatic fever most often occurs in children, with the peak age of incidence occurring between 5 and 15 years old. Most initial attacks in adults take place at the end of the second and beginning of the third decades of life. Although recurrent attacks have occurred in the fifth and sixth decades of life. Risk factors associated with individual attacks and outbreaks include a low standard of living (especially crowding), lower socioeconomic class, the type of organism and the degree of host immunity to the prevalent serotypes.[2]

Most major outbreaks occur under conditions of impoverished overcrowding where access to antibiotics is limited. Rheumatic heart disease accounts for 25-50% of all cardiac admissions world wide. Regions of major public health concern include the Middle East, the Indian subcontinent, and some areas of Africa and South America. As many as 20 million new cases occur each year. The introduction of antibiotics has been associated with a rapid worldwide decline in the incidence of ARF. Now, the incidence is 0.23-1.88 patients per 100,000 population.[3]

CASE VIGNETTE

Ms. Zis a 15-year-old, Malay female, 54 kg, daughter of a farmer who complains of fever of 3 days duration and pain and swelling over the right knee of one day duration.

HISTORY OF PRESENT ILLNESS:

The patient first noticed that she was having fever 3 days ago. It was sudden onset, low grade, continuous, no chills and rigors, no diurnal variation. It progressively worsened and did not get relieved with paracetamol.

On the third day of fever, there was right knee joint pain and swelling. Pain was sudden in onset and progressively worsened. It was continuous, and worsened with walking and weight bearing. Pain was throbbing in nature. Swelling of right knee joint was also sudden in onset, mild, and no skin changes over the swelling. The swelling worsened on walking and was relieved by resting. No history of palpitation or reduced effort tolerance. No chest pain, no abnormal movement noted over upper limbs. Neither history of pain nor swelling suffered over any other joints.

brain → She did not have URTI shortness of breath and cough. There was no headache, photophobia, vomiting , seizures, rashes or skin lessions

There is no history of travelling or from dengue endemic area

There is no history of dysuria and micturition.. Bowel movement is as usual.

Past Medical history:

When she was a 9-year-old girl, the patient had a similar episode. She had sore throat and high grade fever for 1 week, and subsequently developed a similar knee swelling bilaterally. She also developed cardiac complications and admitted for 1 month. Upon discharge she was referred to National Heart Institute, where echocardiogram was done and she was advised not to exert herself too much or compete in sport activities. On her last follow up in November 2011, she was told that she did not require any invasive procedure.

Past drug history: She is on oral penicillin prophylaxis since the age of 9.

Family history: She was born from a nonconsanginous marriage and she is the youngest from 3 siblings who are all alive and healthy.

CHECK LIST FOR HISTORY TAKING IN ACUTE RHEUMATIC FEVER

* 5-15-year-old

* Fever, history of sore throat

* Migratory polyarthritis of ankle, knee, elbow and wrist joints

* Palpitation, shortness of breath

Physical Examination:

General Examination:

Patient is propped up at 45°, conscious, alert and coorperative. She is pale and not in respiratory distress.

Palms are pale and cool. No clubbing, peripheral cyanosis or stigmata of infective endocarditis. Capillaries refilling time is less than 2 secs.

BP: 110/80 mmHg, RR: 20, Temp: 37° C,

Radial Pulse: 88 bpm, regular, low volume, bilaterally equal.

All the peripheral pulses are felt.

Conjunctival pallor is present, There is no jaundice, central cyanosis, and palpable lymph nodes. There is no pitting oedema in lower limbs.

Cardiovascular Examination

Inspection: No chest deformity observed, no hyperdynamic precordium, sternal bulge, visible pulsations or scar.

JVP is not raised 7 cm from RA. (5cm +2cm)

Palpation: Apex beat is palpable at left 5th IC space at mid clavicular line and is diffuse. No palpable thrills. No parasternal heave.

Auscultation: Normal S1S2 are heard. Apansystolic murmur is heard loudest over the mitral area, grade 3/6, harsh, radiating to the left axilla.

Lungs: Normal breath sounds with no accompaniments. No crepitations are heard.

Abdomen: Soft, moves with respiration. No hepatosplenomegaly.

Investigations:

Throat swab culture: negative,

ASO titre: 400 Todd units

FBC:Haemoglobin: 10.7 g/dl, Total WBC: $12200*10^9/l$, with 80% neutrophils, 15% lymphocyte and 1% eosinophil.

Echocardiography: Mild mitral regugitation by Doppler color flow mapping. Normal chamber size.

Diagnosis: Rheumatic Heart Disease; mild mitral regurgitation, normal sinus rhythm, no pulmonary hypertension; not in failure with acute rheumatic fever (recurrence)

PATHOGENESIS: The pathogenic mechanisms that lead to the development of ARF remain incompletely understood. The pathogenesis has been grouped into three major categories: (1) a toxic effect of streptococcal extracellular products on the host tissues, (2) direct infection by the group A streptococcus and (3) an abnormal or dysfunctional immune response to one or more as yet unidentified somatic or extracellular antigens produced by all group A streptococci.[2] Evidence suggests that elevated immune-complex levels in blood samples from patients with ARF are associated with HLA-B5.[4]

JONES CRITERIA: The most recent modification of the Jones Criteria has been divided into two classes, the "major" and "minor". These include carditis, Sydenham's chorea, migratory polyarthritis, subcutaneous nodules and erythema margiantum.

1. Carditis is a pancarditis involving the pericardium, myocardium, epicardium and endocardium. The carditis is characterized by various signs or symptoms such as sinus tachycardia, a mitral regurgitation murmur, an S3 gallop, cardiomegaly and a pericardial friction rub or pleuritic chest pain.[2,5]

2. Sydenham's chorea is a neurologic disorder consisting of abrupt, purposeless, non-rhythmic involuntary movements, muscular weakness and emotional disturbances. Emotional changes can manifest as transient psychosis or outburst of crying and restlessness. Chorea may have a longer latent period, up to several months from the onset of streptococcal infection.[2]

3. Migratory polyarthritis usually affects the ankles, knees, elbows and wrists over a period of days.[2] Arthritis (which includes pain and swelling) is usually the earliest manifestation of ARF. Joint inflammation is present in several joints, and each joint is inflamed for no more than one week. Radiographs show a slight effusion in the affected joint or it may be unremarkable.[5] Analysis of synovial fluid normally reveals a sterile inflammatory fluid.

4. Subcutaneous nodules are painless, firm nodules, of varying size located over bony surfaces or near tendons. They are present most often in patients with long-standing rheumatic heart disease.[2]

5. Erythema marginatum is an uncommon manifestation which may present as an evanescent, macular, non-pruritic pink or faintly red rash that affects the trunk or the limbs, but not the face. A hot shower may make them more evident.[2]

The minor criteria are nonspecific and include the following: fever, arthralgias, elevated erythrocyte sedimentation rate and C-reactive protein and a prolonged PR interval. The criteria for diagnosis of ARF is either two major criteria, or one major and two minor criteria, plus evidence of a previous streptococcal infection.[6] The latter may be provided by positive throat culture or rapid antigen detection test and/or an elevated streptococcal antibody test.[2]

Minor criteria
* Fever , Arthralgia, Previous acute rheumatic fever or rheumatic heart disease
* Acute-phase reactants
* increase erythrocyte sedimentation rate, C-reactive protein, leukocytosis
• Electrocardiogram—prolonged PR interval

Evidence of streptococcal infection
• Throat culture positive for the bacteria
• Positive rapid antigen detection test results
• Elevated antistreptolysin O titre, Scarlet fever

Clinical Manifestations of Acute Rheumatic Fever

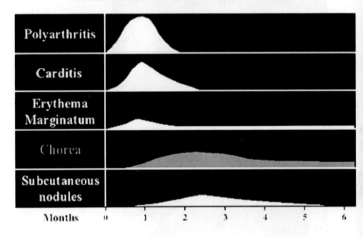

Acute rheumatic fever (ARF) is diagnosed based on clinical manifestations supported by laboratory tests. Usually, a latent period of approximately 18 days occurs between the onset of streptococcal pharyngitis and ARF. This latent period is rarely shorter than 1 week or longer than 5 weeks.

Typically, the first manifestation is a very painful migratory polyarthritis. Often, associated fever and constitutional toxicity develop. Acute attacks usually resolve within 12 weeks.

Ref: T. Duckett Jones[7] have been slightly revised by the American Heart Association (AHA).[8]

Group A streptococcal antigen detection tests are specific but not very sensitive. However, note that children without ARF may have an isolated positive antistreptolysin O (ASO) titer. This may also be found in patients with certain related diseases such as rheumatoid arthritis and Takayasu arteritis. Therefore, rising ASO titers should be combined with a careful clinical evaluation and the discovery of other antistreptococcal antibodies to support the diagnosis of ARF. ASO is found in 80-85% of patients with ARF. the sensitivity of ASO titer (adults with >240 Todd U and children with >320 Todd U) is 80%. The sensitivity of throat culture as evidence of recent streptococcal infection is 25-40%. The sensitivity of an elevated ASO titer in addition to anti-DNAse B or antihyaluronidase is 90%. Acute-phase reactants such as C-reactive protein and ESR are usually elevated and helpful in monitoring disease activity. ECG is helpful for diagnosing carditis and may reveal a prolonged PR interval.[9]

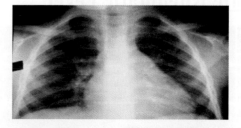

Cardiomegaly due to carditis of acute rheumatic fever.

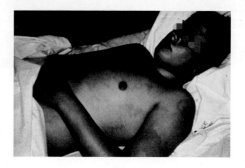

Erythema marginatum, the characteristic rash of acute rheumatic fever.
Pansystolic murmur radiate to left axilla ➔ Mitral regurgitation
Pansystolic murmur radiate to epigastrium ➔Ventricular septal defect
Pansystolic murmur radiate to left sternal edge ➔ Tricuspid regurgitation

COMPLICATION OF ARF:

Rheumatic heart disease is a late and most severe sequela of ARF. It usually occurs 10 to 20 years after the original attack and is a major cause of acquired valvular disease in the world. The mitral valve is most commonly involved, followed by the aortic valve. The classic finding of rheumatic heart disease is mitral stenosis secondary to severe calcification, often requiring surgical intervention. The findings are new or changing valvular murmurs, cardiomegaly, congestive heart failure, and/or pericarditis.[2]

DIFFERENTIAL DIAGNOSIS OF Acute Rheumatic Fever

1. Kawasaki Disease

2. Sepsis, Bacterial

3. Septic Arthritis

4. Systemic Lupus Erythematosus

DIFFERENTIAL DIAGNOSIS OF MITRAL REGURGITATION

Acute	Chronic
Papillary muscle rupture (post-MI)	Rheumatic fever with Mitral valvulitis and sequelae
Chordal rupture/Leaflet flail (MVP, IE)	Myxomatous valve (MVP)
Infective Endocarditis	Endocarditis (healed)
Trauma	Mitral annular calcification
	HOCM with SAM (Hypertrophic obstructive cardiomyopathy with systolic anterior motion of the mitral cusp)
	Dilated cardiomyopathy
	Ischemic (LV remodeling)
	Congenital Mitral valve defects (cleft Mitral valve, AV canal defect)

Based on Harrison's Principle of Internal Medicine.

TREATMENT AND PROPHYLAXIS OF ARF:

There are three goals in the treatment of ARF: (1) symptomatic relief of the clinical manifestations, (2) anti-streptococcal therapy and (3) prophylaxis against future infection to prevent recurrent cardiac disease.

The mainstay for symptomatic relief remains anti-inflammatory agents, most commonly aspirin. The duration of anti-inflammatory therapy should

241

be maintained until symptoms are absent and C-reactive protein (CRP) concentration and erythrocyte sedimentation rate (ESR) have normalized. The CRP and ESR are both elevated during the active rheumatic process and are useful lab tests for monitoring recurrence of inflammation when treatment is being tapered or has been discontinued.[2] Oral aspirin, three tablets of 325 mg each 6 hourly, a total of 3.8 gm daily (60mg/kg). This should be continued until his ESR fallen and then gradually tailed off.[10]

Severe carditis can present with congestive heart failure, cardiomegaly or third-degree heart block. These patients will need to be treated with conventional therapy for heart failure. At times, rheumatic carditis is treated with corticosteroids and aspirin may be added during a steroid taper.[2]

A single parenteral injection of benzathine benzylpenicillin can ensure compliance. The patient should be kept in bed and given 1.2 million units of benzyl penicillin intramusculary after test dose. Oral cephalosporins, rather than erythromycin, are recommended as an alternative in patients who are allergic to penicillin.[10]

* Analgesia is optimally achieved with high doses of salicylates, often inducing dramatic clinical improvement.

* Corticosteroids should be reserved for the treatment of severe carditis. After 2-3 weeks, the dosage may be tapered, reduced by 25% each week. Overlap with high-dose salicylate therapy is recommended as the dosage of the prednisone is tapered over a 2-week period to avoid poststeroid rebound.

* Protracted Sydenham chorea has responded to haloperidol. Chorea requires long-term antimicrobial prophylaxis, even if no other manifestations of rheumatic fever evolve. The manifestations of chorea may be exaggerated by emotional trauma.

* Primary prevention: Eradicate *Streptococcus* from the pharynx, which generally entails administering a single intramuscular injection of benzathine benzylpenicillin.

* The AHA Committee on Acute Rheumatic Fever recommends a regimen consisting of benzathine benzylpenicillin at 1.2 million units intramuscularly every 4 weeks. However, in high-risk situations, administration every 3 weeks is justified and advised at least until 40 years old. High-risk situations include patients with heart disease who are at risk of repetitive exposure.

* Oral prophylaxis, which is less
phenoxymethylpenicillin (penicillin V) or sulfad
in compliant patients. phenoxymethylpenicillin (

CLINICAL DISCUSSION OF THE CASE

LEARNING OUTCOMES

By the end of this case review the student should be able to:

  * take thorough history for symptom analysis regarding acute fever with joints pain associate with or without upper respiratory tract infection.

  * listen the pansystolic murmur at apex of heart and can differentiate among mitral regurgitation, Tricuspid regurgitation, and ventricular septal defect.

  * answer the reasonable provisional diagnosis based on history taking and positive physical examination.

  * list the relevant laboratory investigations, chest X-ray, ECG, and Echocardiography.

  * discuss the principle of management in this patient.

COMMONLY ASKED QUESTIONS

What is the pathogenesis of ARF?

Briefly outline the modified Jones criteria for diagnosis of ARF?

How will you diagnose acute rheumatic fever?

What is the complication of acute rheumatic fever?

Briefly outline the treatment of acute rheumatic fever.

HIGH ACHIEVER QUESTIONS

a. List the differential diagnosis of Mitral Regurgitation.

b. Describe the murmur in the above case scenario and how to differentiate it from tricuspid regurgitation and ventricular septal defect?

MISTAKES

 ...t **competent in distinguishing the characteristic rise in
 ...perature of acute fever and associated symptoms.**. Therefore,
wrongly considering viral fever due to Dengue, Chikungunya fever.

* Unable to differentiate murmurs occuring in mitral regurgitation and
mitral stenosis. Not consdiering pancarditis apart from carditis   in
rheumatic fever.* Not being familiar with antibiotic   prophylaxis
medication and duration of treatment.

REFERENCES

1. Gibofsky A, Zabriskie JB. Clinical Manifestations and Diagnosis of
Acute Rheumatic Fever. *Up To Date Online*, V.13.2,2005.

2. Kaplan E.L.Rheumatic Fever. *Harrison's Principle of Internal
Medicine*. 14th Edition. McGraw Hill, 1998-1309-1311.

3. Chun LT, Reddy DV, Yamamoto LG. Rheumatic fever in children and
adolescents in Hawaii. *Pediatrics*. Apr 1987;79(4):549-52..

4. Yoshinoya S, Pope RM. Detection of immune complexes in acute
rheumatic fever and their relationship to HLA-B5. *J Clin Invest*. Jan
1980;65(1):136-45..

 5. Gibofsky A, Zabriskie JB. Clinical Manifestations and Diagnosis of
Acute Rheumatic Fever. *Up To Date Online*, V.13.2,2005.

 6. Jones Criteria (revised). For Guidance in the Diagnosis of Rheumatic
Fever. *Circulation* 1965; 32: 664.

7. Jones TD. Diagnosis of rheumatic fever. *JAMA*. 1944;126:481-85.

8. Digenea AS, Ayoub EM. Guidelines for the diagnosis of rheumatic
fever: Jones criteria updates 1992. Circulation 87. *Circulation*.
1993;87:302.

9.   http://emedicine.medscape.com/article/333103-overview#a0199
(accessed on 20th May 2012)

10.Nicholas AB, Nicki RC, Brian RW. Chapter 18, Davidson"s Principles
and Practice of Medicine (20th edn)

OVERVIEW

A ventricular septal defect (VSD) is the most common congenital heart defect and accounts for 25% of all congenital cardiac defects. Often it is a constituent of complex cardiac entities such as Tetralogy of Fallot, and may be life-saving in defects such as Transposition of great vessels and tricuspid atresia where mixing of the blood of both sides of the heart is essential for survival.

Although precise reasons for the defect remain unclear, gene mutations and chromosomal anomalies have been shown to result in VSD. About 3 %% of the offspring of a parent with a VSD have a congenital cardiac defect, usually a VSD.

The defect can occur in any portion of the septum, but most are the membranous type. A subpulmonary defect (also known as supracristal) is much more common among Asian populationcompared to the West. The defect may impinge on the aortic sinus and cause aortic insufficiency.

The natural course of the defect depends on the size of the defect. About 30-50% of small defects close spontaneously, usually in the first two years of life. Prognosis after primary surgical repair is excellent, and these patients are considered to be at standard risk for health and life insurance.

HEMODYNAMICS

The size of the defect and the pulmonary vascular resistance determine the magnitude and direction of the shunt. Normally the high fetal pulmonary arterial resistance falls to adult levels by 3-6 months of life, and allows a left-to-right shunting of blood. Thus at birth there is no shunt across the defect and no murmur is heard. Since it is the oxygenated blood from the left side of the heart that is mixing with the deoxygenated blood in the right ventricle and again going to the lungs for oxygenation, there is no cyanosis.

With large defects (more than 50% of the size of the aortic diameter), the pressure in the ventricles equalizes and the magnitude and direction of the shunt depends on the pressure difference between the pulmonary arterial and systemic vascular resistances. Fortunately, in these patients the involution of the media of small pulmonary arterioles is delayed, thus limiting the shunt flow, otherwise the entire systemic flow would empty into the pulmonary circulation. The larger the defect in the septum and lower the pulmonary arterial resistance, greater is the shunt from left –to-right.

The bulk of shunting occurs in systole when both ventricles contract. Hence in a small defect all the shunted blood drains into the pulmonary circulation without flooding the right ventricle. It is the left ventricle that is working extra hard, trying to maintain the cardiac output, and this is the chamber that hypertrophies. As a corollary, if the right ventricle also shows evidence of hypertrophy, the shunt is too large to drain into the pulmonary circulation and hence crowding the right ventricle. If there is evidence of bi-ventricular hypertrophy, the defect is not small.

Left to right shunting increases the amount of blood passing through the right ventricle (if the defect is large enough), pulmonary arteries, left atrium, and left ventricle. If the defect is large, there will also be hypertension of the pulmonary circulation and right ventricle. This causes irreversible pulmonary vascular obstructive disease to develop in children one year of age or older. Repair of the defect after this may be fatal because in presence of increased resistance in the pulmonary circulation, no blood will be able to enter the pulmonary circulation after the repair has reduced the amount of blood shunting across into it.

<u>Types Of Cases For Clinical Examination</u>

<u>OSCE/ SHORT CASE</u>

The student may be asked to examine the cardiovascular system, or only the precordium.

The student should look for growth failure, respiratory distress, signs of congestive cardiac failure and all the signs of a VSD in the precordium. It will be nice if, on the basis of his clinical findings, he can make an assessment of the size of the defect too (whether it is a large defect or not).

LONG CASE

The student should be able to take a detailed history and complete examination of all the systems to look for multiple anomalies/syndromes of which this defect may be a part. History should include the course of the illness and complications.

The student should be able to discuss the value of relevant investigations and principles of management.

CASE VIGNETTE

A nine month old female infant is admitted with complaints of cough, breathlessness and difficulty in feeding for the past three days.

This is her fourth admission since birth for the same complaints.

Differential Diagnosis:

1. Bronchial asthma
2. Recurrent pneumonia (foreign body aspiration, progressive primary complex)
3. Aacyanotic congenital heart defect with congestive cardiac failure

   Respiratory illnesses will have relevant history (positive family history for bronchial asthma, history of contact for tuberculosis), and clinical findings (rhonchi for asthma, anemia, lymphadenopathy, etc for tuberculosis, pneumonia in the same area every time in a case of foreign body aspiration).

HISTORY

A detailed **history of presenting illness** should include:

- Presence/ absence of **fever**.

  Fever denotes an infective pathology. High, continuous fever in a sick-looking child is usually seen in recurrent bacterial pneumonia.

  Bronchial asthma may be precipitated by a viral upper respiratory infection, in which case the child will have a low grade fever, signs of upper respiratory infection, and not appear to be so sick except for the respiratory distress.

  Pulmonary congestion causes the child to be breathless without fever, but superimposed infection (pneumonia) may cause fever, and acyanotic congenital heart disease is a known cause of recurrent pneumonitis.

- **Feeding history:** Is the child able to take feeds well, or, did she take a long time to feed, stopping several times to catch her breath (the suck-rest-suck cycle)?

  Increased volume of blood in the lungs decreases the compliance and increases the work of breathing. Fluid leaks into the interstitial space and alveoli and causes pulmonary edema. Features of heart failure (difficulty in feeding, respiratory distress and wheezing) appear, although the heart (left ventricle) is pumping more blood than normal and is not really failing.

- Student should ask **details of cough and breathlessness**: is it a "productive" cough? Does the cough have a diurnal/postural variation? Does it end in post-tussive vomiting?

  Infants and toddlers are unable to expectorate the phlegm, but the cough sounds "wet", hence labelled as productive cough. Diurnal variation is usually seen in asthmatic patients, the cough being worse late at night/early in the morning.

  The cough may become worse when the infant lies supine because of a post nasal drip. In these cases there will be signs of upper respiratory catarrh.

  In rare cases of congenital bronchiectasis cough may increase in certain posture due to increased drainage of secretions due to gravity.

- Ask the mother if she has noticed **excessive sweating** over the forehead, especially during feeding.

  High output by the left ventricle is maintained by increasing the stroke volume and heart rate. This is achieved by increased activity of the sympathetic nervous system. This leads to sweating and irritability, especially during feeding (exertional dyspnea).

- Student should specifically ask the caretaker about **weight loss** or decreased weight gain.
  The mother is usually worried if her child is not gaining weight inspite of all her care. She will generally compare her with her older siblings and be able to give you an assessment.

- **Regurgitation and vomiting** may occur in severe congestive cardiac failure due to venous stasis that causes congestion in the gastro-intestinal system.

Past History:

Since this is the fourth admission of the infant, a detailed history of all previous admissions is essential. What was the age at first admission? Was she admitted with the same complaints every time? What investigations were done during the past admissions? What were the reports of those investigations (some parents can specify)?

Is the child completely asymptomatic in between the admissions (this includes feeding difficulty, appetite and weight gain)? A completely asymptomatic child in between the attacks favours one of the respiratory pathologies mentioned above.

Birth History:

a) Antenatal history:

This should include details of any event (in each trimester) that could have caused a congenital defect in the child. Specific enquiries should be made about any viral illness (fever with rash), drugs taken, and maternal diabetes, especially in the first trimester. A bad obstetric history (recurrent spontaneous abortions/ still births) support a genetic/ chromosomal abnormality.

Ultrasonographic findings antenatally may be able to pick up the congenital defect.

b) Intrapartum history:

Details of delivery: Student should ask about prematurity, requirement of resuscitative measures, and birth asphyxia.

- Student should ask about feeding difficulties (suck-rest-suck cycle), failure to thrive, and NICU admission.
- The child is acyanotic, but duskiness may appear on crying or during infections.
- Growth and developmental History:
- Approximately 65% of children with congenital heart defect have been found to have delayed development independent of chronic hypoxia. Hence a detailed history of age at which the milestones were achieved should be noted.
- Some children may have delayed gross motor development simply because they are exhausted/ too weak to move. In these

children, fine motor, speech and social developmental milestones will be normal.

- Most symptomatic infants will have decreased growth velocity. In severe cases, the infant may never exceed her birth weight because of poor feeding and increased oxygen and energy demand as the heart and lungs are overworked.
- Dietary History:
- In view of the growth failure these children have, it is important to rule out dietary insufficiency. A detailed history of dietary intake, with special emphasis on calories and protein intake is a must.
- Breast feeding requires the infant to actively squeeze out the milk from the breast, whereas bottle feeds need only to be swallowed and the infant has to exert less. Hence some mothers switch the baby to bottle feeds saying that the baby does not take breast feeds.
- Immunization History:
- All routine immunizations should have been given, and enquiry of this should be made. Influenza vaccine should be given if available
- **Family History:**
- Family history should include three generations, both on the maternal as well as paternal side.

History of consanguineous marriage between parents should be enquired into, as should the presence of cardiac defects, other congenital anomalies, early deaths, and mental retardation in other family members.

- **Socio-economic history:**

This is important in view of the growth failure that the child is having, to rule out undernutrition as a cause.

Systemic Review of symptoms:

- **Respiratory distress**, on exertion, or even at rest, denotes the severity of pulmonary congestion, and indirectly the size of the shunt. Some infants are asymptomatic between the hospital admissions, the only sign being tachypnea, which may be missed by the caretaker. Recurrent respiratory infections are a symptom of increased pulmonary congestion, and support the diagnosis of an acyanotic congenital heart defect.
- **Neurological symptoms** and **other congenital anomalies** may be present as a part of certain genetic/chromosomal defects/syndromes.

Check List for history taking in a case of VSD:

- Age at appearance of initial symptoms
- Exertional dyspnea, including feeding difficulty
- Recurrent symptoms of congestive cardiac failure (tachypnea, dyspnea, reduced intake)
- Growth failure

EXAMINATION

General Examination:

Introduce yourself and obtain consent for examination. Wash hands thoroughly.

Have mother or caretaker close by and expose relevant areas explaining to the child as to what is expected to be done.

Small defects with trivial shunts are usually asymptomatic, and are detected during routine check-ups.

- **Note the general appearance:**

    Irritability is a sign in pediatrics, and denotes the degree of distress. A lethargic child is more seriously ill than one who can show signs of irritation. As she improves, she becomes friendlier. When she smiles at you, it is time to discharge her.

    Failure to thrive is seen in children with moderate – severe VSD because of feeding difficulty coupled with increased oxygen and energy demand by the heart and lungs. Recurrent pneumonia (as mentioned above) also increases the basal metabolic rate, consuming more energy and decreases the appetite.

    Respiratory Distress is present in most children, and its signs should be carefully looked for. Suprasternal recession can be seen by showing the infant a bright coloured toy/light from a torch above his head so that he looks up. Also make a note of intercostal recession, substernal retractions, and nasal flaring.

    Recurrent respiratory distress in an undernourished infant leads to the development of **Harrison's Sulcus.**
    Student should carefully look for **Dysmorphism and other congenital malformations** as VSD is commonly found as a part and parcel of several syndromes.

251

- **Vital Signs:**

  Heart/ pulse rate and pulse volume should be recorded.
  Since the left ventricle has to maintain the cardiac output in spite of some blood draining away into the right ventricle, heart rate (pulse rate) has to increase. Hence tachycardia is usually present.

  Pulse volume is generally normal unless the heart is failing.
  It is difficult to count the pulse rate of an irritable infant. The student should palpate the radial pulse and **all the peripheral pulses** for pulse volume, character and rhythmicity, and count the heart rate.

  Respiratory rate tachypnoea is the first sign to appear and is a sensitive indicator of respiratory compromise. Hence respiratory rate should be counted carefully, for at least 30 seconds in an infant, and at least for a minute in a neonate (to offset the periodic **respiration** they have).

  Temperature should be recorded to confirm/ rule out an infectious pathology.

  Student should always record the **blood pressure** as a baseline value. If it is not possible (the child is very small/uncooperative), look for clinical signs of shock and record them – cold, clammy extremities, feeble/not palpable peripheral pulses, prolonged capillary refill time, lethargic patient.

- **Extracardiac manifestations of cardiac disease:**

  The cardinal signs ofcongestive cardiac failure (raised jugular venous pressure, crackles at the bases of lungs) are difficult to discern in an infant whose neck is small (and the child is irritable) and the lungs are already congested due to the basic illness.

  The **cardinal signs of cardiac failure in infancy** are: tachycardia, tachypnoea, hepatomegaly and cardiomegaly. Hence, in addition to recording her vital signs, the student should also measure and record the size of the liver below the subcostal margin in the midclavicular line. Of course, because of respiratory distress, the liver may also be pushed down, and this should be determined by percussing its upper border and recording the intercostals space in which the upper border is present.

If the primary pathology is a respiratory illness, there will be no cardiomegaly (this can be documented clinically by the shift of apical impulse and radiologically on taking an X-ray of the chest).

Pedal edemais not seen in infants since they are supine. They develop sacral edema, and sudden weight gain.

If a child suspected of VSD has **clubbing or central cyanosis,** she is developing Eisenmenger complex, and that is a grave development.

Examination of the cardiovascular system:

- **Shape of the precordium :**
  A **precordial bulge** is best noted by observing from the foot end of the bed, with your eyes at the same level as the patient's chest. In this position the two hemithoraces can be compared. In a VSD of significant severity, cardiomegaly leads to a bulging precordium.

- Palpation of the heart should begin with the patient in the supine position at 30 degrees. If the heart is not felt in this position, the patient can be examined in sitting posture, leaning forward.
  The apical impulse is rapid and hyperdynamic due to the volume overload. It is shifted inferiorly and laterally,depending on the hypertrophy of the ventricles, which depends on the severity of the shunt.

- A **left parasternal heave** may be noted, indicating right ventricular hypertrophy.

- A **systolic thrill** may be felt over the left lower sternal border. The thrill of a membranous defect is heard best in the left 3rd and 4thintercostals space in the parasternal region. Small defects have a larger pressure difference across them, hence there is greater turbulence in blood flow across the defect, and thrill is more easily palpable.

- **Heart sounds: First heart sound** is diminished in intensityat the left lower parasternal area because of the onset of the murmur. **Second heart sound** is normal in a small defect, but may be loud if the defect is large and pulmonary hypertension is developing.

- Characteristic murmur is a blowing holosystolic murmur heard best over the lower left sternal border. If the defect is small, the murmur is loud, harsh and may end before the 2nd sound presumably because the defect may close during late systole. The murmur of a membranous defect is heard best in the 3rd-4^{th}intercostals space at the sternal border. If the defect is subpulmonic, it is best heard in the 2nd space at the sternal border.

  In a large defect the holosystolic murmur is less harsh because of a lower pressure gradient across the defect. Thrill is then uncommon.

  A mid-diastolic, low-pitched rumble is heard at the apex due to excessive blood flow across the mitral valve.

  If the pulmonary hypertension is at systemic level, there may be virtually no left-to-right shunt, no systolic murmur, the pulmonary component of the second heart sound is very loud, and the patient is mildly cyanosed.

Examination of other systems:

The **respiratory system** is examined to rule out a non-cardiac diagnosis. The presence of pulmonary crepitations most often signifies infection or atelectasis andnot pulmonary edema, but may be due to pressure by the enlarged left atrium on the bronchus.

A detailed assessment of his mental development is a must to look for any associated **developmental anomaly**.

A careful survey of all systems should be made to exclude any **associated congenital anomalies.**

Check list for the examination findings in VSD:

- Small VSD: asymptomatic, discovered accidently with a loud harsh, pansystolic murmur heard best in the left lower parasternal area associated with a systolic thrill. First heart sound may be diminished in intensity, second sound normal.

- Large VSD: a bulging precordium in a malnourished, scrawny infant with hyperdynamic apical impulse and cardiomegaly and a soft pansystolic murmur in the left lower parasternal area. Thrill may be absent, second sound may be loud, and a diastolic murmur may be heard in mitral area.

INVESTIGATIONS

Hemoglobin and hematocrit are important because anemia aggravates the symptoms of volume overload.

An elevated **white cell count** supports the diagnosis of a superimposed infection which may be worsening the cardiac failure.

Chest Radiograph:

In a small VSD it is usually normal.

In a large VSD the chest radiograph shows bi-ventricular hypertrophy, prominence of left atrium and pulmonary artery, and increased pulmonary vascularity. The chamber enlargement is proportional to the size of the shunt.

Electrocardiography

ECG shows evidence of bi ventricular hypertrophy and left atrial P waves.

Echocardiography

Two dimensional echocardiogram and colour Doppler are useful in estimating the size of the defect and calculating the pressure gradient across the defect. This helps determine whether the patient is at risk for the development of early pulmonary vascular disease. It will also show the presence of aortic insufficiency.

CASE SUMMARY

A nine month old female infant is admitted with complaints of cough, breathlessness and difficulty in feeding for the past three days.

This is her fourth admission since birth for the same complaints.

On examination, she has tachycardia, tachypnoea and a hyperdynamic precordium. The apical impulse is felt in the 6th intercostal space in the anterior axillary line. There is a soft holosystolic murmur heard best in the left 3rd & 4th intercostals space in the parasternal area. The second heart sound is loud in the pulmonary area.

Her liver is palpable 4cm below the subcostal margin in the midclavicular line. She also has growth failure. Her weight at nine months is 5.3 kg (birth weight was 3.2kg)

PROVISIONAL DIAGNOSIS

Ventricular septal defect with congestive cardiac failure with pulmonary hypertension.

CLINICAL DISCUSSION

The student should be able to

- Identify a case of congenital acyanotic heart disease on the basis of a conglomerate of tachypnoea, tachycardia, growth failure and repeated hospitalizations
- Identify the holosystolic murmur of VSD.
- outline a plan of management for this patient.

<u>MANAGEMENT</u>

Management of this infant:

1.Assess SPO_2 and provide supplemental oxygen if required.

2. If the infant cannot feed because of tachypnea, set up an intravenous line and give maintenance fluids

3. Send blood counts and culture to rule out infection (since lungs will have crepitations due to pulmonary congestion) and start appropriate antibiotics pending blood reports.

4. Administer diuretics (furesemide intravenously) to reduce pulmonary edema.

5. Administer an ACE-inhibitor to reduce systemic vascular resistance,thus reducing the amount of blood being shunted into the right ventricle

6. Investigate the patient (Echocardiography) to confirm the diagnosis, and take a surgical opinion.

7.Pending surgery, build up the child's nutritional status by providing a diet high in calories and proteins. Give small frequent feeds.

Counseling:

Presence of a cardiac or non-cardiac congenital anomaly in the parents or siblings is a major risk factor.

The incidence of VSD in siblings of a patient is three times more than in general population.

Counselling and treatment options are essential. As the child was admitted with symptoms and shows growth failure these need to be addressed.

Long Term Prognosis:

- If surgery is done early enough, the child regains her position on the growth curve.
- Even with late surgery, she will improve her growth velocity, though she may remain shorter than her siblings.
- Complete right bundle branch block occurs in almost all surgically managed infants younger than 6 months of age but is not of much consequence.

LEARNING OUTCOMES

At the end of this discussion the student should be able to:

- Identify tachypnoea, tachycardia and growth failure with recurrent admissions as indicators of an acyanotic congenital cardiac defect
- Recognize the pansystolic murmur and grade its quality to interpret the size of the defect.
- Identify loud second sound as a sign of pulmonary hypertension.
- identify signs of cardiac failure in infants
- Explain the hemodynamics of a case of VSD

COMMONLY ASKED QUESTIONS

- List the causes of a pansystolic murmur in the lower left parasternal area
- State the signs of cardiac failure in infants
- Name the investigation most useful to clinch the diagnosis and plan surgery
- State the principles of management of a case of VSD

HIGH ACHIEVER QUESTIONS

- State the clinical findings that suggest that it is a small VSD

  Answer: A VSD is considered to be small if:

  o the child is asymptomatic and growing normally
  o the heart size is normal
  o the murmur is harsh, loud and accompanied by a thrill
  o there is no electrocardiographic evidence of ventricular hypertrophy

- Discuss the medical management of a case of VSD
  Answer:
  o Provide a high calorie diet – the energy content of infants' milk can be increased by adding edible oil, or making it more concentrated. A maximum caloric concentration of 27kal/oz is recommended. Making it more energy dense will stress the kidneys, as well as cause abnormal amino acidograms in the blood with deleterious effects on the developing brain.
  o Appropriate antibiotic prophylaxis for bacterial endocarditis
  o diuretics to reduce the volume overload
  o ACE inhibitors to reduce the systemic vascular resistance and thus reduce shunting of blood to the right side by decreasing the pressure gradient across the defect

- How long should one wait for the defect to close?
  Answer: Most small defects close spontaneously by two years of age. However, (as mentioned above in hemodynamics) in significant volume overload pulmonary vascular obstructive disease develops by 1 year of life, and surgical repair is not possible once that happens. Also, the mortality of primary repair now is only 1%. Hence if the defect has not closed by the second half of 1st year of life, it is advisable to close it.

COMMON MISTAKES

- Not being able to identify that the infant is in cardiac failure
- Not being able to differentiate between the ejection systolic murmur of pulmonary hypertension and the pansystolic murmur of VSD in an infant's small chest
- Missing the loud second sound

OVERVIEW

In 90% of term newborns, the ductus closes functionally by 48 hours of life. In preterm newborns it may be patent for a longer period, and in sick newborns with ventilator/circulatory compromise it may remain patent for ~10 days. The mechanism of ductal closure is a complex interaction of the level of arterial oxygen, circulating prostaglandins, genetic predetermination, and unknown factors.

The aortic end of the ductus is just distal to the origin of the left subclavian artery, and the ductus enters the pulmonary artery at its bifurcation. Females with patent ductus arteriosus (PDA) outnumber male patients 2:1. It is also common after maternal rubella infection in early pregnancy. In 10% of patients with other congenital heart lesions a PDA plays a vital role in establishing the much needed communication between the systemic and pulmonary circulations.

In a study conducted by Children Hospital Boston during 1988-2004, there were 544 cases with a primary diagnosis of PDA. Of these, 59% were females, 11% had a specific syndrome, and 2% had respiratory problem. Spontaneous closure of the defect after infancy is extremely rare. Patients with a small PDA can live a normal life, but infective endocarditis or embolism can occur anytime.

HAEMODYNAMICS

In the intrauterine life, venous return from right atrium enters the right ventricle, and onwards into the pulmonary artery. Since the lungs are collapsed, they offer a high resistance, and the blood is shunted through the ductus into the descending aorta. With the first breath the lungs expand, lowering the resistance in the pulmonary circulation. At the same time oxygenation improves. Once the PO_2 of the blood passing through the ductus increases (~50%,), the smooth muscles in its walls contract and the ductus closes. In a preterm infant the smooth muscles are not sensitive to the high PO_2 and the ductus remains patent for some time. The baby is born early, the ductus closes at its preordained time. But not all of them close. The incidence of PDA in preterms well past infancy is greater than in normal population. In a term infant with PDA, the ductal wall is deficient in the muscular layer, and it will not close spontaneously or with drugs. In a preterm no intervention is required during the neonatal life.

In a patent ductus postnatally, since the aortic pressure is higher than that in the pulmonary vascular bed, blood shunts through the ductus from the aorta to the pulmonary artery in all phases of the cardiac cycle. The magnitude of the shunt depends on the size of the ductus and the difference between the systemic and pulmonary vascular resistances. There is excessive blood flow to the lungs, left atrium, left ventricle and ascending aorta, and these enlarge in proportion to the size of the shunt. In a large PDA the pulmonary artery pressure may become equal to the systemic pressure and the patient is at a high risk of developing pulmonary vascular obstructive disease, although this is rare before the first birthday.

TYPES OF CASES FOR CLINICAL EXAMINATION:

OSCE/ SHORT CASE

Student may be asked to examine the cardiovascular system, or the precordium.

In examination of the cardiovascular system, the student should examine the extracardiac manifestations of a cardiac illness, i.e. all the peripheral pulses, jugular venous pulse, respiratory rate and auscultatory signs, hepatomegaly, pedal edema, clubbing and cyanosis. Then examine the precordium.

Examination of the precordium begins with looking for a bulge/ deformity in the shape of thorax, and a hyperdynamic apical impulse which is shifted down and laterally. The student should then proceed to elicit all the physical signs of a PDA (as described below), and also to assess whether the patient is developing a pulmonary vascular obstructive disease.

LONG CASE

The student should be able to take a detailed history and complete examination of the cardiovascular system and all the other systems to look for multiple anomalies/syndromes of which this defect may be a part. Look for growth and developmental delay. History should include the course of the illness and complications. Student should be able to mention relevant investigations and principles of management.

CASE VIGNETTE

An eight month old female infant is admitted with complaints of cough, breathlessness, and poor feeding for the past 4-5 days. She has been admitted thrice in the past with the same complaints.

Differential Diagnosis:

1. Bronchial asthma
2. Recurrent pneumonia (foreign body aspiration, progressive primary tuberculosis)
3. Acyanotic congenital heart defect with congestive cardiac failure.

Respiratory illnesses will have relevant histories (positive family history for bronchial asthma, history of contact for tuberculosis), and clinical findings (rhonchi for asthma; anemia, lymphadenopathy, etc for tuberculosis; pneumonia in the same area of lung repeatedly in a case of foreign body aspiration). Bronchial asthma is a diagnosis made by exclusion, and very rarely before the fifth birthday.

HISTORY

A small PDA may be asymptomatic, discovered accidently. In symptomatic cases, symptoms will be similar to those seen in a case of ventricular septal defect, since both are high pressure shunts from the systemic to the pulmonary circulation.

A detailed **history of presenting illness** should include:

*   Presence/ absence of **fever**.
    Fever denotes an infective pathology. High, continuous fever in a sick-looking child is usually seen in recurrent bacterial pneumonia.

    Bronchial asthma may be precipitated by a viral upper respiratory infection, in which case the child will have a low grade fever, signs of upper respiratory infection, and not look so sick except for the respiratory distress.

    Acyanotic congenital heart disease is a known cause of recurrent pneumonitis. A child with crepitations in the lungs is presumed to have infection superimposed on the pulmonary congestion caused by the increased pulmonary flow.

*   **Feeding history:** Is the child able to take feeds well, or, did she take a long time to feed, stopping several times to catch her breath (the suck-rest-suck cycle)?

    Increased volume of blood in the lungs decreases the compliance and increases the work of breathing. Fluid leaks into the interstitial space and alveoli and causes pulmonary edema and features of heart failure (difficulty in feeding, respiratory distress and wheezing) appear.

- Student should ask **details of cough and breathlessness**: is it a "productive" cough? Does it have a diurnal/postural variation? Does it end in post-tussive vomiting?

  Infants and toddlers are not able to expectorate the phlegm, but the cough sounds "wet", hence labeled as productive cough.

  Diurnal variation is usually seen in asthmatic patients, the cough being worse late at night/early in the morning. In bronchial asthma the cough is in repetitive bouts, with short breaths, in primary tuberculosis there will be other signs of a generalized infection (anemia, lymphadenopathy, visceromegaly)

- History of **cyanosis:** does the child turn blue during crying?

  Some children with pulmonary congestion and high pulmonary vascular resistance will show a dusky color around the oral cavity during crying or during infections.

  If the pulmonary vascular resistance is nearing the systemic vascular resistance, the shunt may become bidirectional, and then gradually reverses over time, with blood flowing from right to left, and cyanosis appears (Eisenmenger physiology). This cyanosis is typically seen in lower limbs (**differential cyanosis**) because the upper limbs and head and neck area receive oxygenated blood via the ascending aorta, while the deoxygenated blood from the reversed shunt flows through the PDA to the descending aorta.

- Ask the mother if she has noticed **excessive sweating** over the forehead, especially during feeding.

  High output by the left ventricle (to compensate for the aortic runoff into the patent ducts) is maintained by increasing the stroke volume and heart rate. This is achieved by increased activity of the sympathetic nervous system. This leads to sweating and irritability, especially during feeding (exertional dyspnea).

- Student should specifically ask the caretaker about **weight loss** or decreased growth velocity. The mother will generally compare her with her older siblings and be able to give you an assessment.

- **Regurgitation and vomiting** may occur in severe congestive cardiac failure due to venous stasis that causes congestion in the gastro-intestinal system.

Past History:

Since this is the fourth admission of the infant, a detailed history of all previous admissions is essential. What was the age at first admission? Was she admitted with the same complaints every time? What investigations were done during the past admissions? What were the reports of those investigations (some parents can specify)? What treatment/ advice were given then?

Is the child completely asymptomatic in between the admissions (this includes feeding difficulty, appetite and weight gain)? A completely asymptomatic child in between the attacks favours one of the respiratory pathologies mentioned above.

In acyanotic congenital heart disease, the lungs are constantly flooded with blood, which causes leakage into the interstitial tissue and some alveolar leakage; hence the child is always tachypnoeic, though this may not be noticed by the caretakers during asymptomatic periods in between.

Birth History:

c) **Antenatal history:**
    This should include details of any events (in each trimester) that could have caused a congenital defect in the child. Specific enquiries should be made about any viral illness (fever with rash), drugs taken, especially in the first trimester and maternal diabetes. A bad obstetric history (recurrent spontaneous abortions/ still births) support a genetic/ chromosomal abnormality. PDA has a high association with complex cardiac defects and with **maternal rubella infection** in early pregnancy.

d) **Intrapartum history:**

    Details of delivery: Student should ask about **prematurity**, requirement of resuscitative measures, and birth asphyxia.

    In preterm newborns the ductus is less responsive to ambient oxygen, and may remain patent till the newborn reaches a post conceptual age of ≥ 37 weeks. However, it does not always close after that, and the incidence of PDA in these children is higher than that found in general population.

e) **Postpartum period:**
Student should ask about feeding difficulties (suck-rest-suck cycle), failure to thrive, and NICU admission.

Preterm newborns generally need intensive care for a while, and the murmur is discovered within days after birth.

Ten percent of PDAs are a part of complex congenital anomalies, and the newborn may have required intensive care for these.

Growth and Developmental History:

A detailed history of ages at which the milestones were achieved should be noted.

Approximately 65% of children with congenital heart defect have been found to have delayed development independent of chronic hypoxia.

Some children may have delayed gross motor development simply because they are exhausted/ too weak to move. In these children, fine motor, speech and social developmental milestones will be normal.

Most symptomatic infants will have decreased growth velocity. In severe cases, the infant may never exceed her birth weight because of poor feeding and increased oxygen and energy demand as the heart and lungs are overworked.

Dietary History:

Breast feeding requires the infant to actively squeeze out the milk from the breast, whereas bottle feeds need only to be swallowed and the infant has to exert less. Hence some mothers switch the baby to bottle feeds saying that the baby does not take breast feeds.

In view of the growth failure these children have, it is important to rule out dietary insufficiency. A detailed history of dietary intake, with special emphasis on calories and protein intake is essential.

Immunization History:

All routine immunizations should have been given, and enquiry of this should be made. Influenza vaccine should be given if available

Family History:

Family history should include three generations, both on the maternal as well as paternal side.

History of consanguineous marriage between parents should be enquired into, as should the presence of cardiac defects, other congenital anomalies, early deaths, and mental retardation in other family members.

Socio-economic history:

This is important in view of the growth failure that the child is having, to rule out undernutrition as a cause.

Systemic Review of symptoms:

Respiratory distress, on exertion, or even at rest, denotes the severity of pulmonary congestion, and indirectly the size of the shunt. Some infants are asymptomatic between the hospital admissions, the only sign being tachypnea, which may be missed by the caretaker. Recurrent respiratory infections are a symptom of increased pulmonary congestion, and support the diagnosis of an acyanotic congenital heart defect.

Neurological symptoms and **other congenital anomalies** may be present as a part of certain genetic/chromosomal defects/ syndromes.

CHECK LIST FOR HISTORY TAKING IN A CASE OF PDA:

- Age at appearance of initial symptoms
- Exertional dyspnea, including feeding difficulty
- Recurrent symptoms of respiratory distress/ cardiac failure (tachypnea, dyspnea, reduced intake)
- Growth failure
- Antenatal history suggestive of rubella

EXAMINATION

General Examination:

Introduce yourself and obtain consent for examination. Wash hands thoroughly.

- Note the **general appearance:**

  Irritability denotes the degree of distress. A lethargic child is more seriously ill than one who can show signs of irritation. As she improves, she becomes friendlier. When she smiles at you, it is time to discharge her.

  Failure to thrive is seen in children with moderate – severe PDA because of feeding difficulty coupled with increased oxygen and energy demand by the heart and lungs. Recurrent pneumonia (as mentioned above) also increases the basal metabolic rate, consuming more energy and decreases the appetite.

  Respiratory Distress is present in most children, and its signs should be carefully looked for. Suprasternal recession can be seen by showing the infant a bright colored toy/light from a torch above his head so that he looks up. Also make a note of intercostals recession, substernal retractions, and nasal flaring.

  Recurrent respiratory distress in an undernourished infant leads to the development of **Harrison's sulcus.** This is a groove formed just above and parallel to the subcostal margins where the diaphragm is attached to the inner surface of the ribs. Recurrent respiratory distress causes forceful diaphragmatic contractions, tugging at the ribs, which thus get molded into a groove/Sulcus.

  If the shunt has become bidirectional, or is being reversed due to the development of pulmonary arterial hypertension, the lower part of the body (excluding the head and neck and the upper limbs) will receive deoxygenated blood. This results in cyanosis, and stimulates the production of erythropoietin. Hence the patient will look **polycythemic** in spite of minimal cyanosis in the upper limbs.

  Student should carefully look for **Dysmorphism and other congenital malformations** as PDA is commonly found as a part and parcel of several complex cardiac defects.

- **Vital Signs:**

  Heart/ pulse rate and pulse volume should be recorded.

  Since the left ventricle has to maintain the cardiac output in spite of some blood draining away into the pulmonary circulation, heart rate (pulse rate) has to increase. Hence **tachycardia** is usually present.

  It is difficult to count the pulse rate of an irritable infant. The student should palpate the radial pulse and **all the peripheral pulses** for pulse volume, character and rhythmicity, and count the heart rate.

  A large PDA will result in **bounding (high volume) pulse** due to the aortic runoff of blood into the pulmonary circulation during diastole. **Pulse pressure** will also be wide for the same reason. The larger is the aortic runoff, wider is the pulse pressure, and more striking are the peripheral pulses.

  Tachypnoea is the first sign to appear and is a sensitive indicator of respiratory compromise. Hence respiratory rate should be counted carefully, for at least 30 seconds in an infant, and at least for a minute in a neonate (to offset the periodic respiration they have).

  Temperature should be recorded to confirm/ rule out an infectious pathology.

  Student should always record the **blood pressure** as a baseline value. If it is not possible (the child is very small or uncooperative), look for clinical signs of shock and record them – cold, clammy extremities, feeble/not palpable peripheral pulses, prolonged capillary refill time, lethargic patient. As mentioned above, there will be a **wide pulse pressure** because of the aortic runoff.

- **Extracardiac manifestations of cardiac disease:**

  The cardinal signs of congestive cardiac failure (raised jugular venous pressure, crackles at the bases of lungs) are difficult to discern in an infant whose neck is small (and the child is irritable) and the lungs are already congested due to the basic illness.

  The **cardinal signs of cardiac failure in infancy** are: tachycardia, tachypnea, hepatomegaly and cardiomegaly. Hence, in addition to recording her vital signs, the student should also measure and record the size of the liver below the subcostal margin in the midclavicular line. Because of respiratory distress, the liver may be pushed down, and this should be determined by percussing its upper border and recording the intercostal space in which the upper border is present.

If the primary pathology is a respiratory illness, there will be no cardiomegaly (this can be documented clinically by the shift of apical impulse and radiologically on taking an X-ray of the chest).

Pedal edema is not seen in infants since they are supine. They develop sacral edema, and sudden weight gain.

If a child suspected of PDA has **clubbing or central cyanosis,** she is developing Eisenmenger complex, and the prognosis is grave. Typically, these patients will have **differential cyanosis.** The fingers and lips will be minimally cyanosed as they receive oxygenated blood from the left ventricle through the ascending aorta, but lower limbs will show obvious cyanosis and clubbing because deoxygenated blood flows to these parts through the PDA into the descending aorta.

Examination of the cardiovascular system:

- **Shape of the precordium :**
  A **precordial bulge** is best noted by observing from the foot end of the bed, with your eyes at the same level as the patient's chest. In this position the two hemithoraces can be compared. In a PDA of significant severity, cardiomegaly leads to a bulging precordium.

- Palpation of the heart should begin with the patient in the supine position at 30 degrees. If the heart is not felt in this position, the patient can be examined in sitting posture, leaning forward.
  The apical impulse is rapid and hyperdynamic due to the volume overload. It is shifted inferiorly and laterally, depending on the hypertrophy of the ventricles, which depends on the severity of the shunt.

- A **left parasternal heave** may be noted, indicating right ventricular hypertrophy.

- A **systolic thrill** may be felt in the left 2nd intercostal space. It may radiate towards the left clavicle or down the left sternal border. It is usually systolic, but **may be felt continuously**

- **Heart sounds:** Heart sounds are difficult to comment upon because of the continuous murmur. **Second heart sound** is normal in a small defect, but may be loud if the defect is large and pulmonary hypertension is developing.

- Characteristic murmur is described as a **continuous machinery murmur** (a motorbike very far away), harsh because of an overlay of clicking sounds (like shaking dice) especially during systolic phase. It is heard best in the left second intercostal space, and can be traced to just under the left clavicle.

  With a large ductus, when there is equilibration of pressures in the pulmonary and systemic circulations during diastole, the diastolic component of the murmur disappears and the student can hear **only the systolic murmur**. This can be confused with the ejection systolic murmur of pulmonary hypertension since both are heard best in the left 2nd intercostals space. But the pulmonary hypertension murmur is an ejection murmur heard best in the parasternal area, while the PDA murmur may be pansystolic in character, and heard more laterally in the same intercostal space. Also, the latter murmur radiates to the clavicle, and the student should make an attempt to trace it up the infraclavicular area. Its quality is also machinery like (with systolic clicks).

  A **mid-diastolic murmur** may be heard in the apical area due to increased blood flow across the mitral valve (functional mitral stenosis).

Examination of other systems:

The **respiratory system** is examined to rule out a non-cardiac diagnosis. The presence of pulmonary crepitations signifies infection more often than cardiac failure.

A detailed assessment of his mental development is a must to look for any associated **developmental anomaly**.

A careful survey of all systems should be made to exclude any **associated congenital anomalies.**

CHECK LIST FOR THE EXAMINATION FINDINGS IN PDA:

- Small PDA:
- Asymptomatic, discovered accidently
- A loud continuous machinery like murmur heard best in the left second intercostal space radiating to the left clavicle
- Associated with a systolic thrill.
- Heart size is normal.
- Large PDA:

o A bulging precordium in a malnourished infant

o Hyperdynamic apical impulse

o Cardiomegaly

o Pansystolic/continuous murmur in the left second intercostal space radiating towards the left clavicle.

o Second sound may be loud

o A diastolic murmur may be heard in mitral area.

INVESTIGATIONS

Chest Radiograph:

Chest radiograph is normal if the defect is small.

In a large PDA the ascending aorta, left ventricle, left atrium, pulmonary vessels are enlarged in proportion to the magnitude of the shunt.

The first chamber to be stressed is the left ventricle, and it hypertrophies first. In large shunts transmitting the systemic resistance to the pulmonary vasculature, pulmonary hypertension develops after sometime, and right ventricle hypertrophies once this happens because it has to pump blood against pulmonary vascular resistance. As a corollary, if only right ventricular hypertrophy is seen, it is untenable with the diagnosis of an isolated, uncomplicated PDA.

Electrocardiography (ECG)

ECG is normal if the PDA is small

If the defect is large, it shows left ventricular hypertrophy.

If the defect is large and pulmonary hypertension has developed, it shows biventricular hypertrophy.

Echocardiography

Two dimensional echocardiogram and colour Doppler are useful in estimating the size of the defect and calculating the pressure gradient across the defect. Absence of a gradient is taken as an evidence of pulmonary hypertension

CASE SUMMARY

An eight month old female infant is admitted with complaints of cough, breathlessness, and poor feeding for the past 4-5 days. This is her 4th admission for the same complaints.

On examination, she has tachypnea and tachycardia. Her pulses are bounding, and she has evidence of cardiomegaly and a hyperdynamic, bulging precordium. There is a harsh, continuous murmur best heard in the left $2^{nd}/3^{rd}$ intercostal space and under the clavicle. Her liver is palpable ~5cm below the right subcostal margin in the midclavicular line. She also has failure to thrive.

PROVISIONAL DIAGNOSIS

A patent ductus arteriosus with congestive cardiac failure.

CLINICAL DISCUSSION

The student should be able to:

- Identify a case of congenital acyanotic heart disease on the basis of a combination of tachypnea, tachycardia, growth failure and repeated hospitalizations

- Identify the continuous machinery murmur of PDA, and to differentiate it from the ejection systolic murmur of pulmonary hypertension heard in the same intercostal space.

- Differentiate clinically between a VSD and PDA on the basis of the peripheral signs and the murmurs

LEARNING OUTCOMES

The student should be able to:

- Explain the Pathophysiology of the signs of PDA, and of cardiac failure in the infant.

271

- Differentiate whether the PDA is large/ small, whether the patient has pulmonary hypertension or not.

- Suggest relevant investigations and outline a plan of management

COMMONLY ASKED QUESTIONS

- List the causes of a continuous/ systolic murmur in the left second intercostal space.
  Answer:
  a) Fallot's tetralogy with pulmonary atresia and collateral circulation will produce continuous murmurs heard all over the chest. With good collaterals, cyanosis may be minimal.
  b) A venous hum
- State the signs of cardiac failure in infants
- Name the investigation most useful to clinch the diagnosis and what one expects to find in them.
- State the principles of management of a case of PDA.

HIGH ACHIEVER QUESTIONS

- How will determine the development of pulmonary hypertension in PDA?
  Answer: If the patient is developing pulmonary hypertension:
  o The episodes of cardiac failure decrease, but her exertional dyspnea increases
  o There is history of the infant developing a dusky hue especially in the lower limbs
  o Cyanosis and clubbing make their appearance in the lower limbs.
  o A left parasternal heave is present, signifying a right ventricular hypertrophy
  o The murmur becomes systolic
  o The second sound becomes loud
  o An additional ejection systolic murmur appears more medially in the left second intercostal space.

- Discuss the management of a case of PDA
  Answer:
  o Treatment of congestive cardiac failure is the only medical management required.
  o Surgical closure is the only definitive treatment, and is advocated for all patients, even those with small defect and no symptoms, because of the threat of infective endocarditis.

- Pulmonary hypertension is not a contraindication as long as cardiac catheterization shows that the shunt is predominantly left to right.
- Transcatheter closure is done by coils or umbrella like devices.

COMMON MISTAKES

- Not being able to identify that the infant is a case of acyanotic cardiac defect
- Not being able to identify that the infant is in cardiac failure.
- Missing the clubbing and cyanosis in the lower limbs of a small infant
- Not being able to differentiate between the ejection systolic murmur of pulmonary hypertension and the systolic murmur of PDA in an infant's small chest.
- Missing the loud second sound

CASE 18: TETRALOGY OF FALLOT
USHA RANI SINGH

OVERVIEW

Tetralogy of Fallow (TOF) is the most common cyanotic congenital heart defect, with an incidence of 3.26 per 10,000 live births, or about 1300 new cases per year in the United States. It is slightly more common in males. Mutations in several genes have been identified in Tetralogy of Fallot. Incidence of Fallot's tetralogy is high in Alagille syndrome, Holt-Oram syndrome, trisomy 21, 18, and 13, but the gene/genes responsible for it are still unidentified. It can also occur as an isolated defect.

Among a selected group of 1538 tetralogy of Fallot patients seen at Children's Hospital, Boston during a 14-year period, 61% had simple tetralogy of Fallot with pulmonary stenosis, 33% had pulmonary atresia, 3% had absent pulmonary valve, and 3% had common atrioventricular canal.

As the name suggests, it comprises of four malformations:

- infundibular pulmonary stenosis,
- a large, unrestrictive ventricular septal defect (VSD),
- dextroposition of the aorta such that the aortic root overrides the VSD,
- right ventricular hypertrophy.

Unrepaired TOF patients develop more cyanosis with passage of time due to progressive infundibular stenosis and right ventricular outlet obstruction. Older children develop complications of prolonged hypoxia and polycythemia, like impaired cognitive development, brain abscess, stroke, and gall stones. These complications are rare now as repair during infancy is the rule. The early mortality of patients repaired in infancy is 3-6%. Late mortality will be known after these patients reach later decades of life.

HEMODYNAMICS:

Venous return from the right atrium enters the right ventricle through the tricuspid valve. From here it should be going to the lungs for oxygenation through the pulmonary artery. But as there is outlet obstruction in the form of subpulmonary stenosis part of it goes into the pulmonary artery onwards to the lungs while the rest is shunted through the aorta which is overriding the VSD. This mixes with the oxygenated blood returning to the heart via the pulmonary veins resulting in the patient having central cyanosis.

TYPES OF CASES FOR CLINICAL EXAMINATION:

SHORT CASE/ OSCE:

Student may be asked to perform a general examination only, or to examine the cardiovascular system.

In general examination student should look for growth failure (anthropometry), cyanosis, clubbing, polycythemia (congested sclera and conjunctiva), respiratory distress, and emphasize the characteristics of the vital signs; normal pulse and blood pressure. Presence of other congenital anomalies should also be looked for.

Examination of the cardiovascular system includes the extracardiac manifestations of a cardiac disease as mentioned above: absence of signs of cardiac failure (pedal edema, raised JVP, hepatomegaly, basal crepitations), and the examination of the precordium.

LONG CASE:

In a long case, a detailed history and examination of the cardiovascular system is expected.

History should include the course of the illness and complications.

Student should be able to mention relevant investigations and principles of management.

CASE VIGNETTE

A four years old boy is brought to the clinic by his parents with complaints of bluish discoloration of lips and breathlessness on exertion since age of four- five months.

Differential Diagnosis:

a)   Tetralogy of Fallot

b)   Transposition of great vessels

c)   Truncus arteriosus

d)   Respiratory distress (pneumonia, bronchiolitis, foreign body aspiration)

Differentiating a cardiac illness from a respiratory one is simple enough:

A congenital cardiac defect is present since birth, whereas the respiratory problem is an acute presentation

There is no audible murmur, no cardiomegaly, and adventitious sounds relevant to the respiratory illness (rhonchi/ crepitations) are audible in a case of respiratory distress.

In case of doubt (in neonatal period or early infancy) the "hyperoxia test" is used to differentiate between the two.

HISTORY

A detailed history of presenting illness should include:

Details of the central cyanosis: age of appearance, whether it is progressive, and whether it becomes worse on crying.

Some children with Fallot'sTetrology may not be cyanotic for the first few months of life because the right ventricular outlet obstruction may be mild, hence little or no right-to-left shunting of blood may occur. These are known as "pink Fallot's".

The sub-pulmonary infundibular narrowing may increase over time, increasing the resistance to flow through the pulmonary circulation, and cyanosis appears then as more deoxygenated blood is shunted across into the aorta.

Increase in pulmonary vascular resistance during crying will also increase the shunting across the VSD and increase the cyanosis.

Children born with transposition of great vessels present early in life (within hours or days)with severe hypoxia and collapse. Their cyanosis is not affected by crying.

Feeding: Ask if, as an infant, was the child able to take feeds well, or, did he take a long time to feed, stopping several times to catch his breath (the suck-rest-suck cycle)?

Some cases of pink Fallot's tetralogy may even have left-to right shunting of blood in early infancy, with pulmonary over circulation, and symptoms of heart failure similar to a VSD.

Patients with truncus arteriosus will present with signs of congestive cardiac failure and a hyperdynamic apical impulse early in infancy.

Child's exercise tolerance: how far can he walk? Does he squat every now and then during walking?

Older children learn to squat as this causes kinking of the femoral arteries, thereby increasing the systemic vascular resistance. This limits the right–to –left shunting across the VSD, enabling a greater proportion of blood to go to the lungs for oxygenation.

Student should ask specifically for history of hypercyanotic spells.

The child becomes distressed for no apparent reason. Crying worsens the cyanosis and hypoxia deepens, aggravating the condition. These occur in the mornings usually.

It is postulated that catecholamine stimulation of right ventricular mechano-receptors increases the right-to-left shunting. These usually occur in those children who have mild/ no clinical cyanosis, since they have not developed compensatory mechanism develops(polycythemia) to tackle severe hypoxia.

Squatting and hypercyanotic spells are the hallmarks of tetralogy of Fallot.

Older patients may have hemoptysis due to rupture of a collateral vessel.

PAST HISTORY:

Student should ask for history of any previous admissions, complications (stroke/ dehydration), and treatment taken, along with response to the treatment. A previous palliative cardiac surgery for the problem will alter the physical findings.

Birth History:

a)Antenatal history:

This should include details of any event (in each trimester) that could have caused a congenital defect in the child. Specific enquiries should be made about any viral illness (fever with rash), drugs taken, and maternal diabetes, especially in the first trimester. A bad obstetric history (recurrent spontaneous abortions/ still births) support a genetic/ chromosomal abnormality.

Ultrasonographic findings Detailed imaging of the fetal heart and fetal echocardiography can detect most heart lesions after 23 weeks gestation.

b)Intarpartumhistory:

Details of delivery: Student should ask about prematurity, requirement of resuscitative measures, and birth asphyxia.

c)Postpartuml period:

Student should ask about feeding difficulties, failure to thrive, NICU admission and cyanosis that deepens on crying.

Transposition of great vessels presents with sudden collapse with minimal signs early in the neonatal period.

Truncus arteriosus presents with cardiac failure in the first couple of m

DEVELOPMENTAL HISTORY:

Patients with chronic cyanosis have been found to have diminished cognitive function;~65% of children with congenital heart defect were found to have delayed development independent of chronic hypoxia. Hence a detailed history of age at which the milestones were achieved should be noted.

Dietary History:

In view of the growth failure these children have, it is important to rule out dietary insufficiency. A detailed history of dietary intake, with special emphasis on calories, protein and iron intake is a must.

Children with cyanotic heart defect have polycythemia, which increases the demand for iron. Iron deficiency results in microcytic erythrocytes, which are rigid and resist deformation in the microcirculation, thus increasing the risk of hyperviscosity symptoms like cerebrovascular thrombosis.Their hematocrit should be maintained at ~65%.

Immunization History:

All routine immunizations should have been given, with the inclusion of influenza vaccine where feasible.

Family History:

Family history should include three generations, both on the maternal as well as paternal side.

History of consanguineous marriage between parents should be enquired into, as should the presence of cardiac defects, other congenital anomalies, early deaths, and mental retardation in other family members.

Socio-economic history:

This is important in view of the growth failure that the child is having, to rule out undernutrition as a cause.

Systemic Review of symptoms:

Respiratory distress, on exertion, or even at rest, denotes the severity of insufficient pulmonary arterial flow.

Recurrent respiratory infections are a symptom of increased pulmonary congestion, and are against the diagnosis of Tetralogy of Fallot, except in the early stages when there may be left-to-right shunting in a pink Fallot, as has been explained above.

Neurological symptoms may be seen in cerebral thrombosis/abscess, or as an independent congenital defect.

Other congenital anomalies, as a part of certain genetic/chromosomal defects/ syndromes may be present.

✓ **CHECK LIST FOR HISTORY TAKING IN FALLOT'S TETRALOGY:**

- Age at appearance of central cyanosis
- Exertional dyspnea (feeding difficulty)
- Squatting episodes
- Hypercyanotic spells

EXAMINATION

General Examination:Introduce yourself and obtain consent for examination. Wash hands thoroughly.

Note the general appearance –

Respiratory distress is seen characteristically after exertion. Children play for a while, and then sit or lie down. Older children will walk a little distance and then stop/ assume a squatting posture for relief.

Failure to thrive is seen in severe untreated patients, where oxygen saturation is chronically <70%,

Mental subnormality and dysmorphic facies may be a part of certain syndromes. As mentioned earlier, delayed development is found in ~65% of patients of congenital heart defects unrelated to hypoxia.

Older children with prolonged cyanosis develop a dusky blue skin, grey sclera with engorged blood vessels. Congested palpebral conjunctiva is seen as a result of polycythemia due to cyanosis.

Vital Signs:

Pulse rate and volume should be recorded, and all peripheral pulses should be palpated: normal in tetralogy of Fallot.

Bounding, high volume pulse with a wide pulse pressure is seen in Truncus Arteriosus.

Signs of respiratory distress should be recorded. Respiratory distress/ hyperpnoea are noted especially after exertion.

Blood pressure should be recorded.

Extracardiac manifestations of cardiac disease:

Central cyanosis is seen in mucous membranes of lips and mouth, in fingers and toe nails. A decrease in systemic vascular resistance during exercise or fever may increase the right-to-left shunt and increase the hypoxia.

Clubbing of fingers and toe nails develop after 3-6 months of age in cases with profound cyanosis.

Signs of cardiac failure (pedal edema, raised jugular venous pulse, basal crepitations in the lungs) should be looked for. If these are found, especially after infancy, a diagnosis of Fallot's tetralogy is unlikely. Student should then check for signs that may suggest a Truncus arteriosus.

JVP, Peripheral pulse and BP

One would expect the jugular venous pressure to be raised in presence of infundibular stenosis, and thus the patient should develop cardiac failure. This does not happen because right ventricle has to raise its pressure only enough to equal the left ventricular pressure, so that it can push its share of blood into the aorta. It thus "bypasses" the obstruction and does not fail.

Further, the ultimate cardiac output is the same as the venous return (part of it going into the pulmonary circulation before reaching the aorta, and the rest reaching the aorta directly). Hence the pulse volume, and blood pressure are normal.

Examination of the cardiovascular system:

• Shape of the precordium :

A precordial bulge is best noted by observing from the foot end of the bed, with your eyes at the same level as the patient's chest. In this position the two hemithoraces can be compared. The right ventricular hypertrophy in TOF is generally moderate, hence the precordial bulge may be mild and easily missed. As mentioned above, the right ventricle does not have to hypertrophy much, so the heart size does not increase much. if left untreated, it does hypertrophy gradually, and signs of right heart failure will develop in older children/adolescents.

In chest radiographs too the heart size is essentially normal; the only evidence of right ventricular hypertrophy being an elevated apex.

The precordium is bulging with cardiomegaly in truncus arteriosus.

• Palpation of the heart should begin with the patient in the supine position at 30 degrees. If the heart is not felt in this position, the patient can be examined in sitting posture, leaning forward.

The apical impulse is normal in position and character in tetralogy of Fallot, (because there is not much increase in the size of heart, the main change being a little concentric hypertrophy of right ventricle), whereas it is hyperdynamic and shifted in truncus arteriosus.

• A left parasternal heave may be noted, indicating right ventricular hypertrophy.

• A systolic thrill may be felt in the left third and fourth parasternal spaces due to turbulent blood flow through the narrow infundibular tract.

• The second heart sound may be single.

• An ejection systolic murmur is heard in the pulmonary area and upper left parasternal area. It may become louder as obstruction increases, but may be inaudible during a hypercyanotic spell when blood flow through the narrow ventricular outflow tract is severely compromised. Thus, more cyanotic patients may have greater obstruction and a softer murmur.

Ejection systolic murmur is heard along the left upper sternal border in truncus arteriosus too, but the cyanosis is minimal (since pulmonary blood flow is adequate) and pulses is bounding.

• The pansystolic murmur expected in a ventricular septal defect is not heard in Fallot's Tetralogy because the VSD is large, unrestrictive, and is overridden by the dextroposed aorta into which both the ventricles discharge their output.

• Sometimes a continuous murmur may be heard because of collateral vessels.

Examination of other systems:

The central nervous system should be examined in detail for signs of neurological deficits, which may be sequelae of past strokes/ cerebral abscesses.

The respiratory system is examined to rule out a non-cardiac diagnosis.

A detailed assessment of his mental development is a must to look for any developmental anomaly.

A careful survey of all systems should be made to exclude any associated congenital anomalies.

CHECK LIST FOR THE EXAMINATION FINDINGS IN TETRALOGY OF FALLOT:

• A normal pulse, normal blood pressure, normal apical impulse in a cyanotic congenital heart disease is suggestive of Fallot's Tetralogy.
• Left parasternal heave.
• Systolic thrill and ejection systolic murmur in upper left parasternal area.

INVESTIGATIONS

Hemoglobin and hematocrit values are elevated in proportion to the degree of cyanosis.
Prolonged prothrombin and coagulation times. Patients with significant cyanosis have diminished coagulation factors, and diminished total fibrinogen.

Chest Radiography shows
• A normal sized heart,
• Decreased pulmonary vascularity,
• Sometimes a right sided aortic arch.
• The apex of the heart is often elevated owing to right ventricular hypertrophy.
• A concave contour along the left upper heart border due to main pulmonary artery hypoplasia or atresia,

The last two features give the cardiac silhouette a so-called boot shape (coeur en sabot), although this may not be apparent in the infant with a prominent thymus.

Electrocardiography (ECG) shows evidence of right ventricular hypertrophy which increases with age as the obstruction worsens. Right atrial enlargement may be seen in severe, untreated, older children. If right ventricular hypertrophy is not seen in ECG, the diagnosis of Fallot's tetralogy is in doubt.

Echocardiography can identify all the anatomic anomalies of tetralogy of Fallot.

This investigation, along with color Doppler will provide all the relevant structural information for planning a surgery:

- The size and extent of the ventricular septal defect
- The location and size of additional muscular ventricular septal defects
- The levels of right ventricular outflow tract obstruction
- The degree of pulmonary valve abnormality
- The pulmonary artery anatomy
- The size and competency of the aortic valve
- The coronary artery anatomy,
- The presence of associated atrial septal defect or a patent ductus arteriosus
- The presence a right aortic arch

CASE SUMMARY

A four year- old male child is brought with complaints of bluish discoloration of lips and breathlessness on exertion since the age of four-five months.

On examination he has central cyanosis and clubbing. He is also seen squatting after walking a little distance. His pulse rate is 98 beats/ minute and he has a left parasternal heave. Apical impulse is palpable in the left 4th intercostals space in the mid-clavicular line, and an ejection systolic murmur is heard best in the pulmonary area.

PROVISIONAL DIAGNOSIS

Tetralogy of Fallot.

CLINICAL DISCUSSION OF THE CASE

Student should be able to:

•   Detect central cyanosis and clubbing in infants

•   Note that pulse rate and volume and apical impulse are normal even though the child has a cyanotic congenital heart disease

Recognize the ejection systolic murmur originating from the pulmonary area.

MANAGEMENT

QUESTION under high achiever includes medical management-reference can be made to that but an outline of management for the average student would complete the picture in a LONG CASE question

LEARNING OUTCOMES

At the end of this discussion the student should be able to:

•   Identify the peripheral signs of a congenital cardiac disease

•   Explain the haemodynamic changes seen in TOF and be able to explainthe pathophysiology of signs and complaints associated with TOF

•   Identify the murmur as an ejection systolic murmur

•   Take a relevant history and make a an appropriate diagnosis on the basis of this coupled with correct clinical findings

•   Suggest relevant investigations for confirming the diagnosis

•   Discuss the principles of management, and,

•   Counsel the parents on treatment options and genetic counselingabout recurrence rates of congenital heart disease

COMMONLY ASKED QUESTIONS

1)   List the four components of Tetralogy of Fallot.
2)   State two investigations that will clinch the diagnosis
3)   Discuss the management of a hypercyanotic spell.
4)   List the complications of untreated tetralogy of Fallot.
5)   Discuss the principles of medical management of a case of Fallot's Tetralogy

6) Prevent dehydration
7) maintain hematocrit at ~65% (low dose iron therapy)
8) prophylaxis for bacterial endocarditis
9) surgical repair

HIGH ACHIEVER QUESTIONS

What should be the optimum hematocrit in a case of cyanotic congenital heart disease?

Answer: Polycythemia secondary to a cyanotic heart lesion is pathologically different from that seen in polycythemia vera. In the latter, an association has been observed between a raised hematocrit and thrombosis. Although this has not been established in a cyanotic congenital heart defect, it is advisable to keep the hematocrit ~ 65%.

How can we maintain hematocrit at this level?

Answer: Phlebotomy with volume replacement and low dose iron therapy will prevent hyperviscosity. Iron deficiency leads to production of microcytic erythrocytes which resist deformation in microcirculation and increase the viscosity of blood, thereby increasing the risk of thrombosis

What is the medical management of a case of Fallot's tetralogy?

Answer:

1) Asymptomatic patients need only appropriate antibiotic prophylaxis for bacterial endocarditis
2) Prevent dehydration as it will increase the viscosity of blood
3) Iron therapy and phlebotomy (see above) with volume replacement
4) Management of a hypercyanotic spell
5) Place the child on mother's shoulders with the knees flexed under the belly
6) Give free flow oxygen
7) give intravenous fluids to increase the venous return
8) I V propanalol to relax the infundibular spasm
9) give morphine to decrease the ventilatory drive and allay anxiety
10) phenylephrine to increase systemic vascular resistance and reduce shunting.
11) maintain temperature and serum glucose levels, as hypothermia and hypoglycemia increase oxygen demand

How can you diagnose Fallot'stetralogy antenatally?

Answer: Fetal echocardiography in early second trimester can diagnose tetralogy of Fallot. Later in gestation, the central pulmonary arteries may appear hypoplastic, consistent with the hypothesis that obstruction to blood flow in the embryonic heart may impair the development of more distal cardiovascular structures. Doppler studies of the ductus arteriosus may show retrograde flow (i.e., from aorta to pulmonary artery) if right ventricular outflow tract obstruction is severe.

COMMON MISTAKES:

1) Missing cyanosis and clubbing in an infant, especially if it is mild
2) Thinking that a case of Fallot's tetralogy should be cyanosed right from birth, hence missing the diagnosis
3) Having the wrong notion that all cardiac cases should have abnormal heart rate and cardiomegaly
4) Not being able to identify the ejection systolic murmur, confusing it with the holosystolic murmur of VSD, especially in a small infant with mild cyanosis.

USHA RANI SINGH

OVERVIEW

Any opening in the atrial septum is described as an atrial septal defect. Ostium secundum defect is the most common one and is usually single. Most often it is asymptomatic with a soft murmur, hence detected in older children. Openings ≥2cm are common in symptomatic older children.

The incidence is 1.0 per 1000 live births. Females outnumber males 3:1. About 50% of children with complex cardiac defects have an atrial septal defect (ASD) associated with it. Majority of isolated ASD cases are sporadic though autosomal dominant inheritance is observed as a part of Holt-Oram syndrome. Here only isolated, uncomplicated ASD is discussed.

The natural course of an atrial septal defect is benign; many patients living for decades before developing any symptoms. Cardiovascular disease acquired in adult life (e.g. systemic hypertension) increases the left ventricular pressure and increases the left-to-right shunt causing an increase in pulmonary vascular pressure. Late complications include congestive cardiac failure, atrial fibrillation and rarely pulmonary vascular obstructive disease. The incidence of atrial fibrillation decreases after early closure, but the risk is not totally eliminated.

HEMODYNAMICS

The degree of left to right shunting of blood depends on the size of the defect, compliance of both the ventricles and the resistance of the pulmonary and systemic vasculature.

Fully oxygenated blood from the left atrium is shunted through the defect and mixes with the systemic venous return and passes into the right ventricle, thence into the pulmonary circulation. Since it is the oxygenated blood that is circulating again and again through the lungs, there is pulmonary congestion and no cyanosis. With large defects, the ratio of pulmonary blood flow to the systemic flow (Qp: Qs ratio) may be 2:1 to 4:1. This increased flow of blood in the right side of the heart results in enlargement of the right atrium, right ventricle and the pulmonary artery. Left atrium may get enlarged, but the left ventricle and the aorta are essentially normal. The reason why pulmonary arterial pressure is normal in spite of the increased flow is the absence of a high pressure communication between the systemic and pulmonary circulations. Over the years pulmonary vascular resistance may increase, and by adulthood the shunt may reverse, producing cyanosis. This is rare before 20 years of age.

Types Of Cases For Clinical Examination

<u>OSCE/ SHORT CASE</u>

The student may be asked to examine the cardiovascular system.

He should emphasize the absence of cardiac failure, or any peripheral extracardiac signs of a cardiac disease. He will find subtle signs of right ventricular overload and functional pulmonary stenosis (described below) with the characteristic wide, fixed split of the second sound..

<u>LONG CASE</u>

The student should be able to take a detailed history which should include the course of the illness and complications. He should look for growth failure (anthropometry) and any other associated anomalies (since approximately 50% of ASDs are a part of complex congenital anomalies). He should be able to plan relevant investigations and suggest an outline for management of the case.

CASE VIGNETTE

A six year old girl is brought to the clinic for a routine preschool check up. On examination, an ejection systolic murmur is heard in the left 2nd intercostal space (grade 2/6).

DIFFERENTIAL DIAGNOSIS

1. Functional murmur
2. Partial anomalous pulmonary venous connection (PAPVC).

A **functional murmur** is due to physiologic conditions as opposed to structural defects in the heart itself. It is found in an otherwise healthy person, is a soft, ejection systolic murmur (< grade 3/6), and changes on change of position.

In **PAPVC** one or more of the pulmonary veins bringing oxygenated blood from the lungs draining into one of the vena cavae or the right atrium. It may occur as an isolated defect or (in about 10% of patients) it may occur with an atrial septal defect (ASD). These patients have symptoms of right-sided overload. Signs and symptoms are same as in ASD and depend on how much of the pulmonary venous return drains into the right atrium. If both ASD and PAPVC are present in the same patient, child is symptomatic earlier. Diagnosis is made by investigations.

HISTORY

Since most murmurs are detected accidently, the history is usually retrospectively taken.

- Since the child will be a little underweight for her age, the student should ask about **effort intolerance**. Ask whether the child can keep up with his peers during play.
- The student should ask the caretaker about any recent illnesses causing **weight loss**, or a history of **decreased weight gain** compared to her other siblings.

PAST HISTORY

- Some children (those with a large defect) may have **recurrent attacks of respiratory distress**; hence this should be specifically asked for. Most normal children have about 6-8 attacks of upper respiratory illness per year, but these are mostly viral, confined to the upper respiratory tract, and resolve spontaneously. These do not affect her growth or weight gain.
- **Growth failure**: student should ask the caretaker if the child has lost weight or there has been a decrease in growth velocity recently. In that case a chronic infection should be looked for.

BIRTH HISTORY

a) **Antenatal history:**
   This should include details of any events (in each trimester) that could have caused a congenital defect in the child. Specific enquiries should be made about any viral illness (fever with rash), drugs taken, especially in the first trimester and maternal diabetes. A bad obstetric history (recurrent spontaneous abortions/ still births) supports a genetic/ chromosomal abnormality.

b) **Intrapartum history:**

   Details of delivery: Student should ask about prematurity, requirement of resuscitative measures, and birth asphyxia.

b) **Postpartum period:**
   Student should ask about feeding difficulties (suck-rest-suck cycle), failure to thrive, and NICU admission. These will generally be found in an ASD associated with other cardiac anomalies (in which case they are detected earlier),

   Since ASD may be a part of complex congenital anomalies, and the newborn may have required intensive care for these.

Growth and D

evelopmental History:

A detailed history of ages at which the milestones were achieved should be noted.

Approximately 65% of children with congenital heart defect have been found to have delayed development independent of chronic hypoxia.

Dietary History

In view of the growth failure these children have, it is important to rule out dietary insufficiency. A detailed history of dietary intake, with special emphasis on calories and protein intake is essential.

Immunization History:

All routine immunizations should have been given, and enquiry of this should be made. Influenza vaccine should be given if available

Family History:

Family history should include three generations, both on the maternal as well as paternal side.

History of consanguinous marriage between parents should be enquired into, as should the presence of cardiac defects, other congenital anomalies, early deaths, and mental retardation in other family members.

Socio-economic history:

This is important in view of the growth failure that the child is having, to rule out under nutrition as a cause.

Systemic Review of symptoms:

Ask for history of **respiratory distress**. Some patients may have tachypnoea due to pulmonary overload, which may be missed by the caretaker in an otherwise asymptomatic child.

Recurrent respiratory infections are a symptom of increased pulmonary congestion, and support the diagnosis of an acyanotic congenital heart defect.

Neurological symptoms and **other congenital anomalies** may be present as a part of certain genetic/chromosomal defects/ syndromes.

CHECK LIST FOR HISTORY TAKING IN A CASE OF ASD

- Usually asymptomatic, discovered accidently
- Effort intolerance
- Recurrent symptoms of respiratory distress/ cardiac failure (in a large defect or older patient)
- growth failure

EXAMINATION

General Examination:

Introduce yourself and obtain consent for examination. Wash hands thoroughly. Have the caretaker close by, and explain to the child what is being done. Expose the relevant areas

Note the general appearance:

Failure to thrive is seen in children with ASD because of increased oxygen and energy demand by the heart and lungs. The student should record the anthropometric measurements, plot them on the relevant growth charts and interpret them.

Recurrent pneumonia/ congestive cardiac failure are rare in children with ASD except those with a large defect. Hence **respiratory distress** is present in children with large defects or those with complex cardiac defects which will therefore be diagnosed earlier.

Student should carefully look for **dysmorphism and other congenital malformations** as ASD is commonly found as a part and parcel of several complex cardiac defects.

Vital Signs:

Pulse rate and pulse volume should be recorded. Pulse volume is normal in patients with uncomplicated ASD, as are all peripheral pulses, which should also be palpated. If there is pulmonary congestion leading to heart failure, there may be tachycardia.

Student should count the **respiratory rate** for at least 30 seconds in all patients older than two months (in those less than 2 months, count for at least 1 minute). Pulmonary congestion due to a large defect may manifest only as **tachypnea** which may be missed by the caretaker.

Temperature should be recorded to rule out infection as a cause of tachypnea.

Blood pressure should be recorded as a baseline parameter.

- **Extracardiac manifestations of cardiac disease**

Since most cases are discovered accidently, no extracardiac signs of a cardiac illness are expected. This should be emphasized by the student. Signs of cardiac failure, clubbing or cyanosis are generally not found in an isolated ASD.

Examination of the cardiovascular system:

Shape of the precordium:

A **precordial bulge** is best noted by observing from the foot end of the bed, with your eyes at the same level as the patient's chest. In this position the two hemithoraces can be compared. In ASD, the child may have a slight precordial bulge (due to right ventricular enlargement) which may be missed unless carefully looked for.

Palpation of the heart should begin with the patient in the supine position at 30 degrees. If the heart is not felt in this position, the patient can be examined in sitting posture, leaning forward. **The apical impulse** is generally normal in patients of ASD. However, in older children, or those with a large defect, it may be shifted laterally due to a right ventricular enlargement.

A left parasternal heave, again a sign of right ventricular enlargement may be present especially if the right ventricular has to handle a large volume load.

Heart sounds: The first heart sound may be normal or loud at the left lower parasternal border.

The characteristic finding in ASD is a **widely split and fixed second sound (the splitting interval unaffected by respiration)** heard best in the pulmonary area.

In a normal child during inspiration (when the intrathoracic pressure is negative) the venous return to the heart increases and more blood flows through the pulmonary valve. Hence it closes later. At the same time, cardiac output decreases (again because of the negative intrathoracic pressure) and the aortic valve closes early; i.e. the splitting of the second sound is wide.

During expiration the reverse occurs. The venous return diminishes (since the intrathoracic pressure is positive) and pulmonary valve closes early, while the cardiac output increases and the aortic valve closes later, thereby narrowing the splitting of the second heart sound.

In the presence of an ASD, variations in systemic venous return during respiration are counterbalanced by reciprocal changes in the flow through the ASD, maintaining total right ventricular flow more or less constant. Hence, the right ventricular diastolic filling is increased constantly in all phases of respiration and the pulmonary valve always closes later. This does not vary with respiration.

There is usually an **ejection systolic murmur** heard best in the left upper parasternal area, due to an increased blood flow across the right ventricular outflow tract into the pulmonary artery (functional pulmonary stenosis). This is a soft/medium pitched murmur, not accompanied by a thrill (maximum grade 2/6).

Examination of other systems:

The **respiratory system** is examined to rule out a non-cardiac diagnosis. The presence of pulmonary crepitations signifies infection more often than cardiac failure.

A detailed assessment of his mental development is essential to look for any associated **developmental anomaly**.

A careful survey of all systems should be made to exclude any **associated congenital anomalies.**

CHECK LIST FOR THE EXAMINATION FINDINGS IN ASD

- Failure to thrive
- Effort intolerance
- Mild precordial bulge with or without left parasternal lift
- Wide, fixed split of the second heart sound

INVESTIGATIONS

Chest RadiographX-ray chest shows enlargement of the right ventricle, right atrium, the pulmonary artery, and increased pulmonary vascularity. It is best seen in the lateral view because right ventricle enlarges anteriorly (behind the sternum).

Electrocardiogram

ECG is normal unless right ventricular hypertrophy has developed later in life.

Echocardiography

It shows

- o   The location and size of the defect,
- o   The right ventricle overload
- o   Abnormal motion of the interventricular septum, which flattens during diastole due to increased flow.

Magnetic Resonance Imaging

MRI is useful in those with inconclusive clinical and echocardiographic findings.

Cardiac catheterization

This is indicated in whom pulmonary hypertension and vascular obstructive disease are suspected.

CASE SUMMARY

A six years old girl is brought for a preschool checkup to the clinic. She weighs 15 kg (71% of the optimum weight), and her height is 90cm (80% of the optimum).

On examination she has a slight precordial bulge, and a fixed, wide split of the second heart sound heard best in the pulmonary area. She also has a grade 2/6 ejection systolic murmur heard in the left 2nd and 3rd intercostal area in the parasternal region.

PROVISIONAL DIAGNOSIS

Congenital heart disease with Atrial septal defect

CLINICAL DISCUSSION

Student should be able to:

- •   Diagnose growth retardation in the patient
- •   Notice the mild precordial bulge
- •   Identify the fixed and wide split second heart sound,
- •   Identify the soft ejection systolic murmur and differentiate it from a functional murmur

LEARNING OUTCOMES

The student should be able to:

- •   Explain the pathophysiology of ASD, and how it differs from other left-to-right shunts (why it is asymptomatic)
- •   Explain the wide split second heart sound

- Suggest relevant investigations and outline a plan of management.
- Understand the importance of examining every child completely, and to look for a cause of failure to thrive.

COMMONLY ASKED QUESTIONS

1. How will you differentiate the ejection systolic murmur of an ASD from a functional murmur?
2. What are the causes of failure to thrive?
3. What investigations are relevant for ASD?
4. What are the causes of an ejection systolic murmur in the left second intercostal space, and how will you differentiate them?

When pulmonary hypertension develops (even in a case of ASD), the second sound becomes loud, and right ventricle hypertrophies (evident in an ECG). Only the early component of the systolic murmer may be heard wirh pulmunary hypertension. Other peripheral signs of hyperdynamic circulation will be present.

In pulmonary stenosis, the second heart sound is soft, and there is no clinical evidence of pulmonary vascular congestion. Right ventricular hypertrophy is present in these cases

HIGH ACHIEVER QUESTIONS

5. What is the mechanism of the wide, fixed split in the second heart sound?

Answer: (explained under the examination findings above)

6. Should an asymptomatic ASD be closed surgically?

Answer: Smaller defects are followed up in small infants for a few years, because many of them will close spontaneously, especially those ≤ 3 mm in diameter. If shunting persists, or the defect is ≥ 5 mm, it should be closed.

7. Why should an asymptomatic defect be treated surgically?

Answer: The primary reason for closing the defect is to prevent pulmonary vascular obstructive disease. If it is closed before the age of 40 years, it also reduces the incidence of atrial fibrillation. Defect is closed either surgically or by a catheter – delivered device.

COMMON MISTAKES

8. Missing the case altogether

9. Not being able to interpret failure to thrive
10. Missing the wide fixed split 2nd sound
11. Missing the murmur

Partial anomalous pulmonary venous return to the systemic venous circulation has many of the physiologic characteristics of an atrial defect and in fact is often associated with such a defect.

OVERVIEW

Rheumatic fever is considered a delayed autoimmune response in a genetically predisposed individual to group A β hemolytic streptococci. The incidence of rheumatic fever in developing countries is about 150 per 100,000 population, with mortality rates as high as 8 per 100,000 from heart involvement, compared with less than 1 per 100,000 and less than 2 per 100,000 respectively, in developed countries. In Malaysia, a prevalence study of rheumatic heart disease in primary school children in Kelantan revealed a prevalence rate of 0.11 per thousand. The reported incidence of first attack was 15.8/ 100,000 per year and recurrent attack of 5.38/100,000 per year

The commonest age when the child gets the first attack of rheumatic fever is 5-15 years. It is rare below the age of three years. The average latent period between the attack of pharyngitis and rheumatic fever is about two weeks. For reasons unknown, mitral valve is the commonest to be damaged, followed by the aortic valve, and then the tricuspid valve. Pulmonary valve is rarely affected. If mitral valve is not involved, diagnosis of rheumatic heart disease is in doubt. If it occurs before the age of five years, it is more severe and chronic.

TYPES OF CASES FOR CLINICAL EXAMINATION:

OSCE/SHORT CASE

Student may be asked to examine the cardiovascular system, or only the precordium.

In examination of the cardiovascular system, the student should examine the extracardiac manifestations of a cardiac illness, i.e. all the peripheral pulses, jugular venous pulse, blood pressure, respiratory rate, pedal edema, clubbing and cyanosis. Then examine the precordium, and auscultate the chest (for respiratory and cardiac findings) and look for hepatomegaly.

LONG CASE

The student should be able to take a detailed history to establish the diagnosis of a cardiovascular disease and to differentiate it from pulmonary disorders. A complete examination of the cardiovascular system and all the other systems is done meticulously to look for complications like cardiac failure, infective endocarditis and systemic embolization. He should also look for growth retardation. Student should be able to suggest relevant investigations and principles of management.

CASE VIGNETTE

A fifteen years old girl is admitted with history of cough and breathlessness for the past three weeks. She was admitted with pain and swelling of both knee joints about three years ago, and was discharged after three weeks with advice to take some tablets daily. She has defaulted on her medication for the past two months as she thought she was cured and did not need the drugs.

DIFFERENTIAL DIAGNOSIS

1. Rheumatic heart disease with cardiac failure
2. Bronchial asthma
3. Community acquired pneumonia
4. Infective endocarditis

The hallmark of bronchial asthma is a history of recurrent attacks. There is usually a positive family history of asthma/ other allergic disorders. Patient may also have evidence of eczema/inhalant allergen sensitization, a good response to bronchodilators and asymptomatic periods in between with normal growth.

Community acquired pneumonia is preceded/accompanied by fever.

Past history of hospital admission due to pain in both knee joints with advice to take some tablets daily is suggestive of rheumatic fever.

A child with fever, cardiac murmurs, arthralgia, and raised ESR can be either reactivation of rheumatic fever or infective endocarditis. Differentiation is difficult and observation for a few days along with relevant investigations is required. In recurrence of rheumatic activity, especially with prolonged, indolent carditis, the Duckett Jones criteria cannot be applied.

HISTORY

A detailed **history of presenting illness** should include:

*   Presence/ absence of **fever:**

Fever denotes infection. High continuous fever is seen in bacterial pneumonia. Viral pneumonia or that caused by atypical pathogens will have low grade fever. Bronchial asthma is often precipitated by viral upper respiratory tract infection with low grade fever.

Fever may accompany rheumatic activity, but cardiac failure without fever may also be the sign of renewed rheumatic activity.

- Details of **cough and breathlessness:**

Is the cough productive/non-productive? Is it more at night? Does it disturb her sleep?

Is the breathlessness more on exertion? Or on lying down? Does she wake up at night with sudden breathlessness (paroxysmal nocturnal dyspnea)? Does she sleep propped up with pillows?

Productive cough with fever supports the diagnosis of pneumonia.

Cough with pink frothy sputum and severe dyspnea indicates pulmonary edema.

Cough becoming worse at night suggests bronchial asthma, but in cardiac failure also cough increases on lying down. However, there is no diurnal variation in cardiac failure.

Student should specifically ask history suggestive of **paroxysmal nocturnal dyspnea (PND).** The patient will sleep for a few hours, and then wake up with sudden breathlessness, gasping for air. After about an hour (during which she is sitting upright), she becomes comfortable and goes back to sleep. Normally during upright posture (in the daytime) fluid collects in the dependent part (the lower limbs) even without cardiac failure/ overt edema. When we lie down at night this fluid gets absorbed, increasing the intravascular volume which a normal heart is able to handle. In early left-sided cardiac failure, this causes pulmonary congestion and patient wakes up with dyspnea.

Specific history of **orthopnoea** should be taken. The patient becomes more dyspnoic on lying supine. It suggests left heart failure or bronchial asthma. Orthopnoea may be preceded by dry cough and may be accompanied by a wheeze.

The student should ask about **pedal edema.** The patient may not notice overt edema, but may be able to tell you that her footwear becomes tight towards evenings.

A failing heart causes activation of sympathetic-adrenal system. This causes sympathetically mediated renal vasoconstriction which activates the rennin-angiotensin-aldosterone mechanism with increased retention of sodium and water. The Increased preload increases the capillary venous pressure, and this causes leakage of fluid into the interstitial compartment, especially in the dependent parts of the body (lower limbs around the ankles in an upright person, and in the sacral area if the patient is bed-ridden).

- Student should ask for history of **palpitations,** which may be caused by arrhythmias or sympathetic overdrive.

Past History

The student should enquire about symptoms suggestive of rheumatic fever in the past. In more than half the cases, history suggestive of rheumatic fever may not be forthcoming.

- Ask for **migratory polyarthritis.** It involves the large joints (knees, ankles, elbows and wrists), and migrates from one joint to another in a few days. The joints are red, swollen and tender, and movements are painful. At least two or more joints should be involved to label it as "polyarthritis". Once it subsides there is no residual deformity. For this reason it is said "rheumatic fever licks the joints but bites the heart".
- Previous attacks of **carditis** may be missed by the patient unless she sought medical help then. Alternatively, she may remember suffering from fatigue, breathlessness and palpitations at that time.
- Student should specifically enquire whether the patient had **Fever** during the attacks of joint pains/ palpitations.
- Enquiry about **chorea** should be made specifically.
- Details of any previous admissions, investigations done and their reports (if known to the patient or her caretaker) should be asked for and noted.

Growth and Developmental History:

If the patient has had recurrent attacks of rheumatic fever, she is likely to be stunted. Hence a detailed history of growth should be taken.

Dietary History and Socio-economic History

These are important in view of the stunting of growth. Also, rheumatic fever is a disease of the lower socio-economic class.

Systemic Review of symptoms:

Respiratory distress is a sign of failing heart, and denotes the severity of pulmonary congestion.

Abdominal pain may be due to hepatomegaly, or pericardial effusion or inflammation of the abdominal serous surfaces.

Check List for History Taking In A Case Of Chronic Rheumatic Heart Disease

- Exertional dyspnoea / PND/ orthopnoea
- Palpitations
- Swelling over feet/ ankles
- Joint pains
- Cough/sputum/ hemoptysis
- Abdominal pain
- Fever

EXAMINATION

General Examination:

Introduce yourself and obtain consent for examination. Wash hands thoroughly. Have the caretaker close by, and explain to the child what is being done. Expose the relevant areas as you need to examine them.

- **General appearance**
  Is the patient comfortable, or in **respiratory distress**? Note the signs of respiratory distress.

  Irritability/ confusion are signs of cerebral hypoxia and denote severe respiratory distress.

  Growth failure: The student should measure her weight and height and record it.

- **Vital Signs:**

  Pulse rate and volume should be recorded.

  Tachycardia is a sign of carditis/ cardiac failure, and recording it on a daily basis will tell you whether the carditis/cardiac failure is responding to treatment or not. Pulse will be rapid and of low volume when myocardial contractility is compromised.

  In mitral insufficiency pulse is high volume. If mitral stenosis is the dominant lesion, pulse will be low volume due to a low cardiac output.

Student should check for irregularity of the pulse.

All **peripheral pulses** should be palpated. Absence of a peripheral pulse may indicate thromboembolism. In such a case, look carefully for signs of impending gangrene.

Respiratory rate is an indicator of pulmonary congestion, and indirectly of cardiac failure. This should also be recorded daily to monitor the progress of disease.

Blood Pressure is low in cardiac failure. Hence this also forms a part of daily monitoring of the progress of the disease.

Temperature: if fever is present, either there is superadded infection (pneumonia), or it is a part of reactivation of rheumatic activity, or development of infective endocarditis.

Pedal edema: Is seen by applying pressure for about 10 seconds over the medial malleolus, and noticing a "pit" or indentation created by displacement of fluid.

Jugular venous pulse (JVP) in the right side of the neck is seen with the patient's head raised at an angle of 45^0 Normal JVP is about 6-8 centimetres measured above the right atrium (i.e. the vertical height above the manubrium sternum). It is raised in congestive cardiac failure denoting the increased preload or venous congestion.

The student should examine the nails and mucosa for **anemia,** as this can worsen the heart failure.

Clubbing and cyanosis are not found in a case of chronic rheumatic heart disease.

Chorea usually occurs alone, though rarely it can occur as a part of acute rheumatic activity. It consists of semi-purposeful, uncontrolled movements, aggravated by stress that disappears during sleep.

Student should look for **signs of infective endocarditis**, like splinter hemorrhages, clubbing and pallor, Janeway lesions, Osler's nodes.

Examination of the cardiovascular system:

- **Shape of the precordium :**

A **precordial bulge** is best noted by observing from the foot end of the bed, with your eyes at the same level as the patient's chest. In this position the two hemithoraces can be compared. The presence of a bulge indicates long standing disease.

Mitral stenosis (MS) causes an obstruction in blood flow from the left atrium to left ventricle. There is therefore an increase in pressure within the left atrium, which is transmitted to the pulmonary vasculature, and right side of the heart (so there is right ventricular hypertrophy). In this case, a left parasternal heave may be noticed (described below). However, mitral stenosis often coexists with mitral regurgitation which may cause left ventricular hypertrophy also.

- Locate the **apical impulse.** It is hyperdynamic due to the volume overload in severe mitral regurgitation, and the apex may be shifted down and laterally in left ventricular dilatation and hypertrophy. In pure MS, there is right ventricular hypertrophy which causes the displacement of the apical impulse laterally in the fifth intercostal space.
- **A left parasternal heave** is palpable in the lower left parasternal region in long standing mitral valve disease due to right ventricular hypertrophy as a consequence of chronic pulmonary hypertension.
- **A systolic thrill** may be palpable at the apex in a case of mitral regurgitation, and a **diastolic thrill** if mitral stenosis is present.
- The **Pulmonary component of the second heart sound** may be palpable in the left second intercostal space in severe pulmonary hypertension.
- **The first heart sound** at the apex is loud in mitral stenosis, but soft in regurgitation, when it may be buried in the pansystolic murmur. If both the lesions co-exist the intensity of the 1st heart sound depends on the dominance of the underlying lesion.
- The **second sound** is loud in the pulmonary area if pulmonary hypertension has developed.
- The murmur of MS is a low-pitched, rumbling, **mid-diastolic murmur** heard in the mitral are. It does not radiate, and is best heard with the bell of the stethoscope with the patient in left lateral position. A presystolic accentuation is heard if there is no atrial fibrillation. It is preceded by the **opening snap** which is heard just after the second sound at the apex or medial to the apex.
- A **holosystolic murmur** at the apex that radiates to the axilla is pathognomonic of mitral insufficiency. The characteristic murmur is at least grade 3/6.

- If the patient has developed pulmonary hypertension, an **ejection systolic murmur** will be heard in the left 2nd intercostal space.
- Patients with mitral valvular lesions with pulmonary hypertension may develop functional tricuspid insufficiency (TR) due to dilatation of right ventricle, and a **pansystolic murmur** may be heard in the left lower parasternal region. This may be confused with the murmur due to MR. However,a TR murmur is confined to the left lower parasternal area, increases in intensity and duration during inspiration and is accompanied with prominent V wave in the jugular venous pulse.

  Mitral stenosis takes years to develop, whereas insufficiency may be seen in acute rheumatic fever also because of dilatation of the valve ring due to myocarditis. This murmur disappears as carditis resolves. The organic murmur appears later.

Examination of other systems:

Respiratory system should be examined for crepitations at the base of the lungs and for pleural effusion (usually right-sided). Lungs should also be examined to exclude pneumonia as the primary diagnosis.

Abdomen should be examined to see the **size of liver**, which may be increased due to right heart failure. Normally up to 2 centimetres of liver is palpable below the subcostal margin in the midclavicular line. More than this denotes hepatomegaly. It may be pushed down due to pulmonary congestion. Hence the upper border of liver should be percussed and the intercostal space where its upper margin is present should be recorded. The span of a normal liver is 8-9 centimetres. Any increase in size beyond this denotes hepatomegaly.

In acute cardiac failure hepatomegaly is soft and tender due to acute congestion, while in chronic/ recurrent heart failure liver fibrosis sets in and hepatomegaly is firm and non-tender.

Neurological Examination for evidence of chorea and stroke (due to thromboembolism due to atrial fibrillation).

Check List for the Examination Findings in Chronic Rheumatic Heart Disease

- Tachycardia , with high volume pulse in MR, low volume in MS
- Irregular pulse in atrial fibrillation

- Tachypnea/exertional dyspnea
- Raised JVP
- Pedal edema
- Locate and discern the type of apical impulse
- Left parasternal heave
- Systolicl/diastolic thrill
- Palpable/loud second sound
- Murmurs over the precordium
- Crepitations in bases of lungs
- Tender, soft, hepatomegaly
- Evidence of infective endocarditis

INVESTIGATIONS

Electrocardiography

ECG is normal in mild cases.

In severe MR, it shows a prominent bifid P wave, left ventricular and atrial hypertrophy, and right ventricular hypertrophy if pulmonary hypertension has developed.

In severe MS, the P wave is notched and prominent, and evidence of right ventricular hypertrophy is seen. Atrial fibrillation is a common late manifestation.

Roentgenography

X-ray chest shows prominence of left atrium and left ventricle in MR.

In Mitral stenosis, chest radiography shows left atrial enlargement and prominent pulmonary artery, with increased size of right heart chambers. In severe obstruction the apices of lungs show greater perfusion (reverse of normal) due to redistribution of pulmonary flow.

Echocardiography

Echocardiogram shows left atrial and left ventricular enlargement, and thickened mitral valve, and Doppler studies demonstrate the severity of regurgitation in MR.

In MS, thickening of the mitral valve with narrowing of the orifice is seen along with left atrial enlargement. Doppler studies can estimate the pressure gradient.

Investigations Important For Management of the Patient

Full blood count to rule out infections

ESR/CRP to document presence/absence of rheumatic activity

Liver function tests, renal function tests, serum electrolytes (before commencing therapy)

Urine routine and microscopic examination to look for hematuria (for bacterial endocarditis)

CT scan if stroke is suspected

CASE SUMMARY

A fifteen years old girl is admitted with history of cough and breathlessness for the past three weeks. She was admitted with pain and swelling of both knee joints about three years ago, and was discharged after three weeks with advice to take some tablets daily. She has defaulted on her medication for the past two months as she thought she was cured and did not need the drugs.

On examination she is in respiratory distress, has tachycardia and tachypnea. Her JVP is raised. She is lying in bed with two pillows under her head. She also has bilateral pitting pedal edema.

Examination of the cardiovascular system reveals a precordial bulge with a hyperdynamic precordium. The apex beat is palpable in the 7th intercostal space 2cms lateral to the midclavicular line. There is a left parasternal heave. A systolic thrill is palpable at the apex. On auscultation in the apical area a pansystolic murmurs is heard at the apex along with a low pitched diastolic murmur. The pansystolic murmur radiates to the axilla. The 2nd sound is loud in the pulmonary area.

Examination of other systems reveals crepitations in the bases of both lungs, and a tender palpable liver measuring 5cms below the subcostal margin in the midclavicular line.

CLINICAL DISCUSSION

The student should be able to
- Elicit a relevant history of past attack/s of rheumatic fever
- Detect a raised JVP, pedal edema, tachycardia and respiratory distress
- Identify the various murmurs and know how to interpret them.

LEARNING OUTCOMES
The student should be able to

- Explain the pathophysiology of rheumatic valve disease
- Explain the pathophysiology of cardiac failure and the pathogenesis of all the clinical signs found in a case of chronic rheumatic disease
- Suggest relevant investigations, and interpret them
- Outline a plan of management of such a case.

COMMONLY ASKED QUESTIONS

- What are the causes of a pansystolic murmur over the precordium?

Answer: a) Ventricular septal defect

b) Mitral insufficiency

c) Tricuspid insufficiency

- What is paroxysmal nocturnal dyspnea? Why is the patient not dyspnoeic during the daytime?

- What is the pathogenesis of edema in a case of cardiac failure?

- What is the differential diagnosis of a patient presenting with edema?

Answer: a) When hepatic failure is the cause of anasarca, it usually begins form the abdomen (ascites) because of increased pressure in the lymphatics draining the area. The patient looks extremely cachexic, except for the distended abdomen ("a lemon on toothpicks").

b) In anasarca due to a renal pathology, the edema begins from the soft tissue around the eyes and is generally more early in the morning.

c) in a case of cardiac failure, the edema begins from the lower limbs (pathogenesis described above)

- Outline a plan of management for this patient.

Answer:

o Assess the oxygenation (SPO_2) and provide oxygen inhalation if necessary

- o Elevate the head end of the bed

- o Send relevant investigations

- o Administer diuretics to reduce the preload

- o ACE-inhibitors to reduce the systemic resistance (afterload) so that less blood returns to the left atrium

- o Administer digoxin for increasing myocardial contractility

- o Advise bed rest, salt restricted diet

- o Monitor vitals, weight, urine output and ESR to document response

- o Patient education on the importance of

  - secondary prophylaxis against fresh attacks of rheumatic fever

  - Regular antenatal check up whenever she has pregnancy, because the blood volume increases and she may develop frank left heart failure.

HIGH ACHIEVER QUESTIONS

- What are the signs of pulmonary hypertension?

Answer:

- o Left parasternal heave

- o 2nd sound becomes loud/palpable

- o An ejection systolic murmur appears in the 2nd left intercostal space

- o **Graham Steel murmur** in the pulmonary area. This is a systolic-diastolic murmur caused by pulmonary hypertension combined with dilatation of the pulmonary valve ring.

- Is rheumatic fever a familial disease?

  Answer: Familial incidence of rheumatic fever has been mentioned, but laboratory evidence is not conclusive

- List the complications of mitral valve insufficiency and stenosis

Answer: a) atrial fibrillation

b) infective endocarditis

c) right heart failure

d) ventricular arrhythmias

- When do you label a mitral stenotic lesion as severe?

  Answer:

  o Long duration of the diastolic murmur with presystolic accentuation

  o Duration between the 2nd sound and opening snap is shortened

- Where is the blood clot formed for embolization to occur?

  Answer:

  It is formed in the left atrium in only mitral stenosis.

- What is the significance of opening snap?

  Answer:

  An opening snap signifies that the mitral valve is still pliable and surgical repair is possible. If the valve gets calcified, the snap disappears and the valve has to be replaced.

- Can a patient of Mitral stenosis develop hoarseness of voice?

  Answer:

  He can develop hoarseness of voice due to compression of left recurrent laryngeal nerve between the aorta and the enlarged left atrium.

COMMON MISTAKES

- Not eliciting the history of previous attacks of rheumatic fever
- Missing a raised JVP, anemia, tachypnea
- Missing the loud 2nd sound
- Missing the irregular pulse
- Missing the murmur of MS, especially as it disappears after exercise

The appearance of congestive heart failure in a rheumatic child is always interpreted as evidence of active disease and, by implication, involvement of the myocardium as well as the valves. When there is valvar regurgitation sufficient to cause congestive heart failure, surgery may be needed and may be life-saving, despite associated myocardial damage. When in doubt, surgery is probably the best choice because any myocardial problem is only aggravated by the valvar abnormality. The idea that cardiac surgery is specifically prohibited in the face of active rheumatic disease is no longer tenable

CASE 21: INFECTIVE ENDOCARDITIS
NANDAKUMAR

OVERVIEW

In patients with infective endocarditis (IE), the history is very variable. Fever and chills are the most common symptoms; anorexia, weight loss, malaise, headache, myalgia, night sweats, shortness of breath, cough, or joint pains are often the regular symptoms complained of.

Infective endocarditis (IE), may present with signs of congestive heart failure due to valvular insufficiency. Approximately 20% of the cases present with focal neurologic complaints and stroke syndromes(Embolic stroke). Other obvious reasons may be due to intracerebral hemorrhage and multiple micro abscesses.

Dyspnea, cough, and chest pain are common complaints seen in intravenous drug users. This may be due to the predominance of tricuspid valve endocarditis and secondary embolic showering of the pulmonary vasculature. In such circumstances, signs of pulmonary infection or infarction are frequent occurrences.

Signs of systemic septic emboli are more commonly associated with mitral valve vegetations. Signs of congestive heart failure, such as distended neck veins, frequently are due to acute left-sided valvular insufficiency.

The patient should be questioned regarding invasive procedures carried out on him and drug use that may be causing the bacteremia. Most sub-acute disease is caused by *Streptococcus viridans* infection and is related to dental disease. In 85% of patients, the symptoms of endocarditis appear within two weeks of dental or other invasive procedures.

Cases for Examination

IE may be presented as LONG CASE or OSCE. The the former a general approach including history and physical examination is required with a throughful approach in requesting for relevant investigations especially when complications supervene.

In the OSCE specific instructions would be given to test the student in demonstrating skills in cardiovascular examination,neurological and other systems.

CASE VIGNETTE:

A 35 year old, unemployed gentleman who is HIV positive is admitted to the hospital with the following complaints:

He had sore throat for a week following which he developed a low grade fever which has been persistent till the current consultation. Fever is low grade and not associated with chills and rigors. There is no headache, flu like symptoms , cough or photophobia.

The patient has been having shortness of breath on exertion and palpitations for the past three weeks but there is no chest pain or leg oedema.

He also complains of abdominal pain and diarrhoea (3-4 episodes a day) which is preceded by food intake and nausea. Vomitus is not bile stained and is of variable in amount. There is no blood in the vomitus and is not projectile.

There is also urgency and frequency of micturition. Arthralgia has been noticed over the past three weeks limited to 2-3 joints. They are asymmetrical and there is no swelling.

PAST MEDICAL HISTORY
1. HIV positive, diagnosed 10 years ago , currently he is on HAART (Highly active anti-Retroviral therapy) T.Stocrin 1 tab, T. Tenofir + Emtricitabine 1 tab
2. Tuberculosis, diagnosed a few months ago, currently on maintenance therapy, Rifampican 450mg OD, Isoniazide 300mg OD, Piramzinamide 10mg OD

PAST SURGICAL HISTORY /ALLERGY HISTORY: NIL
FAMILY HISTORY
Parents, 5 siblings and 3 children are all healthy.

SOCIAL HISTORY
1. Smoker, since the age of 15 years old till now (20 years), five sticks per day
2. Intravenous drug abuser, started 5 years ago. Active IVDU, last injection taken- yesterday – Right inguinal route – using heroin

Note:

- In a typical case scenario as illustrated the student is expected to perform a thorough evaluation exhibiting correct techniques so as to detect positive clinical findings to establish the diagnosis. Examination of the cardiovascular and neurological systems would be performed following the techniques described in other relevant cases.

- The social history as illustrated in this case could easily affect a student to be judgmental. This must be avoided totally. All the complications of IVDU other than IE highlighted here (hepatitis etc) would apply as the student is expected to be holistic in his approach.

GENERAL PHYSICAL EXAMINATION

Patient appears to be lying comfortably on a semi-reclined bed. He is thin built, does not appear to be in any respiratory distress. On a closer look of the nails, - clubbing is present over all 10 digits, splinter hemorrhages are seen on the left ring and middle finger, and on all the fingers over the right hand. No Osler's nodes seen

General appearance:
Describe the appearance as shown here: He is pink, no pallor, capillaries refilling time is around 2 seconds
Palm: - No Janeway lesions, palm is pink, warm and dry
Pulse: - 86 bpm, regular rhythm, good volume, no specific character appreciated, no radio-radial delay
Needle prick injuries can be seen over the flexor of both arms.
Multiple petechial 'rashes' over the upper and lower limbs (see Figure1).

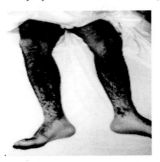

Fig 1:Middle-aged man with a history of intravenous drug use who presented with severe myalgias and a petechial rash. He was diagnosed with right-sided staphylococcal endocarditis.

Blood pressure: 120/80 mmHg
Eyes: No sub conjunctival pallor, no icterus, no hemorrhage spots over the sub conjunctiva, no Roth spots
Oral cavity: Hydration is good, poor oral hygiene, mulitiple carious tooth , no petechial hemorrhage over mucous membrane
No cervical lymphadenopathy, No pedal edema elicited.

313

CARDIOVASCULAR EXAMINATION

Inspection: No chest deformity observed, no previous surgical scars, no apex beat appreciated

JVP was raised 11cm from RA. (5cm +6cm)

Palpation: Apex beat is at the 5[th]intercostal space, midclavicular line (not shifted), no thrills felt in all 4 auscultatory area, no parasternal heave

Auscultation: Normal S1S2 are heard at the 4 auscultatory areas. **Pan systolic murmur** is heard loudest over the tricuspid area, no radiation of the murmur is appreciated. Murmur increases on inspiration, no added sounds, no pericardial rub is heard.

RESPIRATORY EXAMINATION

No evidence of pulmonary emboli, cyanosis or unequal chest movement

ABDOMINAL EXAMINATION

The abdomen is flat, soft and non tender on palpation.

No organomegaly and non-pulsatile liver.

Note:

At the end of having taken a thorough history and performing a physical examination , the student should be able to suggest relevant investigations. It would be prudent to state which investigations are diagnostic in nature and which are requested to evaluate complications and assist in management.

Positive findings for Infective Endocarditis in the above clinical scenario are as follows:

Fever for 2 weeks, Arthralgia for 2 weeks, Upper respiratory tract symptoms , and Shortness of breath

Splinter hemorrhages seen on the left ring and middle finger and on all the fingers over the right hand.

clubbing present over all 10 digits

Multiple petechial rashes over the upper and lower limbs.

JVP was raised 11cm from RA. (5cm +6cm)

Pan systolic murmur was heard loudest over the tricuspid area.

BLOOD CULTURE:

Positive for *Staphylococcus aureusin .Two different samples taken on Day 1 & Day 2.*

Echocardiography

Vegetations over tricuspid valve, mild-moderate tricuspid regurgitation with PASP 24mmHg with trivial Mitral regurgitation.

NOTE: *There are two major and three minor criteria in the above case which fulfills the Duke criteria and confirms the patient's diagnosis as Right Sided Staphylococcal Endocarditis*

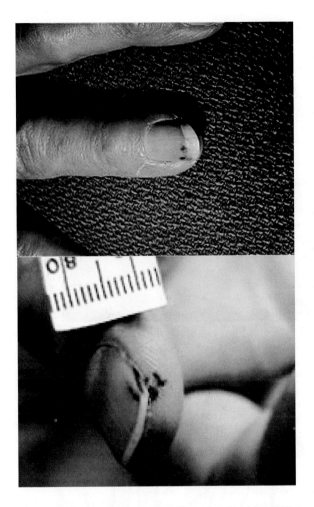

Fig 2:Splinter Hemorrhages: Non-blanching, linear reddish-brown lesions found under the nail bed

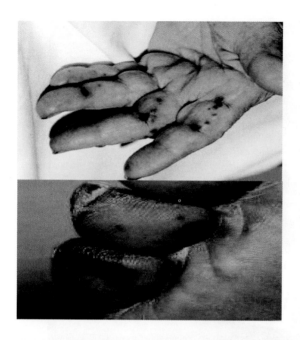

Fig 3:Janeway Lesions: Erythematous, blanching, non-painfulmacules on palms and soles

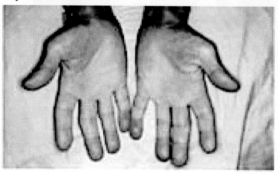

Fig 4:Osler's Nodes: Pink, Painful, Pea-sized,Pulp of the fingers/toes.

DIFFERENTIAL DIAGNOSES

- Atrial Myxoma
- Cardiac Neoplasms, Primary
- Endocarditis
- Lyme Disease
- Polymyalgia Rheumatica
- Reactive Arthritis
- Systemic Lupus Erythematosus

Note: A Student may anticipate other clinical signs that include the following.

He /she should be competent in discussing the basis of the signs detected (see OVERVIEW).
In a LONG CASE, questions may be asked on these complications.

- Stiff neck, Delirium, Paralysis, hemiparesis, aphasia
- Conjunctival hemorrhage, Pallor, Gallops,
- Cardiac arrhythmia
- Pericardial rub, Rales, Pleural friction rub
- Splenomegaly

Types of Infective endocarditis

Acute infective endocarditis
 Sub-acute native valve endocarditis
Intravenous-drug-abuse infective endocarditis
Prosthetic valve endocarditis
Pacemaker infective endocarditis
Bacteria-free infective endocarditis
Nosocomial infective endocarditis

Infective Endocarditis- Causative Organisms

Staphylococcus aureus infection is the most common cause of IE, including PVE, acute IE, and IVDA IE.

Approximately 35-60.5% of staphylococcal bacteremias are complicated by IE. And associated with valvular problems.The mortality rate of *S aureus* IE is 40-50%.

Streptococcus viridians: Accounts for 50-60% of cases of subacute disease. Most clinical signs and symptoms are mediated immunologically.

Streptococcus intermedius group: Accounts for 15% of streptococcal IE cases. *It*can actively invade tissue and can cause abscesses.

Abiotrophia: 5% of subacute cases of IE are due to this and associated with large vegetations that lead to embolization and a high rate of post-treatment relapse.

Group D streptococci: Most cases are subacute.The source is the gastrointestinal or genitourinary tract.It is the third most common cause of IE.

Group B streptococci: Acute disease develops in pregnant patients and older patients with underlying diseases (eg, cancer, diabetes, alcoholism).The mortality rate is 40%.

Pseudomonas aeruginosa: This is usually acute, except when it involves the right side of the heart in IVDA IE. Surgery is commonly required for cure.

HACEK

(ie, *Haemophilusaphrophilus, Actinobacillusactinomycetemcomitans, Cardiobacteriumhominis, Eikenellacorrodens, Kingellakingae*)These organisms usually cause subacute disease.They are the most common gram-negative organisms isolated from patients with IE.

Fungal: These usually cause subacute disease.The most common organism of both fungal NVE and fungal PVE is *Candida albicans*.

Multiple pathogens (polymicrobial) Pseudomonas *and enterococci are the most common combination of organisms.*It is observed in cases of IVDA IE. The cardiac surgery mortality rate is twice that associated with single-agent IE.

Note:

- *At the end of establishing the diagnosis the student is expected to outline clinical management. Again a holistic approach is expected in undergraduate examination considering the underlying social problem in addition to suggest specific management of infective endocarditis.*

- *Clearly this patient's management should also reiterate the management of TB and assessment and treatment of both HIV and its complications.*

- *A high achiever student would be expected to recognize and discuss adverse drug reactions, drug interaction and compliance to therapy.*

- **Treatment of Infective Endocarditis: Tailor therapy to results of susceptibility testing.**
    - Use parenteral drugs.
    - Plan for prolonged courses of antibiotics.
    - Be vigilant for adverse drug effects.
    - Use bactericidal agents.
    - Synergistic combinations are useful.
    - Monitor levels of aminoglycosides.

Antibiotics are the mainstay of treatment for infective endocarditis (IE). Goals to maximize treatment success are early diagnosis, accurate microorganism identification, reliable susceptibility testing, proper monitoring of toxic antimicrobial regimens, and aggressive surgical management of correctable mechanical complications.

Penicillin G is used for IE caused by S viridans or S bovis (0.1 mcg/mL)

Vancomycin is the drug of choice for patients who are allergic to penicillin, who have streptococcal endocarditis, & with methicillin-resistant S aureus (MRSA) IE, and beta-lactam–resistant gram-positive IE infections. The duration of treatment is 4 weeks in penicillin-susceptible streptococcal IE and 4-6 weeks for staphylococcal infections, prosthetic valve infections.

Gentamicin is an aminoglycoside used in combination therapy to attain bactericidal activity against enterococci and resistant streptococcal species, and for prosthetic staphylococcal IE.

Streptomycin is an aminoglycoside antibiotic that has bacteriocidal activity. It may be used for the treatment of streptococcal or enterococcal endocarditis.

Ampicillin and sulbactam (Unasyn) is a drug combination consisting of a beta-lactamase inhibitor with ampicillin. It interferes with bacterial cell wall synthesis during active replication.

CeftazidimeCeftazidime is a third-generation cephalosporin with broad-spectrum, gram-negative activity, including against pseudomonas. It is inhibiting cell wall biosynthesis.

Ceftriaxone (Rocephin) is given as once-daily treatment of S viridans or HACEK (ie, H aphrophilus, Aactinomycetemcomitans, C hominis, E corrodens, K kingae) IE. It is a third-generation cephalosporin with broad-spectrum gram-negative activity

Cefepime (Maxipime) is a fourth-generation cephalosporin with gram-negative coverage comparable to ceftazidime, but it has better gram-positive coverage and rapidly penetrates gram-negative cells.

Rifampin (Rifadin) is used in the treatment of staphylococcal infections associated with a foreign body, such as a prosthetic heart valve.Specifically, it interacts with bacterial RNA polymerase but does not inhibit the mammalian enzyme

COMMONLY ASKED QUESTIONS:

1. Briefly outline the pertinent aspects of counseling and in a patient who is an IVDU who is HIV positive so as to avoid infecting his spouse.

Answer: See case discussed under Ethics and confidentiality.

Fear and denial are the most common obstacles to HIV testing among those acknowledging that they have been at risk. The number of new cases of AIDS acquired from heterosexual intercourse is greater than from homosexual activity. Patients should therefore be encouraged to accept HIV testing in a wider range of settings than is currently the case.

Universal HIV testing is recommended in all the following:

- Those attending sexual health clinics.
- Antenatal services.
- Termination of pregnancy services.
- For those diagnosed with tuberculosis, hepatitis B, hepatitis C and lymphoma.
- All patients presenting for healthcare where HIV enters the differential diagnosis
- All patients diagnosed with a sexually transmitted infection.
- All men who have disclosed sexual contact with other men.

- All female sexual contacts of men who have sex with men
- All patients reporting a history of injecting drug use.
- All men and women known to be from a country of high HIV prevalence (>1%) - see up-to-date UN AIDS list in 'Internet and further reading' section, below.
- Blood donors.
- Dialysis patients.
- Organ transplant donors and recipients.
- Members of staff with a needle stick injury.

If the patient is still uncertain about wanting a test, give time to consider and return. They may wish to talk anonymously in confidence to a trained telephone advisor on one of the national helplines. These are the Sexual Health Information Helpline.

The pre-test discussion is meant to clear issues raised by the patient about the test and HIV infection. Written information is useful. Such issues often include:
- Risk and lifestyle.
- Benefits of knowing HIV status and treatment possibilities.
- What tests are available and which is recommended.
- The window period for testing.
- Seroconversion.
- The difference between HIV and AIDS.
- Confidentiality.

The post-test discussion for individuals who test HIV positive

This needs to be done with care and consideration that befits the importance of such a result.
- Follow good clinical practice when breaking bad news:
- Give the result face to face in a confidential environment.
- Give the information and result in a clear and direct manner.
- Use an appropriate confidential translation service if there are any language difficulties.
- Any individual testing HIV positive for the first time should be seen by a specialist (HIV clinician, specialist nurse or sexual health advisor.
- The specialist will address:Assessment of disease stage,Treatment plan, Partner notification

2. What are the criteria for diagnosing infective endocarditis in this patient according to the Duke's criteria?

Duke Criteria for Infective Endocarditis (IE)

Major criteria:

A. Positive blood culture for Infective Endocarditis

1- Typical microorganism consistent with IE from 2 separate blood cultures, as noted below:

- viridans streptococci, Streptococcus bovis, or HACEK* group, or

- community-acquired Staphylococcus aureus or enterococci, in the absence of a primary focus

  or

2- Microorganisms consistent with IE from persistently positive blood cultures defined as:

- 2 positive cultures of blood samples drawn >12 hours apart, or

- all of 3 or a majority of 4 separate cultures of blood (with first and last sample drawn 1 hour apart)

  B. Evidence of endocardial involvement

  1- Positive echocardiogram for IE defined as :

  oscillating intracardiac mass on valve or supporting structures, in the path of regurgitant jets, or abscess, or new partial dehiscence of prosthetic valve or

  2- New valvular regurgitation (worsening or changing of pre-existing murmur)

Minor criteria:

- Predisposition: predisposing heart condition or intravenous drug use

- Fever: temperature > 38.0° C (100.4° F)

- Vascular phenomena: major arterial emboli, septic pulmonary infarcts, mycotic aneurysm, intracranial hemorrhage, conjunctivalhemorrhages, and Janeway lesions

- Immunologic phenomena: glomerulonephritis, Osler's nodes, Roth spots, and rheumatoid factor

- Serological evidence of active infection with organism consistent with IE

- Echocardiographic findings: consistent with IE but do not meet a major criterion as noted above

- Possible IE
  - 2 major
  - 1 major and 3 minor

- 5 minor
- Rejected IE
  - Resolution of illness with four days or less of antibiotics

☞ *Note*: This patient fulfils the Duke's criteria for the following reasons:

Blood culture: Positive for Staphylococcus aureus in 2 different samples taken on Day 1 & Day2.Echocardiography shows vegetations over tricuspid valve, mild-moderate tricuspid regurgitation   with PASP 24mmHg with trivial Mitral regurgitation.

Also showing minor criteria such as fever for 2 weeks, arthralgia for 2 weeks, upper respiratory tract symptoms , splinter hemorrhages seen on the left ring and middle finger and on all the fingers over the right hand, clubbing present over all 10 digits, multiple petechial rashes over the upper and lower limbs.

JVP was raised 11cm from RA. (5cm +6cm)

3. What Laboratory Investigations will you do in a case of Infective endocarditis?

o   FBC to determine -Anemia of Chronic Disease in 50-80%
o   ESR "almost always" elevated.
o   May be normal in those with CHF.
o   Urinalysis:
  - o   Gross or microscopic hematuria
  - o   Casts in glomerulonephritis
  - o   Bacteriuria and pyuria
o   Elevated BUN and Creatinine
o   Rheumatoid factor present in 50%

4. What is the pathophysiology of neurological complications seen in infective endocarditis?

Pathophysiology:

o   Turbulent blood flow disrupts the endocardium making it "sticky"
o   Bacteremia delivers the organisms to the endocardial surface
o   Mechanical and inflammatory lesions promote adherence of the organisms to the endocardial surface
o   Eventual invasion of the valvular leaflets
o   Endothelial disruption leads to the release of sub endothelial factors (extracellular matrix proteins, thromboplastin, and tissue factors) that promote coagulation. Pathogens associated with IE bind to the resultant coagulum, and initiates tissue factor production, resulting in **progressive enlargement of "infected vegetation".**

o   Subsequent local extension causes tissuedamage and thismay result in abscess formation andseptic emboli may disseminate to remote organs, notably the brain, spleen, and kidney, with corresponding resultant clinical sequelae.

The incidence of CNS complications in infective endocarditis varies by organism (*Staphylococcus* species, 54%; *Enterococcus* species or *Streptococcus viridans*, ≥19%) and by location (mitral valve with *Staphylococcus aureus*, 87%). *Staphylococcus* species classically lead to embolization and often cause hemorrhage within the first 48 hours
Stroke: 15-50% of the CNS manifestations are due to embolic occlusion and/or stroke.
Half of patients with cerebral emboli also have systemic emboli.
Infectious aneurysms: Mycotic aneurysms (Mushroom shaped) occur in 15% of patients with infective endocarditis. A leak of a mycotic aneurysm can produce meningeal irritation and cause secondary aseptic meningitis
Intracranial hemorrhage: The prevalence of hemorrhage in CNS involvement of is 3-7%.
Seizures: Focal seizures may indicate an embolic etiology, whereas generalized seizures can result from meningitis.
Immune complex vasculitis: usually with streptococcal endocarditis.

5. What are the potential complications of infective endocarditis?

- Myocardial infarction, pericarditis, cardiac arrhythmia
- Cardiac valvular insufficiency
- Congestive heart failure
- Aortic root or myocardial abscesses
- Arterial emboli, infarcts, mycotic aneurysms
- Arthritis, myositis
- Glomerulonephritis, acute renal failure
- Stroke syndromes
- Mesenteric or splenic abscess or infarct

6. Discuss briefly the indications for surgery in infective endocarditis?
Approximately 15-25% of patients with IE eventually require surgery.

- Congestive heart failure refractory to standard medical therapy
- Fungal IE (except that caused by *Histoplasmacapsulatum*)
- Persistent sepsis after 72 hours of appropriate antibiotic treatment

- Recurrent septic emboli, especially after 2 weeks of antibiotic treatment
- Rupture of an aneurysm of the sinus of Valsalva
- Conduction disturbances caused by a septal abscess
- Kissing infection of the anterior mitral leaflet in patients with IE of the aortic valve

7. List the most frequently detected microbes? (State two common microbes implicated in Infective endocarditis and choice of antibiotics for treatment)

o *Staphylococcuaureus* infection is the most common cause of IE, including PVE, acute IE, and IVDA IE. Approximately 35-60.5% of staphylococcal bacteremias are complicated by IE. & associated with valvular problems. The mortality rate of *S aureus* IE is 40-50%..

o *Streptococcus viridians*:Accounts for 50-60% of cases of subacute disease. Most clinical signs and symptoms are mediated immunologically.

Treatment:

o Penicillin G is used for IE caused by S viridans or S bovis (0.1 mcg/mL)

o Vancomycin is the drug of choice for patients who are allergic to penicillin, who have streptococcal endocarditis, & with methicillin-resistant S aureus (MRSA) IE, and beta-lactam–resistant gram-positive IE infections. The duration of treatment is 4 weeks in penicillin-susceptible streptococcal IE and 4-6 weeks for staphylococcal infections, prosthetic valve infections.

8. List the conditions where you will advise antibiotic prophylaxis?
High Risk: Prophylaxis Recommended

Prosthetic cardiac valves, including bio prosthetic and homograft valves

Previous bacterial endocarditis

Complex cyanotic congenital heart disease (e.g., single ventricle states, transposition of the great arteries, tetralogy of Fallot)

Surgically constructed systemic pulmonary shunts or conduits

Moderate Risk: Prophylaxis Recommended

Acquired valvular dysfunction (eg, rheumatic heart disease)

Hypertrophic cardiomyopathy

Mitral valve prolapse with valvular regurgitation and/or thickened leaflets

Other conditions:

Respiratory Tract

Tonsillectomy

Violation of respiratory mucosa.

Rigid bronchoscopy.
Gastrointestinal Tract
Esophageal sclerotherapy or stricture dilation
ERCP
Biliary surgery
Violation of intestinal mucosa
GU Tract
Prostate surgery
Cystoscopy
Urethral dilatation.

TAKE HOME MESSAGE:

- Incidence decreases significantly after initiation of effective antibiotics.
- IVDA and the elderly are at greatest risk of developing IE.
- A thorough but timely evaluation (including serial blood cultures and an echo) is crucial to accurately diagnose and treat IE.
- Beware of life-threatening complications.

References:

1. Karchmer AW. Infective endocarditis. In: *Braunwald's Heart Disease: A Textbook of Cardiovascular Medicine.* 7th ed. WB Saunders Co; 2005:1633-1658.
2. Karchmer AW. Infective endocarditis. In: *Harrison's Principles of Internal Medicine.* 16th ed. McGraw-Hill; 2005:731-40.
3. A)Lerner PI, Weinstein L. Infective endocarditis in the antibiotic era. *N Engl J Med.* Feb 17 1966; 274(7)
   B)Lerner PI, Weinstein L. Infective endocarditis in the antibiotic era. *N Engl J Med.* Feb 3 1966; 274(5)
   C)Lerner PI, Weinstein L. Infective endocarditis in the antibiotic era. *N Engl J Med.* Jan 27 1966; 274(4):199-206; 259-66; 388-93 contd.
4. Miró JM, del Río A, Mestres CA. Infective endocarditis in intravenous drug abusers and HIV-1 infected patients. *Infect Dis Clin North Am.* Jun 2002;16(2):273-95, vii-viii
5. Murdoch DR, Corey GR, Hoen B, Miró JM, Fowler VG Jr, Bayer AS, et al. Clinical presentation, etiology, and outcome of infective endocarditis in the 21st century: the International Collaboration on Endocarditis-Prospective Cohort Study. *Arch Intern Med.* Mar 9 2009; 169(5):463-73.
6. Mylonakis E, Calderwood SB. Infective endocarditis in adults. *N Engl J Med.* Nov 1 2001;345(18):1318-30.

CASE 22: VALVULAR HEART DISEASE
RIFDY MOHIDEEN

OVERVIEW

Valvular heart disease remains common in many countries, despite a decrease in prevalence of rheumatic fever due to a rise of degenerative valve diseases. Rheumatic heart disease however remains an important predisposing factor yet in the developing countries. Aortic and mitral valves are the two most common valves affected. The chronicity of the valvular lesions becomes a fertile ground to practice cardiovascular examination techniques and also serves as a popular clinical examination topic. Students may be tested on a number of formats including long case, short case or OSCE.

CASE VIGNETTE:

A 46-year-old man presents with progressively increasing dyspnoea on exertion and fatigue for the past two years. He also has orthopnoea, and paroxysmal nocturnal dyspnoea. On examination, he is propped up on two pillows but has no cyanosis with warm peripheries and no pedal oedema. The pulse is 88 beats/min regular and bounding, blood pressure is 166/70 mm Hg and jugular venous pressure 3 cm above sternal angle. The apex is diffusely enlarged and felt at the left sixth intercostal space, 2 cm lateral to the mid-clavicular line. On auscultation, first heart sound is normal and the second aortic sound is soft and a high-pitched early diastolic murmur is heard at the third left intercostal space. At the apical region a short mid-diastolic murmur is heard with no thrill The lung bases are clear.

The clinical features are suggestive of a middle aged man with symptomatic chronic valvular heart disease. The diagnosis should be confirmed and underlying cause established, the extent of the disease and physiological disturbance assessed and functional disability should be determined to plan treatment strategy.

HISTORY OF THE PRESENTING COMPLAINT

- Shortness of breath: Establish when it was first noticed and the rate of progression
- Paroxysmal nocturnal dyspnoea: Are you awakened suddenly by difficulty in breathing or coughing? Do these symptoms improve when you sit up or walk? (suggestive of left ventricular dysfunction)
- Orthopnoea: Do you find it more comfortable to sleep or rest in bed with several pillows? (suggestive of heart failure)

- Chest pain: Do you have any pain or discomfort in the chest? Does it occur at rest or with activity? (suggestive of angina)
- Palpitations: Do you experience your heart racing or skipping a beat? If so find out when it occurs, how long does it last and what else occurs with it. (suggestive of arrhythmias)
- Syncope: Have you experienced lightheadedness or blackouts (suggestive of arrhythmias)
- Excessive sweating: Do you have profuse sweating and does it occur at night? (seen in severe valve involvement)
- Swelling of feet: Do your feet swell? (occurs in the severe lesions)

PAST MEDICAL HISTORY
- Previous admissions (determine if these were for worsening symptoms such as heart failure, arrhythmias, angina, infective endocarditis or for investigations)
- History of rheumatic fever (Have you had painful swollen joints during childhood? Have you received penicillin prophylaxis?)
- History of other joint diseases (Pain and swelling of large joints, backache – ankylosing spondylitis and Reiter syndrome)
- History of hypertension (How long and if there was any difficulty in controlling blood pressure)
- History of asthma (for beta-blocker use), allergy to drugs (angioneurotic oedema following ACEI)
- Were you ever told by the doctor that an abnormal heart sound is heard? When was it?

FAMILY HISTORY
- Size of family and children
- Are there any family members having heart valve problems? (Marfan's syndrome, rheumatic heart disease – rare)

SOCIAL HISTORY
- Employment history: current and past employment and ability to continue work
- Income: able to afford hospital visits, medication and possible purchase of heart valve on personal funds. Check if insured and how much of the medical expenses are covered.
- Alcohol: quantify and assess if dependent
- Smoking: quantity and duration of use

TREATMENT HISTORY
- Obtain a list of drugs the patient is taking and the dosage (esp. diuretics, vasodilators, beta-blockers)

- Inquire if on penicillin prophylaxis or on anticoagulants
- Check adherence to therapy
- Assess if follow up is satisfactory

✓ **CHECK LIST FOR HISTORY IN VALVULAR DISEASE**
- Assess current and past cardiac symptoms and comorbidities (e.g. diabetes, COPD, renal disease)
- Inquire on patient's lifestyle to detect progressive changes in the daily activity and functional disability in an objective manner
- Review possible underlying causes (e.g. rheumatic heart disease)
- Review if current medications are appropriate and adequate with special reference to penicillin prophylaxis and anticoagulation
- Assess the quality of the follow up and check adherence to medication
- Assess patient's understanding of the illness

EXAMINATION

- Explain to patient what you intend doing before starting to examine
- Make sure the curtains are drawn and males should ask for a chaperone when examining a female patient
- Position patient for adequate viewing of jugular veins
- Expose the chest adequately

GENERAL EXAMINATION

- Observe patient. Note if well, dyspnoeic or distressed. Count respiratory rate
- Note if there is head bobbing (de Musset's sign)
- Examine eyes for unequal pupils (Argyll-Robertson pupil)
- Inspect tongue for pallor, plethora and cyanosis
- Check for systolic pulsation of uvula (Muller's sign)
- Inspect neck for prominent carotid pulsations. (Corrigan's sign)
- Inspect hands for clubbing, Osler's nodes and arachnodactyly
- Check for Quincke's pulse (visible capillary pulsations below the nail when it is pressed distally)
- Inspect lower limb for oedema
- Examine the back for tenderness over sacroiliac joints and sacral oedema

CARDIOVASCULAR AND OTHER SYSTEM EXAMINATION

- Examine radial pulse for rate, regularity, volume, character (collapsing); time with femoral pulse (need to competently execute how you look for collapsing pulse)
- Examine the contralateral radial pulse at the same time. Note if any inequality in pulse characteristics (rarely aortic regurgitation is seen in aortic dissection)
- Examine all other accessible peripheral pulses for volume, pulsation and bruits (carotids, femoral, popliteal, dorsalis pedis, posterior tibial arteries)
- Listen over femoral artery for a pistol-shot sound (placing the stethoscope lightly over the artery)
- Check for a Duroziez sign (to and fro murmur heard distally on compressing the femoral artery proximally with the bell of the stethoscope)
- Inspect jugular veins; measure height and observe waveform
- Measure blood pressure (note widened pulse pressure) (should lying and standing BP be included)
- Localise and characterise apex (heaving, thrusting) & determine tracheal position at the same time
- Feel for a left parasternal pulsation
- Feel for thrills over the precordium; time with carotid pulse. Grade thrills if present
- In auscultation is it necessary to mention the postions the patient should take for listening to the pulmonary area
- Auscultate for heart sounds (identify first, second & additional sounds). Note if the sounds are normal, soft, loud, split or single
- Auscultate for murmurs; note timing, site best heard, loudness, radiation, character, variation with posture, position and other manoeuvres. Use the bell for low-pitched sounds and the diaphragm for high-pitched sounds.
- Auscultate for an early diastolic murmur with the patient leaning forward with breath held in expiration using the diaphragm of stethoscope
- Auscultate for a mid-diastolic murmur by tuning the patient to the left and using the bell of the stethoscope
- Auscultate lung bases for crepitations and check for dullness.
- Palpate liver for enlargement and pulsation; note other features
- Palpate the spleen for enlargement; note other features
- Examine other systems (respiratory, nervous, musculoskeletal, abdomen) depending on the instructions, case format (OSCE, long case etc.), relevance and availability of time.

- Thank the patient at the end of the examination and cover patient up

✓ **CHECKLIST FOR EXAMINATION FINDINGS IN AORTIC REGURGITATION**

- General examination: visible carotid pulsation (Corrigan's sign), rhythmical head bobbing with each heartbeat (de Musset's sign)
- Pulse: Bounding with collapsing in character, femoral arterial pistol-shot pulse, Duroziez's sign
- Blood pressure: Wide pulse pressure (what difference do we accept?)
- Apex: Displaced to left, with a diffuse heave
- Left parasternal heave in the presence of pulmonary hypertension
- Heart sounds: Normal S1, soft A2, S3
- Murmurs: Soft blowing early diastolic murmur best heard at the base of heart and down the left or right of the sternum (use diaphragm of stethoscope, lean patient forward with the breath held in expiration); Early diastolic murmur best heard at the apical area or axilla (rare; Cole-Cecil murmur); Ejection systolic murmur along the right parasternal area radiating to neck (does not always indicate valvular aortic stenosis); Mid-diastolic murmur at apex (Austin Flint murmur)

INVESTIGATIONS

- ECG: LVH (diastolic overload pattern), left atrial enlargement
- Chest radiograph: enlarged left ventricle, dilated ascending aorta, aortic valve calcification, pulmonary venous congestion
- Echocardiography: LV vigorously contractile and dilated; thickened aortic valve cusps; aortic root may be dilated; flutter of anterior leaflet of mitral valve; regurgitant jet on Doppler study
- Cardiac catheterization: to exclude coexistent coronary artery disease: Left ventricular angiography and aortic root angiography to exclude aortic root disease.
- Additional investigations may be required to identify the underlying aetiology (e.g. radiography of the sacroiliac region and spine for ankylosing spondylitis, syphilitic serology)

CASE SUMMARY

This middle aged man with cardiac symptoms of left ventricular dysfunction has typical signs of aortic valve regurgitation. He has no clinical features of infective endocarditis or arrhythmias. The diagnosis should be confirmed on echocardiography and presence of other valvular involvement should be excluded in view of the presence of other murmurs. The degree of left ventricular impairment should also be assessed.

CLINICAL CASE DISCUSSION

Starts with the summary of the patient which highlights the symptoms and abnormal signs

The functional disability in terms of NYHA classification should be stated.

The appearance of symptoms in chronic aortic regurgitation (also in other valvular disease) signifies the failure of the adaptive and compensatory mechanism of both volume and pressure overload. The symptomatic phase usually heralds a progressive decline of left ventricular function. The full benefit of surgical correction of the regurgitant valve lesion, at this stage cannot be expected.

Medical therapy should be aimed at symptomatic relief and at reducing the progression of the valvular lesion and left ventricular dysfunction. The benefit of vasodilators is unproven. However, angiotensin converting enzyme inhibitors are considered to be the drug of choice in chronic severe aortic regurgitation with left ventricular dysfunction. The diagnosis should be confirmed and underlying cause established, the extent of the disease and physiological disturbance assessed and functional disability should be determined to plan treatment options.

The follow up and repeat echocardiography should be more frequent in the severe form of aortic regurgitation who are at the threshold for intervention and less intense in the mild to moderate lesion who are managed medically.

LEARNING OBJECTIVES

By the end of this case review the student should be:student should be able to

1. Elicit a focussed history in a patient with suspected valvular disease
2. Perform a complete examination of the cardiovascular system and detect the abnormal physical signs
3. Explain the clinical features on a physiological and pathological basis
4. Make a clinical diagnosis or provide a differential diagnosis based on the history and examination findings
5. Select the relevant investigations that would confirm the diagnosis, assess overall cardiac status and be useful in overall management of the patient
6. List the common causes of valvular diseases (aortic regurgitation)
7. Discuss the principles of management of valvular disease (aortic regurgitation)
8. Discuss the indications for surgical treatment including valve replacement
9. Discuss preventive measures against infective endocarditis
10. Communicate to the patient about the nature of the illness, general and specific preventive measures including dental health and safety and risks of everyday and leisure-related activities

CAUSES OF CHRONIC AORTIC REGURGITATION

Common	Less common
Rheumatic heart disease	Ankylosing spondylitis, rheumatoid arthritis
Bicuspid valve	Syphilitic aortitis
Hypertension	Giant cell aortitis
Marfan syndrome	Osteogenesis imperfecta
Idiopathic dilatation of the aorta	Ventricular septal defects with Prolapse of an aortic cusp
Calcific degeneration	Ehlers-Danlos syndrome
Myxomatous degeneration	Reiter's syndrome

COMMONLY ASKED QUESTIONS

1. What are the characteristic physical signs of aortic regurgitation?
Characteristic of aortic regurgitation

- Blowing early diastolic murmur,
- displaced apex,
- wide pulse pressure and peripheral signs are.

2. Why is it necessary to auscultate the patient leaning forward with the breath held in expiration?
Leaning the patient forward brings the aorta close to the chest wall.
During expiration the AR murmur is accentuated and as the high-pitched murmur resembles the vesicular breath sounds, holding the breath helps to distinguish one from the other.

3. How is the presence of a mid-diastolic murmur (Austin Flint murmur) in aortic regurgitation explained?
The regurgitant jet of blood from the aorta in this lesion impinges on the anterior leaflet of the mitral valve which is prevented from opening completely and thereby producing a mid-diastolic murmur.

4. How do you explain the presence of a mid-systolic murmur in aortic regurgitation?
This murmur occurs as a result of the ejection of a large stroke volume caused by the regurgitation of blood from the aorta and should not be confused with aortic stenosis.

5. How is the diagnosis confirmed?
Doppler echocardiography and colour flow mapping can identify the regurgitant jet (jet height and area) and assess the severity (pressure half-time of aortic spectral display, size of effective regurgitant orifice). Echocardiography can also detect the causes such as bicuspid and other abnormalities in valves, dilated aortic root, aortic dissection and vegetations.

6. When is surgery generally indicated in aortic regurgitation?
Indications for surgery (aortic valve replacement) are when the patient is symptomatic but in an asymptomatic person , evidence of increasing heart size on radiography or echocardiography showing a left ventricular end-systolic dimension (LVESD) of 55 mm or greater. The size of the aortic root is a factor for diseases of the aorta that are associated with aortic regurgitation.

7. What are the life-threatening complications of valvular disease (aortic regurgitation)?

- Acute left ventricular failure,
- Infective endocarditis
- Ventricular tachycardia

8. What are the general factors that should be taken into consideration before valve surgery is considered?

General factors such as life expectancy, quality of life, patient's wishes, local resources and surgical expertise of the centre should be carefully considered prior to the procedure. Informed consent from the patient (and family) should be taken after the risks and benefits of the surgical procedure are explained.

DISTINCTION LEVEL QUESTIONS

1. How do you assess the severity of aortic regurgitation?

The following factors should be taken into consideration when the severity is assessed:

- Length of murmur,
- Enlargement of heart,
- Evidence of left ventricular failure,
- ECG evidence of left ventricular hypertrophy,
- Echocardiographic LV cavity size,

Pressure half-time of aortic spectral display, size of effective regurgitant orifice and height and area of regurgitant jet on colour flow Doppler echocardiography.

2. Under what condition does the pulse pressure in aortic regurgitation get narrowed?

When heart failure complicates aortic regurgitation, the diastolic blood pressure increases narrowing the pulse pressure.

3. What causes of AR are more likely when the early diastolic murmur is best heard to the right of the sternum?

The early diastolic murmur when located to the right of the sternum occurs with a dilated aorta, which is seen in conditions such as syphilitic aortitis, Marfan syndrome and dissecting aneurysm of aorta as opposed to rheumatic aortic regurgitation, which is best heard to the left of the sternum.

4. What is a Cole-Cecil murmur?

This is seen rarely when the early diastolic murmur is best heard at the apical area or axilla.

RED FLAG ENCOUNTERS

335

The following are situations that may be overlooked:

- Failure to auscultate the patient in the sitting position with the patient leaning forward and holding the breath in expiration resulting in failure to detect the murmur
- Failure to turn patient to the left to identify additional murmurs when present (e.g. an apical diastolic murmur)
- Failure to check blood pressure or interpret the wide pulse pressure

MUST KNOW FACTS OF AORTIC REGURGITATION

- Often asymptomatic, till late in the natural history of the lesion
- Common cause of collapsing pulse and wide pulse pressure
- The murmur can be missed if patient is not examined in the seated position
- Leads to progressive decline in left ventricular function
- Require valve replacement in the asymptomatic stage for optimal outcome; appearance of symptoms may be too late for valve therapy
- Is a risk factor for infective endocarditis and should receive preventive treatment prior to high risk procedures

SECTION 3: ABDOMEN

SAROJ JAYASINGHE

OVERVIEW

Histopathologically cirrhosis is defined when the liver develops widespread fibrosis leading to distortion of its architecture and nodule formation. Often there is hepatocyte injury or necrosis.

Pathogenesis is due to the cytokines released by Kuppfer cells and hepatocytes in response to cell injury (e.g. from ethanol). These compounds transform the stellate cells in the space of Disse to myofibroblast like cells that are capable of producing collagen. As a result of the distorted architecture there is increase in the resistance to blood flow leading to portal hypertension and opening of porto-systemic vascular shunts (e.g. gastro esophageal varices). The fibrosis also hinders close contact between blood and functioning hepatocytes and concurrent cell injury and necrosis leads to liver cell failure. A proportion of these patients develop hepatoma after several years of cirrhosis.

Clinical presentation of cirrhosis is highly variable and range from asymptomatic (e.g. when cirrhosis is found during abdominal surgery), to isolated organomegaly (e.g. splenomegaly) or associated with complications: features of portal hypertension (e.g. upper gastrointestinal bleeding and ascites), liver failure (e.g. oedema, encephalopathy), spontaneous bacterial peritonitis (SBP). When features of liver failure are seen we describe the clinical status as "hepatic decompensation" (in contrast to compensated liver disease when there are no clinical features of liver cell failure).

In Malaysia and some areas of South East Asia, the main cause of cirrhosis is chronic viral hepatitis (due to virus C or B infection). This scenario is changing s due to increasing numbers due to non-alcoholic steato-hepatitis (NASH) and excessive chronic ethanol intake. Other causes include autoimmune hepatitis (common in females) and biliary cirrhosis (e.g. primary biliary cirrhosis which is an autoimmune disorder, or arising from long standing obstruction to the biliary tree).

Rare hereditary causes include primary hemachromatosis (i.e. iron overload), alpha$_1$ Antitrypsin deficiency and Wilson's disease (i.e. copper overload from absent or low caeruloplasmin).

Note that iron overload can be acquired (e.g. in chronic haemolysis) and that hepatitis A and E do not lead to cirrhosis.

Types of Cases for Clinical Examination

i. *OSCE, short or long: Man with abdominal distension and oedema.*

The student should be able to take a focussed history and demonstrate competency in examination of the abdomen: observe for distension of abdominal veins (e.g. caput medusa), flank fullness, abdominal distension and status of umbilicus (e.g. eversion); palpate for organs (liver, spleen and kidneys); percuss for free fluid (e.g. horseshoe shaped dullness, shifting dullness and fluid thrill); and auscultate for hepatic bruit, splenic rub.

The student should volunteer to examine the inguinal region (for hernia) and male genitals (for testicular atrophy).

ii. *Long case or OSLER*

The student should aim: (a) to take a detailed history inclusive of alcohol intake, drugs that lead to cirrhosis (e.g. INAH given for TB), blood transfusions, IV drug use and sexual habits (for hepatitis B or C infection); and a family history (e.g. for Wilson's disease) (b) demonstrate clinical competencies in general examination and of the relevant systems; and (c) show clinical reasoning skills in managing the patient.

CASE VIGNETTE

A 55-year-old male, with no known past-medical history presents with a 3–month history of ankle swelling. There is a symmetrical swelling of both feet, ankles to mid-leg level. He has also noticed abdominal distension of apprximately 2 months duration.

DIFFERENTIAL DIAGNOSIS

- Cirrhosis (decompensated)
- Right heart failure (e.g. congestive cardiac failure or cor-pulmonale)
- Renal causes such as nephrotic syndrome
- Malnutrition
- Rarely GI causes such as malabsorption or loss of proteins from gut and internal malignancies

HISTORY TAKING

HISTORY OF PRESENTING ILLNESS

- Swelling of ankles and abdominal distension. Usually painless. May be less when waking up (because patient lies down the swelling subsides). The abdominal distension is progressive and may be uncomfortable.

- Those relevant to cirrhosis: Constitutional symptoms such as anorexia, nausea, yellowish discoloration, pruritus, vague RHC discomfort, fatigue, weakness, low grade fever, impotence and diarrhoea.

- Symptoms of advanced cirrhosis: altered sleep pattern, drowsiness, confusion seen with encephalopathy, malena or haematemesis from bleeding varices.

- Relevant negative features that help to rule out other causes for the clinical presentation.
    - Absence or minimal history of shortness of breath on exertion, no cough or wheeze (seen in congestive cardiac failure (CCF) or cor-pulmonale)
    - No history of facial puffiness and haematuria (as in nephrotic syndrome or acute glomerulonephritis)
    - Relatively good protein intake with no bowel symptoms to suggest malabsorption
    - No history of severe anorexia, loss of weight, change in bowel habits, haemoptysis that could suggest internal malignancies

PAST MEDICAL HISTORY

- Some have a relevant past history that indicate the presence of complications: such as hematemesis or malaena (from gastroesophageal varices); episodes of abdominal pain with fever (spontaneous bacterial peritonitis); drowsiness or coma (encephalopathy). Jaundice may indicate alcoholic hepatitis or sudden decompensation or the onset of illness due to acute hepatitis B. Note that hepatitis C infection does not give an acute hepatitis. There may be a history of blood transfusions that have led to hepatitis B or C infection.

FAMILY HISTORY

- Rarely, there is a family history: persons with primary hemachromatosis and Wilson's disease

SOCIAL HISTORY

- Alcohol intake. This is very important and a detailed history must be taken with an attempt to quantify the amount of alcohol (e.g. as units) and to see if the person is a problem drinker (e.g. using CAGE questionnaire).
- Features relevant to identify hepatitis B and C infection: history of IV drug use and sharing of needles; sexual history: visits to commercial sex workers, sexual orientations and contacts, use of condoms; tattoos and acupuncture from poorly qualified practitioners.

SURGICAL HISTORY

- History of surgery requiring blood transfusions (hepatitis B or C)

SYSTEMIC REVIEW OF SYMPTOMS

Urinary symptoms (e.g. dysuria, frequency, haematuria) , bowel symptoms (e.g. loose stools, constipation), respiratory symptoms (e.g. cough, shortness of breath, hemoptysis), symptoms attributable to the nervous system (e.g. headache, peripheral numbness)

EXAMINATION

Professionalism:

Introduce yourself, obtain consent, position patient ideally lying down, suitably undressed and request for a chaperone when you are examining for areas such as groins (e.g. for testicular atrophy)

Physical examination:

Observe the patient from the foot of the bed and comment on obvious abnormalities

- Appearance: oedema, pallor, glossitis, jaundice, clubbing (a feature of cirrhosis), Dupuytren's contracture, gynaecomastia, and loss of axillary hair (be aware of variations according to ethnicity) from liver cell failure, cachexia, and abdominal distension (from ascites).
- Note special skin changes: spider naevi, telengiactasia, and palmar erythema

- State whether patient is conscious, alert, oriented and look for hepatic flaps (asterixis). You could also state whether there is fetor hepaticus.
- State the relevant negative findings: lack of dyspnea (which may be seen in CCF), and lack of facial puffiness with per-orbital oedema that is a feature of nephritic and nephrotic syndrome.

Chest- look for features of cor pulmonale and CCF (e.g. elevated jugular venous pressure). With ascites the patient can develop a pleural effusion.

Abdomen –This is the crucial part of the examination.
State degree of abdominal distension (mild limited to flank fullness , moderate or tense with shiny skin); status of umbilicus (normal, flat or everted), distension of abdominal veins (e.g. caput medusa).
Examine by palpation for organs (liver, spleen and kidneys). You may need to perform 'dipping' if there is tense ascites because the liver and spleen will be drowned and "under water").
Percuss for free fluid (e.g. horse-shoe shaped dullness, shifting dullness and fluid thrill); and auscultate for hepatic bruit (a feature of hepatoma).
Examine inguinal areas for hernia (cause by ascites) and testes for atrophy. (The latter is probably caused by decreased metabolism of female sex hormones by the liver and also accounts for gynaecomastia, loss of axillary hair, spider naevi, telengiactasia, and palmar erythema).

Professionalism: Thank the patient, place him in previous position he was in and re-dress patient.

Note:

The student would have a prioritized list of investigations to assist in confirming the diagnosis of cirrhosis. He would also be prepared to discuss investigations that are relevant for determining the complications arising from the condition.

Clinical reasoning in requesting for relevant investigations is expected.

As has been mentioned under 'Hepatoma', the ultrasound is a useful equipment in imaging the architecture of the liver and the biliary tree and in determining pathology. Interpretation of liver function tests and questions on hepatitis screening can be expected in a long case or in the OSPE test.

INVESTIGATIONS

- Full blood count: Patients may have thrombocytopenia due to hypersplenism. This can progress to pancytopenia. Anaemia could also be from GI bleeding from varices (as a result of portal hypertension), oozing from portal gastropathy, and peptic ulcers (more common in persons with cirrhosis than in the general population). If the bleeding is chronic the anaemia is hypochromic microcytic. Chronic liver disease on its own leads to macrocytosis.

- Liver Function Tests: Tests specific for liver diseases: With chronic liver disease the serum albumin will be decreased witha prolonged prothrombin time (or INR). The serum bilirubin may be elevated. The liver enzymes (AST, ALT, and alkaline phosphatise) may be normal or mildly elevated.

- Other metabolic abnormalities include hyperglycemia or hypoglycaemia, hyponatraemia and hypokalaemia.

- Ultrasound of abdomen is very sensitive to detect ascites. Liver is enlarged in early stages of cirrhosis (be ready to discuss why this happens). With advancing cirrhosis the fibrosis contracts and shrinks the liver. Echogenicity also increases and there may be nodularity.

- CT if done may show the nodularity.

- Definitive diagnosis is by liver biopsy (done percutaneous or trans-jugular) It will show fibrosis with cell necrosis (especially around portal, with distortion architecture and nodule formation. Be ready to discuss (a) the procedure (b) the complications anticipated and (c) taking informed consent.

- Tests to confirm cause of cirrhosis:
  Infective causes: Hepatitis B: Hepatitis BsAg, anti HBc, and coinfection with Hepatitis D by checking for anti-HDV. Hepatitis C: antibody against hepatitis virus C (anti- HCV)
  Autoimmune: anti-smooth muscle antibodies, antinuclear antibodies, anti-live/kidney microsomal antibodies
  Hemachromatosis: high ferritin levels, serum iron, total iron binding capacity
  Wilson's disease: low caeruloplasmin levels, high urinary copper excretion

COMMON QUESTIONS

1. How would you treat a patient with cirrhosis?

The fibrosis in cirrhosis is often irreversible, and treatment is directed to complications: portal hypertension and ascites. Portal hypertension leads to variceal bleeds, a main cause of mortality. Prevention is by reducing the portal pressure (by using oral propranolol) and by banding large varices or those that have bled (through an upper GI endoscope). Rarely trans-jugular intrahepatic portosystemic shunt (TIPS) is done to reduce portal pressure. Portosystemic shunt surgery is rarely done with the advent of TIPS.

2. Name the common complications of cirrhosis

Portal hypertension, ascites, and hepatic encephalopathy.

3. How would you manage the complications such as variceal bleeding, encephalopathy and ascites?

Variceal bleeding Endoscopic treatment is the most important treatment. Ideally banding (or ligation) is done, though some centres still do sclerotherapy. Octreotide or somatostatin can be used intravenously to acutely reduce portal pressure and reduce bleeding. Direct pressure on the varices (i.e. balloon tamponade) can be performed using the Sengstaken tube. Rarely trans-jugular intrahepatic portosystemic shunt (TIPS) is done to reduce portal pressure. With the advent of TIPS, portosystemic shunt surgery is rarely done.

Encephalopathy

Remove precipitants (e.g. correct hypokalaemia, treat infections and discontinue any sedatives). Lactulose results in acidification of the colon, and diarrhea and the goal is to have 2-3 soft stools daily. Oral metronidazole also helps. Other agents include rifaximine. Neomycin, a poorly absorbed antibiotic is limitedly used in the short term, (because long-term use leads to nephrotoxicity). Zinc supplements, albumin infusions and LOLA (L-ornithine L-aspartate given to stimulate the urea cycle and thereby reduce ammonia levels) are useful. Broad spectrum antibiotics (e.g. ceftrioxone) are used routinely because of sub-clinical bacteremia. In the terminal phase, mannitol may help to reduce cerebral oedema. Nursing care should be optimised to prevent pressure sores, aspiration and malnutrition.

Ascites

Restrict salt, oral spironolactone, oral furosemide and monitor weight, abdominal girth, serum creatinine and electrolytes, and urine output. The goal to achieve 0.5 Kg per day weight loss in those without oedema, while 1 kg/day is safe if there is oedema. Refractory ascites may require large volume paracentesis and intravenous infusions of albumin. TIPS can also be used to reduce portal vein pressure thereby facilitating control of ascites. SBP should be treated with intravenous antibiotics (e.g. Cefotaxime). Prevention of SBP will require prophylactic antibiotics (e.g. co-trimoxazole or norfloxacin).

HIGH ACHIEVER QUESTION

1. How would you manage resistant ascites?

Resistant ascites is when ascites does not respond to salt restriction, high doses of diuretics (spironolactone and frusemide) and intravenous albumin.

Such patients often require large volume of ascites fluid to be removed by paracentesis. About 5 to 15 litres could be removed safely. Those on diuretics or with mild renal impairment may benefit from infusions of albumin in order to prevent dangerous depletion of the intravascular compartment.

The procedure gives immediate relief from abdominal discomfort, anorexia, or dyspnea, and reduces risk of the rate complication of umbilical hernia rupture. LeVeen shunts (plastic tubing that connects the peritoneal cavity to the internal jugular vein via a pumping chamber) could be used to return peritoneal fluid to the intravascular compartment. Main problems includes blockage, infection, sepsis and DIC. Rarely TIPS is performed to reduce portal pressure. Liver transplantation remains the definitive treatment.

2. How is prognosis of liver cirrhosis assessed ?

There are two main scoring systems:

Child-Pugh classification (using presence / absence and severity of encephalopathy, serum bilirubin levels, serum albumin level, prothrombin time, and presence / absence and severity of ascites);

Model for End-stage Liver Disease- MELD score: uses serum bilirubin, INR and serum creatinine levels.

These scores are used to recommend liver transplantation.

Death is often due to hepatorenal syndrome when renal failure develops in the presence of cirrhosis with ascites.

3. What is the hepato-renal syndrome?

This is a continuum where renal dysfunction is observed in patients with cirrhosis. It reverses with improvement in hepatic function (e.g. after liver transplantation) and there are no observable histological changes in light microscopy (i.e. it is a functional renal failure, rather than acute tubular necrosis). The reason is due to vasoconstriction of large and small renal arteries and impaired renal function. Diagnosis is by finding a creatinine clearance <40mL/min or serum creatinine >1.5 mg/dL, 24-hour urine volume is <500 ml and urine sodium <10 mEq/L, in the presence of serious liver disease.

4. How should one screen for hepatomas in patients with cirrhosis?

The best strategy is to screen patients with cirrhosis at intervals of 6 months using ultrasound of abdomen. Hepatomas are more common in those with underlying haemochromatosis and alpha-1 antitrypsin deficiency and less common or rare with primary biliary cirrhosis and Wilsons disease.

RED FLAG ENCOUNTERS

Areas where students tend to fall into trouble are:

- Not doing a thorough general examination relevant to the patient
- Not detecting ascites or organ enlargement
- Not turning the patient towards you when examining for a spleen
- Not listening to a hepatic bruit
- Giving unlikely causes for cirrhosis
- A few rules of thumb: biliary cirrhosis is always accompanied by jaundice, males hardly ever get primary biliary cirrhosis, alcohol use is extremely rare among Muslims

MUST KNOW FACTS ABOUT CIRRHOSIS

- ✓ It can be asymptomatic
- ✓ Hepatitis A virus and E virus do not lead to cirrhosis
- ✓ Pathogenesis of the clinical features of cirrhosis
- ✓ Clinical presentations and management complications of cirrhosis
- ✓ Tests and interpretation
- ✓ Basic management principles

OVERVIEW

Hepatoma occurs when the primary hepatocellular cancer (HCC) arises from hepatocytes (in contrast to the more common secondary deposits in the liver that are from cancers in other sites such as the bowels). HCC usually arises in a cirrhotic liver (from any cause of cirrhosis) or rarely without any underlying cirrhosis (fibrolamellar hepatocellular carcinoma). They present as a single nodule or multiple nodules. Spread within the liver and to lymph nodes is common, while lung and bone metastases are rare

Clinical presentation ranges from asymptomatic (e.g. when it is detected during ultrasound examinations) to rapid and sometimes painful enlargement of the liver. Most have features of cirrhosis: organomegaly (e.g. splenomegaly), features of portal hypertension (e.g. upper gastrointestinal bleeding and ascites), and liver failure (e.g. oedema, encephalopathy). A rare acute presentation is intra-abdominal bleeding (and resultant abdominal pain, pallor and shock) due to hepatic rupture.

Globally hepatitis B virus infection is the commonest cause for hepatoma. With the change in dietary habits, these global trends are changing because of the rapid increase in the numbers affected by non-alcoholic fatty liver disease. Since non-alcoholic steatohepatitis (NASH) can progress to cirrhosis and ultimately to hepatoma, the epidemiological pattern is likely to undergo change.

Note:

The student would be expected to be well conversant in discussing the anatomy of the liver, its vascular supply and the biliary tree. As ultrasonography remains a readily available and sensitive imaging modality, it is used to scan all 8 segments of the liver, to demonstrate location of the tumor. Ultrasonic imaging is useful in management of HCC when surgical resection and tumor embolization are indicated ; both aspects requiring a good knowledge of liver anatomy.

Types of Cases for Clinical Examination

OSCE, short or long: Man with abdominal distension.

> The student should be able to take a focussed history (especially in relation to underlying cirrhosis), and demonstrate competency in examination of the abdomen.

In the case of hepatoma palpation of liver, and ability to present the characteristics are important: size of nodule, consistency, tenderness and presence or absence of a bruit.

The student is expected to mention the presence or absence of the signs described under cirrhosis: palpation liver, spleen and kidneys; percussion for free fluid.

Long case or OSLER

The student should aim:
(a) to take a detailed history as described in the chapter in cirrhosis and describe aspects specific to hepatoma (pain and discomfort in the right hypochondrium, low grade fever, anorexia, loss of weight, development of jaundice)
(b) demonstrate clinical competencies in general examination and of the relevant systems
(c) show clinical reasoning skills in managing the patient.

CASE VIGNETTE

A 56-year-old male gives a 2–month history of pain in the right hypochondrium. He has past history of abdominal distension and lower limb swelling intermittently for 12 months in the past and had been treated for a liver problem several times.

DIFFERENTIAL DIAGNOSIS

- Development of hepatoma
- Cirrhosis with worsening of liver failure
- Malignancy with secondary deposits in the liver
- Since he gives a history of liver disease, the other differential diagnosis are less likely: right heart failure (e.g. congestive cardiac failure or cor-pulmonale), renal causes such as nephrotic syndrome, and malnutrition

HISTORY TAKING

HISTORY OF PRESENTING ILLNESS

- Dull pain in the right hypochondrium (RHC) due to stretching of the pain sensitive liver capsule from the enlarging tumour. Pain is often in the RHC because hepatomas are more likely in

the right lobe. If it arises in the left lobe, the symptoms are localized in the epigatrium.
- Other manifestations include low grade fever, anorexia, loss of weight, and development of jaundice.
- There may also be painless swelling of ankles and abdominal distension. The abdominal distension is progressive and may be uncomfortable.

PAST MEDICAL HISTORY

- Some patients may have no a relevant past history. Others would give features suggestive of cirrhosis and its complications or its causes: hematemesis or malaena (from gastroesophageal varices), episodes of jaundice, or a history of blood transfusions.

- Specifically ask if patient is aware of the results of ultrasound examinations done on him or blood tests. (Hepatomas are increasingly being detected during surveillance in those with cirrhosis: ultrasound scans of abdomen and serum alpha feto-protein levels now constitute part of wellness examination).

FAMILY HISTORY

- Rarely, there is a family history: in persons with hemachromatosis.

SOCIAL HISTORY

- This is similar to the chapter on cirrhosis: history should include details on alcohol intake; history of IV drug use and sharing of needles (for hepatitis B or C infection); sexual history and tattoos and acupuncture from poorly qualified practitioners

SURGICAL HISTORY

- History of surgery requiring blood transfusions (hepatitis B or C) and upper GI endoscopies

SYSTEMIC REVIEW OF SYMPTOMS

- ➤ Those relevant to cirrhosis: Constitutional symptoms such as lethargy; symptoms of advanced cirrhosis: altered sleep pattern, drowsiness, confusion seen with encephalopathy, malena or haematemesis from bleeding varices

> History of severe anorexia, loss of weight, change in bowel habits, haemoptysis that could suggest internal malignancies

EXAMINATION

Professionalism:

Introduce yourself, obtain consent, position patient; ideally lying down, suitably undressed and request for a chaperone when you are examining for areas such as groins. Ask patient if he is having pain in any part of the body, especially in the abdomen before palpation.

Physical examination:

Observe the patient from the foot of the bed and comment on obvious abnormalities

- Appearance: state the features seen in cirrhosis: oedema, pallor, jaundice, clubbing, gynaecomastia and loss of axillary hair, cachexia, and abdominal distension (from ascites), and skin changes (e.g. spider naevi, telengiactasia, and palmar erythema). Patients may have low grade fever or rarely have polycythaemia or hypoglycemia.
- State whether patient is conscious, alert, oriented and look for hepatic flaps.
- You may state the relevant negative findings, especially the absence of certain features that suggest a primary malignancy such as thyroid nodules, lymphadenopathy, testicular lumps, and bowel masses (and breasts in the case of females).

Chest- Examine for features of lung malignancy (e.g. collapse or mass lesion in the lungs, or a pleural effusion).

Abdomen –This is the most important part of the physical examination.
State features described in the chapter on cirrhosis: degree of abdominal distension and whether there is a visible mass in the hypochondrium. If it is from the liver, it will also move with respiration.
Look for biopsy scars.
Examine by palpation for organs (liver, spleen and kidneys) with particular attention to the liver. If you feel a nodule, state size, shape, whether tender (taking care not to hurt the patient), consistency (firm or hard), demarcation of margins (well defined or ill-defined), smoothness of surface, and any pulsations felt.
Percuss for free fluid and also for liver span at the mid-clavicular line.
Auscultate carefully for a hepatic bruit using the bell of the stethoscope.

Examine inguinal areas for hernia (cause by ascites) and testes for atrophy.

Professionalism: Thank the patient, place him in previous position he was in and re-dress patient.

INVESTIGATIONS

In the long case you would have developed a list of investigations. Be prepared to prioritise the investigations so as to establish the diagnosis. Learn to separate the list for diagnosis and management (complications and treatment)

Be familiar with the typical ultrasound appearances of hepatoma (primary and secondary as you may be asked to comment on pictures of ultrasound)

- Patients may have features related to cirrhosis: thrombocytopenia, anemia, macrocytosis. There may be neutrophilia.
- Rare manifestations include hypoglycaemia, and erythrocytosis.
- As with chronic liver disease, the serum albumin is decreased and prothrombin time (INR) prolonged. The serum bilirubin can be very high when the biliary tree is obstructed by the tumour or in the terminal phases when most of the liver is replaced by tumour. AST and ALT is often mildly elevated, while alkaline phosphatase levels increase proportionately more.
- Ultrasound of abdomen is very sensitive to detect hepatomas. Liver often shows increased echogenicity due to underlying cirrhosis. There may be a single nodule or multiple nodules. Spread within the liver and to lymph nodes is common, while lung and bone metastases are rare.
- Contrast enhanced CT will demonstrate increased vascularity of the hepatomas.
- MRI may detect smaller lesions and angiography useful in special circumstances.
- Tumour marker: high levels of serum alpha – feto proteins (AFP). This is usually normal in fibrolamellar hepatocellular carcinoma
- Liver biopsy of nodule shows cells similar to rapidly dividing hepatocytes.
- Tests to confirm cause of underlying cirrhosis: especially infective causes: Hepatitis B surface antigen, antibody against hepatitis virus C, and hemachromatosis: high ferritin levels

351

PRINCIPLES OF TREATMENT

 Note:

The student is expected to discuss management especially in a long case. Concepts of management should include short and long term management. Aspects of continued care in terminal disease are expected to be discussed.

Management of symptoms are essential as with any condition, especially pain control. Nausea and vomiting are managed with anti-emetics (e.g. domperidone, metoclorpramide or ondansetron). Fever responds to paracetamol. One must be careful to use NSAIDs because of the underlying cirrhosis, and thrombocytopaenia.

Specific treatment depends on severity if underlying cirrhosis (e.g. assessed using Child Pugh Turcotte classification) and size of tumour. Small tumours can be resected while those with cirrhosis or with multiple hepatomas benefit from liver transplant. The treatment of choice for non-cirrhotic patients is resection. Cirrhotic livers when resected have a high chance of liver failure and therefore transplantation offers the better option. Other methods include percutaneous ablation (with either ethanol or radiofrequency-RFA), transarterial chemoembolization (TACE) or chemotherapy.

Long-term or palliative care forms an important facet in the treatment of hepatomas that are not amenable to surgical resection or recur after therapy. The student must be familiar with the 'analgesic ladder'. This offers a simple framework where we increase dose frequency, dosage, and type of analgesic (non-opioid or opioid; and in the latter codeine, morphine, fentanyl) in a step-wise progressive manner to achieve pain relief (e.g. beginning with milder opioids, skin patches of fentanyl and proceeding to regular or patient controlled intravenous or subcutaneous morphine).

The 'serious illness' news must be broken to the patient in a compassionate and professional manner. Patient education on symptom control and therapeutic options are essential for proper care.

The prognosis of hepatomas are poor, often because by the time of detection, most are not resectable. Those that are resectable can be classified according to the TNM classification. The prognosis in those that are unresectable is determined mainly by the state of the liver, rather than the tumour size.

RED FLAG ENCOUNTERS

Areas where students tend to fall into trouble are:

- Not doing a thorough general examination
- Not detecting the nodule
- Not listening to a hepatic bruit
- Mistaking the enlarged liver for another lump (e.g. stomach)

MUST KNOW FACTS ABOUT HEPATOMA
- ✓ Commonest cause globally is hepatitis B infection
- ✓ A cancer that can be prevented by a vaccine (by vaccination against hepatitis B)
- ✓ It can be asymptomatic
- ✓ Basic management principles

DISTINCTION LEVEL QUESTION

1. What are the prevention strategies?

Primary prevention is available in the form of vaccination against hepatitis B. This will effectively prevent one of the main causes of hepatoma. The other strategy is to screen patients with cirrhosis at 6 monthly intervals to detect subclinical hepatoma. Screening is done using ultrasound of the abdomen. AFP levels are not beneficial in screening of cirrhotics to detect early disease.

2. What is the pathogenesis of hepatoma?

With regeneration in cirrhosis, there is a higher chance of mutations that lead to hepatoma formation. The genetic make-up and the environmental triggers may play a role. In the case of hepatitis B virus, hepatocellular carcinoma can develop even without cirrhosis because the DNA virus integrates in the host genome. In contrast, HCV which is a RNA virus does not get integrated to the host genome and carcinoma sets in the presence of cirrhosis.

3. What is the utility of AFP in hepatoma?

It is a tumour marker produced by the tumour cells or regenerating hepatocytes. High serum levels are seen with heptomas but it is usually normal in fibrolamellar hepatocellular carcinoma. It is not too sensitive (only 40-64% sensitive) because some hepatomas do not produce AFP it. AFP levels are also elevated in chronic active hepatitis C and in other conditions (e.g. recovery stage following injury to hepatocytes, and seroconversion following hepatitis B infection). The specificity of the diagnosis increases when the serum values are high (e.g. above 400 ng/ml) in the appropriate clinical setting with compatible radiological findings.

CASE 25:   CHRONIC HEPATITIS
SAROJ JAYASINGHE

OVERVIEW

Chronic hepatitis (CH) is defined as the presence of hepatic inflammation for more than 6 months. An important cause for this is Autoimmune Hepatitis (AIH) when there is inflammation of the liver due to an autoimmune process. There is injury and death of hepatocytes. The process can lead to a chronic hepatitis and cirrhosis. Infections with hepatitis B or C virus (HBV and HCV) too can cause a chronic hepatitis. Clinical presentation ranges from asymptomatic, to acute hepatitis with jaundice and fever, to cirrhosis. Other causes include drugs (such as isoniazid, methyl dopa, methotrexate), hemachromatosis and Wilson's disease.

Types of Cases for Clinical Examination

i.   *OSCE, short or long: Female with jaundice and abdominal distension.*

The student should be able to take a focussed history and demonstrate competency in examination of the abdomen. In the case of AIH you must mention the presence or absence of jaundice, acne, straie, hirsuitism, and signs described under cirrhosis: palpation of liver, spleen and kidneys; percussion for free fluid.

ii.   *Long case or OSLER*

The student should aim:
(a) to take a detailed history as described in the chapter in cirrhosis and describe aspects specific to AIH (progress of jaundice, oligomennorhea, acne, low grade fever, anorexia, arthlagia, skin rashes, features that help to distinguish the different causes). In the case of infective causes (hepatitis B and C) the history should highlight social history: IV drug use and sharing of needles, sexual history and tattoos and acupuncture from poorly qualified practitioner
(b) demonstrate clinical competencies in general examination and of the relevant systems; and
(c) show clinical reasoning skills in managing the patient.

CASE VIGNETTE

A 32-year-old female presents with a 9–month history of progressive lethargy, low grade fever, discomfort in the right hypochondrium with associated jaundice for 6 months. She also has abdominal distension and lower limb swelling intermittently for the last 2 months.

DIFFERENTIAL DIAGNOSIS

- AIH
- Chronic hepatitis due to HBV or HCV
- Cirrhosis with worsening of liver failure

HISTORY TAKING

HISTORY OF PRESENTING ILLNESS

- History of jaundice must be taken in detail. The duration, progress and depth must be described. You must also mention whether there is pruritus, which is a feature of biliary obstruction (seen with primary biliary cirrhosis).
- There can be discomfort in RHC due to stretching of the pain sensitive liver capsule from the hepatic inflammation.
- Other features of AIH .include describing the type of fever (usually low grade fever), anorexia, arthralgia, loss of weight, acne, oligomennorrhoea or absent periods.
- There may also be painless swelling of ankles and abdominal distension.

PAST MEDICAL HISTORY

- Some patients may have no relevant past history.

- Jaundice may indicate the onset of illness due to AIH or acute hepatitis B. HCV infection does not give an acute hepatitis.

- There may be a history of blood transfusions that have led to HBV or HCV infection.

- Some would give features suggestive of liver cell failure or rarely even portal hypertension: hematemesis or malena.

- Ask for a history of chronic medication. Isoniazide (INAH) used in tuberculosis leads to chronic liver disease. Other drugs include methyldopa and methotrixate.

FAMILY HISTORY

- Rarely, there is a family history of other autoimmune disorders such as SLE. A family history may be seen with primary hemachromatosis and Wilson's disease.

SOCIAL HISTORY

- In order to rule out HBV and HCV infection you need to specifically mention about a history of IV drug use and sharing of needles, sexual history and tattoos and acupuncture from poorly qualified practitioners. Even though this case is a female, it is best to rule out alcohol induced liver disease which could mimic most forms of cirrhosis or chronic hepatitis.
- Ensure that you ask for herbal preparations that could include hepatotoxins and alcohol.

SURGICAL HISTORY

- History of surgery requiring blood transfusions (HBV and HCV) and upper GI endoscopies for assessment of varices (which indicates the presence of portal hypertension).

SYSTEMIC REVIEW OF SYMPTOMS

- ➢ Those relevant to any form of hepatitis: constitutional symptoms such as lethargy and anorexia. Mention features seen with cirrhosis and liver failure: oedema and ascites, altered sleep pattern, drowsiness, confusion seen with encephalopathy, malena or heamatemesis from bleeding varices from portal hypertension,

When presenting a case, it is important to state why other possible differential diagnoses are considered by the presence or absence of specific symptoms.

EXAMINATION

Professionalism:

Introduce yourself, obtain consent, position patient ideally lying down, suitably undressed and request for a chaperone when you are examining for areas such as groins. Ask patient is she is having pain in any part of the body, especially in the abdomen.

Physical examination:

Observe the patient from the end of the bed and comment on obvious abnormalities

- Appearance: Features common to any form of fairly aggressive CH include jaundice, fever and oedema.
- With advancing disease or cirrhosis there is loss of axillary hair, cachexia, and abdominal distension (from ascites), and skin changes (e.g. spider naevi, telengiactasia, and palmar erythema).
- A few features are more specific for AIH: acne, striae, hirsutism, pallor (sometimes severe with associated autoimmune haemolysis), and 'Cushingoid' features.
- State whether patient is conscious, alert, oriented and look for hepatic flaps.
- You may state the relevant negative findings: lack of features of alcoholism: e.g. parotid enlargement.

Chest- Look for features of an effusion associated with ascites.

Abdomen –This is the most important part of the physical examination.
State features described in the chapter on cirrhosis: degree of abdominal distension and whether there is a visible mass in the hypochondrium.
Examine by palpation for organs (liver, spleen and kidneys) with particular attention to the liver. If you feel the liver, check for upper border by percussion, state span in centimetres at the mid-clavicular line, state consistency (firm or hard) and tenderness (usually absent or mild, unlike with acute viral hepatitis when it is more tender and soft), demarcation of liver margin (usually well defined), smoothness of surface (usually smooth), and any pulsations felt (not felt unless there is transmission from the aorta in the thin person).
Percuss for free fluid.
Auscultate carefully for a hepatic bruit using the bell of the stethoscope.
Examine inguinal areas for hernia (caused by ascites) and testes for atrophy.

Professionalism: Thank the patient, place him in previous position he was in and assist to re-dress patient if requested.

INVESTIGATIONS

- Patients may have the following features: thrombocytopenia, haemolytic anemia, reticulocytosis.
- As with chronic liver disease, the serum albumin will be decreased and prolongation of prothrombin time (INR),

elevated serum bilirubin, with moderate to very high levels of AST, ALT (usually in the hundreds if there is acute inflammation), and an elevated alkaline phosphatase.

- Ultrasound will confirm that the liver is enlarged with increased echogenicity. With superadded cirrhosis the fibrosis contracts and shrinks the liver.
- Liver biopsy will show typical features of inflammation with predominantly lymphocytic and plasma cell infiltration, and cell necrosis. With progression to cirrhosis there will be fibrosis, distortion architecture and nodule formation.
- Serological tests will confirm AIH: Antinuclear antibody (ANA), Anti–smooth muscle antibody (ASMA), Anti–liver-kidney microsomal antibody (anti–LKM-1), and antibodies against soluble liver antigen (anti-SLA).
- Tests for other causes of CH, especially infective causes: HBsAg, antibody against hepatitis virus C, RNA for HCV.
- Hemachromatosis: high ferritin levels, serum iron, total iron binding capacity.
- Wilson's disease: low caeruloplasmin levels, high urinary copper excretion

MANAGEMENT

A holistic approach is warranted. Exhibit skills in disclosing 'serious illness news' and discuss issues related to psychological aspects as depression would an accompanying component especially in the presence of overt clinical manifestations (jaundice, liver failure, ascites etc).
Be realistic about results of definitive treatment and prognosis.

TREATMENT

Treatment will depend on the cause.

The use of antivirals (e.g. interferon-alfa) in the case of underlying hepatitis B or C infection is established. There appears to be a place even in the presence of superadded cirrhosis.

HBV: If the virus gets incorporated into the genome, cure in chronic HBV becomes impossible. Treatment is recommended for patients with evidence of ongoing inflammation (i.e. high aminotransferase–ALT), chronicity (high levels for 3-6 months), and active infection (high viral load as evidenced by hepatitis B virus DNA levels, and positive hepatitis B e antigen [indicating active viral replication]). Main drugs are interferon alpha (IFN-a) and lamivudine. Interferon is given subcutaneously 3 times a week for 4 months. An alternative is pegylated IFN-a 2a. Lamivudine is given orally.

HCV: Cure is possible. Antiviral drugs are recommended for those with elevated ALT levels with evidence of HCV (positive HCV antibody and serum HCV RNA test) and compensated liver disease (i.e. no ascites or encephalopathy). Treatment includes the use of interferon alpha often with ribavirin. Other drugs include boceprevir and telaprevir (protease inhibitors).

AIH: Biopsy is essential prior to starting treatment for AIH. The main stay of treatment is corticosteroids (e.g. prednisolone 1 mg /kg/day). It is indicated if there is disease activity (elevated liver enzymes). Inactive cirrhosis, and decompensation per se are not indications for corticosteroids. Increasingly a combination of prednisolone and azathioprine is being employed, followed by azathioprine alone for maintenance. The latter is withdrawn only after checking on biopsy and once liver enzymes normalize. It is common for treatment to continue for 1.5 to 2 years.

Symptomatic treatment consists of paracetamol for fever. Nausea and vomiting (especially with flares in disease activity) may require intravenous fluids and antiemetics. Most patients tolerate a normal diet. A high protein and high caloric diet is necessary to combat hypercatabolism associated with inflammatory response and steroids. Those with superadded cirrhosis may develop ascites when a low-salt diet and diuretics may be prescribed.

Patients must be educated and advised regarding need to adhere to long periods of treatments with potential side effects.

Cirrhosis indicates irreversibility and definitive treatment should include liver transplantation. Infection of the grafted liver is seen when transplantation is done on patients who had hepatitis B or C. This is despite undetectable viruses in peripheral blood, and is believed to be from reservoirs in mononuclear cells, spleen and other organs.

PROGNOSIS

Prognosis depends on the cause of chronic hepatitis, severity of inflammation, and the stage it was detected.

About 5 – 10% of adults with hepatitis B infection progress to develop chronic hepatitis. In the case of hepatitis C, it is as high as 85%. About 20% of those with chronic hepatitis will develop cirrhosis.

In the case of hepatitis B, complete eradication is possible, unless the virus is incorporated in to the genome. In hepatitis C, virus is not eliminated completely and therefore the goal is to have a sustained virological response where the virus is not detected in the blood for 6 months, indicating that its growth is suppressed. The response to drugs depend on the genotype (or strain) of virus.

Autoimmune hepatitis usually responds to drug therapy. Treatment failures could be offered liver transplantation. Hepatoma is less common in cirrhotics due to AIH, compared to cirrhosis from hepatitis B or C.

RED FLAG ENCOUNTERS

Areas where students tend to fall into trouble are:

- Not eliciting a history of autoimmune disorders or risk factors for hepatitis B or C virus infection
- Not ruling out alcohol induced liver disease.
- Not doing a thorough general examination
- Not detecting the features that suggest AIH (e.g. acne, striae)

MUST KNOW FACTS

- ✓ It can be asymptomatic
- ✓ Antivirals are used for CH due to hepatitis B or C virus.
- ✓ Corticosteroids are the mainstay in treatment of AIH
- ✓ CH leads to cirrhosis in a proportion of patients
- ✓ Basic management principles (i.e. supportive care)

DISTINCTION LEVEL QUESTION

What are the common types of AIH ?

There are three main types in this heterogenous group of disease based on antibody markers, age, sex, gamma globulin elevation, HLA association, steroid response and progression to cirrhosis. . .

Type I AIH are often in females (around 40 years) and have a high frequency of autoimmune disorders such as Hashimotos' thyroiditis, rheumatoid arthritis, and Grave's disease. They have high titres of ANA and ASMA.

Type II is seen often in children, and they have has anti–LKM-1 without ANA and ASMA.

Type III do not have the above antibodies, but have antibodies against soluble liver antigen (anti-SLA). Histologically all three types are similar.

What are the side effects of interferon?

- Flulike symptoms
- Gastrointestinal: nausea and vomiting
- Hematological: especially neutropenia, thrombocytopenia
- Neuropsychiatric: headaches, depression, irritability
- Cardiovascular: hypotension or hypertension
- Metabolic: hypothyroidism and hyperthyroidism

CASE 26: HEPATOSPLENOMEGALY

SANGEETA POOVANESWARAN

OVERVIEW

Hepatosplenomegaly implies the simultaneous enlargement of both the liver and spleen. This can occur as the result of a variety of causes ranging from infection, haematological disorders, connective tissue diseases or portal hypertension due to chronic liver disease.

As hepatosplenomegaly can occur in a variety of diseases it is a commonly asked examination question and students should be familiar with:

- Clinical detection of this abnormality
- Techniques of examination
- Examine other but related structures or organs

Be prepared to discuss differential diagnosis for an abdominal mass in the upper abdomen (upper right and left quadrant masses).

 **Note: Types of Cases for Clinical Examination**

1. **OSCE, short or long: Patient with distended abdomen**

Aim is to take a focused history, exhibit clinical competency in examination of abdomen for hepatosplenomegaly and detection of clinical signs of chronic liver failure.

May need to volunteer to examine other sites for third space fluid loss, lymphadenopathy.

2. **Long case or OSLER**

Aim is to take a detailed history to assess underlying cause of hepatosplenomegaly and exhibit clinical competency in examination of the relevant systems (respiratory, cardiovascular, haematological or gastro-intestinal system).

CASE VIGNETTE

A 35-year-old man, presents with a 10 day history of fever, jaundice, nausea and abdominal discomfort. He has recently been on holiday to India.

DIFFERENTIAL DIAGNOSIS

Infections:

- Malaria (given the recent history of travel to India, this diagnosis must be considered, mild hepatospenomegaly can occur usually after one week of fever),
- Viral hepatitis (important to note that patient usually presents with jaundice and fever, mild hepatomegaly may be present although splenomegaly is less common),
- Infectious mononucleosis (this presents with fever and there may be lymphadenopathy, pharyngitis in addition to hepatosplenomegaly; jaundice is rarely seen),
- Cytomegalovirus infection, typhoid

Haematological disease: myeloproliferative disorders, lymphoproliferative disorders (leukaemia, lymphoma), haemolytic disorders (thalassaemia)

Liver disease:
Chronic liver disease with portal hypertension: chronic active hepatitis. Alcoholic liver disease (alcoholic hepatitis)

Rare causes are: systemic lupus erythematosus, sarcoidosis (jaundice is unusual), amyloidosis , pernicious anaemia, sickle cell anaemia (an enlarged spleen is unusual) and Gaucher's disease. (jaundice is unusual)

HISTORY OF PRESENTING ILLNESS

- Ask specific questions about fever (typical history with chills and rigors which subsides with profuse sweating; paroxysms of fever will depend on the type of malaria)
- Ask specific questions related to jaundice- duration, pruritis, colour of urine and stools, and abdominal pain.
- If abdominal pain is present, the location, exacerbating and relieving factors.
- Ask about specific symptoms associated with nausea eg. fever, weight loss, loss of appetite

- For viral hepatitis it is important to take a detailed history of risk factors eg. blood transfusion in the last 6 months, tattoos, intravenous drug use, sexual history, and recent intake of seafood.

Symptoms of chronic liver disease

- In lymphoproliferative disorders, the patient may have constitutional symptoms like weight loss, lethargy; also they may have other symptoms related to the disease like lymphadenopathy and anaemia.

PAST MEDICAL HISTORY

- Previous admissions with similar symptoms
- Thalassemia- anaemic symptoms requiring blood transfusion

FAMILY HISTORY

- Exclude inherited conditions e.g. thalassemia, Wilson's disease

SOCIAL HISTORY

- Sexual history as risk of spread of viral hepatitis B and C infection
- Employment history (e.g. medical related field, working with children) as this has implication if patient is a Hepatitis B and C carrier. Also, if patient is unemployed, need to ask about financial support, e.g. from family or is he homeless
- If he is married or has children , need to assess risk of transmission
- Do consider other infectious diseases that would be considered in management viz. risk taking behaviour and HIV AIDS, STI .
- Alcohol intake – as chronic alcohol abuse can have similar clinical presentation

SURGICAL HISTORY

- Situations where patient may have had blood transfusion

DRUG HISTORY

- Methyldopa, methotrexate and isoniazid are possible but rare causes (if case scenario is of a previously well person, then this won't be relevant).

SYSTEMIC REVIEW OF SYMPTOMS

Need to assess for each system, relating to hepatitis symptoms, as well as to exclude other differentials
e.g. SLE- rash, joint pains, infectious mononucleosis – sore throat, rash
When presenting a case, it is important to state why other possible differential diagnoses are considered by the presence or absence of specific symptoms.

✓ CHECK LIST FOR HISTORY IN HEPATOSPLENOMEGALY

1. Identify underlying cause eg. infective cause vs non-infective cause
2. In viral hepatitis- need to assess for other risk factors eg. Tattoos, blood transfusion
3. Detailed history on symptoms especially relating to gastro-intestinal symptoms

EXAMINATION

Professionalism: Introduce yourself, obtain consent, position patient ideally lying flat, suitable undressing of garment for abdominal examination (from infra mammary region to just above the genitalia) and have a chaperone.

Inspection:

Observe the patient from the end of the bed and comment on obvious abnormalities

Appearance – pale, jaundiced, cachexic looking, nutritional status, abdominal distension

Respiration- tachypnoea, use of oxygen therapy, use of accessory muscles

Abdomen- obvious swelling, symmetry of swelling

Hands- comment on absence/presence of clubbing, leuconychia, palmar erythema, Duputryen's contracture (for this student needs to feel for thickening of fascia before commenting), hepatic flap

Arms- spider naevi, bruising, purpura, needle marks, pigmentation, scratch marks

Neck, face and chest- palpate for supraclavicular and cervical lymph nodes, look for anaemia, jaundice and xanthelesma in eyes, pallor of tongue, spider naevi in upper chest and face, axilla for hair loss and acanthosis nigricans (which is seen as part of NAFLD), gynaecomastia

ABDOMEN

Inspection:

Inspect for movements, obvious mass, presence of any visible veins and visible peristalsis.

Palpation:

Before palpation ask the patient if there are any areas of tenderness

Student must either kneel on the floor or sit on a chair before proceeding to palpation of abdomen

Palpate all nine regions and if any tenderness/mass is obvious comment on characteristics. Perform both light and deep palpation with patient breathing through mouth.

Check for Murphy's sign, palpable gallbladder (as patient has jaundice)

For examination of liver, spleen and kidneys, palpate and percuss/ ballot for each organ individually.

Percussion:

Assess presence of ascites by looking for shifting dullness.

When patient is rolled to the side, assess for pitting oedema in sacral region.

Professionalism: Thank patient at the end of examination, position patient in same position as prior to start of examination, re-dress patient.

 **CHECK LIST FOR COMMENTING ON HEPATOSPLENOMEGALY**

Hepatomegaly:

- Size- demonstrate location of upper and lower border, and measure length
- Surface-smooth, firm, nodular (smooth in hepatitis, craggy in hepatoma)
- Edge- smooth, irregular
- Tenderness
- Movement with respiration-downwards
- Non-pulsatile

Splenomegaly:

- Size- demonstrate location of lower border, if not palpable , comment on percussion of Traube space
- Surface-smooth, firm,
- Edge- smooth, irregular, splenic notch
- Tenderness
- Movement with respiration- diagonally

State other factors that differentiate it from a kidney- non-ballottable, cannot get above it

 *Note : Professional approach*

Executing the motions for enlargement of the liver and spleen using the correct techniques alone is not sufficient as more marks are given for the correct findings.

INVESTIGATIONS

1. Thick and Thin blood film- malarial parasites
2. Liver function tests- obstructive (raised alkaline phosphatase) vs hepatitis jaundice (raised transaminases), liver function(low serum albumin)
3. Clotting screen- (delayed prothrombin time)
4. Renal function tests (pre- renal failure due to dehydration from prolonged fever with nausea)
5. Urine- for bile pigments
6. Imaging- ultrasound scan or CT scan to assess architecture of liver, spleen, check for portal hypertension
7. ESR and CRP may be elevated
8. If negative for malaria then must consider other differentials such as viral hepatitis (serology for A,B,and C),lymphoproliferative and myeloproliferative disorders (blood film, bone marrow biopsy, CT scan for staging),other serology- EBV antibodies, for haemolysis (serum haptoglobin, reticulocyte count and Coomb's test)

 Note:

In discussing investigations consider the objective of requesting for such.
In the OSCE setting mention those that would be essential for confirming the diagnosis of hepatosplenomegaly. Then shift to investigations that

would be needed for determining the cause of hepatosplenomegaly and management of this case.

CASE SUMMARY

A 35-year-old man, who has recently returned from a holiday in India, presents with a 10 day history of fever, jaundice, nausea and abdominal discomfort. On examination, he has a fever of 38 degree Celcius, tachycardia but is normotensive. He is jaundiced and is sweating. There is a 14 cm enlarged tender liver and a mildly enlarged spleen, 2cm below the costal margin. Ascites and stigmata of chronic liver disease are however not present.

The most likely diagnosis is malaria.

CLINICAL DISCUSSION OF THE CASE

LEARNING OBJECTIVES

1. Able to classify causes of hepatosplenomegaly
2. Make a diagnosis based on the history and clinical examination findings
3. List the investigations in determining the cause of jaundice with hepatosplenomegaly
4. State the differential diagnosis for hepatosplenomegaly
5. To examine for stigmata of chronic liver disease
6. To examine the abdomen in systematic manner
7. Present investigations in logical manner and explain rationale for performing the investigations
8. Outline the management principles in malaria

COMMONLY ASKED QUESTIONS

1. Describe how you would approach a patient with hepatosplenomegaly?

2. What is the likely differential diagnosis in this case?

3. What investigations would you perform in this patient?

4. How do you confirm the diagnosis of malaria?

5. How would you manage this patient?

6. Explain the mechanism of jaundice in malaria

7.   What are the life-threatening complications of malaria?

DISTINCTION LEVEL QUESTION

1. Why would viral hepatitis B be unlikely in this case based on history and clinical examination?

There is lack of risk factors for transmission of hepatitis.Clinical examination does not have any evidence of venipuncture marks to indicate intravenous substance abuse. In viral hepatitis, patients typically present with fever and jaundice. Rarely is there hepatomegaly and usually if present it may be 1-2 finger breath enlargement below the costal margin. Splenomegaly rarely is present and if so, it is usually mild with dullness in the traube space. However, it is an important differential diagnosis to consider.

2. In what situations can a liver be palpable but not enlarged?

Increased diaphragmatic descent, presence of emphysema with an associated flattened diaphragm, thin person with a narrow thoracic cage, presence of a palpable Riedel's lobe.

RED FLAG ENCOUNTERS

This highlights the possible areas where the student can find himself in trouble by possible omissions or overlooking the examination findings.

- Mistaking spleen for kidney
- Not examining abdomen in a systematic manner
- Unable to differentiate obstructive and hepatitic jaundice from clinical history and examination

MUST KNOW FACTS OF HEPATOSPLENOMEGALY

1.   There are multiple causes and eliciting specific symptoms and signs in history and examination will help to identify the likely underlying cause.

2.   Hepatosplenomegaly in the setting of a short history of fever and jaundice, think of infective causes like malaria, viral hepatitis and infectious mononucleosis

3.   If there are no other signs except anaemia, think of myeloproliferative or lymphoproliferative causes, if stigmata of chronic liver disease present, think of cirrhosis of the liver with portal hypertension.

4.   Tests and interpretation

5.   Basic management principles

CASE 27: MASSIVE SPLENOMEGALY
SANGEETHA POOVANESWARAN

OVERVIEW

Massive splenomegaly is a term used to describe a spleen that extends into the left lower quadrant or pelvis or which has crossed the midline of the abdomen. Splenomegaly may also be defined by its weight or largest dimensions. If it weighs 400-500 g it indicates splenomegaly and if it weighs more than 1000 g it is massive splenomegaly. Splenomegaly is considered as moderate if the largest dimension is 11-20 cm, and massive if the largest dimension is greater than 20 cm.

As splenomegaly can occur in a variety of disease pathologies it is a commonly asked exam question and students should be familiar with clinical detection of this abnormality, techniques of examination for enlarged spleen and examination of related sites. Be prepared to discuss differential diagnosis for an abdominal mass in the upper abdomen (upper left quadrant masses).

DIFFERENTIAL DIAGNOSIS

Haematological disorders- myelofibrosis, leukaemia, polycythaemia vera, essential thrombocytopenia, lymphoma
Inherited conditions – thalassaemia major, Gaucher's disease
Infections- visceral leishmaniasis (kala azar), malaria

Types of Cases for Clinical Examination

OSCE, short or long: Patient with distended abdomen

Aim is to take a focused history, exhibit clinical competency in examination of abdomen for splenomegaly.

Long case or OSLER

Aim is to take a detailed history to assess underlying cause of splenomegaly and exhibit clinical competency in examination of the relevant systems (respiratory, haematological or gastro-intestinal system).

CASE VIGNETTE

A 12-year-old boy is admitted for blood transfusion. His main symptoms currently are lethargy, breathlessness and palpitations on moderate exertion. He also has had a distended abdomen for many years, however, recently he has been experiencing significant discomfort.

Splenomegaly can occur in the setting of various pathologies, however, massive splenomegaly in Malaysia, is usually seen in myeloproliferative disorders,leukaemia, lymphoma, thalassemia and chronic malaria (tropical splenomegaly syndrome).

The thalassaemias are a heterogeneous group of genetic disorders with defective synthesis of one or more globin chains. Data from the 2009 Malaysian Thalassaemia Registry showed that there were 4,541 registered patients with β thalassaemia of which 3,310 consist of the transfusion dependent β thalassaemia major and HbE β thalassaemia patients.

HISTORY TAKING

HISTORY OF PRESENTING ILLNESS

- Ask specific questions related to anaemia- lethargy, palpitations, breathlessness, dizziness, cardiac symptoms to suggest overload.
- Ask specific questions regarding blood transfusion requirements- frequency, amount, side-effects, and transfusion reactions. Use of iron chelation therapy- frequency, side-effects encountered.
- Ask about abdominal pain and associated symptoms
- Ask about growth and development eg. Development of secondary sexual characteristics, height (student must be able to plot height and weight on centile chart and interpret the chart)
- Symptoms related to extra-medullary haematopoiesis- headaches, bone pain, hepatomegaly.
- Need to exclude neoplastic cause of splenomegaly- ask about lymphadenopathy, night sweats, weight loss, fever, chills, easy bruising such as epistaxis and gingival bleeding

PAST MEDICAL HISTORY

- Previous admissions with similar symptoms of anaemia or that related to thalassemia (recurrent infection, organ function for iron overload)

FAMILY HISTORY

- As it is an autosomal recessive condition, ask about affected family members (student must be able to draw a family tree)

SOCIAL HISTORY

- School/university- grades, attendance, social problems at school, bullying, isolation

  In an older patient:

- Employment history – if he has already started to work, ask about problems faced, frequent absences

- If he is married or in a relationship- ask about psycho-social issues, concerns about having children with thalassemia

SURGICAL HISTORY

- Situations where patient may have had increased need for blood transfusion

DRUG HISTORY

- Ask about iron chelation therapy (oral or subcutaneous), vitamin C supplementation

SYSTEMIC REVIEW OF SYMPTOMS

Need to assess for each system, relating to thalasaemia, as well as to exclude other differentials for massive splenomegaly
eg. Gaucher's disease, myeloproliferative conditions, lymphoma.

When presenting a case, it is important to state why other possible differential diagnoses are considered by the presence or absence of specific symptoms.

Check List for History in Massive Splenomegaly

- ✓ Identify underlying cause eg. Inherited conditions vs malignancy vs infection

- ✓ In thalassemia- need to assess for signs of developmental delay (both physical and psychological)

EXAMINATION

Professionalism: Introduce yourself, obtain consent, position patient ideally lying flat, suitable undressing of garment for abdominal examination (from inframammary region to just above the genitalia), have a chaperone.

It is important to note that although the focus of the clinical examination may be to comment on splenomegaly, it is important to also comment on clinical features related to thalassaemia which are present and also relevant negative signs.

Inspection: Observe the patient from the end of the bed and comment on obvious abnormalities

- Appearance – pallor, jaundice, cachexia, nutritional status, abdominal distension, height, weight, obvious pain/distress

- Respiration- tachpnoea, use of oxygen therapy, use of accessory muscles (patient may have cardiac failure due to iron overload)

- Abdomen- obvious swelling, symmetry of swelling

1. Hands- comment on absence/presence of clubbing, leuconychia, palmar erythema, duputryen's contracture (for this student needs to feel for thickening of fascia before commenting), hepatic flap

2. Arms- spider naevi, bruising, purpura, needle marks, pigmentation, scratch marks

3. Neck, face and chest- palpate for supraclavicular and cervical lymph nodes (this may be present in CML and lymphoma), anaemia and jaundice.

   In thalasaemic patient, hepatomegaly may also be present therefore it is important to comment on absence or presence of clinical features relating to liver failure (gynaecomastia, spider naevi), development of secondary sexual characteristics and stature.

4. Abdomen

   Inspection:

   - inspect for movements, obvious mass, present, any visible veins, visible peristalsis.

   - In thalassaemic patients look out for bruising and injection marks in abdomen to suggest injection site of iron clelation therapy or patient may be on insulin (due to iron overload).

374

Palpation:

- Before palpation ask the patient if there are any areas of tenderness

- Student must either kneel on the floor or sit on a chair before proceeding to palpation abdomen

- Palpate all 9 regions and if any tenderness/mass is obvious comment on characteristics. Perform both light and deep palpation with patient breathing through mouth.

- Check for Murphy's sign, palpable gallbladder (as patient has jaundice)

- For examination of liver, spleen, kidney, palpate and percuss/ ballot for each organ individually.

- Start low when examining the spleen and be gentle during palpation. Even though, it may be very clear that the patient has splenomegaly, it is important to still go through the motions of ruling out a palpable kidney (perform bimanual palpation, check for ballotment, feel for the splenic notch)

Percussion:

- Assess presence of ascites by looking for shifting dullness.

- When patient is rolled to the side, assess for pitting oedema in sacral region.

5. Legs

- Pitting oedema

Based on the history, especially in Long Cases/OSLER, it is important to assess and other abnormalities noted in a thalassaemic patient (eg. Frontal bossing, thalassaemic facies, short stature, pigmentation due to iron overload, cardiac failure, secondary sexual characteristics, hepatomegaly may also be present)

Professionalism: Thank patient at the end of examination, position patient in same position as prior to start of examination, re-dress patient.

CHECK LIST FOR COMMENTING ON SPLENOMEGALY

Splenomegaly:

- ✓ Size- demonstrate location of lower border, if not palpable , comment on percussion of traube space

- ✓ Surface-smooth, firm,

- ✓ Edge- smooth, irregular, splenic notch

- ✓ Tenderness

- ✓ Movement with respiration- diagonally

- ✓ State other factors that differentiate it from a kidney-non-ballottable, cannot get above it

Professional approach

Executing the motions for enlargement of the spleen using the correct techniques alone is not sufficient as more marks are given for the correct findings especially in the senior years of training.

INVESTIGATIONS
1. Full blood count- check for anaemia (including low MCV and MCH), white cell and platelet count (if hypersplenism develops then there will be leucopenia, neutropaenia and thrombocytopenia)
2. Peripheral blood film- marked anisocytosis, poikilocytosis (including fragments and tear-drop poikilocytes), hypochromia and microcytosis. Basophilic stippling, Pappenheimer bodies and target cells.
3. Serum ferritin levels 9this is usually monitored every 3-6 months)
4. Liver function tests- raised bilirubin, transaminases and reduced albumin
5. Clotting screen- may be abnormal due to liver involvement
6. Qualitative haemoglobin electrophoresis (this test would have been done at time of diagnosis)
7. Imaging to assess for iron overload (MRI of heart and liver)
8. In lymphoproliferative and myeloproliferative disorders (blood film, bone marrow/ lymph node biopsy, CT scan for staging)
9. ESR and CRP may be elevated

10. In discussing investigations consider the objective of requesting for such. In the OSCE setting mention those that would be essential for confirming the diagnosis of splenomegaly. Then shift to investigations that would be needed for determining the cause of splenomegaly and management of this case.

CASE SUMMARY

This 12-year-old boy who has been having regular blood transfusions presents with lethargy, breathlessness and palpitations on moderate exertion for 1 week duration. He also has a distended and tender abdomen. On general inspection, he has frontal bossing and thalassaemic facies, he is short in stature and has signs of delay in development of secondary sexual characteristics. He is pale and jaundiced. Abdominal examination reveals pigmentation and bruising from iron chelation therapy. He has hepatomegaly and massive splenomegaly.

This patient has transfusion dependent thalassaemia and is on iron chelation therapy.

CLINICAL DISCUSSION OF THE CASE

LEARNING OUTCOMES

Students should be able to:

- Define mild, moderate and massive spenomegaly.
- State the differential diagnosis for splenomegaly.
- To examine for signs of thalassaemia
- To examine the abdomen in systematic manner
- Present investigations in logical manner and explain rationale for performing the investigations
- Outline the management principles in thalassaemia
- Discuss holistically the management of the patient with regards to psycho-social issues especially in a long case

COMMONLY ASKED QUESTIONS

1. Describe how you would approach a patient with spenomegaly?
2. What is the likely differential diagnosis in this case?
3. What investigations would you perform in this patient?

DISTINCTION LEVEL QUESTION

1. What does hypersplenism mean?
Splenomegaly with persistent leucopenia and thrombocytopenia.

2. When is splenectomy indicated?
Splenectomy is indicated if there is increased transfusion requirements which is 1.5 times than usual or exceeding 200 - 250 ml/kg/yr of pure red blood cells; if there is evidence of hypersplenism as documented by splenomegaly with persistent leucopaenia or thrombocytopaenia or massive splenomegaly causing discomfort and risk of infarct or rupture from trauma.

RED FLAG ENCOUNTERS

This highlights the possible areas where the student can find himself in trouble by possible omissions or overlooking the examination findings.

Mistaking spleen for kidney
Not examining gastro-intestinal system in systematic manner
Unable to identify cause of massive splenomegaly from clinical history and examination with features typical of thalassaemia

MUST KNOW FACTS OF MASSIVE SPLENOMEGALY

- There are multiple causes and eliciting specific symptoms and signs in history and examination will help to identify the likely underlying cause.
- Rarely does massive splenomegaly occur in isolation, usually there is anaemia, hepatomegaly, jaundice, thalassaemic facies or lymphadenopathy which will help in identifying the underlying pathology.
- If there are no other signs except anaemia and lymphadenopathy, think of myeloproliferative or lymphoproliferative causes as they are the commonest cause of massive splenomegaly.
- When clinical signs of thalassaemia are present, it is important to check for all signs relating to thalassaemia eg. developmental delay

CASE 28: HEPATOSPLENOMEGALY WITH LYMPHADENOPATHY

SANGEETA POOVANESWARAN

OVERVIEW

Hepatosplenomegaly with lymphadenopathy implies the simultaneous enlargement of both the liver and spleen with localized, regional or generalized lymphadenopathy.

When presented with such a case the differential diagnosis is one of malignancy either lymphoma or chronic lymphocytic leukaemia. Other conditions rarely present with just these 3 signs in isolation and usually have other associated signs.

Types of Cases for Clinical Examination

    i.   OSCE, short or long: Patient with distended abdomen

Aim is to take a focused history, exhibit clinical competency in examination of abdomen for hepatosplenomegaly and lymphadenopathy.

May need to volunteer to examine other systems to rule out other possible differential diagnosis..

    ii.   Long case or OSLER

> Aim is to take a detailed history to assess underlying cause of hepatosplenomegaly with lymphadenopathy and exhibit clinical competency in examination of the relevant systems (respiratory, cardiovascular, haematological, musculoskeleta or gastro-intestinal system).

CASE VIGNETTE

A 65-year-old man, presents with abdominal distention and non-tender swellings in the neck and axilla. He denies fever, rash, joint pain. Clinically he appears pale but is not jaundiced.

Differential diagnosis

- Lymphoma : Hodgkin's or non- hodgkin's lymphoma
- Leukaemia: chronic lymphocytic leukaemia (CLL)

Rare causes are: infectious mononucleosis, cytomegalovirus infection, brucellosis, leptospirosis

HISTORY TAKING

HISTORY OF PRESENTING ILLNESS

- In lymphoma, patients may present with localized, regional or generalized painless lymphadenopathy, constitutional or B symptoms (fevers, night sweats or weight loss), occasionally pruritis and pain following ingestion of alcohol at sites of lymphadenopathy. In non- hodkin's lymphoma there may be extra-nodal involvement (eg. skin).

- In CLL, there may be fever, weight loss, fatigue, bleeding, history of recurrent infections.

- In infectious mononucleosis, there may be fatigue, fever, sore inflamed throat and tender lymphadenopathy.

- In CMV infection, patient is usually only symptomatic in immunocompromised states, so ask about chronic illness, long term use of immunosuppressive medication and HIV status. Associated symptoms include fever, malaise, night sweats, joint pain and symptoms specific to site of infection eg. pneumonia, reduced vision,encephalitis , diarrhoea.

- In brucellosis, there may be animal contact or ingestion of unpasteurized dairy products, fever, sweats, weight loss, joint pains, fatigue.

- In leptospirosis, there may be history of contact with urine of infected rodents eg. swimming in rivers, flooding. Associated symptoms are fever, headaches, muscle aches, vomiting, diarrhoea, photophobia and reduced appetite.

PAST MEDICAL HISTORY

- usually none, unless previous diagnosis of lymphoproliferative disorder or immuno-compromise.

FAMILY HISTORY

- nil

SOCIAL HISTORY

- If suspecting immunicompromise- need to ask about high risk behaviour/ blood transfusion

- If suspecting leptospirosis/leptospirosis- ask if any other family or friends are affected

SURGICAL HISTORY

- Situations where patient may have had blood transfusion

DRUG HISTORY

- long term immunono suppressive medication

SYSTEMIC REVIEW OF SYMPTOMS

Need to assess for each system, to rule out infective systemic pathologies eg. infectious mononucleosis – sore throat, rash

When presenting a case, it is important to state why other possible differential diagnoses are considered by the presence or absence of specific symptoms.

CHECK LIST FOR HISTORY IN HEPATOSPENOMEGALY WITH LYMPHADENOPATHY

- ✓ Identify underlying cause eg. infective cause vs non-infective cause

- ✓ painless vs non-painless lymphadenopathy

- ✓ Presence or absence of other symptoms

EXAMINATION

Professionalism: Introduce yourself, obtain consent, position patient ideally lying flat, suitable undressing of garment for abdominal examination (from inframammary region to just above the genitalia), have a chaperone.

In the course of discussion new information related to other infectious diseases like AIDS, or malignancy may be elicited. Be prepared to discuss the sensitivity of presenting such information and be cautious of confidentiality of disclosing information.

INSPECTION:

Observe the patient from the end of the bed and comment on obvious abnormalities

Appearance – pale, jaundiced, cachexic looking, nutritional status, abdominal distension

Respiration- tachpnoea, use of oxygen therapy, use of accessory muscles

Abdomen- obvious swelling, symmetry of swelling

Hands- comment on absence/presence of clubbing, leuconychia, palmar erythema, duputryen's contracture (for this student needs to feel for thickening of fascia before commenting), hepatic flap

Arms- spider naevi, bruising, purpura, needle marks, pigmentation, scratch marks

Neck, face and chest- examine oral cavity for phaprygitis, tonsillar lymphadenopathy, gum bleeding,palpate for supraclavicular, cervical and axillary lymph nodes, anaemia, jaundice and xanthelesma in eyes, pallor of tongue, spider naevi in upper chest and face, axilla for hair loss and acanthosis nigricans (which is seen in obesity, acromegaly, diabetes, gastric cancer), gynaecomastia

ABDOMEN

Inspection:

inspect for movements, obvious mass, present, any visible veins, visible peristalsis.

Palpation:

Before palpation ask the patient if there are any areas of tenderness

Student must either kneel on the floor or sit on a chair before proceeding to palpation abdomen

Palpate all 9 regions and if any tenderness/mass is obvious comment on characteristics. Perform both light and deep palpation with patient breathing through the mouth.

For examination of liver, spleen, kidney, palpate and percuss/ ballot for each organ individually.

Palpate for inguinal lymphadenopathy

Percussion:

Assess presence of ascites by looking for shifting dullness.

When patient is rolled to the side, assess for pitting oedema in sacral region.

LEGS

Pitting oedema

 *Note: Based on the history, especially in Long Cases/OSLER, be wary of the need to examine other systems eg dermatology if rash present, musculoskeletal system if arthralgia or myalgia present.*

Professionalism: Thank patient at the end of examination, position patient in same position as prior to start of examination, re-dress patient.

✓ **CHECK LIST FOR COMMENTING ON HEPATO-SPENOMEGALY AND LYMPHADENOPATHY**

Hepatomegaly:

1. Size- demonstrate location of upper and lower border, and measure length
2. Surface-smooth, firm, nodular (smooth in hepatits, craggy in hepatoma)
3. Edge- smooth, irregular
4. Tenderness
5. Movement with respiration-downwards
6. Non-pulsatile

Splenomegaly:

1. Size- demonstrate location of lower border, if not palpable , comment on percussion of traube space
2. Surface-smooth, firm,
3. Edge- smooth, irregular, splenic notch
4. Tenderness
5. Movement with respiration- diagonally
6. State other factors that differentiate it from a kidney- non-ballottable, cannot get above it

Lymphadenopathy:

1. examine all lymph node groups in a systematic manner
2. size
3. location
4. surface and edge-hard, rubbery,matted, well circumscribed
5. mobility
6. tender or non-tender

☞ *Note: Executing the motions for enlargement of the lymph nodes, liver and spleen using the correct techniques alone is not sufficient as more marks are given for the correct findings especially in the senior years of training.*

INVESTIGATIONS

1. Full blood count- check for anaemia and infection
2. Blood film- abnormal cell morphology eg excessive lymphocytes
3. Liver function tests- raised transaminases, bilirubin level, protein, albumin
4. Clotting screen- assessment of liver function
5. Renal function tests
6. LDH and beta2- microglobulin- for monitoring response
7. lymph node biopsy- diagnostic for lymphoma. Aid in diagnosis of CLL and other infective causes
8. bone marrow biopsy/trephine for diagnosis and staging of CLL and lymphoma
9. Imaging- CT scan for staging of CLL and lymphoma
10. Serology-EBV antibodies, CMV antibodies, brucella and leptospirosis
11. Blood cultures if fever is present for diagnosis of brucella and leptospirosis, although nowdays serology is the most popular investigation tool
12. ESR and CRP may be elevated in both malignancy and infection as such non- specific
13. In discussing investigations consider the objective of requesting for such. In the OSCE setting mention those that would be essential for confirming the diagnosis of hepatosplenomegaly with lymphadenopathy. Then shift to investigations that would be needed for determining the cause of hepatosplenomegaly with lymphadenopathy and management of this case.

CASE SUMMARY

A 65-year-old man, presents with abdominal distention and non-tender swellings in the neck and axilla. He denies fever, rash, joint pain. Clinically he is anaemic but not jaundiced. He has hepatospenomegaly with non-tender lymphadenopathy in the axilla and cervical region bilaterally.

The most likely diagnosis is a haematological malignancy either lymphoma or chronic lymphocytic leukaemia.

CLINICAL DISCUSSION OF THE CASE

Students should be able to:

- state the differential diagnosis for hepato-splenomegaly with lymphadenopathy and mention why infective causes are unlikely due to lack of other associated symptoms/signs.
- to examine the abdomen in systematic manner
- present investigations in logical manner and explain rationale for performing the investigations
- discuss holistically the management of the patient with regards to a malignant disease including terminal life care especially in a long case

COMMONLY ASKED QUESTIONS

1. Describe how you would approach a patient with hepatospenomegaly with lymphadenopathy?

2. What is the likely differential diagnosis in this case?

3. What investigations would you perform in this patient?

DISTINCTION LEVEL QUESTION

1. How would you break bad/serious news to a patient?

Preparation/setting the scene:
Ask the patient to come in with a relative/close friend, allow enough time to speak to the patient without any interruptions, have a nurse present,
Sharing the information:
Summarize the history/investigations to date and ask the patient to explain in their own words what they think is going on and what symptoms they are currently experiencing since the last time you met them, assess the patient's understanding first and gauge how much the patient wishes to know, give warning signs first that difficult information is coming, do not give too much information at one go, do not use jargon, give small amount of information and check if the patient understands what you are telling them before proceeding with more information, read non-verbal clues from the patient, allow patient opportunity to ask questions, encourage expression of feelings.
Planning and support:
Identify patient's concerns and address them, explain to patient what would be the plan in management and the timeframe, give hope but also be realistic, emphasize importance of quality of life
Follow up and ending session:

Summarize what has been discussed, allow patient to ask questions and check patient's understanding of information received, don't rush the patient, offer to see the patient again if there are any further questions, provide written information of treatment plan or phone numbers of support group/ nurse in charge so that questions can be addressed.

RED FLAG ENCOUNTERS

This highlights the possible areas where the student can find himself in trouble by possible omissions or overlooking the examination findings.

1 .Mistaking spleen for kidney
2. Not examining gastro-intestinal system in systematic manner
3. Failure to examine for lymphadenopathy

MUST KNOW FACTS OF HEPATOSPLENOMEGALY WITH LYMPHADENOPATHY

- ✓ There are multiple causes and eliciting specific symptoms and signs in history and examination will help in identifying the likely underlying cause.

- ✓ If there are no other signs except anaemia, think of myeloproliferative or lymphoproliferative causes, if infective signs/symptoms or other systemic manifestations are present like arthralgia, myalgia or rash think of unusual infections like leptospirosis, brucellosis etc.

- ✓ Tests and interpretation

- ✓ Basic holistic management principles of malignancy, not just treatment with chemotherapy and/or radiotherapy but also psycho social issues.

CASE 29: ASCITIS
SANGEETA POOVANESWARAN

OVERVIEW

Ascites is a term used to describe pathological accumulation of fluid in the peritoneal cavity. Ascitic fluid can accumulate as a transudate or an exudate. Transudates are a result of increased pressure in the portal vein (>8 mmHg, usually around 20 mmHg), *e.g.* due to cirrhosis, cardiac failure or nephrotic syndrome, while exudates are actively secreted fluid due to inflammation or malignancy.

As a result, exudates are high in protein, high in lactate dehydrogenase, have a low pH (<7.30), a low glucose level, and more white blood cells. Transudates have low protein (<30g/L), low LDH, high pH, normal glucose, and less than 1 white cell per 1000 mm³. Clinically, the most useful measure is the difference between ascitic and serum albumin concentrations. A serum to albumin gradient (SAAG) of less than 1.1 g/dl (11 g/L) implies an exudate and if the SAAG is more than 1.1g/dl then it is a transudate.

As ascites can occur in a variety of disease pathologies it is a commonly asked exam question and students should be familiar with clinical detection of this abnormality, techniques of examination and volunteer to examine other but related sites. Be prepared to discuss differential diagnosis for ascites.

Types of Cases for Clinical Examination

OSCE, short or long: Patient with distended abdomen

> Aim is to take a focused history, exhibit clinical competency in examination of abdomen for ascites and detection of clinical signs of chronic liver failure.

> May need to volunteer to examine other sites for third space fluid loss, hepatosplenomegaly, cardiac failure, lymphadenopathy.

Long case or OSLER

> Aim is to take a detailed history to assess underlying cause of ascites and exhibit clinical competency in examination of the relevant systems (respiratory, cardiovascular, haematological or gastro-intestinal system).

CASE VIGNETTE

A 45-year-old man, who is an intravenous drug abuser, presents with early satiety and abdominal discomfort. Clinically, he is jaundiced and his abdomen is distended and there is bilateral leg swelling.

Differential diagnosis for ascites

- Transudate: cirrhosis, cardiac failure, nephrotic syndrome, hepatic venous occlusion, constrictive pericarditis, kwashiorkor
- Exudate: cancer (peritoneal carcinomatosis or metastases), peritoneal tuberculosis, pencreatitis

Rare causes are: vasculitis, hypothyroidism, Meig's syndrome.

Causes of cirrhosis: alcohol, post-viral (B,C), idiopathic, drugs (methyldopa, chloropramazine, isoniazid, nitrofurantoin, propylthiouracil, methotrexate, amiodarone), autoimmune chronic hepatitis, Haemochromatosis, Wilson's disease, primary sclerosing cholangitis, primary biliary cirrhosis.

HISTORY TAKING

HISTORY OF PRESENTING ILLNESS

- Cirrhosis is present in three-quarter of cases with jaundice or ascites and in one-quarter with abdominal pain, acute bleeding or encephalopathy.
- Ask specific questions related to jaundice- duration, pruritis, colour of urine and stools, fever, and abdominal pain. If abdominal pain is present enquire for the location, exacerbating and relieving factors
- Ask specific questions regarding IV substance abuse- duration, sharing of needles, type of substance abuse
- Ask about specific symptoms associated with nausea eg. fever, weight loss, loss of appetite
- Important to take a detailed history on other risk factors eg. blood transfusion, tattoos, sexual history, travel history, and seafood.
- Symptoms of chronic liver disease, also loss of libido, impotence
- In lymphoproliferative disorders, the patient may have constitutional symptoms like weight loss, lethargy; also they may have other symptoms related to the disease like lymphadenopathy and anaemia.

PAST MEDICAL HISTORY

- Previous admissions with similar symptoms of hepatitis or jaundice including contacts
- Complications eg. history of encephalopathy, portal hypertension (ascites, variceal bleeding), gallstones
- Blood transfusion history- for surgery or anaemia (in thalassaemia)
- History of diabetes, cardiac failure or arthropathy (haemochromatosis)

FAMILY HISTORY

- Exclude inherited conditions eg. thalassaemia

SOCIAL HISTORY

- Alcohol intake
- Tattoos
- Sexual history / preference
- Employment history (eg. medical related field, working with children) as this has implication if patient is a Hepatitis B and C carrier. Also, if patient is unemployed, need to ask about financial support, eg. from family or is he homeless
- If he is married or has children , need to assess risk of transmission
- Do consider other infectious diseases that would be considered in management ie. Risk taking behaviour and HIV AIDS, STI .
- Overseas travel eg. acute hepatitis

SURGICAL HISTORY

- Situations where patient may have had blood transfusion

DRUG HISTORY

- For chronic active hepatitis: methyldopa, isoniazid, nitrofurantoin Treatment previously eg. protein restriction, fluid restriction, alcohol abstinence, steroids, lactulose, neomycin

SYSTEMIC REVIEW OF SYMPTOMS

Need to assess each system for symptoms of chronic liver disease, and also to exclude other differentials e.g. Cardiac failure, nephrotic syndrome

When presenting a case, it is important to state why other possible differential diagnoses are considered by the presence or absence of specific symptoms.

CHECK LIST FOR HISTORY IN ASCITES

- ✓ Identify cause for ascites ie. Is it related to portal hypertension or not (exudate vs transudate)

- ✓ Identify underlying cause of cirrhosis eg. infective cause vs non-infective cause

- ✓ In viral hepatitis- need to assess for other risk factors eg. Tattoos, blood transfusion

- ✓ Detailed history on symptoms especially relating to chronic liver disease

EXAMINATION

Professionalism: Introduce yourself, obtain consent, position patient ideally lying flat, suitable undressing of garment for abdominal examination (from inframammary region to just above the genitalia), have a chaperone.

In the course of discussion new information related to other infectious diseases like AIDS, syphilis and other STI may be elicited. Be prepared to discuss the sensitivity of presenting such information and be cautious of confidentiality of disclosing information.

Inspection:

Observe the patient from the end of the bed and comment on obvious abnormalities

- Appearance – pale, jaundiced, cachexic looking, nutritional status, abdominal distension

- Respiration- tachpnoea, use of oxygen therapy, use of accessory muscles

- Abdomen- obvious swelling, symmetry of swelling

Hands- comment on absence/presence of clubbing, leuconychia, palmar erythema, duputryen's contracture (for this student needs to feel for thickening of fascia before commenting), hepatic flap

Arms- spider naevi, bruising, purpura, needle marks, pigmentation, scratch marks, tattoos

Neck, face and chest- palpate for supraclavicular and cervical lymph nodes, anaemia, jaundice and xanthelesma in eyes, pallor of tongue, spider naevi in upper chest and face, axilla for hair loss and acanthosis nigricans (which is seen in obesity, acromegaly, diabetes, gastric cancer), gynaecomastia

Abdomen

Inspection:

Inspect for movements, obvious mass. If present, any visible veins, visible peristalsis.

Palpation:

Before palpation ask the patient if there are any areas of tenderness

Student must either kneel on the floor or sit on a chair before proceeding to palpation abdomen

Palpate all 9 regions and if any tenderness/mass is obvious comment on characteristics. Perform both light and deep palpation with patient breathing through mouth.

Check for Murphy's sign, palpable gallbladder (as patient has jaundice)

For examination of liver, spleen, kidney, palpate and percuss/ ballot for each organ individually.

Percussion:

Assess presence of ascites by looking at fullness at the flanks, everted umbilicus, presence of shifting dullness (percuss with your fingers parallel to the level of fluid) and fluid thrill. If ascites is gross, use the 'dipping method' to feel the liver and spleen.

When patient is rolled to the side, assess for pitting oedema in sacral region.

6.   Legs

Pitting oedema

Look carefully for signs of chronic liver disease, signs of encephalopathy, signs of portal hypertension (splenomegaly, ascites, oedema, caput medusae), signs of bleeding (malaena).

Consider hepatocellular carcinoma (in haemachromatosis and cirrhosis due to hepatitis B and C).

In young patients consider Wilson's disease and look carefully for Kayser-Fleischer rings.

Consider end stage primary biliary cirrhosis, if there is deep jaundice, scratch marks and xanthelasma, particularly in a woman,.

Examine the cardiovascular system to exclude severe right heart failure, tricuspid regurgitation or constrictive pericarditis.

Professionalism: Thank patient at the end of examination, position patient in same position as prior to start of examination, re-dress patient.

CHECK LIST FOR COMMENTING ON ASCITES

- Check for stigmata of chronic liver disease
- Look for signs of underlying cause of ascites
- Ascites- inspect flanks, umbilicus, shifting dullness and fluid thrill

Professional approach

Executing the motions for assessment of the liver and spleen and presence of fluid using the correct techniques alone is not sufficient as more marks are given for the correct findings especially in the senior years of training.

INVESTIGATIONS

- Viral Serology for Hepatitis A,B,C

- Full blood count- check for anaemia (this may be due to chronic disease, blood loss, folate deficiency, bone marrow depression, hypersplenism, haemolysis or sideroblastic anaemia). Round macrocytes are common in alcoholics. Leucopenia and thrombocytopenia occur in hypersplenism.

- Liver function tests- obstructive (raised alkaline phosphatase) vs hepatitis jaundice (raised transaminases), liver function (albumin) Clotting screen (especially albumin and prothrombin index gives an idea of prognosis)

- Renal function tests to exclude hepatorenal syndrome

- Ascites fluid examination following paracentesis

  - ✓ Serum to ascites albumin gradient

  - ✓ Blood- malignancy or recent invasive test

  - ✓ Turbid or white fluid-infection or chylous ascites

  - ✓ Cell count-if raised suggestive of spontaneous bacterial peritonitis

  - ✓ pH< 7.35- spontaneous bacterial peritonitis or systemic acidosis

  - ✓ lactate- increased in spontaneous bacterial peritonitis

  - ✓ amylase- elevated in pancreatic ascites

  - ✓ adenosine deaminase- increased in tuberculous ascites

  - ✓ cytology- for malignant cells

  - ✓ culture- for spontaneous bacterial peritonitis

- Imaging- ultrasound scan or CT scan to assess architecture of liver, spleen, check for portal hypertension

- ESR and CRP may be elevated

- If hepatocellular cancer is suspected- alpha fetoprotein levels (AFP)

 NOTE:

In discussing investigations consider the objective of requesting for such. In the OSCE setting mention those that would be essential for confirming the diagnosis of ascites. Then shift to investigations that would be needed for determining the cause of cirrhosis and management of this case.

CASE SUMMARY

A 45-year-old man, who is an intravenous drug abuser, presents with early satiety and abdominal discomfort. Clinically, he is malnourished, unkempt, jaundiced with stigmata of chronic liver disease. He has ascites and bilateral pitting leg oedema.

The most likely diagnosis is liver cirrhosis secondary to viral hepatitis.

CLINICAL DISCUSSION OF THE CASE

LEARNING OBJECTIVES

Students should be able to:

- state the differential diagnosis for ascites.
- state the risk factors for viral hepatitis.
- to examine for stigmata of chronic liver disease
- to examine the abdomen in systematic manner
- present investigations in logical manner and explain rationale for performing the investigations
- outline the management principles in cirrhosis
- discuss holistically the management of the patient with regards to risk taking behaviour beyond viral hepatitis especially in a long case

COMMONLY ASKED QUESTIONS

1. Describe how you would approach a patient with ascites?
2. What is the likely differential diagnosis in this case?
3. What relevant investigations would you perform in this patient?

DISTINCTION LEVEL QUESTION

1. How would you manage a patient with cirrhosis and ascites?

The most important treatment is sodium restriction and diuretics. Fluid restriction is usually not needed unless serum sodium drops below 130 mmol per liter. If the abdomen is tense, ascitic fluid should be removed to relieve shortness of breath, to diminish early satiety and to prevent pressure related leakage of fluid from the site of previous paracentesis.
Serial monitoring of urinary sodium concentration helps to determine optimal dose of diuretic; doses are incrementaly increased until a negative

sodium balance is achieved. The most effective diuretic combination is spironolactone with frusemide. Ninetypercent respond to this therapy.

In diuretic resistant ascites, therapeutic paracentesis with infusion of salt free albumin is helpful. Other treatment options are peritoneovenous shunting, transjugular intrahepatic portosystemic stent shunt (TIPS), liver transplantation.

2. How should ascites due to high serum to ascites albumin gradient (SAAG) be managed?

They do not respond to salt restriction or diuretic therapy. Regular paracentesis and treatment of underlying pathology is the management.

 Note:

Although the case presented is that of cirrhosis related to hepatitis, (80% of ascites are due to cirrhosis), the student should be competent to discuss the mechanisms involved in fluid retention and the proposed effect of portal hypertension. Consequently the student shoud be prepared to discuss the role of the kidneys in salt and water retention. The student should also be competent to discuss ascites due to CCF, malignancies and pancreatic ascites (of alcoholism).

RED FLAG ENCOUNTERS-

This highlights the possible areas where the student can find himself in trouble by possible omissions or overlooking the examination findings.

- Unable to pick up stigmata of chronic liver disease
- Not examining gastro-intestinal system in systematic manner
- Unable to explain investigation to identify cause of ascites (transudate vs exudate)

MUST KNOW FACTS OF ASCITES

✓ There are multiple causes of ascites and eliciting specific symptoms and signs in history and examination will help to identify the likely underlying cause.

✓ Able to identify stigmata of chronic liver disease

✓ Tests and interpretation

✓ Basic management principles

OVERVIEW

Acute glomerulonephritis (AGN) refers to a broad category of renal disease of glomerular origin that is either primary with renal manifestation or caused by a secondary disease with the kidney been one of a multisystem involvement. AGN is characterised by generalised glomerular inflammation, resulting from an antigen-antibody reaction which activates a number of systems including the complement cascade, cytokines and coagulation factors.

The term is a pathological process which may present as one of the following clinical manifestations: acute nephritic syndrome, nephrotic syndrome, rapidly progressive glomerulonephritis and acute renal failure.

Post-streptococcal glomerulonephritis (PSGN) is the most common cause of acute nephritic syndrome and occurs as sporadic cases or in epidemic outbreaks which is now uncommon. The incidence of PSGN, has declined worldwide, but remains prevalent among the poor in developing countries. The acute mortality is low but causes significant morbidity. The risk of developing AGN is higher with skin infection than with pharyngitis.

Long Case or OSLER

AGN manifested through one of the renal syndromes is a commonly given Long Case. The candidate should take a detailed history of the presentation, detect the presence of complications (e.g. rapidly progressive glomerulonephritis) and exclude a secondary systemic illness (e.g. infective endocarditis). During clinical examination, the candidate should demonstrate clinical competence in correct and accurate measurement of blood pressure and jugular venous pressure and detect the presence of any extra-renal manifestations. The candidate should also be able to discuss the rationale of the choice of investigations, plan of management and follow up.

CASE VIGNETTE

A 17-year-old female student, previously healthy is admitted with a history of puffiness of face and swelling of ankles of two days duration. She has noticed passing dark coloured urine in smaller than normal quantities. She feels fatigued and has lost appetite. Two weeks ago, she developed an itchy skin rash over the hands and wrists for which she took anti-histamines.

On examination, there is puffiness over eyes, mild pedal oedema, no pallor, pulse 70 beats per minute, blood pressure 160/100 mmHg, jugular venous pressure 6cm above sternal angle; apex beat normal, normal heart sounds and lungs clear. Abdomen and nervous system examination is normal.

The clinical features are suggestive of acute nephritic syndrome in a young girl with recent-onset swelling of feet, facial puffiness with the passage of small quantity of dark urine. The blood pressure and jugular venous pressure is raised. Other renal conditions such as acute renal failure, chronic renal failure and nephrotic syndrome should also be considered.

Investigations should be done to confirm the clinical suspicion, exclude systemic causes and assess renal function prior to devising a treatment strategy.

DIFFERENTIAL DIAGNOSIS

- Acute nephritic syndrome
- Acute renal failure
- Chronic renal failure
- Nephrotic syndrome

HISTORY OF THE PRESENTING COMPLAINT

- Passing dark urine: Check if the urine is smoky (AGN), cola – like, tea-coloured or frank bloody. Make sure that it is not due to dietary articles (e.g. beetroot, food colouring etc.), drugs and dyes.
  Check on the time relationship to urination (if throughout the passage of urination it could come from kidney or ureter (AGN); if at the beginning it may suggest from the anterior urethra and end of the stream may suggest a bladder condition)
- Puffiness of eyes: Find out is this is worse in the morning. Other causes include angioneurotic oedema and hypothyroidism.
- Abdominal and lumbar pain: Onset of pain (sudden or slow build up), location and radiation (dull loin pain in AGN, loin to groin-ureteric colic), character (dull, sharp or colicky –Henoch Schönlein purpura (HSP)), aggravating and relieving factors, previous similar episodes
- Swelling of feet: The swelling is mild to moderate
- Quantity of urine; check if there is reduction in the output

- Associated symptoms: fever (PSGN, SLE, infective endocarditis (IE)), visual disturbance (hypertensive encephalopathy), nausea and vomiting (uraemia)
- Sore throat: check if throat symptoms occurred about 1-3 weeks prior to illness and if treatment was taken
- Skin infection: if itchy over hands (scabies) and legs in the preceding 3-5 weeks

REVIEW OF SYSTEMS

- Uremic symptoms: (fatigue, loss of appetite, pruritus, weight loss, excessive thirst and excessive passage of urine)
- Shortness of breath: Establish when it was first noticed and the rate of progression (due to hypertension)
- Paroxysmal nocturnal dyspnoea: Are you awakened suddenly by difficulty in breathing or coughing? Do these symptoms improve when you sit up or walk? (suggestive of left ventricular dysfunction)
- Orthopnoea: Do you find it more comfortable to sleep or rest in bed with several pillows? (suggestive of left ventricular dysfunction)
- Pain and swelling of joints: Is it only pain (common with SLE) or with swelling?
- Skin rashes: impetigo (following scabies), purpura (HSP), vasculitic (SLE, vasculitis)

PAST MEDICAL HISTORY

- Previous episodes of painless haematuria (IgA nephropathy)
- Previous admissions (determine if these were for abdominal pain, haematuria or hypertension)
- History of hypertension (how long was it known and how was it detected first time)

FAMILY HISTORY

- Size of family, deaths and illnesses.
- Are there any family members known to have kidney problems? If yes, find out details including symptoms, follow up and diagnosis. Draw family tree and indicate affected members going back to three generations.
- Are there any family members having high blood pressure or been on dialysis?

SOCIAL HISTORY

- Educational progress: if relevant
- Social class
- Income: able to afford hospital visits, medication if required on personal funds. Check if insured and how much of the medical expenses are covered.

TREATMENT HISTORY

- Obtain a list of drugs the patient is taking and the dosage

CHECK LIST FOR HISTORY

- Assess current and previous renal symptoms
- Assess if there complications have already developed (e.g. rapidly progressive glomerulonephritis)
- Assess if the hypertension is severe
- Check if skin or throat infection preceded current symptoms
- Check for presence of systemic diseases (e.g. IE, SLE)
- Check family history for similar illness
- Assess patient's understanding of the illness

EXAMINATION

PROFESSIONALISM

- Explain to patient what you intend doing before starting to examine
- Make sure the curtains are drawn and males should ask for a chaperone when examining a female patient
- Position patient with arms at the sides and adequate exposure of abdomen with genitals covered
- Get patient to empty the bladder before starting to examine

GENERAL EXAMINATION

- Observe patient. Note if well, tachypnoeic.
- Note complexion (sallow in uraemia)
- Inspect skin for impetigo (hands), purpura (legs and buttocks-HSP) and other maculopapular rashes, scalp for hair loss (SLE)
- Inspect tongue for pallor
- Inspect throat for tonsillar enlargement and redness
- Examine neck for cervical lymphadenopathy (residual pharyngitis)

399

- Inspect feet and legs for oedema
- Examine joints for swelling and tenderness (small joints – SLE, knees –HSP)

CARDIOVASCULAR EXAMINATION

- Examine radial pulse for rate, regularity, volume and character.
- Inspect jugular veins; measure height and observe waveform
- Measure blood pressure (average two recordings ; take third reading if there is significant difference between first two)
- Localise and characterise apex (heaving) & determine tracheal position at the same time
- Auscultate for heart sounds (identify first, second & additional sounds) and murmurs (infective endocarditis); Check for pericardial rub (SLE, uraemia)
- Auscultate lung bases for crepitations (pulmonary oedema, Goodpasture syndrome) and check for dullness (pleural effusion)

anriglomerular basement membrane antibodies - f alveolar membrane.

ABDOMINAL EXAMINATION

- Observe for abdominal fullness
- Note any surgical scars, puncture marks (attempted renal biopsy), and striae (previous steroid use)
- Palpate liver for enlargement and tenderness (congestion due to volume overload); note other features
- Palpate the spleen for enlargement; note other features, measure size ((infective endocarditis, SLE)
- Examine for loin tenderness. Watch patient's facial reaction
- Palpate the lower abdomen for a distended bladder (significant if patient had attempted to empty prior to examination)
- Percuss flanks for free fluid and check for free fluid by rolling over patient to one side
- Examine other systems (respiratory, nervous, and musculoskeletal) depending on the instructions, case format (OSCE, long case etc.), relevance and availability of time.
- Nervous system examination should focus on higher functions and fundal examination (hypertensive changes and papilloedema)
- Thank the patient at the end of the examination and cover patient up

CHECKLIST FOR EXAMINATION FINDINGS IN ACUTE GLOMERULONEPHRITIS

- General examination: pallor, impetigo, maculopapular, purpuric or vasculitis rash
- Enlarged tonsils and pharyngeal redness
- Pedal oedema
- Pulse; relatively slower rate (due to acute rise in blood pressure)
- Jugular venous pressure elevated
- Blood pressure: elevated
- Apex: displaced to left, and heaving
- Heart sounds: S3
- Added sounds: pericardial rub
- Murmurs: murmur (IE, SLE)
- Crepitations over lung bases, dullness of lung bases
- Ascites
- Joint swelling and tenderness (SLE)
- Hypertensive optic fundal changes and papilloedema

INVESTIGATIONS

Note: Aim of investigations is to confirm the diagnosis, assess complications and evaluate response to treatment.

Students should be able to explain relevance of investigations along these lines and also be aware of cost-benefit of investigations

- Full blood count; normocytic normochromic anaemia (partly dilutional), mild leucocytosis
- Serum creatinine/blood urea; usually elevated
- Serum electrolytes; raised serum potassium may occur
- Urine for albumin and deposits: albumin trace to 2++, dysmorphic red cells, red cell casts
- Arterial blood gases (if moderate to severe renal impairment is present)
- Ultrasound scan of abdomen: absence of small kidneys excludes chronic renal disease, corticomedullary demarcation blurred
- ECG: left ventricular hypertrophy (LVH) indicates long standing hypertension
- Chest radiograph: enlarged heart shadow, pulmonary congestion

- Echocardiography: LVH and normal LV function, vegetations (IE, SLE), pericardial effusion
- Renal biopsy: rarely needed but may show features of endocapillary glomerulonepritis
- Complement levels (C3 & C4): low C3 levels in PSGN, SLE and IE ; normal in HSP, C4 levels usually normal
- Serum IgA: increased in HSP
- Evidence of preceding streptococcal infection: rising anti-streptococcal O-titre (ASOT) or raised >200 IU/ml, anti-DNAse)
- Throat culture: positive in about 25% of cases
- Additional investigations may be required to identify systemic conditions (e.g. pANCA,cANCA, ANA, anti-dsDNA, blood culture-infective endocarditis)

CASE SUMMARY AND CLINICAL DISCUSSION OF THE CASE

This young girl 17-year old, with oliguria, haematuria, oedema and hypertension has features of acute nephritic syndrome. Clinical examination confirms presence of moderately elevated blood pressure and intravascular fluid retention. There is no clinical evidence of a systemic disorder. There is no evidence of complications of AGN. The diagnosis should be confirmed on blood and urine investigations, which will also exclude other conditions which may present similarly.

MANAGEMENT

The principles of management of this patient are as follows:
- Bed rest
- Fluid restriction and monitoring of intake and output
- Salt restriction
- Prompt treatment of throat or skin infection with antibiotics. Penicillin is the drug of choice
- Antihypertensive therapy, choosing drugs that are both effective and safe when renal impairment is present (nifedipine, captopril, metoprolol; if urgent consider using labetalol, sodium nitroprusside, hydralazine)
- Loop diuretic for oedema, raised blood pressure and pulmonary congestion
- Close monitoring of blood pressure, fluid intake and losses, renal function and electrolytes
- Dialysis (haemodialysis or peritoneal) if hyperkalemia or uraemia develops
- Renal biopsy if rapid deterioration of renal function occurs or a renal manifestation of a systemic disorder is suspected

LEARNING OUTCOME

The student should be able to

- Elicit a focussed history in a patient with haematuria and oedema
- Perform a complete examination of the cardiovascular system and abdomen
- Detect the physical signs present, particularly puffiness around eyes, elevated jugular veins and raised blood pressure
- Explain the clinical features on a physiological and pathological basis
- Make a clinical diagnosis or provide a differential diagnosis based on the history and examination findings
- Select the relevant investigations that would support the diagnosis, assess renal function and exclude systemic causes
- List the common causes of haematuria and explain how to differentiate one cause from the other based on the history
- Discuss the principles of management of AGN
- Discuss appropriate nutritional, fluid and electrolyte management
- Discuss the choice of antihypertensive medication in this condition
- Describe the complications of AGN and how to suspect these at an early stage
- Communicate to the patient about the nature of the illness, general and specific preventive measures including follow up and prognosis.

COMMONLY ASKED QUESTIONS

What are the common complications of PSGN?
Pulmonary oedema, acute renal failure, hypertensive encephalopathy, nephrotic syndrome, chronic renal failure, rapidly progressive glomerulonephritis

What is the prognosis in an uncomplicated episode of PSGN?
The prognosis is usually excellent for the great majority of patients with full recovery of renal function. Persistent proteinuria and presence of comorbid conditions may lead to chronic renal failure.

Name the antibodies that are present in PSGN patients?
Anti-DNA antibodies, antiCiq antibodies, anti-neutrophil cytoplasmic antibodies (ANCA), cryoglobulins and rheumatoid factor are present in some patients.

What is the significance of dysmorphic red cells and red cell casts in urine?

These doughnut shaped red cells with spheroidal protrusions are characteristically of glomerular origin. Rarely these may be present after renal biopsy or passed out with urine in patients with renal tumours. Red cell casts are another feature present in the urine sediment that suggests that the bleeding has occurred at the glomerular level and are then casted in the tubules with mucoprotein.

When should a renal biopsy be done in post-streptococcal glomerulonephritis?

Usually a renal biopsy is not indicated for the diagnosis but may be required under the following circumstances.

- Rising serum creatinine (to exclude RPGN)
- Persistent oliguria
- Proteinuria is in the nephrotic range
- Serum complement level is normal
- Serum complement level remains low after recovery (usually back to normal by one month)

DISTINCTION LEVEL QUESTIONS

Name TWO new blood investigations that improve the diagnosis of a streptococcal aetiology in PSGN?

Two new antigens have been implicated in PSGN; nephritis associated plasmin receptor (NAPlr), and streptococcal pyrogenic exotoxin (erythrotoxin) B (SPEB) and its zymogen precursor (zSPEB). Antibodies to these are present long after the illness is subsided and provides a test with improved specificity over the traditional ASOT estimation. However, these are not widely available at present for routine testing.

RED FLAG ENCOUNTERS

The following are situations that may be overlooked:

- Failure to consider AGN in the differential diagnosis
- Poor technique in measurement of blood pressure
- Fails to detect raised jugular venous pressure
- Failure to check the optic fundi for hypertensive changes
- Misses clinical features of a treatable systemic disorder

MUST KNOW FACTS OF ACUTE GLOMERULONEPHRITIS

- Most common glomerular syndrome seen in clinical practice
- May be subclinical but the common presenting features are acute onset haematuria, oedema and hypertension in a young person is characteristic
- Onset of AGN after impetigo is much later than after pharyngitis
- Majority of patients fully recover from the acute episode.
- Several life threatening complications such as acute pulmonary oedema, acute renal failure and hypertensive encephalopathy may occur in the acute phase of the illness.
- Chronic renal failure is an uncommon squeal of AGN

CASE 31: NEPHROTIC SYNDROME
RIFDY MOHIDEEN

OVERVIEW

Nephrotic syndrome (NS) is a grouping of renal and laboratory manifestations that can be caused by primary renal disease or a number of secondary causes.

The common secondary causes are diabetes mellitus, lupus, amyloidosis, viral infections and pre-eclampsia. The main clinical and laboratory features are heavy proteinuria, peripheral oedema, hypoalbuminemia and hyperlipidaemia. Additionally lipiduria and evidence of hypercoagulability are seen.

The main pathological process is increased glomerular permeability of the glomeruli to large molecules, such as albumin but other plasma proteins too, are lost in the process. Proteinuria is typically heavy exceeding 3.5 g/24 hrs. Serum albumin is often below 25 g/L. The metabolic consequences of proteinuria are infection especially to Streptococcus pneumonia, Haemophilus influenza and E.coli; hyperlipidemia, hypocalcemia with bone changes, hypercoagulability and hypovolumia. Patients with NS are prone to infection due a variety of causes apart from loss of immunological proteins. Ascitic fluid is a goo media for infection . The use of immunosuppressive agents and a lowered perfusion by the spleen due to hypovolumia have been suggested as reasons.

Oedema in lower limbs, ascites , pleural effusion are related to hypoalbuminemia. The resulting fall in serum albuminuria due to proteinuria reduces oncotic pressure and causes intravascular volume depletion. Activation of the renin-angiotensin-aldosterone and sympathetic nervous systems causes sodium retention leading to oedema.

The prevalence varies significantly by the age of onset and underlying causes. The prognosis and treatment vary dramatically depending on the underlying aetiology.

Types of Case for Examination

NS is a commonly given as a LONG CASE. The candidate should take a detailed history of the presentation, check out if complications have already developed (e.g. venous thrombosis) and look out for a secondary cause (e.g. amyloidosis). During clinical examination, the candidate should demonstrate presence of oedema, fluid collection in abdomen and chest and look out for clues of a secondary cause. The candidate should also be able to discuss the rationale of the choice of investigations, plan of management and follow up.

CASE VIGNETTE

A 20-year-old female undergraduate, who was previously healthy presents with a history of puffiness of face and swelling of ankles of two weeks duration. She has noticed passing urine that is frothy but in normal quantities as before. There is no dysuria or haematuria. She also complains of abdominal distension and had loss of appetite. There is no history of allergy or long term use of medications.

On examination, there is puffiness over eyes, oedema of lower limbs up to the knees, no pallor, pulse 80 beats per minute, blood pressure 120/70 mmHg, jugular venous pressure 2cm above sternal angle, apex beat normal, normal heart sounds and reduced breath sounds on the right lower zone. Abdomen is distended with flank dullness which shifted on turning patient to the right. Nervous system examination is normal.

The clinical features are suggestive of nephrotic syndrome, with significant swelling of lower limbs, facial puffiness with the passage of normal quantities of frothy urine. The blood pressure and jugular venous pressure are normal. Other renal conditions such as nephritic syndrome, chronic renal failure, chronic liver disease and should also be considered. Rarely protein-losing enteropathy may present with oedema

Investigations should be done to confirm clinical suspicion, exclude systemic causes and assess renal function prior to devising a management strategy .

Differential diagnosis

- Nephrotic syndrome
- Chronic renal failure
- Acute nephritic syndrome
- Chronic liver disease
- Protein-losing enteropathy

History of the presenting complaint

- Passing frothy urine: Check if the urine is foamy or frothy and if this is persistent. Frothy urine is a sign of protein in the urine.
- Colour of urine; check if dark urine has been bloody or dark in colour. Make sure that it is not due to dietary articles (e.g. beetroot, food colouring etc.), drugs and dyes.

Check on the time relationship of passing dark urine to urination (if throughout the passage of urination it could come from kidney or ureter (AGN); if at the beginning it may suggest from the anterior urethra and end of the stream may suggest a bladder condition. Frank haematuria is not usually associated with nephrotic syndrome except when renal vein thrombosis supervenes)

- Quantity of urine; Check if there is change in the quantity; often this remains unchanged in the early stages but oliguria may occur when intravascular volume diminishes following use of diuretics
- Puffiness of eyes: Find out is this is worse in the morning. Other causes include angioneurotic oedema and hypothyroidism.
- Swelling of feet: The swelling is mild to moderate. Usually this worsens at the end of the day and improves somewhat is the morning.
- Abdominal distension or fullness: May occur with fluid collecting in the peritoneal cavity.

Review of systems

- Abdominal, flank and loin pain; Pain in these locations may indicate additional complications such as renal vein thrombosis or peritonitis.
- Uremic symptoms: (fatigue, loss of appetite, pruritus, weight loss, excessive thirst and excessive passage of urine)
- Shortness of breath: Establish when it was first noticed and the rate of progression (due to accumulation of fluid in pleural cavity, heart failure)
- Pain and swelling of joints: Is it only pain (common with SLE) or with swelling?
- Skin rashes: macular-papular rash (SLE), purpura (amyloidosis), vasculitic (SLE, vasculitis)
- Occult malignancy: Loss of weight, cough, fever, dark stools

Past medical history

- Previous episodes of facial puffiness and limb swelling ()
- Previous admissions (determine if these were for oedema, haematuria or hypertension)
- History of hypertension and diabetes (how long was it known and how was it detected first time)
- History of previous infections (hepatitis B & C, HIV)

Family history

- Size of family, deaths and illnesses.
- Are there any family members known to have kidney problems? If yes, find out details including symptoms, follow up and diagnosis. Draw family tree and indicate affected members going back to three generations.
- Are there any family members having high blood pressure or been on dialysis?

Social history

- Educational progress: if relevant
- Income: able to afford hospital visits, medication if required on personal funds. Check if insured and how much of the medical expenses are covered.

Treatment history

- Obtain a list of drugs the patient is taking and the dosage (bisphosphonates, gold, penicillamine, NSAIDs, lithium carbonate)

Check list for history

- Assess current and previous renal symptoms
- Exclude other causes of oedema (cardiac, liver and malabsorptive)
- Determine if there complications have already developed (e.g. thrombosis) Renal vein Thrombus → loin pain
- Determine if the hypertension and haematuria is present (poor prognostic features)
- Check for presence of systemic diseases (e.g. SLE)
- Check family history for similar illness
- Assess patient's understanding of the illness

Examination

Professionalism

- Explain to patient what you intend doing before starting to examine
- Make sure the curtains are drawn and males should ask for a chaperone when examining a female patient
- Position patient with arms at the sides and adequate exposure of abdomen with genitals covered
- Get patient to empty the bladder before starting to examine

General examination

- Observe patient. Note periorbital swelling, moon-faced (steroid use)
- Note complexion (sallow in uraemia)
- Inspect skin for maculopapular rashes, scalp for hair loss (SLE), bruising (amyloidosis)
- Inspect tongue for pallor (uraemia)
- Inspect nails (white horizontal bands in hypoalbuminemia)
- Inspect feet, legs and sacrum for oedema
- Examine the buttocks for eruptive xanthomata
- Examine joints for swelling and tenderness (small joints – SLE)

Cardiovascular examination

- Examine radial pulse for rate, regularity, volume and character.
- Inspect jugular veins; Usually jugular veins are not elevated in NS; if elevated consider cardiac failure, pericardial effusion or advent of acute or chronic renal failure
- Measure blood pressure (average two recordings; blood pressure usually normal)
- Localise and characterise apex (exclude cardiac cause for oedema and systemic amyloidosis)
- Auscultate for heart sounds (identify first, second & additional sounds) and murmurs (SLE); Check for pericardial rub (SLE, uraemia)
- Auscultate lung bases for dullness (pleural effusion)

Abdominal examination

- Observe for abdominal fullness
- Note any surgical scars, puncture marks (renal biopsy, peritoneal dialysis), and striae (previous steroid use)
- Palpate liver for enlargement and tenderness (congestion due to heart failure); note other features
- Palpate the spleen for enlargement; note other features, measure size (SLE, amyloidosis)
- Percuss flanks for free fluid and check for free fluid by rolling over patient to one side. Palpate for a fluid thrill if shifting dullness is present.
- Examine the genitalia for oedema when severe

- Nervous system examination may find clinical clues of secondary causes; peripheral neuropathy (diabetes, amyloidosis), retinopathy (diabetes and hypertension)
- Examine other systems (respiratory, nervous, and musculoskeletal) in detail depending on the instructions, case format (OSCE, long case etc.), relevance and availability of time.
- Thank the patient at the end of the examination and cover patient up

Checklist for examination findings in nephrotic syndrome

- General examination: puffy facies, moon-faced (if on steroids), white band in nails, eruptive xanthomata, bruising
- Extensive limb oedema
- CVS: normal jugular venous pressure, blood pressure and apex with no murmurs unless complicated with chronic renal disease or secondary causes
- Chest: dullness of lung bases
- Ascites

Investigations

Note ordering the list of investigations the student should be considering confirming the diagnosis of NS, determining a cause (primary or secondary) and assess complications mentioned.

The criteria for a diagnosis of NS :

- Proteinuria (>85% albumin)   >3.0-3.5 g/24 hours
- Spot urine protein:creatinine ratio >300-350 mg/mmol
- Serum albumin <25 g/L
- Severe hyperlipidemia (total cholesterol >10 mmol/L)
- Peripheral oedema

Specific investigations are directed to the presenting symptom. For example if the patient has no evidence of a pleural effusion (shortness of breath) then a chest radiograph would be low on the list. Similarly a renal ultrasound may be indicated if renal function is abnormal . If the cause of NS is diabetes , then a host of investigations for complications of diabetes is warranted apart from what is listed below.

Relevant investigations include:

- Full blood count; anaemia may be seen (loss of transferrin and eythropoietin)

- ESR: usually elevated irrespective of underlying cause
- Serum creatinine/blood urea; usually normal
- Serum electrolytes; usually normal, low serum sodium or potassium in cases of aggressive diuresis; raised serum potassium following therapy or advent of renal failure
- Urine for albumin and deposits: albumin 2 to 4++++, fatty casts, oval fat bodies, red cells (in some pathologies such as membrano-proliferative glomerulonephritis and renal vein thrombosis)
- Urine spot protein:creatinine ratio: correlates to the amount of protein/day excretion (>300 mg/micromol, is diagnostic for nephrotic-range proteinuria)
- Urine for Bence Jones proteins: if multiple myeloma is suspected
- Lipid panel; elevated total and LDL cholesterol and lipoprotein(a) fraction, normal or low HDL, raised triglycerides
- Blood glucose and HbA1c
- Renal ultrasound: large kidneys, also seen in amyloidosis, HIV, diabetes
- Doppler renal ultrasound; renal vein thrombosis
- ECG: left ventricular hypertrophy (LVH) indicates long standing hypertension
- Chest radiograph: evidence of pleural effusion
- Echocardiography: indicated if systemic amyloidosis is suspected
- Renal biopsy: often needed unless in minimal chain nephropathy
- Additional investigations may be required to identify systemic conditions (e.g. ANA, anti-dsDNA, hepatitis B & C serology, HIV testing)

Case summary and clinical discussion of the case

This young 20-year-old girl with gross oedema, pleural effusion and ascites has heavy proteinuria suggestive of nephrotic syndrome. Absence of hypertension and haematuria are good prognostic features. There are no clinical features of a secondary cause but this has to be excluded by investigation. There is no evidence of complication. The diagnosis should be confirmed on blood and urine investigations, which will also exclude other similar presenting features.

MANAGEMENT

The principles of management of this patient are as follows:
Would some general principles be helpful for a holistic approach before the list below?

Primary glomerular disease and some specifics like role of steroids for minimal change and risk of relapse; expectant management with anti-inflammatory agents in amyloidosis, why ACEIs an ARB are good for hypertension, why IV albumin , prophylactic antibiotics are of no value. Mention of common immunosuppresants (could be in the question)

- Fluid restriction and monitoring of intake and output
- Daily weight on chart
- Salt restriction to less than 100mmol/day (Prevent Na retenth.
- Protein intake: limit intake to 0.8–1 g/kg/d, with a preference for vegetable and fish proteins
- Diuretics; judicious use to avoid rapid intravascular volume depletion and electrolyte imbalance; loop diuretics can be combined with potassium-sparing diuretics
- Intravenous salt-poor albumin is of doubtful benefit
- ACEIs: on large doses to reduce albuminuria, may be combined cautiously with angiotensin receptor blockers for additional effect
- Antihypertensive therapy: if required choose drugs that are reduce proteinuria (ACEIs, ARBs, non-dihydropyridine calcium channel blockers)
- Statins: for severe hyperlipidaemia
- Anticoagulation: if thrombosis is only confirmed and in severe membranous glomerulonephritis
- Prophylactic antibiotics: no evidence of usefulness
- Treat underlying secondary cause (e.g. steroids, immunosuppressive agents for SLE)
- Treat underlying glomerular pathology (steroids for minimal change GN)
- Close monitoring of weight, proteinuria, blood pressure, fluid intake and losses, renal function and electrolytes

Note: In a LONG CASE (OSLER) communication skills would be evaluated as to breaking serious illness news, how prognosis is discussed especially in this case where she is young and she would require a series of investigations which would be both invasive and non-invasive. The candidate should be able to take informed consent for renal biopsy and discuss effect of drugs on ovarian and reproductive function.

Learning outcome

The student should be able to

- Elicit a focussed history in a patient with gross oedema
- Perform a complete general examination and relevant system examinations
- Detect the physical signs present, particularly puffiness around eyes, oedema, ascites and pleural effusion
- Explain the oedema and proteinuria (frothy urine) on a physiological and pathological basis
- Make a clinical diagnosis or provide a differential diagnosis based on the history and examination findings
- Select the relevant investigations that would confirm the diagnosis, assess renal function and exclude systemic causes
- List the common causes of nephrotic syndrome and explain how it differs from acute nephritic syndrome by its clinical features
- Discuss the principles of management of NS
- Discuss appropriate nutritional, fluid and electrolyte management
- Discuss the choice of medications that reduces proteinuria in this condition
- Describe the complications of NS and how to suspect these at an early stage
- Communicate to the patient about the nature of the illness, general and specific therapies that are beneficial, prognosis and follow up measures

Commonly asked questions

Name THREE primary pathological conditions that cause nephrotic syndrome?
Membranous glomerulonephritis, focal segmental glomerulosclerosis, membranoproliferative glomerulonephritis and minimal change glomerulonephritis

What are the reasons for the susceptibility to infections in nephrotic syndrome?
NS causes a urinary loss of immunoglobulins and complement. Additionally, immunosuppressive drugs further increase susceptibility.

What are the factors that increase coagulability in nephrotic syndrome?
There is increased clotting factor synthesis in the liver (factors I, II, V, VII, VIII, X, and XIII), and loss of coagulation inhibitors such as

antithrombin III in the urine. The other prothrombotic risks include hyperviscosity resulting from increased fibrinogen levels, hyperlipidaemia, prolonged immobilization, and use of diuretics.

When should a renal biopsy be done in nephrotic syndrome?
Often a renal biopsy is indicated for the diagnosis in adults. Common indications are as follows:

- age at onset (less than 1 year or more than 10)
- steroid-resistant cases
- gross or persistent microscopic haematuria or presence of red cell casts
- abnormal serologies
- significant persistent renal failure

What are the medications that are associated with nephrotic syndrome?
Bisphosphanates, gold, antimicrobials, NSAIDs, penicillamine, captopril, tamoxifen and lithium

Distinction level questions

Explain why there is hyperlipidaemia in nephrotic syndrome?
The mechanisms underlying lipid abnormalities are multifactorial. These include increased rates of lipoprotein synthesis and defective clearance and catabolism of circulating particles.

Nephrotic syndrome leads to marked upregulation of hepatic acyl-CoA-cholesterol acyltransferase (ACAT), which plays an important part in packaging and secretion of apoB-containing lipoproteins by the liver. There is also down regulation of lipoprotein lipase, VLDL receptor and hepatic triglyceride lipase and upregulation of hepatic acyl-CoA-diacylglycerol acyltransferase, which is the final step in triglyceride synthesis.
HDL subtypes are abnormally distributed, with a reduction of HDL2 and an increase in HDL3 although HDL may be normal or low. These lipid abnormalities puts these patients with NS at higher risk of cardiovascular disease.

Red flag encounters

The following are situations that may be overlooked:

- Failure to consider NS in the differential diagnosis of oedema
- Unable to recall the main clinical and laboratory features of NS
- Fails to detect presence of significant ascites
- Misses a likely underlying secondary cause or clue

Must know facts of nephrotic syndrome

- A common glomerular syndrome seen in clinical practice caused by direct renal injury or a systemic disorder
- NS due to minimal change glomerulonephritis carries the best prognosis and is the most common underlying cause in children
- Important complications include thrombosis, infections and progression to chronic renal failure
- Thrombosis is a well-recognised risk in membranous nephropathy
- Marked hypercholesterolemia is common and require statin therapy
- Chronic renal failure is an important long-term complication

CASE 32: CHRONIC KIDNEY DISEASE WITH END STAGE RENAL FAILURE
VAANI VALERIE VISUVANATHAN

OVERVIEW

Chronic kidney disease (CKD) describes the gradual and progressive loss of kidney function over time. It is divided into 5 stages as depicted in the table below:

Stage	Description	GFR (mL/min/1.73m^2)
1	Kidney damage with normal or increased GFR	>90
2	Kidney damage with mild decrease in GFR	60-89
3	Moderate decrease in kidney function	30-59
4	Severe decrease in kidney function	15-29
5	Kidney failure	< 15 (or dialysis)

Chronic kidney disease is defined as either evidence of kidney damage or GFR< 60mL/min/1.73m^2 for ≥ 3 months. For Stages 1 and 2, calculation of GFR exclusively is inadequate to confirm the diagnosis. Other parameters, for example, proteinuria, haematuria, albuminuria and structural abnormalities of the kidneys should be taken into consideration. Patients in Stages 1, 2 and 3 are relatively well and tend to only develop symptoms as kidney function deteriorates further.

The incidence of chronic kidney disease (CKD) has increased markedly over recent decades. It is estimated that one out of every ten Malaysian has CKD. The common causes of CKD are diabetes mellitus, hypertension, vascular diseases, glomerular diseases (primary or secondary) and urinary tract obstruction.

Types of cases that may be presented for clinical examination:

LONG CASE

OSCE (SHORT AND LONG)

CASE VIGNETTE

A 58-year-old gentleman is seen at the medical out-patient clinic during his regular follow-up. He complains of bilateral ankle swelling and feeling lethargic for the past one month. He is known to have type 2 diabetes mellitus and hypertension for the past 14 years. His blood investigation results are:

	Today	1 year ago
Urea	18mmol/L	15mmol/L (3-9)
Creatinine	321µmol/L	289µmol/L (60-100)
Haemoglobin	9.8g/dL	10.5g/dL
	(MCV 88fL, MCH 29pg)	

Question:

Obtain a detailed history from the patient and perform a focused physical examination.

Differential Diagnoses:

HISTORY OF PRESENTING ILLNESS

- Ankle swelling – duration, extent, aggravating factors, associated symptoms (explore regarding other symptoms of fluid overload eg. shortness of breath, orthopnoea), rule out other causes of ankle swelling (eg. trauma, cellulitis)
- Lethargy – severity, limitation of daily activities, associated symptoms (palpitations, angina)
- Anaemia – other possible causes of anaemia should be explored eg. dietary
  Note: In this patient, lethargy may be due to anaemia, uraemia, pulmonary oedema or a combination of these factors.

SYSTEMIC REVIEW

- Other manifestations of uraemia, for example, pruritus, nausea, restless leg syndrome or easy bruising
- Symptoms of renal bone disease eg. bone pain, fractures
- Urinary symptoms eg. decreased stream strength, hesitancy, haematuria

- Proteinuria (frothy urine) and nocturia – duration
- Symptoms of other systemic disorders which may cause CKD eg. arthritis, photosensitivity

PAST MEDICAL HISTORY

- Diabetes mellitus – glycaemic control, complications (eg. diabetic ketoacidosis, hypoglycaemia), compliance to medications, other end organ damage
- Hypertension – duration, control, complications (eg. hypertensive emergency)
- Cardiovascular disease
- Liver cirrhosis
- Urinary calculi or infections
- Benign prostate hypertrophy
- Other systemic disease eg. systemic lupus erythromatosus, scleroderma

  Note: It is important to ask about history of hypertension during childhood or pregnancy (in females). Be familiar with normal biochemistry variations between men and women (e.g. slight difference in creatinine levels.

SURGICAL HISTORY

- Procedures performed for removal of urinary calculi
- Pelvic surgery (in females)

FAMILY HISTORY

- Polycystic kidney disease (autosomal dominant disorder)
- Diabetes mellitus and hypertension

SOCIAL HISTORY

- Smoking – significantly increases the rate of progression of renal failure
- Alcohol intake
- Financial status – in the event of patient requiring renal replacement therapy in the future
- Family support

MEDICATION HISTORY

- Nephrotoxic medications eg, non-steroidal anti-inflammatory drugs, chemotherapeutics, radio contrast agents

- Necessity of dose adjustment be required for any of the current medications

CHECK LIST FOR HISTORY TAKING

- ✓ Symptoms of uraemia
- ✓ Symptoms of anaemia
- ✓ Symptoms of renal bone disease
- ✓ Symptoms of fluid overload
- ✓ Other symptoms suggestive of renal impairment
- ✓ Identify the possible causative agent of CKD
- ✓ Identify factors that could accelerate the progression of kidney failure
- ✓ Other organs or systems involved
- ✓ Medication history
- ✓ Financial and family support

EXAMINATION

Introduce yourself, confirm the patient's identity and explain that you would like to perform a physical examination. Ensure that you have a chaperone, if required.

General examination and vital signs

Perform a general inspection. Ensure that you do not exhaust the patient if he is dyspnoeic, tachypnoeic or cyanosed. Assess the patient's mental status and look for the presence of a sallow appearance. Patients with severe uraemia tend to be drowsy. Determine if he is anaemic.

Hyperventilation may suggest that patient has metabolic acidosis (Kussmaul breathing). Measurement of blood pressure and assessment of hydration status is essential. Patient may have intractable hiccups, uraemic fetor or uraemic frost (white powdery substance on skin caused by urea precipitates from sweat) due to uraemia.

Nails should be examined for leuconychia, half-and-half nails and clubbing.

The presence of arteriovenous fistulas and the functional status of the fistulas should be commented on. (Functioning fistulas usually have a palpable continuous thrill and evidence of recent puncture, however imaging studies are confirmatory).

Bruises (due to impaired platelet aggregation), scratch marks (secondary hyperparathyroidism leads to calcium deposits which cause pruritus), gouty tophi and carpal tunnel release scars may be present.

uraemia

Asterixis can be elicited by getting the patient to hold his forearms outstretched in front with his wrists hyper-extended.

Bone tenderness would be supportive of increased bone turnover which would be evident in hyperparathyroidism. Osteoarthritis and chronic gouty arthritis should also encourage the student to entertain the possibility of chronic analgesic abuse as a cause of renal impairment.

Head and neck

Conjunctival pallor, xanthelasma and scleral icterus should be looked for in the eyes. Malar rash and mouth ulcers might suggest systemic lupus erythematosus. Microstomia with tight, mask-like skin would be noted in scleroderma.

Jugular venous pressure must be measured with patient satisfactorily positioned. Scars of previous internal jugular dialysis catheter insertion may be noted on the neck.

Abdomen

Inspection for any previous peritoneal dialysis scars (lower abdomen) or nephrectomy scars (loin) should be performed. Transplanted kidneys are usually placed in the iliac fossa and felt as a bulge under the surgical scar. Ascites may be present.

Liver and kidneys may be enlarged and palpable in patients with polycystic kidney disease.

Half of the patients with renal artery stenosis have a renal bruit which is best heard above the umbilicus, 2cm lateral to the midline.

Cardiopulmonary

Locate the apex beat and auscultate the heart. A pericardial rub would suggest pericarditis.

Examination of the lungs should focus on looking for basal crepitation (pulmonary oedema) or reduced breath sounds at the bases (pleural effusion).

Neurological

A neurological examination focusing on complications of diabetes mellitus, e.g. glove and stocking sensory loss and cerebrovascular accident, should be performed.

Fundus

Direct ophthalmoscopy should be performed to look for diabetic and hypertensive changes in the retina.

Digital rectal examination and pelvic examination

This is of utmost importance in males, to assess the size of the prostate gland and to identify malena. Pelvic masses must be sought for among females. Advanced pelvic cancer (cancer of cervix) and recurrent pelvic cancer may cause obstructive uropathy in women.

Note: a thorough physical examination should be performed in this patient as he has diabetes mellitus and hypertension.

CHECK LIST FOR CLINICAL EXAMINATION

- ✓ Signs of impaired renal function
  - Uraemia
  - Fluid overload
  - Hypercalcaemia (secondary hyperparathyroidism)
  - Anaemia
  - Metabolic acidosis
  - AV fistula or previous dialysis
- ✓ Signs to suggest underlying cause of renal impairment
  - Transplanted kidneys
  - Dehydration/sepsis/shock
  - Diabetic/hypertensive retinopathy
  - Liver cirrhosis (Hepato-Renal Synd)
  - Polycystic kidneys
  - Prostate hypertrophy / pelvic mass → obst. uropathy
  - Connective tissue diseases

INVESTIGATIONS

☞ *Note:*

Investigations are done for confirmation of renal dysfunction in assessing the progress of disease and development of complications.

The criteria for diagnosis of CKD need to be fulfilled.

To ascertain chronic kidney damage

Urine analysis

Albuminuria can be detected easily, however, quantification may require a 24-hour urine protein.

Haematuria may be noted as well. In patients with persistent microscopic haematuria, urinary tract malignancy needs to be ruled out.

Albumin : creatinine

Albumin:creatinine(ACR) ratio is the preferred investigation to identify kidney damage and monitor kidney disease. It has greater sensitivity than protein:creatinine ratio(PCR) for detecting low levels of proteinuria and is not influenced by urine concentration.

Imaging of the kidneys

Ultrasonography of the kidneys is useful to look for structural lesions eg. cysts, calculi, tumours.

Hydronephrosis may be detected in the presence of urinary tract obstruction, as well as, the aetiology eg, pelvic mass or retroperitoneal fibrosis.

Serum calcium and phosphate

Vitamin D is hydroxylated to calcitriol(active form) in the kidney. Failing kidney function impairs this process leading to reduced absorption of calcium from the gut and hence, hypocalcaemia. There is concurrent phosphate retention as renal function deteriorates. Hypocalcaemia and hyperphosphatemia trigger parathyroid hormone synthesis (secondary hyperparathyroidism), causing increased bone resorption as the body attempts to correct the hypocalcaemia. Persistently elevated serum parathyroid hormone levels lead to increased bone turnover and lesions, such as, osteitis fibrosa cystica.

Note: Renal osteodystrophy refer to a constellation of skeletal abnormalities, consisting of osteitis fibrosa cystica, osteomalacia and adynamic bone disease.

Hyperkalaemia

Hyperkalaemia usually develops in patients with Stage 4 or 5 CKD, and in those with impaired aldosterone secretion.

Haemoglobin

Anaemia is commonly seen among patients with chronic kidney disease.

The causes for anaemia may be multifactorial consisting of:

- Chronic inflammation
- Poor nutrition causing deficiency of iron, folate or B12
- Decreased synthesis of erythropoietin
- Occult blood loss
- Blood loss through dialysis

Blood gases

Metabolic acidosis develops due to the impaired excretion of endogenous acids in the urine. In Stage 5 CKD, the accumulation of phosphates, uric acid and organic anions contributes to this state.

Chest radiograph

There may be evidence of pulmonary oedema as a result of fluid overload.

INVESTIGATIONS TO ASCERTAIN CAUSE OF KIDNEY DAMAGE

1. HbA1C – to ascertain glycaemic control

2. Liver function test – to rule out hepatorenal syndrome

3. Anti-nuclear antibody, double stranded DNA antibody – if systemic lupus erythematosus is suspected

4. C3 and C4 complement levels – may be decreased in certain types of glomerulonephritis

5. Anti-glomerular basement membrane – present in Goodpasture syndrome

6. Renal artery ultrasound – to diagnose renal artery stenosis

7. Renal biopsy – performed when the cause of the kidney damage is unclear and to determine the degree of disease activity, e.g. systemic lupus erythrematosus.

Note: In this case, the patient's cardiovascular risk factors should be assessed too. A fasting serum lipid, electrocardiogram and echocardiography should be performed.

CASE SUMMARY

This 58-year-old gentleman, who is known to have diabetes mellitus and hypertension, presents with symptoms of fluid retention and anaemia which are both secondary to chronic kidney disease. On examination, he is pale and has bilateral ankle oedema. He has uraemic fetor and uraemic frost. The degree of kidney damage should be assessed by performing a urine albumin:creatinine and calculation of GFR (glomerular filtration rate). A renal ultrasonography should also be performed to assess kidney size and rule out structural lesions.

CLINICAL DISCUSSION OF THE CASE

The patient has a long history of diabetes mellitus and hypertension. As the results imply, the renal impairment is chronic (at least 1 year), clearly not acute kidney failure. The disease needs to be prevalent for > 3 months to be categorized as CKD. He now presents with ankle swelling due to fluid retention and lethargy which may be due to uraemia or anaemia or a combination of both.

☞ Note: Having established the clinical diagnosis, the student is expected to outline a management plan in a LONG CASE. In a long OSCE, specific questions pertaining to management may be asked.

Management

The management of a patient with chronic kidney disease involves:

- Identifying the cause and treating it
- Intervention to slow or halt progression of kidney damage
- Management of complications that arise from kidney damage
- Preparation for renal replacement therapy and referral to nephrologist (if indicated)
- Advanced instructions on resuscitation and further care in terminal disease

Identify cause

The most common causes of CKD would be diabetes mellitus, hypertension and glomerulonephritis. The causative agent in infective causes can be identified from history and relevant investigations, as mentioned.

Slow disease progression

Target blood pressure would be <130/80mmHg in patients with CKD or diabetics with proteinuria.

The American Diabetic Association recommends a target HBA1C of <7% for diabetics with or without kidney disease.

Angiotensin receptor blockers and ACE inhibitors are beneficial, especially in patients who have proteinuria. If a patient is on oral hypoglycemic agents, they should be stopped because reduced renal clearance may lead to hypoglycaemia. Short acting insulin is initiated instead.

Smoking cessation has been proven to slow progression to end stage renal failure and reduce risk of cardiovascular disease.

Hyperlipidaemia should be maintained at target values with the aid of statins.

Nephrotoxic drugs are to be avoided at all costs.

Moderate-intensity exercises should be encouraged to aid in reduction of blood pressure.

Note: Complications may already be present in some patients at the time of presentation and focussed questions based on complications may be asked. The student would be competent is recognizing expected complications from clinical examination.

MANAGEMENT OF COMPLICATIONS

Anaemia

- Haemoglobin level should be maintained >10g/dL
- Correct nutritional deficiencies and initiate erythropoiesis stimulating agents

(Note: The TREAT trial in 2009 revealed that chronic kidney disease patients with diabetes and moderate anaemia but not undergoing regular dialysis, who were administered darbepoetin alfa, an erythropoietin stimulating agent, did not have reduced rates of death, heart failure, myocardial infarction, admission for myocardial ischemia, or end-stage renal disease as compared to the control group)

Renal osteodystrophy

- Calcium supplements and calcitriol are prescribed for hypocalcaemia
- Calcium-based phosphate binders and dietary phosphate restriction are used for reduction of phosphate levels
- Bisphosphanates can be offered for treatment of osteoporosis
- Parathyroidectomy may be required for patients with tertiary hyperparathyroidism (↑ blood Ca)

Hyperkalaemia

- Potassium rich food should be avoided

Fluid overload

- Fluid restriction or diuretics, especially for patients on dialysis with minimal urine output.

Malnutrition

- A protein-controlled diet (0.8-1.0 g/kg/day) is recommended by some. However, patient should be carefully monitored for nutritional deficiencies.

Initiation of renal replacement therapy

Renal replacement therapy should be initiated in patients with estimated GFR < 20mL/min/m^2 in the presence of refractory metabolic acidosis, uraemic symptoms, decline in nutritional status and volume overload not responding to medications.

Kidney transplant from a live donor may be promoted for eligible patients who require renal replacement therapy.

LEARNING OUTCOMES

By the end of this case review the student should be able to:

1. Obtain a relevant history from a patient with chronic kidney disease

2. Identify the causative agent from history

3. Perform a relevant and focused clinical examination of a patient who has chronic kidney disease

4. Discuss the relevant investigations that should be performed and the pathophysiology of the expected findings

5. Discuss the aspects in management

COMMONLY ASKED QUESTIONS

1. What would be the recommended blood pressure target for this patient?
Less than 130/80mmHg

2. How could the progression of kidney damage be slowed in this patient?
The underlying aetiology has to be identified and treated adequately.
Blood pressure is maintained <130/80.
Angiotensin converting enzyme inhibitors and angiotensin receptor blockers reduce the efferent arteriole and degree of proteinuria.
Good glycaemic control and improved lipid profile.
Low impact exercises.
Stop smoking (if patient is a smoker).
Cessation of nephrotoxic medications.

3. State the radiological findings of renal osteodystrophy.
Pathological fractures, osteopenia, coarsened trabecular, Looser zones (pseudofractures), soft tissue calcification, osseous resorption.

4. What are the types of renal replacement therapy available?
Haemodialysis, peritoneal dialysis, renal transplant

HIGH ACHIEVER QUESTIONS

Discuss the indications for urgent dialysis.
Severe uraemia with encephalopathy, pericarditis or neuropathy
Severe fluid overload with pulmonary oedema, no response to medications
Refractory hyperkalaemia (potassium >7mmol/L)
Persistent metabolic acidosis

2. What are the indicators of adequate dialysis in a patient with ESRF undergoing haemodialysis?
Adequacy of dialysis is measured via calculation of Kt/V or urea clearance (amount of urea removed with excess fluid) as suggested by KDOQI guidelines. However, a more subjective approach would be to consider patient's wellness, blood pressure control, fluid balance, left ventricle function, nutritional status and calcium and phosphate balance.

3. How can uraemic pruritus be management?
Adequate dialysis should be ensured. Optimal management of calcium and phosphate level with treatment of secondary parathyroidism can

reduce pruritus. Topical treatments include skin emollients, capsaicin cream and tacrolimus. Naltrexone, an opioid receptor antagonist, and ultraviolet therapy are also beneficial.

COMMON MISTAKES

- Not determining stage and cause of CKD
- Failure to identify and manage factors that are leading to rapid progression of kidney damage
- Not managing complications of CKD
- Failure to prepare patient for renal replacement therapy

EXPECTED LEARNING OUTCOMES

At the end of this review the student is aware of:

1. CKD is increasingly more common, as diabetes mellitus and hypertension are the commoner causes, and hence must be identified among high risk individuals.

2. Calculation of estimated GFR for staging of CKD.

3. Many patients with CKD only develop symptoms when the kidney damage is advanced.

4. Patients with CKD are also at risk for cardiovascular disease and this is the main cause for mortality.

5. There are clear guidelines for renal replacement therapy

6. Counselling patients on long term therapy of CKD

REFERENCES:

1. The National Kidney Foundation Kidney Disease Outcomes Quality Initiative
(KDOQI)
http://www.kidney.org/professionals/KDOQI/guidelines.cfm

2. 2008 Canadian Medical Association Guidelines for Management of Chronic Kidney Disease

SECTION 4:HEMATOLOGY

CASE 33: MYELOFIBROSIS
KOH KWEE CHOY,JAMES

OVERVIEW

Primary myelofibrosis* is also known as Idiopathic Myelofibrosis, Agnogenic Myeloid Metaplasia, Chronic Idiopathic Myelofibrosis and Myeloid Metaplasia. It is one of the conditions categorized under Chronic Myeloproliferative Disorders (CMPD). It is a stem cell disease characterized by proliferation of fibroblasts and excessive collagen production within the bone marrow secondary to abnormal secretion of growth factors by clonal megakaryocytes which ultimately results in bone marrow fibrosis. It is more common in men in their 5th or 6th decade of life.

Failure of haematopoiesis results in symptoms of anemia, increased susceptibility to infections and bleeding. Extra-medullary hematopoiesis results in enlargement of the liver and spleen.

Secondary myelofibrosis may arise from other myeloproliferative disorders such as Essential Thrombocythaemia (ET) and Polycythaemia Rubra Vera (PRV); or from autoimmune disorders, inflammatory conditions, cancer or chronic infections (e.g. tuberculosis, post-radiation, Hodgkin's lymphoma).

Myelofibrosis may eventually become Chronic Myelogenous Leukaemia (CML) or undergo acute transformation into acute leukaemia (usually myeloid). The median life-expectancy from diagnosis is between 3 – 6 years.

Myelofibrosis was first described by Gustav Heuck (1854-1940), a German surgeon.

Patients with myelofibrosis are often good cases for the OSCE. The focus is usually on the examination of the abdomen where the clinical finding of hepatosplenomegaly is the expected outcome. Not infrequently, these patients may also be used in the long case for history taking and clinical examination. As the signs are relatively obvious and easy to find, myelofibrosis is commonly used in postgraduate examinations except perhaps in the area of discussion on its management.

Myelofibrosis is one of the relatively few conditions which presents with moderate to massive splenomegaly. The other conditions being CML, Tropical splenomegaly, Kala-Azar, Gaucher's disease – all of which, with the exception of CML, are relatively uncommon in this part of the world.

CASE VIGNETTE

A 64-year-old man complains of feeling tired over the last 6 months associated with abdominal fullness and a dull ache in the left upper abdomen. Take a detailed history, perform a general examination followed by examination of the abdomen.

History of Presenting Illness

About 20-25% of people with myelofibrosis are asymptomatic.The diagnosis in such is usually incidental (from an abnormal full blood count or incidental finding of an enlarged spleen). The remaining 75-80% of the patients are symptomatic. Some of the common manifestations of myelofibrosis are shown in Table 1.

Table 1: Common presenting symptoms in myelofibrosis

Symptom	Underlying pathology
Fatigue, weakness, syncopal attacks, shortness of breath, palpitations	Anaemia – due to ineffective erythropoiesis, hypersplenism or bleeding tendencies
Early satiety, fullness of abdomen, abdominal distension, pain below ribs	Hepatomegaly and splenomegaly – due to extramedullary hematopoiesis. Pain may be due to splenic infarcts.
Easy bruising or frank bleeding	Thrombocytopenia, platelet dysfunction, peptic ulcer, oesophageal varices and lower gastrointestinal bleeding
Weight loss, night sweats, fever	Hypermetabolic state which may precipitate acute gouty arthritis or renal calculi causing hematuria.
Frequent infections	Leukopenia, humoral immune dysfunction, acute leukaemic transformation
Bone pain	Extramedullary hematopoiesis –

manifestations depend on the site of extramedullary hematopoiesis. Seizures may occur if there are intracranial tumours. Spinal cord compression may occur in epidural space hematopoiesis.

The symptoms of myelofibrosis are not exclusive. Many other conditions present with similar manifestations such as CML, acute leukaemia, chronic liver disease, hepatocellular carcinoma with metastasis to the bones and chronic infections like tuberculosis or histoplasmosis.

Additional manifestations may be present if the myelofibrosis has changed into CML (fever, blurring of vision, and respiratory problems due to markedly elevated WBC count) or has undergone acute leukaemic transformation (fever, bleeding, bone pain, and sepsis).

Past Medical History

Enquire for past history of conditions which may predispose to secondary myelofibrosis such as other chronic myeloproliferative disorders (ET, CML, PRV); lymphoma; chronic infections like tuberculosis; and radiotherapy.

Family History

Family history of Gaucher's disease may be relevant if this condition is suspected.

Travel history

Recent travel to places where malaria and Kala-Azar are endemic (Africa, parts of Europe and Asia, South America) may be relevant to rule out these causes for massive splenomegaly.

Occupational history

Exposure to industrial solvents such as benzene or toluene has been implicated as a risk factor for myelofibrosi

CHECK LIST FOR HISTORY TAKING IN MYELOFIBROSIS

o   Determine the onset of symptoms
o   Enquire about symptoms related to bone marrow dysfunction and extramedullary manifestations of the disease

- o   Rule out other causes presenting with similar symptoms
- o   with transformation of myelofibrosis to CML or acute leukaemia
- o   Take relevant negative family, travel and occupational histories
- o   Determine if there are symptoms associated

EXAMINATION

General examination and vital signs

Introduce yourself to the patient, explain your intentions and obtain consent from the patient before starting the physical examination.

In the general examination, look for signs of anaemia (e.g. conjunctival pallor) and its complications (tachycardia, tachypnoea, raised JVP, peripheral oedema). Look for signs of bleeding such as cutaneous petechiae and ecchymosis. Offer to take the temperature or ask for the temperature chart (infection, sepsis, acute leukaemia) to look for fever. Some patients may have lymphadenopathy.

Examination of the abdomen

Professionalism

Explain to the patient what you are about to do and ask for permission to expose the patient's abdomen. The patient should be lying supine with one pillow under the head. Ideally, the exposure should be from the level of the nipples to mid-thigh level. In practice however, and because of patient's modesty and sensitivity, the area of exposure may have to be compromised especially in female patients. In the latter, exposure from just below the breasts to just above the symphisis pubis should be adequate. Remember to request for a chaperone especially if the patient is female.

Inspection

Carefully look over the entire anterior surface and sides of the abdomen before offering to present the positive signs seen. Look for evidence of abdominal distension, fullness of the flanks (suggesting ascites secondary to portal hypertension), visible veins, pulsations, surgical scars and visible masses. Often the spleen is so big that it is hard to miss the obvious swelling over the left side of the patient's abdomen.

Proceed to the foot-end of the bed and, after instructing the patient to breathe in and out deeply, observe for movement of the abdomen during respiration. Comment on the movement of the abdomen on respiration. Asymmetry in the movement is the expected finding with massive splenomegaly.

434

Palpation

Light and deep palpation should easily confirm the presence of hepatomegaly (present in 60-70% of patients) and massive splenomegaly (>90% of patients). Always palpate the abdomen at the level of the patient's abdomen (the student may have to kneel or seat himself on a chair). Percuss for the upper border of the liver and measure the liver span. Similarly feel for the lower end of the spleen and measure its length from the left hypochodrium. Although the palpable mass is obviously the spleen, the student should not neglect to look for an enlarged kidney with bimanual palpation and determine if the mass is ballotable. Occasionally there may be ascites (in portal hypertension) which can be confirmed by presence of shifting dullness and fluid thrill. During palpation, maintain a steady flow of conversation with the patient, always reassuring the patient and be alert to signs of discomfort or pain experienced by the patient such as facial grimace.

Spleen examination

Do not forget to look for all of the findings associated with an enlarged spleen such as the distance of its inferior border from the left costal margin, the direction of its expansion infero-medially from the left hypochondrium, the presence of splenic notch medially and its absence laterally, its smooth surface, firm consistency and the inability to 'get above' the swelling. It also descends on inspiration. Gentle percussion over the spleen may reveal a tympanic note (due to overlying colonic gas) and auscultation might reveal the presence of a splenic rub.

The size of the spleen may vary from being barely palpable to massive (crossing the midline). Always begin palpating for the spleen from the right inguinal area upwards in the direction of the left hypochondrium. Occasionally the spleen grows inferiorly instead of infero-medially and unless the student palpates the left flank and the left inguinal region, the enlarged downward enlargement of spleen might be missed.

Other systems

Before completing the examination, request for the patient to turn to the left lateral position to look for presence of sacral oedema and surgical scar over the iliac crests indicating a bone marrow aspiration has been performed. Offer to examine the cardiovascular system (look for signs of heart failure), respiratory system (foci of infection, basal crepitations from heart failure) and the nervous system (for neurological deficits if spine involvement is suspected).

Check list for the examination findings in myelofibrosis

- ✓ Look for signs of anemia and its complications
- ✓ Look for bleeding tendencies
- ✓ Look for evidence of sepsis
- ✓ Look for hepatosplenomegaly
- ✓ Examine other related systems: cardiovascular, respiratory and nervous system

INVESTIGATIONS

Table 2: Relevant investigations in myelofibrosis

Investigation	Justification
Full blood count	Anemia (> 60% of patients will have haemoglobin level < 10 g/dL). Leukocytosis (early stage of disease due to hyperactive marrow; very high count may suggests acute leukaemic transformation). Leukopenia (later stage of disease due to marrow scarring). Thrombocytosis or thrombocytopenia.
Peripheral blood smear	Leukoerythroblastic picture with presence of tear drop red blood cells (RBCs), nucleated RBCs and immature cells of myeloid lineage. Megakaryocytes may be seen.
Genetic testing of peripheral blood	May be useful to rule out other myeloproliferative disorders (e.g. testing for the *bcr.abl* gene to exclude CML). *JAK2* test testing for the *JAK2 V617F* mutation (about 50% of myelofibrosis have this mutation).
Bone marrow biopsy.	Bone marrow aspirate is usually disappointing because of 'dry tap' from extensive marrow scarring. Therefore a bone marrow biopsy is preferred and is diagnostic. The biopsy specimen typically shows hypercellular marrow with megakaryocytosis. Other marrow features include extensive fibrosis,

	dysplastic or clustering of megakaryocytes.
Imaging studies	Ultrasound or CT scan of the abdomen confirms liver and splenic enlargements. Skeletal radiographs may show mottled patches where bone density is increased.

CASE SUMMARY

This 64-year-old man presents with symptomatic anemia. On examination there is pallor, hepatomegaly and massive splenomegaly. Taking into consideration his age, the most likely diagnosis is a chronic myeloproliferative disorder. Differential diagnoses include myelofibrosis, chronic myelogenous leukaemia and myelodysplastic syndrome.

CLINICAL DISCUSSION OF THE CASE

The student should be able to:

- Be competent in eliciting relevant history in a patient with myelofibrosis.
- Rule out secondary causes of an enlarged spleen.
- Confidently elicit hepatomegaly and (usually) massive splenomegaly on examination as well as signs of complications (pallor, bleeding, infection, bone pain).
- Offer a reasonable diagnosis of chronic myeloproliferative disorder and its differential diagnoses based on the history and physical examination findings.
- List the relevant investigations in a logical manner with appropriate justifications.
- Discuss the principles of management in this patient.
- Explore important issues related to the care and rehabilitation of a patient with myelofibrosis.

The principles of management include:

- Control of symptoms
    - Blood transfusion may be needed to correct anemia.

- o Platelet transfusion may be necessary if there is bleeding due to thrombocytopenia.
- o Erythropoiesis can be stimulated using androgenic hormones (e.g. Danazol) and erythropoetin.
- o Cytoreductive therapy (for thrombocytosis or leukocytosis) using agents like hydroxyurea or interferon-alfa.
- o Thalidomide with corticosteroids to reduce transfusion dependence.

- • Prevent complications
  - o Low dose aspirin if there is risk of thrombosis.

- • Management of spleen size
  - o Splenectomy or splenic irradiation if there is hypersplenism, severe portal hypertension, frequent need for transfusions or intractable abdominal pain or discomfort. However, post-operative mortality is high with splenectomy and it is associated with higher risk of transformation to acute myeloid leukaemia.
  - o *JAK1/JAK2* inhibitor (ruxolitinib) may help reduce spleen size in some patients.

- • Control of disease progression
  - o High-dose chemotherapy may slow the disease.
  - o Allogenic stem cell transplantation may be curative.
  - o Radiotherapy may alleviate bone pain due to extramedullary hematopoiesis.

LEARNING OUTCOMES

By the end of this case review the student should be:

1. Able to define what is myelofibrosis and its differential diagnoses.

2. Make a reasonable diagnosis based on history and findings from clinical examination.

3. List the relevant investigations in myelofibrosis.

4. Discuss the principles in the management of a case of myelofibrosis

COMMONLY ASKED QUESTIONS

1. What are the causes of anaemia in myelofibrosis?
2. What are the possible causes for bleeding in myelofibrosis?
3. Enumerate some chronic myeloproliferative disorders.
4. Name a few conditions presenting with massive splenomegaly.
5. What are the clinical findings suggestive of an enlarged spleen?
6. What relevant investigations will you perform for this patient?

HIGH ACHIEVER QUESTIONS

QUESTIONS

1. What are the signs suggestive of leukemic transformation of myelofibrosis?
2. What is the hallmark finding in the bone marrow of patients with chronic myeloproliferative disorders?
3. What are some of the poor prognostic factors of myelofibrosis

COMMON MISTAKES

- Neglecting to inspect the abdomen from the foot end of the bed
- Palpation of the abdomen not done at level of the patient's abdomen
- Neglecting to constantly ask if the patient is experiencing pain or discomfort and not looking at the patient's facial expression during palpation of the abdomen
- Neglecting to measure the liver span, the spleen size and performing the bimanual examination to look for palpable kidneys
- Overlooking signs of bone marrow dysfunction (pallor, bleeding, sepsis)
- Neglecting to look for signs of intervention (e.g. bone marrow biopsy scar)
- Missing a spleen which enlarged inferiorly instead of infero-medially

MUST KNOW FACTS ABOUT MYELOFIBROSIS

1. Myelofibrosis is a stem cell disorder and is one of the differential diagnoses of chronic myeloproliferative disorder.

2. Myelofibrosis is essentially a disease of the elderly (above 60 years) and is characterized by hepatomegaly and massive splenomegaly.

3. The manifestations of the disease are associated with bone marrow failure and extramedullary hematopoiesis.

CASE 34: LEUKEMIA
SANGEETHA POOVANESWARAN

OVERVIEW

Leukemia is cancer of the blood or bone marrow. Ninety percent of all leukemia occurs in adults. In Malaysia it is the 7th most common type of cancer in adults and the most common type of cancer in children.

Clinically and pathologically, leukemia is subdivided into a variety of large groups. The first division is between its <u>acute</u> and <u>chronic</u> forms:

> <u>Acute leukemia</u>, which is the most common form in children, is characterized by a rapid increase in the numbers of immature blood cells. Immediate treatment is required in acute leukemia due to the rapid progression of the disease.

> <u>Chronic leukemia</u>, which tends to occur in older people, is characterized by the excessive buildup of relatively mature, but abnormal white blood cells over months or years. While acute leukemia must be treated immediately, chronic forms are sometimes monitored for some time before treatment to ensure maximum effectiveness of therapy.

Additionally, leukaemia can be subdivided according to the type of blood cell that is affected; lymphoblastic or <u>lymphocytic leukemias</u> and myeloid or <u>myelogenous leukemias</u>.

> Acute lymphoblastic leukemia (ALL) is the most common type of leukemia in young children. This disease also affects adults, especially those aged 65 and older. Treatment involves chemotherapy and radiotherapy. The survival rates vary accpording to age: 85% in children and 50% in adults.

> Chronic lymphocytic leukemia (CLL) most often affects adults over the age of 55. Two-thirds of affected people are men. The five-year survival rate is 75%. It is incurable, but there are many effective treatments.

> Acute myelogenous leukemia (AML) occurs more commonly in adults, men being affected more than women. AML is treated with chemotherapy. The five-year survival rate is 40%.

> Chronic myelogenous leukemia (CML) occurs mainly in adults. Treatment is with <u>imatinib</u> which is a tyrosine kinase inhibitor or other drugs. The five-year survival rate is 90%.

OSCE, short or long: Patient with symptoms of anaemia or easy bruising/ bleeding or frequent infections.

Aim is to take a focused history for anaemia, infections and thrombocytopenia; exhibit clinical competency in examination of abdomen for hepatosplenomegaly and lymphadenopathy.

Long case or OSLER

> Aim is to take a detailed history to assess underlying cause of anaemia, frequent infections, thrombocytopenia, hepatosplenomegaly, lymphadenopathy and exhibit clinical competency in examination of the relevant systems (respiratory, cardiovascular, haematological, musculoskeletal or gastro-intestinal system).

CASE VIGNETTE

A previously well 25-year-old woman, presents with a 1 month history of gum bleeding when brushing her teeth, lethargy and spontaneous bruising over her arms and legs. She is noted to be pyrexial and having a cough productive of green sputum. Clinically she appears pale but is not jaundiced and purpura is noted over her arms and legs.

Differential diagnosis

In this case, the patient is presenting with a short history of pancytopenia. It is important to think about malignancies which result in marrow infiltration such as lymphoma and leukaemia, (solid tumour resulting in marrow infiltration is unlikely given that the patient was well previously), aplastic anaemia due to infections such as parvovirus; medication such as carbamazepine, phenytoin, quinine, chloramphenicol; exposure to benzene or ionizing radiation. Immunocompromised patients can present with recurrent infections and may be anaemic due to chronic disease, however, purpura and easy bruising is usually not present and the history will be of a longer duration.

HISTORY TAKING

HISTORY OF PRESENTING ILLNESS

> · In leukemia, normal bone marrow is displaced by abnormal cells as such patients may present with symptoms of

pancytopenia. If thrombocytopenia is present- easy bruising, bleeding, menorrhagia, and /or petichiae are noted .

- If anaemia is present look for lethargy, palpitations, dyspnea and in older patient for heart failure.

- If white cell function is impaired, the following may be present: fever, chills, recurrent infections, sore throat, life threatening diarrhea and opportunistic infections.

- Other symptoms are nausea, flu-like symptoms and weight loss.

- If hepatosplenomegaly is noted the patient may present with abdominal discomfort and distension.

- If the central nervous system is involved, then the patient may present with headaches or neurological symptoms. Lymphadenopathy may be present in CLL.

- In lymphoma, patients may present with localized, regional or generalized painless lymphadenopathy, constitutional or B symptoms (fevers, night sweats or weight loss), occasionally pruritis and pain following ingestion of alcohol at sites of lymphadenopathy. In Non- Hodgkin's lymphoma there may be extra-nodal involvement (eg. skin).

- In patients who are immunocompromised e.g. due to HIV or on immunosuppressive medication, the history will be longer and the patient will have other past medical history.

PAST MEDICAL HISTORY

- Usually none, unless previous diagnosis of lymphoproliferative disorder (lymphoma, leukemia) or immuno-compromise or malignancy from solid tumour which has now lead to marrow infiltration. Human T- lymphotrophic virus is linked to adult T cell leukemia. Down Syndrome is linked to ALL and AML; and Fanconi Anaemia linked to AML.

- If aplastic anaemia is due to medication, then there may be a history of malaria or epilepsy or exposure to benzene or radiation.

FAMILY HISTORY

- Higher risk if twin is affected

SOCIAL HISTORY

- If one is suspecting an immunocompromise state - need to ask about high risk behaviour/ blood transfusion

SURGICAL HISTORY

· Situations where patient may have had blood transfusion

DRUG HISTORY

· Immunono suppressive medication, carbamazepine, phenytoin, quinine, chloramphenicol
· Radiation exposure

SYSTEMIC REVIEW OF SYMPTOMS

Need to assess each system, to rule out pathologies
- e.g.   Infectious mononucleosis – sore throat, rash
  - o   HIV positive cases- recurrent infections, Kaposi sarcoma and other AIDS defining illnesses
  - o   Renal transplant

When presenting a case, it is important to state why other possible differential diagnoses are considered by the presence or absence of specific symptoms.

CHECK LIST FOR HISTORY IN LEUKEMIA

✓ Identify clinical symptoms to confirm pancytopenia
✓ Identify possible causes of pancytopenia- infection, HIV, malignancy, medication, radiation exposure
✓ Presence or absence of other symptoms to suggest extent of disease eg, abdominal discomfort and distension, neurological symptoms

EXAMINATION

Professionalism:

Introduce yourself, obtain consent, position patient ideally lying flat, suitable undressing of garment for abdominal examination (from inframammary region to just above the genitalia), have a chaperone.

In the course of discussion new information related to other infectious diseases like AIDS, or malignancy may be elicited. Be prepared to discuss the sensitivity of presenting such information and be cautious of confidentiality of disclosing information.

Inspection:

Observe the patient from the end of the bed and comment on obvious abnormalities

- Appearance – pallor, jaundice, cachexia, purpura, nutritional status, abdominal distension

  In Down syndrome it is important to comment on the typical features present of the syndrome and then proceed to examine related systems as well. (Appearance- eg. epicanthal skin folds at the inner corner of the eyes, small chin, large protruding tongue, single palmar crease, flat broad face, short neck, etc; Eyes- strabismus, cataract, Brushfield spots; Mental characteristics- delayed speech and fine motor skills; thyroid disorders- hypothyroidism; Gastro-intestinal symptoms due to Hirschsprung disease or reflux; Neurology- epilepsy; Hearing impairment).

- Respiration- tachypnoea, use of oxygen therapy, use of accessory muscles

- Abdomen- obvious swelling, symmetry of swelling

  Hands-comment on absence/presence of clubbing, leuconychia, palmar erythema, duputryen's contracture (for this student needs to feel for thickening of fascia before commenting), hepatic flap

  Arms- spider naevi, bruising, purpura, needle marks (in HIV patients), pigmentation, scratch marks

  Neck, face and chest- examine oral cavity for pharyngitis, tonsillar lymphadenopathy, gum bleeding, gum hypertrophy in AML, palpate for supraclavicular, cervical and axillary lymph nodes, anaemia, jaundice, spider naevi in upper chest and face, axilla for hair loss and acanthosis nigricans (which is seen in obesity, acromegaly, diabetes, gastric cancer), gynaecomastia

  Abdomen

  Inspection:

  - Inspect for movements, obvious mass present, any visible veins, visible peristalsis.
    Palpation:

  - Before palpation ask the patient if there are any areas of tenderness

  - Student must either kneel on the floor or sit on a chair before proceeding to palpation of the abdomen

  - Palpate all 9 regions and if any tenderness/mass is obvious comment on characteristics. Perform both light and deep palpation with patient breathing through the mouth.

- For examination of liver, spleen, kidney, palpate and percuss/ ballot for each organ individually.

- Palpate for inguinal lymphadenopathy
  Percussion:

- Assess presence of ascites by looking for shifting dullness.

- When patient is rolled to the side, assess for pitting oedema in sacral region.

- Legs for pitting oedema

Based on the history, especially in Long Cases/OSLER, be wary of the need to examine other systems eg dermatology if rash is present, musculoskeletal system if arthralgia or myalgia present, respiratory system if chest infection present, neurological system if any neurological symptoms are present.

Professionalism: Thank patient at the end of examination, position patient in same position as prior to start of examination, re-dress patient.

CHECK LIST FOR COMMENTING ON LEUKEMIC PATIENT

Constitutional symptoms:-Weight loss, lethargy, loss of appetite

Anaemia:Symptoms and signs- palpitations, tiredness, dizziness, pallor

Hepatomegaly:

- ✓ Size- demonstrate location of upper and lower border, and measure length
- ✓ Surface-smooth, firm, nodular (smooth in hepatits, craggy in hepatoma)
- ✓ Edge- smooth, irregular
- ✓ Tenderness
- ✓ Movement with respiration-downwards
- ✓ Non-pulsatile

Splenomegaly:

- ✓ Size- demonstrate location of lower border, if not palpable , comment on percussion of traube space
- ✓ Surface-smooth, firm,
- ✓ Edge- smooth, irregular, splenic notch

- ✓ Tenderness
- ✓ Movement with respiration- diagonally
- ✓ State other factors that differentiate it from a kidney-non-ballottable, cannot get above it

Lymphadenopathy:

- ✓ examine all lymph node groups in systematic manner
- ✓ size
- ✓ location
- ✓ surface and edge-hard, rubbery, matted, well circumscribed
- ✓ mobility
- ✓ tender or non-tender

Professional approach

Executing the motions for enlargement of the lymph nodes, liver and spleen using the correct techniques alone is not sufficient as more marks are given for the correct findings especially in the senior years of training.

INVESTIGATIONS

Be ready to discuss relevant investigations to both support the diagnosis and manage the patient.

Full blood count- check for anaemia (MCV and MCH may be normal or reduced if there is also blood loss) and raised white cells (due to presence of blast cells in acute leukaemias; or numerous mature but abnormal white cells in chronic leukemias) and low platelets

Blood film- abnormal cell morphology eg excessive lymphocytes, blast cells

Liver function tests- raised transaminases, bilirubin level, protein, albumin

Clotting screen- assessment of liver function

Renal function tests

LDH and beta2- microglobulin- for monitoring response in lymphoma

lymph node biopsy- diagnostic for lymphoma. Aids in the diagnosis of CLL and other infective causes

bone marrow biopsy/trephine for diagnosis and staging of leukemia and lymphoma

Imaging- CT scan for staging of leukemia and lymphoma, Chest radiograph for detecting consolidation ofpneumonia or congestive cardiac failure due to anaemia

Blood cultures if fever is present for diagnosing inter-current infection

ESR and CRP may be elevated in both malignancy and infection as such it is non- specific

In discussing investigations consider the objective of such a request.. In the OSCE setting mention those that would be essential for confirming the diagnosis of leukemia. Also mention investigations that would be necessary to confirm inter-current infection.

CASE SUMMARY

A 25-year-old woman, who was well epresents with a 1 month history of gum bleeding, lethargy and spontaneous bruising over her arms and legs. She is having pyrexia, anaemia and has purpura over her arms and legs. Gum hypertrophy with bleeding is present. Respiratory examination reveals dullness at the left lower zone, with associated bronchial breathing and coarse crepitations. She has hepatospenomegaly but no lymphadenopathy.

The most likely diagnosis is a haematological malignancy such as acute myeloid leukemia with lobar pneumonia.

CLINICAL DISCUSSION OF THE CASE

Students should be able to:
- state the differential diagnosis for pancytopenia and mention why leukaemia is suspected.
- to examine the abdomen in a systematic manner
- present investigations in logical manner and explain rationale for performing the investigations.
- discuss holistically the management of the patient with regards to a malignant disease including terminal life care especially in a long case

COMMONLY ASKED QUESTIONS

1. Describe how you would approach a patient with pancytopenia?
2. What is the likely differential diagnosis in this case and explain rationale?
3. What investigations would you perform in this patient?

LEARNING OBJECTIVES

By the end of this case review the student should be be able to

- Able to classify causes of hepato-splenomegaly with lymphadenopathy

448

- Make a diagnosis based on the history and clinical examination findings
- List the investigations to confirm diagnosis
- Able to outline basic management principles

DISTINCTION LEVEL QUESTION

1. Briefly describe the challenges in managing a patient with Down Syndrome and acute leukaemia?

Children with Down Syndrome have a 10-20 fold increase risk of developing leukaemia as compared to children without this genetic disorder. Children with Down Syndrome who develop AML have a more favourable outcome due to increased sensitivity to chemotherapy. However, this is not the case with ALL, as they have a poor outcome.

The major challenge is in managing chemotherapy toxicites in patients with Downs. It is not clear why they have more severe toxicities ranging from mucositis, hepatotoxicity, cardiac toxicity and neutropaenic sepsis.

As these patients may already have other organ dysfunction due to the Down chemotherapy doses have to be tailored to the individual case to limit severe toxicities from occurring.

Moreover, these patients may not fully understand the side- effects of treatment and may not come forthcoming in a timely manner. As such, it is important to counsel the patient and their family/ carers extensively and frequently.

2. What is the cancer risk in patients with Down Syndrome?
The incidence of cancers are generally lower in Down patients except for haematological cancers and testicular cancer. This may possibly be due to increased number of tumour suppressor genes

Under high achiever expectation it would be appropriate to add a note of Ph chromosome and another on stem cell transplantation?

RED FLAG ENCOUNTERS-

This highlights the possible areas where the student can find himself in trouble by possible omissions or by overlooking the examination findings.

- Not picking up the clinical signs of pancytopenia
- Not examining gastro-intestinal system in systematic manner
- Failure to examine for lymphadenopathy

MUST KNOW FACTS OF LEUKAEMIA

✓ There are multiple causes and eliciting specific symptoms and signs in history and examination will help to identify the likely underlying cause.

✓ It is important to realize patient may present with very vague symptoms of lethargy or frequent infections or easy bruising/bleeding. There may not be organomegaly or lymphadenopathy. Diagnosis is usually made when full blood count reveals a very high white cell value. However, in an examination setting it is important to suspect leukaemia when the patient presents with symptoms of pancytopenia.

✓ Tests and interpretation

✓ Basic holistic management principles of malignancy; not just treatment with chemotherapy and/or radiotherapy but also psycho social issues.

CASE 35: LYMPHOMA
SANGEETHA POOVANESWARAN

OVERVIEW

Lymphoma is a broad term used to categorise a group of cancers that affect the immune system. They are broadly divided into two groups, namely Hodgkin's and Non-Hodgkin's lymphoma. Lymphoma is the 10th commonest cancer in Malaysia, accounting for 3.2% of all cancers.

CASE VIGNETTE

A 25-year-old lady, with no known past-medical history presents with a 6 –month history of night sweats and weight loss which is associated with a rapidly enlarging masses in the neck and left axilla.

DIFFERENTIAL DIAGNOSIS

- Malignancies eg. Lymphoma, Leukaemia
- Chronic infections. Eg. TB, brucellosis, glandular fever, CMV
- Connective Tissue Disorders- SLE, Rheumatoid Arthritis, Sarcoidosis

HISTORY OF PRESENT ILLNESS

Enquire into:

- Onset, duration and progression of the symptoms viz: night sweats, weight loss and lymphadenopathy
- Lymphadenopathy: non-tender, rapidly enlarging, generalised
- Drenching night sweats and unexplained weight loss of >10% body weight and unexplained fevers >38 Celcius are part of 'B Symptoms in lymphoma'

PAST MEDICAL HISTORY

- Usually patients have no relevant past medical history. However do elicit history of immunodeficiency disorders, e.g. HIV are associated with lymphoma

FAMILY HISTORY

- Rarely there is a family history, but it is important to elicit history of cancers in the family

SOCIAL HISTORY

- Hodgkin's lymphoma is associated with higher social economic status

SYSTEMIC REVIEW OF SYMPTOMS

- Pruritus and alcohol induced pain in the affected lymph nodes are not B symptoms , although they are useful indicators of relapse.
- Constitutional symptoms eg, lethargy, cachexia
- Abdominal distension
- If patient has been started on treatment, it is important to ask about side-effects, eg nausea, vomiting, alopecia, infections.

✓ CHECK LIST FOR HISTORY IN LYMPHOMA

- Areas with generalised lymphadenopathy
- B symptoms
- Abdominal symptoms
- Constitutional symptoms

EXAMINATION

☞ Note: Usually the instruction during an OSCE will be specific e.g. Examine this patient's neck. As soon as decide to examine the lymph nodes, examine the lymph node groups and relevant specific systems to determine underlying pathology

How to begin the examination .

- Observe the patient from the end of bed
- Inspect for obvious abnormality eg. Swelling in neck, sweating, breathlessness, cachexia, lethargy, alopecia (esp. if patient is on chemotherapy), anaemia

1. **Neck and all lymph node groups-**examine the lymph nodes in the neck in a systematic way and comment on abnormalities (submental, submandibular, deep and superficial cervical, occipital, posterior triangle, supra-clavicular, infraclavicular, axillary, epitrochlear, inguinal)
2. **Mouth** –tonsillar lymph nodes; in glandular fever there will be palatal petechial and pharyngitis
3. **Chest-** when looking for systemic spread of lymphoma i.e pleural effusion or changes in keeping with TB (apical fibrosis)

4. **Abdomen** –examine the liver and spleen for systemic involvement of lymphoma.

✓ **CHECK LIST FOR COMMENTING ON LYMPHADENOPATHY**
- Size
- Consistency- rubbery, firm
- Edge- smooth, well-circumscribed, matted
- Non-tender
- Mobility- mobile or fixed to skin or underlying structure
- Non-pulsatile

INVESTIGATIONS
- Patients may have neutrophilia, thrombocytosis and anaemia of chronic disease
- ESR and CRP may be elevated
- LDH is a useful guide for bulk of disease
- Biopsy of lymph node to confirm diagnosis
- CT scan for staging

CASE SUMMARY

A 25-year-old lady, with no known past-medical history presents with a 6 month history of night sweats and weight loss which is associated with a rapidly enlarging mass in the neck and left axilla.

Proceed with examination of this patient's neck and relevant systems.

CLINICAL DISCUSSION OF THE CASE

Professionalism- how to break serious news to patient?

What treatment options are available?
Chemotherapy and radiotherapy- for localised disease i.e. Upto Stage IIA 3-4 cycles of chemotherapy and radiotherapy to the involved nodal groups. For more extensive disease, 6-8 cycles of chemotherapy followed by radiotherapy to residual disease. The exception is for low grade NHL where management is mere observation and treating when symptomatic by using low dose chemotherapy.

THE RELEVANT AREAS OF THE CASE THE STUDENT SHOULD KNOW ARE DISCUSSED

- The students should be able to categorise lymphoma into Hodgkin's and NHL.

- Students should be aware of the B symptoms.
- Students should be able to examine for generalised lymphadenopathy in systematic manner.
- Patient should be aware that prognosis is generally good compared to solid tumours and cure is possible albeit low in Stage IV disease.

COMMONLY ASKED QUESTIONS –

QUESTIONS

1. How would you approach a patient with lymphadenopathy?
2. What is the likely differential diagnosis in this case?
3. What investigations would you perform in this patient?

HIGH ACHIEVER QUESTIONS

1. Describe the histology in Hodgkin's lymphoma?
2. How is Hodgkin's disease staged?
3. How are Non-Hodgkin's disease classified?
4. Name a few side-effects of chemotherapy that this patient may encounter?

RED FLAG ENCOUNTERS

This highlights the possible areas where the student can find himself in trouble by possible omissions or overlooking the examination findings.

- Not adequately exposing the patient for examination of the neck and axillary group of nodes.
- Not being systematic in examining the groups of lymph nodes
- Not being able to correlate history to physical findings

MUST KNOW FACTS OF LYMPHOMA

It is a painless lymphadenopathy
It is associated with B symptoms

LEARNING OBJECTVES

By the end of this case review the student should be:

1. Able to list causes of marrow suppression
2. Make a diagnosis based on the history and clinical examination findings

3. List the investigations to confirm diagnosis
4. Able to outline basic management principles

CASE 36 : HAEMOLYTIC ANEMIA
CHAMPIKA BODINAYAKE

OVERVIEW

Anaemia due to shortened red cell survival is classified as haemolytic anaemia. Haemolytic anaemia results from a variety of causes which could be hereditary or acquired. Haemolysis could result following a defect within the red blood cell (RBC) (intracorpuscular) or outside RBC (extracorpuscular). Common causes of hereditary haemolytic anaemia in the world are thalassaemia and sickle cell anaemia, both resulting from haemoglobinopathy. Geographically sickle cell anaemia is common in areas where malaria was endemic reflecting a probable survival advantage for the abnormally deformed cells from malaria. Haemolysis could result from a variety of reasons acquired in later life and occur in adults from immunological or non immunological causes.

Acute haemolysis could be life threatening. Haemolysis following ingestion of Fava beans in a patient with red cell enzyme glucose 6 phosphate dehydrogenase (G6PD) deficiency is a classical example of acute intravascular haemolysis. Chronic haemolysis has a relapsing course and is generally compensated by increased production of red cells from the bone marrow which gives a classical clinical picture.

Haemolytic anaemia's are a popular exam topic both in the long and short cases.

Case vignette

A 25 year old single female presented with shortness of breath and fatigue for two weeks. Her friends noticed that she was looking pale with yellowish discolouration of eyes. Since childhood she was unable to cope with exertion and avoided sports activities at school. She had hepatitis at the age of nine. Last year she had two episodes of abdominal colic which was treated by her general practitioner who additionally prescribed an oral iron preparation as the haemoglobin was low. There was no fever, weight loss or anorexia. Her urine, bowel habits and menstruation were normal. There was no consanguinity in her family. Her father who died at the age of 45 following pneumonia has had a similar illness in his childhood with anaemia, which apparently recovered following surgery; no further details were available for review. Her mother and two brothers were well. She was not taking any form of medications or illicit drugs. On examination she was pale and conjunctival icterus was present. No lymphadenopathy, fever or purpura was noted. The cardiovascular system examination revealed pulse 90 beats/min regular and bounding, blood pressure 120/70 mm Hg. The cardiovascular system and respiratory system were clinically normal. Examination of the abdomen revealed tenderness over right upper quadrant and a firm palpable spleen of 2cm felt below the left costal margin.

This young female presents with a two week history of anaemia and jaundice. She had poor exercise tolerance noticed previously. Examination reveals firm splenomegaly. Presence of jaundice and splenomegaly in a patient with anaemia points towards haemolytic anaemia. There was a history of 'hepatitis' at age nine, which may be viral hepatitis, but could also mean an episode of haemolysis. She has had two recent episodes of abdominal colic which may be due to billiary colic following pigment gallstones. The long history of poor exercise tolerance, probable previous episode of jaundice, anaemia noted by her general practitioner suggest a hereditary cause. Presence of a chronic haemolysis is further emphasized by the possibility of gallstones. Similar illness in her farther suggests probable autosomal dominant inheritance, and his recovery following a surgery which could be a splenectomy, suggests the diagnosis of hereditary spherocytosis. There is no recent febrile illness, medication or any other identifiable precipitant. Though other hereditary haemolytic anaemia due to haemoglobinopathy or enzymopathy can produce a similar chronic haemolysis, the said inheritance pattern, gender (G6PD deficiency has X linked recessive inheritance hence occur in males) strongly favours a clinical diagnosis of hereditary spherocytosis.

History of the presenting complaint

- Shortness of breath: Establish when it was first noticed and the rate of progression and severity, which indicate the onset duration and severity of anaemia. Chronic haemolytic anaemia is well compensated and the patient may be asymptomatic in contrast to acute haemolysis. Acute breathlessness may indicate rapidly developing anaemia due to acute haemolysis. In a patient with sickle cell anaemia, acute shortness of breath may indicate occlusion of small vessels in the lungs by sickled red blood cells(RBC) leading to ventilatory failure

- Fatigue and loss of energy: These are non specific but common complaint in a patient with anaemia

- Chest pain: Is there any pain or discomfort in the chest on exertion? Angina could be a presenting feature of severe anaemia with or without structural cardiac disease

- Jaundice: Is there yellowish discolouration of eyes? Deep jaundice may indicate obstructive jaundice than haemolysis. In obstructive jaundice there is associated dark urine and pale stools. In haemolytic anaemia the urine colour on voiding is normal but darkens progressively due to the presence of excess amounts of urobilinogen

- Dark urine: Is the urine dark on voiding? In intravascular haemolysis is the urine is red or dark on voiding due to presence of free haemoglobin. In paroxysmal nocturnal haemoglobinuria (PNH) characteristically the urine voided in the early morning is dark which progressively cleared during the day

- Fever: is there associated fever at present or in the recent past? Infections may be etiologically related like malaria, which causes non immune damage to red cells (RBC). Certain infections like mycoplasma can lead to immune mediated haemolysis. Parvovirus infection can precipitate an aplastic crisis in a patient with haemolytic anaemia leading to pancytopenia. Additionally any cause of fever can precipitate haemolysis.

- Bleeding manifestations. In haemolytic anaemia generally no bleeding manifestations are present except in rare instances where presence of purpura or ecchymosis may indicate associated thrombocytopenia. In Evans syndrome both haemolysis and thrombocytopenia occur due to autoimmune destruction of RBC and platelets

- Abdominal pain: recurrent billiary colic may be due to pigment gallstones following chronic haemolysis. Recurrent abdominal pain could be a feature in PNH following venous thrombosis

- Bone pain: In sickle cell anaemia bone pain specially in the fingers is a feature of occlusion of small vessels by sickled red cells

- Acrocyanosis: Does the nose, ears, fingers and toes become blue and painful on exposure to cold? This is a feature in cold agglutinin disease which is an autoimmune haemolytic anaemia common in the elderly, which result from red cell agglutination occurring at low temperatures

- Thrombosis: has the patient had a history suggestive of a thrombotic episode which can occur in PNH

- Leg ulcers: In chronic haemolytic anaemia, as sickle cell anaemia non healing ulcers around the ankle are a feature

- Weight loss, night sweating: These may indicate the presence of a haematological malignancy like lymphoma or chronic lymphocytic leukaemia which can be the cause of haemolysis

- Prolonged march or walking: rarely prolonged march or running can lead to damage to red cells in feet, usually a self limiting condition.

- Presence of prosthetic valves: Mechanical haemolysis can be induced by prosthetic devices but usually clinically not significant

- Race, ethnicity and geographical area of origin: This may give an important clue to the diagnosis. Thalassaemias are widely spread over the Mediterranean and Asian region, whereas sickle cell anaemia is common in Africa

Past medical history

- Similar episodes in the past: If there had been similar episodes in the past were any investigations performed? Most haemolytic anaemia's have a relapsing and remitting course. What are the precipitating factors? Is the patient referred to a specialized centre for follow up?
- History of concurrent disease. In adults haemolysis may be a feature of a multisystem disease like systemic lupus erythematosus (SLE).
- History of surgery such as splenectomy or cholecystectomy. What is the course of illness following splenectomy?
- What is the patients HIV status (if available)?

Family history

- Are there any family members having similar illness?
- It is important to draw a family tree to show the pattern of inheritance. Eg: hereditary spherocytosis has an autosomal dominant inheritance whereas G6PD deficiency is X linked recessive.
- What is the severity of illness in family members? What treatment are they receiving?
- Are the patients children affected?
- Has genetic testing, screening and counselling being performed for the patient and his family?

Social history

- Exposure to drugs and chemicals
- Employment history: current and past employment and ability to continue work
- Income: able to afford hospital visits, medication. Check if insured and how much of the medical expenses are covered
- Travel: travel to malarial areas are important
- Support received from family
- Alcohol: quantify and assess if dependent
- Smoking: quantity and duration of use

Treatment history

- Obtain the details of treatment received
- Blood transfusions: History of blood transfusions from childhood suggests a hereditary cause. Frequency, special cross matching, use of blood warmer, complications following transfusion need to be assessed.
- Medications: Is the patient on steroids/ immunosuppressant? Are there adverse effects like diabetes? Are fertility and pregnancy issues discussed

- If multiple transfusions were given is the patient on iron chelation therapy? If so how often is it performed? Has the patient been screened for ocular complications while on desferrioxamine?
- Has the patient had surgery as splenectomy or cholecystectomy?
- History of vaccination. Has the patient received hepatitis B, pneumococcal, meningococcal and haemophilus vaccines?
- Is lifelong penicillin prophylaxis given after splenectomy?
- Check adherence to therapy
- Assess if follow up is satisfactory

Checklist for history in haemolytic Anaemia

- Assess current symptoms with emphasis on onset, duration, likely cause,
- Assess precipitating factors if any.
- Past medical history with emphasis on similar relapses, billiary colic due to gallstones.
- Presence SLE, malaria, concurrent or recent infections and other relevant illness should be noted.
- Treatment history: special investigations and treatment received. History of surgery as splenectomy or cholecystectomy
- Family history: it is extremely important to obtain details of similar illness in the family which gives a clue to the diagnosis. Drawing a family tree may be appropriate in some situations.
- Assess patients functional disability
- Review if current medications, vaccination, effects due to drugs as steroids.
- Assess follow up, compliance and referral for further treatment.
- Assess patient's understanding of the illness and support received from family

Examination

- Explain to patient what you intend doing before starting to examine
- Make sure the curtains are drawn and males should ask for a chaperone when examining a female patient

General examination
- Observe patient. Note the colour of patient eg: pallor, jaundice and slate grey pigmentation which suggest iron overload
- Observe and detect typical facial appearances- eg:thalassaemic facies with prominence of malar region and frontal bossing,

cushingoid appearance following long term steroids, malar rash and alopecia of SLE
- Examine mucosae for the presence and severity of pallor
- Inspect conjunctivae for icterus
- Examine for lymph nodes in neck, axillae and inguinal regions. The patient may be seated and neck is palpated from behind looking for enlarged groups of lymph nodes in the neck.
- Inspect the throat for tonsillar enlargement and evidence of infection
- Examine hands for shortened digits following bone infarcts (sickle cell anaemia). Look for evidence of arthritis
- Inspect for ulcers around ankle
- Inspect for cutaneous punctures indicative of subcutaneous infusion
- Record height and the weight. Note the presence or absence of secondary sexual characteristics indicating transfusion siderosis related endocrine dysfunction
- Record temperature

Abdomen and other system examination
- Inspect for scars suggesting splenectomy or cholecystectomy
- Palpate for tender areas specially over right hypochondrium
- Palpate for splenomegaly: size and consistency of the spleen should be assessed. Sometimes spleen may be just palpable and percussion over splenic area may reveal increased dullness confirming spenomegaly. If the spleen is large, palpate the splenic notch which is present at the anterior border, and auscultate for a rub over surface of spleen.
- Hepatomegaly: size and consistency of the liver should be noted.
- Presence of intra abdominal masses indicative of enlarged lymph nodes. (lymphoma is well known to be associated with immune mediated haemolysis)
- Ascites: is indicative of cirrhosis and portal hypertension which could arise as a treatment related complication.(chronic iron overload or following transfusion related hepatitis)
- Distended veins over the abdomen and direction of blood flow. These features are indicative of venous obstruction following thrombosis which can be present in haemolytic anaemia associated with PNH
- Cardiovascular system: examine radial pulse with attention to rate rhythm and notice the presence of collapsing pulse
- Elevated JVP
- Blood pressure
- Cardiac apex: displaced to left suggesting cardiomegaly in chronic anaemia

461

- Cardiac murmurs: a systolic flow murmur can be heard over precordium due to anaemia
- Detailed examination of respiratory system and nervous system may be relevant in some cases guided by symptoms but both systems are examined in general for completeness.
- Thank the patient at the end of the examination and cover patient up

Checklist for examination findings in Haemolytic anaemia

- General examination: mucosal pallor, conjunctival icterus, typical facies, skin pigmentation, leg ulcers, purpura, cutaneous puncture marks,surgical scars,arthritis
- Splenomegaly: size, consistency, if large, splenic notch and a rub over surface should be sought.
- Hepatomegaly; size and consistency and span of the liver should be noted
- Palpable gallbladder, right hypochondrial tenderness
- General observations Pulse, blood pressure and temperature
- Secondary sexual characteristics
- Cardiac apex: displaced to left suggesting cardiomegaly in chronic anaemia
- Cardiac murmurs:a systolic flow murmur can be heard over precordium due to anaemia
- Height and weight,BMI

Investigations

The investigations are aimed at the following
1. Confirming haemolysis
2. Finding the cause of haemolysis
3. Detecting complications
   - Complete blood count: Low haemoglobin (Hb), sudden drop in suggests acute haemolysis. Mean cell haemoglobin concentration (MCHC) is high in spherocytosis but mean cell volume (MCV) is low normal due to young RBC in peripheral blood.
   - Reticulocyte count: Elevated count is a feature of haemolysis
   - Serum bilirubin direct and indirect: Indirect fraction increased in haemolysis.
   - Serum lactate dehydrogenase (LDH): Increased in haemolysis
   - Blood picture: Often the blood picture provides a useful clue to aetiology and guides further investigations. Eg: in

sickle cell anaemia many sickled RBC are seen in blood film directing the investigations to confirm the presence of Hb F. Spherocytosis is seen in both HS and autoimmune haemolytic anaemia. In microangiopathic haemolytic anaemia the blood film is characteristic with numerous fragmented RBC

Depending on the above further investigations are planned to identify the cause. Direct antiglobulin test (DAT) also known as Coombs test: positive DAT confirms the presence of auto antibodies directed towards RBC which confirms a diagnosis of autoimmune haemolytic anaemia

- Osmotic fragility test: This measures the ability of resistance of RBC to osmotic shock. In hereditary spherocytosis RBC are less resistant to osmotic shock and than normal RBC, therefore haemolysis starts early and complete at lower concentrations of saline.
- Hb electrophoresis: Demonstrates the presence of different haemoglobins
- High performance liquid chromatography (HPLC):Sensitive method of detecting different haemoglobins in the diagnosis of haemoglobinopathies
- Red cell G6PD assay: low in G6PD deficiency except during acute haemolysis as young RBC contain higher levels of enzyme
- Urine free haemoglobin: Positive in intravascular haemolysis
- Urine haemosiderin: Indicates chronic intravascular haemolysis and is positive in PNH
- Flow cytometry: flow cytometry based analysis of CD55 and CD59 expression of GPI linked proteins in leucocytes is a useful confirmatory test in PNH
- Cold agglutinin titres: elevated titres of anti I, (positive in mycoplasma) anti i (positive in infectious mononucleosis) and anti P antibodies(positive in paroxysmal cold haemoglobinuria) are found in cold autoimmune haemolytic anaemia
- Anti nuclear antibodies: Positive in autoimmune haemolytic anaemia associated with SLE
- Thick and thin blood film for malaria parasite

Detection of complications

- Serum ferritin: grossly elevated in transfusion related iron overload.
- Ultrasound abdomen: splenomegaly, gallstones, and cirrhosis

- Liver function tests: liver dysfunction following iron overload
- ECG:cardiac damage following iron overload
- Chest radiograph
- 2D echo: may detect cardiomegaly and heart failure associated with chronic anaemia or following iron overload
- Radiography: Chest, skull and hands: In haemoglobinopathy characteristic appearances are present in skull and hands following marrow expansion
- MRI scan of heart and liver (ferriscan): This is a special MRI scan which detects transfusion related iron overload
- Hormone assays: Detects endocrinopathy following iron overload

Management of haemolytic anaemia

Management of haemolytic anaemia depends on the cause. Most hereditary haemolytic anaemias like thalassaemia have a chronic course with chronic haemolysis, increased erythropoesis leading to bony changes, growth retardation, gross hepatosplenomegaly and organ dysfunction due to severe transfusion related iron overload. The commonest effects are at heart (dilated or restrictive cardiomyopathy), pancreas (insulin dependent diabetes, liver (cirrhosis) and pitutary (gonadal failure). Hb should be maintained around 9-10.5g/dl by regular transfusions every 2-5 weeks. Iron chelation with subcutaneous desferrioxamine 6 nights /week via an infusion pump is commenced after first 10-20 transfusions or when ferritin is above 1000µg/l. Alternative oral iron chelators include deferiprone and deferisirox which are also shown to be effective.

Sickle cell anaemia in addition to chronic haemolysis, classically exhibits sickling crises which follow occlusion of small vessels during hypoxia, acidosis or infection. Plugging of small vessels in bone produce severe bone pain following infarcts specially in the fingers and toes (dactilitis) in children and femora, humeri, ribs pelvis and vertebrae in adults where active marrow is. Pulmonary sequestration produce sever hypoxia, and is the commonest form of death in adults. Venous obstruction can cause severe pain and loss of function of organs. In children this leads to massive spenomegaly but in adults, following many such episodes ultimately the spleen undergoes infarction and no longer palpable or functioning. Vaso occlusive crises are managed by prompt rehydration, oxygen, analgesia, antibiotics and in some cases blood transfusion. In sever crises exchange transfusion may be needed. Regular transfusion may be needed to suppress HbS to keep below 30%. Bone marrow transplant from an HLA matched sibling is curative but not widely available yet. Red cell enzymopathy such as G6PD deficiency causing acute haemolysis is managed by avoiding precipitating drugs.eg: aspirin, antimalarial, quinolon, sulphonamides. Chronic compensated haemolysis may not need specific treatment Acquired causes of haemolysis are diverse. In autoimmune haemolytic anaemia, an underlying cause like lymphoma, SLE or infection as mycoplama, infectious mononucleosis should be sought. Warm autoimmune haemolytic anaemia is managed with prednisolon 1mg/kg initially and tailing once response is achieved. (Steroids suppress autoantibody formation and macrophage mediated destruction of RBC.) For non respondents further immunosuppression may be tried with cyclophosphamide or azathioprine but will eventually need a splenectomy. Cold autoimmune haemolytic anaemia managed by avoiding exposure to lower temperatures (antibody binding to RBC occurs in low temperatures as 4^0C and haemolysis occur at body temperature). They are generally poorly steroid responsive. An underlying lymphoma should be looked for as a treatable cause. If blood transfusion is needed it should be performed through a blood warmer.

Management of hereditary spherocytosis is discussed under case discussion

Case summary

This 20 yr old female presented with anaemia which is of recent onset, the presence of icterus and splenomegaly suggesting haemolytic anaemia. The cause of haemolysis is more likely to be hereditary considering the long course, presence of gallstones and the history of similar illness in the father. Similar illness in father and his apparent recovery following possible splenectomy points toward hereditary spherocytosis(HS), though other hereditary anaemias cannot be completely excluded.

Clinical discussion of the case

Starts with the summary of the patien highlighting important clues in the history and abnormal physical signs.
Clinical diagnosis should be confirmed by investigations in order to start specific therapy.

The diagnosis of haemolytic anaemia is confirmed by elevated reticulocyte count, serum unconjugated hyperbilirubinaemia and elevated serum lactic dehydrogenase. Following confirmation of haemolysis, further investigations are arranged to confirm a specific cause. Findings in the blood picture guides further investigations. In this patient the most likely clinical diagnosis is hereditary spherocytosis hence investigations are directed towards confirming HS. In hereditary spherocytosis, the blood film reveals microspherocytes. Presence of autoimmune HA is excluded by performing a Coomb's test. Further confirmation of hereditary spherocytosis includes an osmotic fragility test. As most cases of asymptomatic disease is compensated with increased RBC production, no treatment is indicated for such cases. Blood transfusion is indicated for severe cases presenting with acute haemolysis. Patients with chronic haemolysis should be offered a splenectomy which induces a remission and obliviates the need for transfusion. (spleen is the site of destruction of the less deformable spherocytic RBC in hereditary spherocytosis. .

Folic acid prophylaxis 5mg/week is recommended for life for all patients with hereditary spherocytosis. Symptomatic gallstones need a cholecystectomy.

Causes of haemolytic anaemia

	Intra corpuscular defects	Extracorpuscular defects
hereditary	Haemoglobinopathy eg:Thalassaemia, Sickle cell anaemia	Familial haemolytic uremic syndrome (familial HUS)
	Enzymopathy eg: G6PD deficiency	
	Membrane defect eg:Hereditary spherocytosis	
Acquired	Paroxysmal nocturnal haemoglobinuria (PNH)	Autoimmune haemolytic anaemia eg: warm antibody type cold antibody type
		Mechanical destruction
		Drugs and toxins
		Infection related eg:malaria

Learning outcomes

The student should be able to

- Elicit a focussed history in a patient with suspected haemolytic anaemia

- Perform a relevant physical examination and detect abnormal physical signs
- Explain the clinical features on a physiological and pathological basis
- Make a clinical diagnosis or provide a differential diagnosis based on the history and examination findings
- Discuss the common causes of haemolytic anaemia in adults understanding the pathological basis and classification
- Select the relevant investigations that would confirm haemolysis and arrange specific investigations to determine the aetiology and assess the patient for further management.
- Discuss the treatment including medical therapy, blood transfusions, splenectomy and therapy related complications
- Discuss diagnosis, prevention and treatment of complications
- Communicate to the patient about the nature of the illness, the need for long term follow up and support that can be obtained
- Discuss risk for offspring, family screening and genetic counselling

Commonly asked questions

What additional investigations can confirm haemolysis?
- absence of serum haptoglobins
- marrow erythroid hyperplasia
- shortened red cell survival shown by radio labelled assays

What is the pathogenesis of hereditary spherocytosis?'
In hereditary spherocytosis there is deficiency or dysfunction of membrane cytoskeletal proteins such as spectrin, ankyrin, band 3 or protein 4.2 leading to loss of membrane. The RBC surface to volume ratio is reduced producing small spherocytes. These cells are less deformable therefore they are trapped and removed in spleen leading to shortened RBC survival.

What abnormality is seen in the blood film of a patient with hereditary spherocytosis?
- In hereditary spherocytosis the blood film reveals microspherocytes which are small spherical shaped RBC.

How would you differentiate between causes if large numbers of sphrocytes are present in blood film?
Autoimmune haemolytic anaemia and hereditary spherocytosis both show spherocytosis in blood film and are differentiated from each other by finding a positive DAT in autoimmune haemolytic anaemia.

What are the complications of hereditary spherocytosis?
- Haemolytic crises

- Aplastic crises (occur in association with parvovirus infection, which invades RBC precursors and completely switch off RBC production)
- Megaloblastic crises (occur in association with folic acid deficiency due to increased RBC turnover)
- Pigment gallstones (may be present in 50% of cases)

What are the indications for splenectomy in hereditary spherocytosis?
Splenectomy improves RBC survival and is indicated in recurrent severe crises, family history of death from disease, symptomatic cholecystitis and in growth retardation in children.

Distinction level questions

How is the diversity of disease severity explained in hereditary spherocytosis? The diversity in severity is explained by the presence of severe deficiency/ dysfunction or presence of combined deficiency of membrane anchoring proteins namely ankyrin, spectrin, band 3 and protein 4.2

What are the changes present in the blood film following splenectomy in a patient with hereditary spherocytosis?

The blood film will still show spherocytes as well as Howell-Jolly bodies which are present following splenectomy.

Should concurrent cholecystectomy be performed with splenectomy?
In the absence of gallstones concurrent cholecystectomy is not indicated as there is no gallstone formation after splenectomy.

What explanation can be given for the disease recurrence following splenectomy?
If accessory splenic tissues (spleniculi) are left behind there could be recurrence of symptomatic anaemia.

Red flag encounters

The following are situations that may be overlooked:

- Mild icterus may be easily missed unless examination performed under good light.
- Muddy sclera can be mistaken for conjunctival icterus unless the observer is familiar in differentiating either
- Not turning the patient to the right lateral position and using the correct technique to examine may fail to detect a just palpable spleen

Must know facts in hereditary spherocytosis

- Hereditary spherocytosis is usually autosomal dominant inheritance,25% have no positive family history
- Though disease is hereditary, presentation may only occur in adult life
- The defect in hereditary spherocytosis is in the molecules of RBC membrane which forms the cytoskeleton
- Spherocytes resulting from the membrane defect have shortened RBC survival causing chronic haemolysis
- Hereditary spherocytosis is confirmed by osmotic fragility test
- Lifelong folic acid prophylaxis is advised for all cases of hereditary spherocytosis.
- Spleen is the site of destruction spherocytes, hence splenectomy is advised in severe cases.
- Vaccination for specific infections and lifelong penicillin prophylaxis is advised for patients undergoing splenectomy

References

The British Committee for Standards of Haematology homepage. Available from www.bcshguidelines.com Guidelines for the management of hereditary spherocytosis Sep 2011.

Fausi A.S. Harrison's principles of Internal Medicine.17th edition.Mc Graw Hill. 2007.

Hoffbrand A.V Postgraduate Haematology.5th edition. Blackwell publishing. 2005.

SECTION 5:NEUROLOGY

CASE 37: STROKE
KOH KWEE CHOY, JAMES

OVERVIEW

Stroke, also known as cerebrovascular accident (CVA), is an acute neurological injury caused by one of two pathological processes, namely ischaemia or haemorrhage with the former accounting for 80% of cases of stroke. It is the second commonest cause of death worldwide and is the leading cause of adult disability. It is the 4th highest cause of death in Malaysia.

Stroke is one of the commonest conditions used in undergraduate examinations. The examination of the Central Nervous System (CNS) has always been a bane for medical students as it is often perceived as being time consuming or intimidating, and the findings deemed hard to interpret. A good understanding of the 'why' behind each step should make the CNS examination less dreaded and more meaningful.

Types of Cases for Clinical Examination

1. OSCE (short or long)

   In the short OSCE, often students are asked to examine only a component of the neurological deficits present in the stroke patient. For example, students may be asked on just the examination of the cranial nerves while in the long OSCE; generally students are expected to examine a larger component of the neurological deficits present, such as examination of the motor system.

2. Long case or OSLER

   In the long case, detailed history taking is expected from students which, in addition to the presenting complaints, should also explore the premorbid status of the patient, possible causative factors and complications. The student would be expected to perform detailed CNS examination which may include assessment of higher mental function, cranial nerves examination, motor and sensory examinations and cerebellar signs, depending on the history obtained.

CASE VIGNETTE

A 56-year-old man presents with sudden onset of right sided body weakness associated with inability to verbalize. However, he is able to understand spoken words. He has history of diabetes mellitus, hypertension, ischemic heart disease and atrial fibrillation.

Examine this patient's gait and the motor system.

Differential Diagnoses:

   1. Cerebrovascular accident (either ischaemic or haemorrhagic).

   2. Transient ischemic attack (TIA).

   3. Unilateral space occupying lesions such as tumors or infective foci.

History of Presenting Illness

Determining the onset of symptoms is very important. Strokes are typically acute in onset while limb weakness caused by intracranial tumors or infection are typically slow and progressive in nature.

The presence of associated preceding symptoms such as severe headache, vomiting and vertigo suggests vertebrobasilar (brain stem) strokes. Loss of consciousness suggests either a massive middle cerebral artery (MCA) occlusion or vertebrobasilar stroke.

The student should determine if the patient has receptive (sensory or Wernicke's) or expressive (motor or Broca's) dysphasia or both (Global dysphasia) during history taking and this provides vital clues to the location and extend of the lesion in the brain. The Broca's area is located in the left inferior frontal lobe while the Wernicke's area is located in the left superior and posterior temporal lobe.

Immediate complications as a result of stroke such as seizures and head trauma due to a fall might be present.

Past Medical History

History of known risk factors for stroke such as diabetes mellitus, hypertension, hypercholesterolemia, obesity, rhythm disorders, heart problems with and smoking should be elicited. Non-modifiable risk factors such as age, gender and ethnicity may play a role (older age group, males and Asians compared to Caucasians, have higher risk of stroke).

History of neurological deficits which resolved spontaneously, suggestive of transient ischaemic attacks (TIA); leading to the present complaint might be present.

Relevant drug history and compliance to medications are important.

Family History

Rarely, there may be family history of young stroke suggestive of rare hereditary disorders such as arterio-venous malformations (Osler-Weber-Rendu Syndrome) or hypercoagulable states such as antiphospholipid antibody syndrome, Leiden Factor V mutation, and protein C and protein S deficiencies.

Family history of known risk factors for stroke such as diabetes mellitus, hypertension, obesity, hypercholesterolemia and heart diseases may be present.

Social history

Smoking tobacco – calculate the number of pack years (number of cigarette packs/day multiplied by the number of years smoking).

Surgical history

No relevance

Systemic review of symptoms

Symptoms related to underlying risk factors should be explored. For example, constant thirst and frequent urination are suggestive of poorly controlled diabetes mellitus; chest pain, shortness of breath and palpitations in ischaemic heart disease with rhythm abnormality.

It is important, when presenting a case, to mention the differential diagnoses that you have considered and eliminated based on the presence or absence of symptoms from a detailed history taking.

CHECK LIST FOR HISTORY TAKING IN STROKE

- Onset of symptoms
- Assess for vertebrobasilar stroke symptoms
- Ask about known risk factors for stroke
- Explore possible relevant family history

EXAMINATION

The examination of the CNS is long and sometimes tedious but if done systematically and methodically can be very rewarding. Remember that the main objective of the CNS examination is to establish the SITE of the lesion and to discover the underlying aetiology for the stroke.

General examination and vital signs

Begin with the general examination. Introduce yourself, explain your intentions and obtain consent from the patient. During the introduction, perform a quick visual survey of the patient's general condition; note the attitude of the limbs (the weaker side is relatively immobile in comparison to the healthy side); quickly establish if the patient is oriented to his surroundings; discover if he could understand or obey your commands to establish if he has sensory (Wernicke's aphasia) or motor aphasia (Broca's aphasia) or both (Global aphasia); note if there is obvious drooping of the angle of mouth on the contralateral side to the limb weakness.

Proceed with taking the vital signs. In acute stroke, the blood pressure is typically elevated in response to raised intracranial pressure due to expanding oedema in the brain matter (the penumbra) surrounding the stroke. This is known as Cushing Reflex. Irregularly irregular pulse is suggestive of underlying atrial fibrillation. Respiratory rate may be shallow and slow, again due to raised intracranial pressure.

Look for tell-tale signs of underlying risk factors for stroke such as nicotine-stained nails and palmar erythema (smoking), xanthelesma and tendon xanthomas (hypercholesterolemia), and pallor and sallow appearance (diabetes mellitus with renal impairment). In some patients, following an acute stroke, the eyes are deviated contralateral to the side of limb weakness (Prévost's sign).

Cranial nerves examination

Unless specifically asked (in OSCE or long case), performing the full cranial nerves examination may not be necessary in a case of stroke. Instead, careful examination of a few selected cranial nerves (II, III, IV, VI, VII, IX and X) may yield adequate information to help localize the site of the lesion. Because all cranial nerves (except for cranial nerves I and 2)originate from the brain stem at different levels, any cranial nerves abnormality detected could provide clues to the extent of the affected area in the CNS.

Visual deficits, rarely looked for by students, are not uncommon. Contralateral homonymous hemianopia is common in large MCA infarct which can be easily revealed with a careful examination of the visual field using the confrontation test. Examination of the III, IV, VI cranial nerves using the 'H' test will reveal evidence of ophthalmoplegia, which in the case of stroke may suggests gross cerebral oedema or brain herniation compressing these cranial nerves.

By asking the patient to "look up" and observe for forehead wrinkles, "shut your eye-lids against resistance", "puff up the cheeks and blow", "smile" and observe for deviation of angle of the mouth, the student can quickly deduce if the VII nerve palsy is upper motor neuron (UMN) or lower motor neuron (LMN) in origin. Lesion between the cerebral cortex and the internal capsule produces contra lateral UMN facial and limb paralysis ,where as brain stem (Mid brain, Pons and upper medullary) lesion produces ipsilateral cranial nerve paralysis and contra lateral limb paralysis. Thus an internal capsular lesion on left side will produce right UMN facial palsy and paralysis of right upper and lower limbs, while left pontine lesion will result in left LMN facial palsy and paralysis of right upper and lower limbs

Assessment of the IX and X cranial nerves is important as they control the gag reflex which is often affected in the setting of an acute stroke rendering the patient vulnerable to choking and aspiration pneumonia. The IX nerve can be quickly assessed by asking the patient to say "Ah" and observe for the lifting of the soft palate and uvula as well as asking the patient to swallow. Similarly, the X cranial nerve can be assessed with the swallowing test and the quality of speech produced.

Motor system examination

When performing the motor system examination on the patient, the student should keep in mind the homunculus distribution of muscles in the brain (Figure 1).

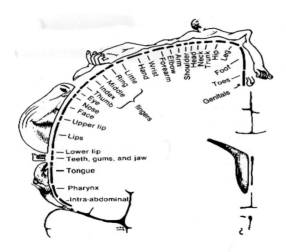

Figure 1: The homunculus

The student should ask two basic questions: 1. "On which side is the weakness" and 2. "Is this a UMN or LMN paralysis?" UMN paralysis is characterized by initial muscle weakness or paralysis, spasticity of affected muscle and hyper-reflexia while LMN paralysis is characterized by muscle weakness, wasting, flaccidity, hypoactivity or absent tendon reflex and fasciculation.

Combining the information gathered from the examination of the motor system with the knowledge of the homunculus should help the student come a reasonable conclusion as to which of the three main vessels supplying the brain, namely the anterior cerebral arteries (ACA), the middle cerebral arteries (MCA) and the posterior cerebral arteries (PCA) is affected. The ACA and MCA are branches of the internal carotid artery while the PCA are branches of the basilar arteries. Stroke involving the PCA are not as common as the other two arteries.

Muscle power is graded from 0 (complete paralysis), 1 (flicker of contraction), 2 (active movement with gravity eliminated), 3 (movement against gravity), 4 (active movement against resistance) and 5 (normal power). By determining the muscle power in the extensors and flexors of the upper and lower limbs in the affected side, the student can quite confidently deduce which of the circulation is affected. For example, if the right upper and lower limbs have complete paralysis (hemiplegia), the site of occlusion is either near the origin of the ACA and MCA affecting a large hemispheric area or at the internal capsule where all the nerve fibres converge into a small area. However, if the right upper limb is weaker compared to the right lower limb, the area supplied by the MCA is ~ted (temporo-parietal lobes).

The student should remember that the patient with stroke may have developed increased muscle tone and spasticity over time (giving rise to 'clasp knife rigidity') and this may interfere with assessment of muscle power. In addition, the flexors are stronger that the extensors in the upper limb while the extensors are stronger than the flexors in the lower limbs.

If the patient is able to walk, observing the gait and arm swing can provide useful clues to the underlying pathology. Ask the patient to walk using not only their regular gait, but also to attempt to walk on their toes, heels and perform tandem walking (one foot in front of the other). Stroke patients typically demonstrate a spastic gait with little or no arm swing.

Sensory system examination

In contrast to the motor system, examination of the sensory system may not be as rewarding with regards to its localizing value in the CNS. A lengthy sensory examination would typically include testing for vibration sense with a 128 Hz tuning fork, proprioception (or joint position sense), pinprick to test for pain sensation, temperature with heat and cold, and light touch. Of these, light touch is the least useful in its localizing value. For example, a patient with diabetes mellitus may not feel light touch because of peripheral sensory neuropathy rather than from a CNS deficit.

To quickly screen for sensory problems, the student need only use one test for each of the two separate sensory pathways, namely the spinothalamic tract which carries impulses related to touch, pain and temperature, and the dorsal column which carries impulses related to vibration and proprioception.

Reflex testing

Before testing for reflexes, the student must keep two important points in mind. Proper positioning and technique are important to obtain the desired results. For example, proper exposure of the arm to watch and feel the tendon move in response to tapping the biceps tendon is essential. Similarly, adequate exposure to facilitate feeling of the quadriceps muscles contraction when testing the patella jerk is important.

Essentially there are only four reflexes that need to be tested, namely, the biceps, the triceps, the knees and the ankles. Each of these reflexes when tested, provide localizing value to different levels of the spinal cord. A patient with UMN stroke has hyperreflexia while LMN stroke has hyporeflexia. When a reflex is absent, ask the patient to perform the Jendrassik manoeuvre to augment the reflex.

Testing the plantar reflex is important although the desired response (up going plantar with dorsiflexion of the big toe and fanning out of the other toes or positive Babinski response) in UMN stroke may not be readily obtainable as it is largely dependent on proper positioning of the foot and the technique used. The student should also keep in mind that, reflexes tend to diminish with repeated testing at any one time and so with repeated testing, the desired response may altogether disappear!

Examination of other related systems

Depending on the underlying aetiopathogenesis of the stroke and the patient's past medical history, examination of the relevant systems may be carried out at the end of the CNS examination.

Fundoscopic examination of the eye may reveal retinal changes secondary to hypertension, diabetes and hypercholesterolaemia.

Cardiovascular examination – look for arrhythmia, evidence of cardiomegaly, carotid bruit, and valvular involvement.

Respiratory system – look for evidence of chronic obstructive airway disease secondary to smoking.

CHECK LIST FOR THE EXAMINATION FINDINGS IN STROKE

Determine which side of the body is weak

Establish if the weakness is UMN or LMN

Assess the cranial nerves, motor and sensory system

Look for evidence of risk factors for stroke

INVESTIGATIONS

In addition to basic diagnostic studies, the following investigations are relevant and essential in the management of a patient with stroke:

Investigation	Justification
Electrocardiography (ECG)	An ECG is essential in all patients with acute stroke to look for arrhythmias that would predispose a patient to embolic events (e.g. atrial fibrillation).
Chest radiography	To look for cardiomegaly, consolidation (pneumonia can predispose to atrial fibrillation), evidence of aspiration, and changes secondary to COAD.

Transcranial Doppler ultrasonography	It is a non-invasive technique to evaluate the patency of intracranial vessels. Carotid ultrasonography or Doppler is useful in defining carotid artery stenosis.
Computed tomography (CT)	CT scan of the brain is done to rapidly rule out or diagnose intracerebral haemorrhage. However, in the first few hours after the onset of symptoms, CT scan may not pick up any abnormality in ischaemic stroke. Combining CT angiography with CT scan can improve the diagnostic value of CT scanning in stroke patients.
Magnetic Resonance Imaging (MRI)	MRI brain can detect changes secondary to ischaemic stroke within 30 minutes of onset.
Echocardiography	Transthoracic and transoesophageal echocardiography can be used to look for intracardiac thrombus or aortic source of emboli.

CASE SUMMARY

This 56-year-old man has evidence of stroke. He has history of diabetes mellitus, hypertension, hypercholesterolemia, atrial fibrillation and smoking. On examination, there is irregularly irregular pulse and right dense hemiplegia and right UMN facial nerve palsy. He also has expressive dysphasia. The most likely diagnosis is thromboembolic stroke affecting the left MCA territory secondary to atrial fibrillation.

CLINICAL DISCUSSION OF THE CASE

The student should be able to

- Establish that the cause of the patient's disability is a left cerebrovascular accident (CVA) based on the history and clinical examination.
- Make a reasonable diagnosis of thromboembolic stroke after evaluating for known risk factors (i.e. atrial fibrillation).
- List the relevant investigations in a logical manner with appropriate justifications for each.

- Discuss the principles of management in this patient.
- Explore important issues related to the care and rehabilitation of a stroke patient.

With the availability of radioimaging studies, the diagnosis of stroke and the differentiation of stroke into thromboembolic and haemorrhagic type are relatively straight forward. However, the subsequent management of a patient with acute stroke is often not as smooth sailing and is often fraught with complication such as aspiration pneumonia, chronic pain, contractures, pressure sores, total dependence on others for activities-of-daily-living and disruption in the immediate social and family structure. Patients who suffered ischaemic stroke has better chance of survival compared to haemorrhagic stroke but the latter, if they survive, have a better chance at regaining functionality.

Post-stroke rehabilitation of patient would include physical therapy, occupational therapy, recreational therapy and speech therapy

The risk of recurring stroke is highest in the first few weeks after the 1st episode and about a quarter of patients with stroke will have a recurrence within 5 years. Risk factors associated with recurrent strokes include:

- Alcoholism
- Atrial fibrillation
- Diabetes mellitus
- Haemorrhagic or embolic stroke
- History of coronary artery disease, carotid artery disease, peripheral artery disease, or TIA
- Older age
- Valvular heart disease

LEARNING OUTCOMES

By the end of this case review the student should be:

1. Able to define stroke.

2. Make a diagnosis based on history and findings from clinical examination.

3. List the investigations in stroke.

4. Discuss the principles in management of stroke.

COMMONLY ASKED QUESTIONS

1. Name two causes for this patient's condition.
2. What is the most likely underlying cause of his condition?
3. What investigations will you perform in this patient

HIGH ACHIEVER QUESTIONS

1. What are the modifiable and non-modifiable risk factors for stroke?
2. What are the risk factors associated with recurrence of stroke?
3. What is Broca's aphasia and Wernicke's aphasia*?
4. What are the risk factors associated with increase short-term and long-term mortality in a stroke patient?
5. What is dyspraxia or apraxia?
6. What does the term 'neglect' mean ?

Pierre Paul Broca (1824 –1880) was a French physician, surgeon, anatomist, and anthropologist. Carl Wernicke (1848 - 1905) was a German physician, anatomist, psychiatrist and neuropathologist.

COMMON MISTAKES

- Wrongly attributing LMN weakness as UMN weakness. These two conditions share only one common factor which is weakness. LMN weakness is flaccid while UMN weakness is spastic in nature. With LMN lesions, deep tendon reflexes are decreased, pathological reflexes are absent and superficial reflexes are present. In contrast, UMN lesions, deep tendon reflexes are increased, pathological reflexes are present and superficial reflexes are absent.
- Neglecting to examine for visual field defects in suspected MCA territory infarct.
- Neglecting to compare the affected side with the opposite healthy side of the body.
- Neglecting to make allowance for stronger muscle power according to the 'handedness' of the patient. Typically, the dominant side of the patient will be about 10% stronger than the corresponding opposite muscle.
- Inadequate exposure when testing for deep tendon reflexes.
- Neglecting to ask the patient to perform the Jendrassik* manoeuvre to augment reflexes when initial reflex testing was unsatisfactory.

- Repeated attempts at reflexes testing which only serve to diminish the response.

Erno Jendrassik (1858 – 1921) was a Hungarian physician whose area of specialty was reflexes.

MUST KNOW FACTS ABOUT STROKE

1. The two commonest causes of stroke are thromboembolism (ischaemic) and haemorrhage with an incidence of 80% to 20%, respectively.

2. Neurological deficits in brain stem stroke are typically 'crossed' (ipsilateral cranial nerve palsy and contralateral limb weakness, (of UMN type).

3. Careful history and systematic clinical examination will reveal the site of lesion.

4. Stroke has defined modifiable and non-modifiable risk factors.

5. Recurrence of strokes is dependent on presence of poor prognostic risk factors.

OVERVIEW

Paraplegia is defined as permanent paralysis of the body caused by injury or disease affecting the spinal cord. It involves loss of sensation and movement in the legs and occasionally involves the entire trunk depending on the level of the injury. Paraparesis denotes partial weakness. The cause of injury may be due to external trauma or internal disease or degeneration. Traumatic injuries are more common in young men while non-traumatic injuries are more common in persons above the age of 50 years

Compared to stroke, paraplegia is less commonly encountered in medical undergraduate examinations. Because most paraplegia cases are traumatic in origin, the students may encounter their first case of paraplegia in the orthopaedic ward rather than in the medical ward. Patients with paraplegia may be used in the OSCE or as long case in the examination. The discussion in this chapter shall be confined to paraplegia from non-traumatic origin, although much of what will be discussed is also applicable for paraplegia from traumatic origin.

CASE VIGNETTE

A 35-year-old woman complains of back pain over the last 2 weeks. She noticesweakness of her lower limbs soon after the onset of the back pain which is associated with tingling sensation in the lower limbs. Over the past 4 days she is no longer able to move her legs, has difficulty in voiding urine and suffers from constipation. She received rabies vaccine about a month ago in preparation for her annual holiday to Bali.

Take a detailed history and perform a neurological examination of this patient's lower limbs.

DIFFERENTIAL DIAGNOSIS

The differential diagnoses of non-traumatic acute or subacute paraplegia may be broadly categorized into:

1. Compressive-disorders of the spinal cord

External (extra-medullary) or internal (intra-medullary) compression of the spinal cord by space occupying lesions (e.g. subdural or epidural abscess, herniated disc or disc prolapse, spondylosis, spinal stenosis, syringomyelia, neoplasms, vertebral abscess or degeneration)

The differences between paraplegia as a result of intra or extra-medullary compressive disorders are shown in Table 1.

Table 1: Differences between intra and extra-medullary compressive disorders causing paraplegia

	Intra-medullary	Extra-medullary
Root pain & vertebral pain	Unusual. late	Common, early
UMN signs	Late	Early
LMN signs	Prominent and diffuse	unusual
Sensory deficit	Dissociated sensory loss (see discussion in 'Sensory System Examination'	Ipsilateral proprioception and vibration sensations loss with contralateral pain and temperature sensations loss
Sacral sparing	Present	Absent
Bowel and bladder disturbances	Early	Late
Spine tenderness	Absent	Present

2. Non-compressive disorders of the spinal cord

2.1 Intra-medullary lesions (within the cord)

a. Vascular disorders compromising the blood supply to the spinal cord (e.g. vasculitis, atherosclerosis, hematoma, decompression sickness, arterio-venous malformations).

b. Inflammatory disorders affecting the spinal cord (e.g. acute transverse myelitis of viral, bacterial fungal origin or post-vaccination or myelitis from chronic disorders like multiple sclerosis).

2.2 Extra-medullary lesions

a. Any conditions which affect the pathway of muscle innervation from the spinal cord (e.g. Guillain-Barre syndrome, periodic hypokalemic paralysis, myasthenia gravis, vitamin B12 deficiency, myositis, myopathy, motor neuron diseases).

b. Lesions affecting areas supplied by the anterior cerebral arteries in the brain (e.g. falx cerebri tumor, metastasis to the brain or cerebral infection).

History of Presenting Illness

First determine if the patient has weakness and *not* fatigue. Although similar, these two conditions are in fact, distinct from each other. The former implies lack of muscle strength (the patient might say she requires extra effort to move her limb) while the latter is a feeling of exhaustion or tiredness as a result of lack of energy (too exhausted to move).

Naturally, traumatic causes of paraplegia should first be ruled out. Ask about history of fall or blunt force trauma to the back. Ask about the onset of paraplegia – whether it is acute (within minutes to hours; e.g. acute transverse myelitis, disc prolapse, anterior spinal artery thrombosis), subacute (days to weeks; e.g. subacute combined degeneration (SACD), subacute transverse myelitis, Pott's disease, spinal cord tumors or abscess) or chronic (months to years; e.g. compression by slowly progressing space-occupying spinal or para-spinal lesions, familial disorders, amyotrophic lateral sclerosis).It is also important to determine if the *upper limbs* are involved as well which would suggest a lesion higher in the spinal cord (e.g. cervical cord).

Ask about her back pain (duration, intensity). Determine if the patient has any history suggestive of girdle pain (unilateral or bilateral thorax or abdominal pain of dermatomal distribution which worsens on coughing, sneezing or valsalva) or root (radicular) pain (unilateral or bilateral shooting pain of dermatomal distribution that radiates to the limbs and aggravated by coughing, sneezing or valsalva) (Table 1).

Determine if the weakness is symmetrical or more on one side compared to the other. Asymmetry (one limb weaker than the other) may be the presenting complaint before the weakness becomes symmetrical. The patient may say one leg felt heavier first before the other leg. This suggests a spinal cord lesion which affects a part of the spinal segment before affecting the segment in total. Ask questions to differentiate if the weakness is distal or proximal (e.g. "Do you trip when you walk?", "Do you have difficulty climbing stairs or getting up from sitting position?", "Are you able to comb your hair?"). Proximal weakness suggests myopathy while distal weakness suggests neuropathy. Ascending paralysis suggests peripheral demyelination disorders such as Gullain-Barre syndrome while weakness which diminishes with exertion and improves with rest suggests myasthenia gravis.

485

Sensory symptoms include feelings of numbness, tingling, burning sensation or cold. Patients with transverse myelitis may complain of areas of skin which are extra sensitive to touch (allodynia).

Fever may be present in paraplegia from infectious origins or may be the presenting symptom complications arising from the paraplegia (e.g. urinary tract infection, infected pressure sores).

Remember to ask about the patient's activities of daily living prior to onset of symptoms which will help to establish her premorbid functional status.

PAST MEDICAL HISTORY

Ask if there is any history of direct trauma to the spine, lifting of heavy weights (intervertebral disc prolapse) or procedures performed on the spine (e.g. epidural anaesthesia for childbirth, spinal surgery).

Ask about possible risk factors for acute transverse myelitis such as preceding viral infections (chicken pox, shingles, herpes simplex), or bacterial infections (otitis media, *Mycoplasma* pneumonia) and recent vaccinations (rabies and chicken pox). Determine if the patient has history of tuberculosis and if present, enquire if she has completed the recommended length of therapy.

Tactfully ask if there is history of any malignancies in the past which, if not completely eradicated, may now manifest as secondaries in the spine.

Enquire about symptoms suggestive of underlying vasculitis or autoimmune disorders which may cause myelitis (e.g. malar rash, photosensitivity, mouth ulcers, and hair loss in Systemic Lupus Erythematosus (SLE); dry eyes and mouth in Sjogren's syndrome). Visual symptoms are important as the paraplegia may be another manifestation of multiple sclerosis which is associated with optic neuritis (hence, the expression: Two different neurological manifestations from two different sites at two different times).

History relating to possible extra-spinal conditions may be important. For example, ascending weakness of the lower limbs post-respiratory tract infection in Guillain-Barre syndrome; weakness after a heavy meal or exercise in periodic hypokalemic paralysis; and headache or visual disturbance in space-occupying lesions of the brain.

Carefully explore if she has underlying conditions associated with atherosclerosis (e.g. diabetes mellitus, hypertension, ischaemic heart disease). Remember to take a menstrual and obstetric history. Recurrent miscarriages may be associated with underlying autoimmune problems (e.g. antiphospholipid syndrome).

FAMILY HISTORY

Although uncommon, there are a number of hereditary conditions presenting with limb weakness (e.g. hereditary spastic paraplegia, Friedreich's ataxia, periodic hypokalemic paralysis.

SOCIAL HISTORY

Smoking is a risk factor for stroke and atherosclerosis. Chronic alcohol consumption is associated with myopathy. Strict vegetarian diet may result in vitamin B_{12} and folate deficiencies.

Once you have gained the patient's confidence, attempt to explore her sexual history. Syphilis is associated with spinal cord problems (tabes dorsalis, meningomyelitis, cerebral or spinal gumma). HIV infection may cause myelopathy, multiple mononeuropathies, and is associated with progressive multifocal leukoencephalopathy which may present with limb weakness.

SURGICAL HISTORY

History of spinal surgery might be relevant.

OCCUPATIONAL HISTORY

Divers and deep sea workers are at risk of decompression sickness (Caisson's Disease) which may present with paralysis.

SYSTEMIC REVIEW OF SYMPTOMS

Carefully ask questions to quickly screen through the other systems which may reveal the underlying cause of the paraplegia. For instance, chronic cough, fever and night sweats suggest pulmonary tuberculosis (TB) with the paraplegia caused by spinal TB (Pott's disease).

Ask about bladder and bowel involvement (urinary retention, overflow incontinence, altered bowel habits, bowel incontinence).

By asking questions in a systematic and logical way, the differential diagnoses for the paraplegia in a patient may be truncated considerably.

CHECK LIST FOR HISTORY TAKING IN PARAPLEGIA

- Onset of symptoms
- Establish that the problem is weakness and not fatigue
- Rule out traumatic causes first as they are more common
- Define the character of the neurological deficit (site, symmetry, strength, sensation)
- Explore possible relevant past medical and family history
- Check for bladder and bowel involvement

EXAMINATION

General examination and vital signs

Before commencing the physical examination, introduce yourself to the patient, explain your intentions and obtain consent from the patient. Be aware that the patient may be in pain. During the introduction, quickly perform a visual survey of the patient's general condition. If the patient fails to rise from the chair when greeted, it may indicate proximal weakness or complete paralysis of the lower limbs. Pallor and ichthyosis suggest SACD. Jaundice, palmar erythema and spider naevi suggest underlying chronic liver disease. Cyanosis may be present in Guillain-Barre Syndrome (GBS) involving respiratory muscles. Lymph nodes enlargement and cachexia suggest possible TB or malignancies. Clubbing may be present (malignancy, chronic liver disease). Pressure sores on dependent areas may be present as a complication of paraplegia. Nicotine-stained finger nails suggest chronic smoking. An indwelling urinary catheter suggests bladder dysfunction.

Proceed with taking the vital signs. Tachypnoea may be present in GBS or myasthenia gravis affecting respiratory muscles. Signs related to underlying causes may be found (e.g. stigmata of chronic liver diseases in myopathy associated with liver cirrhosis; cardiomegaly and aneurysm in tabes dorsalis (very rare)).

Examination of the lower limbs

Remember that the main objective of examining a patient with paraplegia is to establish the SPINAL LEVEL of the lesion and to discover the underlying aetiology for the paraplegia. In order to achieve this, a reasonably good working knowledge of neuroanatomy is essential, namely:

1. Location of motor and sensory nerve tracts and bundles within the spinal cord (Figure 1).

2. Sensory dermatomes and myotomes in the human body (Figure 2; Table 3).

3. Superficial and deep reflexes levels (Table 3).

At first glance, the many nerve tracts with apparently confusing names may seem intimidating but the student should not be overly alarmed. To examine a case of paraplegia, only a few of these tracts are important – namely the pyramidal tract comprising of the anterior and lateral corticospinal tracts (motor fibres); the antero-lateral system (ALS) comprising of the anterior and lateral spinothalamic tracts (pain, temperature and light touch) and the dorsal column (proprioception. touch and vibration).

Briefly, the motor fibres originate from the cerebral cortex to become tightly packed in the posterior limb of the internal capsule before descending to the level of the medulla oblongata where about 80% of the fibres cross to the contralateral side to form the lateral corticospinal tract (LCT). The remaining 20% continue on the ipsilateral side as the anterior corticospinal tract (ACT) which crosses to the contralateral side at the level of the spinal cord. Both the LCT and ACT eventually synapse with motor neurons in the anterior (ventral) horn of the spinal cord. To put it simply, ALL motor fibres on one side of the body is controlled by the opposite cerebral hemisphere.

Both the LCT and ACT are upper motor neurons (UMN) while the motor neurons beginning from the ventral horn are 2nd order neurons which are lower motor neurons (LMN). Therefore, any injury to the spinal cord may produce LMN signs *at* the level of the injury and UMN signs *below* the level of injury.

Sensations are carried in primarily two nerve bundles in the spinal cord – the dorsal column and the ALS. Fibres in the dorsal column do not decussate in the spinal cord while the spinothalamic tracts typically ascend one or two spinal segment before crossing to the contralateral side. What this means in practice is that, unlike the ALS, the dorsal column sensations have no localizing value in a case of paraplegia. Because the fibres in the ALS ascend a one or two segments before crossing the midline to the opposite side, the offending lesion in the spinal cord causing the loss of pain and temperature sensations *is actually one or two segments higher* than what is detected in the clinical examination. The student must also remember that the spinal cord is shorter than the vertebral column, terminating at around T12 vertebral before forming the conus medullaris and cauda equina. A good general indicator for estimating the corresponding vertebral level of a spinal segment is shown in Table 2.

It is worthwhile to note that motor and sensory fibres for the arms, trunk and legs are arranged in a centrifugal (expanding out from centre) pattern with the fibres for the arms located more medially compared to those for the trunk and legs (Figure 1). This knowledge is important trying to determine if a spinal cord lesion arose from within (intramedullary lesions such as syringomyelia, central spinal cord tumors) in which case the arms would first be affected before the legs; or from without (extramedullary lesions such as paravertebral abscess or tumors) where the legs would be affected before the arms.

Table 2: Rule-of-thumb in estimating the vertebral level of a spinal lesion

Segment affected according to sensory examination	Actual vertebral level of lesion
Cervical	Subtract 1
Upper thoracic	Subtract 2
Lower thoracic	Subtract 3
Lumbar 1, 2	T10
Lumbar 3,4	T11
Lumbar 5	T12
Sacral and coccygeal segments	L1

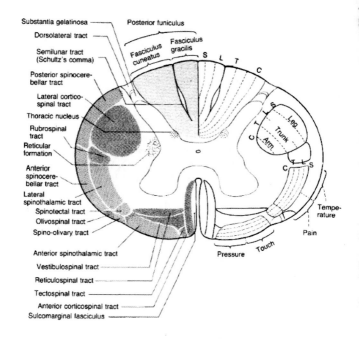

Figure 1: Cross section of spinal cord showing location of nerve tracts and bundles.

Abbreviations: C: cervical; T: thoracic; L: lumbar, S: sacral.

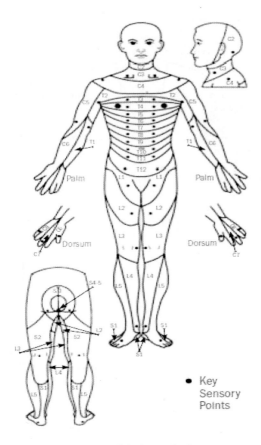

Figure 2: Dermatomes of the human body

Table 3: Corresponding spinal levels of dermatomal, myotomal and reflexes testing

Spinal level	Key sensory area for dermatomal testing	Myotome
C5	Radial antecubital fossa	Elbow flexors (biceps*, brachialis, and brachioradialis*)
C6	Thumb	Wrist extensors (extensor carpi radialis longus and brevis)
C7	Middle finger	Elbow extensors (triceps*)
C8	Little finger	Finger flexors* (distal phalanx—flexor digitorum profundus)
T1	Ulnar antecubital fossa	Hand intrinsics (interossei)
L2	Mid-anterior thigh	Hip flexors (iliopsoas)
L3	Medial femoral condyle	Knee extensors* (quadriceps)
L4	Medial malleolus	Ankle dorsiflexors (tibialis anterior)
L5	Dorsal second/third toe web space	Long toe extensors (extensor hallucis longus)
S1	Lateral heel	Ankle plantar flexors* (gastrocnemius, soleus)

* Commonly tested reflexes

492

Motor system examination

The examination of the patient should ideally be done with the patient lying in supine position. Ensure adequate exposure of the lower limbs while taking care to protect the patient's modesty. Obtain the patient's consent before proceeding. Always have a female chaperone in the room when performing physical examination on a female patient.

Before touching the lower limbs, look for evidence of muscle wasting and if present, whether it is found in the distal (e.g. neuropathy, syringomyelia) or proximal muscles (e.g. myopathy, myasthenia gravis, Duchenne muscle dystrophy).Look closely for fasciculations and abnormal movements.

After ensuring the patient does not have any painful areas in the limbs, passively move the limbs to assess the muscle tone. Table 4 shows the differences between UMN and LMN muscle weakness. Bear in mind that acute UMN weakness may present with flaccidity due to spinal shock but spasticity will take over.

Table 4: Differences between UMN and LMN muscle weakness.

	UMN weakness	LMN weakness
Tone	Spastic (hypertonia)	Flaccid (hypotonia)
Muscle atrophy	Minimal (Disuse atrophy)	Profound
Fasciculations	Absent	Present
Reflexes	Hyper	Hypo
Clonus	Present	Absent

Determine which individual muscle or groups of muscles are affected. By correlating the findings with the myotome distribution (Table 3), the level of the affected spinal segment can be determined (Table 2). For example, if the patient can flex her hips but not extend her knees, the affected spinal segment is between L2 and L3. Grade the power of the muscles from 0 to 5. [0 (complete paralysis), 1 (flicker of contraction), 2 (active movement with gravity eliminated), 3 (movement against gravity), 4 (active movement against resistance) and 5 (normal power)]. Compare muscle power between proximal and distal muscles.

If only LMN weakness is found in the lower limbs, it suggests conditions affecting the ventral horn cells, the nerve root, peripheral nerve, the myoneural junction or the muscle. In other words, the cause is *outside* the spine (extra-medullary causes). If on the other hand, the LMN signs are segmental (confined to a particular spinal segment) and UMN signs are present below that level, it suggests the lesion affects a segment of the spinal cord. Bilateral UMN weakness below a spinal level indicates bilateral corticospinal tracts involvement (e.g. transection of spinal cord). Presence of both UMN and LMN signs at the same spinal level should prompt the student to consider motor neuron disease as a possibility.

Sensory system examination

Before commencing, make sure the patient fully understands what you are about to do as testing for pain and other sensations can be uncomfortable and accurate testing depends on the patient's cooperation. Maintain verbal communication with the patient at all times and observe for signs of discomfort (e.g. facial grimace) in the patient. In contrast to the motor system, examination of the sensory system in a case of paraplegia is often more rewarding in localizing the spinal level of the lesion. The student only needs to test one or two sensations carried by the two separate sensory pathways. For instance, the student can test for pain sensation instead of temperature when evaluating the integrity of the antero-lateral system. The sensory deficits may be present in many forms such as segmental hyper-aesthesia (e.g. spinal cord compression) or hypo aesthesia at or below a spinal level; complete loss of all sensations below a spinal level; or loss of vibration sense or proprioception. Sometimes, the sensory deficit may be 'dissociated' in nature (e.g. loss of pain and temperature below a particular level but dorsal column sensations are intact in syringomyelia expanding anteriorly and laterally). Test for pain using the sharper end of a broken 'orange stick', vibration (with a 128 Hz tuning fork), and light touch using cotton wool. Compare between distal and proximal sites of the extremities, and between right and left side. Follow the dermatomal pattern of the human body when attempting to localize the spinal level (Figure 2). For example, absence of sensation below the level of the umbilicus indicates a lesion at spinal level of T10 which corresponds to T7 vertebra (see Table 1).

Reflex testing

The superficial reflexes (abdominal reflexes, the cremasteric reflexes (in a male), anal reflex and the plantar reflexes) and deep tendon reflexes may provide clues in localizing the spinal level of the lesion. For example, if the abdominal reflexes of the upper quadrants (left and right above the umbilicus) are present while the lower quadrants are absent with bilateral upgoing plantar reflexes, the lesion is at the level of T10. The examination of the anal tone and reflexes is rarely necessary unless exclusive involvement of the sacral nerves is suspected. Deep tendon reflexes are lost at the affected spinal segment but are exaggerated below that level. For example, lesions at L2 and L3 segments produce absent knee jerks with exaggerated ankle jerks.

Examination of the spine

Before concluding the nervous system examination, remember to examine the spine. Look for any deformity (kyphosis, scoliosis), gibbus, paravertebral swelling (tumor, infection); tuft of hair, dimpling or pigmented area (neural tube defects) and restriction in movement of the spine. Ask the patient to bend forward and palpate along the spinous processes for gibbus and tenderness. Also check for paravertebral tenderness or swelling. Finally, look for complications from paraplegia such pressure sores in dependent areas, fever and suprapubic tenderness (from urinary tract infection), deep vein thrombosis and contractures. Offer to examine the upper limbs and fundoscopy.

CHECK LIST FOR THE EXAMINATION FINDINGS IN STROKE

- Establish if the paraplegia is LMN only, UMN only or combined LMN and UMN
- Determine if there is segmental involvement
- Establish the spinal level of the lesion by combining results from examination of the motor and sensory systems and reflexes with the knowledge of the dermatome and myotome.
- Correlate the spinal level with the appropriate vertebral level (Table 2)
- Do not forget the spine

INVESTIGATIONS

In addition to basic diagnostic studies, the following investigations are relevant and essential in the management of a patient with paraplegia (Table 5):

Table 5: Relevant investigations in a case of paraplegia

Investigation	Justification
Plain X-ray of the spine	To look for obvious spinal deformity or lesions (e.g. reduction in intervertebral space, osteophytes, vertebral collapse or destruction, paraspinal mass shadow.

Myelogram (be sure of the spinal level involved)	This contrast study can help differentiate between extradural and intradural lesions. (Be sure the patient has no history of allergy or underlying renal impairment before ordering this investigation).
Plain computed tomography (CT) of the spine	Useful to diagnose intervertebral disc disorders.
Contrasted computed tomography (CT) of the spine	Useful in diagnosing cord compression.
Magnetic Resonance Imaging (MRI) of the spine	MRI with contrast should include several levels above and below the suspected spinal level. Hyperintense lesion seen over several levels (esp. thoracic spine) is suggestive of myelitis. Saggital view is useful in the diagnosis of syringomyelia.
Lumbar puncture and cerebrospinal fluid (CSF) analysis	Performed only if there are *no contraindications*. Raised CSF protein is seen in spinal canal obstruction, malignancy and infections. Pleocytosis (esp. leucocytosis) is present in infections such as abscess and Pott's* disease. CSF cultures to look for infections. CSF immunoglobulin level and protein electrophoresis to look for abnormal activation of the immune system.
Other relevant investigations	Sputum for acid-fast bacilli staining and culture (TB) Lymph node biopsy (TB, malignancy)

Sir Percivall Pott (1714–1788) was a surgeon who trained at St Bartholomew's Hospital, London. He was credited for describing the arthritic changes in tuberculosis of the spine. He was also the first to link cancer with an occupational hazard.

CASE SUMMARY

This 25-year-old woman has subacute onset of paraplegia with bowel and bladder dysfunction. She gives history of recent vaccination with rabies vaccine. On examination, she has symmetrical UMN weakness of her lower limbs and impaired pain and light touch sensation at T8 segmental level which corresponds to T 5-6 vertebral levels. The upper limbs are uninvolved. The knee and ankle jerks are hyperreflexic. Babinski sign is positive. Given the positive history and clinical evidence, the most likely diagnosis is post-vaccination subacute transverse myelitis.

CLINICAL DISCUSSION OF THE CASE

The student should be able to

- Establish that the patient has true weakness as opposed to feeling fatigued.
- With cnfidence rule out trauma as a cause of the paraplegia.
- Rule from careful history taking the myriad causes for paraplegia and make a reasonable diagnosis of post-vaccination as the cause.
- List the relevant investigations in a logical manner with appropriate justifications for each.
- Discuss the principles of management in this patient.
- Explore important issues related to the care and rehabilitation of a paraplegic patient.

The diagnosis of transverse myelitis is often by 'exclusion' after meticulous and systematic investigations fail to detect other causes for the paraplegia (e.g. tumor, infection). Recovery from transverse myelitis may take between 2 weeks to 2 years although most patients do regain some functions within 3 – 6 months. About one third of patients completely recover with little or residual neurological deficits and regaining normal or near-normal sphincter control. Another one third regain partially recover their premorbid functions while the remaining one third do not regain any meaningful functions. In general, the more rapid the onset of neurological deficits, the poorer is the prognosis.

The management of a patient diagnosed with paraplegia should include the following:

- Determining the underlying cause
- Counselling for the patient with regards to the possible cause of her problem as well as the likely prognosis
- Physiotherapy and rehabilitation of the patient
- Steps to prevent complications such as:
    - Techniques to prevent pressure sores
    - Self-catheterization to void urine
    - Regular enema

LEARNING OBJECTIVES

By the end of this case review the student should be:

1. Able to define stroke
2. Make a diagnosis based on history and findings from clinical examination.
3. List the investigations in stroke.
4. Discuss the principles in management of stroke

COMMONLY ASKED QUESTIONS

1. State two causes for this patient's condition.
2. What is the most likely underlying cause of her condition?
3. What relevant investigations will you perform for this patient and why?

HIGH ACHIEVER QUESTIONS

What does 'dissociated sensory loss' mean? How does this happen?

What is the difference between conus medullaris and cauda equina syndrome?

What are the inverted deep tendon reflexes and what are they indicative of?

COMMON MISTAKES

- Mistaking LMN weakness as UMN weakness. These two conditions share only one common factor which is weakness. (See Table 4).

- Successful examination of the sensory system is very dependent on cooperation from the patient. Uncooperative patients who are in pain may not provide the expected feedback, so it may be wise to conduct the examination only when the patient is ready.
- Neglecting to look at the patient to see if she is in pain or is experiencing discomfort as a result of the physical examination.
- Using too much pressure when testing for 'light touch' sensation with the cotton wool.
- Neglecting to ask the patient to perform the Jendrassik*manoeuvre to augment reflexes when initial reflex testing was unsatisfactory. Forgetting to examine the spine.

MUST KNOW FACTS ABOUT PARAPLEGIA

1. Trauma is the commonest cause of paraplegia in young adults.

2. Features of paraplegia may include:

- Vertebral or root pain
- Hyperaesthesia at a spinal level with sensory loss below the level
- Motor loss below the level (UMN weakness)
- Bowel and bladder dysfunction
- Segmental loss of superficial reflexes
- Exaggeration of deep tendon reflexes below the level

Cranial nerve palsies

1. The cranial nerves (CN) consist of twelve nerves that emerge from the ventral surface of the brain, innervating respective structures in the head and neck. Below is a summary of the cranial nerves and their main functions.

Cranial nerve	Function
CN I (Olfactory)	Smell
CN II (Optic)	Vision
CN III(Oculomotor)	Eye movements (all eye movements except, lateral rectus and superior oblique) and pupillary constriction. Parasympathetic innervation to the ciliary and sphincter pupillae muscles
CN IV (Trochlear)	Eye movement (superior oblique)
CN V (Trigeminal) -consists of ophthalmic, maxillary and mandibular divisions	Supplies muscles of mastication Receives sensory fibres from various parts of face
CN VI (Abducens)	Eye movement (lateral rectus)
CN VII (Facial)	Muscles of facial expression and stapedius muscle Transmits parasympathetic impulses to lacrimal and salivary glands (submandibular and sublingual glands) Receives sensory fibres from anterior two thirds of tongue
CN VIII (Acoustic)	Hearing and equilibrium
CN IX (Glossopharyngeal)	Supplies stylopharyngeus muscle Receives sensory fibres from posterior one third of tongue, soft palate, upper pharynx and auditory tube

	Parasympathetic innervation to parotid gland via otic ganglion
CN X (Vagus)	Supplies muscles of larynx and pharynx Parasympathetic fibers to heart, lungs and visceral organs Carries sensory fibers from the recurrent and internal laryngeal nerves (that supply the larynx), posterior pinna and posterior part of meninges
CN XI (Accessory)	Innervates laryngeal, sternocleidomastoid and trapezius muscle
CN XII (Hypoglossal)	Supplies muscles of the tongue

The olfactory epithelium of the nasal chamber is the origin of the first cranial nerve, while the retina is the origin of the second cranial nerve. The Oculomotor and Trochlear nerve originate from the midbrain. CN V, VI, VII and VIII originate from the pons and the last four cranial nerves have the medulla as their origin.

Dysfunction of one of the cranial nerves is referred to as cranial nerve palsy. The common disorders that may cause dysfunction of any of the cranial nerves are:

- Diabetes mellitus
- Multiple sclerosis
- Sarcoidosis
- Systemic lupus erythematosis
- Vasculitides eg. microscopic polyangitis, polyarteritis nodosa
- Tumours
- Infections eg. Lyme disease, HIV, syphilis

Some lesions result in combined cranial nerve palsies, in view of their proximity, for example cerebellopontine angle lesions may cause CN V, VI, VII and VIII palsy.

Types of cases for clinical examination:

Short /long case
OSCE
OSPE

CASE VIGNETTE

A 20-year-old gentleman presents with drooping of the left side of his mouth since waking up in the morning. He has a tingling sensation on the affected side of the face. There is no weakness or numbness of his limbs. He was previously well with no known medical problems.

Obtain a relevant history from the patient and perform a focussed physical examination.

Note: The short introduction suggests facial nerve palsy. The student is expected to confirm this via history and clinical examination, determine whether the other cranial nerves are affected, determine the site of the lesion and suggest a probable cause of the palsy. These would only be possible if the course and innervation of the facial nerve is known.

The facial nerve consists of motor fibers which originate from the facial nerve nucleus in the pons and sensory fibers which arise from nerves intermedius. (The nerves intermedius conveys (1) afferent taste fibers from the chorda tympani nerve, which come from the anterior two thirds of the tongue; (2) taste fibers from the soft palate via the palatine and greater petrosal nerves; and (3) preganglionic parasympathetic innervation to the submandibular, sublingual, and lacrimal glands). The facial nerve leaves the pons through the cerebellopontine angle and enters the petrous temporal bone through the internal auditory meatus accompanied by the vestibulocochlear nerve. It runs a tortuous course through the facial canal and changes direction to form the geniculate *(genu=bend)* ganglion. The geniculate ganglion is formed by the juncture of the nervus intermedius and the facial nerve into a common trunk. The branch which supplies the stapedius muscle is given off from within the facial canal. The chorda tympani then joins the facial nerve in the facial canal. The facial nerve emerges from the stylomastoid foramen and passes through the parotid gland, where it divides into five branches that supply the muscles of facial expression. The five branches are Temporal, Zygotic, Buccal, Mandibular and Cervical.

History of Presenting Illness

- Facial asymmetry – side, onset, progression, movements affected, recurrent, activities of daily living affected, psychological effect on patient
- Other manifestations – incomplete eye closure, reduced eye lacrimation, reduced sense of taste, hyperacusis, facial pain, facial rash(as in Ramsay Hunt syndrome)
- Associated symptoms – tinnitus, deafness, diplopia, headache, reduced sensation over face, speech difficulty, dysphagia (these

symptoms are significant as they would suggest involvement of other cranial nerves and a clue as to the pathology)

- Trauma – recent or remote (fractures of temporal bone)

Past Medical History

- Previous stroke or transient ischaemic attack
- Recent viral illness (Bell's palsy has been associated with herpes simplex infections)
- Other infections eg. otitis media, HIV infection, Lyme disease, leprosy
- Diabetes mellitus ,hyperlipidaemia and hypertension
  - diabetes mellitus may cause mononeuritis
  - Presence of diabetes mellitus and/or hypertension are also risk factors for developing cerebrovascular accidents
- Malignancy
  - tumours of the facial nerve(neuroma) or tumours causing impingement of the facial nerve (parotid gland tumours) especially should be suspected in slowly progressive lesions with involvement of other cranial nerves
- Pregnancy
  - Women develop Bell's palsy more frequently when pregnant
- Connective tissue disease eg. systemic lupus erythematosus, sarcoidosis, Sjogren's syndrome
- Others eg. Gullain Barre syndrome

Past surgical history

- Parotidectomy or otologic procedures

Medication history

- Aspirin or warfarin
- Alcohol dependence

Family history

- A strong family history is found in about 10% of patients with Bell's palsy

Check list for history taking

- ✓ Facial asymmetry – onset, progression, associated symptoms eg, hypolacrimation, loss of taste

✓ Involvement of other cranial nerves (diplopia, deafness, dysphagia)
✓ Cause of palsy (cerebrovascular accident, tumour, mononeuritis, iatrogenic, idiopathic)
✓ Effect on patient – activities of daily living, psychological

EXAMINATION

Introduce yourself to the patient. Explain that you would like to perform a physical examination on him and elaborate on what this would entail.

General examination and vital signs

A few seconds should be spent to inspect the surroundings and the patient. Look for walking aids by the side of the patient that would suggest a lower limb weakness. Is the patient wearing a hearing aid? Patients with severe dysphagia or weakness of bulbar muscles would frequently have a nasogastric tube in situ.

Inspect for facial asymmetry and hemifacial spasm. However, patients with bilateral facial nerve palsy may not have any noticeable asymmetry!

Look for butterfly rash on the face, ptosis and scars on the face.

Facial nerve

Ask the patient to look upwards and raise his eyebrows, observing for asymmetry of wrinkling of forehead. Loss of wrinkling would indicate weakness of the frontalis muscle. In an upper motor neuron (UMN) disorder, there will be sparing of the frontalis muscle because of its bilateral innervation. The UMN lesion would be either in the brainstem or cortex. Lower motor neuron (LMN) lesions cause weakness of both upper and lower parts of the face.

Get the patient to screw his eyes shut tight and attempt to open them. As the patient closes his eyes, look for incomplete apposition of the eyelids. Ability to prise open the eyes indicates weakness of the orbicularis oculi. *(Note: This should be performed gently and the student should inform the patient before trying to prise open the eyes as this may cause some discomfort).*

The buccal, orbicularis oris and zygomatic branches of the nerve can be tested for by getting the patient to puff out his cheeks.

Hyperacussis is tested for by placing a tuning fork in proximity to the ear. If the patient hears it louder on the affected side, a lesion proximal to the stapedius nerve root is suggested. *(Note: This test should only be performed if the eighth cranial nerve is not affected)*

The sensory component is examined for by testing the taste sensation at anterior two thirds of the tongue. Loss of taste would suggest a peripheral lesion proximal to branching of the chorda tympani.

Other cranial nerves

The sixth cranial nerve should be examined as well, since the nucleus of the sixth cranial nerve lies in proximity of the nucleus of the facial nerve in the pons. Involvement of the ipsilateral trigeminal nerve and vestibulocochlear nerve with cerebellar signs would indicate a pathology in the cerebellopontine angle.

Test for sensation on the face along the distribution of the three branches of the trigeminal nerve. The sensory component of the corneal reflex is mediated by the ophthalmic division. Occasionally, loss of the corneal reflex may be earliest presentation of a fifth nerve palsy. The motor division of the fifth nerve supplies the muscles of mastication. First, inspect for any wasting of the temporal and masseter muscles. Then, ask the patient to clench his teeth and palpate for contraction of the masseter. Get the patient to move his jaw from side to side. Assess for weakness of the muscles of mastication by getting the patient to keep his mouth open while gentle force is applied in an attempt to close it.

A sixth cranial nerve palsy leads to weakness of ipsilateral lateral rectus. This causes failure of abduction of the eye and convergent strabismus. There will be diplopia that is maximal on looking to the affected side, with images lying side by side. A cover test can be performed to determine the eye with the pathology.

Test for hearing by covering one ear with a finger and whispering in the other ear. If partial deafness is present proceed to perform the Rinne's and Weber's test to determine the pattern of hearing loss (sensorineural vs conductive). Do not forget to inspect the external auditory meatus and pinna. Examine the ear with an otoscope.

If any of these cranial nerves are affected, proceed to examination of the remaining cranial nerves.

Head and neck

Inspect for enlargement of the parotids and surgical scars of parotidectomy. Palpate over the parotid gland for tenderness. Examination of the cervical lymph nodes might be necessary in some patients.

The limbs

Examine the upper limbs and lower limbs for hemiparesis or hemisensory loss. Look for the typical skin changes of diabetic dermatopathy.

Also, examine for cerebellar signs. The presence of ipsilateral cerebellar signs would suggest an ipsilateral cerebellopontine angle lesion.

Check list for clinical examination

- ✓ General – facial asymmetry, hemifacial spasm, ptosis, scars
- ✓ Facial nerve – frontalis, orbicularis oculi, orbicularis oris, taste in anterior two third of tongue, hyperacusis
- ✓ Trigeminal, abducens and vestibulocochlear nerve
- ✓ Other cranial nerves
- ✓ Head and neck – parotid gland
- ✓ Upper limbs and lower limbs – hemiparesis, hemisensory loss, cerebellar signs

INVESTIGATIONS

1. Magnetic Resonance Imaging (MRI) Brain

An MRI of the brain is useful in the diagnosis of intracranial aetiologies of facial nerve palsy eg. acoustic neuroma.

2. Electrophysiology

Electrophysiology studies are important to determine the extent of nerve disruption and necessity of surgical intervention.

3. Other investigations depend very much on the cause of the facial nerve palsy:

- Fasting blood sugar, fasting serum lipid and electrocardiogram – cerebrovascular accident
- Anti-nuclear antibody and anti- double stranded DNA – systemic lupus erythematosus

CASE SUMMARY

This young gentleman presented with sudden onset of drooping of the left side of his mouth. Examination revealed a loss of wrinkling of the forehead on the left, loss of the nasolabial fold on the left and incomplete closure of his left eye. The fifth, sixth and eighth cranial nerves are intact. There are no cerebellar signs. There are no vesicles seen on the pinna and external auditory meatus. In summary, this young gentleman has a left lower motor neuron facial nerve palsy.

2.2. CASE VIGNETTE

A 65-year-old lady, who is seen at the Medical Out-patient clinic, complaints of seeing double for the past one week. There is no headache or pain of the affected eye.

Obtain a relevant history and perform a focused physical examination of the patient.

History of presenting illness

- Diplopia
    - determine that the patient's understanding of diplopia is the same of the student's understanding of diplopia (many patients tend to refer to the blurring of images as diplopia!)
    - monocular or binocular (monocular causes of diplopia are mainly opthalmological)
    - onset and progression – diplopia that is intermittent with diurnal variation is suggestive of myasthenia gravis, whereas progression of symptoms might suggest an enlarging compressive lesion.
    - Exacerbating and relieving factors – rest improves the diplopia present in myasthenia gravis
    - Associated symptoms – pain on eye movements would indicate an inflammatory cause or aneurysm, ptosis may be present in a third cranial nerve palsy
    - Alignment of images
    - Direction of maximal separation of images is useful in determining the extraocular muscle involved – the images are usually maximally separated when the direction of gaze is the same as the direction of action of the paretic muscle

Systemic review

- Headache – patients with parasellar neoplasms or hemiplegic migraine may present with headache, scalp tenderness when combing hair is a frequent complaint of patients with temporal arteritis
- Weakness, numbness or incoordination of limbs – multiple sclerosis
- Symptoms of hypo- and hyperthyroidism

- Recent trauma

Past medical history

- Diabetes mellitus
- Hypertension
- Multiple sclerosis
- Syphilis

Social history

- Smoking
- Effect of diplopia on occupation and driving

Check list for history taking

- ✓ Diplopia – monocular or binocular, onset, progression, alignment of images, direction of maximal separation, associated symptoms
- ✓ Systemic review – thyroid function, weakness, numbness, incoordination, trauma, headache
- ✓ Medical disorders – diabetes mellitus, hypertension, multiple sclerosis
- ✓ Effect on patient – work

Examination

Introduce yourself to the patient and establish the identity of the patient. Obtain consent to perform a physical examination on the patient.

General examination

A couple of minutes spent on general examination will not be regretted. Look at the bedside table for visual aids. Note walking aids at the bedside.

Examine the head for craniotomy scars (berry aneurysm). Inspect the lower limbs for lesions of diabetic dermatopathy, amputated toes and ulcers.

Third, fourth and sixth cranial nerves

Exopthalmus, proptosis with congested conjunctiva would lead the student to suspect thyroid eye disease.

Examine the eye movements of the patient and look for any opthalmoplegia. Get the patient to inform you when double images are seen. Establish the position of the images and the direction in which the separation is maximal (if the images are side by side, the medial or lateral rectus is most likely impaired).

The cover test is done to establish the paretic extraocular muscle or muscles. This is performed by asking the patient to look in the direction that the two images are maximally separated. Get the patient to close one eye. If the outermost image disappears, it can be concluded that the pathology exists in that eye.

Look for complete or partial ptosis of the ipsilateral eye to suggest a third cranial nerve causing levator palpebrae superioris paresis. If there is complete ptosis, manually elevate the affected eyelid during examination.

Look at the position of the pupils at rest. A third cranial nerve palsy causes pupils that are typically described to be 'down and out' and a divergent strabismus. A sixth cranial nerve palsy leads to divergent strabismus.

Examine the size of the pupils and their reactivity to light. A complete third nerve palsy will cause a ipsilateral dilated pupil that is unreactive to light and accommodation. (Note: Diabetes mellitus and hypertension that cause infarct of the oculomotor nerve, are pupil-sparing and do not affect the pupils. In infarction the centre of the nerve is affected more than the surface, which can still obtain nutrients and oxygen from the cerebrospinal fluid. However, compressive lesions often affect the parasympathetic fibres from the Edinger-Westphal nucleus, as they are situated superficially.)

Always, exclude the presence of ipsilateral fourth cranial nerve palsy when a third nerve palsy is noted. Look for intortion of the orbit by tilting the patient's head towards the affected side.

Other cranial nerves

Examine the fifth cranial nerve by examining facial sensation, corneal reflex and integrity of the muscles of mastication. *(Note: First division of the trigeminal nerve may be involved in Tolosa Hunt syndrome)*

Others

Examine the neck for goitre and enlarged lymph nodes.

Examine the limbs for weakness. *(Note: Weber's syndrome which is caused by a lesion in the midbrain causes ipsilateral third nerve palsy with contralateral hemiplegia)*

Fatigability of the muscles of the limbs suggests myasthenia gravis.

Perform a direct opthalmoscopic examination to look for optic atrophy and measure the blood pressure of the patient.

Check list for clinical examination

✓ Diplopia – position, cover test
✓ Ptosis
✓ Pupils
✓ Trigeminal, abducens and trochlear nerve
✓ Limbs – weakness, diabetic dermatopathy
✓ Head and neck – goitre, lymph nodes
✓ Direct opthalmoscope – optic atrophy
✓ Blood pressure

Case summary

This 65-year-old lady, who has diabetes mellitus and hypertension, presented with sudden onset of painless diplopia. Physical examination revealed a divergent strabismus with the right pupils in a 'down and out' position. The right pupil is unreactive to direct light and accommodation. There is also partial ptosis on the right. In summary, she has a complete right third cranial nerve palsy.

CLINICAL DISCUSSION OF THE CASE

Facial nerve palsy
The causes of lower motor neuron facial nerve palsy are:
- Idiopathic (Bell's palsy) – most common
- Trauma (base of skull)
- Infective – herpes zoster (Ramsay Hunt syndrome), otitis media, Lyme disease
- Tumour – posterior fossa tumours, parotd gland tumours
- Neurological – mononeuropathy (diabetes mellitus, sarcoidosis), multiple sclerosis, systemic lupus erythematosus

Bell's palsy
- An idiopathic acute paralysis of the facial nerve, first described by Sir Charles Bell in 1821
- An association with herpes simplex virus has been suggested by studies
- The onset of symptoms is sudden and it peaks in severity within 48 hours
- Some patients complain of paraesthesia of the face or pain at the back of the ear but there is no involvement of other cranial nerves (as in the case above)

- Management of Bell's palsy includes glucocorticoids and antiviral agents (Acyclovir for five days)
- Artificial tears and eye pads should be prescribed for patients who are unable to close their eyes completely
- Physiotherapy and facial exercises are important
- Surgical therapy is only considered when there is minimal improvement after three weeks and based on electrophysiological studies

<u>Oculomotor nerve palsy</u>

The common causes of a third cranial nerve palsy are:

- Hypertension
- Diabetes mellitus
- Aneurysm of posterior communicating artery (painful)
- Tumours (pituitary adenoma, sphenoid wing meningioma)
- Cavernous sinus thrombosis
- Trauma
- Mononeuropathy (syphilis, multiple sclerosis)

Patients who present with pupil involving third nerve palsy require an urgent Computed Tomography scan of the brain to rule out an aneurysm. An angiogram of the cerebral vessel may be indicated too, if an aneurysm is suspected.

Other relevant investigations include:

- HbA1C– glycaemic control
- Thyroid function test

LEARNING OUTCOMES

By the end of this case review the student should be able to:

1. Take a relevant history from a patient who presents with facial asymmetry

2. Perform physical examination to demonstrate a facial nerve palsy

3. Localise the lesion in a patient with facial nerve palsy

4. Discuss regarding management of Bell's palsy

5. Take a relevant history from a patient presenting with diplopia

6. Perform a physical examination and determine the cause of diplopia

COMMONLY ASKED QUESTIONS

1. What is the Ramsay Hunt syndrome?
Ramsay Hunt syndrome is the reactivation of Herpes zoster virus in the geniculate ganglion of the facial nerve. It is associated with painful, erythematous vesicles in the external auditory meatus and facial nerve palsy.

2. What is Bell's phenomenon?
Bell's phenomenon refers to the upward movement of eyeballs and incomplete eye closure when the patient attempts to close his eye on the side with facial nerve palsy.

3. What is the course of the seventh cranial nerve?
Answer included in discussion above

HIGH ACHIEVER QUESTIONS

1. What are the causes of bilateral facial nerve palsy?
Guiilain Barre syndrome, sarcoidosis, bilateral Bell's palsy, Melkerson-Rosenthal syndrome (a rare disease consisting of a triad of recurrent facial nerve palsy, chronic swelling of the lip and plicated tongue)

2. How should a patient with third cranial nerve palsy secondary to diabetes mellitus be managed?
If diplopia is causing distress to the patient, eye patch can be used. Prism s can be used for milder diplopia. The patient should be supplied with adequate knowledge of the disease and that recovery is usually spontaneous within eight weeks. The patient should be discouraged from driving in the meantime. Glycaemic control should be optimised and co-existent hypertension treated.

3. What are the causes of a dilated pupil?
Oculomotor nerve palsy, optic atrophy, Holmes Adie pupil, mydriatic eyedrops

COMMON MISTAKES

- Not being able to localise the lesion in a patient with facial nerve palsy
- Confusion between upper motor neuron and lower motor neuron features of facial nerve palsy
- Not examining for the integrity of other cranial nerves
- Not elevating the eyelid manually in a patient with complete ptosis

- Unable to differentiate between medical and surgical causes of third nerve palsy via clinical examination

MUST KNOW FACTS ABOUT CRANIAL NERVES PALSY

1. The commonest cause of lower motor neuron facial nerve palsy is Bell's palsy.

2. Lower motor neuron facial nerve palsy usually involves the upper and lower part of the face.

3. An associated sixth nerve palsy with a facial nerve palsy suggests a lesion in the pons.

4. A cerebellopontine angle lesion causes lesions of the fifth, sixth, seventh and eighth nerve.

5. Third nerve palsy causes a divergent strabismus with pupils positioned 'down and out'.

6. Medical causes of third nerve palsy frequently cause pupil-sparing.

7. A sixth nerve palsy causes a convergent sttabismus

References:

Diplopia and eye movement disorders (J Neurol Neurosurg Psychiatry 2004;75(Suppl IV):iv24–iv31

CASE 40: ULNAR NERVE PALSY
AP SINGH

OVERVIEW

OVERVIEW

Leprosy is the second commonest cause of peripheral neuropathy in the world, the first being diabetic neuropathy. Its commonest manifestation is mononeuropathy or mononeuropathy multiplex. Branches of 5th & 7th are also affected either alone or in combination with other nerves. The nerves are affected either by direct infection of peripheral nerves by *Mycobacterium leprae* or it may occur as a part of lepra reaction. Patients of leprosy are usually given as a short case.

 Note:

For a brief of definitions and background reading on peripheral neuropathy kindly refer to the case of Diabetic peripheral neuropathy.

This case could be given as a SHORT OSCE or LONG OSCE.

Based on the examination question the student is expected to demonstrate correct techniques of examination.

He may volunteer to ask pertinent questions. In the interest of time, he may be provided relevant information if no time is allocated for history taking as seen in short OSCE.

CASE VIGNETTE

A 30 year- old expatriate from Nepal is working as a security guard in a factory in Malaysia for past one year. He has sought consultation for numbness of his right 4th & 5th finger of one year duration.

Examine patient's upper limb

 Note:

Based on the chief complaint it is preferable to have a list of differential diagnosis. This would assist in focusing on specific areas and also examine other relevant systems.

Differential diagnosis

1. Ulnar neuropathy.

2. Root compression of C8- T1.

3. Intramedullary lesion e.g. syringomyelia.

PHYSICAL EXAMINATION

The aim is to localize the lesion responsible for numbness of patient's fingers. The lesion could be in the ulnar nerve, C8T1 roots or it could be within the spinal cord interrupting the axons of second order neurons carrying pain, temperature and crude touch. Therefore, it will be a mistake to confine your examination to the right hand only. Since the ulnar nerve, root compression and syrinx may have telltale sign in the skin and skeletal system, do pay attention to other systems or else the diagnosis may be missed.

General examination and vital signs:

- Look at patient's face for any evidence of leprosy (depressed bridge of the nose, loss of eye brows, infiltration of face and ear lobes).
- Look for hypo or hyper pigmented anesthetic patch of skin in gluteal area and back which the patient may be unaware of.
- Look for cafe au lait spots in skin, which has a known association with neurofiromatosis of the spinal nerves causing root compression. A nerve tumour in the above roots will not only cause numbness of little finger but may also produce Horner's syndrome.
- Look for short neck & low hairline, part of a craniovertebral anomaly, especially Arnold -Chiari malformation which has very strong association with syringomyelia. Skeletal abnormality of spine may also be noted.
- Patient's vital sign should be recorded

EXAMINATION OF RIGHT UPPER LIMB AND OTHER RELEVANT AREAS

i. Look for any deformity of fingers, wasting of small muscle of hand with due care of those innervated by ulnar nerve. Pay special attention to hypothenar eminence, 1st dorsal interosseus.

ii. Look for any atrophy , absorption of terminal phalanx, ulcers ,burn marks over tip of fingers(4th & 5th).These findings favour leprosy or syringomyelia.Look for evidence of dysautonomia in the hand /fingers (shiny oedematous skin, loss of hair, change in the colour of skin on elevation or putting the limb in dependant position suggests dysautonomia)

515

iii.   Look for Horner's syndrome. Its presence indicates that sensory & motor findings in the hand are due to root compression in the spinal canal and not in the spinal cord or in the ulnar nerve (neuro anatomy explains these findings)

iv.   Tone in hypothenar as well as other muscles of hand and upper limb should be checked. If the lesion is in ulnar nerve only the hypothenar muscles will feel soft. Power of individual muscles in the hand should be checked. If the lesion is in ulnar nerve, all except the thenar & 2 lateral lumbrical muscles will be weak.

v.   If patient's symptoms are due to syringomyelia all the small muscles of right hand including thenar & lumbricals as well as muscles of fore arm will be weak and hypotonic depending on the size of syrinx .Left hand is also likely to be affected.

vi.   Examine the deep tendon jerks(DTJ). In leprosy these are normal while syringomyelia causes areflexia or reduced DTJ in the upper limb and exaggerated response in the lower limbs with positive Babinski reflex.

vii.   Examine the sensory function .Check for light touch with cotton, thermal with cold and warm water & pain with sharp pin. Check for vibration test with a tuning fork with 128Hz If the sensory deficit is found in the right 5th finger ,medial half of 4th finger and over medial side of volar aspect of palm, lesion is in right ulnar nerve. In leprosy, thermal as well as pain perception is lost first, later all modalities are lost. However in root compression, loss of sensation will be in C8 & T1 dermatome, like ulnar nerve but the motor function will affect not only the muscles innervated by ulnar nerve but also the mediannerve innervated muscles too.

viii.   If it is a syringomyelia or central cord lesion, patient will have dissociated segmental sensory loss not only over upper limb but also over the chest.This is due to interuption of 2nd order axons by the syrinx in spinal cord.

ix.   The student should palpate right ulnar nerve, compare it with the left and feel other superficial nerves e.g. greater auricular, medial, radial, common peroneal and post tibial nerves. Feel for thickened coetaneous nerve around the anesthetic skin patch

Examine other related systems.

CHECK LIST FOR EXAMINATION FINDINGS IN NEURAL LEPROSY

- Examine the muscles of hand.
- Look for extent of sensory deficit
- Look for thickened ulnar nerve at elbow

- Look for anesthetic patch.

Note:In discussing investigations consider the relevance in diagnosis.

The professional aspect of counseling and discussing breaking 'serious illness ' news are also relevant.

The patient should be informed as to how long it takes for some results to come back (e.g biopsy-two weeks).

INVESTIGATIONS TO CONFIRM THE DIAGNOSIS

1. Skin biopsy for mycobacterium leprae

2. Nerve conduction and EMG studies.

The student should be conversant with some complications that can be anticipated with regards ulnar nerve palsy.

Comments on how patient is to be handled (best for outpatient treatment, need for avoiding trophic ulcers etc)

CASE SUMMARY

30 years old Nepali national who presents with numbness of 4th & 5th finger of right hand of one year duration has been found to have thickened and tender right ulnar nerve with a hypopigmented anesthetic patch over his buttock. He has motor and sensory deficit in the distribution of right ulnar nerve.

Provisional diagnosis:

Tuberculoid neural leprosy with dermal patch of leprosy over buttock

CLINICAL DISCUSSION OF THE CASE

The student should be able to:

Recognize ulnar nerve palsy and test small muscles of hand and sensation .

- Appreciate thickened and tender Ulnar nerve
- Establish the diagnosis of leprosy
- List the investigation to confirm the diagnosis.
- Outline the principles of management.

- Explore the issues regarding rehabilitation including reconstructive surgery.

Professionalism and Ethics

- Discuss employment issues in view of him being a foreign national. Ethical issues in confidentiality may arise.
- The student is also expected to be aware of list of notifiable disease and mechanism of notifying health authorities in Malaysia.

LEARNING OUTCOMES

By the end of this review the student should be

1. Able to recognize ulnar nerve paralysis

2. Make a diagnosis of neural leprosy.

3 List the investigations to clinch the diagnosis.

4. Discuss the principles of management of leprosy and effects of nerve damage caused by it.

Suggested answers would be appreciated

COMMONLY ASKED QUESTIONS.

1.What are different types of leprosy? **(Ans:Tuberculoid (TT,BT) leprosy, Borderline (BB,BL)Leprosy and Lepromatous (LL)Leprosy)**

2. Name two diseases associated with thickened peripheralnerves. **(Ans:Neurofibromatosis,Charcot- Mary Tooth (CMT) disease**

3. What is the current treatment regime of leprosy? **(Ans:WHO recommended regimen.Tuberculoid leprosy-Dapsone 100mg/d, unsupervised *plus* rifampicin600 mg/ month supervised for 6 months.Lepromatous leprosy-Dapsone100mg/d *plus* clofazimine50mg/ d unsupervised; and rifampicin 600 mg *plus* clofazimine 300mg monthly supervised for 1 to 2 years.**

4. Discuss the chronic compications of peripheral nerve palsy in leprosy.

HIGH ACHIEVER QUESTIONS

1. What is lepra reaction?**(Ans:Lepra reactions are immunologically mediated inflammatory states and cause considerable morbidity.Two types of reactions have been recognised,Type 1 Lepra reaction is down grading and reversal reaction occurs in Tuberculoid leprosy ,while type 2 reaction occurs exclusively in Lepromatous leprosy manifesting as erythema nodosum leprosum)**

2. How do you stain for *Mycobacterium Leprae*? **(Ans:By ZN staining)**

3. How is *mycobacterium leprae* cultured? **(Ans:Foot pad of mouse)**

4. Which nervefibres are affected first in leprosy? **(Ans:Small myelinated and unmyelinated fibres)** .

5 .Why are deep seated nerves spared in leprosy? (**Ans:** *M.leprae* **grogws best in cooler tissues like skin peripheral nerves anterior chamber of the eyes, upper respiratory tract and testes sparing warmer area like axilla groin and deeper tissues)**

COMMON MISTAKES

1. Not looking for anesthetic skin lesion.

2. Ignoring to look for thickened nerves.

3. Not testing for thermal sensation.

4. Not knowing how to break 'serious illness' news.

CASE 41: A CLINICAL APPROACH TO PERIPHERAL NEUROPATHY

AP SINGH

OVER VIEW

OVER VIEW

Peripheral neuropathy is frequently seen entity in clinical practice. Its prevalence is estimated between 2-8%. Peripheral nerve is broadly divided in somatic and autonomic nervous system. The former includes cranial nerves 3-12 and all ventral and dorsal roots, spinal nerves, plexuses and peripheral nerves. The autonomic nervous system consisting of sympathetic and parasympathetic accompany the peripheral and cranial nerves.

Clinically peripheral neuropathy presents with motor, sensory, autonomic symptoms either alone or in combination. If one individual nerve is affected it is mononeuropathy. When multiple individual nerves are affected at different time interval e.g. days, weeks or months apart, it is mononeuritis multiplex. When multiple nerves are affected simultaneously and symmetrically it is called polyneuropathy. Involvement of root is called radiculopathy and when plexus is affected the term plexopathy (brachial/ lumbosacral).

Clinical manifestation depends on which component of peripheral nerve is predominantly damaged. Motor nerve involvement presents as weakness and wasting the latter becomes obvious in superficial muscles 4-6 weeks later. Sensory symptoms consists of numbness, burning, tingling sensation or losing balance in darkness. In severe cases, patient may seek advice for not feeling any sensation in the affected part. Disturbances of autonomic nervous system can range from impotence, bladder dysfunction, constipation, diarrhoea, sweating disturbances to recurrent dizzy spells and early satiety.

When a patient presents with symptoms of peripheral neuropathy, the medical student (clinician) has to answer the following questions:

(a). Is it mononeuropathy, mononeuropathy multiplex ,polyneuropathy, radiculopathy, or plexopathy?

(b).What is the etiology?

©. Which investigation will clinch the diagnosis?

(d).What can be done for the patient?

(e).What is the prognosis?

The commonest cause of peripheral neuropathy world over is due to diabetes mellitus followed by leprosy, vasculitis, drugs, toxins and hereditary neuropathy. Undiagnosed neuropathy often belongs to hereditary group.

Diagnosis of peripheral neuropathy depends on a thorough history, clinical examination and relevant investigations. There is no substitute to a thorough history. Examination of nervous system will reveal the type of neuropathy, but it is the examination of other systems that gives a clue to the underlying cause.

The investigations that may be required to establish the diagnosis include-blood count, blood biochemistry, serum B12 and folic acid, thyroid function tests serology for HIV,HBV Lyme disease, screening for drugs & toxins, urine for porphobilinogen & delta aminoluvinic acid.Specialized tests for vasculitis and paraproteinemias.

Nerve conduction and EMG are extremely useful investigations.Nerve biopsy is useful in confirming the diagnosis of vasculitis, amyloidosis and adrenoleukodystrophies. Genetic studies have contributed in solving many unresolved etiology.

TYPES OF CASES FOR CLINICAL EXAMINATION

1. OSCE (Short or long)

- In short OSCE, often students are asked to examine cranial nerves3, 4, or 5th.In the long OSCE 7th cranial nerve palsy is kept for examination.
    2. Long case or OSLER

- In the long case, detailed history and neurological as well as systemic examination is expected.

DIABETIC PERIPHERAL NEUROPATHY (As a long case)

OVERVIEW

The disease is defined as presence of symptoms and signs of peripheral nerve dysfunction in diabetic patients after excluding other causes of neuropathy. It is estimated that almost 50% of diabetic -patients may be unaware that they are suffering from peripheral neuropathy. In type 2 diabetes mellitus, patient may present with neuropathy e.g. a foot drop or

3rd cranial nerve palsy & diabetes may be detected at the time of diagnosis while in type 1 diabetes it appears 5-10 years later.

Following are the different presentation of diabetic peripheral neuropathy:

1. Symmetrical motor, sensory or mixed

2. Proximal asymmetrical neuropathy(diabetic amyotrophy)

3 Autonomic neuropathy.

4. Thoraco-abdominal radiculopathy.

5. Mononeuritis ,mononeuritis multiplex

6. Cranial neuropathy.

Peripheral neuropathy in diabetes is associated with considerable morbidity including dysautonomia (postural dizziness, bladder dysfunction, impotence) and non healing ulcers in the feet, which in conjunction with ischemia accounts for 4.3% of non traumatic amputations of limbs in Malaysia.

CASE VIGNETTE

A 65 years old man with diabetes mellitus type 2 of 20 years duration has sought consultation for numbness of feet with non healing ulcers over sole of right foot of three months duration.

Examine the patient with special reference to lower limbs.

Differential diagnosis

1. Diabetes mellitus with polyneuropathy.

2. Diabetes mellitus with mononeuritis multiplex.

3. Cauda equina syndrome.

History of present illness

For how long has he been symptomatic with neurological problem?

Was the onset of illness acute?

How has been the course of disease?

Sensory symptoms:-

Student should ask when he was free from numbness and how the symptoms began. Did it appear in both feet simultaneously or if one foot was affected before the other? Did it ascend proximally towards the knee?. Did he also experience tingling numbness over tips of fingers? Does he experience burning sensation over the soles and if so when it is worse, during night or day time? When he walks in the darkness does he lose balance? Does he feel the sensation of ground has changed from rough to cotton wool?

The hall mark of polyneuropathy is symmetrical and simultaneous appearance of sensory symptoms in the feet , then ascending up to mid thigh. When sensory symptoms reach the knee, numbness starts appearing in the tips of fingers, spreads proximally up to wrist. It is the glove and stocking distribution of sensory symptoms that is typical feature of polyneuropathy

In mononeuritis multiplex, individual nerves will be affected first and then over months and years it will resemble polyneuropathy.

Motor symptoms: Patient may complain that he is unable to hold slippers between his first and second toes and that the bulk of muscles have reduced in legs & feet.

Inability to hold slippers between the toes indicates weakness of interossei. The toes getting caught in the rug suggests weakness of dorsiflexors of feet .Wasting of muscles indicate loss of motor fibres due to axonopathy.

Autonomic symptoms: are poorly interpreted by medical students. Do enquire specifically regarding erectile dysfunction, bladder symptoms, postural dizziness, early satiety, and change in the sweating pattern.

Does he have claudication symptoms in the legs?

The student should enquire how regularly he goes for his medical check up & about drug compliance.

Past Medical History

Since diabetes mellitus can have different pattern of nerve involvement, the student must inquire into motor, sensory and autonomic symptoms in the distribution of individual nerves. Ask the patient did he ever have foot or wrist drop? Did he ever suffer from diplopia and squint? Sometimes symptoms may suggest radiculopathy or carpal tunnel syndrome.

Has he been diagnosed as diabetic retinopathy or nephropathy during an annual medical check up?

Has he suffered from coronary artery disease, or stroke?

Family History

Student should enquire about family history of diabetes in his parents and siblings and also whether they suffered from stroke, heart attack, renal failure and amputations of toes /feet.

Social history

Does he smoke cigarettes (pack per year), consume alcohol (amount of alcohol consumption per week.)?

Surgical history

Has the patient undergone amputation of toes /feet, coronary by pass surgery, laser surgery for the eyes?

Systemic review of symptoms

Symptoms pertaining to poor glycemic control should be enquired. Since peripheral neuropathy, diabetic retinopathy and nephropathy are complications of microangiopathy it is worth finding out whether he has symptoms related to eyes and renal system. The student should ask the patient whether he has been hospitalized for diabetic complications like diabetic ketoacidosis (DKA), hyperglycemic hyperosmolar state (HSS) stroke, coronary artery disease, urinary tract infection, pulmonary tuberculosis or any major illness.

Check list for history taking

- Onset of symptoms, acute or chronic
- Which part of the body was affected first and how much of the symptoms progressed?
- History of drug compliance, control of blood sugar ,lipid and and blood pressure.
- Ask consumption of alcohol & tobacco smoking.
- Has he suffered from non healing ulcers over feet, amputation in the past?
- Any symptoms pertaining to any other system should also be enquired.

While presenting the case think of possible differential diagnosis and confirm or exclude them by appropriate history and examination findings.

EXAMINATION

Examination of sensory system requires proper tools and good examnaton technique. Patient's cooperation is essential. Repeated testing tires the patient and findings may be misleading. Clinical evaluation of sensory function in diabetic neuropathy requires 10-g Semmes-Weinstein monofilament for pressure sensation,128 Hz tuning fork for vibration perception, pin/sharp wooden tooth pick & good knee hammer.

General examination

Introduce yourself as a medical student, explain the purpose of examination and obtain his consent. Clean your hands with lotion /soap and water before examining the patient.

Observe the general appearance. Record his pulse, & BP in supine and two minutes after standing position(To detect dysautonomia). Ask whether he feels dizzy on standing and note if there is any drop in blood pressure(Fall of >20 mmHg systolic BP suggests dysauonomia). Note if there is any change in the pulse rate in supine and two minutes after standing posture.In dysautonomia the patient has resting tachycardia and pulse does not increase on standing.

Record his height and weight & calculate BMI. Look for pallor which could be part of CKD.

Since this patient's main concern is numbness of feet and non healing ulcer over his sole, examine the lower limbs and upper extremities more carefully.

Patient should remove his shoes and socks .Expose both lower extremities up to upper thigh and the upper extremities should also be exposed.

Look at the soles for any ulcer /callosities. Note the precise location of ulcer, whether it is foul smelling and discharging. Measure the size of ulcer and note whether it is tender and if the bone is exposed. Check for evidence of osteomyeltis, deformity of joints (Charcot's joint), hammer toes & clawing of toes.

Look for infection in toe webs and nails. Observe any change in the colour of skin suggesting any impending gangrene. Do the feet appear cold? Feel the dorsalis pedis, posterior tibials, popliteal and femoral arteries. Look for evidence of dysautonomia in the form of dry cracked skin over feet, absence or excessive sweating & loss of hair from legs.

Examine the nervous system for evidence of old stroke, peripheral neuropathy

Quickly check orientation in time, space and person, attention span including recent and remote memory.(When did he come to hospital and how did he reach the ward).Assess his speech for comprehension and verbal expression.

Check the motor system by looking carefully for any wasting of muscles in upper and lower limbs. Check for tone and muscle power at shoulder, elbow ,wrist and hand grip, small muscles of hand, hip, knee, ankle and small muscles of feet. Ask your self does this patient has evidence of old hemiparesis? Look for Upper Motor Neuron Sign.Check for loss of sensation in one half of body which may suggest an old lacunar infarct in the contralateral thalamus.Diabetic patients may manifest features of old hemiparesis and peripheral neuropathy at the same time.

Proceed to examine for evidence of diabetic peripheral neuropathy

Although this patient's symptoms are confined to legs only but look for signs of paresis of the 3rd, 6th & 7th cranial nerves.

Now look for evidence of neuropathy in the limbs.

Motor

Is there wasting of any muscles in distribution of any specific nerve. Check for any wasting of muscles of feet, legs, thighs, hand and forearm, Assess the tone & the muscle power (MRC grading of muscle power, 0 to-5 Grades?)

Sensory

Use monofilament and apply pressure over different parts of sole and observe patient's response. If he does not appreciates the touch proceed proximally to determine the upper level until he feels normal sensation

Next check vibration over big toe, malleolus and tibial tuberosity until the sensation is perceived as normal. Elicit ankle and knee jerks, if absent resort to Jendrassik's maneuver. Lastly check for pain sensation.

After examining the lower limbs, check all these modalities in the upper limbs also.

Examine for Romberg sign , gait & bladder incontinence or fullness.

In polyneuropathy, the student will find blunted sensation in stocking & glove distribution.

Examine the other systems to find out co morbid conditions namely, cardiac failure, lungs for evidence of old pulmonary tuberculosis. Palpate the abdomen for organomegaly and renal tenderness. Check the eyes for cataract & examine the fundi for retinopathy.

CLINICAL DISCUSSION OF THE CASE

The student should be able to

- establish that the cause of patient's disability is due to diabetic neuropathy and ischemia of foot.
- differentiate between different varieties of diabetic peripheral neuropathy.
- list the relevant investigation for appropriate management.
- discuss the principles of management.
- advice regarding care of his feet and measures to prevent recurrence of ulcers.

The risk factors of foot ulcers are: peripheral neuropathy, peripheral vascular disease, poor glycemic control, cigarette smoking, recurrent trauma to the feet and improper use of foot wear.

Patient should be advised for yearly check up for detecting neuropathy. He/she should be advised to wash feet every evening and check with a mirror under sole to look for callosities and ulcers. Wear soft well fitting shoes outdoor as well as inside the house.

The diabetic peripheral neuropathy can be prevented by maintaining good glycemic control.

LEARNING OUTCOMES

By the end of this case review the student should be able to:

1. Identify neuropathy in a diabetic patient.

2. Make a diagnosis of diabetic polyneuropathy

3. List the relevant investigation for diagnosis and management.

4. Discuss the principles of management

Commonly asked Questions

1. Name different varieties of peripheral neuropathy in a diabetic patient.

2. How will you distinguish between polyneuropathy and mononeuritis multiplex?

3. Which cranial nerves may be affected in diabetes mellitus?

4. Can neuropathy be the first manifestation of type 2 diabetes mellitus?

HIGH ACHIEVER QUESTIONS

1. Which diabetic neuropthies are painful? (Answer—3rd and 6th cranial nerve palsy, acute thoraco lumbar neuropathy, acute symmetrical distal sensory polyneuropathy)

2. Why is pupil spared in 3rd nerve palsy due to diabetes mellitus? (Answer : The artery supplying the 3rd nerve runs through the centre of the nerve. When it is thrombosed ,it affects the fibres supplying medial,superior,inferior recti, inferior oblique & levator palpebrae superioris.The papillary constrictor fires which are most superficial escape, as it derives its nutrition from CSF and blood during its course in the cavernous sinus.

3. What are the two different mechanisms of neuropathy in diabetes mellitus?

(Answer : Infarction of nerves due to micro angiopathy, clinically manifesting as mononeuropathy & due to metabolic changes associated with hyperglycemia presenting as poly neuropathy).

4. What is the role of nerve biopsy in diagnosis of neuropathy due to diabetes mellitus?

(Answer : There is no role for nerve biopsy in the diagnosis of diabetic neuropathy)

5. What is diabetic amyotrophy and state its prognosis? (Answer:It is proximal asymmetrical neuropathy due to infarction of femoral nerve, manifesting with pain in the thigh & weakness of quadriceps muscles.Onset is usually acute / subacute, first on one side then on the other, Prognosis is fairly good but may take two years to improve.)

6. What are gastro intestinal manifestations of dysautonomia?(Answer : Difficulty in swallowing, early satiety, bloating sensation, constipation & nocturnal diarrhoea.)

COMMON MISTAKES

1. Not knowing the basic neuroanatomy and physiology of the peripheral nervous system and unable to undestand symptoms and signs

2. Not using proper tools for examining the sensory system.

3. Inadequate exposures of the limbs while testing for deep tendon jerks.

4. Forgetting to look for dysautonomia.

5. Not testing for Romberg sign and gait.

6. Not palpating the peripheral nerves for thickening and tenderness. A diabetic patient may suffer from leprosy as well.

CASE 42: PARKINSONISM
KOH KWEE CHOY, JAMES

OVERVIEW

James Parkinson* was the first to describe a condition he called *'paralysis agitans'* which was later to become known as Parkinson's disease. Parkinson's disease (PD) is characterized by the triad of **T**remors, **R**igidity, **A**kinesia and **P**ostural instability (mnemonic: TRAP). Parkinsonism encompasses a group of nervous system disorders with similar presentations to Parkinson's disease. Unlike PD, there is often a specific cause in Parkinsonism, such as certain drugs or chronic exposure to toxic chemicals or metals.

PD is one of the most common neurodegenerative disorders in the world with an annual incidence of 4-20 cases per 100,000 and prevalence of 100-180 per 100,000. Males have a slight predominance over females (1.3:1) and the condition is more common amongst those in their 6th decade of life.

Despite the advances in neuroimaging studies, the diagnosis of PD is still dependent on careful history taking and physical examination. Separating PD from Parkinsonism and other tremor disorders remain a diagnostic challenge.

*James Parkinson (1755 – 1824) was an apothecary (a role now served by pharmacists or dispensers) and surgeon.

Patients with Parkinsonism may be used in the medical undergraduate examination under the theme of 'Tremor disorders'.

Types of Cases for Clinical Examination

1. LONG OSCE

The student may be asked to assess the gait of a patient with Parkinsonism and then examine the relevant systems based on the characteristics of the patient's gait.

2. LONG CASE OR OSLER

Detailed history taking is expected from students which, in addition to the presenting complaint, should also explore the premorbid status of the patient, possible causative factors and complications. The student would be expected to perform relevant physical examination on a patient who presents with tremor disorder.

CASE VIGNETTE

A 62-year-old man presents with progressive worsening of hand tremors over the last 6 months which is more pronounced on his right hand. This has made it difficult for him to perform tasks which he used to be able to do easily such as eating and writing. His wife complains that her husband seems to have 'slowed down' a little in terms of carrying out his activities of daily living.

Take a detailed history, examine the patient's gait and then perform the relevant physical examinations based on the patient's gait.

DIFFERENTIAL DIAGNOSES:

It is essential to differentiate between the variants of Parkinsonism and other tremor disorders because the management and prognosis of each of these are different. The differential diagnoses of tremor disorders are shown in Table 1.

Table 1: Differential diagnoses of tremors disorders and their characteristics.

Tremor	Character	Tone	Reflexes
Essential tremor	Relatively common in those above 60 years old; usually bilateral, progressive. Absence of extrapyramidal signs.	Normal	Normal
Cerebellar dysfunction	Unilateral or bilateral depending on cause. Intention tremor, exaggerated by movement. Other cerebellar signs may be present (e.g. ataxia, nystagmus)	Hypotonic	Pendular knee jerk

Extrapyramidal	Includes PD and Parkinsonism. In PD, the tremor is classically resting pill-rolling of the hand and is exaggerated by inattention. It is usually unilateral and may affect the head or lower limbs.	Cogwheel or lead-pipe rigidity	Normal

---

Parkinsonism may be classified into:

1. Idiopathic Parkinson's disease (PD)

2. Parkinsonian Syndromes:

- Progressive supranuclear palsy (PSP)/Steele-Richardson-Olszweski Syndrome
- Dementia with Lewy bodies
- Normal pressure hydrocephalus
- Vascular Parkinsonism (VP)
- Multi-system atrophy (MSA)/Shy Drager syndrome
- Drug-Induced Parkinsonism (DIP)
- Corticobasal degeneration

The undergraduate medical student is not expected to know in detail the different entities under Parkinsonism Syndromes although knowledge of salient features of these conditions may be advantageous.

HISTORY OF PRESENTING ILLNESS

The diagnosis of PD and Parkinsonian Syndromes is mainly clinical through meticulous and detailed history taking and careful physical examination. Therefore, the student must attempt to ask discriminative questions during history taking. In late stages of Parkinsonism, the patient himself may not be able to provide the history due to cognitive dysfunction or dementia in which case the history may have to be taken from the care-giver.

First, determine if the patient truly has Parkinsonian features. Ask about associated symptoms prior to the onset of tremor, which the patient may not have noticed until highlighted, such as general aches and pains, changes in handwriting or general slowing down in movement.

Next enquire regarding the tremor. On which hand was the tremor first noticed. Is the other hand or the feet involved as well? Tremor is the presenting complain in about 2/3 of patients although less than half (42%) have tremor alone without rigidity or bradykinesia. Ask if the tremor is more noticeable at rest or during movement. Ask if the tremor becomes worst if the patient gets emotional or anxious (essential tremor). If a patient presents with akinesia or rigidity *without any* tremor, the student must entertain the possibility of a diagnosis other than PD. On the other hand, if the patient *only* has tremor without any gait problems, always think of the possibility of essential tremor. Ask how the tremor has impacted his activities of daily living – is he able to eat, write, and clean himself?

Determine if he has associated rigidity and bradykinesia by asking if he has difficulty in maintaining his posture, difficulty in walking and stopping, difficulty in getting out of bed or getting up from a seated position and whether he has any postural instability. Ask if he has had frequent falls due to the instability.

Next ask if he has any features suggestive of autonomic dysfunction (a hallmark feature of MSA) such as feeling faint when rising from sleep or from sitting, urinary dysfunction (retention or incontinence) and impotence. Bradykinesia and rigidity are symmetrical in MSA and resting tremor is less common. MSA is usually encountered in younger (5th decade) males.

Ask if the patient has visual symptoms such as diplopia, blurring of vision and photosensitivity. Ask specifically if the patient has difficulty looking down (vertical downward palsy) which is a hallmark of PSP. Patients with PSP are typically males in their 7th decade of life and usually present with postural instability and falls. There is symmetrical bradykinesia and rigidity. Cognitive or behavioural and dysarthria are common. Tremor is a less common feature.

PAST MEDICAL HISTORY

History of known risk factors for stroke such as diabetes mellitus, hypertension, hypercholesterolemia, obesity, rhythm disorders, heart problems with and smoking should be elicited. There is evidence to suggest a link between cerebrovascular diseases with Vascular Parkinsonism (VP). Ask if there is history of CNS infection or intracranial tumor (normal pressure hydrocephalus).

SURGICAL HISTORY

History of head trauma, cranial surgery, and frequent falls (subarachnoid hemorrhage), may be important in the development of Normal Pressure Hydrocephalus.

FAMILY HISTORY

Although the majority of patients with PD have no family history of Parkinsonism, a small subset of patients with younger onset has positive family history. Familial cases of PSP have also been reported. Patients with essential tremors usually have positive family history.

SOCIAL HISTORY

Smoking and alcohol consumption is associated with ischaemic stroke which may be a factor in VP. Alcohol consumption improves tremor in Essential Tremor. Decreased libido may be a sign of autonomic dysfunction or depression.

OCCUPATIONAL HISTORY

Occupation (e.g. boxing resulting in repeated head trauma) may be a risk factor. Parkinson's disease has been linked to exposure to chemicals associated with farming and exposure to certain metals such as manganese, copper, lead, iron, mercury, zinc, and aluminium.

DRUG HISTORY

Ask if the patient has any psychotic problems and is on neuroleptics. Both phenothiazines and non-phenothiazines can induce Parkinsonism. Other offending drugs associated with Parkinsonism are antiemetics such as metoclopramide; antiepileptics such as sodium valproate and antihistamine used for motion sickness such as cinnarizine.

✓ CHECK LIST FOR HISTORY TAKING IN PARKINSONISM

- Determine if the patient truly has features of Parkinsonism
- Explore for possible subtle symptoms preceding onset of tremor
- Attempt to characterize the tremor, bradykinesia and rigidity
- Is there autonomic dysfunction?
- Are there any visual disturbances?
- Family history
- Relevant social, occupational and drug history

EXAMINATION

The patient with Parkinsonism may be distressed by his own inability to control the tremors. The wise student would keep this in mind and tries to minimize the patient's discomfort during the physical examination.

General examination and vital signs

Introduce yourself to the patient, explain your intentions and obtain consent from the patient. During the introduction, perform a quick visual survey. Note the lack of or loss of facial expression (mask-like facies), the unusually oily and sweaty skin (autonomic dysfunction), and the low volume monotonous quality of his speech. Look for infrequent blinking of the eyes. There might be drooling of saliva in late stage of the disease.

Proceed to measure his blood pressure, both in the upright and supine position (look drop in systolic and diastolic blood pressure and for wide pulse pressure – autonomic dysfunction).

Features of Parkinsonism

Request the patient to sit up from lying position. Note if he has difficulty rolling in bed and rising from the bed. Ask if he experiences any postural faintness (autonomic dysfunction).

Note the presence of hand tremor – on which hand is it present and if the other hand and feet have tremors as well. Tremors are usually asymmetrical in PD, present at rest and diminish on movement. The classical description is that of pill-rolling movement between the thumb and the index finger with a frequency of 4-6 Hertz. Distract the patient by asking him to *"repeatedly subtract 7 starting at 100"* and watch if the tremor becomes worst. Sometimes, tremor may be seen in the patient's head and jaw.

Present the patient with a pen and a piece of paper and ask him to write his name. Note if there is any micrographia (small cramped handwriting).

Assess the muscle tone by flexing and extending the patient's arm. The characteristic lead-pipe rigidity (due to increased muscle tone) is felt. Rotate the wrist joint and feel for cogwheel rigidity which is tremor superimposed onto lead-pipe rigidity. Repeat with the other arm. PD affects the upper body more than the lower body, so the same rigidity may not be so apparent if the lower limbs are examined.

Next, request the patient to stand up. Note the stooping posture (flexion of neck, trunk and limbs). Although some clinical manuals suggest giving the patient a little nudge at this point to look for propulsion and retropulsion, it is an unwise move and may cause the patient to fall. The student may, instead, inform the examiner that he is aware of these signs without performing them.

Ask the patient to walk. Look for the classical signs of Parkinsonism such as difficulty in initiating movement (start hesitation), loss of arm swing (on the affected side), short shuffling steps, and festination (as if the patient is hurrying to catch up with his centre of gravity – be careful as the patient may fall). On turning around, the patient turns 'en bloc' – the patient keeps his neck and trunk rigid and takes multiple small steps to accomplish the turning.

Allow the patient to return to the examination table and be seated. If there is time, request to perform the following:

1. Examination of the eyes – look for ophthalmoplegia, vertical downward gaze palsy, impaired pupillary light reflex, reduced blinking lid retraction, and absent Bell's phenomenon (all features of PSP).

2. Perform a glabella tap. The patient continues to blink with each tap instead of stopping.

3. Examination of the motor and sensory system.

4. Assess for cerebellar signs.

5. Perform a mini-mental test (to screen for dementia, a late sign in PD). Be aware that up to 40% of patients with PD have depression especially in the early stages of their condition.

6. Look for features of thyroid dysfunction.

✓ **CHECK LIST FOR THE EXAMINATION FINDINGS IN PARKINSONISM**
- Vital sign – look for evidence of postural hypotension
- Head – mask-like facies, eye signs, glabella tap, head and jaw tremors, oily and sweaty skin
- Trunk – truncal rigidity
- Tremor – asymmetry, resting type, exaggerated by distraction
- Posture – stooping, dystonia may be present
- Gait – characteristic loss of arm swing, shuffling steps, start hesitation, festination, turning en bloc
- Look for features of Parkinsonian Syndromes
- Screen for dementia and depression

INVESTIGATIONS

The diagnosis of Parkinson's disease and Parkinsonism is mainly clinical. Imaging studies have limited diagnostic value except to rule out other possible causes of the symptoms. For example, an MRI brain may be ordered to rule out intracranial tumor or stroke. Positive emission tomography, if available, may be of value in the diagnosis of PD by allowing assessment of the dopaminergic system.

CASE SUMMARY

This 62-year-old man presented with progressively worsening tremor of the right hand. On examination, he has features suggestive of Parkinson's disease such as mask-like facies, low volume monotonous speech pill-rolling resting tremor and characteristic posture and gait. In the absence of features of Parkinsonian Syndromes in the history and physical examination, the most likely diagnosis is Idiopathic Parkinson's disease.

CLINICAL DISCUSSION OF THE CASE

The student should be able to

- Take a detailed and reliable history utilizing discriminative questions to attempt to diagnose PD from Parkinsonian Syndromes
- Rule out other possible causes of his symptoms through good history taking and physical examination
- Elicit the classical signs of Parkinson's disease
- Look for signs of Parkinsonian Syndromes
- Explore important issues related to the care and rehabilitation of a patient with Parkinsonism
- Know the pharmacological management of Parkinson's disease

The management of PD and other associated health problems (e.g. dementia, dysphagia, depression, sleep disturbances, hypotension, and constipation) requires a multidisciplinary approach which includes:

1. Pharmacological approach

- Anticholinergics (e.g. benztropine, orphenadrine)
- Carbidopa/Levo-dopa
- COMT inhibitors (e.g. Entacapone)
- Dopamine agonists (e.g. Bromocriptine)
- MAO-B inhibitors (e.g. Selegiline)

- NMDA receptor blocker (e.g. Amantadine)

Long term management of PD requires careful and frequent adjustments of medications and doses.

2. Surgical approach

- Stereotactic deep brain stimulation

3. Exercise and physiotherapy

4. Nutritional support

5. Speech and language therapy

6. Educational support

7. Occupational therapy

8. Social and welfare support

LEARNING OUTCOMES

By the end of this case review the student should be:

1. Able to define paraplegia.
2. Make a reasonable diagnosis based on history and findings from clinical examination.
3. List the relevant investigations in paraplegia.

COMMONLY ASKED QUESTIONS

1. What is the underlying pathology of Parkinson's disease?

2. How is rigidity different from spasticity?

3. Describe the principles of management of Parkinson's disease.

HIGH ACHIEVER QUESTIONS

1. What do you understand by the term 'Parkinson Plus Syndromes?

2. What are Lewy Bodies?

3. Name some eye signs seen in PSP.

4. Based on the Hoehn-Yahr Staging Scale, at which stage is your patient in and what is its significance?

COMMON MISTAKES

- Mistaking essential tremors for tremors of Parkinsonism
- Ignoring the red flags which suggest an alternative diagnosis of PD:
  - Absence of tremor at the time of diagnosis
  - Symmetrical presentation
  - Early dementia or psychosis
  - Early onset of autonomic dysfunction
  - Ophthalmoplegia and vertical gaze palsy
  - Early onset of falls
  - Babinski sign positive
  - Little or no response to Levo-dopa

MUST KNOW FACTS ABOUT PARKINSONISM

1. Parkinson's disease is one of the commonest neurodegenerative disorders in the world.

2. The diagnosis of PD and Parkinsonian Syndromes is based on careful history taking and clinical examination. Initiation of drug therapy for early Parkinson's disease is delayed until the patient develops functional disability.

4. There are no blood tests available that can be used for diagnosis of Parkinson's disease or Parkinsonian Syndromes.

CASE 43: CEREBELLAR SIGNS
KOH KWEE CHOY,JAMES

OVERVIEW

The cerebellum*is part of the brain which is distinct from the cerebral hemispheres. It is located underneath the cerebral hemispheres, just posterior to the brain stem at the level of the pons and is connected to the latter via 3 pairs of peduncles. It processes signals received from the spinal cord (spinocerebellar tract) and the cerebral cortex (frontopontocerebellar fibres), and coordinates the fine tuning of muscle movement. It also plays an important role in cognitive functions such as language or speech regulation and attention. Consequently, any damage to the cerebellum will result in disorders involving posture, equilibrium and motor function

Cerebellum (Latin: little brain)

Patients with cerebellar signs are not uncommonly encountered in the OSCE or the long case.

1. OSCE

The student may be asked to examine the patient's gait and elicit several cardinal signs of cerebellar dysfunction.

2. LONG CASE

What strikes you: VERTIGO and UNSTEADY GAIT

The student may be asked to take a detailed history of a patient complaining of vertigo and unsteady gait.

The aim would be to explore the possible underlying aetiology for the cerebellar dysfunction in addition to performing a general physical examination and demonstrating the cerebellar signs in the patient.

CASE VIGNETTE

A 48-year-old man presents to the emergency department soon after a fall. There was no loss of consciousness before or after the fall. He complains of increasingly unsteady gait over the last few months. He has no known preceding illnesses but admits to consuming excessive amount of alcohol for the past 15 years.

Examine the patient's gait and based on the finding, proceed to examine the relevant systems.

DIFFERENTIAL DIAGNOSIS:

Remember that cerebellar signs are merely signs and not a diagnosis in itself. The signs are manifestation of a disease or disorder that has affected the cerebellum.

The differential diagnoses of cerebellar diseases are many but they can be conveniently classified into two broad categories:

1. Congenital/Hereditary causes

- Friedreich's ataxia
- Arnold-Chiari malformation
- Spinocerebellar degeneration
- Wilson's disease

2. Acquired causes

- Cerebrovascular accidents (CVA)
- Drug induced (e.g. alcohol, anticonvulsants)
- Trauma
- Multiple sclerosis
- Space-occupying lesions (SOL)affecting the cerebellum or adjacent structures (tumors, abscess, granulomas)
- Paraneoplastic syndrome
- Hypothyroidism

HISTORY OF PRESENTING ILLNESS

Causes for the fall

In obtaining the history from a patient who had a fall, it is important to explore the many possible causes which can result in a fall such as cardiovascular events (e.g. arrhythmias, vasovagal attack, postural hypotension, myocardial infarction), hypoglycaemia, and neurological causes (e.g. stroke, transient ischemic attack, seizures (TIA)). As such, questions should be targeted at symptoms suggestive of these possible causes (e.g. aura before seizures; palpitation, chest pain and sweating in myocardial infarction, post-seizure drowsiness, rapid resolution of neurological deficits in TIA).

More about the abnormal gait

Once these causes are ruled out, determine the onset of the unsteady gait and its progression. Ask if the patient also noticed any tremors, abnormal limb movements, slurring of speech, difficulty in maintaining upright

541

position when sitting or standing up and tendency to fall to one side. Ask if he experiences any headache (SOL) or fever (infective causes).

PAST MEDICAL HISTORY

 **Bear in mind:**

- Trauma
- Subdural haematoma
- Neurological deficits

Ask if there is any history of trauma, frequent falls (chronic subdural haematoma), previous episodes of neurological deficits (multiple sclerosis), treated cancers and endocrine problems (e.g. hypothyroidism).

FAMILY HISTORY

Although uncommon, there are a number of hereditary conditions presenting with ataxia (e.g. Friedreich's ataxia, Wilson's disease).

SOCIAL HISTORY

Note alcohol intake and smoking

Chronic alcohol consumption is associated with cerebellar degeneration. Present the amount as of alcohol consumed by the patient as 'Units' per week (One unit is equivalent to half a pint of ordinary strength (3-4%) beer). The upper limit for men is 21 units per week while it is 14 units per week for women. Smoking is a risk factor for stroke and atherosclerosis.

SURGICAL HISTORY

Not relevant

OCCUPATIONAL HISTORY

Enquire about the patient's occupation as his condition may affect his ability to work.

DRUG HISTORY

Anticonvulsants (e.g. phenytoin sodium) are associated with cerebellar dysfunction.

✓ **CHECK LIST FOR HISTORY TAKING IN A PATIENT WITH CEREBELLAR SIGNS**

- Onset of and progress of presenting symptoms
- Associated symptoms – frequent falls, unsteady gait, vomiting, vertigo, tremors.
- Underlying cause – alcohol, drugs, infection, trauma, multiple sclerosis, cancers, CVA, hereditary causes.
- Family history – Spinocerebellar degeneration, Friedreich's ataxia, Wilson's disease

EXAMINATION

Anatomical Correlates

As with other examination of the nervous system, the aim of the physical examination is to try and localize the site of the lesion affecting the cerebellum. Thus, the findings from the examination of the patient may help point to the site of the lesion in the cerebellum.

The cerebellum can be divided into two hemispheres joined by a central vermis (Figure 1). Lesions affecting the vermis may produce severe gait and truncal ataxia. The patient may not be able to maintain a sitting or standing position even with support. If the lesion extends further, there may even be 4th cranial nerve involvement, marked nystagmus, vertigo and vomiting.

Lesions affecting the hemispheres give rise to ipsilateral limb ataxia characterized by intention tremor, past pointing, hypotonia and the rebound phenomena. In lateral lesions, nystagmus is less marked compared to lesions affecting the vermis.

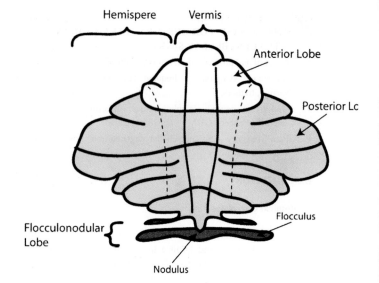

Figure 1: Anatomical subdivisions of the cerebellum

Examination for cerebellar signs

Introduction and setting the scene

Note the speech

Politely introduce yourself to the patient, explain your intentions and obtain consent from him. Notice the quality of his speech. Cerebellar lesions produce sluggish (dysarthria) or staccato speech. Ask him to pronounce words like "baby hippopotamus" or "British constitution". His speech would sound jerky, sometimes even explosive with syllabic emphasis. A patient with cerebellar signs may often be distressed by what they perceive as their own 'clumsiness', therefore the student should aim to minimize as much as possible the discomfort felt by the patient. This can be achieved by not making the patient shift his position too frequently. In other words, the student should try to gather maximum information while requiring the least effort from the patient.

Testing the gait

First ask the patient to stand up and walk. Observe his gait and coordination. Patients with vermial lesion would find it hard to maintain an upright position (truncal ataxia) and would tend to fall backward. The patient may stand with his legs far apart or may say he is too scared to stand up. On attempting to walk, the patient tends to reel towards the affected side (ipsilateral lesion) or from side to side (bilateral lesions). The classical broad based unsteady gait is noted. Because the patient's gait is unsteady, the student should always be near the patient in case he falls.

Romberg's sign

Before asking the patient to sit down at the edge of the bed, get the patient to stand with his feet together and then close his eyes momentarily. Alleviate his anxiety by reassuring him that should he fall, you are there to support him. A patient with cerebellar lesion tends to 'wobble' or sway when the eyes are closed. This is known as Rombergism or pseudo-Romberg sign which is not a true positive Romberg's test. The latter is seen in impaired proprioception sense.

Examine the eyes

With the patient seated with his legs dangling over the edge of the bed, proceed to examine his eyes. Note if there is the characteristic sign of Wilson's disease (Kaiser-Fleischer ring). Next ask the patient to follow your finger with his eyes and look as you move your finger to the patient's extreme left or right. Observe for nystagmus in his eyes which would be more pronounced towards the side of the lesion. See if there is any ophthalmoplegia (4th cranial nerve involvement).

Past pointing

Next, carefully instruct the patient to place the tip of the index finger of one hand on his nose tip before attempting to touch your upright index finger held at arm's length away from him in a rapid fashion. Look for intention tremors (increasing tremors on approaching the target) and past pointing (his finger overshoots the target). Repeat with the other side. Intention tremors and past pointing are cerebellar signs. Be aware that this test may be confounded by factors such as patient's age (senile tremors), poor eyesight, alcohol or sedative consumption and associated muscle or joint disorders. Also give allowance for the non-dominant side to perform less efficiently than the dominant side.

Testing the hands

Next, ask the patient to rapidly supinate and pronate one hand upon the other hand or the thigh. It is easier to do this by first demonstrating this to the patient and asking him to follow. Repeat with the other side. Dysdiadochokinesia (*Greek: "dys (bad)-(diadocho) reciprocal-(kinesia) movement"*) is the inability to rapidly perform alternating movements, in this case supinating and pronating the hand.

Tone

Passively move the upper limbs to assess the tone (hypotonia). Ask the patient to extend both upper limbs in front of him and close his eyes. Rapidly press one hand down and release and watch for rebound phenomena. The affected side will reveal the patient's inability to halt the rebound of the hand on release.

Deep tendon reflexes and leg examination

Before asking the patient to lie down, elicit the patellar reflex in both lower limbs. The leg on the affected side will swing several times before stopping (the leg only swing once before stopping in a normal reflex). This is known as the pendular reflex which is pathognomonic for cerebellar disorders.

Finally, with the patient lying supine on the bed, demonstrate to the patient the heel-shin-test by passively lifting his right leg, touching the heel of that leg to the top of the shin of the opposite leg before sliding the heel along the shin down to the foot. Repeat with the other side. A patient with cerebellar lesion will not be able to perform this test efficiently on the affected side. Bear in mind that the interpretation of this test is subjective to the patient's ability to comprehend your instructions, whether he has any ipsilateral weakness (e.g. concomitant stroke) and the presence of any muscle, nerve or joint disorders.

Go beyond that expected by asking if you could do more:

Before concluding the examination, ask to examine the fundus (papilledema); cranial nerves (particularly the V, VII and VIII nerves for cerebropontine angle tumors); motor and sensory neurological examination (e.g. multiple sclerosis); evidence of malignancies (e.g. lymph nodes, chest, organomegaly); signs of hypothyroidism and signs of Friedreich's ataxia.

Systemic examination

Examination of the relevant systems may be warranted (e.g. stigmata of chronic alcoholic liver disease).

 CHECK LIST FOR THE EXAMINATION FINDINGS IN A PATIENT WITH CEREBELLAR SIGNS
- ✓ Broad based gait
- ✓ Pseudo-Romberg's sign
- ✓ Nystagmus on lateral gaze
- ✓ Slurred or staccato speech

- ✓ Dysdiadochokinesia
- ✓ Intention tremors and past pointing
- ✓ Hypotonia
- ✓ Pendular reflexes
- ✓ Impaired heel-shin test

INVESTIGATIONS

Often the diagnosis of cerebellar disorder can be made from careful history taking and from clinical examination. However, investigations may be necessary to determine the underlying cause of the cerebellar disorder. In addition to routine haematological and biochemistry including the liver functions tests, other relevant tests may be done.

Investigation	Justification
Plain and contrasted computed tomography (CT) of the brain	May be able to reveal cerebellar atrophy (especially in parasaggital view) or presence of space occupying lesions like tumor or abscess.
Magnetic Resonance Imaging (MRI) of the brain	MRI is superior to CT brain in delineating soft tissue lesions (e.g. tumors, ischemia) and is the preferred radioimaging modality.
Screening for malignancies	Relevant screening tests to look for possible malignancies which may cause cerebellar syndrome (e.g. paraneoplastic syndrome)
Ultrasonography of the liver	To look for evidence of liver cirrhosis secondary to chronic alcohol consumption.
Thyroid function test	To rule out hypothyroidism
Relevant genetic tests	To rule out hereditary disorders
Relevant screening tests for multiple sclerosis	Relevant imaging tests, lumbar puncture and evoked-potential tests

| Relevant investigations for Wilson's disease | Low ceruloplasmin and serum copper; high urine copper level; liver biopsy; genetic testing |

CASE SUMMARY

This 48-year-old man, with progressive unsteady gait over several months presents after a fall. On examination, he exhibits classical cerebellar signs of nystagmus, dysarthria, intention tremor, past pointing, dysdiadochokinesia, impaired heel-shin test, pendular knee jerk and broad based gait. In view of his chronic alcohol consumption and absence of other risk factors, the most likely diagnosis is cerebellar degeneration secondary to alcohol.

CLINICAL DISCUSSION OF THE CASE

The student should be able to

- Rule out the possible causes for the fall sustained by the patient through careful history taking
- Establish chronic alcohol consumption as the most likely cause
- Discuss and rule out the differential diagnoses of cerebellar signs
- Demonstrate the classical signs of cerebellar disorder
- Discuss the principles of management in this patient.
- Explore important issues related to the care and rehabilitation of a patient with cerebellar signs

The management of a patient presenting with cerebellar signs should include the following:

- Determining the underlying cause and removal of the offending cause if possible
- Appropriate antibiotics and surgical intervention may be necessary for infection and SOL
- Counselling for the patient regarding the cause of his problem
- Appropriate measures for hereditary disorders (e.g. chelating agents for Wilson's disease)
- Physiotherapy and rehabilitation of the patient

LEARNING OUTCOMES

By the end of this case review the student should be:

1. Differentiate between Parkinson's disease and Parkinsonism.
2. Make a reasonable diagnosis based on history and findings from clinical examination.
3. Discuss the principles in management of Parkinson's disease

COMMONLY ASKED QUESTIONS

1. Name four differential diagnoses in a patient with cerebellar signs.
2. What is the most likely underlying cause of his condition?
3. What relevant investigations will you perform for this patient and why?

HIGH ACHIEVER QUESTIONS

1. What is Friedreich's ataxia?
2. What is spinocerebellar degeneration? How does it differ from Friedreich's ataxia?
3. What does the term 'motor learning' mean and what is the role of the cerebellum in motor learning?

COMMON MISTAKES

- Mistaking tremors from other disorders as intention tremors (e.g. Parkinsonism, senile tremors, drug-induced tremors)
- Causing excessive discomfort to the patient with a poorly executed flow of physical examination (e.g. asking the patient to lie down, then sit up, then lie down again, then stand and walk)
- Neglecting to ask the patient to perform the Jendrassik manoeuvre to augment reflexes when initial reflex testing was unsatisfactory.
- Mistaking pseudo-Romberg for positive Romberg's test.
- Forgetting to perform the pendular reflexes.

MUST KNOW FACTS ABOUT CEREBELLAR SIGNS

1. The common causes of cerebellar signs are chronic alcoholism and multiple sclerosis.

2. There is NO paralysis in cerebellar dysfunction.

3. Classical features of cerebellar signs include (mnemonic: **VANISHED**)

- **V**ertigo
- **A**taxia
- **N**ystagmus
- **I**ntention tremor
- **S**lurred (or **S**taccato) speech
- **E**xaggerated broad based gait
- **H**ypotonic reflexes
- **D**ysdiadochokinesia

CASE 44: MUSCULAR DYSTROPHY
KOH KWEE CHOY, JAMES

OVERVIEW

Muscular dystrophies are a group of hereditary disorders affecting mainly the skeletal muscles. It is characterized by progressive weakness and degeneration of these muscles. In some cases, non-skeletal muscles such as cardiac muscles and other organ systems are also involved. Muscular dystrophies are one of the differential diagnoses of hereditary myopathies which include channelopathies (e.g. hypo or hyperkalemic periodic paralysis), congenital myopathies, metabolic myopathies (e.g. Glycogen and Lipid Storage Disorders), mitochondrial myopathies (e.g. MELAS - Mitochondrial encephalomyopathy, lactic acidosis, and stroke) and myotonias.

Compared to stroke, paraplegia, cerebellar disorders and cranial nerves examination, muscular dystrophies are, arguably, the least likely to be used for the undergraduate medical examination. It remains very much the domain of postgraduate medicine. Nevertheless, it is not uncommon to encounter muscular dystrophy in the long case where the emphasis is on history taking.

There are many types of muscular dystrophies. Some of the common types of muscular dystrophies with their characteristic presentations are detailed in Table1.

CASE VIGNETTE

A 16-year-old boy presents with progressive weakness of the lower limbs over the past 2 years. He used to be very active in athletics especially in the high jump and the 400 meter- run but had to quit these sports due to the weakness. He has a cousin from the paternal side with similar complaints.

INSTRUCTIONS:

Take a detailed history and perform a neurological examination of this patient's musculoskeletal system.

Table 1: Types and characteristic presentations of common muscular dystrophies

Muscular dystrophy (MD)	Inheritance pattern	Characteristics
Duchenne's* MD	X-linked recessive	Most common. Primarily affects boys with early onset at around 3-5 years old. Unable to walk by early adolescence. Cardiomyopathy common.
Becker's** MD	X-linked recessive	Similar to Duchenne's MD but less severe, presents in late childhood or early adulthood.
Facioscapulohumeral MD (Landouzy - Dejerine***)	Autosomal dominant	Onset in adolescence and as the name suggests, mainly affects muscles of the face, arms, legs, shoulders and chest. Symptoms may vary between mild to severely disabling.
Myotonic MD (Myotonia Dystrophica)	Autosomal dominant	Most common adult form characterized by muscle spasms. Muscle weakness is characteristically distal. Other associated features include visual disturbance (cataract), cardiac muscle disorders and endocrine disorders.
Limb-girdle MD (Erb's	Autosomal	A group of disorders

MD)	recessive	characterized by weakness of muscles moving the shoulders and hips. The onset may be in childhood, adolescence or in adulthood. They are characterized by symmetrical progressive proximal muscle weakness.
Emery-Dreifuss**** MD	Mainly X-linked	Characterized by joint deformities and muscle contractures presenting in early adolescence, and cardiac abnormalities (conduction defects and arrhythmias).

* Guillaume-Benjamin Duchenne, a French neurologist, first described the condition in 1861.

** Becker Muscular Dystrophy is named after the German doctor Peter Emil Becker, a German physician.

***French physicians, Louis Landouzy and Joseph Dejerine, first described the condition in 1884.

**** Fritz E. Dreifuss, a German-born, American neurologist et al, first described the condition in 1961.

Table 2: Acquired myopathies

Endocrine myopathies (e.g. thyrotoxic myopathy, diabetic myopathy, Cushing's disease)

Toxic or drug-induced myopathies (e.g. statin –induced myopathy, chronic alcoholism, corticosteroids)

Inflammatory myopathies (e.g. dermatomyositis, polymyositis)

Infections (e.g. HIV, Toxoplasmosis, Lyme's disease)

Connective tissue diseases (e.g. rheumatoid arthritis, systemic lupus erythematosus (SLE), polyarteritis nodosa)

HISTORY OF PRESENTING ILLNESS

Despite advances in diagnostic tests, the diagnosis of muscular dystrophy (MD) is still largely dependent on thorough history taking and physical examination. A meticulous history should allow the medical student to offer a reasonable preliminary diagnosis which, together with findings from the physical examination, will lead ultimately to the correct clinical diagnosis. This is because some muscular dystrophies have such characteristic features that a bedside diagnosis is usually possible.

Muscle weakness may be the presenting complaint for any number of disorders affecting the motor unit (anterior horn cell, motor nerve, neuromuscular junction and the muscle fibres) and therefore the first task of the medical student is to determine the *site* of the lesion. Once it has been established that it is indeed primarily a muscle disease (and not for instance, a motor neuron disease, peripheral neuropathy or a neuromuscular junction disorder), the next task is to determine if the condition is a hereditary or acquired disorder. Some examples of acquired myopathies are shown in Table 2.

Early onset of symptoms in childhood suggests more severe forms of MDs (Duchenne's, Becker's) while later onset (adolescence or adulthood) suggests less severe forms (Facioscapulohumeral MD (FSHMD), Limb-girdle MD (LGMD), Emery-Dreifuss MD (EDMD), Myotonic MD). In contrast, toxic myopathy and episodic weakness (e.g. periodic hypokalemic paralysis) typically have acute onset; conditions like dermatomyositis and polymyositis have subacute onset while endocrine myopathies develop over weeks or months.

The gender of the patient provides an important clue as a number of the MDs are X-linked disorders and thus primarily affect males (Duchenne's, Becker's, EDMD).

The presenting symptoms vary depending on the types of muscular dystrophy. Determining which groups of muscles are affected may provide clues as to which type of MD is present. Some MDs affect all muscle groups (Duchenne's & Becker's MD) while others characteristically affect only certain groups of muscles (FSHMD and LGMD). The patient usually presents with complaints of weakness and/or fatigue.

ASSESSING SEVERITY

Assess the severity of muscle weakness by asking questions related to activities of daily living. Muscle weakness in MDs often begins in the lower limbs and may be proximal (e.g. Duchenne's and Becker's MDs) or distal (FSHMD, EDMD and Myotonic MD). The patient may complain of inability to walk on heels or toes, climbing stairs, rising from seated position and jumping. Over time, the progressive muscle weakness may result in unsteady gait and frequent falls. Involvement of facial muscles (inability to whistle, drooling, drooping eyelids), shoulder girdle muscles (difficulty to comb hair) and pelvic girdle muscles (unsteady gait) suggests FSHMD.

In late stages, muscles of the neck, trunk and distal muscles of the limbs may also be involved leading to spinal deformity, poor hand grip and wrist or foot drop. In addition to weakness, the patient may also complaint that his muscles have "become smaller" (atrophy). Paradoxically, pseudohypertrophy of the calves are seen in Duchenne's and Becker's MDs.

MDs are characterized by *absence of* muscle pain or tenderness and cramps. Indeed, the medical student should immediately consider other alternative diagnoses if a patient presents with predominantly muscle pain or tenderness with very little muscle weakness. On the other hand, muscle contractures are a feature of EDMD and LGMD while myotonia (impaired relaxation after forceful contraction) is a feature of Myotonic MD. In the latter, the patient may say he has difficulty relaxing his hand after gripping something tightly (e.g. handshake, opening jars, buttoning and unbuttoning).

PAST MEDICAL HISTORY

Some acquired causes of myopathies can be quickly eliminated from the differential diagnoses by enquiring about history of endocrine disorders (e.g. thyroid, adrenals, and diabetes), autoimmune disorders (e.g. rheumatoid arthritis, SLE) and renal impairment; all of which may present with muscle weakness.

FAMILY HISTORY

As MDs are hereditary disorders, scrutinizing the family history may yield valuable clues to the type of MD the patient has. The patient's family tree should be explored to include previous generations if possible, as some MDs (e.g. FSHMD and Myotonic MD) may be so variable that immediate affected family members may be asymptomatic. The student should look out for possible patterns of transmission, whether autosomal dominant, autosomal recessive or X-linked. Questions regarding the presence of muscle weakness in other family members should be clearly and specifically framed. For example, instead of asking, "Are there any other members with weakness in your family?", the student should instead ask if anyone in the family requires walking aids, who are they and how are they related to the patient, their gender, the onset of the problem, family members with skeletal deformities and if there are any children, particularly boys, affected at a young age or at adolescence.

SOCIAL & OCCUPATIONAL HISTORY

History of chronic alcohol consumption is important to rule out alcohol related myopathy. Travel and sexual histories may be relevant if an infective aetiology is suspected (e.g. HIV). Occupational history is particularly relevant in MD with adult onset as the progression of the disease may not only impact the patient's ability to work but also in the management of any. At times, a change of occupation may be warranted.

DRUG HISTORY

The patient should be asked regarding the use of medications associated with muscle weakness such as corticosteroids, statins, colchicine and anti-retroviral agents (e.g. Zidovudine). Ask if the patient consumes liquorice which is associated with hypokalemic paralysis or indulges in illicit drug use such as heroin and cocaine.

SYSTEMIC REVIEW OF SYMPTOMS

In late stages when the respiratory muscles are affected, the patient may even present with symptoms of respiratory insufficiency (shortness of breath, decreased effort tolerance) which may be complicated by pneumonia. Early symptoms of respiratory muscle involvement include frequent waking at night, feeling of non-restful sleep, daytime somnolence and poor concentration.

The student should also explore if there is any cardiac involvement. The commonest cardiac presentations are congestive heart failure and rhythm disorders. The patient may present with shortness of breath, swelling of dependent areas, decreased effort tolerance and syncopal attacks.

Rarely, patients with Duchenne's or Becker's MDs may pass red or dark-colour urine (myoglobinuria due to rhabdomyolysis) with or without fever which may be complicated by acute renal tubular necrosis. Dysphagia and visual disturbances are features of Myotonic MD

 CHECK LIST FOR HISTORY TAKING IN MUSCULAR DYSTROPHY
o   Determine the onset of symptoms
o   Establish if the condition is a hereditary or acquired disorder
o   Determine which groups of muscles are involved and whether distal or proximal muscles are affected

- o Enquire if there is associated muscle pain or tenderness, contracture or spasms
- o Rule out conditions affecting the motor unit presenting as muscle weakness (anterior horn cell, motor neuron disease, neuromuscular junction disorders)
- o Rule out endocrine and connective tissue diseases
- o Take detailed family history and look for patterns of transmissions
- o Take detailed social, occupational, travel, sexual and drug histories
- o Check for involvement of other organ systems – respiratory, cardiovascular and urogenital

EXAMINATION

General examination and vital signs

Introduce yourself to the patient, explain your intentions and obtain consent from the patient before starting the physical examination. If local custom allows it, offer to shake the patient's hand. The gesture offers an opportunity to assess if the patient has myotonia, in which case, the patient may show a delay in releasing his hand grip.

During the conversation with the patient, do a quick visual survey of his face and facial expressions. Presence of frontal baldness (high hair line), bilateral cataracts, wasting of temporalis and masseter muscles, ptosis, lack of facial expression, a thin neck (swan-like due to sternocleidomastoid atrophy) and speech difficulty suggests Myotonic MD. A lilac rash around the upper (and sometimes lower) eyelids (heliotrope rash) suggests Dermatomyositis. Cognitive impairment may be present in Duchenne's MD.

Examination of the motor system

When assessing muscle power in a patient presenting with myopathy, the student should bear two important points in mind, namely:

    i.   Whenever possible, test all muscle groups *against gravity* in order for accurate assessment of muscle weakness which may otherwise escape notice

    ii.   Test these muscles *bilaterally.*

Professionalism

Ask permission from the patient to expose the neck, shoulders and upper limbs (in female patients, a cloth may be tied around the trunk to cover her bosoms).

A chaperone must be present.

Inspection:

- Look for evidence of wasting in the neck muscles (sternocleidomastoid), the shoulder girdle and the upper arms (FSHMD, LGMD). In the lower limbs, exposure should at least be at mid-thigh level to allow proper evaluation for muscle atrophy.
- Carefully note if the calves are paradoxically larger than normal (pseudo-hypertrophy). Bear in mind that in early stages of muscular dystrophy, muscle mass may be normal before onset of atrophy but the muscles will be hypotonic.
- Note the presence of any contractures (EDMD).
- Determine if there is presence of muscle pain or tenderness (suggestive of myositis) before proceeding to assessment of muscle power.
  - Muscle power is graded from 0 (complete paralysis), 1 (flicker of contraction), 2 (active movement with gravity eliminated), 3 (movement against gravity), 4 (active movement against resistance) and 5 (normal power). An expanded scale for assessment of muscle power such as the Medical Research Council (MRC) of Great Britain grading scale may be used to further fine-tune the assessment of muscle power but the usual 0-5 grading scale should be sufficient for undergraduate level.
- Assess the power of muscles involved in movement of various joints in the upper and lower limbs.

Table 3 shows the movements to be tested in different joints.

Table 3: Assessment of movements in various joints in muscular dystrophy

Joint	Movements to be tested	Comments
Neck	Flexion and extension	Test flexors in supine position and extensors in prone position
Shoulder	Abduction, internal and external rotation	Test abduction in upright position
Elbow	Flexion and extension	

Wrist	Flexion and extension	
Fingers and thumb	Flexion, extension and abduction	
Hip	Flexion, extension and abduction	Test flexion in seated position. Test abduction in lateral decubitus position
Knee	Flexion and extension	Test extension in seated position. Test flexion in prone position
Ankle	Dorsiflexion, plantar flexion, inversion and eversion	
Toes	Flexion and extension	

Testing the muscle groups

Because of the need to test muscle groups against gravity whenever possible, the student may have to break away from the traditional method of testing all muscle groups of one joint before moving to the next joint. Instead the student may have to perform these assessments depending on the position of the patient. In order to minimize discomfort to the patient, the student may choose to first examine the patient in the supine position where the neck flexors and the internal and external rotators of the shoulders can be assessed before asking the patient to assume a lateral decubitus position for assessing the hip abductors and finally asking the patient to lie prone for assessment of neck extensors weakness (a feature of Myotonic MD) and knee flexors against gravity.

Next, the patient may be asked to be seated with the legs dangling from the edge of the bed. In this position, the shoulder abductors, flexors and extensors of the elbow, wrist, fingers and thumb, ankle and toes as well as the hip flexors may be assessed. In addition, abduction of fingers and ankle inverters/everters can also be assessed. Examination must be done on *both sides* of the body.

Finally, if possible, request the patient to get off the bed and squat before attempting to get up from the squatting position. Gower's sign is seen in severe proximal myopathy in which the patient may have to literally use his/her hands to climb up him/herself. This is a classical sign in Duchenne's MD. If the patient could be made to walk, the gait may provide useful clue to the presence of pelvic girdle weakness.

In muscular dystrophy, there is characteristically *no* sensory deficit and the *deep tendon reflexes are normal.*Ask to examine the patient's back and look for scapulae winging (serratus anterior and trapezius muscles weakness) and any spinal deformity (kyphosis, scoliosis, kyphoscoliosis, lordosis).

Examining related systems

Before completing the examination, offer to examine the following related systems:

1. Cardiovascular system: rhythm abnormalities, cardiomegaly and signs of heart failure
2. Respiratory system: breathing rate, use of accessory muscles, evidence of infection
3. Eyes: bilateral cataracts, ophthalmoplegia, ptosis

✓ **CHECK LIST FOR THE EXAMINATION FINDINGS IN MUSCULAR DYSTROPHY**
- ✓ Determine the muscle groups involved and symmetry of involvement
- ✓ Whenever possible assess muscle power against gravity and bilaterally
- ✓ Establish if the muscle weakness is proximal or distal
- ✓ Look for presence of characteristic features of some types of muscular dystrophy
- ✓ Sensory deficit are characteristically absent while deep tendon reflexes are normal
- ✓ Do not forget the back and the spine
- ✓ Examine other related systems: cardiovascular, respiratory and eye.

INVESTIGATIONS

Often at the end of a comprehensive history taking and physical examination, a fairly accurate diagnosis of the type of muscular dystrophy can be made.

Laboratory studies can then be ordered to aid in making the final diagnosis (Table 4)

Table 4: Relevant investigations in muscular dystrophy

Investigation	Justification
Creatinine kinase (CK)	CK is markedly elevated in Duchenne's and Becker's MDs but may be modestly elevated or normal in other MDs (LGMD, FSGMD, Myotonic MD).
Electrophysiological studies comprising of nerve conduction studies (NCS) and electromyography (EMG).	NCS are typically normal in MDs while EMG can help to confirm the presence of myopathy.
Muscle biopsy	Allows histo-pathological diagnosis of the condition.
Molecular genetic studies	Genetic testing using peripheral blood DNA can confirm the diagnosis which may negate the need for muscle biopsy.
Relevant investigations to rule out other causes of myopathy	For example, relevant screening tests for endocrinopathy and connective tissue diseases can be done.
Urine myoglobin	Done if suspected myoglobinuria
ECG and Echocardiography	For assessment of cardiac status and to detect rhythm abnormalities
Arterial blood gas	If respiratory compromise is suspected

CASE SUMMARY

This 16-year-old boy has a primary muscle disorder characterized by predominantly symmetrical proximal muscle weakness in all muscle groups. There is no sensory system involvement and the deep tendon reflexes are preserved. There is no evidence for cardiac or respiratory systems complications. Taking into account the age of onset of symptoms, the positive family history and characteristic clinical findings, the most likely diagnosis is Becker's Muscular Dystrophy.

CLINICAL DISCUSSION OF THE CASE

The student should be able to:

- Establish that the patient's condition is a myopathy and not from lesions of other sites in the motor unit.
- Establish that the disorder is hereditary in nature as opposed to acquired myopathic disorders.
- Offer a reasonable diagnosis of the type of muscular dystrophy based on the history and findings of the physical examination.
- List the relevant investigations in a logical manner with appropriate justifications for each.
- Discuss the principles of management in this patient.
- Explore important issues related to the care and rehabilitation of a patient with muscular dystrophy.

Competency in breaking serious illness news

In a counselling station where the diagnosis is given, the student can be tested for his competency in breaking serious illness (bad) news. Elements of the following need to be shared in counselling.

There is no cure for muscular dystrophies and therefore the goal of therapy is mainly symptomatic. The student must be able to show empathy when dealing with patients with incurable conditions like muscular dystrophy as the diagnosis and prognosis may be hard for the patient to accept.

The management of a patient diagnosed with muscular dystrophy should include the following:

- Confirming the type of muscular dystrophy by performing relevant investigations.

- Counselling for the patient with regards to the diagnosis as well as the likely prognosis.
- Physical therapy can help to maintain muscle strength and function as well as reduce contractures.
- In late stages, patients may require aids for mobility such as leg braces or wheel chairs.
- Surgical intervention may be necessary for correction of deformities, contractures and spinal abnormalities.
- Cardiology referral may be necessary for management of abnormal rhythm and cardiomyopathy. Pacemaker insertion may be necessary.
- Ophthalmology referral for early intervention of cataract (Myotonic MD) can save the patient's sight.
- Corticosteroids are used in Duchenne's MD to delay rate of muscle wasting.
- Vaccinations may be considered to reduce risk of recurrent pneumonia in patients who have respiratory muscle involvement.
- Genetic counselling for patients who consider starting a family.

LEARNING OUTCOMES

By the end of this case review the student should be:

1. Able to demonstrate the cerebellar signs
2. Make a reasonable diagnosis based on history and findings from clinical examination.
3. List the relevant investigations
4. Discuss the principles in management of a patient with cerebellar signs

COMMONLY ASKED QUESTIONS

QUESTIONS

1. What is the most likely diagnosis?
2. Based on the history and physical findings, what is the most likely type of muscular dystrophy the patient has?
3. What does myotonia mean?
4. What relevant investigations will you perform on this patient?

HIGH ACHIEVER QUESTIONS

1. What is the explanation for pseudohypertrophy of the calves in muscular dystrophy?

2. What are the issues involved in counselling a patient with muscular dystrophy?

3. How do the various types of muscular dystrophies differ in their patterns of muscle weakness?

COMMON MISTAKES

- Wrongly attributing muscle weakness due to lesions in other sites of the motor unit (e.g. ventral horn, motor neuron, neuromuscular junction) as myopathy which is a primary muscle disorder. Not spending enough time exploring the relevant family history in order to establish the hereditary pattern of the disease.
- Neglecting to look for characteristic features of various muscular dystrophies during the physical examination.
- Not testing muscle groups against gravity and therefore misses any significant muscle weakness.
- Not examining both sides of the body.
- Forgetting to examine the back, the spine and other associated systems (cardiovascular, respiratory and eye).

MUST KNOW FACTS ABOUT MUSCULAR DYSTROPHY

1. Muscular dystrophies are group of hereditary disorders primarily affecting the skeletal muscles and in some cases, other organ systems.

2. Most MDs have distinctive hereditary patterns. Some MDs have distinctive clinical features which makes bedside diagnosis possible.

4. MDs are incurable disorders and management is mainly symptomatic.

CASE 45 : GULLIAN BARRE SYNDROME
AP SINGH

OVERVIEW

Guillain-Barre Syndrome(GBS) is an acute inflammatory demyelinating polyradiculoneuropathy (AIDP).Amongst all peripheral neuropathy, its clinical presentation is unique, often mistaken for acute transverse myelitis, acute myopathy or acute disorders of myoneural junction. Untreated, it carries a heavy mortality due to respiratory failure. Even with treatment mortality and morbidity is considerable. Despite ventilatory support, plasmapheresis and immunoglobulin therapy about 5% die at the end of a year, 10% are left with severe disability and mild disability is seen in another 10 -15 % cases. Only 60 -70% have full recovery. The disease results from an acute immune response following a viral or acute bacterial infection of gastrointestinal by *Campylobacter jejuni* and not infrequently following vaccination against Rabies(Neural vaccine), H1 N1 or Hepatitis B

Types of Cases for Clinical Examination

1. OSCE (Short or long)

In the short OSCE, the student may be asked to examine the sensory system or cranial nerves while in long OSCE complete examination of motor system may be requested.

2. Long Case or OSLER

In long case, detailed history taking is expected from students covering the course of illness, possible cause, complications, effect and contribution of pre morbid conditions.Student should be able to examine neurological system in detail and also the other systems, plan investigations (diagnostic & for overall management of the case) and know the principles of treatment.

CASE VIGNETTE

A 30 years old Malay gentleman has sought consultation for rapidly progressing weakness of all four limbs for the last one week along with tingling & numbness of both hands & feet .He has difficulty in breathing since this morning.Ten days before the onset of neurological illness he suffered from upper respiratory tract infection.

DIFFERENTIAL DIAGNOSIS (DD) :

1. Guillain –Barre Syndrome (GBS)
2. Acute transverse myelitis
3. Hypokalemic paralysis
4. Acute toxic myopathy

The aim of detailed history in a neurological case is to know

(a)The physiological deficit (motor, sensory, visual, sphincter, speech disturbance &, alteration in level of sensorium etc).

(b)The site of lesion in neural axis (cerebral hemispheres, brain stem, spinal cord, peripheral nerves, myoneural junction & or muscles)

(c) The probable cause.

(d) Complications due to the neurological illness.

HISTORY OF PRESENTING ILLNESS

(a) Find the physiological deficit & probable site of lesion

- Patient should be encouraged to narrate the story of his illness. It is useful to ask when he was in good health to do his daily chores. This gives an idea about the onset of illness. Dramatic onset points to a traumatic and sudden vascular insufficiency. Acute and subacute onset over a day to few weeks suggests infectious, inflammatory, demyelinating disease or exposures to toxins/ chemicals or metabolic disorders. Gradual onset, slowly progressive illness points to space occupying lesions, degenerative or nutritional deficiency syndrome. All the diseases mentioned in the differential diagnosis have an acute onset.

- Course of illness should be enquired. For instance in GBS, the symptoms do not progress beyond four weeks and if the patient continues to worsen, possibility of other disease like Chronic Inflammatory Demyelinating Polyneuropathy (CIDP) should be thought of, while in traumatic and vascular etiology the disease reaches its nadir in a day or two and remains static or improves there after. If there is history of remissions and relapses, it points to primary demelinating disorder (multiple sclerosis) or steal syndrome due to vascular malformation

- Since the main complaint of this gentleman is weakness, the student should enquire into symptoms which will help to differentiate upper motor and lower motor neuron lesion.

Stiffness of limbs points to Upper Motor Neuron (UMN) lesion, loss of muscle bulk and fasciculation suggests Lower Motor Neuron(LMN) lesion. He should ask whether weakness is equal in proximal and distal muscles. Proximal weakness points to myopathy and radiculopathy while predominant distal weakness suggests peripheral neuropathy & UMN lesion (There are exception to this rule).Lastly the student should clarify where did the weakness first appear .Did it appear first in the legs and ascended up to involve the trunk and upper limbs? Has it affected both sides equally? If answer to above questions is in affirmative it points to GBS. Descending paralysis favours a variant of GBS (Miller Fischer syndrome).

- This gentleman had sensory symptoms in the form of tingling & numbness in hand and feet indicating involvement of peripheral nerves or the sensory tracts in the spinal cord. The student must ask the upper limits (ankle knee or mid thigh) of sensory disturbances over limbs or has it extended to the trunk. Sensory symptoms confined to limbs in stocking & glove distribution suggests polyneuropathy, while a distinct level over trunk (below neck, nipple, epigastrium, umbilicus & groin) suggests lesion of sensory tracts in spinal cord i.e. a diagnosis of myelopathy.

- The student must ask the patient whether there is any problem in voiding urine. Retention of urine in a quadriplegic patient points either acute transverse myelitis (due to disruption of descending bladder fibres which run along the medial side of corticospinal tract) or it could occur in GBS due to dysautonomia (dysfunction of parasympathetic fibres arising from the intermediate horn of S2, S3, S4 segment of spinal cord & exiting along with corresponding motor nerve roots)which supply the detrusor muscles of bladder. Findings of UMN sign in lower limbs favor acute transverse myelitis as the cause of urinary retention while LMN signs in the lower limb along with other features of dysautonomia indicate GBS.

- This patient complained of difficulty in breathing, suggesting possible weakness of respiratory muscles, in view of widespread motor weakness. Diaphragm & intercostals muscle weakness is frequent occurrence in GBS rather than transverse myelitis.

- To distinguish between transverse myelitis and polyradiculoneuropathy the student must enquire whether muscles of head & neck have also been affected or not. Weakness of facial, ocular, pharyngeal & neck muscles are inconsistence with diagnosis of transverse myelitis because these are supplied by cranial nerves located in brain stem and not by spinal nerves. On the other hand quadriplegia accompanied by paralysis of cranial nerves with stocking & glove anesthesia favors GBS.

(b)Probable cause of patient's neurological problem

- The student should now try to find the cause of patient's illness. History of upper respiratory infection, diarrhoea, vaccination, in the preceding weeks is consistently associated with GBS.HIV infection during early phase of seroconversion can present with GBS. Occasionally this follows surgical intervention This young man suffered from a viral infection (URTI) a week before & remained symptom free for almost a week before developing the neurological illness, suggesting that the infective agent has caused indirect damage & that the neural axis has not been invaded by it. Patient should be asked about having received any vaccine in the preceding weeks (anti rabies neural vaccine, H1 N1 vaccine & hepatitis B vaccine).Do inquire about diarrhoea. Infection with *Campylobacter jejuni* has been consistently associated with GBS.

- The student must enquire history of fever at the onset of illness .It suggests an infective etiology(e.g. West Nile, EV70 viral infection, poliomyelitis and rabies, tuberculosis, acute epidural abscess should be considered). All the above diseases are the cause of myelitis rather than GBS. As a matter of fact, the diagnosis of GBS should not be entertained if the neurological illness begins with fever.

PAST MEDICAL HISTORY

- An enquiry should be made discretely regarding HIV infection as GBS & acute transverse myeltis is a recognized association.
- Has patient suffered from similar illness in the past? Recurrent attacks of generalized muscle weakness raises suspicion of hypokalemic periodic paralysis. Use of laxative and diuretics can precipitate hypokalemic paralysis
- Past history of tuberculosis & malignancy are relevant in this case.

FAMILY HISTORY
- The student should enquire whether friends or family members who had dinner together suffered from similar illness (C jejuni)
- Recurrent attacks of acute quadriparesis in family members suggests hypokalemic periodic palsy / porphyria

SOCIAL HISTORY

- Tobacco smoking (number of pack years) and alcohol consumption should be asked including the quantity and duration.

SURGICAL HISTORY

- Surgical intervention in the preceding week has been linked to GBS

SYSTEMIC REVIEW OF SYMPTOMS

- Palpitation, syncope, constipation and unexplained diarrhoea raise the suspicion of dysautonomia. Presence of breathlessness and ineffective cough indicates significant weakness of respiratory muscles.
- Student should know that alteration in level of sensorium could be due to hypoxia or hyponatremia secondary to SIADH (syndrome of inappropriate ADH secretion), a complication of GBS & should specifically enquire about it.

CHECK LIST FOR HISTORY TAKING IN GUILLAIN–BARRE SYNDROME.

- Onset of symptoms
- Ascending motor weakness.
- Sensory symptoms
- Autonomic disturbances if any
- Absence of fever at the onset of illness.
- History of URTI /diarrhoea/ vaccination, a few weeks preceding the illness

**While presenting a case of polyradiculoneuropathy appropriate history should be taken to support or exclude disorders of muscles, myoneural junction, & transverse myelitis.

EXAMINATION

General examination & vital signs

- Introduce yourself and obtain consent for examination. During history taking you must have noted respiratory distress if any (his inability to speak full sentence in a single breath indicates lack of strength in respiratory muscles).

- Note whether he is changing position of his limbs .Note his mentation and alertness.
- Record his vital signs. Temp is usually normal in all the conditions mentioned in the DD. Presence of fever indicates lurking infection either in lungs (aspiration pneumonia) urinary tract infection, deep vein thrombosis. BP and pulse may fluctuate due to dysatonomia. Respiratory rate, depth of respiration, chest expansion and breath holding time should be recorded. If possible vital capacity should be measured.
- Check the scalp and pubic hair for tics. Tick paralysis mimics GBS.
- Check the colour of urine in the bag. Port wine colour urine may be due to porphyria which is another cause of polyradiculopathy mimicking GBS.
- Look for telltale signs of HIV infection in the oral cavity and skin.

Neurological examination

- Check his orientation in time place and person His attention span and recent memory by asking when did he come to hospital and who brought him. This should be corroborated with medical documents/ attendant.
- Speech may be hypophonic in view of weak diaphragm
- Cranial nerves(CN) should be checked carefully.Ocular movements are usually normal. However pupils may be large and show poor reaction to light due to dysautonomia In GBS bilateral 7th 9th 10th &11th are involved often.
- Motor system – look for the bulk, tone, power fasciculation, coordination. The muscle power should be graded from 0-5 on Medical Research Council (M RC) grading. Determine whether weakness is equal or different in proximal and distal muscles of limbs. In GBS, patient will have symmetrical LMN signs while in transverse myelitis UMN signs (Tone is spastic, DTJ exaggerated, Babinski is positive) are seen. Proximal weakness is generally more prominent than distal weakness in GBS.

- Sensory function should be assessed for fine touch, vibration and pain. Joint position may be tested but it is affected in severe lesions. It is important to check the distribution of sensory impairment. Stocking and glove hypoesthesia / anesthesia suggest polyneuropathy while a distinct level over trunk favours transverse myelitis.

- Deep tendon jerks(DTJ) should be tested by exposing the muscle & positioning the limb in correct position. If the DTJ are absent, repeat the test during reinforcement (Jendrassik maneuver). GBS is LMN lesion due to polyradiculoneuropathy all DTJ are absent even on reinforcement. In transverse myelitis all DTJ, caudal to spinal lesion will be brisk. However, acute transverse myelitis in spinal shock despite UMN lesion behaves like LMN lesion until the shock passes off in 3 -6 weeks time and may be mistaken for GBS.It is the presence of a distinct sensory level over the trunk that favours the diagnosis of acute transverse myelitis. In myopathy & myoneural junction disorders DTJ are normal until very late phase of the illness and there is absence of sensory disturbance.

- Plantar reflex should be tested & its response noted. In transverse myelitis Babinski is positive while in GBS it is flexor(provided grade 2/5 power is present in the leg muscles & foot is kept in a position with gravity eliminated)

- Sphincter disturbances may be seen in acute transverse myelitis as well as in GBS but never in myopathy and myoneural junction disorder.

- Spine should be checked for gibbus, deformity and tenderness. Gait should be checked if patient is ambulant and any abnormality noted. In myelopathy spastic gait is seen.

Examination of other related system

- Check the lungs for aspiration pneumonia, cardiovascular system for dysautonomia. Look for bed sores and deep venous thrombosis.

Check list for the examination findings in GBS

- Hypotonic, areflexic, symmetrical motor deficit.
- Sensory impairment in stocking & glove distribution.
- Features of dysautonomia may be present.
- Check for respiratory muscle weakness.
- Any complication due to GBS namely aspiration pneumonia & deep venous thrombosis.

INVESTIGATIONS

Diagnostic tests

1.Cerebrospinal fluid - shows albumino cytological dissociation classically in second to third week. The cell counts are with in normal range (except HIV associated)while protein is raised to 1-2 gm/dl. The practical implication is that in the first week of illness the CSF may be normal.

2. Nerve conduction velocity (NCV) & Electromyogram (EMG) study. In the first seven to ten days it may be normal. Thereafter it shows demyelination & axonopathy.

3. Spirometry should be done on admission as a baseline and later whenever respiratory muscle weakness is suspected. If the vital capacity falls to 25 ml/ kg body weight ventilatory support becomes mandatory.

4. Serum electrolytes. Serum potassium <2.5 mmol / L may mimic GBS. Serum sodium may also be reduced due to inappropriate ADH secretion (SIADH)

5. HIV serology

6. Serology for *Campylobacter jejuni*

Tests required for management of the case

1. ECG for cardiac arrhythmia (due to dysautonomia.)

2. Radiograph of the chest to pick up aspiration pneumonia

3. Blood count, and biochemistry (sugar, urea, creatinine, LFT)

4. Urine for porphobilinogen.

CASE SUMMARY

This 30 years old Malay gentleman developed acute onset ascending paralysis of all four limbs over period of seven days. On examination he had symmetrical hypotonic, areflexic paralysis of all the four limbs with blunted sensation in stocking and glove distribution. He had in addition bilateral lower motor facial, 9th, 10 and neck muscle weakness. His respiratory muscles were also weak. He had features of dysautonomia.

Provisional diagnosis: Guillain-Barre syndrome (Acute inflammatory demyelinating polyneuropathy)

CLINICAL DISCUSSION OF THE CASE

The student should be able to

- Differentiate UMN from LMN lesion
- Recognize that the sensory impairment in glove and stocking distribution is the hall mark of polyneuropathy.
- Distinguish myopathy, myoneural junction diseases, polyneuropathy and myelopathy from each other on the basis of history and relevant signs.

LEARNING OUTCOMES

By the end of this case review the student should be:

1. Able to identify motor and sensory symptoms & signs of polyneuropathy.
2. Make a diagnosis on the basis of history & clinical findings.
3. List the investigations for diagnosis.
4. Discuss the principles of management

COMMONLY AQSKED QUESTIONS

1. Name two causes of GBS.

2. Name two investigations which clinch the diagnosis of GBS.

3. Name one modality of treatment that improves muscle power & reduces hospital stay.

HIGH ACHIEVER QUESTIONS

1. How do you clinically distinguish GBS from acute transverse myelitis? (**Answer mentioned in the text**)

2. What are the other forms of GBS?

(Ans: AcuteMotorAxonal Neuropathy(AMAN) and Acute Motor-Sensory Axonal Neuropathy (AMSAN).It is due to destruction of axolemma by the autoantibodies associated with *Campylobacter Jejuni* infection.Prognosis is poor.)

3. What are the poor predictors of GBS? **(Ans: Old age,rapid onset of severe quadriplegia, need for early ventilation and acute axonal form of the disease)**

4. What are causes of death in GBS? **(Ans: Respiratory failure, aspiration pneumonia dysautonomia, pulmonary thrombo embolism)**

5. What are indications of immunoglobulin administration and its dose? **(Ans: Motor weakness <grade 2, rapid onset of illness, impending respiratory failure. The total dose of Immunoglobulin is 2 gm / Kg body weight to be divided over 5 days and administered intra venously over 6 to 8 hours daily).**

COMMON MISTAKES

- Not taking proper history to find out physiological deficit.
- Inability to distinguish UMN signs from LMN signs in presence of spinal shock.
- Neglecting to compare the DTJ with its counterpart and not resorting to reinforcement when it is absent.
- Unfamiliarity with the pattern of sensory loss and its anatomical correlation
- Not testing the sensory function with proper tools.
- Not looking for the signs of dysautonomia

SECTION 6 :RHEUMATOLOGY

CASE 46 : SYSTEMIC SCLEROSIS (SCLERODERMA)
SHIVANAN THIAGARAJAH & ESHA DAS GUPTA

OVERVIEW

Systemic sclerosis (SSc) or Scleroderma is an uncommon disorder known to have a clinical spectrum ranging from limited to generalized disease, non-systemic to systemic involvement having and aetiology related to environmental factors and autoimmune rheumatic disease. The term scleroderma is derived from the Greek words *skleros* (hard or indurated) and *derma* (skin). Robert H. Goetz first described in detail the concept of scleroderma as a systemic disease in 1945; he introduced the term progressive systemic sclerosis to emphasize the systemic and often progressive nature of the disease. This chronic multisystem disorder is characterized clinically by accumulation of connective tissue resulting in thickening of the skin and multisystem structural and functional abnormalities (gastrointestinal tract, lungs, heart, and kidneys). It has a higher female preponderance.
The risk of systemic sclerosis is 4-9 times higher in women than in men.

- According to the American College of Rheumatology (ACR) criteria, classification of systemic sclerosis requires one major criterion or two minor criteria. One *major criterion or two minor criteria have a sensitivity of 97% and specificity of 98%*

- Major criterion:
  - o Proximal scleroderma characterized by symmetric thickening, tightening, and induration of the skin of the finger and the skin that is proximal to the metacarpophalangeal or metatarsophalangeal joints.
  - o These changes may affect the entire extremity, face, neck, and trunk.

- Minor criteria
  - o Sclerodactyly is characterized by thickening, induration, and tightening of the skin, limited to only the fingers.
  - o Digital pitting scars or a loss of pulp from the finger pad as a result of ischemia, depressed areas of the fingertips or a loss of digital pad tissue.
  - o Bibasilar pulmonary fibrosis including a bilateral reticular pattern most pronounced in basilar portions of the lungs on standard chest radiograph.

These densities may assume the appearance of diffuse mottling or a honeycomb lung and are not attributable to primary lung disease.

Pathology: Three main abnormalities observed are:
- i) Vasculopathy – there is extensive endothelial injury leading to dysfunction. Raynaud's phenomenon is a clinical manifestation of vasculopathy and vasomotor dysfunction.
- ii) Inflammation – there is an increased inflammatory process that leads to further vascular damage and multisystem disorder.
- iii) Fibrosis – this is the hallmark of scleroderma leading to the main cause of morbidity and mortality. There is excess deposition of collagen and extracellular material that deposits in vessels and organs leading to multisystem disorder.

The limited and diffuse lesions are distinguished clinically by extent of skin involvement. Scleroderma is classified based on the diagram below.

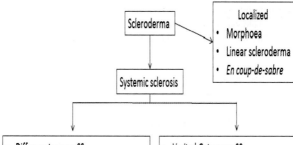

Note: The student should understand the pathological basis of SSc and comprehend the role of investigations that relate to the underlying dysfunction. Such meaningful learning would avoid depending on recall and also assist in giving reasons for requesting for specific investigation.

Types of cases for clinical examination:
1) Short /Long OSCE – Clinical recognition of dermatologic manifestations are common. The student should be able detect characteristic skin changes over face, chest and extremities and explain the findings.
2) As systemic involvement is possible, examination instructions would direct student to examine particular systems
3) OSPE – Pictures of classical scleroderma (spot diagnosis), Laboratory investigation for interpretation e.g. Chest radiograph for lung involvement, radiological changes in soft tissue (calcinosis etc.)
4) Long Case – Students would be expected to take a detailed history and perform a thorough clinical examination eliciting the multisystem involvement of the disease

CASE VIGNETTE

A 35-year-old lady, presents with a history of numbness and pain of the hands especially in cold weather. She has noticed that her hand becomes pale and cold and after a while becomes red and painful. She has been having this for the past 3 years. Recently, she is having difficulty in swallowing. She also feels that the skin over her face and extremities are tight. She has been diagnosed with hypertension and has been told that there is some 'renal impairment'.

HISTORY OF PRESENTING ILLNESS

Note: Clinical presentations in SSc may vary from patient to patient but 95%have Raynaud's phenomenon. A good systemic review must be done to look for the multisystem involvement of the disease.

Raynaud's phenomenon
- Ask the patient about changes of skin color over the hand and feet when exposed to cold
- Ask the patient about pain and numbness over hand and feet
- Ask if there are skin ulcers especially over the digits.70% of the patients have this on the onset of the disease and 95% of them eventually develop during the course of the disease.

Note: The patient will complain of episodic changes in hand. Usually there is pallor or cyanosed due to intense vasoconstriction. The hands become cold and patient may experience numbness. When blood flow returns sluggishly there is cyanosis and finally there is reactive hyperemic phase which results in pain and tingling sensation. The phenomenon is precipitated by cold exposure. The intense vasoconstriction may cause ulcers of the digital pulps.

The student is expected to discuss the basis of Raynaud's phenomenon based on the pathophysiology (vasculitis).

Skin manifestation
- Ask about swelling of extremities and face.
- Ask about tightening of skin over extremities and face.

Note: Oedema (swelling) occurs in the early phase which results from small vessel endothelial injury and increased permeability. Increased amounts of collagen produced in the subcutaneous tissue is followed by fibrosis. The skin becomes atrophic and progressively binds to underlying tissue making the skin tight and shiny. The extent of skin lesion will distinguish diffuse and limited cutaneous sclerosis. Changes most often begin in the fingers (sclerodactyly) and hands and may spread to involve more proximal tissues, including the trunk and face. The lower extremities often are less severely involved.

- Ask if she has noticed any rash over face and body.

Note: Telangiectasia is local collection of dilated loops of small blood vessels in the skin. Telangiectasia have a tendency to bleed at sites prone to trauma.

Musculoskeletal Features
- Ask about swelling, and stiffness of the fingers and knees

Note: inflammatory arthritis can occur early in the disease, but typical joint involvement is limited to synovial fibrosis.

- Ask if there is muscle weakness
- Ask for symptoms of carpal tunnel syndrome

Note: severe skin involvement causes muscle weakness due to disuse atrophy. There may also be myopathy and myositis with scleroderma.

PAST MEDICAL HISTORY
- Usually no significant past history

SURGICAL HISTORY
- Nonspecific – may have past history of surgery for complication of disease

FAMILY HISTORY
- Family history if present, increases risk.

SOCIAL HISTORY
- Ask if patient can eat , clothe and bath herself
- Ask about her occupation – symptoms may be affecting work

- Ask about support at home.
- Ask about home conditions: type of house , type of toilet , availability of basic necessities

Note: It is important to take a detailed social history and occupational history to determine functional limitation. Scleroderma is a progressive disease with multi-organ involvement. Patient will develop functional limitation as the disease progress. Assessment of living condition shows that you are a holistic and caring doctor.

DRUG HISTORY
- Take a history of over- the- counter drugs and analgesic use.
- Take history of traditional medication use.

Note: Remember the patient may have been seen by other doctors or may have seen a traditional practitioner.

SYSTEMIC REVIEW OF SYMPTOMS

Gastrointestinal tract
- Ask patient about dysphagia and reflux symptoms

  Note: Esophageal motility dysfunction occurs when collagen replaces smooth muscle in the lower two-thirds of the esophagus. Esophageal strictures and ulceration, can occur resulting from reflux. Hoarseness may occur due to acid reflux with vocal cord inflammation or fibrosis
- Ask about dyspepsia symptoms

Note: Dysmotility of stomach give rise to delayed gastric emptying time
- Ask patient about diarrhoea and constipation

Note: small bowel involvement leads to reduced intestinal movement and intermittent cramping, diarrhea, and bacterial overgrowth giving rise to malabsorption syndrome

Pulmonary & Cardiovascular Manifestations
- Ask patient about shortness breath at rest and reduced effort tolerance
- Ask patient about chronic cough
- Ask patient about heart failure symptoms
- Ask patients about palpitations
- Ask the patient about chest pain

Note: Fibrotic proliferation that occurs in peribronchial and perialveolar tissues causes progressive interstitial lung disease. Pulmonary hypertension results from fibrosis and narrowing of pulmonary arteries. Scleroderma can cause cardiomyopathy producing congestive cardiac failure, arrhythmias, and conduction disturbances (Prolonged QT interval, Heart blocks). Fibrotic involvement of small myocardial vessels may result in angina.

Renal Involvement
- Ask about headaches, blurring of vision and nausea. (malignant hypertension)

Note: Acute renal failure can occur with scleroderma renal crisis. Fibrotic damage to arteries of the kidney coupled with vasoconstrictive stimulus results in a massive renin-angiotensin release. This leads to malignant hypertension and microangiopathic hemolytic anemia. This can lead to chronic renal failure and death if left untreated.

Neurologic involvement
Note: Fibrotic entrapment neuropathies of the median and trigeminal nerves may occur.

Eye & Mouth
- Ask for dry mouth and eyes

Note: there can be coexistence of Sjögren's syndrome or patient may have fibrosis of lacrimal and salivary ducts.

Constitutional:
- Ask about fatigue and weight loss

Note: A good candidate must always try to determine patients preconceived ideas about the illness and understand - concerns and expectation.

Check list for history taking
- ✓ Get a history of Raynaud's phenomenon(key feature of systemic sclerosis)

- ✓ Get a history of joint involvement

- ✓ Identify multisystem complications of the disease (systemic review)

- ✓ Get a history of dysphagia, reflux ,and dyspnoea

- ✓ Determine the functional status of patient

- ✓ Determine patient concerns

EXAMINATION

Introduce yourself and explain to the patient you would like to examine her.

General inspection

General inspection gives an idea of the patient's functional disability. Also look around the room to get clues about functional disability (e.g. walking frame/ stick).

In scleroderma you must look for:
- General nutritional status
- Anemia and jaundice
- Signs of respiratory distress (patients may have restrictive lung disease , lung fibrosis, heart failure)

Inspect the hands:
- Tight smooth shiny skin of the hands with sausage shaped fingers (sclerodactyly)
- Evidence of Raynaud's phenomenon
- Nail fold infarcts raged cuticles
- Digital ischemia with ulceration
- Infarction and pulp atrophy (amputations of the digit)
- Pseudo clubbing (due to overhanging nail over the atrophied pulp of the finger)
- Dilated nail folds capillaries (telangiectasia)
- Vasculitic rashes at the finger tips.
- Calcinosis – subcutaneous calcium deposits in the digits and finger tips

Double pinch test –pinch the area between two adjacent interphalangeal joints then pinch the skin of the dorsum of your own hand for direct comparison

Inspect the face for

- Tight smooth shiny skin over the face
- Beaked nose
- Small mouth (microstomia) and Perioral furrowing/ puckering
- Telangiectasia
- Alopecia
- Pallor and jaundice
- Comment on speech abnormalities when talking to patient

Note: Sclerosis of frenulum limits mobility of tongue
Note: Avoid using descriptions like bird-like mouth during presentation as it may be offensive to the patient.

Inspect the trunk and legs for vasculitis, telangiectasia and ulcerations, vitiligo.

Note: Vitiligo is a sign of autoimmune disorder.

Complete examination by looking for organ specific complication:

Blood pressure:
- Malignant hypertension can occur with renal disease. If BP is high, a fundoscopy must be done.

Cardiovascular examination:
- Patient may have pulmonary hypertension , look for parasternal heave , palpable 2nd heart sound and tricuspid regurgitation (pansystolic murmur louder on inspiration)

Respiratory examination:
- Interstitial fibrosis, look for fine end inspiratory and bibasal crackles

Eyes & mouth
- Look for dry eyes and mouth due to either coexistent Sjögren's syndrome or ductal fibrosis

Endocrine
- Look for – signs of hypothyroidism (may coexist as this may also be of autoimmune disorder)

Functional status of patient
Check patient's daily functions by asking her to imitate actions:
- Buttoning and unbuttoning shirt
- Holding a cup
- Turning a door knob or using a key to open a lock
- Combing hair and ability to bath self

Note: These functions are very important because you can gauge the patient's ability to take care of herself and it shows that you are determining the patient's level of activity and quality of life.

Check list for clinical examination
- ✓ Look at general condition of patient
- ✓ Examine hand and face for skin changes and other signs of scleroderma
- ✓ Look for beaked nose, small mouth (patient cannot put her 3 fingers into her mouth)
- ✓ Raynaud's Phenomenon
- ✓ Tightness of the skin
- ✓ Telegiectasia
- ✓ Subcuticular calcinosis
- ✓ Try to differentiate diffuse and limited systemic sclerosis by the extent of involvement
- ✓ Look for complications of disease – focused examination
- ✓ Asses functional status

INVESTIGATIONS

Note: The investigations must reflect on the pathophysiology of disease and help confirm the diagnosis, assess systemic involvement (complications) and in ascertaining progress of illness and response to treatment.

Blood Investigations:
- Full blood count – scleroderma is a chronic disease with multi-organ involvement, hence look for anemia.
- ESR and -CRP may be high
- ANA is positive in 90-95% of cases
- Serum electrolytes and liver function test – Liver function may be deranged. Chronic renal failure rarely occurs in scleroderma.
- Urine full examination - microscopic examination (UFEME) to look for proteinuria.
- Thyroid function test – hypothyroidism may occur with scleroderma

Respiratory investigation
- Chest radiograph – A baseline radiograph serves to compare x-rays during progression of disease. Look for fibrotic changes. Changes are only seen in advanced disease (may require a (HRCT, high resolution computer topography scan).
- Lung function test – restrictive lung disease

Cardiac investigations
- ECG – hypertensive changes, conduction defects

- Echocardiogram – Look for effects of pulmonary hypertension - (Doppler) , pericarditis , and myocarditis (may need MUGA scan)

GI investigations
- Barium swallow examination for dysphagia
- Endoscopy

Autoimmune panels
- Anti-nuclear antibody (ANA) – present in 90%-95% of affected patients with speckled or centromere pattern.
- Topoisomerase I antibodies (Scl-70) - present in approximately 30% of patients with diffuse disease but absent in limited disease. If present it is often associated with pulmonary fibrosis.
- Anticentromere antibodies- present in about 45%-50% of patients with limited disease.
- RNA polymerase I and III – present in about 20% of diffuse systemic sclerosis , assiation with renal disease.

CASE SUMMARY

This 35-year old lady has sclerodactyly evidenced by thickened tight shiny skin over her hands till elbow. She also has involvement of the face with microstomia and perioral puckering. She has limited systemic sclerosis. There is marked dysphagia and reduced mobility of her fingers manifested by difficulty to button her clothes. She also has Raynaud's phenomenon as evidenced by pain and colour changes in the fingers when exposed to cold. This patient has developed renal failure along with hypertension.

Note: When presenting the case always try to present the positive findings (lesion), the aetiology and the functional status. In some cases complication of the disease and of treatment should also be reported.

MANAGEMENT

Professional aspects of how 'serious illness news' should be broken would evaluated as this is a chronic and progressive disease disorder.

With such disclosure comes psychological aspects of the disease like depression due to disease and a marked drop in quality of life. Occupation may also be affected. The student is expected to consider all these factors in drawing a management plan.

Specific to the case:

a) Nonpharmacological treatment

Patient education and support; patient needs to be counseled on scleroderma. Familiarize patient to the symptoms and natural course of disease as well as how we are going to manage it. Patents must understand that the disease is progressive and involves multi organ systems.

b) Physical therapy and occupational therapy – Designated exercise program to maintain posture and range of motion. Occupational therapy is aimed at rehabilitation and teaching patients how to maximize their limitations so that they can still care for themselves.

Specific management:

a) Raynaud's phenomenon

i) Patient should be advised to avoid cold

ii) Patient should be advised against smoking

iii) Medications: calcium channel blockers, prostacyclin, sildenafil

iv) In severe cases, surgical sympathectomy may be required when ....

b) Skin

i) Topical emollients

ii) Methotrexate in diffuse disease

iii) D-penicillamine, cyclophosphamide

c) Esophagitis / dyspepsia

i) Patient should be advised raise head on lying down in bed and not to sleep soon after meals. She should avoid NSAIDS

ii) Medication : proton pump inhibitors (PPI) , motility agents (metoclopramide)

d) Pulmonary fibrosis

i) Pulmonary rehabilitation

ii) Corticosteroids and immunosuppressive drugs (cyclophosphamide)

iii) Bosentan, (a dual endothelin receptor antagonist) for pulmonary hypertension

e) Dysrhythmias and conduction defects - Depends on underlying rhythm may need medication or pacemaker

f) Pulmonary hypertension

i) Long term oxygen therapy

ii) Medications(endothelial receptor antagonist (Bosentan),prostaglandins, diuretics)

g) Heart failure and -Diuretics / ACE inhibitors

h) Renal disease – Manage hypertension especially with ACE inhibitors

NOTE: The student should be well versed in discussing the commonly used drugs, its profile and their safety. A variety of new agents are now available but not all are approved by the Drug Control Authority. Cost – benefit ratios and close consultation with rheumatologist is vital

Learning Outcomes

By the end of this case review the student should be able to:

- Take a good history of the scleroderma manifestation especially Raynaud's phenomenon.
- Able to recognize multi-organ involvement of scleroderma
- Examine the skin and focused specific organ r complications
- Formulate the appropriate investigations and explain rationale for performing them.
- Outline the principles of management.

COMMONLY ASKED QUESTIONS

QUESTIONS

4. What is CREST syndrome?
   Limited systemic sclerosis which manifest as
   C-calcinosis
   R-Raynaud's phenomenon
   E-Esophegeal dysmotility
   S-Sclerodactaly
   T-Telangiectasis

5. What are the differences between limited systemic sclerosis and diffuse systemic sclerosis?
   They can be differentiated based on extent of skin involvement. In limited systemic sclerosis Raynaud's phenomenon may precede skin changes my many years. It also manifests as CREST syndrome (see above). However gastrointestinal disorders and pulmonary hypertension commonly occurs but are not in CREST. Diffuse systemic sclerosis involves skin changes above elbows or knees or involving the trunk. Typically occurs within one year of onset of Raynaud's phenomenon.

6. What is scleroderma renal crisis?
   Commonly occurs in diffuse systemic sclerosis. It is characterized by an abrupt onset of severe hypertension (headache, blurring of vision) and accelerated oliguric renal failure (nephritic picture). This leads to flash pulmonary edema, heart failure pulmonary and pericardial effusion. There

is also microangiopathic hemolytic anemia (MAHA) and thrombocytopenia. This is treated with angiotensin converting enzymes (ACE)

DISTINCTION LEVEL QUESTION

1. What is the prognosis in scleroderma?

   The estimated 5 year mortality in scleroderma ranges from 34%-73%. Survival correlates best with the clinical disease subtype (diffuse cutaneous and limited cutaneous) and extent of organ involvement.

   The limited cutaneous subset carries a 10-year survival rate of 71%.

   The diffuse cutaneous subset carries a 10-year survival rate of 21%.

   Pulmonary hypertension is a major prognostic factor for mortality.

2. What are the possible causes for anaemia in scleroderma?

   - *Chronic disease /chronic renal failure - Anaemia of chronic disease*
   - *Iron deficiency secondary to blood loss – bleeding from esophagitis, stomach ulcers*
   - *B12 and folate deficiency – malabsorption*
   - *Microangiopathic hemolytic anaemia- malignant hypertension and scleroderma renal crisis*
   - *Bone marrow suppression – secondary to medications like methotrexate and other immunosuppressive drugs*

3. What is mixed connective disorder?

   Mixed connective-tissue disease (MCTD) an overlap syndrome with clinical features of systemic lupus erythematosus (SLE), scleroderma, and myositis. There is a distinctive antibody against U1-ribonucleoprotein (RNP).

COMMON MISTAKES

- Not asking the patient if he is in pain before examining the patient. It reflects badly on the candidate if pain is caused to the patientduring examination

- Not assessing functional status of patient

- Not looking for complications of the disease

- A good student will go one step higher and look for complications of treatment

MUST KNOW FACTS OF SCLERODERMA

- ✓ Scleroderma is progressive disease with multisystem involvement

- ✓ Recognize the subtypes of limited and diffuse systemic sclerosis

- ✓ Raynaud's phenomenon

- ✓ Investigations including autoimmune panels specific to the disease

- ✓ Basic management principles

Reference

1. Harrison's Principles of Internal Medicine, 17th edition, chapter 316, Systemic Sclerosis (Scleroderma) and Related Disorders by J Varga.
2. Fries R, Shariat K, von Wilmowsky et al. Sildenafil in the treatment of Raynaud's phenomenon resistant to vasodilatory therapy. *Circulation*. Nov 8 2005;112(19):2980-5.

CASE 47 : ANKYLOSING SPNDYLYTIS
SHIVANAN THIAGARAJAH & ESHA DAS GUPTA

OVERVIEW

Ankylosing spondylitis (AS) is a chronic systematic inflammatory disorder of unknown aetiology that primarily affects the axial skeleton (sacroiliac joints and spine). The name is derived from Greek roots 'ankylos'- meaning 'stiffening of the joints' and 'spondylos' –meaning spinal vertebra. Other clinical manifestations of the disease include peripheral arthritis, enthesitis and extra-articular organ involvement.

AS is grouped into seronegative spondyloarthropathies which is genetically linked (human leukocyte antigen [HLA] class-I gene *HLA-B27*). The disease has a male to female prevalence of approximately 3:1 and usually begins in the second or third decade.

Types of cases for clinical examination:
5) Short /Long OSCE – Examination of the spine.
6) OSPE – Radiographs showing sacroiliitis/ bamboo spine
7) Long case – Students would be expected to take a detailed history and perform a focused clinical examination of a patient who presents with chronic back pain and suggest management

CASE VIGNETTE

A 33-year-old man, with no known past-medical history presents with a history of a chronic low back pain for last 2 years. For the past 3 months the pain is increasing in severity especially after waking up in the morning. His sleep is disturbed due to back pain. He finds some relief after exercise.. He works as a lorry driver. Lately he finds it very difficult to drive long distances.. He denies any history of injury and also denies any history of fever. He is worried that he may not be able to work. He had an older brother who suffered backache and has died after a motor vehicle accident.

HISTORY OF PRESENTING ILLNESS

Back pain and stiffness
- History of back pain and stiffness that is progressive in nature.
- Pain is usually diffuse involving sacroiliac joint and lumbar spine. There may be radiation of pain down both buttocks which may present as 'alternating buttock pain'.

- Symptoms typically worsen during rest but improve with exercise Patient may experience stiffness and pain that awakens them in the early morning. (a distinctive feature from mechanical back pain)
- Onset of symptoms is usually insidious occurring over months or years but generally at least 3 months before presentation.
- Stiffness may last up to 30 minutes in the mornings
- Intermittent flares can occur between periods of remission.
- Osteoporosis occurs in up to half of patients with Ankylosing spondylitis, which increases the risk of spinal fracture.

Peripheral joint involvement: Along with the back pain, the patient may have arthritis of the peripheral joints in his limbs. Distal arthritis may occur in 1/3 of patients and usually is asymmetrical oligo-arthritis which less likely involves the small joints of hand and feet.

PAST MEDICAL HISTORY
- Usually no significant past history. History of diarrhoea is important as inflammatory bowel disease (IBD) may be coexisting with AS.

SURGICAL HISTORY
- Patient may have history of frequent motor-vehicle accidents due to restricted lateral vision due to cervical spine stiffness.
- History of hip fractures due to osteoporosis.

FAMILY HISTORY
- Family history (first degree relative with AS) increases risk.

SOCIAL HISTORY
- Occupation – symptoms may affect work.
- Determine the level of disability
- Activities of daily living may deteriorate
- Ask about the patient's social support network.
- Smoking and alcohol intake

Note: It's important to take a detailed social history and occupational history to determine functional limitation. As described in the case vignette -his disease is affecting his job. Issues related to insurance and work place compensation need to be factored in management.

DRUG HISTORY

- Take a history of 'over the counter drug' and analgesic use.

- Take history of traditional medication use.
- Evaluate 'quality of life' indices

Note: Remember patient is having symptoms for several years and may have well have tried a variety of treatment prior to seeing you.

SYSTEMIC REVIEW OF SYMPTOMS

Constitutional symptoms
- Fatigue is a common symptom seen in (60%).
- Fever, anorexia and weight loss occurs during periods of active disease.

Extra articular manifestation
- Enthesitis: - inflammation of the site of insertion of ligaments and tendons to bones occur in AS (e.g. Achilles tendonitis and plantar fasciitis).Enthesitis can cause extra-articular bony tenderness.
- Eye involvement– anterior uveitis, iriitis (red eye 25%-30 %); usually unilateral.
- Lung involvement - apical pulmonary fibrosis (decreased effort tolerance)
- Heart involvement- Aortitis eventually presents as aortic regurgitation (early diastolic murmur), arrhythmias (palpitation)
- GI involvement (IBD)– diarrhoea
- Rash- Psoriatic arthritis may present as AS.

Depression
- Always asses the possibility of coexisting depression as chronic back pain and limitation of function can be disabling and affects quality of life.

Note: A good candidate must always try to determine patients preconceived ideas about his disease and understand his concerns and expectation.

Check list for history taking

✓ Determine the nature of back pain

✓ Ask about the type of onset, acute or insidious

✓ Progress of the pain. Progressive back pain is suggestive of malignancy or AS

✓ Character of the pain and radiation of the pain if any

✓ Exacerbating and reliving factors (rest exacerbates and exercise relieves)

✓ Alarm symptoms if any

✓ Identify extra articular complications of the disease (systemic review)

✓ Determine the functional status of patient

✓ Determine patient's concerns

EXAMINATION

Professionalism

Introduce yourself and explain to the patient you would like to examine him.

Rheumatology assessment follows *look, feel* and *move.*

Chaperone may be needed

General Inspection

General inspection gives an idea of the patient's functional disability. Also look around the room as it can give you clues (e.g. walking frame/ stick). In AS you must look for:

- General nutritional status.
- signs of respiratory distress (patients may have restrictive lung disease , apical fibrosis)
- question mark posture – this is caused by caused by loss of lumbar lordosis and fixed kyphoscoliosis with extension of cervical spine
- protuberant abdomen which occurs due to diaphragmatic breathing

- any other joint swelling or deformities (may have peripheral oligo arthritis)

Note: It's important to always ask the patient if he/she is in pain before touching or moving any joints.

Spine examination:

Look:
- Swelling, skin changes deformities.
- Loss of normal thoracic kyphosis and lumbar lordosis.

Feel:
- Palpate vertebral body for tenderness and palpate for muscle spasm.

Movement:
- Always test active movement first. This will tell you the normal range of movements for the patient.

Movement of cervical spine:
- Ask patient to touch his chin on chest (flexion). Ask patient to touch his ear to shoulder (lateral flexion). Ask patient to rotate neck to right and left.
- The movements may be restricted.

Note: Cervical spine is affected late in the disease

Movement of thoraco-lumbar spine
- Ask patient to bend forward and touch the toes with knees kept straight (forward flexion).
- Ask patient to lean backward (extension).
- Ask patient to slide the right hand down the right leg as far as possible without bending forward. The same is done for the opposite (Lateral Flexion)
- Ask patient sit on a chair. With the pelvis fixed ask patient to turn the head, shoulder and upper torso to each side (rotation).
- *It is important to fix the pelvis in order to test the rotation of the spine as a good range of motion of the hip joints can compensate the loss of spinal mobility.*

Note: *Flexion is usually contributed by lumbar spine and rotational movement, from thoracic spine*
Forward and lateral flexion are lost early in AS
The aim of testing movement is to show that there is restriction of spinal movement overall.

Schober's test: It tests the degree of lumber flexion. (See Fig. 1)

- A mark is made at the level of posterior iliac spine on the vertebral column (L5) .Place one finger 5cm below this mark and another finger at about 10cm above this mark. Ask the patient to touch his toes without bending the knees. If the increase in distance between the two fingers on the patients spine is less than 5cm then this is indicative of a limitation of lumbar flexion.

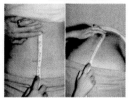

Fg 1: Aschber's test

(Occiput to wall distance

- As the cervical spine is extended along with thoracic kyphosis, the patient cannot touch the wall with his occiput when the patient's heel and back are against the wall (upper thoracic and cervical limitation)

Proceed to look for associated complications:

Remember the As

Anterior uveitis / iriaitis – redness of eye

Apical lung fibrosis- fine end inspiratory crepitation at upper zones

Aortic regurgitation (4%) - mid diastolic murmur

Atrio-ventricular nodal heart block (10%) - irregularity of pulse (ask for ECG to be done)

Arthritis- swelling or pain of joints

Achilles tendonitis and plantar fasciitis- foot pain and tenderness on palpation)

Abdominal (IBD) - increased microscopic evidence of bowel inflammation; increased prevalence of Crohn's disease.

Check list for clinical examination
- ✓ Examine spine following look, feel, and move to demonstrate restriction of movement
- ✓ Schober's test
- ✓ Look for Arthritis of peripheral joints
- ✓ Look extra articular manifestation AS

INVESTIGATIONS

Students should request for relevant investigations and give reasons for any test asked for. Data interpretation may be required especially in a LONG CASE and at OSPE

Blood Investigations:
- Full blood count – Baseline FBC gives an idea about inflammation. Anti TNF may affect WBC and hemoglobin counts.
- Base line electrolytes and liver function test – Patients are usually put on NSAIDS which may affect renal function. Treatment with anti TNF may affect liver function.
- Inflammatory markers (CRP, ESR) – This is an inflammatory disease and the markers will give an idea on control of disease.
- HLA B27

Radiographs (x-ray):

Overall bony morphology and subtle calcifications and ossifications may be demonstrated well radiographically. The diagnosis may be reliably made if the typical radiographic features of ankylosing spondylitis are present.

Sacroiliitis occurs early in the course of ankylosing spondylitis and is regarded as a hallmark of the disease.

- Anterior posterior view of sacroiliac joints along with postero-anterior and lateral radiographs of lumbar spine are important views
- Radio graphically, sign of sacroiliitis include
  1) narrowing of joint space, subchondral (changes are usually asymmetrical)
  2) Bony erosions on the iliac side of the joint
  3) Subchondral sclerosis with bony proliferation
- In the spine, the early stages of spondylitis are manifested as small erosions at the corners of the vertebral bodies surrounded by sclerosis and is called Romanus lesion
- Squaring of the vertebral body is another characteristic feature
- Syndesmophyte formation, that is ossification of the outer fibers of the annulus fibrosis leads to bridging of the corners of one vertebra to another causing 'bamboo spine'

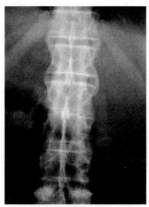

Fig. 2: Bamboo Spine

- Chest radiograph – look for upper lobe fibrosis (may require a (HRCT) high resolution computer topography scan).
- May investigate for secondary osteoporosis

CASE SUMMARY

This patient has Ankylosing Spondylitis (aetiology) as evidenced by a question-mark posture due loss of lumbar lordosis and a fixed kyphosis with extension of the cervical spine (lesion). Spinal movements are restricted as there is limited flexion and lateral movements of the cervical spine (functional status).

Note: When presenting the case always try to present the positive findings (lesion), the aetiology and the functional status. It some cases complication of the disease and complication of treatment should also be reported.

CLINICAL DISCUSSION OF THE CASE

The issues in this case are:

- **Ankylosing spondylitis with functional disability**
- **Disabling pain**
- **Affecting his occupation as a driver**

How would you manage a patient with Ankylosing Spondylitis?

Management of AS can be divided into:

Non pharmacological

Patient education – patient needs to be counseled on Ankylosing Spondylitis. Familiarize patients to the symptoms and natural course of disease as well as how he is going to be managed.

Regular exercise - helps reduce the symptoms and may slow the progress of the disease. Swimming is a good option.

Physical therapy – designated exercise program to maintain posture and rage of motion.

Psychological and professional issues: Serious illness news need to be broken to patient (chronic disabling disease) and liaison psychiatry if warranted.

Pharmacological. NASIDS- Improve pain and increase mobility of patient. Daily use has shown to slow don progression of disease.

Anti TNF: (e.g. infliximab) – shown to rapidly and profoundly reduce symptoms and sustain reduction of clinical and laboratory parameters of disease activity.

LEARNING OUTCOMES

By the end of this case review the student should be able to:
- Take a good history of backache and pick up symptoms that suggest inflammation.
- Able to recognize associated clinical manifestation of Ankylosing Spondylitis
- Examine movement of spine and perform the Schober's test.
- Outline the principles of management

Formulate the appropriate investigations explain rationale for performing them

COMMONLY ASKED QUESTIONS

QUESTIONS

What are the other forms of seronegative arthritis that also present with back pain?

Back pain (sacroiliitis) is commonly seen in Reiter's syndrome, psoriatic arthritis, and intestinal arthropathy

What is the differential diagnosis that needs to be ruled out when diagnosis AS is made?

Psoriatic arthritis – pitting of nails and psoriatic plaques. Psoriatic arthritis often involve small joints unlike AS (arteritis mutilans)

Diffuse idiopathic skeletal hyperostosis (DISH) – hyperostosis process in DISH is similar to AS sacroiliac joints are typically spared. Syndesmophyets in DISH is non-marginal as opposed to marginal Syndesmophyets in AS

Mechanical back pain – usually worse on movement as oppose to AS. Patient never wakes up from bed due to pain. No stiffness or constitutional symptoms involved.

Spondyloarthropathy associated inflammatory bowel disease (IBD) - may be a part of AS. Many patients don't present with IBD symptoms until many years after onset of arthropathy

Reiter's syndrome – triad of arthritis, uveitis and urethritis in men or cervicitis in women

What is the genetic association that are found in seronegative arthropathy

HLA B27 (90% association with AS)

DISTINCTION LEVEL QUESTIONS

What are the poor prognostic signs for AS?

Poor prognostic indicators include peripheral joint involvement, young age of onset, elevated erythrocyte sedimentation rate (ESR), and poor response to nonsteroidal anti-inflammatory drugs (NSAIDs).

What is the prognosis of AS?

Life expectancy is reduced in AS attributed to aortic valve disease, amyloidosis and complication of fractures. Most common cause of morbidity is hip arthritis and osteoporosis

What is the diagnostic criteria for AS

Modified New York criteria (1984) which consist of the following:

   a.   A history of inflammatory back pain

   b.   Limitation of motion of the lumbar spine in both the sagittal and frontal planes;

   c.   Limited chest expansion, relative to standard values for age and sex;

d.   Definite radiographic sacroiliitis.

The presence of radiographic sacroiliitis plus any one of the other three criteria is sufficient for a diagnosis of definite AS.

A patient with Ankylosing Spondylitis brought to emergency department after a minor motor vehicle accident. He complainss of neck pain. Radiograph spine shows advanced AS changes with bamboo like spine but no fracture is seen. What other investigation is warranted. Give reasons?

Do an MRI of cervical spine. Patients with advance d AS with bamboo spine can have fractures through the fused disc space leading to unstable cervical spine and risk of myelopathy. This condition is difficult to be recognized on plain radiograph and a more sensitive tool is needed.
Patients with bamboo spine have higher incidences of whiplash injury and prone to accidents due to restricted lateral vision

COMMON MISTAKES

- Not asking the patient if he is in pain before examining the patient. It reflects badly on the candidate if pain is caused to the patient.
- Not asking the patient to do active movement before attempting passive movement.
- Not looking for associated extra -articular involvement

MUST KNOW FACTS

- ✓ Seronegative arthropathy involving mainly the spine

- ✓ Back pain and stiffness improves with exercise

- ✓ Has extra articular involvement

- ✓ Radiographic features of AS

- ✓ Basic management principles

Reference:

1.Harrison's PRINCIPLES OF INTERNAL MEDICINE (Seventeenth Edition) (Quote chapter , pages, authors, editor and publisher and year
2.Oxford Textbook of Medicine 4th edition (March 2003)
3.John H Klippel,Paul A Dieppe ;Rheumatology (second edition)
4.Stephen Hoole; Cases for PACES (second edition)
5.Douglac C Macdonald ; Success in PACES (second edition)

CASE 48 : RHEUMATOID ARTHRITIS
SHIVANAN THIAGARAJAH & ESHA DAS GUPTA

OVERVIEW

Rheumatoid arthritis (RA) is a chronic autoimmune systemic inflammatory polyarthritis of unknown cause. The name 'Rheumatoid Arthritis' was coined by British physician Sir Alfred Garrod in 1859. The hallmark feature of this condition is persistent symmetric polyarthritis (due to synovitis) that affects mainly the hands and feet causing joint destruction and deformity. Other joints may be involved.

The rheumatoid disease process in the joints is characterized by synovitis (inflammatory effusion and cellular exudate into the joint space), which leads to damage of tendons, ligaments, cartilage, and bone in and around articulating surfaces of the joint. Long tendons (palms, wrists, ankles, and feet) are lined by synovial membrane are also involved in the inflammatory process resulting in damage, fibrosis and rupture.Consequently this causes malfunction and deformities of the affected joints.

Extra-articular involvement of organs such as the skin, heart, lungs, and eyes etc are also seen in rheumatoid arthritis.

RA is extremely heterozygous with regards to severity and progression. Women are affected by RA approximately 3 times more often than men but these differences diminish in the older age groups. Most of the patients have a waxing and waning course typical of the disease whereas in a small group of patients, the disease may progress rapidly to cause early destruction of the joints and deformity.

Management of this disease requires a multidisciplinary approach.

Types of cases for clinical examination:

      1.   Short /Long case

      2.   OSPE – X-ray or picture of 'rheumatoid hands'.

      3.   Long case – students would be expected to take a detailed history and perform a focused clinical examination of a patient who presents with joint pain.

CASE VIGNETTE

A 34-year old pianist presents with pain in the small joints of her hands of 2 months duration. She finds it difficult to play piano as she cannot move her finger joints freely and she also complains of difficulty in making a fist due to stiffness especially after waking up in the morning. This lasts for an hour. Recently she noticed some firm swelling on both her elbows. She has no fever or rash.

Obtain a full history from patient and perform a focused physical examination

History of Presenting Illness

- Onset– The typical case of rheumatoid arthritis begins insidiously, over weeks to months.
- Presence of stiffness in the joints, accompanied by pain and tenderness in the joint.

Patterns of joint involvement

- Usually polyarticular and bilateral symmetrical.

- Most frequently are the proximal interphalangeal (PIP) and metacarpophalangeal (MCP) joints of the hands, the wrists, and small joints of the feet - metatarsophalangeal (MTP) joints.

- The shoulders, elbows, knees, and ankles may also be affected.

- The distal interphalangeal (DIP) joints are spared.

- With the exception of the cervical spine, the spine is unaffected.

pain
stiffness
swelling
deformity
instability of thejt.

Characteristics of Rheumatic Symptoms

- Joint pain $> 30min$
- Morning stiffness (usually more than half an hour). It denotes inflammatory nature of origin as the stiffness becomes better with movement. (*unlike O A - worst w mov*)
- Joint swelling – (Joint pain with swelling constitutes arthritis, whereas joint pain without swelling is termedarthralgia.)
- Joint deformity

 Note: It is important to realize that joint deformity occurs late in disease.

- Instability of joints

Systemic Review

Note: There can be multi-organ involvement in RA.

A good systemic review is important to detect complications of disease and treatment.

Skin Involvement
- Palmar erythema
- Raynaud's phenomenon- Ask about skin changes, pain and altered sensation triggered by cold or emotion.
- Rheumatoid nodules- found in extensor surfaces, and areas of trauma (notable in elbow)

Note: Nodules are not specific to RA but useful for diagnosis and prognosis. It's usually seen in seropositive disease and has is a poor prognostic sign.

- Vasculitis – there may be purpuric rash that resolves spontaneously.

Constitutional symptoms:
- Fever, weight loss, fatigue, lethargy and anorexia – It gives an idea about systemic involvement and control of disease. It also can occur during episodes of acute flare

Note: Constitutional symptoms may affect the patient's quality of life. The RA patient may be too tired to perform daily chores.

Pulmonary involvement
- Pleurisy- presents with pleuratic chest pain
- Pleural effusion – presents with deceased effort tolerance and shortness of breath
- Pulmonary fibrosis – can occur as a part of disease or secondary to treatment (methotrexate)
- Rheumatoid pulmonary nodules – usually asymptomatic, may be mistaken for malignancy on chest radiograph .

Ophthalmic involvement
- Scleritis and scelomalacia – this occurs secondary to rheumatoid vasculitis and presents with painful eye.
- Dry eye – this occurs secondary to Sjögren Syndrome.

Note: Uveitis and conjunctivitis are not features of RA

Cardiovascular involvement

- It's important to asses for symptoms of ischemic heart disease. RA is associated with increased rate of cardiovascular disease most likely due to systemic inflammatory response.
- Pericarditis – presents as chest discomfort .

Neurological involvement

- Entrapment neuropathy – Carpal tunnel syndrome commonly occurs.
- Peripheral neuropathy- glove and stocking distribution
- Mononeuritis multiplex – acute onset of motor neuropathy

Note: Involvement of neuropathy signify aggressive vasculities and confers a poor prognosis .

- Cervical myelopathy - atlanto axial subluxation. Ask patient about pain, weakness and altered sensation of neck, upper limbs and lower limbs.

Fractures

- Generalized inflammation promotes osteoclastic activity causing periarticular osteoporosis. Inactivity, nutritional deficiency and treatment with steroids further increase the risk of fracture.

Infections

- Patient is at an increased risk of infection due to use of immunosuppressive drugs
- Infections may trigger flares

Complication of steroids

- Cataract , skin changes , diabetes , fractures , weight gain , hypertension.

Note: Patient may be on steroids prescribed by general practitioners or may be taking traditional medications containing steroids for several years.

Depression

- Patients with rheumatoid arthritis become debilitated by pain and fatigue and may experience psychological depression, anxiety, and loss of self-esteem, which require additional medical treatment and psychological support

Past Medical and Surgical History

- History of recent infection (D/D of other causes)
- Ask about operations for carpal tunnel syndrome and joint replacements.

Family History

- History of the same type of arthritis in the family

Social history

- Smoking
- An assessment of activities of daily living
- Occupation- patient's job may require use of fine function of hands. Is the patient still able to work?
- Alcohol intake- patients may be using alcohol to self-medicate pain and depression
- Financial burden and family support

Medication history

- Over the counter drug and analgesic use.
- Traditional medication use.

Note: Remember the patient may have seen other doctors or may have seen a traditional practitioner. They may be taking medications that contain steroids or analgesic that may lead to many complications.

Check list for history taking
- ✓ Mode of onset (acute verses insidious)
- ✓ Duration of morning stiffness
- ✓ Number of joints affected
- ✓ Symmetrical involvement
- ✓ Joints affected (small versus big)
- ✓ Aggravating and relieving factors
- ✓ Extra-articular manifestations
- ✓ Family history
- ✓ Determine the level of disability
- ✓ Activity of daily living
- ✓ A good social history
- ✓ Ask about the patient's social support network

EXAMINATION

Introduce yourself and explain your intentions to the patient. Ask about the painful joints and obtain permission to examine.

General inspection

General inspection gives an idea of the patient's functional disability. Also look around the room as it can give you clues (e.g. walking frame/ stick).

Examine the joints following look, feel, move technique.

Examination of the hands:

Look:

Place both the hands on a pillow. Compare both the hands. Inspect the palmer as well as dorsal aspects of the palms.

(While inspecting do not hold the patient's hands, allow the patient move the hands)

 Look for

- Symmetrical involvement
- Swelling of MCP, PIP and wrist joints with sparing of DIP joints.
- Deformity- swan neck, Boutonniere
- Z deformity of the thumb (caused by rupture of thumb flexors) and ulnar deviation of the fingers.
- Subluxation of the small joints.
- Palmer Erythema (a sign of active RA)
- Nail fold infarct if any
- Rule out other nail changes of Psoriatic Arthritis
- Signs of carpal tunnel syndrome
- Rheumatoid nodule at the elbow

Note: Deformities may not be present in most well treated patient as it occurs late in disease.

- *'Swan neck' – hyperextension of PIP joint and fixed flexion of DIP joint-caused by interossei contracture and shortening of the extensor tendon*
- *'Boutonniere' –flexion of the PIP joint and extension of the DIP joint- caused by division of the extensor head with volar slipping or rupture of the tendon.*

Feel for

- Increased temperature of the joints
- Feel for all MCP, PIP, wrist joints between your thumb and forefingers for the tenderness and swelling

- It is usually 'boggy' swelling of the small joints (signifies synovial thickening)
- Feel for the ulnar styloid which may be floating due to destruction of underlined ligament (piano key sign)
- Tenderness of the joints

(Must always maintain eye contact with the patient and be very gentle as not to cause discomfort to the patient)

Move

- Test for power grip (ask the patient to squeeze your fingers)
- Ask to open and spread the fingers apart
- Ask to do the 'prayer sign'(wrist dorsiflexion) and reverse 'prayer sign' (palmar flexion)
- Ask the patient to put the hands behind the patient's head
- Look for thumb movement (opponens, abductors, lexors of the thumb to look for medial nerve entrapment)
- Assessment of function can be done by asking patient to :
i) Squeeze your hand – power grip
ii) Unbutton shirt / pick up coin – precision grip
iii) Turning door knob , pretend to use key

Note: Active assessment of function shows the examiner that you are determining the patient's welfare and functional needs.

Examination of other joints: Namely elbows, shoulder, feet, ankles, knees and hips for inflammation and synovitis.

Systemic Examination:

Skin Examination:
- Raynaud's phenomenon- looks for pulp infarcts
- Vasculitis – look for purpuric rash over the body. Look at the tip of the fingers for vasculitis.

Note: It is important to look for nail changes (pitting and onycolysis) and psoriatic plaques over the extensor surfaces, elbows, back of the ears, scalp and around the umbilicus.

Psoriasis is the main differential diagnosis of RA.

Ophthalmic involvement
- Scleritis and scelomalacia – red eye
- Dry eyes -Sjögren Syndrome.

Pulmonary involvement
- Pleurisy- plural rub

- Pleural effusion – <u>reduced chest wall expansion</u>, <u>dull percussion node</u>, <u>reduced air entry</u>.
- Pulmonary fibrosis – Fine end inspiratory crepitations.

Cardiovascular involvement
- Pericarditis – pericardial rub.

Neurological involvement
- Entrapment neuropathy – Carpal tunnel syndrome
- Peripheral neuropathy- glove and stocking distribution
- Mononeuritis multiplex – acute onset of motor neuropathy
- Cervical myelopathy - atlanto axial subluxation.

Haematological
- Anaemia- pallor, angular stomatitis
- Felty's syndrome- Splenomegaly

Check list for clinical examination
- ✓ Symmetrical arthropathy
- ✓ Warm and boggy swelling of the joints
- ✓ Tenderness of the joints
- ✓ Sparing of the DIP joints
- ✓ Wasting of the small muscles of the hand
- ✓ Palmer erythema
- ✓ Nail fold infarcts
- ✓ +/- vasculitic skin lesion
- ✓ Various deformities
- ✓ Rheumatoid nodule
- ✓ Movements of the hands
- ✓ Look for systemic involvement

INVESTIGATIONS

Blood Investigations:

- Full blood count
- i) Anaemia (may be microcytic, macrocytic or normocytic).
- ii) Platelet (increased in inflammation, reduced in Felty's syndrome, autoimmune involvement)
- iii) WBC (raised in acute flare and infection, reduced in Felty syndrome immunosuppression and sequestration.

- Electrolytes and liver function test – Baseline needed before starting treatment. Methotrexate and anti TNF may affect liver function. Globulin will be raised in active disease.

- Inflammatory markers (CRP, ESR) – This is an inflammatory disease and the markers will give an idea on control of disease.

- Hepatitis B and Hepatitis C serology: this is a prerequisite before starting biologics as it may cause flare of hepatitis.

- Rheumatoid factor: Positive in 65% of cases. Whereas may be falsely positive in elderly.

- Anti-citrullinated protein antibodies: Has high specificity for Rheumatoid arthritis.

Note: Anti CCP is an important marker for diagnosis and confers poor prognosis in RA. It's a marker for erosive disease.

Radiological
- X ray of the affected joints: look for soft tissue swelling, narrowing of the joint space, periarticular osteopenia, and bone erosion.
- X ray of cervical spine if suspected atlanto axial involvement. May need to proceed to do MRI depending on symptoms
- Chest X ray – A baseline radiograph serves to compare x-rays during progression of disease. Look fibrotic changes (may require a (HRCT) high resolution computer topography scan).

Special investigations:
Note: Remember that there can be multiple organ involvement in RA; so relevant investigations should be tailored towards symptoms. (e.g. Lung function test, ECG , Endoscopy etc.)

CASE SUMMARY

This 34 year old lady, a pianist, has Rheumatoid Arthritis affecting the hands as evidenced by symmetrical polyarthropathy affecting her proximal interphalangeal joints and metacarpophalangeal joints and sparing of distal interphalangeal joints. Her joints are swollen, tender and there is reduced range of movements. She also has rheumatoid nodules on her elbow. Her daily living activities are restricted as she is unable to button her clothes. She also has difficulty playing the piano.

CLINICAL DISCUSSION OF THE CASE

A summary of the history and examination findings should be stated. A likely diagnosis is then proposed with supporting factors explained. Then, a reasonable list of relevant investigations should be compiled for further discussion.

How would you manage a patient with RA?

The main aims of management of RA include
1. Symptom relief (pain relief)
2. Physical function maintenance (through, physical therapy, occupational therapy)
3. Prevention of structural damage to joints (early institution of DMARDS)
4. Restore and maintain quality of life (the ultimate goal is to allow the patient to pursue normal work, domestic, and social life)
5. Manage complications arising from disease and treatment of disease.

This is achieved through a multidisciplinary approach which includes the physician other medical and health-care professionals, including specialist nurses, physiotherapists, occupational therapists, and social workers.
Non pharmacological

- Patient education – Inform the patient of the diagnosis and the natural disease progression. RA is a potentially disabling disease and the aim will be to prevent joint deformity and loss of function. Patient will have their own perceptions and concerns about joint disease. It is important to listen to the patient emphatically and allay any misconceptions about their disease.
- Physical therapy and occupational therapy– exercise program to maintain posture and rage of motion. Occupational therapy is aimed at rehabilitation and teaching patients how to maximize their limitations so that they can still care for themselves. The therapist also can help to change home gadgets to suit her.
- Joint protection - provides the patient with techniques and recommendations for the prevention of joint overuse and the avoidance of biomechanical torques that excessively bend the joint
- Support group: Patients will do well when they are able to interact and share experiences with other patients with RA. It keeps patient motivated and generate a positive outlook in dealing with their disease

Pharmacological

Analgesic

- Analgesic like NASIDS/ COX 2 inhibitors –produce symptomatic relief and reduce inflammation of joints .

Note: NSAIDS can cause, GI ulcers, interstitial nephritis and increase risk of cardiovascular morbidity .

DMARDS

- Disease modifying anti rheumatic drugs (DMARDS) –delay disease progression and reduce subsequent disability when introduced early in disease.

Note: DMARDS can cause bone marrow suppression and skin rash. This is some specific side effects of particular DMARDS.

- Hydroxychloroquine- retinal toxicity and maculopathy
- Sulphasalazine- leukopenia, pancytopenia, haemolysis, hepatitis
- Methotrexate- bone marrow suppression (folate deficiency), pulmonary fibrosis, hepatitis , (kena bg dṣn folate)
- Penicillamine – drug induced lupus , nephrotic syndrome .
- Leflunomide- myelosuppression , hepatitis , diarrhoea , alopecia
- Cyclosporine - hypertension, renal toxicity , dyslipidaemia , hyperuricemia

- Glucocoticoids-is used to reduce active disease and whilst waiting for DMARDS to take action. Associated with much complication in long term use.

Biologics

Biologic therapy should only be instituted by a rheumatologist. Patients should fulfil criteria based on guidelines before subjecting patients to their use.

- Anti TNF – Etarnacept, infliximab
- Anti CD20 – Rituximab
- Interleukin 1 receptor antagonist -anakinra

Note: Beware of TB and atypical pneumonia resulting from use of Anti TNF.

Surgical

Surgical interventions can be introduced to limit disability. Some commonly performed surgeries are as below .

- Decompression of carpal tunnel
- Reconstructive arthroplasty- hip, knee, shoulder elbow and small joints of hand.
- Corrective arthrotomies of metatarsals
- Stabilization of cervical spine
- Tendon release and transfer
- Arthrodesis

LEARNING OUTCOMES

By the end of this case review the student should be able to:
- Take a detailed history of a patient who presents with joint pain.
- Identify deformities of Rheumatoid Arthritis.
- Perform a relevant and focused clinical examination of a patient who has Rheumatoid Arthritis
- Discuss the differential diagnosis of polyarticular involvement
- Discuss the principles of management of Rheumatoid Arthritis

Differential Diagnoses: Basically the differential diagnoses of polyarthritis are:

1. Undifferentiated seronegative polyarthritis (fails to meet classification criteria for RA. Up to 20 per cent of cases may evolve into RA)
2. Psoriatic arthritis/other seronegative spondylo arthritis (10 percent of psoriatic arthritis will have an RA-like distribution (MCPs, PIPs, wrists).
3. Systemic lupus erythematosus(Chronic non deforming inflammatory polyarthritis)
4. Nodal osteoarthritis (Elderly age of onset. Distal interphalangeal joints may be involved. Swellings are bony))

COMMONLY ASKED QUESTIONS

What are the poor prognostic indicators of Rheumatoid Arthritis?
- *Age younger than 30 years*
- *Insidious onset and high disease activity at onset (high ESR , CRP)*
- *High levels of Rheumatoid factor and presence of anti cyclic citrullinated peptide Ab (Anti CCP)*
- *Rheumatoid nodules*
- *Early bone erosions in X-ray (within 1 year)*

- *Extra articular manifestations and systemic symptoms (vasculitis)*
- *Large number of involved joints*
- *Persistent activity despite 1 year of treatment (high ESR/ CRP, active joint symptoms)*

What is Rheumatoid Factor(RF) ?

RF are antibodies against the Fc portion of IgG. These, in simple terms are antibodies against antibodies. They are not specific to RA. They can be seen in low titres during repeated acute infections and found in other chronic inflammatory conditions (e.g. SLE, scleroderma). About 5% of normal population and about 25% of elderly people has positive RF.

What is Sjögren's syndrome?

Sjögren's syndrome is an disorder of the immune system presenting with dry eyes (keratoconjunctivitis sicca) and dry mouth (xerostomia) . Sjögren's syndrome is often associated with connective tissue disorders like RA and SLE . It is also commonly seen in autoimmune conditions like thyroid disease, myasthenia gravis and autoimmune hepatitis.

What is the new classification criteria for Rheumatoid arthritis By ACR /EULAR?

ACR/EULAR 2010 classification criteria for Rheumatoid Arthritis	
JOINT DISTRIBUTION (0-5)	
1 large joint	0
2-10 large joints	1
1-3 small joints (large joints not counted)	2
4-10 small joints (large joints not counted)	3
>10 joints (at least one small joint)	5
SEROLOGY (0-3)	
Negative RF AND negative Anti CCP	0
Low positive RF OR low positive Anti CCP	2
High positive RF OR high positive Anti CCP	3
SYMPTOM DURATION (0-1)	
<6 weeks	0
≥6 weeks	1
ACUTE PHASE REACTANTS (0-1)	
Normal CRP AND normal ESR	0
Abnormal CRP OR abnormal ESR	1
Patient needs to have 6 points and above for RA.	

What is the 1987 American Collage Rheumatology Criteria for RA?

Summary of 1987 ACR classification criteria for Rheumatoid Arthritis
• Patients must have four of the seven criteria:
• Morning stiffness lasting at least 1 hour*
• Swelling in three or more joints*
• Swelling in hand joints*
• Symmetric joint swelling*
• Erosions on x-ray of hand
• Rheumatoid nodules
• Positive serum rheumatoid factor.
• *Must be present at least six weeks.

Note: It is important to understand that these are classification criteria and not diagnostic criteria. Diagnosis is still based on clinical findings . The EULAR criteria helps pick up early RA so that treatment can be instituted early as opposed to the 1987 ACR criteria.

DISTINCTION LEVEL QUESTION

What are the causes of anaemia in RA?

- *Iron deficiency* – *(microcytic hypochromic) – due to gastrointestinal blood loss from NSAIDS*
- *Megaloblastic anemia* – *(macrocytic anaemia) Pernicious anaemia can occur in RA. Patient on methotrexate can have folate deficiency.*
- *Anemia of chronic disease* – *can occur due to RA. Inflammatory mediators suppress erythropoiesis*
- *Felty's Syndrome Hypersplenism secondary to RA causes sequestration of RBC*
- *Bone marrow suppression /Aplasia – may occur secondary to drugs like Gold, Penicillamine*

What is Felty's syndrome ? (hypersplenism 2° RA)
This is a condition where a patient with rheumatoid factor positive rheumatoid arthritis has splenomegaly, anaemia, leucopoenia and thrombocytopenia as well as leg ulcers. Splenomegaly causes sequestration of RBC, WBC and platelets. Splenectomy ameliorates hypersplenism.

What are the respiratory complications / features of rheumatoid arthritis?

- *Upper airway – cricoarytenitis (may present with stridor)*
- *Pleura – may cause pleural effusion, pleurisy*
- *Bronchioles – (BOOP) bronchiolitis obliterans organizing pneumonia*

- *Lung parenchyma - Pulmonary fibrosis (may occur due to Ra or due to treatment with DMARDs(e.g. Methotrexate)*
- *Infiltration – Rheumatoid nodules can be seen in lung*

Note: Cryptogenic fibrosing alveolitis is associated with RA. Clubbing, cyanosis and fine inspiratory crepitations are then features.

What is the neurological manifestation of RA?
- *Peripheral neuropathy (glove and stocking distribution)*
- *Entrapment neuropathy – carpal tunnel syndrome*
- *Mononeuritis multiplex*
- *Cervical myelopathy - atlanto axial subluxation*

COMMON MISTAKES

- Not asking the patient if she is in pain before moving the patient. It reflects badly on the candidate if pain is caused to the patient.
- Not assessing functional status of patient
- Not looking for complication of the disease
- Not approaching investigations and management systematically
- A distinction student will go one step higher and look for complications of treatment

MUST KNOW FACTS ABOUT RHEUMATOID ARTHRITIS

- ✓ Joint symptoms in RA
- ✓ Joints involved in RA
- ✓ Associated extra articular complications in RA
- ✓ How to differentiate RA from other polyarthropathies
- ✓ Investigations and their rational
- ✓ Basic management principles

Reference:

1. Barton A, Worthington J. Genetic susceptibility to rheumatoid arthritis: an emerging picture. *Arthritis Rheum*. Oct 15 2009;61(10):1441-6.
2. Lipsky PE. Harrison's Principles of Internal Medicine. In: Isselbacher KJ, Braunwald E, Fauci AS, et al. *Rheumatoid arthritis*. 17th ed. New York, NY: McGraw-Hill; 1994:1648-55.

CASE 49 : POLYARTICULAR GOUT (CHRONIC TOPHACEOUS GOUT)
SHIVANAN THIAGARAJAH & ESHA DAS GUPTA

Since the time of the Greeks, gout was considered as the "disease of the kings," primarily because its association with a diet rich in meat and alcohol . The word gout was initially used by Randolphus of Bocking, around 1200 -1300AD. It is derived from the Latin word gutta, meaning "a drop" (of liquid). In 1679 the Dutch scientist Antonie van Leeuwenhoek first described the microscopic appearance of urate crystals. In 1848 English physician Sir Alfred Baring Garrod realized that this excess uric acid in the blood was the cause of gout,but the pathophysiology of acute gouty arthritis was not described fully until 1962.

Gout is a disorder of purine metabolism resulting in hyperuricaemia either by overproduction or under secretion of uric acid, which in turn deposits as urate crystals in the joints or bursae. The higher the serum uric acid level and the longer it remains elevated, the greater the amount of crystal deposit in joints and tissue.

Gout is characterized by attacks of acute inflammatory severe arthritis usually involve a single joint. The 1st metatarsophalangeal joint (podagra) is typically affected but can also occur over ankle, foot, knee, wrist, elbow and small joints of hand. Lower limb is more affected that upper limb and in the order of heel, ankle, knee. Gout is typically of remitting and relapsing in nature. With recurrent attacks joint show signs of damage with varying degrees of synovitis that clinically manifesting as restricted movement, crepitus and deformity.

Untreated gout evolves slowly through four clinical phases:

i) Asymptomatic hyperuricaemia

ii) Acute gout- acute self-limiting (2 weeks) mono articular arthritis

iii) Intercritical gout-periods between attacks that patients are asymptomatic. Patient may have recurrent attacks and either same joint or more joints are involved

iv) Chronic tophaceous gout- there is poly articular arthritis with crystal deposits ('tophi')

v) Uric acid nephropathy

Gout has a male predominance (male: female, 4:1). Prevalence of gout rises with age and increasing serum urate concentration. It starts to affect men in their fourth decade but women usually are affected after 65 (estrogen has protective uricosuric effect).

When gout presents with polyarticular involvement it needs to be differentiated from rheumatoid arthritis, generalized nodal osteoarthritis, psoriatic arthropathy and xanthomatosis .

Types of cases for clinical examination:

Short /long case – Examine this patient's hands and feet

OSPE – Picture of urate crystals , picture of podagra ,X-ray of gouty joint

Long case – Students would be expected to take a detailed history and perform a focused clinical examination eliciting the multisystem involvement of the disease

---

CASE VIGNETTE

A 38-year-old man, presents with acute painful swelling of his hands and feet on waking up early in the morning. He says he had dinner with his friends previous night. In the past he has had recurrent episodes (4-5 times per year) of toes and ankle swelling. Each episode leaves him in severe pain for couple of days but then resolves completely. He remembers the left big toe was affected the very first time after having a hearty meal for his cousin's wedding. He usually buys medication from a pharmacy when these episodes occur. He has done a recent medical checkup as a prerequisite of changing job and was found to have impaired fasting glucose, dyslipedemia and mild hypertension. He is not on treatment but was advised on diet modification and weight loss.

HISTORY TAKING

HISTORY OF PRESENTING ILLNESS

Hand joint swelling

- Ask patient which joints are affected (small or large)?
- Ask if the distribution symmetrical or not?
- Ask the sequence of joint involvement and which joints are involved?
- Ask how long he has the symptoms?
- Ask if there is stiffness and duration of stiffness? (will occur inflammatory condition like RA but also can be a feature of mechanical problem)
- Ask if there is swelling or redness and if the joints feel hot? (denotes inflammation / acute flare)
- Ask if there is any recent trauma? (trauma can precipitate gout)
- Ask if there is skin rash or nail changes? (rule out psoriatic arthropathy)
- Ask about precipitating and relieving factors? (gout *aggravated after a high purine meal or drugs like diuretics*)

Note: the main aim of taking a joint history is to differentiate between the different polyarticular arthritis (e.g. rheumatoid arthritis, osteoarthritis, psoriatic arthritis,

- Ask patient about functional limitation. Can the patient do activities of daily living (eating, bathing, dressing) independently?
- Ask if there is a progressive change in affected joint shape (Deformities)?
- Ask if patient has a feeling that joint is 'giving way' or 'coming out' (instability)?
- Ask if there is any change in sensation over the joint?

Note: there can be neuropathic pain or paraesthesiae in nerve entrapment or damage from ischemia.

PAST MEDICAL HISTORY
- Patient may be having a past history of mono articular acute gout typically affecting the big toe. These attacks are usually self-limiting. This if left untreated may progress to chronic tophaceous gout.
- Metabolic syndrome- hypertriglyceridemia low high density lipoprotein, hypertension, obesity and diabetes are known associations.
- Chronic renal failure reduces excretion of uric acid and hence serum uric acid becomes high.
- Ask patient about renal colic. Hyperurecimia may lead to nephrolithiasis
- Ask patient about previous treatment and visits to doctors.

SURGICAL HISTORY
- History of ureteric colic or nephrolithiasis.

FAMILY HISTORY
- Family history may increases risk.

SOCIAL HISTORY
- Ask about occupation and is symptoms may be affecting work?
- Alcohol intake also can precipitate gout. Always quantify the intake of alcohol .check for dependence with CAGE assessment. *(CAGE; cut down , angry ,guilty , eye opener)*
- Ask about diet as high purine diet (e.g. meat, shellfish, liver) which may precipitate acute attacks.

Note: It's important to take a detailed social history and occupational history to determine functional limitation. It is always advisable to enquire about financial burden and the social support of the patient. Acute attack is usually precipitated by acute illness, trauma, surgery, purine rich food and alcohol

DRUG HISTORY

- Take a history of over the counter drug and analgesic use.
- Take history of traditional medication use.
- Take history of diuretic use (especially thiazide)
- Take a history of traditional medication.

Note: remember patient may have seen other doctors or may have seen a traditional practitioner. Patient with gout often may have renal disease which can be made worse by traditional medication or analgesics.

SYSTEMIC REVIEW OF SYMPTOMS

Etiology of secondary gout:

i) Myeloproliferative disorders/ Lymphoproliferative disease : (anemia , constitutional symptoms, lymphadenopathy)

ii) Hemolytic anemia : (anemia , jaundice , recurrent transfusions)

Note: Remember gout can also occur from increased production of urate in conditions like (myeloproliferative disorders, lymphoproliferative disorders, tumor lysis syndrome and chronic hemolysis)

Endocrine

Ask for symptoms of hypothyroidism

Ask about symptoms of diabetes (polyuria , polydiposia, polyphagia)

Note: hypothyroidism causes reduced uric acid excretion

Renal

Ask about renal colic

Ask about blood in the urine

Ask about symptoms of chronic renal failure (fatigue , nausea , vomiting)

Constitutional symptoms:

Ask about constitutional symptoms (fever, weight loss, fatigue, lethargy, anorexia) as it may give a clue about sinister underlying pathology. Fever is common with acute gouty attack.

Depression:
Note: many patient may feel depressed due to disfigurement or pain . This may have significant impact on disease and well being of patients. Patients who are depressed are less likely to adhere to management.

Note: a good candidate should take thorough systemic review in order to differentiate other rheumatologic and autoimmune disorders. The systemic review should include eye symptoms, skin rash, Raynaud's phenomenon, cardiac symptoms, respiratory symptoms, gastrointestinal symptoms and urinary symptoms .

Note: A good candidate must always try to determine patients preconceived ideas about his disease and understand his concerns and expectation.

Check list for history taking
- ✓ Take a thorough history of joint disorder to differentiate gout from the other polyarticular arthritis
- ✓ Get a history of recurrent acute gout that is untreated
- ✓ Identify factors associated with gout (metabolic syndrome, renal disease, obesity)
- ✓ Identify history of renal calculi
- ✓ Identify etiology of secondary hyperuricemia (alcoholism , heamatological malignancy , drugs)
- ✓ Determine the functional status of patient
- ✓ Determine patient's concerns

EXAMINATION

Introduce yourself and explain to the patient you would like to examine him.

General inspection
General inspection gives an idea of the patient's functional disability. Also look around the room as it can give you clues (e.g. walking frame/ stick).

In Gout you must looks for:
- Look at general nutritional status. Comment on obesity
- Look for anemia /plethoric appearance (polycytemia rubra vera)

- Look for sallow appearance and any evidence of chronic renal failure or dialysis (AV fistulas, peritoneal dialysis catheter or scars of previous internal jugular catheter or femoral insertion)
- Look for signs attributed to chronic alcohol use or liver damage(palmar erythema, dupytren's contracture, bilateral parotid enlargement)
- Look for signs attributed to diabetes (diabetic dermopathy)

Look
- Look for swelling of small joints of the hand (asymmetrical)
- Look for joint deformity/ damage – note any restricted movement, crepitus, deformity
- Look for tophi (crystal deposits) which are irregular firm translucent nodules , principally around extensor surfaces of fingers, hands, the ulnar surface of the forearms, olecranon bursae. They are also found in the Achilles tendons, first metatarsophalangeal joints
- Always look at the cartilaginous helix of the ear where you may find tophi.
- Look for 'chalky' appearance of crystals beneath the skin.
- Look for ulcerated swelling discharging material which is white and gritty
- Look for local inflammation /active arthritis (erythema, warm , tender)
- Look for wasting of the intrinsic muscles of the hands

Note: Florid tendon xanthomata can resemble tophaceous gout but it can be distinguished by the following:

i) *There will be no active arthritis in tendon xanthomata*
ii) *There is no involvement of bursa or the pinna in tendon xanthomata*
iii) *Tendon xantomata is attached to tendons and not joints like in gout*
iv) *The xanthomata deposits are yellow as compared to the chalky deposits of gout*

Feel and Move
- Feel the affected joints for swelling (synovitis, effusion , crepitation)
- Feel joints for increased temperature and tenderness (active arthritis)
- Examine movement of joints (reduced range of movement)

Functional status of patient

Check patient's daily functions by asking her to imitate actions of

- Button/ unbutton shirt
- Holding a cup , holding a pen
- Turning a door knob / using a key
- Combing hair /bathing self

Note: This is very important because you can gauge the patient's ability to take care of him and it shows that you are looking into patient's welfare actively.

To complete examination:

- Request to check patient weight height and waist circumference (obesity)
- Request to check patient Blood Pressure and do fundoscopy examination (hypertension)
- Request to check urine dipstick for glycosuria, hematuria (kidney stones)

Note: attempt must be made to differentiate between acute gout and chronic inactive gout . Usually the acute gout will present with pain. Some patients may have fever , cellulitis ,joint effusion and bursitis. The later is usually painless. When dealing with monoarticular acute gout, always rule out septic arthritis as it also presents as monoarthritis.

Check list for clinical examination
- ✓ Look at general condition of patient
- ✓ Look for tophi deposits
- ✓ Examine for acute gouty arthritis
- ✓ Look aetiology of gout – focus examination
- ✓ Examine functional status

INVESTIGATIONS

Blood Investigations:

- Full blood count – baseline panel needs to be done to exclude infection. Hematological malignancies (lymphoma, leukemia) may present with gout.
  Note: WBC count may be raised in acute gouty attack.
- Electrolytes and liver function test –Chronic renal failure commonly can lead to hyperuricaemia and conversely urate nephropathy and nephrolithiasis can derange renal function.

- Urine full examination and microscopic examination (UFUME) to look for proteinuria or blood suggesting renal disorder.
- Fasting Blood sugar and Fasting Lipid profile – Patient of metabolic syndrome have higher incidence of hyperuricaemia. hypertriglyceridemia and low high-density lipoproteins are associated with gout
- Serum uric acid level- May be increased in acute / chronic gout. However cannot be used to confirm or exclude gout. Clinical correlation is important. *In one tenth of patients uric acid remains normal during acute attack.*
- Erythrocyte sedimentation rate (ESR) – this is usually is elevated during acute attacks.

Specific Investigations

Joint fluid microscopy and culture:

– Joint fluid aspiration and examination under polarized light microscope is still the gold standard. It will show negatively bifringent crystals of mono sodium urate in the synovial fluid. Uric acid crystals appear as needle-shaped negative birefringent, intracellular and extracellular crystals under polarizing light.

The joint fluid should be sent for analysis, cell count and differential count, Gram stain, culture as well to rule out septic arthritis when in doubt.

Joint radiographs

X-rays of affected joint or joints with established disease may show punched-out erosions or lytic areas with overhanging edges. There may me soft tissue swelling denoting the tophus.

Note: there may be no radiographic changes in new onset or acute gout

Ultrasound Kidney

Urate crystals are radiolucent. In the event that creatinine is derange or there are symptoms suggestive of renal stones an ultrasound needs to be done to exclude it .

CASE SUMMARY

This patient has chronic tophaceous gout affecting his hands and his feet. There is asymmetrical swelling affecting the small joints of the hands with tophi exuding chalky material along with marked deformity. The joints are tender, and erythematous suggesting there is an acute inflammation .There is also presence of tophi on the extensor aspects of the forearms, the left olecranon bursae, the left pinna of the ear as well as the small joints of is feet. He is unable to do fine movement of his hands due to pain. He is suspected of having metabolic syndrome as evidenced by history of hypertension, hypeglycaemia and dyslipidaemia.

CLINICAL DISCUSSION OF THE CASE

How would you manage a patient with gout?

Non pharmacological

- Patient education – gout is a chronic disease which requires understanding and patient's active involvement in the management.
- Advice lifestyle modification :
    - i) Gradual weight loss
    - ii) Reduction in alcohol consumption(more with beer and wine)
    - iii) Avoid precipitating purine rich food
    - iv) Increased water intake
- Physical therapy and occupational therapy– exercise program to maintain posture and rage of motion. Occupational therapy is aimed at rehabilitation and teaching patients how to maximize their limitations so that they can still care for themselves.
- Manage associated hypertension dyslipidemia and diabetes mellitus

Pharmacological Acute attack

- i) NSAIDS – Indomethacin
- ii) Colchicine
- iii) Intra articular steroids
- iv) Systemic steroids (especially in renal insufficiency hepatic dysfunction, heart failure or hypersensitivity to NSAIDS)

Asymptomatic hyperuricemia should generally not be treated. However, patients with levels higher than 660 µmol/l .who overexcrete uric acid are at risk for renal stones and renal impairment; therefore, renal function should be monitored in these individuals. The goal of therapy is to lower serum uric acid levels to approximately below 360 µmol/l .

- Prophylactic agents against gouty attacks

i)   Xanthine oxidase inhibitor-Allopurinol, Febuxostat

ii)   Uricosuric acid agents- probenecid, sulfinpyrazone

☞ Note: In case of renal impairment uricosuric agents should not be used. Xanthine oxidase inhibitor should not be started during acute attack.It may be started at least 2 weeks after the acute attack. Otherwise there is danger of continuation of the attack. Whereas while on Allopurinol the patient develops another attack,it is not necessary to stop Allopurinol.

Surgical management

Surgery may be indicated for tophaceous gout complications in the following circumstances

    i)   infection,
    ii)   joint deformity, loss of function (arthroplasty)
    iii)   compression symptoms
    iv)   Intractable pain,
    v)   cosmetic reasons

LEARNING OUTCOMES

By the end of this case review the student should be able to:
- Take good history gout.
- Able to differentiate between acute gout and chronic gout
- Examine the skin and focused specific organ for complications
- Formulate the appropriate investigations explain rationale for performing them.
- Outline the principles of management.

COMMONLY ASKED QUESTIONS

What are the factors that can trigger a gout attack?
1)   *Foods – red meat, sweetbreads, sea food, sardine, solid internal organs (brains, kidney) ,anchovies fructose-rich foods*
2)   *Alcohol ingestion- especially beer*
3)   *Drugs – Thiazide diuretics, aspirin, cyclosporine, anti-tuberculosis drugs (pyrazinamide and ethambutol)*

4) *Dehydration and fasting- catabolic state increase urate production and ketoacidosis promotes joint deposition in joints*
5) *Trauma or surgery – catabolic states produce urate*
6) *Sepsis – catabolic state increases urate and lactic acidosispromotes joint deposition in joints*

What is the target uric acid level in a patient with Gout?
Uric acid should be kept below 360 μmol/l .

What is Pseudogout?
Acute arthritis caused by deposition of calcium pyrophosphate dihydrate crystals in the joints. These are weakly positively birefringent rhomboid shaped crystals under polarized light. The joints that are often affected wrist, knee, shoulder or polyarticular .

DISTINCTION LEVEL QUESTION

What are the indications for allopurinol?
i) *Recurrent episodes of acute gouty attacks (more than 3 times a year)*
ii) *Presence of tophaceous deposits (Chronic tophaceous gout)*
iii) *Presence of urate nephropathy*
iv) *Presence urate nephrolithiasis*
v) *Cytotoxic chemotherapy or radiotherapy for lymphoma or leukaemia*

How is the presentation of gout in elderly patients different?
i) *There is more likely polyarticular involvement.*
ii) *Higher proportion of women (when age >80)*
iii) *More likely to involve small joints of fingers*
iv) *Tophi develops early in the course of illness*
v) *Higher association with renal disease and diuretic use.*

How do you manage urate nephropathy?
1) *Increase urine output - increase water intake more than 2.5 liters per day*
2) *Increase urine pH – prevent precipitation of urate stones (potassium citrate / Sodium bicarbonate)*
3) *Decrease serum urate– using allopurinol and limiting intake purine intake*

COMMON MISTAKES

- Not asking the patient if he is in pain before moving the patient. It reflects badly on the candidate if pain is caused to the patient.

- Not assessing functional status of patient
- Not looking associated condition with gout

MUST KNOW FACTS OF GOUT

- ✓ Gouty arthritis common presentation (monoarticular , polyarticular)
- ✓ Recognize associated conditions that increase risk of gout
- ✓ Recognize gouty tophi and its common sites
- ✓ Investigations for gout (recognize gouty crystals under microscope)
- ✓ Basic management principles

REFERENCE

1) **Weinberger A**. *Gout, uric acid metabolism, and crystal-induced inflammation. Curr Opin Rheumatol1995;7:359–63.*

2) **Hadler N**, *Frank WA, Bress N, Robinson DR. Polyarticular gout. Am J Med1976;56:715–19.*

3) **Cohen MG**, Emmerson BT. Gout. In: Klippel JH, Dieppe PA, eds. *Rheumatology*. 2nd ed. London: Mosby; 1998:8:14.1.

CASE 50 : SYSTEMIC LUPUS ERYTHEMATOSUS
SHIVANAN THIAGARAJAH & ESHA DAS GUPTA

OVERVIEW

Systemic Lupus Erythematosus(SLE) is an autoimmune inflammatory disease with multisystem involvement and of unknown etiology. There is excessive autoantiboby production some of which cause cytotoxic damage, while others precipitate immune complex formation resulting in immune inflammation. It comes under 'connective tissue disorder' as mostly the connective tissues are affected.

The term 'lupus' a Latin word for wolf, was first used in 18th century. It is thought that the term was such as the rash resembled a wolf bite. Laurent Theodor Biett a Swidish dermatologist and his student Cazenave gave first historical account of lupus in 1833.Then it was considered as a dermatological condition. In 1872 Moritz Kaposi described the systemic nature of SLE. Current understanding of SLE has evolved after discovery of LE cell by Hargraves in 1948.

SLE is characterized by multisystem microvascular inflammation with the generation of autoantibodies. Although the specific cause of SLE is unknown, multiple factors are associated with the development of the disease, including genetic, racial, hormonal, and environmental factors. The development of autoantibodies involves a defect in apoptosis that causes increased cell death and a disturbance in immune tolerance.

The main factors are thought to be:

1. Genetic predisposition (more incidence among twins, racial difference)
2. Environmental influence (Sun light,drugs)
3. Hormonal (more among ladies)

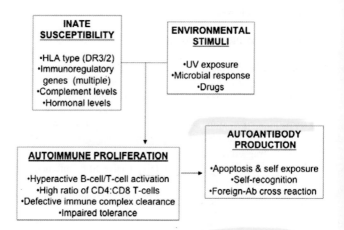

SLE frequently starts in women of childbearing age, and the use of exogenous hormones has been associated with lupus onset and flares, suggesting a role for hormonal factors in the pathogenesis of the disease. The female to male ratio is at 9:1 during the childbearing years.

Types of cases for clinical examination:

8) Short /long case – Examine this patient's face and proceed.
9) OSPE – Pictures of classical butterfly rash (spot diagnosis) , Laboratory investigation for interpretation
10) Long case – Students would be expected to take a detailed history and perform a focused clinical examination eliciting the multisystem involvement of the disease

---

2. CASE VIGNETTE

A 30-year-old lady, presents with joint swelling and stiffness, and extreme fatigue for past 3 months. She first noted stiffness in her fingers in the morning and after activity such as typing on the computer. About 2 months ago she noticed swelling in her fingers and wrists along with fever. She describes the pain as intermittent, most notable in the morning and after activity involving her hands and knees. She complains of tiredness and fatigue the whole day and on questioning she admits of facial rash after sun exposure.

HISTORY TAKING

HISTORY OF PRESENTING ILLNESS

Note: SLE presentations may vary from patient to patient but most patients have either joint or skin manifestation. A good systemic review must be done to look for the multi system involvement of the disease.

Constitutional symptoms

- Ask about easy fatigability and tiredness (active SLE, may suggest anaemia)
- Ask about on and off fever (active SLE, infection due to autoimmune state)
- Ask about weight changes (weight loss, sometimes weight gain due to steroid intake)

Musculoskeletal symptoms

- Ask about joint pain, swelling of small joints of the hands, wrists, knees (90%)
- Ask if there is muscle weakness

Note: arthritis or arthralgia may be asymmetrical, and pain may be disproportionate to swelling

There is no permanent deformity of the joints.

Skin manifestation (95%)

- Ask about malar rash, (an erythematous rash over the cheeks and nasal bridge) specially after sun exposure
- Ask about excessive loss of the hair (alopecia) Ask about other types of rash/lesion like livedo reticularis, oral ulcer (active SLE)
- Ask about discoid rash, any maculopapular rash elsewhere.
- Ask about duration of these symptoms and what has been done so far.

Raynaud's phenomenon

- Ask the patient about changes of skin color over the hand and feet
- Ask the patient about pain and numbness over hand and feet
- Ask if there are skin ulcers especially over the digits.

Note: patient will complaint of episodic changes in hand. Usually there is pallor or cyanosed due to intense vasoconstriction. The hands become cold and patient may experience numbness. When blood flow returns sluggishly there is cyanosis and finally there is reactive hyperemic phase which results in pain and tingling sensation. The phenomenon is <u>*precipitated by cold exposure, vibration, or emotional stress*</u>*. The intense vasoconstriction may cause ulcers of the digital pulps.*

PAST MEDICAL HISTORY
- Exacerbation and remission of the disease
- History of previous thrombotic complication, eg DVT
- Migraine
- **History of miscarriages**
- *Note: All of these may signify presence of antiphopholipid syndrome*

SURGICAL HISTORY
- Nonspecific – may have past history of surgery for complication of disease

FAMILY HISTORY
- Family history increases risk.

SOCIAL HISTORY
- Ask about Occupation – symptoms may be affecting work
- Ask about support at home.
- Ask about home condition , type of house , type of toilet , availability of basic necessities
- Ask about smoking

Note: It's important to take a detailed social history and occupational history to determine functional limitation. SLE is a progressive disease with multi-organ involvement. Patient will develop many system involvement as the disease progress. Assessment of living condition shows that you are a holistic and caring doctor.

DRUG HISTORY
- Take a history of over the counter drug and analgesic use.
- Take history of traditional medication use.
- Take history of contraceptive pills
- Take history of other drugs which may cause lupus like syndrome.

Note: remember patient is may have seen other doctors or may have seen a traditional practitioner.

SYSTEMIC REVIEW OF SYMPTOMS

Renal features (50%)
- Ask about history of swelling of the feet(nephropathy)

- Ask about recent onset of hypertension(renal insufficiency)

Note: Biopsy studies demonstrate some degree of renal involvement in most patients. Glomerular disease usually develops within the first few years of SLE onset and is often asymptomatic.

Neuropsychiatric features
- Ask about presence of headache (migraine)
- Ask about history of seizure, forgetfulness or mood changes, cognitive problem.
- Ask about history of stroke or TIA (presence of antiphospholipid syndrome)

Note: Though only seizure and psychosis are included among the diagnostic criteria of SLE there may also be delirium, transverse myelitis (due to CNS cerebritis and vasculitis). Migraine headaches may be linked to antiphospholipid syndrome. Neuropsychiatric feature may be due to true encephalopathy, neurological damage, medication effects, depression, or some other unclear process

Pulmonary features
- Pleurisy- present with pleuratic chest pain
- Pleural effusion – present with deceased effort tolerance and shortness of breath

Note: Shortness of breath in SLE may be due to many other causes. Pulmonary embolism, lupus pneumonitis, chronic lupus interstitial lung disease, pulmonary hypertension, alveolar hemorrhage, or infection may be related to lupus disease.

Cardiovascular Features
- It's important to asses for symptoms of ischemic heart disease. SLE is associated with increased rate of cardiovascular disease likely as a result of systemic inflammatory response.(coronary vasculitis)
- Pericarditis – presents as chest discomfort .
- <u>Libman-Sacks endocarditis</u> may manifest as infective endocarditis
- Heart failure features

Note: Accelerated ischemic coronary artery disease is associated with SLE and may present as atypical angina.

Hematologic features
- Symptoms related to anaemia
- A history of recurrent early miscarriages may be clue to lupus or isolated antiphospholipid antibody syndrome

Note: A good candidate must always try to determine patients preconceived ideas about his disease and understand his concerns and expectation.

Check list for history taking

- ✓ Get a history of Raynaud's phenomenon
- ✓ Identify multisystem complications of the disease (systemic review)
- ✓ Determine the functional status of patient
- ✓ Determine patient concerns

EXAMINATION

Introduce yourself and explain to the patient you would like to examine her.

General inspection
General inspection gives an idea of the patient's functional disability. Also look around the room as it can give you clues (e.g. walking frame/ stick).

In SLE you must look for:
- General nutritional status.
- Anemia and jaundice
- Vital signs (hypertension may suggest renal disease)
- Signs of respiratory distress (patients may have restrictive lung disease , lung fibrosis, heart failure)
- Lymphadenopathy
- Swollen legs (lupus nephropathy)
- Look for AV fistulas, peritoneal dialysis catheter or scars of previous internal jugular catheter or femoral insertion. (renal complication)

Skin and mucous membrane findings
- Malar rash – a butterfly-shaped rash, typically spares the nasolabial folds (as folds are depressed area and sun does not reach there)
- Photosensitive rash is in sun-exposed areas of the face, arms, or hands(often macular or diffusely erythematous)

- Discoid rash –a raised coin shaped rash with central depression may create scarring (usually on the face, behind the ears and scalp)
- Alopecia - often causes hair loss at the temporal regions.
- Raynaud phenomenon - blue, white, and red color change at the distal digital tips on exposure to cold.
- Look carefully at the buccal mucosa for painless mouth ulcer
- Nail fold infarcts raged cuticles
- Digital ischemia with ulceration
- Vasculitic rashes at the finger tips and hands.

Musculoskeletal

- Arthritis of the proximal interphalangeal (PIP) and metacarpophalangeal (MCP) joints of the hands as well as the wrists.
- Jaccoud arthropathy -nonerosive hand deformities and tendonitis (10% of patients).
- Abnormal gait and hip pain; may be due to avascular necrosis of femoral head (complication of glucocorticoids).

Cardiopulmonary findings

- Tachypnea
- Pleuropericardial friction rubs
- Signs of pleural effusions (dullness on percussion, reduced vocal resonance, reduced vesicular breath sound)
- Systolic murmurs (presence of Libman-Sacks endocarditis)
- Loud P2 heart sound (pulmonary hypertension)

Neurological findings

- Spastic paraparesis should raise consideration of transverse myelitis.
- Focal neurologic deficits may represent stroke, transient ischemic attack (TIA), or mononeuritis.

Eye findings

- Perform funduscopic examination to detect 'cytoid bodies'(soft exudate a disc space away from the optic disc and is due to retinal infarct)
- Check for Sjogren's Syndrome

Note: a good candidate will be able to pick up sign of complication of treatment (e.g. steroid use)

Complete examination by looking for organ specific complication:

Functional status of patient
Check patient's daily functions by asking her to imitate actions of
- Button/ unbutton shirt
- Holding a cup
- Turning a door knob / using a key
- Combing hair /bath self

Note: This is very important because you can gauge the patient ability to take care of her and it shows that you are looking into patients welfare actively.

Check list for clinical examination
- ✓ Look at general condition of patient
- ✓ Examine hand & face for skin changes and other signs of SLE
- ✓ Look for mouth ulcer
- ✓ Look for photosensitive and malar rash
- ✓ Look for alopecia
- ✓ Look for nail fold infarcts
- ✓ Look for joint disorder
- ✓ Look at the ankle for presence of edema
- ✓ Look for complication of disease – focus examination
- ✓ Asses functional status

INVESTIGATIONS

Blood Investigations:
- Full blood count – SLE is a chronic disease with multi-organ involvement look for anemia. There also may be leukopenia, lymphopenia, and thrombocytopenia.
- **Inflammatory markers** :ESR and C-reactive protein (CRP) (Disease activity increases mainly ESR but when infection complecated=s the disease, CRP goes up.)
- Complement levels Low C3 and C4
- Liver function tests may be abnormal with Lupoid Hepatitis
- Renal profile to check for kidney involvement
- Urine for protein and casts.(to detect renal involvement)

Autoimmune panels

- ANA - Screening test; sensitivity 95%
- Anti-dsDNA - High specificity; sensitivity only 70%
- Anti-Sm - Most specific antibody for SLE; only 30-40% sensitivity
- Anticardiolipin and Lupus anticoagulant –To check for antiphospholid syndrome

Chest radiograph To monitor lung disease

Renal biopsy When neccesary

CASE SUMMARY

This patient has arthritis of the small joints of the hands along with photosensitive rash on her face. She also has intermittent fever along with increased tiredness and fatigue.

Note: When presenting the case always try to present the positive findings (lesion), the aetiology and the functional status. It some cases complication of the disease and complication of treatment should also be reported.

CLINICAL DISCUSSION OF THE CASE

How would you manage a patient with SLE?

The management of a patient with SLE is individualized

- c) Non pharmacological
  Patient education and support – patient needs to be counseled on SLE. Familiarize patients the symptoms and natural course of disease as well as how we are going to manage it. Patents must understand that the disease is progressive and involves multi organ systems. A patient support group may be helpful.
- d) Physical therapy / occupational therapy – designated exercise program to maintain posture and rage of motion.
- e) Avoidance of sunlight-patient should be counseled on avoiding the sun as this may trigger the disease. She should use sun block of more than 30 SPF(sun protecting factor)

The patient should be referred to a Rheumatologist or a Physician for the treatment.

f) Hydroxychloroquin an anti malarial drug should be the mainstay for all the patients with SLE. Studies have proved its safety and efficacy.

Antimalarials may work through numerous proposed mechanisms in SLE, mediating subtle immunomodulation without causing overt immunosuppression. They are useful in preventing and treating lupus skin rashes, constitutional symptoms, arthralgias, and arthritis. They also help to prevent lupus flares and have been associated with reduced morbidity and mortality in SLE patients followed in observational trials.

g) Joint and skin involvement only may not require systemic steroid therapy. NSAID may show required benefit.

h) Serious organ involvement requires systemic steroid therapy under close supervision.

i) Cyclophosphamide and Mycophenolate may have benefit with renal and CNS disease

They also have steroid sparing effect. There are other immunomodulatory drugs.

Learning Outcomes

By the end of this case review the student should be able to:
- Take a good history and systemic review of SLE.
- Able to recognize multi-organ involvement in SLE
- Examine the skin and focused specific organ for complications
- Formulate the appropriate investigations explain rationale for performing them.
- Outline the principles of management.

COMMONLY ASKED QUESTIONS

- What is the diagnostic criterion for SLE?

According to 1997 American College of Rheumatology revised criterion 4 out of the following 11 should be positive.

1. Malar rash
2. Discoid rash (red, scaly patches on skin that cause scarring)
3. Serositis: Pleurisy or pericarditis
4. Oral ulcers (includes oral or nasopharyngeal ulcers)

5. <u>Arthritis</u>: nonerosive arthritis
6. <u>Photosensitivity</u> (exposure to ultraviolet light causes rash)
7. Blood—hematologic disorder—<u>hemolytic anemia</u> (low <u>red blood cell</u> count) or <u>leukopenia</u> (white blood cell count<4000/µl), <u>lymphopenia</u> (<1500/µl) or <u>thrombocytopenia</u> (<100000/µl)

   Hypocomplementemia is also seen, due to either consumption of C3 and C4 by immune complex-induced inflammation or to congenitally complement deficiency, which may predispose to SLE.
8. Renal disorder: <u>More than 0.5 g per day protein in urine</u> or cellular <u>casts</u> seen in urine under a microscope
9. <u>Antinuclear antibody</u> test positive
10. Immunologic disorder: Positive <u>anti-Smith</u>, anti-ds DNA, <u>antiphospholipid antibody,</u>
11. Neurologic disorder: <u>Seizures</u> or <u>psychosis</u>

7. What are the common causes of death in SLE?
   The most common causes of death are <u>renal failure</u> and intercurrent infections, followed by diffuse central nervous system disease.

8. What are the skin manifestations of SLE?
   Butterfly rash, periungal erythema, nail fold telengiectasia, alopecia, livedeo reticularis, hyperpigmentation, urticaria, purpura, discoid lupus with scaring alopecia.

DISTINCTION LEVEL QUESTION

3. What do you know about drug induced SLE?

   <u>Drug-induced lupus erythematosus</u> is a <u>reversible</u> condition that usually occurs in people being treated with certain drugs. Drug-induced lupus mimics SLE. However, symptoms of drug-induced lupus generally disappear once the medication is withdrawn. The most common offending drugs are <u>procainamide, isoniazid, hydralazine, quinidine,</u> and <u>phenytoin. Anti-Histone antibody</u> is present in drug induced SLE.

4. What are the patterns of lupus nephritis?
   According to International Society of Nephrology 2003 Revised Classification of SLE Nephritis:

Class I   Minimal mesangial

Class II Mesangial proliferative

Class III : Focal proliferative

Class IV : Diffuse proliferative

Class V : Membranous

Class VI : Advanced sclerosing

5. What is Overlap Syndrome?

   An overlap syndrome is with clinical feature of systemic lupus erythematosus (SLE), scleroderma, and myositis. There is presence of a distinctive antibody against U1-ribonucleoprotein (RNP).

6. What is neonatal lupus?

   Neonatal lupus is the occurrence of SLE in an <u>infant</u> born from a mother with SLE, most commonly presenting with a rash resembling <u>discoid lupus</u>, and sometimes with systemic abnormalities such as <u>heart block</u> or <u>hepatosplenomegaly</u>. It is associated with mothers who carry the <u>Ro/SSA</u> antibody

COMMON MISTAKES

- Not asking the patient if he is in pain before moving the patient. It reflects badly on the candidate if pain is caused to the patient.
- Not assessing functional status of patient
- Not doing proper systemic review
- Not looking complication of disease
- A distinction student will go one step higher and look for complication of treatment

MUST KNOW FACTS ABOUT SYSTEMIC LUPUS ERYTHEMATOSUS

- ✓ SLE is progressive disease with multisystem involvement
- ✓ Diagnostic criterion
- ✓ Raynaud's phenomenon
- ✓ Investigations including autoimmune panels specific to the disease
- ✓ Basic management principles

Reference

4) Wallace DJ, Hahn BH (eds): *Dubois' Lupus Erythematosus*, 7th ed. Philadelphia, Lippincott Williams & Wilkins, 2006
5) *Harrison's Principles of Internal Medicine, 17th edition*, chapter 313, Systemic Lupus Erythematosus, by BH Hahn.

SECTION 7 : ENDOCRINOLOGY

CASE 51 : DIABETIC FOOT

DR. KYAW MIN

OVERVIEW

Diabetes mellitus (DM) is a serious debilitating and deadly disease causing significant mortality and morbidity globally. Worldwide, the number of diabetic patients was estimated to be 135 million in 1995, 154 million in 2000, and it is expected to reach 300 million in year 2025. The projected increase in the developed countries is 42% but in the developing countries like Malaysia, the increase is estimated to be 170 %. [1]

In Malaysia, the reported prevalence (First National Health and Morbidity Survey; NHMS 1) of DM was 6.3% in 1986, 8.2% in 1996 (NHMS 2; prevalence in Kelantan was 10.5%), and WHO estimated that by 2030, Malaysia would have a total number of 2.48 million diabetes (prevalence of 10.8%), compared to 0.94 million in 2000, which represents a 164% increase![1]

In Malaysia, the prevalence rate has been reported to have increased from 6.3% in1986 to 14.6% in 1996. Fifteen percent of patients with diabetes mellitus will developa lower extremity ulcer during the course of their disease. The prevalence of foot ulceration in patients attending a diabetic outpatient clinic in Malaysia has been reported as 6%. Diabetic foot complications pose a substantial problem in theMalaysian diabetic population. They are a major source of morbidity, a leading cause of hospital bed occupancy and account for substantial health care costs and resources. Foot complications have been found to account for 12% of all diabetic hospital admissions.[2]

Foot complications result from a complex interplay of ischaemia, ulceration, infectionand diabetic Charcot's joint. They can be reduced through appropriate preventionand management.

Diabetic foot ulcers, as shown in the images above (it is from Google image), occurs as a result of several factors, such as mechanical changes in conformation of the bony architecture of the foot, peripheral neuropathy, and atherosclerotic peripheral arterial disease, all of which occur with higher frequency and intensity in the diabetes.

Non enzymatic glycosylation predisposes ligaments to stiffness. Neuropathy causes loss of protective sensation and loss of coordination of muscle groups in the foot and leg, both of which increase mechanical stresses during ambulation.

neuropathy → loss of protective sensation & mechanical stresses during ambulation.

CASE VIGNETTE

Ms. SM is a 58-year-old, housewife, 54 kg, who complains of wound in right plantor region of foot for 4 days duration with shortness of breath for 2 days duration. She has Diabetes Mellitus (DM) for the last 7 years. She is on insulin two times per day together with Metformin. She has no past history of surgery. She gives a history of being adniited 6 months ago for chest pain and has been having shortness of breath (SOB) for the last 2 months.. She has systemic hypertension (HPT) and dyslipidaemia (DL) for 10 years.

HISTORY OF PRESENT ILLNESS

The patient first noticed that the the wound started with blisters in the upper part of plantar region of right foot. Two days ago it became worsen with peeling off of skin. It resulted in a 5cm x 3cm sized wound which started bleeding and serious fluid was oozing out of it. She applied some cream on the wound, but it never got better.

She started feeling numbness of feet since diagnosis diabetes mellitus which has worsen after the wound formation. The numbness is worse on the right foot. She did not feel any pain in the foot or wound area.

Shortness of Breath (SOB) became worse after she felt numbness in the feet. It progressively increased in intensity on the day of admission especialy at night. It was also associated with chest tightness, fatigue, and dry cough. She sufferes from orthopnoea (used 3 pillows beneath her head during sleeping), paroxysmal nocturnal dyspnoea and dyspnoea on exertion. The SOB was relieved by rest. The SOB was not associated with chest pain, profuse sweating orfever. Her micturation is normal. There was no nocturia, dysuria or urinary incontinence. Bowel movement is as usual. She had loss of appetide. During bathing especially head shower, she needs to hold to something strong beside her because she fells a sense of imbalance.

FAMILY HISTORY

Her mother passed away with uncontrolled DM and her father passed away due to old age. Her sibblings are healthy except her elder sister who has DM. She had three children and all of them were delivered via spontaneous vaginal delivery .

MENSTRUAL HISTORY

She attained her menopause at age of 54 years which was 4 years ago.

SOCIAL HISTORY

She had no history of smoking, alcohol drinking or betel nut chewing. She stays in single storey house with 3 rooms and 2 persons staying in it. Her husband was a farmer and is adequate financially.

LIFE STYLE

She is on a well balanced diet with reduced salt and sweet intake but sedentary life style with no regular exercises.

Check list for history taking in Diabetic Foot

- ✓ History of presenting foot complaints and duration

- ✓ Numbness of lower limbs and imbalance of body during shower

- ✓ Duration of diabetes, management and control

- ✓ Cardiovascular, renal, ophthalmic evaluation & other co morbidities *Cnaero & mrero*

- ✓ Social history – alcohol / tobacco / occupation / dietary habits

- ✓ Current medication and antibiotic use

- ✓ Allergies

- ✓ Past Medical & Surgical history

- ✓ Cultural habits – walks barefoot / wets feet at work / wear socks / walks alot

- ✓ Patients' perception of Diabetes Mellitus, necessity of weight and diet control

- ✓ Able to afford diabetic drugs

Physical Examination:

General Examination: Patient is well conscious, not in any kind of distress, lying down comfortably with 2 pillows under her head and the bed is slightly elevated. There is a uninary catheter fixed, IV canula present on her left dorsum of hand.

Palms are moist, pale and warm. No clubbing, koilonychia, peripheral cyanosis or fungal infection. Capillary refilling time is less than 2 secs. There are mild fine tremors present in her hands.

BP: 152/90 mmHg, RR: 20/min, Temp: 37° C,

Radial Pulse: 80 bpm, regular, low volume, bilaterally equal. There is no collapsing pulse. The lower extremities pulse, DPA and PTA can not be felt.

Conjunctival pallor is present and there is no jaundice, central cyanosis, and palpable lymph nodes.

Oral cavity: dental hygiene is poor. There are dental carries and only few tooth present. There are no angular stomatitis, glossitis, or central cyanosis,

There is bilateral pitting oedema up to knee level in lower limbs. The toe nails are infected by fungus.

Cardiovascular Examination

Inspection: No chest deformity observed, no sternal bulge, visible pulsations or scar.

JVP is 8 cm from RA. (5cm +3cm)

Palpation: Apex beat is palpable at left 6th IC space lateral to mid clavicular line and heaving in character. Mild parasternal heave.

Auscultation: Normal S1S2 are heard. No murmur in all the four areas. Heart rate is 80 bpm.

Respiratory system examination

Inspection: Her chest is moving symmetrical. There are no chest wall deformaties or scars.

Palpation: Trachea in mid-position. Normal and equal chest expansion on both sides. Tactile fremitus and vocal fremitus normal and equal.

Percussion: Normal

Auscultation: Normal breath sounds with no accompaniments. There are mild bibasal crepitation and mild generalised rhonchi present.

Abdomen: Soft, moves with respiration. No hepatosplenomegaly.

Central Nervous System Examination

Patient is well, conscious and orientated.

Lower limbs:

- Fine touch cannot be felt below knee in both legs.

- Crude touch cannot be felt in right leg below knee but can be felt slightly in left leg.

- Pain sensation cannot be felt in right leg below knee but can be felt slightly in left leg.

- Vibration sense cannot be felt in both legs.

- Possition sense cannot be felt in both legs.

Local examination

Site: upper part of plantar region of right foot.

Size: 5cm x 3 cm

Apperance: bleeding and serious fluid is exuding from the ulcer

Check list for physical examination in Diabetic Foot

* Evaluation of vascular status of the foot and leg:

- Pulses (dorsalis pedis, posterior tibial, popliteal, femoral)

- Capillary return (normal ≤ 3 seconds)

- Venous filling time (normal ≤ 20 seconds)

- Presence of edema

- Temperature gradient

- Colour changes: Cyanosis, dependent rubor, erythema

- Changes of ischemia: Skin atrophy; nail atrophy, abnormal wrinkling,diminished pedal hair

* Evaluation of neurological status of the foot and leg:

- Vibration perception: Tuning fork 128 Hz

- Pressure & Touch: Cotton wool (light), Monofilament (5.07) 10gm (SemmesWeinstein)

- Pain: Pinprick, using sharp and blunt tool (e.g. Neurotip)

- Two-point discrimination

- Temperature perception: hot and cold

- Deep tendon reflexes: ankle, knee

- Clonus testing

- Babinski test

- Romberg's test

* Site, size, duration, odour and type of drainage

* Ulcer/s at the dorsal portion of the toes and on the plantar aspect of the metatarsal heads and the heel.

* Skin & nail problems – sweaty feet / fungal infections / skin disease / blisters/ Ingrown toenails

* Features of Charcot's joint

* Limited joint mobility – active and passive movements

* Tendo - Achilles contractures / equines / foot drop

* Gait evaluation

* Muscle group strength testing

* Plantar pressure assessment

Investigations

FBC:

Haemoglobin: 10.7 g/dl, Total WBC: 14.78 $[10^3/\mu L]$ with neutrophil leucocytosis, RBC 3.69 $[10^6/\mu L]$, HGB: 8.4 (g/dl),

HCT: 25.4%, MCV: 68.8 (Fl), MCH: 22.8 [pg], MCHC: 33.1 (g/dl)

BUN: 27.9, Na^+ 136, K^+ 3.5, Cl^- 101, HCO_3 25, Creatinine: 647, Total CK: 307

RBS: 20.6 mmol/l

Cardiac enzymes: raised LDH

ECG: pathological Q in Lead III and LVH^+

Diagnosis:

Poorly controlled Diabets Mellitus, Diabetic foot ulcer with acute coronary syndrome with congestive cardiac failure

AETIOLOGY OF DIABETIC FOOT

The aetiology of diabetic ulceration includes neuropathy, arterial disease, pressure, and foot deformity. Diabetic peripheral neuropathy, presents in 60% of diabetic persons and 80% of diabetic persons with foot ulcers, confers the greatest risk of foot ulceration; micro-vascular disease and suboptimal glycemic control contribute.

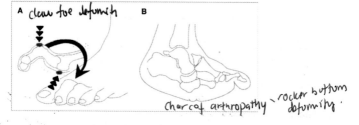

Common foot deformities resulting from diabetes complications: A) claw toe deformity (increased pressure is placed on the dorsal and plantar aspects of the deformity as indicated by the triple arrows); and B) Charcot arthropathy (the rocker-bottom deformity leads to increased pressure on the plantar midfoot).

Clayton W, Elasy TA. Clinical. Diabetes 2009; 27(2): 52-58. 7.[3]

Wagner's Classification of Diabetic Foot Ulcers[4]

Grading	Features
0	Pre-ulcer. No open lesion. May have deformities, erythematous areas of pressure or hyperkeratosis
1	Superficial ulcer. Disruption of skin without penetration of subcutaneous fat layer.
2	2Full thickness ulcer. Penetrates through fat to tendon or joint capsule without deep abscess or osteomyelitis.
3	Deep ulcer with abscess, osteomyelitis or joint sepsis. It includes deep plantar space infections, abscesses, necrotizing fascitis and tendon sheath infections.
4	Gangrene of a geographical portion of the foot such as toes, forefoot or heel.
5	Gangrene or necrosis of large portion of the foot requiring major limb amputation.

Another useful classification, which uses grading as well as staging, is TheUniversity of Texas Diabetic Wound Classification. The inclusion of staging makes this classification a better predictor of outcome.

University of Texas Diabetic Wound Classification[5]

Stages	Example of classification
Stage A: No infection or ischaemia	Stage A
Stage B: Infection present Stage	- Grade 0 ≥ Epithelialized wound
Stage C: Ischaemia present –	- Grade 1 superficial wound
Stage D: Infection and ischaemia present	- Grade 2 penetrates to tendon/ capsule .
	- Grade 3 penetrate to bone / Jt
Grading	
Grade 0: Epithelialized wound – Grade 1: Superficial wound Grade 2: Wound penetrates to tendon or capsule	

Grade 3: Wound penetrates to bone or joint	

TREATMENT Diabetic Foot Ulcer

In this patient optimal control of diabetes, good control of hypetension and hyperlipedemia following CPG guidelines with management of congestive cardiac failure are essential apart from treating the foot ulcer. The focus of the treatment subsequrntly is on diabetic foot ulcer.

Proper treatment of diabetic foot ulcers can lower the incidence of lower limb amputations. The aim is to obtain wound closure as soon as possible and to prevent recurrence. The pathophysiology of diabetic foot ulcer would be the basis of the specifics outlined below.

Principles of Treatment[6]

    i.   Debridement of necrotic tissue: Surgical debridement is an important and effective procedure in the management of diabetic foot ulcers. Diabetic foot abscesses requires immediate incision and drainage. Osteomyelitic bones, joint infection or gangrene digits require resection or partial amputation.

    ii.   Wound care: the ulcer is covered to protect it from trauma and contaminants. Hyperbaric oxygen therapy is available in certain centers in Malaysia and is used as an adjunctive treatment for hypoxic diabetic foot ulcers.

    iii.   Reduction of plantar pressure (off-loading): This involves reducing the pressure to the diabetic foot ulcer, thus reducing the trauma to the ulcer and allowing it to heal. This is an essential component of ulcer healing. Treatment in the acute phase consists of using off loading modalities to reduce stress, like crutches, wheelchair, and walker, total contact cast

    iv.   Treatment of infection: Infection in a diabetic foot is usually secondary to ulceration

    v.   Vascular management of ischaemia: Vascular supply to the affected limb should be assessed early and if impaired,vascular reconstruction surgery (if feasible) should be performed prior to definitive surgical management.

    vi.   Medical management of co-morbidities: Chronic foot ulcers are usually associated with areas of increased peak pressurewhere off loading and wound care techniques are not effective. These ulcers are best treated surgically which includes removal of infected bone or joints. Such operations include metatarsal head resections, partial calcanectomy, exostectomy,sesamoidectomy and digital arthroplasty. (CPG)

vii. Surgical management to reduce or remove bony prominences and/or improve soft tissue cover

viii. Preventing ulcer recurrence: This will require a multidisciplinary approach with committed dedicated professionals including podiatrist, orthopaedic surgeon, vascular surgeon, endocrinologist / physician,infection control nurse and others including cardiologist, nephrologist and neurologist. Patient education is of utmost importance and these include instructions in foot hygiene, daily inspection, proper footwear, identification and early treatment of new lesions. Other preventive measures include proper and regular podiatric management of calluses and in grown toe nails therapeutic footwear with high toe box and pressure relieving insoles and consideration of surgical procedures.

CLINICAL DISCUSSION OF THE CASE (LEARNING OUTCOMES)
By the end of this case review the student should be able to:

- ✓ take thorough history for symptom analysis regarding foot ulcer associated with chronic DM.

- ✓ Must be able to elicit the signs related to peripheral arterial disease and peripheral neuropathy.

- ✓ justify probable provisional diagnosis based on history taking and positive physical examination.

- ✓ answer the two types of classification of DFU (Diabetic Foot Ulcer).

- ✓ list the relevant laboratory investigations, chest X-ray, and ECG,

- ✓ discuss the principles of management in this patient.

COMMONLY ASKED QUESTIONS

Discuss the aetiology and pathophysiology of Diabetic foot ulcer

Briefly outline the Wager and University of Texas Diabetic Wound Classification for Diabetic foot ulcer

How will you diagnose in a patient with Diabetic foot ulcer?

What are the complications of Diabetic foot ulcer?

What is acute Charcot's foot?

Briefly outline the management of Diabetic foot ulcer.

[Handwritten margin notes: Charcot foot → loss of proprioception, loss of pain sensation, loss of sensation, leprothy/mechanical trauma]

HIGH ACHIEVER QUESTIONS

- Briefly state how diabetic foot ulcers can be prevented? Diabetes is a lifelong problem, therefore patients must be educated. The following principles should be followed:

- Patient education and the need for daily foot inspection and early intervention to thepatient

- Diet modification and tight control of hyperglycemia are essential.

- Foot care: Regular podiatric visits for foot examination, debridement of calluses, toe nail care and foot care risk assessment; leading to early detection and aggressive treatment of new lesions.

- Therapeutic Shoes: Adequate room at toes and depth to protect from injury, custom molded shoes, well-cushioned walking sneaker and special modifications.

- Reduction of plantar pressure (off loading) Surgery: Correction of structural deformities like hammertoes, bunions, prevention of recurrent ulcers over deformity with high peak pressure areas has to be done if cannot be accommodated by therapeutic footwear.

COMMON MISTAKES

- ✓ Not competent in distinguishing the signs related to peripheral arterial disease and peripheral neuropathy, hence missing DPA, PTA, possition sense and vibration sense.

- ✓ Unable classify diabetic foot ulcer

- ✓ Weakness in understanding of pathophysiology of diabetic foot ulcer

- ✓ Not familiar with antibiotic medication and duration of treatment in treating infected diabetic foot ulcers.

- ✓ Poor knowledge concerning prevention and risk reduction of reoccurence diabetic foot ulcer

REFERENCES

1.http://www.acrm.org.my/norm/default.asp?page=/norm/diabeticFootHan d) (Accessed on 20th June 2012)

2. Khalid BAK (1998) Status of Diabetics in Malaysia. In World book of Diabetes in Practice; Elsevier Science Publishers (3) 341-342.7

3. Clayton W, Elasy TA. A review of the pathophysiology, classification, and treatment of foot ulcers in diabetic patients. Clinical. Diabetes 2009; 27(2): 52-58. 7.

4. Wagner WF (1981). The dysvascular foot: a system of diagnosis and treatment. J Foot Ankle 2:62-1221.

5. Lavery LA, Armstrong DG, Harkless LB (1996) Classification of diabetic foot wounds. J Foot Ankle Surg 35:528-31.

6. CPG Management of Diabetic Foot. August 2004.MOH/P/PAK/84.04 (GU)

CASE 52 : DIABETES AND DIABETIC COMPLICATIONS
S. NANDAKUMAR

OVERVIEW

Diabetes mellitus (DM)is now a major global public health problem. The incidence and prevalence of diabetes are escalating especially in developing and newly industrialized nations. About 90% of all cases of diabetes in developed and developing countries are type2 DM.

The etiology of type 2 diabetes mellitus appears to involve complex interactions between environmental and genetic factors. The disease develops when a Diabetogenic lifestyle (i.e. excessive caloric intake, inadequate caloric expenditure, obesity) is superimposed on a susceptible genotype.

The body mass index (BMI) at which excess body weight, hypertension and pre-hypertension are associated with greaterer risk. A large population-based, prospective study shows that an energy-dense diet may be a risk factor for the development of diabetes that is independent of baseline obesity.

Metabolic syndrome:

Often a person with abnormal glucose tolerance (IGT or diabetes) will be found to have at least one or more of the other cardiovascular disease risk factors such as hypertension, central (upper body) obesity, and dyslipidaemia. This clustering has been labeled diversely as the metabolic syndrome, Syndrome X, or the insulin resistance syndrome

Secondary diabetes may occur in patients taking glucocorticoids or when patients have conditions that antagonize the actions of insulin (e.g., Cushing syndrome, acromegaly, pheochromocytoma etc).

Classified by aetiology: (Presently accepted WHO classification)
- Type 1
- Type 2 (Lean- Obese- MODY)
- Gestational diabetes
- Other specific types
- I G T

Major risk factors
- Age greater than 45 year (Recent studies show increasing frequency in young individuals)

- Weight greater than 120% of desirable body weight
- Family history of type 2 diabetes in a first-degree relative (e.g., parent or sibling)
- History of previous impaired glucose tolerance (IGT) or impaired fasting glucose (IFG)
- Hypertension (>140/90 mm Hg) or dyslipidemia (HDL cholesterol level < 40 mg/dL or triglyceride level >150 mg/dL)
- History of gestational diabetes mellitus
- Polycystic ovarian syndrome (which results in insulin resistance)
- Evidence supports the involvement of multiple genes in pancreatic beta-cell failure and insulin resistance.
- Accumulating evidence suggests that depression is a significant risk factor for developing type2 diabetes.

International Expert Committee Recommends: (Diagnostic criteria)

	NORMAL:	**HYPERGLYCAEMIC**
DM CATEGORY:		
FBS < 5.6(100) >7.0 mmol/L		5.6-6.9
2 Hr PP < 7.8(140) >11.1 mmol/L		7.8-11.1

We must decide on two values at the time of diagnosis.

Occurrence in Malaysia

With further industrialization plus modernization and life style changes, by 2010, Asia was projected to have 138 million diabetic sufferers.

Diabetes prevalence rate in Malaysia has risen much faster than expected, almost doubling in magnitude over the last decade.

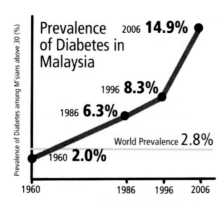

Prevalence of Diabetes in Malaysia

- Prevalence of Diabetes among M'sians above 30 (%)
- 2006 **14.9%**
- 1996 **8.3%**
- 1986 **6.3%**
- World Prevalence **2.8%**
- 1960 **2.0%**

1960   1986   1996   2006

- About 54% of the adult population is either obese or overweight, compared to only 24.1% 10 years ago.
- High sugar intake (which also causes obesity) among Malaysians is one of the contributing factors to the high incidence of diabetes. We consume 26 teaspoons of sugar a day and are the eighth highest sugar users in the world.
- The disease is dangerous because it can also affect the patient's vital organs like the heart, kidneys, nerves and eyes. Of all lower extremity amputations, 40-70% is related to diabetes.
- It is estimated that there are 13,000 kidney patients undergoing dialysis and every year 2,500 people join the ranks of end-stage renal failure patients.
- Another major health concern is that 4 out of 5 people with diabetes will die of heart disease (the number 1 killer in the country).
- Six new cases of stroke occur every hour in Malaysia.
- There is growing evidence that High Fructose Corn Syrup (HFCS), a cheap substitute for sugar used in processed foods and drinks may facilitate insulin resistance, and eventually leads to Type 2 diabetes. HFCS is widely used in a wide range of foods such as jams, chocolate, cakes, packed fruit juices, soft drinks, beverages, energy drinks, sauces, snacks and soups.

CASE VIGNETTE:

Mr. X , 48 year old male, currently not working (previously was a businessman) is admitted on 23 May 2012 for a chief complaints of incoherent speech of – 3 day-duration and shortness of breath of one day duration

He is also disorientated to time, place and person on admission.

History of present illness:

Breathlessness on exertion, and he sleeps on 2-3 pillows due to orthopnea; presence of paroxysmal nocturnal dyspnea. No chest pain or cough or vomiting. There are ulcers present on left big toe, both right and left sole of foot.

Past Medical History: Diabetes mellitus – 25 years and diagnosed to have diabetic foot, nephropathy, retinopathy and sensory-motor neuropathy with medications.

Has been a hypertensive for the pastf 6 months ,controlled with medications and at the same admission diagnosed to be end stage renal failure, ischemic heart disease, and pleural effusion

Previous admission to HSAH – 3 times in 1 month and treated for catheter related sepsis. Amputation of right 4th and 5th toe in 2003.

Vision: Left eye no vision, Right eye: visual acuity = 3/60

Drug History:

- T. Aspirin 150mg OD
- T. Hematinics II/II OD
- T. Calcium carbonate 500mg
- T. Felodipine 5mg OD
- T. Frusemide 80mg BD
- T. Lovastatin 20mg OD
- S/C Humulin 30/70 22 unit am/11 unit pm.

There is a strong family history of diabetes mellitus and hypertension.

Social history: A chronic smoker for 3 years, smokes 40 sticks per day, drinks alcohol for the last 3 years

General Examination:

Patient is looking very confused and drowsy, placed in a 45 degree propped up position, looking cachexic. The pulse rate: is 120 beats per minute, low volume, irregular rhythm. All peripheral pulses are palpable. Blood pressure: 163/84mmHg, Respiratory rate: 22 per minute

Clinical Examination:

Scars are seen at the site where AVF was done,anemic and not jaundiced, JVP raised.

Oral cavity is normal, no lymph nodes palpable, pitting pedal edema noticed up to scrotum level

Palpable pedal dorsalis pulse and posterior tibialis pulse.

Systemic Examination: Cardiovascular system

o   Pericardial rub best heard on tricuspid
o   Systolic murmur best heard on mitral
o   Gallop rhythm heard on aortic
o   Visible and palpable thrill on left sternal edge
o   Shift of apex beat laterally
o   Apex beat is weak and tapping in nature.

Respiratory system: Normal, GIT: Normal CNS: Signs and symptoms related to peripheral sensory motor neuropathy

Investigations:

o   DXT : 6.2
o   Echo (done on 3 June 2012): impaired LV systolic function @ EF 47.9 global hypokinesia
     Dilated RA,LA & LV/LVH, MR by CRM, TR severe by CFM (EPASP 63 + 20 minutes)
     Pericardial effusion seen (NDE 0.6cm – 1.7cm)
o   Electrolyte values: cK+ : 2.5, cNa+ : 110, cCa2+ : 0.47
o   Metabolite values: cGlu : 2.5mmol/L, cLa : 1.6mmol/L
o   Full blood count (2/6): Hb : 8.9, PLT : 177, TWC : 13.7
o   Renal Profile (31/5): Na: 136, K : 9.4, Cl: 96, Urea : 31.2,Creat : 866, Mg : 1.07, PO4 : 1.8 Total Ca : 1.89
o   Liver Function Test (31/5): Total protein : 6.9, Albumin : 14, Globulin : 4.7, Total Bilirubin : 53, Direct Bilirubin : 42, Indirect Bilirubin : 1.1, ALT : 21, ALP : 462
o   Viral screening (23/5): Hepatitis B antigen : weakly reactive, Hepatitis C antibody : weakly reactive, HCV particle agglutination test not detected, HIV : non reactive
     Culture results (23/5): MRSA Staphylococcus aureus sensitive to vancomycin, linezolide and rifampicin.

Provisional Diagnosis:

o   Diabetes mellitus and Hypertension with nephropathy, neuropathy and retinopathy
o   End stage renal failure with dialysis
o   Catheter related sepsis – MRSA
o   Diffuse cerebrovascular disease
o   Diabetic Foot ulcers

> ○   Ischemic heart disease with cardiac failure & pericardial effusion

Questions:

1. Why does type 2 diabetes develop?

- Insulin resistance
- Relative insulin deficiency
- Genetic association
- Environmental factors

Pathophysiology: Following genetic factors that contribute type 2 DM

Glucokinase Variants
Gross increase in pro-insulin to insulin ratio
Deficient Action of Insulin on Target Tissues
Genetic Susceptibility Factor has been identified in Mitochondrial DNAnti Insulin Receptor antibodies

2. How does hyperglycemia promote atherosclerosis?

- Multifactorial causes as follow:
- Modifications of lipoproteins (e.g. glycation of LDL)
- Glycation of arterial wall proteins
- Formation of advanced glycation end-products
- Stimulation of insulin secretion
- Stimulation of protein kinase C.

Note:

- *Framingham data with 20 year follow-up on patients aged 45 to 74, revealed that diabetics had a 2-3 fold increase in clinically evident atherosclerotic disease. Women diabetics were equal to male diabetics in terms of CAD mortality. There was a loss of normal female cardiovascular protective benefit.*
- *In the United Kingdom prospective diabetes study (UKPDS), in an 8 year follow up with newly detected diabetes, 30% had high LDL-C; low HDL-c while 50% had systolic hypertension.*
- *While treating hypertension always keep a lower target for diabetic patients than non-diabetic patients: 130/85 vs. 140/90*
  Dyslipidaemia in DM: Most common abnormality is ↓s HDL and ↑s Triglycerides.

- *A low HDL is the most constant predictor of CV disease in DM*

3.   **Briefly state how you would evaluate a diabetic patient. List all the relevant Investigations you would do on follow up?**

- o BMI
- o Tooth and gums
- o Retinal examination
- o Peripheral pulses & orthostatic hypotension
- o Foot exam
- o Insulin injection sites
- o Peripheral neuropathy
- o Fungal infection of skin, nail
- o Vibratory sense
- o Other system examination for any complications

Investigations:

- Urea/ creatinine/ Electrolytes
- Urine albumin/24 hour urinary protein
- FBS/2hr PPBS/HbA1c
- Lipid profile
- ECG/stress test/ECHO (if indicated)
- Thyroid function tests (once a year)
- Fundoscopy

6. Describe the common eye complications in uncontrolled diabetic patients?

A. Eye Complications – **Cataracts:**
- o Non enzymatic glycation of lens protein and subsequent cross linking
- o Sorbitol accumulation could also lead to osmotic swelling of the lens

B.Retinopathy (stages)

- **Background:** characterized by Micro aneurisms, Scattered exudates, Hemorrhages (flame shaped, Dot and Blot), Cotton wool spots (<5) and Venous dilatations.

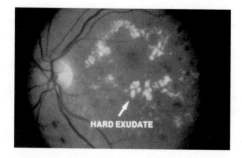

- **Pre-proliferative**

- **Proliferative:** New vessels formation, Fibrous proliferation , Hemorrhages (preretinal, vitreous)

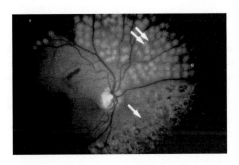

Advanced diabetic eye disease:

o   Rubeosis iridis (neovascularization iris)

o   Neovascular glaucoma

o   Retinal detachment with or without retinal tears (see fig.,)

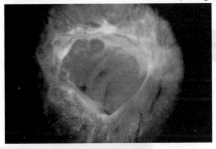

D.**Maculopathy**

E.**Glaucoma**

7. Classify the different stages of diabetic nephropathy?

Diabetic Nephropathy (DN)

About 20 – 30% of patients with diabetes develop end stage renal failure. Advanced glycosylation end products (AGEs) over years of hyperglycemia can contribute to renal damage.

Stage I: This stage is usually not clinically evident. The initial basement membrane thickening and glomerular permeability leads to altered pressures and function within the glomerular capillaries causing leakage of proteins, particularly albumin.

Stage II: Renal lesions are found on biopsy

Stage III: Blood pressure usually starts to increase once fixed albuminuria exists.

Stages I – III is reversible

Stage IV: Overt nephropathy (> 300mg/24h, positive u dipstick) and kidney damage is irreversible at this stage and renal function deteriorates on average at a rate of 1mL per month. Without treatment uremia and death occur in 7 – 10 years. About 15% of newly diagnosed patients are already in this stage because of late diagnosis.

Stage V: ESRD characterized by ↑ blood urea and creatinine levels, hyperkalaemia and fluid overload

Screening for Nephropathy:

o   U. Albumin: Creatinine ratio (spot sample)
o   24hr Albumin excretion rate
o   Early morning Albumin concentration (spot sample)
o   Dipstick for Microalbuminuria

Note: Microalbuminuria (if urinary albumin excretion is >30 mg/24hr) indicates an increased risk for progression to overt nephropathy.

8. Describe the various types of neuropathy that can affect diabetics?

o   Sensorimotor neuropathy (acute/chronic)
o   Autonomic neuropathy
o   Mononeuropathy
o   Proximal motor neuropathy

Sensorimotor Neuropathy:

o   Patients may be asymptomatic / or complain of numbness, paresthesia or pain
o   Feet are mostly affected, hands are seldom affected
o   In Diabetic patients sensory neuropathy usually predominates

Complications of Sensorimotor neuropathy:

o   Ulceration (painless)
o   Neuropathic edema
o   Charcot arthropathy
o   Callosities

Autonomic Neuropathy: Affects the autonomic nerves controlling internal organs

- Peripheral
- Genitourinary —neuropathic bladder
- Gastrointestinal - gastroparesis, dm diarrhea.
- Cardiovascular - post -hypo

Symptomatic	Subclinical abnormalities
—Postural hypotension	Abnormal pupillary reflexes
Gastroparesis	Esophageal dysfunction
Diabetic diarrhea	Abnormal cardiovascular reflexes ?
Neuropathic bladder	Blunted counter-regulatory responses to hypoglycemia
Erectile dysfunction	
Neuropathic edema	Increased peripheral blood flow
Charcot arthropathy	
Gustatatory sweating (sweating on the forehead, face, scalp & neck after ingesting food) gustatory	

Mononeuropathies: Cranial nerve palsies (most common are n. IV, VI, VII)   4, 6, 7

Entrapment Neuropathies:
- Carpal tunnel syndrome (median nerve)
- Ulnar compression syndrome
- Meralgia paresthetica (lat cut nerve to the thigh)
- Lat Popliteal nerve compression (drop foot)
  - **Diabetic amyotrophy:** This syndrome is known by several names, including diabetic proximal motor neuropathy and diabetic polyradiculoneuropathy. Patients typically present with pain and weakness in the proximal large muscles of the legs and pelvic area. Muscle wasting may be unilateral or bilateral
- **Screening for Neuropathy:**
- 128 Hz tuning fork for testing of vibration perception and 10gm Semmers monofilament
- & Nerve conduction studies
-

What are the infections that may be specific to diabetes?

- Pneumococcal infection carries a higher risk of death in diabetic than non diabetic patients
  (S pneumoniae, S aureus, H influenzae)
- Acute bacterial cystitis: more common in diabetic women; *E coli, Proteus*
- Emphysematous pyelonephritis: Emergency nephrectomy often required; *E coli, gr- bacilli*
- Perinephric abscess: surgical drainage usually required; *E coli, Gr-bacilli*
- Necrotizing fasciitis: High mortality; emergency surgery required; *Gr neg.bacilli, anaerobes, Group A streptococci*
- Mucormycosis: Strong association with DKA; emergency surgery required
- Invasive otitis externa: Prompt ENT consultation required; *Pseudomonas aeruginosa*
- Emphysematous cholecystitis: High mortality; gallstones in 50%; emergency cholecystectomy required; *Gr- bacilli, anaerobes*

MACRO VASCULAR COMPLICATIONS:

Macro vascular Damage Affects Large Arteries:

- v Coronary Arteries
- v Carotid/Cerebral Arteries
- v Lower Extremity Arteries

& Macro vascular Damage Causes:

- v Angina, Myocardial Infarction, Sudden Death, Strokes
- v Poor Healing from Wounds or Infections & Amputations

10. Enumerate the major patho physiological factors occur in CVS of diabetic patient:

- Accelerated atherosclerosis
- cardiac autonomic neuropathy
- intrinsic diabetic cardiomyopathy
- Myocardial fragment shows – arteriolar hyalinization leads to myocardial fibrosis
- Diastolic dysfunction
- Systolic dysfunction

11. What are the common surgical complications in diabetes mellitus?

- Furuncle & Carbuncle
  Perianal abscess
- Necrotizing fasciitis
- Fournier's gangrene

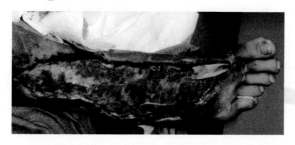

Fig: Necrotizing fasciitis-Mixed organisms responsible & rapidly spreading infection

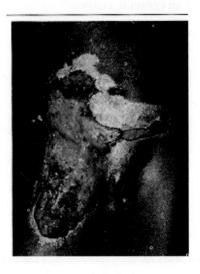

Fig: Fournier's gangrene- Severe infection involving scrotum, perineum & abdominal wall

Take home message:

- ➢ The high body mass index (BMI) especially the abdominal obesity is a marker for the future development of type2 DM.
- ➢ While treating hypertension always keep a lower target for diabetic patients than non-diabetic patients: 130/85 vs. 140/90.
- ➢ HbA1C is thought to reflect average glycemia over 3 months and has strong predictive value for diabetes complications. A1C testing should be performed routinely in all patients with diabetes.Microalbuminuria is an indication for screening for possible vascular disease and aggressive intervention to reduce all cardiovascular risk factors.
- ➢ Tight glucose control prevents the development of diabetic nephropathy.
- ➢ Lowering blood pressure slows the progression of decline in renal function and improves patient survival.
- ➢ ACE inhibitors preserve renal structure and function independent of their effect on systemic blood pressure.

CASE 53: ACROMEGALY
SAROJ JAYASINGHE

OVERVIEW

Acromegaly is observed when there is a characteristic phenotype due to excess secretion of growth hormone (GH) from a tumour arising in the anterior pituitary. The hypersecretion should be after puberty (in contrast to gigantism which is seen with excess growth hormone before puberty). GH stimulates liver cells to produce IGF-I (insulin like growth factor -I) which stimulates growth in almost all cells.

The tumour in a majority (>95%) is due to a pituitary adenoma that is autonomous and independent of the hypothalamus (i.e. GHRH-independent). The adenoma is often (about 80% of the time) a macroadenoma (>1 cm), and less commonly a microadenoma (< 1 cm).

Symptoms are insidious and rarely due to the pressure effects of the tumour. The excess GH leads to soft tissue swelling and enlargement of extremities with increase in ring and/or shoe size. There are coarsening of facial features with prognathism and macroglossia. Increased sweating is a feature, but its relevance as a symptom in the warm tropics can be a problem. An increased incidence of arthritis (from osteoarthritis) and obstructive sleep apnea are seen. Glucose intolerance or frank diabetes mellitus, hypertension, and cardiovascular disease, hypercalcuria, and hypertriglyceridemia are other complications. Rarely congestive heart failure supervenes due to uncontrolled hypertension or to a specific GH induced cardiomyopathy. There is an increased incidence of colonic polyps and adenocarcinoma of the colon

Pressure effects of the tumour can lead to headaches and visual field defects, with the latter depending on which part of the optic nerve is compressed. Most patients with visual field defects have headache. The headache is continuous, bifrontal, or unilateral frontal on the side of the tumor. In some instances, pain is localized to the midface. Rarely the tumor erodes laterally into the cavernous sinus, which contains the first and second divisions of the trigeminal nerve. This results in pressure effect on the optic chiasma giving rise to a bitemporal hemianopia. Rarely damage to the pituitary stalk might cause hyperprolactinemia (because this will lead to a loss of inhibition of prolactin secretion by the hypothalamus). Co-secretion by the tumour itself can also account for high prolactin levels. Rarely, damage to normal pituitary tissue can cause deficiencies of glucocorticoids, sex steroids, and thyroid hormone.

Types of Cases for Clinical Examination
OSCE, short or long:

Students should know the questions that should be asked to elicit the non-specific symptoms associated with acromegaly. Often the case would require you to describe the typical phenotype of acromegaly.

Long case or OSLER

The student should aim to (a) to take a detailed history, including past history and family history of endocrine tumours; (b) demonstrate clinical competence in general examination and of the relevant systems; and (c) show clinical reasoning skills in managing the patient.

CASE VIGNETTE

A 35-year-old male, presents with a history of headache and -medical history of treatment for hypertension for 3 months. He also complains of a 12–month history of excessive tiredness and lethargy. On further questioning he describes a change in his facial appearance. He has the characteristic facies seen in acromegaly with a blood pressure of 150 / 100 mm Hg. The rest of the cardiovascular, respiratory and abdominal examination are normal. Other than bitemporal hemi-anopia (noted on visual fields examination) his neurological system examination is normal.

DIFFERENTIAL DIAGNOSIS

- Acromegaly
- Hypothyroidism (the coarse facial features could be confused with acromegaly, though in hypothyroidism there is no prognathism and the coarseness is from thickening of subcutaneous tissue, whereas in acromegaly its due to growth of the bones)

HISTORY TAKING

HISTORY OF PRESENTING ILLNESS

Symptoms are insidious. The diagnosis should be identified from the characteristic facies because symptom analysis is unlikely to be helpful. On rare occasions the patient may volunteer and state that his facial features have changes (e.g. the facial features have become thicker, the jaw more prominent and space between teeth have widened) or the shoe sizes have increased or ring become tighter (the latter of course happens even with obesity). Once acromegaly is suspected, you should ask for arthritis (especially large joint osteoarthritis), snoring (for obstructive sleep apnea), polyuria and polydypsia (diabetes mellitus), angina (cardiovascular disease), renal colics (hypercalcuria) dyspnoea and oedema (congestive heart failure) and bleeding PR (colonic polyps and adenocarcinoma of the colon). This patient's history of hypertension should be further questioned because of the young age of hypertensive onset (therefore do not forget to ask about symptoms arising from chronic kidney disease or phaeochromocytoma), and he should be specifically questioned as to the presence of hyperlipidemia.

The headache should be described in detail. It can be due to the pressure effects or erosion of surrounding dura mater and bone. The pain in these situations is typically continuous, bifrontal, or frontal on the side of the tumor. In some instances, pain is localized in the midface. Features of increased intra-cranial hypertension (early morning headache) tend to be rare or are masked by the local effects of the enlarging tumour.

PAST MEDICAL HISTORY

- Rarely, acromegaly is a part of the Multiple Endocrine Neoplasia 1 and associated with the presence of parathyroid and pancreatic tumours. Goitre is also well known.

FAMILY HISTORY

- There may be a family history of tumours close to thyroid gland (i.e. parathyroids) or pancreatic tumours.

SOCIAL HISTORY

- Ask about alcohol intake and smoking.

SYSTEMIC REVIEW OF SYMPTOMS

- Weight gain may be a feature. Other less common features are: those of carpel tunnel syndrome, and constipation from secondary hypothyroidism; renal colics (hypercalciuria); angina; osteoporosis; impotence and low libido (from secondary hypogonadism) and rarely galactorrhoea from high serum prolactin

SURGICAL HISTORY

- Surgery for other tumours (e.g. parathyroid, colonic adenomas) are relevant. Prior surgery for acromegaly should be specifically asked for, because the trans-sphenoidal approach may not leave obvious scars.

EXAMINATION

Professionalism:

Introduce yourself, obtain consent, position patient ideally lying down, suitably undressed and request for a chaperone when you are examining, especially because you need to look for features of secondary hypogonadism (due to pressure effects on the pititutary).

Physical examination:

Inspection

Observe the patient from the end of the bed and comment on the typical facies of acromegaly: frontal bossing; thickening of the nose; macroglossia and prognathism. There may be a multinodular goitre. Note enlarged extremities (e.g. sausage-shaped fingers) and skin tags (a possible marker for colonic polyps).

Chest- are there features of cardiomegaly (from organomegaly due to increased GH) or congestive cardiac failure (e.g. elevated jugular venous pressure)?
Kyphoscoliosis is seen in 5 % of cases

Abdomen –There can be enlargement of the liver (due to excess GH) from organomaegaly). Look for sparse hair in the groin. Testicular atrophy is another feature to look for (using a pair of gloves and in the presence of a chaperone).

Neurology – Tumour effects on optic chiasm can lead to bitemporal hemianopia detected on visual confrontation in visual field examination. Ophthalmoscopy may reveal optic atrophy or unilateral papilloedema from the tumour extending and pressing on an optic nerve. Increased intracranial pressure leading to bilateral papilloedema is rare. Cranial nerve palsies (III, IV and VI) are rare. There may be evidence of proximal muscle weakness (i.e. difficulty in getting up from a squatting position).

Note:

The student should be competent in performing a complete visual field and ophthalmoscopic examination and report the findings to explain the defects present in the patient.

Though cranial nerve palsy is uncommon he should attempt to show how they are examined, unless he is dissuaded from doing so due to time constraints.

Musculoskeletal system- osteoarthritis of the knees and cervical spondylosis are known to occur

All the rudiments of good techniques of joint examination should be demonstrated, as is done in orthopaedic examination. These examinations are only relevant if the joints are affected.

Professionalism: Thank the patient, place him in previous position he was in and re-dress patient.

INVESTIGATIONS

Growth Hormone
There is little diagnostic value in random serum GH measurement, because of episodic secretion of GH which has a short half-life. A better measure is the inability of glucose to suppress GH seen in acromegaly. One protocol used is to measure two baseline GH levels prior to ingestion of 75 g of oral glucose, and take additional GH measurements at 30, 60, 90, and 120 minutes. Those with acromegaly do not suppress GH concentration below 2 ng/mL.

IGF-1
Because IGF-I has a longer half-life it is used to screen for acromegaly, and to monitor the efficacy of therapy. Prolactin levels may also be elevated. Since pituitary adenomas are associated with deficiencies of other pituitary hormones, evaluation of adrenal, thyroid, and gonadal axes are important.

In acromegaly there is an increase in the levels of the IGF-1 binding protein (IGFBP-3). This is also useful in diagnosis and monitoring after treatment.

Other hormones secreted by the anterior pituitary:
Screening is done to detect effects of the tumour on ACTH, TSH. FSH and LH secretion. Though these individual hormone levels could be assayed, their prolonged low levels can have effects on the axis (especially ACTH-adrenal, TSH-Thyroid and gonadal axes). These effects can lead to low end-organ hormone levels (e.g. low levels of cortisol, T4, and testosterone). These levels respond to stimulation by the respective pituitary hormone (e.g. ACTH- the Synacthen test-in the case of low cortisol). Hyperprolactinameia). Serum prolactin levels are also high because of damage to the pituitary stalk or by co-secretion by the tumour.

Visual fields and Snellen's chart for visual acuity forms part of the evaluation.

Imaging

X-rays of the pituitary region have now been replaced by CT and MRI. MRIs are the most sensitive in imaging the pituitary gland, hypothalamus and show the surrounding structures better (e.g. optic chiasm and cavernous sinuses).

Rarely no lesion is seen on MRI. In such instances ectopic GHRH induced acromegaly should be considered where tumour arises from sites like lungs, kidneys or pancreas. Appropriate imaging will be required to detect these, starting from the simplest such as chest X-ray, abdominal ultrasound to more sophisticated ones such as MRI or CT of thorax.

Screening for other complications of acromegaly may be required:
- diabetes mellitus
- hypertension, and cardiovascular disease (ECG and ECHO)
- hypercalcuria (urine and X-rays / ultrasound of renal tract)
- hypertriglyceridemia (fasting lipids)
- appropriate X-rays for osteoarthritis

MANAGEMENT

In the long case, develop a management plan based on the case. Consider the complications listed and develop a management plan for all problems seen in the patient.

TREATMENT

Goals are to reduce symptoms caused by the local effects of the tumor and those due to excess GH/IGF-I production.

- Surgical treatment: This is the first-line option
- Medical treatment: Those who are unable to undergo surgery or have residual disease are given medical therapy for residual disease (e.g. octreotide).
- Radiation treatment is generally reserved for refractory cases.

 Note:

Surgical approaches evoke anxiety in patients and these need to be addressed when consent is obtained

Completeness of excision is evaluated on GH and IGF-1 measurement. Consistently elevated GH and IGF-1may require radiotherapy. Response to radiotherapy is not as efficient as surgery.

Postoperative hypopitutitarism is a well recognized complication that needs to be dealt by giving replacement hormones. Loss of libido, impotence, (and amenorrhoea and subfertility in the female) could occur from the effects of the tumour on FSH and LH secretion or following surgery.

COMMON QUESTIONS

1. **What is the histopathology of the pituitary adenomas?**
   Histologically they range from acidophil adenomas, densely granulated GH adenomas, sparsely granulated GH adenomas, somatomammotropic adenomas, and plurihormonal adenomas. Rarely acromegaly may result from an ectopic pituitary tumor or ectopic production of GH by other tumors (eg, cancers of the pancreas or lung).

2. **What is the prognosis in acromegaly?** The prognosis depends on the extension of the tumour (e.g. leading to problems such as erosion into the cavernous sinus) or more commonly due to effects such as hypertension, obstructive sleep apnoea, and susceptibility to stresses such as infections due to hypopitiutarism.

HIGH ACHIEVER QUESTIONS

1. Discuss briefly the modalities available for treatment of acromegaly?
Transsphenoidal hypophysectomy rapidly improves symptoms caused by the tumour's mass effects and reduces GH/IGF-I concentrations. Remission depends on the initial size of the tumor (it is higher with microadenomas than with macroadenomas), the GH level, and the skill of the neurosurgeon.

Medical treatment: Somatostatin and dopamine analogues and GH receptor antagonists are the mainstays. Bromocriptine and cabergoline are dopamine agonists induce tumour shrinkage, but with limited effectiveness. Tumours cosecreting prolactin respond better to these dopamine agonists.

Somatostatin inhibits GH secretion and long-acting analogues are available, but are extremely expensive. Octreotide, a somatostatin analogue that inhibits GH secretion and shrinks the tumour, is used extensively. Pegvisomant, is a GH receptor antagonist that normalizes IGF-I.

Radiation treatment reduces or normalizes GH/IGF-I levels, but patients develop panhypopituitarism. Therefore it is used as an adjuvant for large invasive tumors and when surgery is contraindicated.

2. What is pituitary apoplexy and how will you recognize it?

Pituitary apoplexy is when there is bleeding into the tumour. It is a neurosurgical emergency. Patients present with acute, severe headaches sometimes with meningism (stiff neck, photophobia), and diplopia and ophthalmoplegia. Routine CT scans may miss the presence of blood or a mass within the sella and MRI is more sensitive. There can be features of panhypopituitarism.

3. What is the pathogenesis of hypertension in acromegaly?

The exact mechanism of hypertension in acromegaly is unclear. Several mechanisms have been proposed: a direct anti-natriuric effect of GH or IGF-1; insulin resistance in acromegaly inducing renal sodium absorption; an increase in the sympathetic tone inducing hypertension.

RED FLAG ENCOUNTERS

Areas where students tend to fall into trouble are:

- Missing or not examining for subtle signs: large tongue, thickened fingers, OA, or cardiomegaly.
- Not doing a thorough neurological examination (e.g. visual fields)
- Not being clear about the tests to diagnose the condition
- Not being clear about the modalities available to treat

MUST KNOW FACTS ABOUT ACROMEGALY

- ✓ It is often asymptomatic
- ✓ Photographic records show gradual changes of soft tissue
- ✓ Physiology of GH secretion
- ✓ Pathogenesis of the clinical features
- ✓ Clinical presentations and treatment
- ✓ Tests to detect the tumour and GH excess

CASE 54: GRAVES DISEASE
SAROJ JAYASINGHE

OVERVIEW

Graves Disease is an autoimmune disorder where there is hyper functioning of the thyroid gland. It is mediated by antibodies (Thyroid-stimulating immunoglobulins-TSIs) that attach and activate thyroid stimulating hormone (TSH) receptors on thyroid glandular cells. This leads to growth of the thyroid gland, increased iodine uptake, and synthesis of thyroid hormone by the thyroid follicles. In addition to thyrotoxicosis, these and other auto-antibodies have an effect on extra ocular skeletal muscles and tissues in the orbit (ophthalmopathy), and tissues in the pre-tibial part of the lower limbs (dermopathy).

Clinical features are mainly due to the effects of excess circulating thyroxine and the autoimmune disorder that accompanies the illness. Excess thyroxine induces a raised cellular metabolic rate and up-regulation of the sympathetic nervous system. Raised metabolic rate induces an increase in the body requirements for oxygen, energy and has the ability to raise body temperature (and thereby sweating). Skin manifestations include a warm, moist and sweaty skin. There can be thyroid achropachy which is similar in appearance to clubbing. Thyrotoxicosis induces fine tremors of the out-stretched hands, proximal muscle weakness, easy fatigability, and in some periodic paralysis. Recent studies have shown an imbalance of autonomic system in the heart, with increased sympathetic and decreased vagal modulation of the heart rate. This leads to palpitations (from tachycardia) and dysponea. Tachycardia may be accompanied by collapsing pulse (from vasodilatation). The cardiovascular abnormalities can become more serious with atrial fibrillation, high output heart failure and cardiomyopathy. There can be increased bowel motility with increased frequency of bowel movements. Females may experience irregular menstrual periods and decreased menstrual volume, while males may develop gynaecomastia and impotence. Restlessness, anxiety, irritability, and insomnia are other features.

Eye Manifestations

Eye manifestations occur because thyrotropin receptors are highly expressed in fat and connective tissue of patients with Graves ophthalmopathy. Smoking is highly correlated with the development of ophthalmopathy. These lead to swelling of muscles, their weakness, and infiltration of the confined orbit by inflammatory cells. The resulting muscle weakness manifests as diplopia and ophthalmoplegia. The inflammatory response acts like a space occupying lesion within the orbit thus displacing the eye ball forwards (i.e. proptosis) and also gives rise to diplopia. There can be conjunctival injection and chemosis. Thyrotoxicosis, irrespective of the cause leads to retraction of the upper lid due to hyperstimulation of the sympathetically innervated Mueller muscle in the upper lid. When the patient looks downward, the upper lid gets held back and lag behind the movement of the globe (lid lag). A complete ophthalmologic examination, including retinal examination (for optic atrophy or rarely papilloedema) is indicated. Skin changes or dermopathy are characterized by tissues in the pre-tibial part of the lower limbs resembling an orange peel in color and texture.

Associated Autoimmune Disorders

Graves disease is associated with several other autoimmune disorders such as pernicious anaemia vitiligo, type-1 diabetes mellitus, Addison disease, myasthenia gravis, Sjogrens syndrome, rheumatoid arthritis, and SLE.

Clinical presentation is variable and range from asymptomatic, mild systemic features (e.g. mild smooth goitre, loss of weight and increased appetite), to florid state. The latter is characterized by a smooth goitre with bruits indicating vascularity. Systemic features include low grade fever, loss of weight, and increased appetite. The metabolic effects on the cardiovascular system leads to tachycardia, widened pulse pressure and even collapsing pulse, atrial fibrillation, and a high output cardiac failure.

Types of Cases for Clinical Examination

OSCE or short case: Female with a history of weight loss with a goitre

The student should be able to take a focussed history and demonstrate competency in examining the goitre: confirm the presence of an enlarged thyroid by asking patient to swallow and observing the movement of the gland (ensure the patient is given a glass of water); palpate while standing behind the patient for the surface (smooth in Graves, or nodular in multinodular goitre), consistency (usually firm in Graves), presence of thrills and a pulsatile gland (indicative of vascularity), and cervical lymph nodes; checking for retrosternal extension by showing you can get below the gland at the supra-sternal notch (i.e. if the gland extends below the sternum, one cannot get below the gland); auscultating for thyroid bruits (from a vascular superior thyroid artery).

Look for features of thyrotoxicosis.

Hands: fine tremors, warm peripheries, and achropachy;

CVS: tachycardia, collapsing pulse, or irregularly irregular pulse (AF) with varying pulse volume, displaced cardiac apex which is hyperdynamic (i.e. high amplitude), widened pulse pressure (on measuring BP);

Eye signs: proptosis, lid lag, lid retraction, ophthalmoplegia, conjuctival injection and chemosis;

Skin changes: dermopathy of pre-tibial part resembling an orange peel.

The student should volunteer to examine the abdomen (some patient have mild splenomegaly) and NS (for optic atrophy or papilloedema, and hyper-reflexia, and proximal myopathy: difficulty in getting up from a squatting position)

Long case or OSLER

The student should take a detailed history on (a) the systemic features from increased body metabolic rate outlined above with special mention on weight loss, appetite, warm intolerance, excess sweating, fatigue; (b) the features from up-regulation of sympathetic system: palpitations, dyspnoea; (c) those due to a goitre: progress in size, any pain, dysphagia, dysphonia and attacks of chocking: (d) features of ophthalmopathy: diplopia, irritation or pain in eyes, prominence of eyes; (e) dermopathy: characteristic thickening of skin over shins; (f) other autoimmune diseases: vitiligo, diabetes etc.

Physical examination should be comprehensive and specifically look for the points noted under OSCE or Short Cases.

CASE VIGNETTE

A 45-year-old female, with no known past-medical history presents with a 6 –month history of loss of weight, increased appetite, intolerance to warm weather and palpitations. On closer questioning she also mentions a slight prominence of her neck. She appears thin with mildly prominent eyes, and has fine tremors of hands. Her pulse is irregularly irregular with a rate of about 95 beats per minute and a blood pressure 110 / 60 mm Hg (sitting).

DIFFERENTIAL DIAGNOSIS

- Graves disease
- Diabetes mellitus
- Anxiety state

HISTORY TAKING : HISTORY OF PRESENTING ILLNESS

Points in the history include details on the loss of weight (was the patient weighed?) If so, what was the decrease? Or was it that others mentioned that there was visible weight loss? Or did the clothes become loose?); increase in appetite and intolerance to warm weather.

Palpitations should be explored to find out if it is sustained (e.g. sinus tachycardia or AF) or in episodes (paroxysmal AF or SVT). Ask about onset (abrupt in paroxysmal tachycardias while sinus tachycardia will be gradual), and waning (again the abruptness indicates as with the onset), rapidity of the felt beat, associated syncope or chest pain, and passage of larger volumes of urine (suggesting SVT).

The prominence in the neck should be assumed to be a thyroid gland and the student should ask about the progress in size, pain, and pressure symptoms such as dysphagia, dysphonia and attacks of chocking.

The student should be able to describe presence or absence of systemic features such as fatigue, dyspnoea, periodic weakness (i.e. periodic paralysis) and proximal weakness (i.e. proximal myopathy).
Symptoms due to ophthalmopathy should be asked for: diplopia, irritation or pain in eyes, prominence of eyes. Dermopathy is rarely symptomatic.
Anxiety, irritability and short-temper are other features that the patient may have.

PAST MEDICAL HISTORY

- Other autoimmune diseases may be seen: depigmentation (i.e. vitiligo), type-1 diabetes mellitus, and a history suggestive of Addison's disease, myasthenia gravis, Sicca syndrome (in Sjogrens), arthritis, (e.g. rheumatoid arthritis), and skin rashes (e.g. SLE).

FAMILY HISTORY

- There may be a family history thyroid disease or autoimmune diseases.

SOCIAL HISTORY

- Though in most parts of Asia females do not smoke or take alcohol, it is prudent to ask about these habits.

- Other less common features of thyrotoxicosis could be asked here: frequent stools and even diarrhea, shortness of breath, irregular or infrequent periods.

EXAMINATION

Professionalism:

Introduce yourself, obtain consent, position patient ideally lying down, suitably undressed and request for a chaperone, especially when you are examining the areas such as precordium.

Attention should be paid to placing the patient on a chair with you sitting infront of her for examination of the eyes, thyroid gland and neck.

Physical examination:

Follow the instructions in this station . In an OSCE you may be asked to examine the neck and face (eye signs), hence it is best the patient is examined sitting.

On the other hand you may be asked to demonstrate the 'collapsing pulse' and characteristics of the peripheral pulse. In this instance the patient may be lying down.

In a long case the execution of the examination should be systematic and smooth without tiring the patient because of the several movements required in examining the relevant systems.

A normal sequence of events in a long case would be:

- Begin with hands (evidence of tachycardia, characteristics of pulse, any atrial fibrillation, collapsing pulse), tremors (outstretched hand and paper placed on top), nails ('clubbing', onycholysis), palmar erythema

- Neck: inspect from front (sitting in front of patient) then from side, mention swelling and if scar from previous surgery is present. Look for movement of gland during swallowing (water to be provided).

- Demonstrate other eye signs as mentioned below.

- Palpate from behind (inform patient you will be examining the neck), feel for both lobes and isthmus. Note any swelling or nodules, consistency, shape, mobility, tenderness, and if it moves with swallowing (glass of water to be provided). Look for exophthalmos by peering from above the forehead while standing behind.

- Examine cervical lymph nodes systematically. Palpate for thrills and also feel for the carotid arteries.

- Auscultate the thyroid gland for vascularity (bruit).

If the patient is lying when encountered, observe the patient from the foot of the bed and comment on obvious abnormalities

- Appearance: thin and staring appearance from lid retraction and proptosis.
- Observing the goitre and its characteristics (e.g. lack of obvious nodules)
- Presence or absence of pre-tibial myxoedema
- Thyroid achropachy, fine tremor and palmar erythema

Feel the pulse: Are the hands warm and sweaty? Is the pulse regular? What is the rate? (i.e. is there a tachycardia?). Is there a collapsing pulse? Is it irregularly irregular? (as in AF).

Examine closely for the goitre: confirm its presence by asking patient to swallow and observing the movement of the gland; move behind the patient and explain you are going to palpate the neck and begin to palpate for the surface of the gland (is it smooth or nodular?); Is it firm as in Graves' disease? Are there thrills or does the gland pulsate? Is there cervical lymphadenopathy? Check for retrosternal extension and auscultate for thyroid bruits.

Once these features suggest thyrotoxicosis, proceed to look for lid retraction and lid lag, which are seen with any cause of thyrotoxicosis. Then look for features of Graves' ophthalmopathy: proptosis, ophthalmoplegia, conjuctival injection and chemosis.

Chest- look for features of cardiomegaly with a hyperdynamic apex. Elevated jugular venous pressure will indicate the presence of congestive cardiac failure from thyrotoxic cardiomyopathy.

Abdomen – Splenomegaly may be seen with Graves' disease.

Neurology – There may be evidence of proximal muscle weakness (i.e. difficulty in getting up from a squatting position) and hyper-reflexia.

Professionalism: Thank the patient, place him in previous position he was in and re-dress patient.

INVESTIGATIONS

These could be classified for convenience:
Tests to confirm Graves' disease

Diagnosis of thyrotoxicosis is by showing high serum free T4 (FT4) and T3 (FT3) with low TSH levels. Rarely there is elevated FT3 with normal FT4 (T3-toxicosis).

Note

The student should be able to interpret results of thyroid function and give reasons in relation to the hormonal feedback system to explain the abnormal results.

T3 thyrotoxicosis is seen in the elderly and presents with clinical and laboratory evidence of of hypermetabolism in the presence of low or normal T4 and TSH. This is typically seen in hyperfunctioning solitary nodule (which secreted T3).

Autoimmune nature of the illness is demonstrated by the presence of thyroid antibodies (anti-microsomal antibodies, anti-thyroglobulin antibodies and anti thyroid-stimulating immunoglobulins-TSIs). It is the latter one which suggests Graves' disease.

Thyroid histology
- Rarely a FNAC is done and it shows hyperplastic glandular tissues with a lymphocytic infiltration.

Imaging
- Ultrasound of the thyroid gland will show a smooth goitre and doppler studies will confirm increased vascularity.
- Radio-isotope uptake will show a high uptake, but diffuse. It will also pick up retrosternal extension of the gland.
- CT or MRI of orbits is required for evaluation of proptosis. This is done especially if there is a suspicion of a tumour.
- The pressure effects of the gland and retrosternal extension should be looked for with a soft tissue X-ray of neck and a chest X-ray focusing on the thoracic inlet. These are now superseded by CT scans.

Other metabolic and immune effects
- Metabolic effects are mainly on the heart and therefore the ECG is essential to diagnose sinus tachycardia, AF, ventricular or atrial ectopics, and SVTs. Even a 24-hour ECG is required if

paroxysmal SVT and AF are suspected. ECG may show features of ventricular hypertrophy. Echocardiogram is indicated to confirm the diagnosis of high-output cardiac failure and cardiomyopathy.

- Ultrasound of abdomen may detect splenomegaly.
- Autoimmune tests are indicated if associated autoimmune diseases are suspected: e.g. antinuclear antibodies for SLE, rheumatoid factor for rheumatoid arthritis.
- Hyperglycaemia without frank diabetes can be seen due to the insulin antagonistic effects of thyroxine. Hyperglycaemia from associated type-1 diabetes is also possible
- Full blood count: The haematology results are unremarkable (though there may be a normocytic anemia, low-normal to slightly depressed total WBC count with relative lymphocytosis and monocytosis, and a slightly depressed platelet count).

Investigations are requested in a cost effective manner and students should avoid providing a list without giving the reasons for such requests. Graves'disease is diagnosed from clinical presentation in most instances although hormonal investigations are requested for. Please note that thyroxicosis is confirmed when the free T4 is clearly elevated, and under these circumstances assaying for free T3 is not useful. Free T3 is indicated when free T4 is not above normal reference level and the serum TSH is low.

MANAGEMENT

Student should focus the management based on the disease. He should be able to discuss outpatient management as best option exhibiting knowledge on the effects of drugs and expected response especially when the patient is distressed with palpitations and having an arrhythmia.

A discussion of the options available with the patient (drug, radioactive iodine or surgery) is vital for decision making.

TREATMENT

Treatment is to control symptoms and correct the thyrotoxic state. Symptoms are mainly due to adrenergic system hyperfunction (e.g. palpitations, tremors, and anxiety) and best treated with beta-adrenergic blockade (e.g. propranolol or atenalol). The thyrotoxic state can be corrected by using antithyroid drugs that block the synthesis of thyroid hormones, or by slow destruction of part of the hyperactive gland with radioactive iodine. Surgery to remove part of the gland can also be offered, especially as it improves the cosmetic appearance.

Antithyroid medication

Carbimazole is the drug which is often used. It is a prodrug and is converted to methimazole; the latter is preferred in the US. They inhibit thyroid hormone synthesis.

Propylthiouracil (PTU) is another antithyroid drug that is available, and in addition to inhibiting synthesis, reduces the peripheral conversion of T4 to T3, and therefore has an advantage in thyroid storm (see below). PTU is preferred during pregnancy and lactation as concentrations of methimazole are higher in breast milk. It is also preferred during 1st trimester as its embryotoxic effects are less.

Antithyroid drugs are usually given for 1-2 years to induce a sustained remission of the disease. The drug effect is monitored using FT3 and FT4 levels.

Side effects:

Patient safety is paramount and students should be familiar with the common side effects of anti-thyroid drugs.

Fever and rashes are known side effects. The more serious side effects include risk of agranulocytosis (0.2 to 0.5%) which should be detected early (by explaining to patient to stop the drug at the first sign of a sore throat or fever and reporting to the closest health facility). Monitoring by checking on WBC is not helpful to detect the onset of agranulocytosis because the fall in counts is dramatic. Stopping the drug reverses the neutropenia and rarely recombinant granulocyte colony stimulating factor is required.

Hepatitis is increasingly being recognized: in general PTU is associated with transaminase elevation (and rarely acute liver failure and fatal hepatitis) while carbimazole and methimazole cause a cholestasis. Monitoring of liver enzymes at least for the first 6 months is recommended with PTU.

Potassium iodide is used to reduce vascularity of gland prior to surgery (given 2-3 weeks prior to surgery). They are useful as an adjunct and reduce T4 production. Oral contrast agents (ipodate or iopanoic acid) also inhibit conversion of T4-to-T3 and therefore used during thyrotoxic storm.

Radioactive iodine (RAI)

RAI is commonly used in the US. It used especially when there is large thyroid gland when surgery is declined with high levels of thyroxine, and high titers of TSI. It can be performed as an outpatient, and those on antithyroid drugs must discontinue treatment for at least 2 days prior.

RAI induced hypothyroidism from destruction of the gland can occur. Monthly monitoring is required to identify the onset of hypothyroidism, at which stage life-long T4 replacement is required.

Rarely RAI precipitates thyroid storm by releasing thyroid hormones, and also worsens Graves' ophthalmopathy. The latter could be prevented by a course of steroids for 2-3 months, tapered off before RAI.

The absolute contraindication for radioiodine is pregnancy.

Note:

The student should be able to assist patient in decision making highlighting the advantages and disadvantages of treatment options. He should be aware as to the value of radioiodine therapy and surgery as options to antithyroid drug treatment.

The need for life long thyroxine therapy especially in radioactive ablation (and surgery) is well known. Newer options of thyroid artery embolization may not be relevant for normal discussions.

Management of anxiety is not well addressed in OSCE, and log cases but may be relevant when the patient is bothered by these symptoms.

COMMON QUESTIONS

1. Describe the treatment of Graves' ophthalmopathy

Artificial tears, sunglasses, eye patches, nocturnal taping of eyes and elevating head at night are adequate for mild-to-moderate ophthalmopathy. These prevent exposure keratitis and symptoms. If there is severe ophthalmopathy treatment includes high-dose prednisolone, orbital radiotherapy, or orbital decompression by surgery.

2. How does thyroid storm present?

It is seen typically in those untreated or partially treated and often precipitated by surgery, infection, or trauma. Patients may present with nausea and vomiting, and associated hypermetabolic features: fever or hyperpyrexia, tachycardia, tremulousness, agitation, psychosis and even coma with hypotension.

HIGH ACHIEVER QUESTION

1. How will you manage thyroid storm?

The condition must be clinically recognized and treated without delay even before laboratory confirmation. Patient should be on a cardiac monitor, intubated if comatosed, given supplementary oxygen and fluid resuscitation commenced aggressively (e.g. normal saline). Temperature should be brought down with cooling measures and antipyretics (with paracetamol, because aspirin decreases protein binding of T3 and T4 and can increase their free levels). Only in the setting of subacute thyroiditis is aspirin indicated.

Propranolol and / or digoxin should be given though atrial fibrillation may be refractory to rate control.

Intravenous glucocorticoids (e.g. large doses of dexamethazone) are indicated as it inhibits production of T4 and decreases peripheral conversion from T4 to T3.

PTU or carbimazole or methimazole should be given in large doses. PTU has a theoretical advantage of inhibiting peripheral conversion of T4 to T3 in addition to its inhibition of T4 synthesis. Blocking the release of preformed thyroid hormone is done by iodide administration, but should be delayed until 1 hour after the antithyroid drugs to prevent block the utilization of iodine to synthesise new T4. If necessary these drugs can be given via NG tube.

2. How would you manage Atrial Fibrillation in a patient with Graves's disease?

The same principles of managing AF with other conditions apply.

Rate control is by using any of the following drugs: a beta blocker (e.g. propranolol); or when beta blockers are contraindicated a calcium antagonist (e.g. verapamil or diltiazem); or digoxin.

Beta blockers have the added advantage of improving symptoms. Beta-blockers and calcium antagonists should be cautiously used in severe heart failure as they are negative inotropes.

Warfarin is recommended to prevent embolic phenomena (especially strokes).

Nearly two third revert to sinus rhythm after 8-10 weeks of euthyroid state. After 3 months the chances of reversion are low and therefore cardioversion is recommended. Structural lesions of the heart that contribute to continuing AF (e.g. mitral stenosis) must be ruled out with an echocardiogram. The patient must be anticoagulated for at least 3 weeks prior to, and for 4 weeks post procedure to minimize the risk of embolization

3. What is sub-clinical hyperthyroidism?

This is when there is low TSH with normal FT3 and FT4. A minority of these patients could develop overt hyperthyroidism. Those with sub-clinical hyperthyroidism are at higher risk of developing AF and osteoporosis. Beta blockers or methimazole are recommended by some authorities.

4. What are the principles of managing Graves' during pregnancy?

PTU is preferred to methimazole during pregnancy and lactation, as concentrations of methimazole are higher in breast milk. It is also preferred during 1st trimester as its embryotoxic effects are less.

Propranolol is best avoided because of the effects on fetal growth. Radioactive iodine is absolutely contraindicated.

5. What is periodic paralysis and what is its link to Graves? Young adults from the Southeast Asia seem to have a genetic susceptibility to develop hypokalaemic periodic paralysis associated with thyrotoxicosis, especially Graves. It could present as an emergency with rapid onset of weakness, and thyrotoxicosis may be mild. High carbohydrate diet, sleep, alcohol and infections are known to precipitate the condition. Treatment is with intravenous or oral potassium. Propranolol also has a place in treatment and prevention.

6. Do you know about drug induced thyroid disorders? Amiodorone and lithium are two well known drugs that lead to hypo or hyperthyroidism. Interferone (e.g. used for hepatitis C) and therapeutic irradiation of the neck lead to hypothyroidism. Iodine when given in areas with endemic goitre due to iodine deficiency (often with a multinodular goitre) is known precipitate hyperthyroidism (Jod Basedow phenomenon)

RED FLAG ENCOUNTERS-

Areas where students tend to fall into trouble are:

- Omission in examining for dermopathy, palmar erythema and achropachy
- Not doing a thorough examination of the thyroid gland (e.g. not looking for retro-sternal extension)
- Missing the bruit over the gland
- Incomplete examination for ophthalmopathy
- Not being clear about the tests to diagnose the condition
- Confusing the appropriate management of the patient (e.g. mistakes in the duration of treating with anti-thyroid drugs)

MUST KNOW FACTS ABOUT GRAVES' DISEASE

- ✓ It can be asymptomatic or present with subtle symptoms and signs
- ✓ Pathogenesis of the clinical features of Graves disease
- ✓ Clinical presentations and management of Graves disease
- ✓ Tests of thyroid function and their interpretation

CASE 55: CUSHINGS SYNDROME
VAANI VALERIE VISUVANATHAN

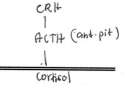

CRH
↓
ACTH (ant. pit)
↓
Cortisol

OVERVIEW

Cushing's syndrome is a hormonal disorder that occurs following prolonged exposure to elevated levels of cortisol hormone. The source of excess cortisol may be exogenous or endogenous.

Normally, cortisol production by the adrenal glands is carefully regulated by the adrenocorticotropic hormone (ACTH) which is secreted by the anterior pituitary gland. Corticotropin-releasing hormone (CRH) from the hypothalamus stimulates the secretion of ACTH. For example, as a response to stress, the neural stimuli lead to release of CRH in the hypothalamic-hypophysial portal venous circulation. This stimulates ACTH secretion into the systemic circulation and hence secretion of cortisol by the adrenal glands. When levels of cortisol are elevated, cortisol binds to its receptors on the hypothalamus and anterior pituitary, producing an inhibitory effect on the release of CRH and ACTH. This is referred to as the negative feedback inhibition.

The normal cortisol production has a Circadian rhythm, which is ACTH dependent, with levels peaking in the early morning and at a nadir at night. This rhythm may be disrupted by physical and psychological stress.

The main physiological functions of cortisol are:

- Increases blood glucose levels by stimulating gluconeogenesis in the liver
- Suppresses humoral immune response and B cells antibody production
- Maintains blood pressure
- Inhibit secretion of sodium while encouraging potassium excretion into urine (mineralocorticoid effect)

Therefore, a patient with Cushing's syndrome may present with:

- Central obesity – limbs appear thin compared to the torso. It is suggested that fat cells around the waistline are more sensitive to cortisol compared to fat cells located elsewhere, hence the development of central obesity in Cushing's syndrome.
- Moon-like face
- Recently diagnosed diabetes mellitus and hypertension
- Thin skin and easy bruising– due to cortisol induced collagen loss

- Hyperpigmentation – only occurs when there is excess ACTH
- Violaceous striae – reddish-purple striae , unlike those that occur in pregnancy and obesity
- Proximal muscle weakness – catabolic action on protein metabolism
- Menstrual irregularities – due to suppression of other pituitary hormones
- Hypothyroidism
- Hirsutism and acne – masculinizing effects seen in female patients is due to excess of androgens _prevent Na excretion_
- Hypokalaemic alkalosis with sodium retention – excess cortisol interacts with mineralocorticoid receptors
- Depression or psychosis
- Osteoporosis – attributed to impaired osteoblastic bone formation, mainly affecting axial bones

Exogenous glucocorticoids intake is the most common cause of Cushing's syndrome. This may be iatrogenic in some cases. Endogenous excess of cortisol is due to Cushing's disease in about 80% of cases. Cushing's disease refers to ACTH producing pituitary tumour causing Cushing's syndrome. The other causes of endogenous Cushing's syndrome are ectopic production of ACTH (by small cell carcinoma of lung or carcinoid tumours), adrenal adenomas, adrenal hyperplasia and CRH producing tumours.

Pseudo-Cushing's syndrome is a condition commonly described among patients who are alcohol dependent, have poorly-controlled diabetes, eating disorders or depressed. They exhibit signs and abnormal hormone levels as seen in Cushing's syndrome but there is no abnormality of the hypothalamus-pituitary-adrenal axis. Cessation or treatment of the underlying disorder will lead to resolution of their symptoms, signs and abnormal laboratory results.

Types of cases for clinical examination:

- Short /long case
- OSCE
- OSPE

CASE VIGNETTE

A 45-year-old lady is seen at the medical out-patient clinic. She complains of recent weight gain, especially noted around her abdomen and face. She also complains of difficulty standing up from a sitting position.

Take a relevant history from this patient and perform a focussed physical examination.

HISTORY OF PRESENTING ILLNESS

- Weight gain – quantify change in weight (if possible), period over which weight change was noted, parts of body most noticeably affected, appetite and food intake, explore causes of weight gain in general eg. smoking cessation, change in diet.
- Weakness – movements affected, activities of daily living affected eg. climbing stairs, assess effect on occupation

☞ Note: The clear history of central obesity and proximal weakness points heavily towards Cushing's syndrome, therefore, the student would be expected to recognize these clues and proceed to take a history as suggested below

SYSTEMIC REVIEW

- Skin changes – easy bruising, purple stretch marks, hyperpigmentation, skin infections, poor wound healing, acne, increased hair in androgen dependent areas eg. chin
- Lethargy
- Mood changes
- Amenorrhoea, infertility, decreased libido
- Impotence (in males)
- Headaches, visual problems, galactorrhoea and polyuria may occur in patients with pituitary tumours
- Bone pain and fractures
- Cough and haemoptysis – suggestive of lung carcinoma

PAST MEDICAL HISTORY

- Glucocorticoids are often prescribed for various medical disorders (anti-inflammatory effect), eg. rheumatoid arthritis, bronchial asthma, myasthenia gravis
- Have blood pressure and blood sugar levels been more difficult to control recently

MEDICATION history

- The importance of obtaining history of previous prolonged (> 1 month) glucocorticoid usage cannot be stressed enough!
- Traditional medications
- Alcohol dependance(? Pseudo Cushing's syndrome)

SOCIAL HISTORY

- Explore the psychological effects of acne/obesity on the patient
- Smoking history

Check list for history taking

- ✓ Symptoms of Cushing's syndrome eg. moon face, striae, obesity (be sensitive to the psychological effects)
- ✓ Causes of Cushing's syndrome eg. medications, autoimmune disorders, mass effect of pituitary tumours
- ✓ Exclude pseudo Cushing's syndrome – alcohol dependency, poorly controlled diabetes mellitus, depression
- ✓ Possible complications – hypertension, infection, osteoporotic fractures

EXAMINATION

Introduce yourself to the patient and confirm her identity. Explain that you would like to examine her and acquire a chaperone, if necessary.

General examination and vital signs

Take a few seconds to observe for features of moon-like facies, facial plethora, male pattern balding, truncal obesity with sparing of the limbs, facial hair, acne and purpura. Also, look for poorly-healing wounds, xanthelasma, acanthosis nigricans (velvety hypigmentation at skin folds) and fungal infections at skin folds and nails. Look for ankle oedema.

Fat deposition in the supraclavicular and interscapular regions are common. *(Note: The student should refrain from using the terms 'buffalo hump' and 'obese' in front of the patient)*

Examine the pupils for cataract, usually present in exogenous glucocorticoids usage.

Look for signs of autoimmune diseases eg. rheumatoid hands, malar rash.

Inspect the oral cavity for oral thrush and buccal hyperpigmentation.

Take the blood pressure of the patient.

Chest

There may be kyphosis and spine tenderness due to vertebral collapse. Examine the chest for hyperinflation and wheeze, which may suggest underlying bronchial asthma or chronic obstructive lung disease, usually treated with steroids. The presence of bronchial breathing or lung collapse could be due to an ACTH producing lung carcinoma.

Abdomen

Purplish striae which, is most commonly observed over the abdomen, buttocks, thighs and upper arms would be evident. If pseudo Cushing's syndrome is suspected, look for signs of chronic liver disease cause by alcohol abuse.

Neurological

Examine for proximal muscles weakness. Most patients would be unable to stand up from a squatting position unaided.

Bitemporal hemianopia would be present in a pituitary tumour that is impinging on the optic chiasma.

Hypothyroidism would cause hyporeflexia.

CHECK LIST FOR CLINICAL EXAMINATION

- ✓ General – moon face, suprclavicular and interscapular fat pad, acanthosis nigricans, fungal infections, oral thrush, buccal hyperpigmentation, ankle oedema, hirsutism, kyphosis
- ✓ Eyes – cataract, visual field
- ✓ Upper limbs – arthropathy, nail infections, purpura, thin skin, proximal weakness
- ✓ Chest – hyperinflation, wheeze, bronchial breath sounds, lung collapse
- ✓ Abdomen – central obesity, purple striae
- ✓ Blood pressure

INVESTIGATIONS

Investigations can be divided into investigations performed to confirm the presence of Cushing's syndrome and investigations to determine the cause of Cushing's syndrome.

Investigations to confirm Cushing's syndrome

1. 24-hour collection of urinary free cortisol

At least 2 measurements are required for this test that is used as an initial screening tool.

A value that is 3 times the upper limit of normal suggests Cushing's syndrome.

Mildly elevated values may suggest pseudo Cushing's or Cushing's syndrome and require further evaluation.

2. 1mg overnight Dexamethasone suppression test

1mg of Dexamethasone is administered at 11pm and blood sample for serum cortisol is taken at 8am the following morning. This is an alternative screening test.

3. Low dose Dexamethasone suppression test

This test is beneficial to distinguish patients with Cushing's syndrome from those with pseudo Cushing's.

0.5mg of Dexamethasone is administered every 6 hours (starting from 8am) for 48 hours and the serum cortisol is measured after that. Failure to suppress serum cortisol suggests Cushing's syndrome.

4. Late night serum and salivary cortisol

Normally, cortisol levels are lowest at late night. Serum or salivary cortisol level measured at 11pm in patients with Cushing's syndrome would be elevated as the circadian rhythm is altered.

5. Other investigations which are relevant include:

- Fasting blood sugar – impaired sugar control
- Serum electrolytes – hypokalaemia
- Blood gases – metabolic alkalosis
- DEXA – bone density measurement

Investigations to determine the cause of Cushing's syndrome

1. Plasma ACTH

If Cushing's syndrome is confirmed, and the plasma ACTH level is undetectable or low in the patient, an adrenal pathology should be suspected. ACTH independent Cushing's syndrome may be due to adrenal adenomas, adrenal carcinomas or adrenal hyperplasia.

2. High dose dexamethasone suppression test with CRH

This test is useful to distinguish Cushing's disease from ectopic ACTH production. 2mg of dexamethasone is administered every 6 hours for 48 hours. Serum cortisol will be suppressed by more than 50% of baseline in patients who have Cushing's disease. The second component of the test involves measurement of plasma ACTH and cortisol after administration of CRH. Pituitary tumours are responsive to CRH, and the suppressed ACTH and cortisol at the end of the dexamethasone suppression test should rise following administration of CRH.

3. Magnetic Resonance Imaging of pituitary

In ACTH dependent Cushing's syndrome, contrast enhanced MRI of the pituitary gland is mandatory. Unfortunately, small microadenomas may not be visualised.

4. Inferior petrosal sinus sampling

Inferior petrosal sinus sampling is a useful procedure in patients with Cushing's syndrome, in whom the diagnosis remains elusive. The procedure entails bilateral catheterization of the inferior petrosal sinus and samples taken from both these catheters. Elevated ACTH levels in the samples would confirm the diagnosis of Cushing's disease.

5. Computed Tomography (CT) scan of Abdomen

A CT abdomen is performed if an adrenal pathology is suspected.

6. Chest radiograph

Chest radiograph is performed to look for lung masses if ectopic ACTH producing lung carcinomas are suspected.

7. Hormone assays

If a pituitary tumour is present other hormones secreted by the anterior pituitary has to be assessed. Thyroid function test, Follicle stimulating hormones, luteinizing hormone, prolactin and growth hormone levels should be determined.

CASE SUMMARY

This patient has presented with recent weight gain and proximal muscles weakness. She is known to have bronchial asthma and has been prescribed oral steroids intermittently during acute exacerbations. Examination revealed thin skin with multiple ecchymoses, fat accumulation at interscapular and supraclavicular region, acanthosis nigricans, moon-like face and central obesity. There are violaceous striae noted on the abdomen and weakness of proximal muscles of the limbs. Based on the history and clinical findings, my diagnosis is Cushing's syndrome. I would like to complete my examination by measuring the blood pressure and doing a urine dipstick test for glycosuria.

CLINICAL DISCUSSION OF THE CASE

Management

The management in the case of exogenous glucocorticoids causing Cushing's is obviously to gradually cease the usage of glucocorticoids and introduce steroid-sparing agents in patients who require immunosuppression.

The treatment for endogenous Cushing's syndrome is surgical resection of the tumour i.e. transphenoidal resection of pituitary tumours and adrenalectomy for adrenal tumours.

If surgery has failed or declined by the patient, medications that inhibit sterodogenesis may be beneficial. Medications frequently used are ketoconazole and metyrapone. An alternative option for patients who have failed surgery is pituitary irradiation.

The hyperglycaemia and hypertension that accompanies Cushing's syndrome should be treated and complications such as hypertensive retinopathy screened for.
Depilatory creams can be prescribed for patients with hirsutism and psychiatry referral may be necessary for some with depression.

LEARNING OUTCOMES

By the end of this case review the student should be able to:
1. Take a relevant history for Cushing's syndrome
2. Attempt to determine cause of Cushing's syndrome and complications from history and physical examination
3. Understand what meant by 'Cushing's disease' and pseudo Cushing's
4. Elicit typical features of Cushing's syndrome
5. Discuss the necessary investigations to confirm Cushing's syndrome and to determine the cause
6. Discuss management plans of the patient

COMMONLY ASKED QUESTIONS

1. What is the significance of hyperpigmentation that occurs in some patients with Cushing's syndrome?
Hyperpigmentation of the palmar creases and buccal mucosa usually occurs in patients with increased ACTH (ACTH dependent Cushing's

syndrome). This is because Melanocyte Stimulating Hormone is one of the by-product of ACTH synthesis.

2. How can patients be screened for osteoporosis?
Dual energy X-ray absorptiometry (DEXA) of the hip and lumbar spine is the most commonly used screening test for osteoporosis

HIGH ACHIEVER QUESTIONS

headache
bitemporal hemianopia
hypo pit.

1. What is Nelson's syndrome?
In the past, bilateral adrenalectomy was the preferred treatment for patients with Cushing's disease. This resulted in enlargement of the pituitary tumour due to loss of negative feedback inhibition. The compilation of features resulting from the local effects of the macroadenoma i.e. headache, bitemporal hemianopia and hypopituitarism is referred to as Nelson's syndrome.

2. In patients on prolonged exogenous steroids, why must the steroids be stopped gradually?
Chronic exogenous steroids lead to suppression of the hypothalamic pituitary axis causing secondary adrenal insufficiency. Abrupt withdrawal of steroids will cause acute adrenocortical failure (adrenal crisis).

COMMON MISTAKES

- Not recognising the signs and symptoms of Cushing's syndrome
- Confusion between the terms Cushing's disease and Cushing's syndrome
- Failure to address complications of Cushing's syndrome
- Not familiar with relevant investigations to confirm Cushing's syndrome and determine cause
- Misdiagnosis of pseudo Cushing's as Cushing's syndrome

MUST KNOW FACTS ABOUT CUSHING'S SYNDROME

1. 90% of Cushing's syndrome is due to exogenous glucocorticoid usage

2. 90% of patients with endogenous Cushing's syndrome have Cushing's disease

3. Other anterior pituitary hormones may be affected in Cushing's disease

4. 24-hour urine cortisol is a screening test for Cushing's syndrome

5. Low dose dexamethasone test is used to distinguish pseudo Cushing's from Cushing's syndrome

6. High dose dexamethasone test is used to distinguish Cushing's disease from other causes of endogenous Cushing's syndrome

References:

1. The Endocrine Society's Clinical Guidelines

CASE 56 : HYPOTHYROIDISM
SAROJ JAYASINGHE

OVERVIEW

Hypothyroidism is when there is deficient thyroid hormone secretion. It is most commonly due to failure of the thyroid gland (primary hypothyroidism), or rarely due to pituitary or hypothalamic disease (secondary hypothyroidism).

Primary hypothyroidism is caused by autoimmune thyroiditis (e.g. Hashimoto's thyroiditis), iodine deficiency, following ^{131}I treatment for hyperthyroidism, following total thyroidectomy (for thyroid carcinoma) and congenitally (e.g. due to a hypoplastic thyroid gland). Tumours and Sheehan's syndrome are the common causes for secondary hypothyroidism.

A majority are asymptomatic or have minimal non-specific symptoms and a high degree of clinical suspicion is required to detect the disease. Symptoms include lethargy, mild weight gain with poor appetite, cold intolerance, constipation, dry hair and skin, hair loss, hoarse voice, poor memory, depression, dyspnoea, and menorrhagia.

Physical signs include non-pitting ankle oedema, dry skin, and coarse facial features including large tongue and periorbital puffiness. There can be loss of lateral aspects of eye brows and pallor. A goiter may be palpable. Some develop features of carpel tunnel syndrome. More characteristic features are bradycardia, mild diastolic hypertension, and slow relaxation of deep tendon reflexes (e.g. ankle jerk). The apex may be shifted due to pericardial effusion and heart sounds soft. Pleural effusions and ascites are rare. Rarely patients present in a stuperous state with hypothermia and respiratory depression (myxedema coma).

In those with secondary hypothyroidism, features of hypopituitarism (e.g. amenorrhea) or the causative disease (e.g. pressure features of a pituitary tumour) tend to mask the hypothyroid features.

Types of Cases for Clinical Examination

OSCE, short or long:

This is an uncommon case for OSCE or short cases. However, students should be familiar with questions that should be asked from patients in whom they suspect hypothyroidism (see above for symptoms).

The student should be competent in examining the thyroid gland and cervical lymph nodes, and in demonstrating slow relaxation of deep tendon reflexes (e.g. ankle jerk) and looking for the clinical signs mentioned above.

Long case or OSLER

The student should aim to (a) to take a detailed history, including past history and family history of treatment for thyroid disorders; (b) demonstrate clinical competence in general examination and of the relevant systems; (c) show clinical reasoning skills in managing the patient, (d) be able to interpret thyroid function tests and the physiological basis.

CASE VIGNETTE

A 45-year-old female, with a past-medical history of treatment for hypertension, presents with a 12–month history of excessive tiredness, lethargy, low mood, and ankle swelling. On further questioning she describes nocturnal cramps of lower limbs. Her work output in office has suffered because of forgetfulness, and she dislikes to stay in air-conditioned rooms. There is mild pallor, facial puffiness, and non-pitting swelling of both ankles. She has also noticed abdominal distension of 3 months duration and there is menorrhagia. The ankle jerk relaxation appears to be delayed.

DIFFERENTIAL DIAGNOSIS

- Hypothyroidism
- Cirrhosis (decompensated)
- Right heart failure (e.g. congestive cardiac failure or cor-pulmonale)
- Renal causes such as nephrotic syndrome

HISTORY TAKING

HISTORY OF PRESENTING ILLNESS

- Swelling of ankles which is painless, associated with tiredness and lethargy. The symptoms are non-specific. During history taking the student may notice the hoarseness of voice with the slow monotonous speech.
- Closer questioning will reveal that the patient has put-on weight, is constipated and has mennorrhagia.
- Relevant negative features that help to rule out other causes for the clinical presentation.

- o Absence of cough or wheeze (seen in congestive cardiac failure (CCF) or cor-pulmonale)
- o No history of facial puffiness and haematuria (as in nephrotic syndrome or acute glomerulonephritis)
- o Relatively good protein intake with no bowel symptoms to suggest malabsorption and no history of severe anorexia, loss of weight, change in bowel habits, haemoptysis that could suggest internal malignancies

PAST MEDICAL HISTORY

- There may be a past history of thyroid disease (e.g. Graves disease or radio-iodine treatment for thyrotoxicosis). In the case of Graves, the gland may become atrophied due to effects of anti-thyroid antibodies. Hypothyroidism is a well known to follow radio-iodine treatment given for Graves.

- Drugs that lead to hypothyroidism include amiodorone (used in ventricular tachycardia) and lithium (for manic-depressive disorders).

- Mild hypertension and hypercholesteraemia are well known to occur due to hypothyroidism

FAMILY HISTORY

- There may be a family history of goitre, thyroid disease or autoimmune diseases.

SOCIAL HISTORY

- It is always prudent to ask about alcohol intake, and smoking. Excess goitrogens (e.g. cassava and cabbage).

SYSTEMIC REVIEW OF SYMPTOMS

- Other less common features of hypothyroidism could be asked here: cramps, features of carpel tunnel syndrome, and ataxia.

SURGICAL HISTORY

- Surgery for multinodular goitre or total thyroidectomy for thyroid carcinoma lead to hypothyroidism.

SYSTEMIC REVIEW OF SYMPTOMS

- Urinary symptoms (e.g. oliguria), dry skin, and symptoms attributable to the cardiovascular system (e.g. angina).

EXAMINATION

Professionalism:

Introduce yourself, obtain consent, position patient ideally lying down, suitably undressed and request for a chaperone when you are examining.

Ensure you have all equipment for examination available including measuring tape. Explain to the patient what you intend to perform in examining the neck and other systems.

Plan your examination as to whether she would be seated on a chair in front of you for examination of the neck, and then to transfer her to the bed for examination of the other systems. The cervical lymph nodes should also be examined after examining the thyroid gland.

Physical examination:

Observe the patient from the end of the bed and comment on obvious abnormalities

- Appearance: oedema, pallor, dry skin, coarse features with thick lips, periorbital fullness, hair loss over lateral eye brows, large tongue, and rarely there is xanthelesma from hypercholesteraemia, and carotinaemia with a yellowish tinge to the skin without jaundice.
- Note any hoarseness of voice and monotomous or slurred speech
- State whether patient is conscious, alert, and oriented.
- State the relevant negative findings: lack of orthopnea, (which is seen in CCF), and lack of facial puffiness with per-orbital oedema that is a feature of nephrotic syndrome.
- Examine closely for the goitre (see chapter on Graves disease): Confirm goitre by requesting patient to swallow and observe movement of the gland; move behind the patient and explain you are going to palpate the neck and begin to palpate for the surface of the gland (is it smooth or nodular?); Is the consistency hard? (as in de Queverines thyroiditis). Check for retrosternal extension.

Feel the pulse: Are the hands cold? (-hypothermia can be diagnosed with a thermometer that can measure low temperatures). Is there a bradycardia?

Chest- look for features of corpulmonale and CCF (e.g. elevated jugular venous pressure).

Abdomen –There can be abdominal distension (from lax abdominal muscles and obesity) . Rarely free fluid could contribute to the distension.

Neurology – There may be evidence of proximal muscle weakness (i.e. difficulty in getting up from a squatting position). The characteristic feature is a slow relaxation of the jerks, most easily demonstrated in the ankle jerk and knee jerks. Other features include those of carpel tunnel syndrome (thenar muscle wasting with sparing of adductor policis and sensory impairment on the palmar aspect of the first 3 digits and radial half of the fourth digit) and cerebellar dysfunction (ataxia, past-pointing, and dysdiadokokinesia)

Note:

The traditional technique in examination of the neck has been with the patient sitting comfortably on a chair with the examiner in front, while examination of the thyroid gland is done with the examiner standing behind the patient. However, some have adopted the anterior approach even for the thyroid examination. In either method the student should show competency in positioning the patient with good lighting to enhance visualization of the neck.

The neck should be in the neutral position or slightly extended. Extending the neck is advantageous as it stretches the overlying tissues and permits better evaluation of the thyroid. Making the patient swallow sips of water would demonstrate the thyroid gland moving upwards.

The examination should also include a side view of the neck where the contour of the neck is better visualized. Systematically scan the entire neck from the cricoid cartilage to the supra-sternal notch, looking for swellings. All lumps must be measured with a measuring tape.

Palpation is done as described under Graves' disease. Begin by locating the isthmus between the cricoid cartilage and suprasternal notch using one hand to displace the sternomastoid muscle while palpating the thyroid gland with the other. Ask the patient to sip some water as you proceed with palpation.

Comment on both right and left lobes of the thyroid, isthmus and any retrosternal extension. Complete palpation by systematically examining the cervical chain of lymph nodes.

Professionalism: Thank the patient, place her in previous position she was in and exit so that patient may re-dress herself.

INVESTIGATIONS

- Diagnosis of hypothyroidism is by showing high TSH with low serum free T4 (FT4) and T3 (FT3). In patients with classical clinical features and high TSH, there is no necessity to do free T4 or free T3 levels.
- Autoimmune nature of the illness is demonstrated by the presence of thyroid antibodies (anti-microsomal antibodies, anti-thyroglobulin antibodies).
- Rarely a FNAC is done and it shows hypoplastic glandular tissues with a lymphocytic infiltration suggestive of Hashimoto's thyroiditis....
- Ultrasound of the thyroid gland will show a smooth goitre and radio-isotope uptake will show low uptake
- If there is a large goitre (which is rare) pressure effects of the gland and retrosternal extension should be looked for. A soft tissue X-ray of neck and a chest X-ray focusing on the thoracic inlet would help though CT scans will give better resolution.
- Metabolic effects are mainly on the heart and therefore the ECG is essential to diagnose sinus bradycardia with low voltages in all leads. Echocardiogram is indicated to confirm cardiomyopathy, which is a rare feature.
- Ultrasound of abdomen may detect free fluid.
- Autoimmune tests are indicated if associated autoimmune diseases are suspected: e.g. antinuclear antibodies for SLE, rheumatoid factor for rheumatoid arthritis.
- Hypoglycaemia and hyponatraemia can be seen, especially when an infection supervenes. Hypercholsteraemia is a characteristic finding.
- Blood counts and blood film may show macrocytes and normochromic anaemia. Rarely there is accompanying pernicious anaemia that could contribute to promote a megaloblastic anaemia. Increased blood loss from excessive periods can produce a picture of iron deficiency anaemia (i.e. hypochromic microcytic).

Note:

With the symptoms presented in this case all the classical features of hypothyroidism are apparent and laboratory investigations would be consistent with a diagnosis of primary hypothyroidism (i.e. from autoimmune thyroiditis). This could be confirmed with the presence of antithyroid antibodies. If there was evidence of a surgical scar in the neck or history of radioiodine ingestion then one should consider the hypothyroidism to be secondary to loss of functioning thyroid gland tissue.

TREATMENT

Hypothyroidism is treated with regular daily dose of levothyroxine (LT4), usually life-long. A small dose (25 ug) is used in the elderly and those with ischaemic heart disease. Others are started with 50 to 100 ug. Symptomatic improvement is seen in 3-5 days and reaches a plateau after 4-6 weeks. It may take several months for TSH to normalize because of slow re-adaptation of the hypothalamic-pituitary axis. Monitor treatment with symptoms and TSH levels. Once stable, at least yearly TSH could be used to monitor progress. Hypercholesteraemia and mild hypertension normalize with treatment.

In the unlikely situation where symptoms are rather vague but suggestive of hypothyroidism an algorithmic approach would be useful based on TSH levels: If TSH is normal then it is best repeated after six months. In the event it is slightly elevated TSH levels (5 to 10 mU/L) subclinical disease is suspected. It may then be justified to perform free T4 before initiating replacement therapy.

COMMON QUESTIONS

1. Describe the treatment of those pregnant and having untreated hypothyroidism

Treatment with T4 is essential to prevent morbidity associated with pregnancy: spontaneous abortion, low birth weight, impaired cognitive development, and fetal mortality. Diagnosis and monitoring is done by using TSH levels. A higher dose of T4 (about 30% higher that is required by the patient in the non-pregnant state) is required, especially in the first and second trimesters. For those diagnosed previously, serum TSH should be measured every 4 weeks during the first half of pregnancy and every 6 weeks thereafter. Post-partum, the dose can be reduced after about 6 weeks.

2. What is subclinical hypothyroidism?

This is when there is elevation of TSH (usually between 5 to 10 mIU / mL) with normal FT3 and FT4. A higher than normal proportion of persons progress to overt hypothyroidism. There is controversy on the need for treatment, and it should be on a case-by-case basis. Those with high serum cholesterol and hypertension seem to benefit. Some would treat those with TSH (5 to 10 mIU / mL) and goitre or positive antithyroid peroxidase antibodies, as these patients have the highest rates of progression to overt hypothyroidism.

HIGH ACHIEVER QUESTIONS

1. How will you detect myxedema coma?

Patients usually give a history of symptoms of hypothyroidism preceding the event. The event is could be precipitated by an infection. However, despite an infection, hypothermia is usually present. A special thermometer is required to check low temperatures.

Other features include:

- extremities cold, with non-pitting oedema of the hands and feet
- cool, pale, dry, scaly, and thickened skin; dry and brittle nails; sallowness due to carotenemia
- hypotension or shock,
- bradycardia with decreased pulse pressure : normal systolic pressure, elevated diastolic pressure
- periorbital, non-pitting edema and coarse features of face with macroglossia and enlargement of the tonsils, and coarse or thinning hair
- enlarged thyroid or not palpable or scar suggesting previous thyroidectomy
- low respiration rate and pleural effusions, consolidation (that precipitates myxoedema coma)
- soft heart sounds, diminished apical impulse, enlarged heart, and pericardial effusion
- distended abdomen secondary to ileus and/or ascites
- confusion, stupor, obtundation, and coma; slow speech, seizures, reflexes with a slow relaxation

2. What is the treatment of myxedema coma?

It is a life threatening condition. Thyroid replacement is using intravenous T4, (about 500 mcg as a bolus loading dose can be given followed by 100 mcg 24 hours later and then 50 mcg daily IV or PO). Use of intravenous T3 is controversial and has a higher frequency of adverse cardiac events.

- Mechanical ventilation if respiratory acidosis/hypercapnia/hypoxia is significant

- Since there is a possibility of adrenal insufficiency, corticosteroids are given *after* collecting blood for cortisol level
- Re-warm slowly using ordinary blankets and a warm room
- Treat possible associated infection with empirical antibiotics after obtaining blood and urine cultures.
- Correct hyponatremia if present
- Correct hypoglycemia with intravenous dextrose
- Treat hypotension with cautious administration of normal saline
- Myocardial infarction may be the precipitating event in older patients and therefore serial ECGS and cardiac troponins are important. In this group, institute thyroid replacement at low doses.

RED FLAG ENCOUNTERS

Areas where students tend to fall into trouble are:

- Missing or not examining for subtle signs such as coarse skin, coarse features, large tongue, bradycardia, ataxia
- Not doing a thorough examination of the thyroid gland (e.g. not looking for retro-sternal extension)
- Not being clear about the tests to diagnose the condition and how to monitor progress
- Not clear about treatment of special groups: elderly, those with coronary artery disease, pregnant mothers

MUST KNOW FACTS ABOUT HYPOTHYROIDISM

- ✓ It is often asymptomatic
- ✓ Pathogenesis of the clinical features of hypothyroidism
- ✓ Clinical presentations and treatment of hypothyroidism
- ✓ Tests of thyroid function and their interpretation

OVERVIEW

It is now incumbent on medical graduates to be able to practice ethically and professionally. The 'hidden curriculum' of medical ethics, moral values, duty of care and professionalism are now being expressed explicitly in most medical education curricula in view of the need to ensure medical graduates can work through ethical dilemma when it arises and seek assistance in case they are unable to resolve ethical issues in the course of their clinical care of patients.

Confidentiality is essential in medical practice and the patient-doctor contractual relationship needs to be sustained except in certain situations where then law and the Court rule that information of a confidential nature needs to be released.

OSCE –LONG OSCE

Case that rests on ethical and professional issues can be included in OSCE counselling stations.
The student would be observed for his ability to recognize and discuss ethical and professional issues given a case scenario .

Simulated patients may be involved in 'role play'.

Two scenarios can be presented:

    i.   The patient who wants to be tested for sexually transmitted disease
    ii.   The third party seeking health information of a patient.

In the case given below the question could be focussed on counselling skills of the doctor involving the treatment of the patient during a long case . On the other hand, a simulated patient may take the role of a friend of the doctor who asks for information on health matters pertaining to his future son-in law. The setting could be in the consultation room or in a public place in the latter.

CASE SCENARIO:

You are the physician working in a small district hospital where you are well received as a leader in the community. Mr ARM is the son of a local leading politician . He is 26 years old and consults you about the risk of a venereal disease and perhaps HIV following unprotected sexual intercourse related to his high risk behaviour. He is confirmed to have gonorrhoea which responds to antibiotics. He is also tested for HIV infection. A rapid test for HIV is negative.

Mr. KTM meets you casually over coffee and excitedly invites you to his daughter's engagement to Mr. ARM. Both you and MR KTM know Mr ARM's father and have attended several of his parties as he is the local Member of Parliament. In the course of their conversation, Mr.KTM enquires if you know of any information of the health status of Mr ARM. He feels he can prepare his daughter better if he has such information.

(Case is adapted from Reference 1)

QUESTIONS

1. How would you counsel Mr. ARM on HIV testing ?
2. Discuss the ethical dilemma in this case and outline the steps in ethical decision making.

Suggested Answers:

1. HIV Testing

It is imperative that testing for infectious diseases should be done confidentially and all information pertaining to the process should not be divulged to third parties. Being the leading physician in the small district hospital you will have specific protocols that your staff should adhere to.

Note:

In the UK several legislations like the Access to Medical Records Act 1988, Data Protection Act 1984 and Access to Health Records Act 1990 allows patients to access their records. In Malaysia medical record keeping varies a great deal and may not be stored such that they can be retrieved easily (see Discovery and Pre-action Discovery for Malaysia).

The patient (Mr ARM) is concerned about HIV infection above that of other sexually transmitted infection (Gonorrhoea). His concerns implies the need to test for HIV infection.

A great deal of confidentiality is warranted in managing sexually transmitted infections. However, the management cannot be confined to the patient alone as several other aspects need to be factored in e.g disclosure to health authorities so as to contain the infection, contact tracing and treatment, if possible protecting vulnerable parties (spouse and partners).

Infections like gonorrhoea and syphilis and caused by bacteria and complete treatment is possible. HIV infection , on the other hand is not curable and other factors need to be considered which medical student needs to be conversant in.

It is good practice to do both pre-and post test counselling in all sexually transmitted infection especially HIV infection.

Pretest and postest procedures

The patient needs to be counselled about the reliability of the tests available, the significance of both rapid test and Western Blot test.

He should also be informed about the 'window period' as you explore further about his risk taking behaviour and how the disease is possibly contracted , the number and frequency of unprotected exposures he has had and results of any previous tests ,if done.

After the patient is well informed , consent needs to be taken for HIV testing . This process prepares him for any eventualities as when the test results return either negative or positive.

Post test process involves information as to when the results will be available and what steps are to be taken or available should HIV be negative or positive.
He would be informed on the need for continued care and treatment should he be HIV positive and the his prognosis if he is HIV positive.

Disclosure to other parties

He will be counselled on disclosure to other parties who may be at a risk of contracting the disease should he not take standard precautions should he be HIV positive.

Notification to health authorities and the COURT does not tantamount to breach of confidentiality. Mr. ARM is informed of this provision in the law of the country.

Note:

There is considerable debate about disclosure of medical information to third parties. This would also apply to HIV positive status. It is fundamental ethical practice that all aspects of the patient's HIV status need not be disclosed.

However, two conditions (under common law) permit disclosure:

i.   That there is a real risk to vulnerable persons (in this case his future bride)

ii.   That the only way to protect such vulnerable persons from contracting the disease is by such disclosure (in this instance this would be operational if Mr. ARM does not reveal his HIV status, if he is positive) .

In Malaysia, the Charter for Doctors (on HIV/AIDS) clearly states 'that patients who are HIV positive shall be encouraged to inform the attending doctor of their HIV status and that this information will be restricted to medical professionals and authorized personnel on a need-to know basis'.

With regards to Evidence Act 1950 , the Act does not appear to 'protect the confidentiality of communication between doctor and his patient!'. Disclosure is required ' if public interest demands'. This implies that the law, as it stands , does not recognize confidentiality between patient and doctor. This is well exemplified by the case, Public Prosecutor v Dato Seri Anwar Ibrahim & Anor [2001] 3 MLJ 193 where the court used the case of W v Egdell . The Court firmly held that 'there is no privilege under the law for a doctor to refrain from disclosing what transpired between him and his patient (see reference 2) .

2.   Ethical Dilemma

Breach of confidentiality is unprofessional and breaks the contract in the doctor-patient relationship.

However, as explained above the Court may require the physician to disclose materials that are pertinent in law.

Infectious diseases are governed by law as Notification of Diseases. Doctors need to be aware of the list of infectious diseases that may pose a public problem and potentially cause an epidemic in the community. Such infections need to be notified to the health authorities within a stipulated period. HIV falls under that list .

However, when such notification is essential the patient should be told about the need for notification.

Ethical Dilemma in disclosure of health information to a third party

Clearly it is not professional to discuss Mr ARM's consultation and tests with Mr KTM despite his noble intentions of wanting to inform his daughter who is due to be given in marriage to Mr ARM (1). Preserving patient's confidentiality is the duty of a physician.

Although Mr ARM has gonorrhoea you, as a physician would not know if he has other transmissible infections like clamydia and herpes; tests you may not have done or are privy to results of such tests. these. Hence you would not have all information about transmissible infections of Mr. ARM. Even if you had , you are not morally and professionally obliged to divulge such to Mr. KTM.

You could however advice Mr KTM that his daughter, being the prospective bride, could freely discuss with Mr ARM about such health information and prepare herself for the eventual union in marriage (1).

Would it be right for you as a doctor, not divulge information , should Mr ARM prove to be HIV positive?   Herein lies the dilemma. As a responsible physician you would advise Mr ARM to inform his future spouse about the implication of a positive HIV test so as to protect her against the infection.

Should Mr KTM's daughter , on the other hand , consult you about other health matters as a patient .eg. contraception or related advice in view of the impending marriage, you may want to share the need to discuss issues related to sexually transmitted infection including HIV with her future husband (1).

Again if Mr ARM is HIV positive and does not reveal his status to his future bride, you may be justified in divulging such information to Mr KTM's daughter.

Courts of law have been kind in situations like this where a breach in confidentiality for the protection of a vulnerable person is concerned (Mr KTM's daughter) (see conditions for disclosure above).

i.   What should you then do?

Protection of vulnerable persons against HIV infection would be a responsibility you should uphold.

You should call up Mr ARM and inform him of his responsibilities to sexual partners and if he has informed Mr KTM's daughter about the treatment and tests he has had. If he fails to inform Mr. KTM's daughter of his HIV status (if he is HIV positive) you are obliged to inform her about risk of contracting the disease should she plan to have un protected sexual contact with him.

ii.   The Ethical Decision Making Model

The medical profession is governed by the Code of Conduct and should adhere to Good Clinical Practice. Medical graduates need to be competent in recognizing ethical dilemma and be aware of resolving ethical issues using an ethical decision making model.

Several decision making models are available. The following steps are adopted from the work of Stadler (1986) and Kitchner (1984). The American Counselling Association has developed 'A Practitioner's Guide to Ethical Decision Making' which makes useful reading for students.

Steps to follow in Ethical Decision Making are:

Identify the problem

- ✓ Sexually transmitted infection (STI) in your patient
- ✓ Divulging information
- ✓ Breach of confidentiality
- ✓ Doctor-patient relationship (fidelity, nonmaleficence, justice)

Refer to Code of Ethics

- ✓ Look up the Medical Code of Ethics and see if you could overcome the dilemma
- ✓ If unable to resolve , go through the rest of the steps

Determine the Nature and Dimensions of the Dilemma

- ✓ Refer to the fundamentals of ethics (beneficence, justice, non-maleficence, fidelity)
- ✓ Which principle applies here ?
- ✓ Always look at local and current views in the country
- ✓ May need to consult professional bodies for advice

In the case discussed, confidentiality will be breached if information of STI is divulged.

However, innocent parties may suffer (contract STI and HIV) if you, as a medical practitioner , did not take any action even through your are aware of such potential consequences.

- Decide on a potential course of action
  - ✓ When in a dilemma, it is worth talking through the possible courses of actions
  - ✓ Need to retain anonymity of the parties concerned when discussing the options with other professionals in deciding potential action.

- ✓ In the case presented , you would take the role of a judge, listing the pros and cons of identified actions so as to make decisions.
- Determine what would be the potential consequences of all options and then determine the course of action
  - ✓ If you were silent in not revealing the status of HIV and high risk behaviour of Mr ARM , another party may potentially suffer
  - ✓ If you did reveal all information to others (including to Mr. RTM, the future father –in-law) you are not following the Code of Ethics.
  - ✓ As you look at all options and consequences it becomes clearer as to which action or combination of actions should be best to follow.
- Ponder over and evaluate the selected course of action

Three simple tests would impact on the actions selected:

- a. Test of justice (would you treat others in the fashion you have decided, given the same consequences?)
- b. Test of publicity (would you have been comfortable if all the circumstances of the case was put up on 'facebook' or the media?
- c. Test of universality (would you recommend the same course of action to another doctor given the same circumstances?)

If you are able to accept the consequences mentioned under these three tests then you may consider implementing this course of action (justifiable that you need to protect the innocent bride from STI, not discuss and reveal confidential matter pertaining to health of Mr ARM with Mr RTM, even though you are good friend, using Code of Good Clinical Practice, by requesting Mr ARM to discuss and inform his partners about his HIV status and if he fails, using the Charter governing role of practitioner , to take the next course of action.

- Implement the course of action

Ethical dilemmas can be complex but need to be resolved as one needs to take the best course of action. The case mentioned may be complicated when the patient tells you that being the son of a local prominent politician , he would rather, you keep all matters of his health confidential.

The student will often meet such ethical dilemma in clinical practice. By working though several clinical scenarios, he/she would be in a better position in taking the appropriate course of action . The patient-physician relationship is unique in that confidentiality cannot always be absolute. There are times when information needs to be revealed . This usually applies in situations when the patient may cause serious harm to either himself or to others (try working this out in this case!).

It would be prudent to make a claim that information related to Mr ARM's STI will be kept confidential but he must also be informed that there are limitations to this and give the reasons for such.

✓ Whatever the course of action you have taken is not only in the best interest of the patient but would be deemed the best judgement (as in protecting innocent parties from getting infection with HIV should the patient continue to maintain risk taking behaviour) . It would also be good clinical practice for the doctor to follow up on the case so as justify the course of actions and evaluate the consequences of such actions.

MUST KNOW FACTS:

✓ Basic tenets of professionalism and the five moral principles i.e autonomy, beneficence, non-maleficence, justice and fidelity
✓ Basic counselling techniques
✓ Confidentiality and limitations
✓ The steps of an Ethical Dilemma Decision on making model
✓ The Court and Laws governing divulging confidential information of patients

RED FLAG

➢ Not exhibiting professional aspects of greeting and engaging with patient in the OSCE 'Ethics Station'
➢ Being judgemental in the course of conversation
➢ Taking paternalistic approach in decision making
➢ Not closing a conversation at the end of counselling

1. **Reference**
   Dickens BM, Cook RJ, Kismodi E. The UNESCO Chair of Bioethics . Reproductive Health Case Studies : Case 8 Pg 20-21

2. Public Prosecutor v Dato Seri Anwar Ibrahim & Anor [2001] 3 MLJ 193

Puteri Nemie Jahn Kassim. Confidentality and Access to Medical Records in: Law and Ethics Relating to Medical Profession. International Law Book Services ,Petaling Jaya. Pp 180-185.

Code of Ethics . American Counselling Association.

3.   http://www.counselling.org/Files/FD.ashx?guide=cf94c260=c9
      6a-4c63-9f52-309547d60dof

Distributed by CSH Book Store
28, Jln TTC 15, Taman Teknologi Cheng,
Cheng, 75250 Melaka.
H/P : 012-392 8388.
E-mail : seanhoon@hotmail.com

Unipress Medical
KL/PJ:
35, Jalan SS 15/5A,
47500 Subang Jaya Selangor.
(Opposite SJMC)
Tel   : 03-5638 2893
Fax : 03-5638 5973

Penang:
86, Jalan Air Itam,
10460 Georgetown, Penang.
(Near Penang General Hospital and
Infront of the old Dato Keramat Market)
Tel   : 04-2263 263
H/P: 016-332 9630
www.unipressmedical.com